Religion, Space, and the Atlantic World

The Carolina Lowcountry and the Atlantic World
Sponsored by the Program in the Carolina Lowcountry
and the Atlantic World of the College of Charleston

RELIGION, SPACE, AND THE ATLANTIC WORLD

EDITED BY

John Corrigan

The University of South Carolina Press

Published by the University of South Carolina Press
Columbia, South Carolina 29208

www.sc.edu/uscpress

Manufactured in the United States of America

26 25 24 23 22 21 20 19 18 17
10 9 8 7 6 5 4 3 2 1

Library of Congress Cataloging-in-Publication Data
can be found at http://catalog.loc.gov

ISBN 978-1-61117-796-1 (hardcover)
ISBN: 978-1-61117-797-8 (ebook)

This book was printed on recycled paper
with 30 percent postconsumer waste content.

CONTENTS

ACKNOWLEDGMENTS

I gratefully acknowledge the support of the National Endowment for the Humanities, Florida State University, Indiana University–Purdue University Indianapolis, and the Virtual Center for Spatial Humanities. Thanks to Molly Reed for assistance organizing gatherings of the Working Group on Religion and Space in the Atlantic World, Shawntel Ensminger for editing assistance, and John Crow for drawing maps. It has been a pleasure to work with Jim Denton and Linda Fogle at the University of South Carolina Press and an honor to have this book included in the press's Atlantic World list. David Bodenhamer and Trevor Harris, as always, offered invaluable criticisms and suggestions from the beginning. I thank three anonymous readers, whose critically astute, detailed suggestions helped me improve the introduction and guided other contributors in their revisions. I also thank Edward Blum, Bret Carroll, Yvonne Chireau, Edward Gray, Paul Harvey, Sylvester Johnson, Tracy Leavelle, Darrin McMahon, and Amanda Porterfield for their readings of parts of the manuscript and/or their conversation in helping me think through an assortment of issues addressed in this book.

Introduction

At a banquet in ancient Thessaly, the Greek poet Simonides of Ceos (556–468 B.C.) chanted a lyric to a roomful of celebrants during a dinner convened to honor their host, Scopas. According to Greek storytellers, when Simonides stepped outside a short time later, the roof of the house collapsed, all were killed, and the bodies were crushed beyond recognition. Called upon to help identify the victims, Simonides subsequently was able to name the dead by recalling the places they had sat at the table. His "method of loci," later referred to as "the memory palace," was reported by Cicero: "He inferred that persons desiring to train this faculty (of memory) must select places and form mental images of the things they wish to remember and store those images in the places, so that the order of the places will preserve the order of the things, and the images of the things will denote the things themselves, and we shall employ the places and images respectively as a wax writing-tablet and the letters written on it."[1]

The relationship between memory and location discussed by Cicero, Quintilian, and other ancients, and exploited in the academic practice of memorization in medieval Europe, has been investigated recently by researchers who have begun to refer to "spatial learning" as an aspect of human brain activity located largely in the hippocampus.[2] Brain science proposes that the mental organization of our activity in the world and the recall of events has much to do with our experience of space. The spatial organization of knowledge is not just a trick of the Greek poet but a hard-wired process that affects the manner in which persons engage the world and make sense of it. That spatially enabled practice of mnemonics encompasses not only the business of storing thoughts, but as Yadin Dudai and Mary Carruthers recently have suggested in *Nature,* it also frames creative and future-oriented thinking.[3] Spatial thinking is not a sideline to other kinds of thinking but is closely interwoven with them, playing a crucial role in the human practice of world-making through the mental production, organization, archiving, and alteration of knowledge.

To think spatially as a historian or academic humanist is to take seriously the degree to which persons' experience of space influences the manner in which they make sense of their lives. Over the course of the past few decades, researchers in various disciplines have made strong contributions to our understanding of how space is constructed in culture. We have learned much about the ways in which cultural boundaries are established, contested, and erased; how power has spatial referents; how our engagement of the spaces of everyday life shapes our lives in unexpected fashion; and how the territories of body, society, and nation can be reimagined. Such research has proven fundamental to the work of many historians. At the same time it has had the effect of distracting us from thinking more seriously about the manner in which our engagement of physical space—in the sense of Euclidean space, within which we as embodied individuals are situated—influences our lives. In the last decade or so, scholarship has begun to reassess the importance of physical space and to estimate how our lives within it are recognizably wrought.

As scholars increasingly have turned their attention to geographic space, a promising avenue of historical investigation is developing at the intersection of (1) research that focuses on the cultural construction of space and (2) studies that stress the direct influence of natural and built physical environments on human lives. From the former we can glean insight into how space is conceived in ways that represent cultural ideals and social predicaments, and from the latter we can learn to appreciate how a coastline, mountain range, piazza, skyscraper, or vast desert set terms for how persons think about their lives and direct their behavior. Spatial thinking joins an awareness of physical environment to culturally derived notions of space as a mirror of social order and power. Such an approach blends attentiveness to what the seating places at Scopas's table reveal about social status, emotional relationships, and religious and political traditions with judgments about the relation of actors to the physical environment.

Research that is attentive to spatiality, then, recognizes the cultural construction of space while remaining wary of taking such constructions as accurate diagrams of physical environment—a virtue historically modeled by Copernicus. A "spatial humanities"[4] advances interpretation by framing historical actors within a broad range of spatial instances, such as the Silk Road, a soccer stadium, the Atlantic world, Times Square, an operating room, the Taj Mahal, or an island. It is inclined to interpretation that is informed by the discovery of patternings and correlations within and across spatial planes, three-dimensional shapes, or coordinate points, alongside interpretation arising from theory-driven analyses of ideologies of space. It asks hard questions, for example, about how we are to understand interpretive claims of "bilocal" and "polylocal" identities when persons actually experience space through physical bodies that can occupy only one space at a time.[5] Similarly, the spatial humanities can prompt rethinking of historical interpretation of how the development of local economic theory, for example, was conditioned by proximity to mineral and biological resources, waterways and terrain suited to trade, and defensible space.[6] And the spatial humanities can lead to rethinking how the words we use to describe our lives are spatially conditioned. The experience of place and the mental images we locate there build, as Cicero observed, a story of our lives, as we "employ the places and images respectively as a wax writing-tablet and the letters written on it."

The Space of the Atlantic World

The Atlantic world as a space defined by four continents and the ocean they share has proven a useful prompt for historians whose interests were not well served by previous historiography. Over several decades the notion of an Atlantic world has grown to include research about colonialism and empire, large-scale migration, networks of commerce, the interplay of ideologies, cultural hybridities, and resistance and revolution.[7] In the simplest terms, it is about the creation of communities, their deterioration and/or erasure, and their subsequent reinvention and rebuilding. In thinking about that, we identify metropoles and peripheries, but note as well the multicentered reality of the Atlantic world. During the seventeenth and eighteenth centuries, it was a dynamic environment, characterized by the circulation through it of people, ideas, commerce, navies. Unexpected discoveries constantly were made, while expected discoveries, such as the Garden of Eden or the Fountain of Youth, were never realized. Accidents of weather, warfare, and disease set the course for the history of the Atlantic World as much as the execution of detailed plans for domination and colonization. The names of people were changed—especially in the case of the African slave trade—as were the names of places. Sites that previously bore no European name were made new by colonists, as, for example, in the case of the English in North America: New England, New Hampshire, New York, New London, New Brunswick, and New Jersey, to name a few. As the English influence in that region increased, other place names were Anglicized, and their original Algonquian (and other tribes') meanings—which described the terrain—were lost in the process: Congamuck Ponds (Nipmuck) for "long fishing place"; Mystic River (Pequot-Mohegan) for "great tidal river"; Massapeag (Mohegan) for "place at the large cove"; Cos Cob (Mohegan from *Cassacubque*) for "high rocks"; Housatonic River (Mahican) for "beyond the mountain"; and Skungamug River (Nipmuck) for "eel-fishing place." Within the space we refer to as the Atlantic world, there were also many discreet spaces, whether they were "eel-fishing" places, the deck of a ship, ancient burial sites, the home of a god, a forest, a village, or the "horse latitudes" of the Atlantic Ocean where the wind might not blow. These spaces could be networked through the efforts of explorers and the machinery of colonization, which linked the four continents in various ways. Such linkages were subject to constant rearrangement as the requirements of empire changed from year to year. Spaces on the four continents (and ocean) also were joined into conglomerates through the histories of the people who had lived there for centuries. The lived boundaries of communities large and small, the imagined relationships between sea and shore, mountain and valley, and the ordering of spaces given in mythologies were all matters of deep background everywhere in the Atlantic world. Such classification and regulation of space was also subject to change, but that change proceeded less rapidly.

The social and political dynamics of the Atlantic world coalesced as the outcomes of competition among a range of constituencies that included European nations and indigenous populations in Africa and the Americas. The British Atlantic, for example, developed against the ongoing challenge of French, Spanish, Portuguese, and Dutch exploration and colonization, and as part of an agenda to dominate Native Americans and people in and from Africa. At times trading partners and political allies who served as models for each other, the various nations involved in the colonization of Africa and the Americas, at other times charted their courses in response to frictions among themselves; and they developed policies and practices to frustrate the plans of nations whose interests collided with their own. Traders, including Africans and Native Americans, in addition to the campaigns of political brokers and conflicts with national enemies, played crucial roles in the shaping of the Atlantic as well. They exercised significant control over timetables of colonization and commerce through either their willingness to collaborate or the resistance they offered. The diversity of the actors involved in the activities of exploration, commerce, settlement, warfare, government, religion, and the fashioning of a material culture was key to the dynamics of the Atlantic world. Lastly, taking again the example of the British, there were places such as Canada, India, and Australasia where different kinds of experiments in populating space and building colonial regimes led to comparisons that affected British operations in North America. In sum, there were complex forces at work in the Atlantic world that continuously shaped and reshaped perceptions of its boundaries, its spatial connectedness or unconnectedness, the relations of colonies to Europe and to one another, and the contact of colonists with indigenes.[8]

The process of colonialism in the Atlantic took place over centuries and developed an assortment of emphases that depended on the changing situations in European countries and their respective claims overseas. The importance of religion varied from place to place. Unlike the Spanish, the British government did not require religion to be a central part of its project. Where Spain sent padres on most of the voyages to the New World and arranged for the Roman Catholic Church to work hand in glove with the military and trade initiatives of the Crown, the British in North America and Africa were less inclined to conceive of religion as part of the official government role in colonization. The case in New France, in turn, was an experimental blending of official state involvement and free-agent initiative on the part of missionaries and their overseers. Protestant and Catholic missionaries from these European states, and others, arrived on three continents and managed to advance in some measure the cause of Christianity among Africans and Native Americans. At times church and state could be coordinated in a specific locale, regardless of the extent of official governmental oversight of a colony, as in the case of seventeenth-century New England. Even there, however, religion was a project that proceeded in fits and starts, with many a reversal and frequent internal disputes as different religious groups competed for a beachhead in the new territories. The Christian religion brought by missionaries and, more consequentially, by colonists could take any number of forms, depending on the broader field of political and social factors in a dynamic colonial setting.

The concept of an Atlantic world has been central to the work of historians for several decades; and in spite of the fact that the concept frequently has been criticized, redefined, and altered, it remains well established in historical writing because its practical advantages are continuously borne out in studies large and small.[9] Scholars make use of the concept of Atlantic world in different ways, however. The manner in which many historians and literary studies scholars have investigated the Atlantic world in recent years evidences space as an organizing principle of research (the "Atlantic world"), but it does not always indicate a commitment to "thinking spatially" in the interpretation of events. Space itself, while presumably defining the topic of study, frequently is placed on a back burner as far as interpretation is concerned. In much scholarship the Atlantic world, like Machu Picchu, the Loire Valley, Vietnam, the Sandwich Islands, the Ottoman Empire, Hong Kong, or the Nile, serves the purpose of a container—geographically molded and to some extent chronologically sized—that holds area-specific data of various sorts. The methodology deployed to interpret that data actually might only in passing have to do with physical geography, spatial metaphors, mapped behaviors, the arrangement of built environments, landscapes of various sorts, and so forth. Just because the Atlantic world is a spatial concept has not meant that those who study it have concerned themselves with space as a primary category of analysis. Some have written about legal space, racial space, gender space, or status space in general. Surprisingly few, however, have directly addressed how persons living in the Atlantic world conceptualized space, how they deliberately or accidentally created place and represented it, or how they enacted in their behaviors experiences of intersections among physical geography, body, and social boundary. Many who have written about the Atlantic world have pursued agendas that have led to clearer understandings of what historian John Elliott described as "the creation, destruction and re-creation of communities as a result of the movement across and around the Atlantic basin, of people, commodities, cultural practices."[10] But an area of study so steeped in critical theory about imperialism, comparativism, and the global, and so defined by a consideration of space—where there is ongoing debate about what land masses or bodies of water are included or excluded, about where the lines are drawn and how porous or impermeable they are, about currents, weather, and flora, fauna, and the time/space relationship itself and how it changes—has developed characteristic emphases without having much of a discussion of space itself.[11]

The Location of Religion

The essays in this collection do not together make up a "theory" of space. They do not define all that we should be thinking about when we think about the space of the Atlantic world. Rather, they illustrate some of the salutary consequences of rethinking ways in which religion has been located in Atlantic space. Although the focus here is primarily on the Americas, the essays in this volume also reference Africa, Europe, the Mediterranean, and the Pacific in their relations to the Americas and to broader Atlantic world networks. Represented here are explicit and implicit arguments for expansive views of the geography of the Atlantic world, for its artificialities and mutabilities, and for its utility when precisely defined. These essays all in one way or another are concerned with the locations and movement of persons, ideas, texts, institutions, rituals, power, and status in and through space and how that was experienced, imagined, and embraced or disdained by historical actors. Religion is the common thread, and the spatial issues that are discussed in these essays are all framed with respect to religious history and largely with respect to Christianity.

Most of the essays here emerged from the "Working Group on Religion and Space in the Atlantic World," an initiative of the Virtual Center for Spatial Humanities undertaken with support from the National Endowment for the Humanities, Florida State University, and Indiana University–Purdue University at Indianapolis. Over the course of several gatherings in Indianapolis and Tallahassee, a diverse group of scholars evaluated the possibilities for prioritizing spatial issues in studying religion in the Atlantic and for incorporating digital technology, including spatial analytic technologies, into historical and textual research on religion in the Atlantic world. The outcome of that project is the current volume, which is organized into four sections: "Maps," "Distance," "Design," and "Identities." The essays that are included in these sections vary in their approaches to space. Some stress physical geography such as topology or hydrology; others address built environment; some discuss conceptualizations and metaphors of space; some are primarily concerned with texts and maps; and some discuss the making and maintenance of place. They represent several areas of study, including history, literature, archaeology, architecture, religious studies, folklore, and geography, but also illustrate how a focus on space can serve as a platform for interdisciplinary approaches.

The studies in part 1, "Maps," focus on spatial boundaries, their absence or ambiguity, and their redrawing. In her analysis of the *Narrative* of Olaudah

Equiano, Elizabeth Maddock Dillon discusses three kinds of space—geographical, conceptual, textual—and demonstrates the ways in which they are interrelated. Equiano, who is well-known for his writing about Christian identity and evangelical salvation history, traveled extensively throughout the Atlantic world as a slave and a free man, and in an assortment of roles. His reports of his travels evidence his experience of a "multiplicity of geographical realities," the interwovenness of spatial registers of distance and closeness (or intimacy), the alternation of the absence and prevalence of conceptual space, and the Atlantic world as a space of "colliding and competing spatial regimes" of deterritorialization and reterritorialization. Most important, Equiano's experience of the Atlantic is of a space that is neither uniform nor inert but rather is volatile, fluid, heterogeneous, and subject to revision. His writing expresses his sense not only of spaces as habitable, or empty, or oppressive; it also glimpses the uneven physical geography of freedom itself. In her deep mapping of the text of the *Narrative,* Dillon offers a critical perspective on historiography and literary studies that tend to imperial views of space as apolitical and closed, and she suggests pathways to creating a more complex view of the Atlantic that might escape the gravity of that literature. Most important, she demonstrates how knowledge is framed in and by space, and how text, imagination, and geography are intertwined.

While Dillon's analysis of Equiano's *Narrative* is teeming with linkages between different kinds of space, it is not always geographical boundaries and their intersections that are the most revealing guides to the cultural dynamics of a place. Space commonly is defined through the imposition of grids, quadrilaterals, pathways, or other such forms, and generally mapped in such a way as to represent the extent of human activity there; but it is also the case that a certain kind of deliberate representation of space as empty—or at least uninhabited—likewise is a process that imposes order. Mappings of North America were accomplished in various ways, including by missionaries, whose agendas for Christianization and the transplantation of institutional power to the Americas informed their representations of space and people. George Edward Milne describes how some mappings of space in North America were accomplished through collaborations between missionary clergy and their friends at court, noting how French missionaries served as cartographic consultants to the king and in turn how both sides benefited from that arrangement. The missionaries wrote Native American religion out of the territory they explored by choosing not to chart native sacred spaces. Milne notes the silences within maps, the disregard by second-wave proselytizers of Indian accounts of the locations of demons or spirits (in spite of the recognition of those spaces by first-wave missionaries). As they replaced such spaces with silences and as they likewise marked Indian settlements with the barest clusters of dots, clergy helped shape a view of North America as constituted by vast expanses of unmarked territory ripe for settlement. Clergy in turn benefited through royal regard for their work and, over time, recognition of their role as scientists whose rational gaze upon the land was welcomed and encouraged. Missionaries demystified the space of North America by emptying it of subjectivities and personalities, and where they did not cartographically erase Native American religions and cultures, they participated in another spatial gymnastic—namely, remaking the image of Native Americans as descendants of "lost" peoples of Mediterranean origins (the same "Lost Tribes" discussed by Brandon Marriott in his essay), whose rational civility needed only be reawakened through educative exposure to European ways of life.

The politics of religious expansion sometimes determined another approach to mapping, one characterized by comprehensive detailed gridding and marking of space. Such an approach to space in Atlantic world seaports such as New York had much to do with the manner in which religious communities developed over time in those places, each religious group influencing the other as they competed for turf. Like the pathways through a small settlement that Steven A. Wernke and Lauren E. Kohut trace in their analysis of religious change in an Inka village, the streets of New York played a central role in the ways in which religious communities coalesced, engaged each other, and were altered. Kyle B. Roberts notes in his study of religion and space in early nineteenth-century New York that the imposition of a grid pattern of streets by the Commissioners Plan of 1811 facilitated the rapid Protestant migration northward from Bleecker Street to 50th Street, to new residential neighborhoods and houses of worship. That same plan likewise ensured that isolation of religious groups, one from another, would not be possible in New York. Jews and Roman Catholics might have been left downtown, but the ease of travel in a straight line (on omnibuses and railroads) enabled the kind of mixing of persons from different religious backgrounds that would make for a dynamic and shifting religious environment, even as opportunities for removing to less heterogeneous areas improved. As Roberts observes, "isolation was not an option" in "ethnically and religiously heterogeneous Atlantic World cities." The space of New Netherlands, which under the Dutch had been ordered symbolically, was transformed by religion, immigration, and the advent of commerce on a massive scale in the early nineteenth century, much as in other Atlantic ports.

Space imagined as empty, as shifting, or as highly clarified by boundary—all such schemes (as Dillon's research reminds us) encoded various understandings of distance. The essays in part 2, "Distance," explore how the organization of space was driven by religious interests but also how religion itself adapted to spatial ordering and reordering initiated by other cultural authorities and how distance was variously perceived by the parties involved. How vast were the territories mapped by Father Paul du Poisson? How far was New Orleans from Québec, London from Jamaica, the Bight of Biafra from Bahi'a? The research here addresses in various ways the theme of distance and in the process remarks on often overlooked aspects of the religious world of the Atlantic. It is important to bear in mind that European missionaries' thinking about time and space was as much shaped by their everyday experiences in the mission field as by geographical knowledge that had been collected by explorers and organized by church officials into estimations of distance, calculation of routes, and the identification of target populations. Luca Codignola reminds us that the Americas were not privileged in Roman Catholic plans for missionizing and that in fact in the early seventeenth century the Americas trailed Asia, the Middle East, and central Africa in terms of their priority in the business of Propaganda Fide. The Atlantic world that scholars have studied so closely since the late twentieth century barely existed for church bureaucrats at that time, comparatively speaking. Codignola notes, moreover, that the activities of Catholic missionaries on the ground in America formed in them a mental geography that vastly underestimated the distance from the Americas to Asia, confused the similarities and differences in climate of one region vis-à-vis another, strangely imagined local demographics, and otherwise peculiarly construed space and time. Missionary time and space were reckoned in more complex ways than as chronological time or physical distance, and the Roman geography of the Atlantic developed along lines that illustrate how spatial locations could be imagined as near to each other or as far apart, depending upon the agendas of those who discussed them.

The point made by Codignola that the Vatican looked eastward before it looked across the Atlantic resonates with some recent criticism of the concept of an Atlantic world by Peter A. Coclanis.[12] The point is reiterated by Brandon Marriott, who suggests how the space of the Atlantic was diminished in the imaginations of some persons and how the eastern Mediterranean was conceptually interwoven with the Americas. He notes that religious thinking about the space of the Atlantic was shaped in part by religious and ethnic communications networks that extended into territories not typically located by historians within an Atlantic world. Marriott's tracking of the emergence of the story of Native Americans as remnants of the Lost Tribes of Jews indicates how the reporting of events in the eastern Mediterranean and Middle East could converge in Western Europe with accounts of life in the Americas. The seventeenth-century emergence of a popular understanding of North American Indians as distant Jews had to do as much with the transmission of stories westward to Amsterdam from the Levant as it did the eastward transit of writings of Protestant missionaries in New England (and Spanish padres in South America). Marriott analyzes how the intertwining of various Jewish and Christian networks transmitting ideas about the Lost Tribes established the framework for locating the descendants of those tribes in the New World and equally in Arabia. In that process, space was compressed by the religious imagination, which placed disparate communities together as a related people even though those various populations were separated by vast distances. A shared religious orientation towards time and space—the eschatological visions of Jews and Christians—advanced the intertwining of ideas about the Lost Tribes and enabled the refinement and enrichment of interpretation about the history of American indigenes. The resulting religious vision made the distant Americas seem closer in space and coordinated in time.

In the same way that Marriott asks us to look eastward from Europe to understand fully the networking of religious ideas in the Atlantic, Richard J. Callahan, Jr., proposes that we should look westward from the Atlantic, to the Pacific, to understand how New England whalers were religiously oriented to the sea. Callahan observes that historians have yet to explore fully the manner in which the space of the ocean itself, rather than as a connector defined by the land masses that it touched, required certain kinds of religious orientations—to both space and time—that differed markedly from life on land. Noting that the history of whaling is intertwined with religious history, he also observes that the Christian traditions that were manifested in the seamen's churches in ports were present on board ships alongside popular initiation rituals, moral rephrasings, burials at sea, the engagement of such quasi-religious techniques as mesmerism, and the curious building of memorials to dead sailors on islands halfway around the world from their homes. Callahan also notes how the enormous space of the sea could be reduced to almost nothing in the imaginations of sailors—an indication, alongside others, of how memory, belief, and geography collaborated in the spatial thinking of whalers. His analysis also clarifies the ocean as a vast liminal space in which experimentation with mesmerism and other novel metaphysical technologies framed the religious perspectives of sailors right alongside Christian doctrine.

The lives of Callahan's sailors were profoundly conditioned by the fact of their physical situatedness on wooden ships built to hunt whales on the oceans. Whale boats were homes at sea for those who sailed them. Actual physical design—the construction of built environment—has a central role in the creation of place. It also brings consequences for the creation and maintenance of community and for the imagining of relations between religious people and the supernatural figures they care about. In part 3, "Design," are some examples of how the construction of boundary, pathway, and network in the physical environment is related to religious life. One approach is to consider how individuals are directed in their movements through space by those in power who have laid out the arteries for persons' passage from one location to another (walking, travel by horse, by canal, and so forth). In their analysis of the reordering of space in an Inka settlement in the Andean highlands, Steven A. Wernke and Lauren E. Kohut frame the everyday lives of the inhabitants as prospective converts to Christianity. The Spanish church and Crown, working together in the securing of empire in the Americas, placed supreme importance on restructuring the spaces of everyday life in indigenous settlements as a means to establishing a social order resonant with Spanish values and goals. That project was made explicit in writings by Spanish commentators and planners. In reading the archaeological record at Malata, a first-generation post-conquest site, Wernke and Kohut identify the transition from Inka to Spanish layout of the settlement. That transition is represented in the siting of the Spanish chapel, public buildings, and plaza in such a way as to materially impress upon persons the "surveillance power" of Crown and church. Pathways were arranged as feeders to a main artery that efficiently delivered persons into the plaza in an official way and in so doing reinforced the panoptic gaze of the church and state. Just as important, the creation of new networks of travel through the site skirted the Inka ceremonial sites, thereby reducing awareness in everyday life of those sites and reducing their power. The enforcement of a "spatial hegemony" in the transition of Malata to a missionary *doctrina* was undertaken through a planning process that fostered "unmediated relationships" between households and the Spanish religious and governmental institutions.

In the colonized territories of the Atlantic world, like-minded religious persons lived with one another in communities physically built to foster certain desired traits and ideals among members. Spanish colonial towns, the various *reducciones* (as we have seen in the Warner/Kohut research), the New England "holy commonwealths," and other styles of built settings for community—including, arguably, the plantation itself[13]—all shaped the religious practice and agendas of those who inhabited and, especially, administrated them. In highly migratory settings, such as all such Christian communities were in the Atlantic world outside of Europe and North Africa, the design of the physical spaces of community and belonging were significant as well for their markings of space as outposts on the periphery. For example, the transplantation of the female religious cloister from France to North America represented an attempt to organize space in New Orleans and Québec along lines that had deep roots in the religious practice of French nuns. As Jan Noel demonstrates, however, the making of place in the New World required recognition that the politics, demographics, and trading culture of emerging North American port cities differed from the circumstances of city life in France, and especially from Paris, where life in the cloister had not changed in centuries. Noel describes how the cloister evolved as Ursuline and Augustinian nuns came to terms with their failures in missionary endeavors to Native Americans and began to take on a more active role in the commercial, educational, care-related-service, and managerial aspects of public life. While remaining cloistered—officially "within the walls"—they developed skill in cultivating relationships with government leaders, wealthy sponsors, and even military conquerors, all of which were calibrated to enable them to retain their cloistered properties and way of life while still projecting authority derived from their conservation of tradition. The religious space of the "well-constructed box" in North America proved resilient, offering autonomy and solidarity for religious women and serving as a point of reference for social stability as nuns took on larger roles in the broader community. In certain respects, then, the evolving American cloister acquired a profile different from its analogues in France.

Some Christian religious spaces in the Americas were the result of deliberate spatial ordering, of the transplantation to New France of the stone-walled convent or the arrangement of buildings around a plaza. Sometimes, however, spatial design comes accidentally, or at least surprisingly, and when that happens, religious authorities might devise ways in which to exploit emergent anomalies in the interest of conserving tradition and extending their power. We see aspects of that process in Sing D'Arcy's mapping of the space of the Christian house of worship in its transformations during the Spanish Reconquista and during the colonization of Mexico on the other side of the Atlantic. D'Arcy explains how the emergence of the *iglesia-salón,* or church hall, in Iberian architecture was shaped by the possession of mosques after the defeat of Muslims and their renovation and reconsecration as Christian churches. In that process of renewal, the Spanish Baroque emerged most strikingly in interior design and decoration. All the *máquinas*—the artifices of *retablos,* sacramental chapels, *camarines,* organ cases, and ephemerae—were refined in such a way as to constitute a grand theater of stimulation of wonder and awe. This "suite of machines," a kind of integrated rhetoric of structure within the *iglesia-salón,* made its way to the New World, but there it took a distinct form as part of the Ibero-American Baroque, a style that was deeply rooted in the spatial realities of urban life in places such as Mexico City. The colonial Spanish cities, laid out in mathematically patterned grids, differed from Iberian cities with their winding alleyways, random public spaces, and odd contours. The new spatial context was crucial, allowing the Mexico City Cathedral, placed beside the *Zócalo,* its steps both separating and joining church and square, to serve as a "nexus of civic and sacred mediated by a facade" in the Spanish Christianopolis. Like the New York described by Kyle Roberts, where street layout had consequences for the religious settling and resettling of Manhattan Island, urban design that relied upon the gridding of streets, as D'Arcy observes, prompted a rethinking of the strategic ends of siting the most important cathedral in Mexico.

Noel's study of the French cloister suggests the adaptability of the nuns who lived within it. Far from France, they nevertheless disciplined themselves to behave as though they were still intimately engaged with the traditions of the home country. Nevertheless, a sense of distance from home was inevitable in their practice of tradition, and they adjusted their expectations in ways that proved advantageous to fashioning an understanding of themselves as a community on the margins of empire. The walled cloister provided a physical environment that helped them remember transatlantic spatial continuities and enabled their adaptation. In certain instances, North American religious groups experienced more complex challenges in understanding their relation to their European roots. Both distance and design typically played a role in such cases. The studies in part 4, "Identities," address more specifically how removal from one space to another prompted religious communities to rethink who they were and where they belonged. Such rethinkings typically were difficult. The fledgling communities of Methodists in Ontario and Québec that are the subject of Todd Webb's research experienced a strong sense of spatial isolation from British Wesleyans even as they sought to build closer relationships with leaders there. With communication networks rudimentary at best and the supervisory bureaucracy of the missionary societies unreliable in its attentions to Canada, some Methodists in Canada came to feel abandoned by their community on the other side of the Atlantic. The distance was too far, the engagement between parties irregular and ambiguous, and the built environment lacking in representations of what it meant to be British. The coalescence of a transatlantic British Wesleyan church in the 1860s was too little and too late to prevent Canadian Methodists from reimagining themselves as "better" Britons than their brethren overseas. They fashioned a sense of their community as superior to their British counterparts, imagining themselves to represent a way of life that was an improvement on Britain. Some even considered their Britishness at risk through continued collaboration with the metropole. What sometimes has seemed a Canadian Methodist exceptionalism emerged in the nineteenth century through Canadian Methodists' reflections on their distance, geographically and culturally, from Britain and from a sense of isolation that developed alongside their fidelity to an idea of what it meant to be truly British. Cultural space, sometimes, could be dramatically reimagined when a community was distant from familiar physical space.

Connections between state and religion were present in all territories of the early Atlantic world and colonial Christian communities early on tended to understand themselves largely in terms of their collaboration with a territorially defined state. Increasingly, however, there were exceptions to that tendency, not only because of political revolutions or consequences of isolation (such as Webb's Canadian Methodists experienced) but because of broader, deeper changes in the political and social organization of Europe. One of the most important changes in the organization of Christian churches in the Atlantic world was the gradual transition from the scheme of *cuius regio eius religio,* an artifact of the Peace of Augsburg (1555) and the Peace of Westphalia (1648), which recognized the religion of the ruler of the state as the religion of the realm. Even before the full consequences of transition from the old order were fully felt, the migration of Christian groups from one location to another around the Atlantic was complex because of the necessity of coming to terms with weak spatial identity, and therefore ambiguous religious authority, on the periphery of empire. The weakening of the scheme of *cuius regio eius religio* compounded the challenge. As Elizabeth Lewis Pardoe points out, Lutheran clergy in the eighteenth-century British colonies in North America had no prince to look to in order to frame a program of local ministry. In that fluid environment, Lutherans cobbled together from a combination of missionary initiatives, personal circumstances, political negotiations, and accidents a sense of where to found congregations and how to sustain them. Absent the controlling narrative of spatial identity (that is, the territory of the religious state), clergy "had to reshape colonists' spatial assumptions about religious practice." She shows that process to be an unpredictable drama rich in incidents of random conversions, racial prejudices, adultery, doctrinal debate, haggling over money, fisticuffs, illegitimate births, best intentions, and congregations meeting haphazardly in barns. In the end—after half a century of experimentation in what Henry Muhlenburg called "this strange, wild country!"—an area designated "Pennsylvania and the Adjacent States" was settled upon as the spatial framework for the Evangelical Lutheran Ministerium, and the "place" of religion coalesced apart from the legitimating oversight of a civil ruler of that place.

Other religious communities in the British North American colonies also found ways to maintain themselves in a new place. That project frequently involved unexpected experiences of space as shared with other religious groups, which, of course, was not only a colonial matter, but in the colonies there could be complicating factors. Seeking to come to terms with the requirement for establishing appropriate relationships between the religious body and the body politic in colonial North America—especially in places such as the British middle colonies, where there was a diversity of Christianities—communities sought to map conceptually the relationships among those many groups. The spread of Christianity through the Atlantic world prompted Protestant Europeans and Euro-Americans to refine their thinking about relationships between members of a religious group who were dispersed among variously emplaced religious communities as those memberships were extended over great distances. Heather Miyano Kopelson demonstrates how we can glimpse in the spatial thinking of Puritans and others varying conceptualizations of the interconnectedness of persons in the religious body and the body politic. Kopelson points out that the popular spatial image of Christians living together as a "body of Christ" represented an understanding of persons joined in community that was continually transformed through divine grace. The body of Christ above all was a salvific community, and relations between communities of baptized persons contained by that body—Quakers, Baptists, Catholics, and others—were dynamic, so that the Body of Christ was characterized by variability, relativity, activity, and contingency. The ideal of the body politic, on the other hand, was grounded in a view of social order in which stasis and hierarchy were the characteristic features. The interplay between those two models, and especially the tension between them, framed an assortment of problems that emerged with the growth of population and commerce in the Atlantic. Were baptized slaves, for example, in the body or out of the body? Could the two spatially defined models of relationships between persons be integrated, or were they set intractably against each other? Kopelson outlines this key aspect of the spatial thinking of colonial Americans and notes how attention to notions of the body of Christ enables us to see more clearly some of the "deep contingency" of colonial life.

Religion and Space

The distinctive contributions made by the scholars who have contributed to this volume can be assessed more fully when read against the background of some previous approaches to the study of religion and space. Like most intellectual turns in the humanities, the study of space has proceeded in fits and starts. Among historians the tendency has been to experiment with integrating GIS (Geographic Information Systems) technology into research, and there have been successes on that front.[14] Scholars working in the field of literary studies, broadly considered, increasingly have experimented with GIS in spatially framing data digitally mined from large corpora, also with promising results. Neither historians nor literary scholars, however, have fully availed themselves of the contributions made by another academic tribe, the geographers. Only occasionally has research in the humanities critically comprehended the rich aggregated literature of geographers, who in the latter part of the twentieth century made impressive strides in generating language to analyze space and place and in integrating analyses of social structuration with metric demographic, commercial, and legal data, while redirecting the field to an awareness of the importance of gender, race, and ethnicity, and the significance of authorial voice in the discussion of geographies.[15]

Taken together, the geographical research accomplished over recent decades has amounted to a hothouse of ideas ripe for transplantation into the neighboring academic vineyards of the humanities. Humanities researchers as a whole, for all their recent discussion of space, remain inclined to mine from familiar critical and theoretical texts within their own fields to gain an edge in interpretation. Philosophers, historians, religion researchers, those working in literary studies, and classicists, among others, have returned to Heidegger, for example, as they have thought more about space. They have reread Durkheim. The writings of Walter Benjamin and Gaston Bachelard have appeared on seminar reading lists. Spatial interpretations that referenced Marx, Simmel, and Freud have proliferated. Tellingly, humanities scholars initially embraced the spatial turn as a call to scrutinize the manner in which spatial metaphors were involved in the construction of *mentalité* and the practice of everyday life. Consequently, physical geography remained underrecognized as metaphors of space came under more serious investigation. That tendency toward decrypting metaphor was one indication of the collateral flow of academic currents, illustrated elsewhere by the late-twentieth-century surge of interest in study of the body, where the fashion was for conceptualizing the body largely as a field upon which were engraved social realities and various regimes of power. The body as blood, bone, and brains—which was the framework for a nascent cognitive science among other initiatives—had not yet enthused humanities researchers. In short, in 1980 the angle of approach to space among humanities scholars had more in common with George Lakoff and Mark Johnson's *Metaphors We Live By* than with Anne Buttimer and David Seamon's *The Human Experience of Space and Place,* both of which appeared that year, or even vis-à-vis the humanities-friendly treatment of space by Henri Lefebvre in *La Production de l'Espace.*[16] Most humanities scholars appeared to have minimal interest in what geographers were doing.

Humanities scholars who have experimented with new perspectives on space, and especially physical space, have benefited by overtures made to them by geographers. In the 1970s geographers—Yi-Fu Tuan and Edward Relph, especially—began to throw lines to colleagues in the humanities by actively bending the genre of geographical writing toward the humanities and in the process reconceptualizing human geography in a way that would find an audience among those working in humanities disciplines.[17] While such undertakings require time to sink into academic discourses, they helped seed research in several branches of the humanities. Among the many noteworthy forays into a more complex study of space that subsequently emerged in humanities scholarship, the historian William Cronon's *Nature's Metropolis: Chicago and the Great West,* which appeared in 1991, substantially incorporated the insights of academic geographic literature and broke ground for serious discussion of the necessity for integrating complex analysis of physical space into humanities research. The multidisciplinary writer Jared Diamond offered another example, *Guns, Germs, and Steel: The Fates of Human Societies* (1997), which attracted praise and criticism alike for its sharp focus on the environmental (physical) aspects of the development of societies. More recently, the importance of space has been stressed by Barry Cunliffe in *Europe Between the Oceans: 9000 BC–AD 1000* (2008), a historical interpretation that foregrounds geographic features in the development of European cultures, which has been commended (perhaps too simply) as illustrative of how "geography is destiny."[18] In literary studies, Franco Moretti's groundbreaking *Atlas of the European Novel, 1800–1900* (1998), with its one hundred maps and inclination to quantification, charted the distribution of books in space and time as a way of analyzing the development of literary forms.[19]

In the specific case of religious studies scholarship, the weak engagement with cutting-edge geographic research is striking. There are exceptions,[20] but many religious studies scholars remain invested in an intellectual agenda bearing the residue of theological partisanships (although rarely explicit) and therefore are less active in engaging geographic literature about space and place that does not converge with traditionally phenomenological, literary, and ritual-studies approaches to religious history that were forged in collaborations with nineteenth- and twentieth-century theological vocabularies. Among religious studies scholars, including those whose research takes a historical approach, there has been much discussion about space—more than fifty papers delivered at the 2013 annual meeting of the American Academy of Religion were about space—alongside publication of a number of creative analyses of religion and space in delimited social contexts. But we should ask why much of that scholarship has not been as involved in the core concerns of the spatial turn as have some other parts of the humanities.

The hesitation of religious studies scholars to directly and systematically address the importance of space was noticed by Lonnie D. Kliever in 1977.[21] Since then, some researchers in the field have experimented with the new emphasis on geography, environment, and physical space, but much academic writing about religion remains committed to a specific project of "theorizing religion and space" that has developed from the work of Mircea Eliade, who made "sacred space" central to religion. Drawing on the writings of geographer Pierre Deffontaines, and with an eye to Durkheim, Marcel Mauss, and Gerardus van der Leeuw, Eliade argued that humans represented space as sacred through their organization of it in terms of centers and peripheries and that they maintained it in ritualized remembering, performing stories about how it came to be. What his contemporary Eric Isaac called "the urge to put heaven on earth" and detailed as a process by which "hallowed sites" were created in the ongoing ritual overlay onto space of the "cosmic pattern" Eliade understood as the natural practice of "*homo religiosus.*" In Eliade's phenomenological approach to religion and space, persons ritually responded to "the sacred" in such a way as to mark space and time, in some cases designating sites where the sacred was present and in other cases inventing calendars marking its recurrence in cycles. In simple terms, the world for Eliade was divided into the sacred (that is, the meaningful, the powerful) and the profane; humans had profound encounters with a transhistorical sacred; and communities organized space around sacred centers, or *axes mundi.*

At times, academic writing about "sacred space" has appeared to be more about asserting that there is such a thing as sacred space than about critically analyzing its contents. Put another way, proposals for understanding religious emplacements have missed opportunities for advancing critical spatial analysis when they have assumed that there is prior agreement about the existence of a kind of deep transhistorical phenomenon of "sacred space." Criticism of the notion of human contact with a reified "sacred" resulting in the detection of sacred space has prompted religion scholars to look elsewhere for theoretical support in analyzing religion and space. In the early 1970s Larry Shiner pointed out that Eliade's theory of sacred space (and its redeployment by religion scholars who embraced it) missed the component of "human spatiality." Shiner endeavored "to show how the typical polarity of sacred and profane space has been overdrawn to the point of obscuring the actual character of human spatiality in its manifold dimensions." Anticipating by several decades the emergence of scholarly interest in "lived religion," Shiner proposed that religion scholars had gotten distracted from thinking productively about "lived space," pointing out that "only by walking through a building or a city square do we come to sense its spatiality." Drawing on Merleau-Ponty and again foreshadowing the late-twentieth-century writing of Michel de Certeau and Bruno Latour, Shiner described human space as "kinesthetic because it is composed of pathways for movement—the enclosure of the house or factory, the piazza, the street, the gateways, or simply the gaps between the trees of a park or the flower beds of a garden. Human space is this separation of things which gives the possibility of movement, of coming closer and bringing closer, of a 'here' and 'there.'"[22]

Shiner's call for joining the study of religion to an appreciation for "human spatiality" and "lived space" prompted some to rethink Eliade's notion of sacred space. One writer who has been important in that regard is Jonathan Z. Smith, whose *To Take Place: Toward Theory in Ritual* (1987) joined a critique of the idea of "the sacred" to a proposal that space was made sacred by ritual. Sacred space, in other words, was not an absolute, independent of human conceptualizations of it. All conceptualizations of space as sacred are cultural artifacts, socially constructed and, as such, contingent and arbitrary. In the interest of distancing himself from some of the phenomenological freight of the term "sacred space," Smith wrote instead about place. For Smith, human activity in ritual makes "place": "Human beings are not placed, they bring place into being."[23] Smith's view of ritual accordingly is one that divides space into that which is meaningful and purposeful and that which is meaningless and accidental (although there is creative tension between them), with the presence or absence of ritual activity being the determinant.[24] While tacking away from certain aspects of Eliade's theory, Smith nevertheless retains others. As ritual studies researcher Ronald Grimes noted, Smith's theory relies both on metaphorical and geographic understandings of space, but unevenly so, so that in the end "metaphorical emplacement is more determinative than geographical place." Because conceptualized space is more important than physical, geographical space, "Smith's theory disembodies ritual," a central aspect of religious practice.[25] Viewed as part of a larger field of humanities scholarship, Smith's privileging of metaphorical space accorded with the similar late-twentieth-century trend in the study of the body mentioned above.

Although Smith does not directly reference Michel de Certeau's discussion of space in *The Practice of Everyday Life* (1984), Smith's theory of ritual and the making of place has much in common with Certeau's emphasis on the role of practice in creating place (called "space" by Certeau, confusingly, for Anglophone readers, inverting the usual reference to space/place).[26] Just as Smith's rituals as they unfolded with respect to remembered stories made place, so also do Certeau's human actors in the city navigate through space in such a way as to layer it with interlocking itineraries, or "narratives," that accomplish something similar. There are important differences between the two, however. In *The Practice of Everyday Life,* Certeau does not theorize "meaningful" place as opposed to "meaningless" space, and there is no dividing the world into sacred and profane. Against a backdrop of recent social thought and geographical discussions among European researchers,[27] Certeau prefers to speak of place as a locative order of the "proper." Tradition, law, and power are located there, as well as "discipline," in the Foucauldian sense.[28] Space (what Smith would call "place") is conceptualized as a network of antidiscipline, a field of tactics, where actors in their everyday practice confront, recast, and undermine disciplinary strategies. The realm of law and power is represented and experienced largely as coherent and stable, while space (for example, Smith's "place"), as it is continuously made and remade by human navigators as they move through it, is about the variability, accidents, and contingencies of daily practice: "Space is a practiced place. Thus the street geometrically defined by urban planning is transformed into a space by walkers."[29] Walkers in the city do not in their habitual but evolving engagement of that space create it as meaningful apart from the discipline that already structures it. As actors, they practice their lives always in relationship both to place (power and law) and to the space they make with others on a daily basis. What matters, in short, is Certeau's proposal of the interrelationship of physical geography (built and unbuilt environment), social structuration (such as economic or gender orders), actors' conceptualizations of place and space, and the purposeful or experimental activity of humans as they move physically in space.[30]

The most promising studies of religion in which space plays a prominent role are moving away from a preoccupation with the notion of sacred space. Spatial thinking as it has developed within the humanities as a whole in recent decades, like thinking about the body, has become richer and more nuanced as it has incorporated a view of space that takes physical geography seriously. This is not to say that the project of human geography represented by the writings of Tuan, Relph, and others has disappeared. It has not. Rather, in the humanities, spatial thinking increasingly is in evidence as collaboration between theories that stress physical environment and approaches that foreground human conceptualizations of space—and their linguistic and imagistic expressions. Among religion scholars, some forays in that direction remain linked to earlier concerns about the sacred and sacred space, but in more complex fashion. Veikko Anttonen, reading Durkheim, Mary Douglas, and W. Richard Comstock, has written about the difficulties posed by phenomenological approaches to religion that rely on the category of "the sacred." He has proposed a kind of cognitive science approach that focuses on body and territory as categories that are present preconceptually and serve as a foundation for coalescence of the category of the sacred, which is understood as "boundary" and is managed by ritual.[31] Thomas A. Tweed has proposed a similar model, offering it as a theory of religion, which he defines in spatial tropes of crossing and dwelling, and with the implication that religion is experientially diasporic. While moving away from older notions of the sacred, Tweed's thinking still plays on the line between a view of religion as grounded in engagement of the "suprahuman" and as a kind of creative, even subversive, spatially defined behavior. "As spatial practices," wrote Tweed, "religions designate where we are *from,* identify whom we are *with,* and prescribe how we move *across.*"[32] Kim Knott likewise has been ambitious in incorporating a spatial approach to the study of religion. In *The Location of Religion,* she outlines a methodology for the study of religion that synthesizes recent scholarship in the humanities and social sciences, especially recent geographical research. Her methodology is grounded in the claim that the body is the "source" of space and in the recognition of the various dimensions of space, including the physical, social, and mental, and the intersections among them. Demonstrating how spatial thinking can lead us to clearer understandings of the physical exercise of power in religion as well as to the conceptual formation of space and its representation in religion, she models an approach that observes the diachronic extensiveness of religion at the same time that it analyzes patterns visible synchronically. In short, her work is not a theory of religion—and it differs from most previous work on religion and space on that point—but rather a kind of critical inventory of tools and a blueprint for their application to the study of religious locales.[33]

Times in Space

The concept of an Atlantic world is largely the creation of historians, including literary historians, who define their approaches by relating chronologies. That is, they are concerned with diachrony, cause and effect, change over time, how we got from there to here. For those whose historical research focuses on religion, there are some added twists. Eschatologies, salvation histories, karmic cycles and omega points, the rise and fall of ancient religious institutions, the refinement or decay of theological standpoints, and mythologies about the creation of the universe all have been at the core of what religion scholars study. Time is at the center of historical writing about religion, then, for obvious reasons, but space is emerging more visibly alongside it. "The great obsession of the nineteenth century," wrote Foucault, "was, as we know, history: with its themes of development and of suspension, of crisis, and cycle, themes of the ever-accumulating past, with its great preponderance of dead men and the menacing glaciation of the world. The nineteenth century found its essential mythological resources in the second principle of thermodynamics—The present epoch will perhaps be above all the epoch of space."[34] Whether we need or should want an "epoch of space" is debatable. But by thinking spatially and conducting our research utilizing perspectives that arise from that orientation, we position ourselves to better advance our understanding of religious people, practices, and institutions in the Atlantic world.

PART ONE

MAPS

A Sea of Texts

The Atlantic World, Spatial Mapping, and Equiano's *Narrative*

Elizabeth Maddock Dillon

Writing has nothing to do with signifying. It has to do with surveying, mapping, even realms that are yet to come.

Gilles Deleuze and Félix Guattari, *A Thousand Plateaus,* 4–5

The "Atlantic World" is a spatial concept. Literally, the "Atlantic" is an ocean, and in recent years, historians and literary scholars have increasingly called upon this ocean to define the field of study in which they work. Scholars who might once have worked in the areas of early American literature or British imperial history have traded a politically and nationally delimited field for a spatially and geographically defined one. There are many good reasons for this development, not least of which is the challenge and excitement of constructing a field imaginary in which the nation-state does not (for those who work in prenational American contexts, for instance) anachronistically organize the canon of meaningful works and the shape of intellectual inquiry. And indeed, the "Atlantic world" is a term that seems to catch at the lived reality of the many people, goods, ideas, biota, and texts that circulated between and among Europe, Africa, and the Americas in the period of European colonization of the Americas, as well as in later periods—periods that may, in turn, be productively viewed in terms of the neoimperial and/or postcolonial national cultures accreted on the bones of this (Atlantic) colonial history. But what are the ramifications of turning to a *spatial* term to define a field of history and literature? More broadly, we might ask, what is the relation of Atlantic *space* to the humanities work being performed under the rubric of its title?

Atlantic Space

This essay offers some exploratory thoughts about the relation between space and the discipline of Atlantic literary and textual studies in particular. The term

"Atlantic" currently appears to have many meanings: the Atlantic in the "Atlantic world" is an ocean, an economy, a cultural network, an imperial territory, and a map of diasporic dispersal, among other things. David Armitage's useful three-part taxonomy of Atlantic history points to divergent methodologies that have taken shape within the field: Armitage distinguishes circum-Atlantic history (which is transnational, focusing on cultures and histories created by oceanic travel), trans-Atlantic history (which is international, focusing on comparing discrete nations around the Atlantic), and cis-Atlantic history (which is national or regional, focusing on specific sites as they exist within an Atlantic context).[1] Armitage's schematization indicates that divergent spatializations are encompassed in the field of Atlantic studies, but all of these spatializations presuppose the coherence of a shared geographical map—that is, they presuppose a standard cartographic notion of the Atlantic as a spatially homogenous field. This notion of space—one based on an ontology of "the God's eye view of space as dead, static, closed, and representationally fixed," as the geographer Matthew Sparkes puts it—has increasingly come under scrutiny in the field of critical geography.[2] Building on critical understandings of space as multivalent and open-ended, this essay attends more closely to the unevenness that inheres within Atlantic space, pursuing, in particular, Doreen Massey's account of space as "the product of interrelations . . . as the sphere therefore of coexisting heterogeneity"[3] within an eighteenth-century Atlantic register.

The phrase "coexisting heterogeneity" is an apt descriptor of Olaudah Equiano's self-presentation in the title of his well-known autobiography, *The Interesting Narrative of the Life of Olaudah Equiano, or Gustavus Vassa, The African. Written by Himself* (1789). The contrapuntal staging of his African name ("Olaudah Equiano"), his European name ("Gustavus Vassa," a name enjoined upon him by a slave master), and the designation "African" within the title points to the coexistence of competing and not easily reconcilable identities: in short, the title indicates, there is not a way to inscribe Equiano's name that is singular and reducible to one language, one cosmography, one nomenclature. Equiano's text narrates the author's extensive travels—both forced and free—within an eighteenth-century Atlantic world geography: born in Africa, sold in the slave yards of Barbados, forced to labor in the fields of Virginia, purchased by a captain in the British Royal Navy, baptized in London, battle-tested under fire in waters off France and Canada, beaten almost to death in the streets of Savannah, Georgia, freed while working as a merchant/sailor in the Caribbean, employed as a hairdresser in London and on ships traveling to locations from Smyrna to Greenland, hired to oversee slaves on a Mosquito Coast plantation, and ultimately destined for renown in England as an advocate for the abolitionist cause—Equiano's narrative repeatedly crisscrosses the Atlantic Ocean. Indeed, in its textual and spatial coverage of key sites and narratives of the Atlantic

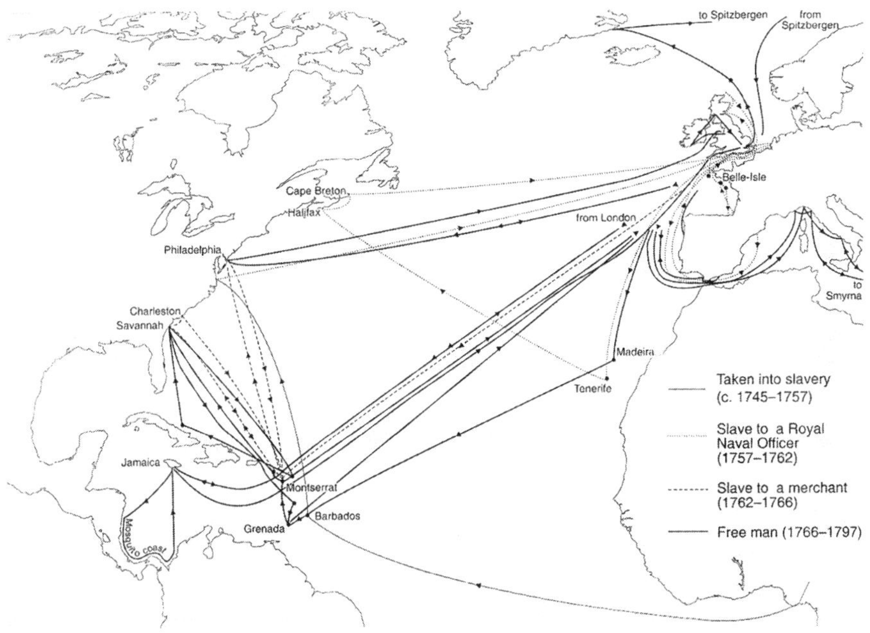

Fig. 1. Map of Equiano's travels as described in the *Narrative,* created by Professor Miles Ogborn and Edward Oliver, School of Geography, Queen Mary University of London. I am grateful to Miles Ogborn for permission to republish this map which appears in his book, *Global Lives* (Cambridge University Press, 2008), as well as on a website about Equiano authored by Brycchan Carey: http://www.brycchancarey.com/equiano/map1.htm.

world, his text exemplifies the contours of the eighteenth-century Atlantic world: a map of the routes of Equiano's travels (see fig. 1) thus sketches out a geography that gives material substance to the concept of the Atlantic world. Yet the map of Equiano's routes of travel, much as it helpfully materializes the Atlantic-ness of Equiano's life for us, nonetheless tends to flatten out the very heterogeneity of identity that Equiano asserts in the title of his narrative. In other words, the spatial register of the map—which depicts the Atlantic Ocean and its littoral as a unified field—tends to erase the disjunctive nature of the language Equiano himself employs to describe the experience of inhabiting the uneven terrain of the Atlantic world. How might one map, then, an Atlantic unevenness in such a way as to register the spatial nature of irreconcilable cosmologies, of forced encounter, of "coexisting heterogeneity" that informs Equiano's *Narrative,* and, more broadly, the vast body of texts that the eighteenth-century Atlantic world generated?

What follows takes Equiano's *Narrative* as a case study for considering some of the possibilities of textual mapping that new technologies offer us as a means of understanding the Atlantic world and its competing and uneven spatialities. This essay (and this volume) grows out of a working group on the topic of religion, the Atlantic world, and Geographic Information Systems (GIS); more broadly, the working group's concern is with spatial thought, mapping technologies, and the humanities. Given that the mapping technology of GIS has largely been the purview of positivist scholarship, something of a conceptual wall separates much existing GIS work from scholarship in the humanities: as John Corrigan has argued, GIS scholarship "privileges disambiguation," whereas humanities scholarship values the "multivalent, equivocal, and protean."[4] As such, the contrast between the flatness of the map of Equiano's travels and the linguistic richness of Equiano's multivalent title sketched out above would seem to serve as evidence of precisely the conceptual wall that enables humanities scholars—especially those invested in textual and literary analysis (including myself)—to dismiss positivist mapping technologies (including standard cartography and GIS) as ontologically insufficient tools of analysis. And yet a number of factors mitigate against such a dismissal, first among which is the spatial nature of the field of the Atlantic world that humanities scholars have recently turned to—a spatial nature that mapping technologies are inarguably well positioned to explore. Second among the important reasons for turning to technologies such as GIS for analyzing Atlantic world texts is the fact that vast digitization projects of these texts are now underway in the humanities. As such, the nature of the text itself has changed; databases of texts are now available for analysis that are too large for a single individual to read but that digital tools can parse in potentially meaningful and generative ways. Looking closely at the relations of text and space in Equiano's *Narrative* demonstrates that forms of mapping using positivist technologies such as text-mining and GIS might indeed provide insight into the unevenness and heterogeneity of the eighteenth-century Atlantic world and the spatial dimensions of that field.

Textual Space

The online catalog of one major research library reveals that twelve separate electronic editions of Equiano's *Narrative* are now available for download and immediate viewing on the computer screen of those with access to the library's resources. While not all institutions will have as many editions available, such a catalog demonstrates that Equiano's *Narrative* can be found in multiple forms in the databases of eighteenth-century English and colonial American texts compiled and marketed by Readex (Archive Americana), Gale Cengage (Eighteenth Century Collections Online), and Proquest (African Writers Series, Literature Online), all of which are increasingly widely available. An electronic edition of Equiano's *Narrative* is also available through Project Gutenberg, a dataspace that digitizes texts not under copyright and makes them available for free. In addition to these electronic editions, at least fifteen different print editions of Equiano's *Narrative* have appeared during the past decade. Clearly, Equiano's *Narrative* is in wide circulation at the moment and is in particularly heavy rotation in the college classroom. Notably, however, the widespread presence and availability of electronic editions of a text such as Equiano's *Narrative,* in addition to standard print editions aimed at the college market, is a recent development and one that has likely already changed the way the text is viewed and analyzed in the classroom by students.[5]

Why is reading an electronic edition of the text different from reading it on paper? Most obviously, the mode of navigating an electronic text is significantly different from that of perusing a printed text: rather than turning to a given page, one navigates to a page or passage by means of a numerical or keyword search. Thus, for instance, if a student using an electronic edition of the text is asked to turn to the page on which Equiano recounts the moment of purchasing his freedom from slavery, he or she might well perform a keyword search on the term "freedom" or "free"—a search that would return a list of passages from the *Narrative* that uses these terms. While such a search could (and likely would) be narrowed with additional keywords and/or phrases to locate the precise moment when Equiano is legally freed, the list of passages that include the words "freedom" and "free" is, nonetheless, intriguing and analytically suggestive. Indeed, this series of passages, read as a group (as a student might, while paging through these passages on the electronic screen), suggests that the moment of acquiring freedom is not singular for Equiano but rather, appears repeatedly in different discursive forms across the *Narrative.*

A brief look at a few of these passages gives one a sense of the range of discursive fields in which the term "freedom" operates for Equiano. Equiano's legal release from slavery occurs in the seventh chapter of the book when Equiano pays the purchase price of forty pounds to his master, who then presents him with manumission papers. Equiano has rather emphatically chosen to *purchase* his freedom rather than to escape from slavery (despite numerous opportunities to do so), and, accordingly, at this point in the narrative he casts his freedom from slavery in terms that are embedded in the discourse of the market—namely the discourse of capital accumulation: "[My master] thought by carrying one little thing or other to different places [on board ship] to sell I might make money. [He indicated] that he also intended to encourage me in this by crediting me with half a puncheon of rum and half a hogshead of sugar at a time; so that, from being careful, I might have money enough, in some time, to purchase my freedom; and, when that was the case, I might depend upon it he would let me have it for forty pounds sterling money, which was only the same price he gave for me" (chapter 6).[6] Here, the master trades in both slave bodies and hogsheads of sugar, and Equiano himself enters into this trade and system of credit to purchase his freedom. Freedom is, then, a matter (in Equiano's words) of becoming the "master of a few pounds" (chapter 6) as much as, or more so, than a matter of escaping the violence and/or oppression of the master and the system of Atlantic race slavery in general. Intriguingly, however, immediately after Equiano purchases his manumission papers, he resorts to a different account of his freedom. Namely, this account associates freedom with his African nativity: when he is manumitted, he describes himself as "being as in my original free African state" (chapter 7). In this instance the "state" of freedom is geographically associated with Africa as a site external to the institution of Atlantic race slavery—a site physically and temporally "original" or prior to Equiano's captivity and enslavement. In a number of subsequent passages, however, the term "free man" becomes associated with the threat of being returned to slavery without recourse to law: traveling in South America, Equiano is set upon by a ship owner named Hughes, who intends to enslave him despite his knowledge that Equiano is legally free. Equiano writes, "I simply asked [Hughes] what right he had to sell me? but, without another word, he made some of his people tie ropes round each of my ancles [*sic*], and also to each wrist, and another rope round my body, and hoisted me up without letting my feet touch or rest upon any thing. Thus I hung, without any crime committed, and without judge or jury; merely because I was a free man, and could not by the law get any redress from a white person in those parts of the world" (chapter 11). Here, Equiano is condemned to a form of torture because he is a "free man"—that is, he is a free *black* man in the Atlantic world who is therefore never unproblematically guaranteed the right of legal freedom to which whites have access. In this passage, as in a number of similar ones, being a "free man" is shorthand for being black and constantly subject to the threat of violence and captivity, particularly while on land in America. And in a final passage that might be added to a list of heterogeneous discourses of freedom, Equiano uses the word "free" in relation to Christianity. "By free grace," he writes, "I was persuaded that I had a part in the first resurrection" (chapter 10). In this instance, freedom is associated with religion in a racially and geographically unmarked fashion: strikingly, then, a universal right to freedom seems most available to Equiano under the sign of religion rather than, say, under the sign of law, commerce, or human rights.

As this very brief canvassing of these passages suggests, a conceptual and physical geography of freedom emerges with particularly clarity with the assistance of an electronic analysis (that is, keyword searching) of the text. Reading the digital edition of the *Narrative* in this fashion allows one to home in on something like a geography of freedom—an uneven geography of freedom at that—and to do so in a way that might be more difficult to accomplish while reading a print edition of the text. Perhaps more important, this example of keyword reading indicates the extent to which different textual media invite different modes of reading *and* the extent to which different modes of reading, in turn, may generate new and different kinds of insight into a given text. Indeed, digital modes of reading (such as keyword searching) are the inevitable counterpart of digital texts. And given that digital texts are increasingly the medium in which both research scholars and students consume eighteenth-century Atlantic world texts, it befits readers and scholars to turn their attention to useful ways of theorizing and understanding the possibilities of digital reading.

Mapping Equiano's *Narrative*

One of the possibilities opened up by digital reading and digital analysis of texts is not simply that of compiling (keywords, for instance) but that of mapping—generating visual and spatial data regarding the "geography" of a text. Building on the example just explored—namely, the notion that freedom is associated with a conceptual and physical geography in Equiano's text—one may propose a threefold model of textual geography that, in its multivalent account of space, provides a means of attending to uneven ontologies of spatialization in Equiano's text. Three identifiable spatial registers appear in Equiano's *Narrative* that are related but nonetheless distinct: (1) geographical space, (2) conceptual space, and (3) textual space. Geographical space corresponds roughly to the map of Equiano's travels visible in figure 1—namely, the physical locations that Equiano describes visiting and inhabiting during the course of his life. Conceptual space, in turn, includes not only the geographical locations that Equiano inhabits but also those to which he makes reference in his *Narrative*—that is, locations that appear within Equiano's prose but that he does not actually inhabit or visit at the time he discusses these places. Textual space, finally, refers to space within a text—specifically, the spatial divisions between chapters, paragraphs, sentences, and words. Thus, for instance, one might speak of a phrase or a trope as occurring at the beginning or end of a text, or at the beginning or end of a paragraph: these terms imply a geography that does not correspond to a world outside the text but rather to the spatial nature of the material text itself. Each of these three registers is operative in Equiano's text and while they are conceptually distinct, they occur simultaneously within the text. Only the first register—geographical space—corresponds to the positivist understanding of space that those working in GIS typically deploy; however, the second two spatial registers (conceptual space and textual space) are clearly present within the text and provide information that can be mapped in visual forms as well. Further, the categories of conceptual space and textual space correspond directly to the written and textual nature of the *Narrative*—that is, to the abstract and referential nature of a text (the ability of a text to conceptualize space that is elsewhere) and to the material nature of the text itself (its own formal and hence spatial nature as a text). The advantage of a mapping technology such as GIS lies precisely in its capacity to visually present layers of information in relation to one another: GIS enables data sets to be juxtaposed and interlayered such that new knowledge emerges from understanding the *relation* of different forms of data—whether this be (as might more typically be the case with GIS) the relation between climate factors, human and/or animal populations, and spatial divisions of land or (in the case of Equiano's *Narrative*) the relation between uses of the word "freedom," narrative development, and physical movement within the Atlantic world.

Mapping Equiano's text with the use of GIS, I aimed both to delineate the three forms of space just outlined and to layer these mappings so that aspects of the text might be read in a new way. I have generated a series of maps in which the spatial schemas proposed—geographical space, conceptual space, and textual space—appear in relation to one another. Using GIS, I created a layer of the map delineating geographical space and a layer of the map delineating conceptual space for each of the twelve chapters of Equiano's *Narrative*.[7] (In figures 2–12, note that geographical space is depicted in black tones marked with white bullets and conceptual space in dark grey tones marked with black bullets.) This series of maps allowed me to trace the transformation within the *Narrative* of geographical and conceptual space in relation to the unfolding of textual space—that is, the unfolding of the narrative across twelve sequentially ordered chapters. To connect the geography of the Atlantic world with the conceptual content of the *Narrative* (namely, with concepts such as "freedom"), I have used text-mining software to generate a list of the most often used statistically unusual words in each chapter and a numerical index for the increased frequency of these words in relation to a standard English language corpus.[8] This list of words thus indicates what topics receive particular attention from Equiano. The words on this list have then been grouped into categories to identify and quantify the main concepts that emerged from the list of statistically unusual words. In other words, on the basis of the list of statistically unusual words derived from text-mining, I generated a series of categories suggested by the words themselves.[9] The categories are these: comfort/success/pleasure, commerce, family, freedom, justice/human rights, maritime, military/war, race/identity group, religion, slavery, and sorrow/punishment/duress. Then I manually coded the words in the lists into categories and aggregated the numerical data associated with individual words into numerical data associated with conceptual categories. I mapped this data in relation to textual space, using bubble charts to display the relative frequency of key concepts in each of the twelve chapters of the *Narrative*. These charts are juxtaposed with the GIS maps of geographical and conceptual space in figures 2–12.

These maps aim to explore the coincidence of physical, textual, and conceptual geographies of Atlantic space and ideas in Equiano's *Narrative*. What, then, emerges from these juxtapositions of divergent spatial registers? The most obvious finding concerns the overwhelming prominence of "maritime" discourse, or language involving sailing and being at sea (including words such as "ship," "vessel," "captain," "sea"). On the one hand, such a finding should not come as a surprise: Equiano describes being subject to the Middle Passage as an enslaved child and then spends much of his life employed as a sailor—whether as a slave to a Royal Navy Officer, a slave to a commercial ship owner, or later as a free man with training as a hairdresser/sailor hired to man ships in the maritime-based Atlantic economy. However, the prominence of maritime discourse does auger for something of a new understanding of the *Narrative,* given that the text is largely understood as a *slave* narrative (and not, for instance, a maritime narrative). Moreover, recent scholarly attention has focused in large part on the question of whether Equiano was, in fact, born in Africa as he states in the *Narrative,* or whether he was born in South Carolina, as some evidence might seem to suggest.[10] This heated and divisive scholarly debate mirrors to some extent the division in Equiano's title alluded to above: namely, the divide between Equiano's African identity (as Olaudah Equiano) and his European identity (as Gustavus Vassa). The prominence of maritime discourse would seem to suggest that these oppositional accounts have in part missed the mark of the *Narrative* itself, in which a maritime identity becomes key to negotiating and dismantling the very binaries of identity—free/enslaved, African/European— in which critics of the text have traded.

A closer look at the mapping of maritime discourse across the space of the text indicates that this language functions in a manner akin to the "switch word" described by Freud—a switch word that, like a railroad switch, enables a shift between two or more separate tracks of thought or discourse. A switch word—or in this instance, a "switch discourse"—thus serves as a hinge or nodal point linking divergent discursive threads. In the first chapter of Equiano's *Narrative,* maritime discourse does not appear at all: rather, notions of family and home dominate (fig. 2). When maritime discourse does appear in the second chapter, it is associated with Equiano's enslavement and with his experience of the Middle Passage: in this chapter, he describes seeing a large, ocean-going ship for the first time, being forced into the ship, and being taken to Bridgetown, Barbados, where he is sold as a slave (fig. 3). Unsurprisingly, a high degree of misery (evident in the predominance of the language of sorrow/punishment/duress) is associated with the emergence of maritime discourse in this chapter. But maritime discourse shifts its affective associations in the third chapter when Equiano is enslaved to an officer in the Royal Navy and effectively becomes a cabin boy on a commercial ship: whereas the language of sorrow and duress predominated in the second chapter, the blossoming of maritime discourse in the third chapter is coupled with a decrease in sorrow and a marked increase in the language of comfort, pleasure, and success (fig. 1.4).

The juxtaposition of the maps of the first three chapters (figs. 2–4) is thus particularly illuminating about the relation among space, freedom, and happiness,

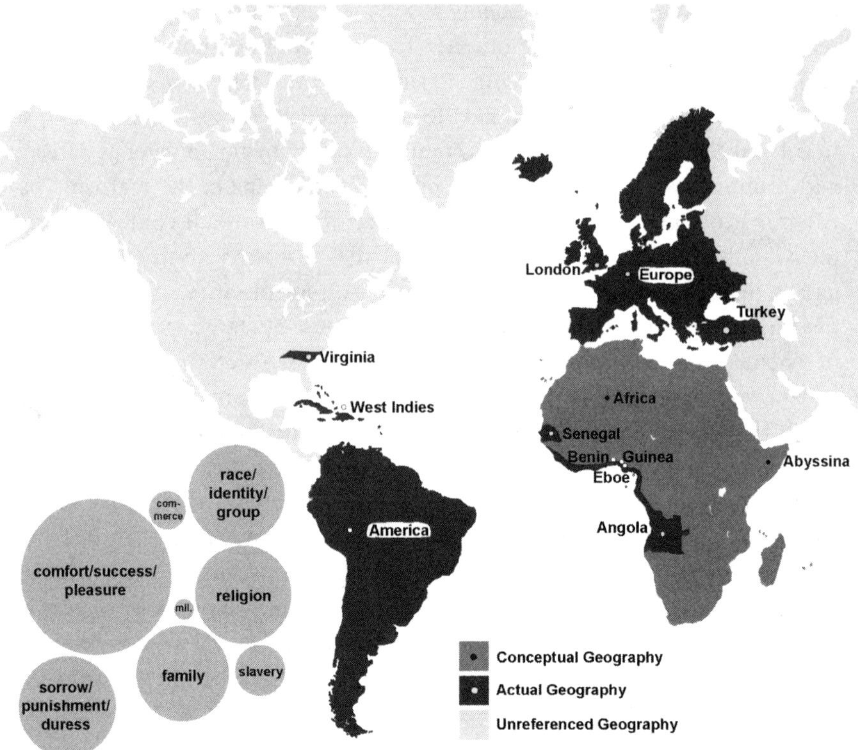

Fig. 2. Map of chapter 1: Equiano's childhood in Africa. Geographical space is depicted in black tones marked with white bullets, and conceptual space in dark gray tones marked with black bullets. Bubble charts indicate relative predominance of discursive categories.

in part because freedom and happiness are not entirely correlated with the experience of being legally enslaved or free but are correlated with ways of inhabiting space and modes of mobility. Specifically, the size of Equiano's world decreases dramatically when he is enslaved: the map of the world for the second chapter is populated by far fewer places than is the map of the first chapter, despite the fact that the physical distance covered by Equiano in his travels in this chapter is greater than that in the first chapter. Notably, there is *no* conceptual space on the map of the second chapter, as compared to the expansive conceptual mapping of the world that occurs in the first chapter. As such, it would seem that the experience of being enslaved is one that causes Equiano's conceptual world to shrink to the point of disappearance. Intriguingly, however, in the third chapter, his world becomes considerably larger: both the geographical (black-coded layer) and the conceptual map (dark gray-coded layer) of Equiano's world are repopulated with place names. Although he is still enslaved aboard a ship in the third chapter, his

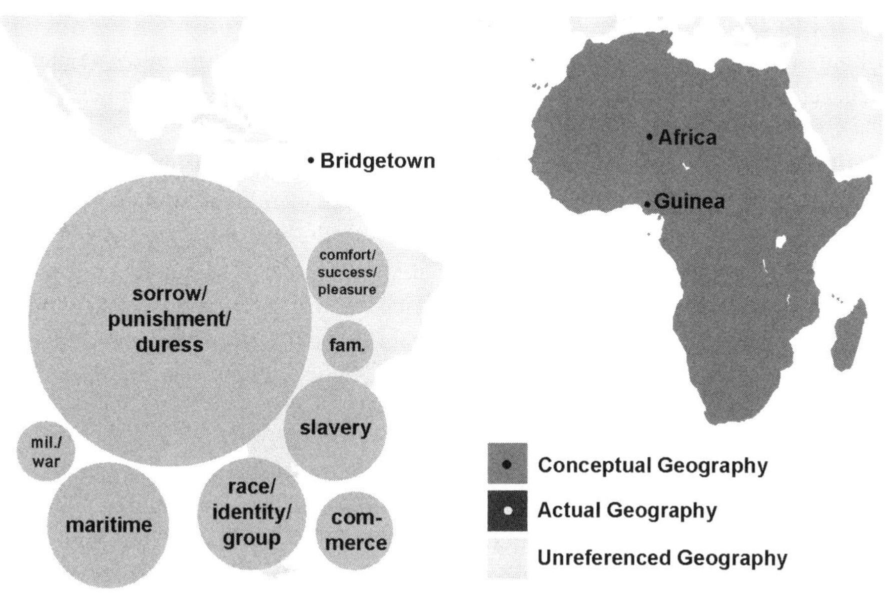

Fig. 3. Map of chapter 2: enslavement and middle passage.

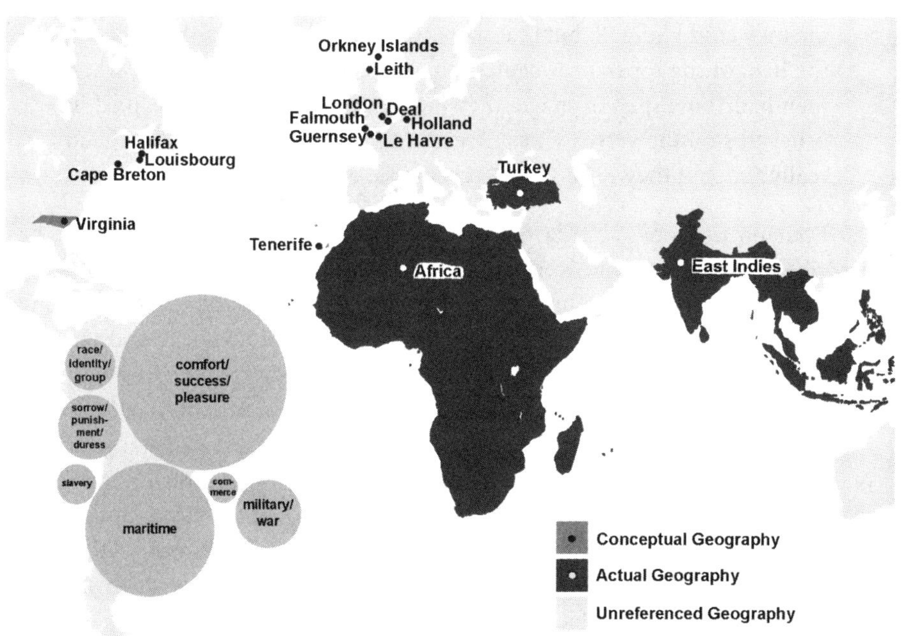

Fig. 4. Map of chapter 3: Equiano is sold to a captain in the Royal Navy; works on board commercial and naval ships as cabin boy.

role as a cabin boy for an officer in the Royal Navy, as opposed to a slave in the hold of a ship, has transformed maritime space from a nonworld into a habitable space: from within this *habitable* space, Equiano is able to conjure a much larger world around and beyond himself.

The Middle Passage, then, is mappable in figure 3 as a scene of what might be called "unworlding." In this chapter, the map of the world that Equiano inhabits, both geographically and conceptually, shrinks to the space of a few sites: Africa and Bridgetown. Accordingly, the slave ship, which carries Equiano across the Atlantic, becomes a sort of vortex into which the world (envisioned much more robustly in the previous chapter) disappears. Indeed, within the text, Equiano describes the slave ship itself as a non-place. Upon encountering the European sailors into whose hands he is sold upon arriving at the African coast, he writes:

> I could not help expressing my fears and apprehensions to some of my countrymen: I asked them if these [Europeans] had no country, but lived *in this hollow place* (the ship): they told me they did not, but came from a distant one. 'Then,' said I, 'how comes it in all our country we never heard of them?' They told me because they lived so very far off. I then asked where were their women? had they any like themselves? I was told they had: 'and why,' said I, 'do we not see them?' they answered, because they were left behind. I asked how the vessel could go? they told me they could not tell; but that there were cloths put upon the masts by the help of the ropes I saw, and then the vessel went on; and the white men had some spell or magic they put in the water when they liked in order to stop the vessel. I was exceedingly amazed at this account, and really thought they were spirits. (chapter 2, emphasis added)

Equiano describes the slave ship as a "hollow place," which is to say, he describes it as a place that is not a place—a place that is empty of the characteristics of life, home, or country. It is difficult for him to credit the very being of the European men who seem to have no country and no social and familial world (in the form of women, for instance): the white men are men without place and without substance; they are "spirits" in Equiano's eyes. And indeed, Equiano's description of the ship echoes the writer Édouard Glissant's evocative description of the slave ship as an abyss, or "nonworld," experienced by the captive in the Middle Passage. Glissant wrote, "What is terrifying partakes of the abyss, three times linked to the unknown. First, the time you fell into the belly of the boat . . . the belly of this boat dissolves you, precipitates you into a nonworld from which you cry out . . . the most petrifying face of the abyss lies far ahead of the slave ship's bow, a pale murmur. . . . Is this boat sailing into eternity toward the edges of a nonworld that no ancestor will haunt?"[11] Glissant's imagining of the "nonworld" of the Middle Passage resonates, in turn, with recent research by Stephanie E. Smallwood on the Middle Passage in which she argued that the geography of the concept of a "middle passage" relies on a European ontology: if Europeans understood the Atlantic crossing as a passage between two fixed points and known bodies of land, enslaved Africans did not share this understanding of the geography of the sea voyage they were forced to endure. For the enslaved African, Smallwood wrote, the voyage to America was an "experience of motion without discernible direction or destination," and, as such, was "perhaps the antithesis of a 'middle' passage with all that phrase implies about a smooth, linear progression leading to a known end."[12]

A comparison of the maps of the first two chapters (figs. 2 and 3) demonstrates precisely this evaporation of knowledge and secure location in the world: in the first chapter, Equiano's early world is defined largely in terms of family, religion, and larger racial and national identity groups, but this grounding, as it were, is one that locates Equiano squarely within a more expansive geography such that his conceptual world extends far beyond the geographical world he inhabits. To be sure, Equiano is narrating this account of his childhood from the perspective of the adult who pens the *Narrative:* accordingly, the geographies that materialize in these chapters are less accounts of the actual world that Equiano knew as a child in Africa (which would not likely have included locations such as London, Turkey, and Virginia) than his evocation of that world and his childhood consciousness from the perspective of an adult living in England. Nonetheless, in his memory of the experience of enslavement, it is notable that, as figure 3 indicates, Equiano's experience of the Middle Passage involves not simply a loss of family and comfort, but a disrupted spatial ontology: in the chapter describing the Middle Passage, the larger world ceases to exist from within the "hollow place" or the "nonworld" of the slave ship. If, for the European sailor, the "middle passage" traces the line between two points of land in the homogenous space of a map of the Atlantic littoral, then, for the African captive, the Middle Passage marks an ontological break: a movement from habitable space to an unfathomable, empty space.

In the third chapter, the map of the world returns and is heavily populated by the geographical locations Equiano visits while on board naval and commercial ships, *and* by a larger conceptual geography that includes Africa, Turkey, and the East Indies (see fig. 4). Significantly, this geography is associated with a burgeoning of maritime discourse together with a discourse of pleasure (as opposed to the high degree of sorrow evident in the previous chapter). The restoration of place and pleasure to Equiano thus does not occur by means of finding a new home on land—that is, the reterritorializing of the world that occurs in this chapter does not occur because Equiano has found a new grounding on land and made a new home in America. Nor does it occur because he is freed from slavery. Both in Barbados, where he is sold into slavery, and in Virginia, where he works briefly as a field laborer, life continues to have a quality of unreality for Equiano. The larger horizons of the world only return to Equiano when he is once again on board a ship crossing the Atlantic (enslaved to a naval officer), but in this case, the ship becomes a place rather than a non-place. In this chapter, he describes arriving on board a merchant ship after being sold (for the second time) to one Captain Pascal in Virginia: "When I arrived [at the shore] I was carried on board a fine large ship, loaded with tobacco, &c. and just ready to sail for England. I now thought my condition much mended; I had sails to lie on, and plenty of good victuals to eat; and every body on board used me very kindly" (chapter 3). Rather than a "hollow place," the ship in this instance becomes a source of life—a container for the stuff of life, including food, a bed, and, significantly, social relations. Once on board the ship, Equiano relates, "I soon enjoyed myself pretty well, and felt tolerably easy in my present situation. There was a number of boys on board, which still made it more agreeable; for we were always together, and a great part of our time was spent in play" (chapter 3). The image of play is particularly resonant here: far from being the scene of extreme privation and social death, the ship in this case is the scene of *play*—a term that connotes a claiming of space through physical, social, and imaginative modes of collective belonging.

Further, when Equiano boards this ship, its destination—England—is already a place in Equiano's conceptual geography despite the fact that he has never been there: he speaks with confidence of the destination of the ship in a way that was not possible when he left the shores of Africa. And indeed, in a telling phrase later in the chapter, Equiano describes visiting a naval ship in London that has the aspect of a "little world": "The Royal George was the largest ship I had ever seen; so that when I came on board of her I was surprised at the number of people, men, women, and children, of every denomination; and the largeness of the guns, many of them also of brass, which I had never seen before. Here were also shops or stalls of every kind of goods, and people crying their different commodities about the ship as in a town. To me it appeared a *little world,* into which I was again cast without a friend, for I had no longer my dear companion Dick" (chapter 3, emphasis added).

As this passage indicates, even in the face of the loss of what had become a sustaining social relation (his friendship with the cabin boy, Dick), the ship retains the aspect of a world—a place populated by people with recognizable social identities (familial, religious, economic), who are engaged in social interactions in which Equiano shares. The ship thus shifts from being the space of a nonworld, inhabited by spirits, to a space that is itself a world, and a world in which Equiano feels increasingly at home.

A number of points are worth underscoring here. First, a larger spatial world is made available to Equiano in relation to his immersion in a maritime environment that is associated with commerce and the military rather than with the slave

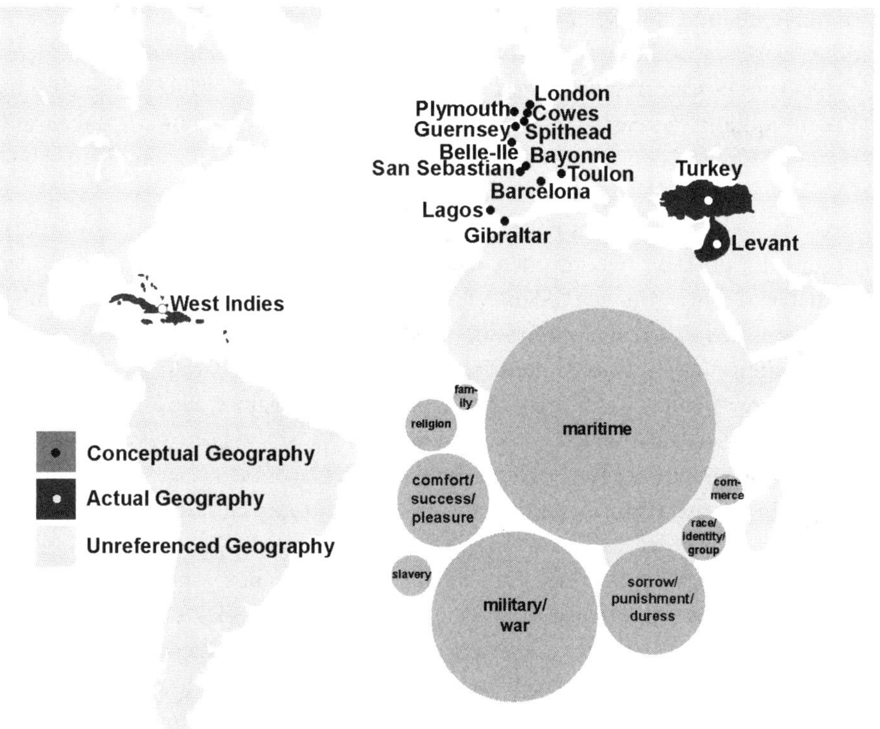

Fig. 5. Map of chapter 4: Equiano works as an enslaved cabin boy for a captain in the British Royal Navy on ships engaged in fighting the French in the Seven Years' War.

trade. As such, a mobility associated with the maritime world enables him to move from one discursive world (slavery), to another (military and commerce): this pattern continues in chapter 4, as is visible in figure 5, where the association between maritime and military discourses remains particularly strong, and in chapters 6 and 7 (figs. 7 and 8), where an association between maritime and commercial discourses emerges as more dominant. Second, Equiano's ability to view a larger world is predicated on establishing a sense of territorialization or belonging within a domestic space: whereas the slave ship is the scene of unworlding and social death that eradicates both domestic and worldly space, the ships he later inhabits grant him a modicum of social identity and belonging such that he is able to reconceive a larger world and achieve mobility within this world. It is in this sense that maritime discourse is a "switch word": it conveys Equiano into social death and out of it as well. Associated with the Middle Passage, maritime discourse is solely privative (as in chapter 2); but when associated with commerce, labor, and employment (as in chapters 3–11), maritime discourse becomes fundamental to Equiano's ability to switch from one world—that of slavery—to other worlds, whether military, commercial, religious, or abolitionist.

Geographical mobility, when grounded in the "little world" of the ship in which Equiano increasingly forges his identity as a skilled sailor, a speaker and reader of English, and "almost an Englishman," thus provides not simply the ability to move through physical space but the ability to move through conceptual space as well. As historians have demonstrated, eighteenth-century black sailors occupied a position that afforded access to forms of wellbeing that were rarely available to slaves who worked on plantations. Summarizing this research, Philip Morgan noted, "As cribbed, confining, and dangerous as shipboard life was, seafaring offered mobility and the opportunity to broaden horizons. . . . Maritime slaves were the most cosmopolitan of men. . . . Furthermore, life afloat generally afforded better treatment than plantation labor. Yes, the lash was still ubiquitous, but opportunities were greater too—the chance of cash wages, the ability to engage in private ventures, and even exposure to literacy and book-reading were all more likely."[13] In Equiano's case, these claims are wholly accurate: Equiano learns to speak, read, and write English on board a ship; he learns labor skills that augment his market value and his capacity to exert control over the conditions of his employment (even as a slave); and he eventually engages in trade such that he is able to acquire money and purchase his freedom. However, the mapping of Equiano's text with GIS allows an increased insight into the nature and meaning of mobility for a black mariner such as Equiano: first, comparing the experience of crossing the Atlantic in the Middle Passage to that of his crossing the Atlantic as a cabin boy (figs. 3 and 4) indicates that it is not simply mobility that generates success and freedom, but also mobility from a position of social identity like that afforded by the "little world" of the ship. This social identity attenuates the social death imposed by slavery and allows mobility to have the effect of enlarging rather than diminishing the surrounding world. Second, one can see that mobility of this sort is both conceptual and geographical, or *ontological* and geographical: what Equiano masters on board ships (in addition to the forty pounds that allow him to purchase his freedom) is a capacity to move between and among heterogeneous worlds and discourses, including worlds that are English and African, Christian and non-Christian, colonial and metropolitan, military and civilian, and enslaved and free.

An analysis of figures 6–11 reveals another interesting pattern: after each chapter in which mobility is high (registered in terms of the number of place names—both geographical and conceptual—populating the map) and in which maritime discourse dominates (chapters 4, 6, and 9), one sees in the subsequent chapter a relative depopulation in place names, coupled with the marked rise of a new mode of discourse (chapters 5, 7, and 10). In other words, an uptick in maritime discourse and mobility in one chapter is followed, in three instances,

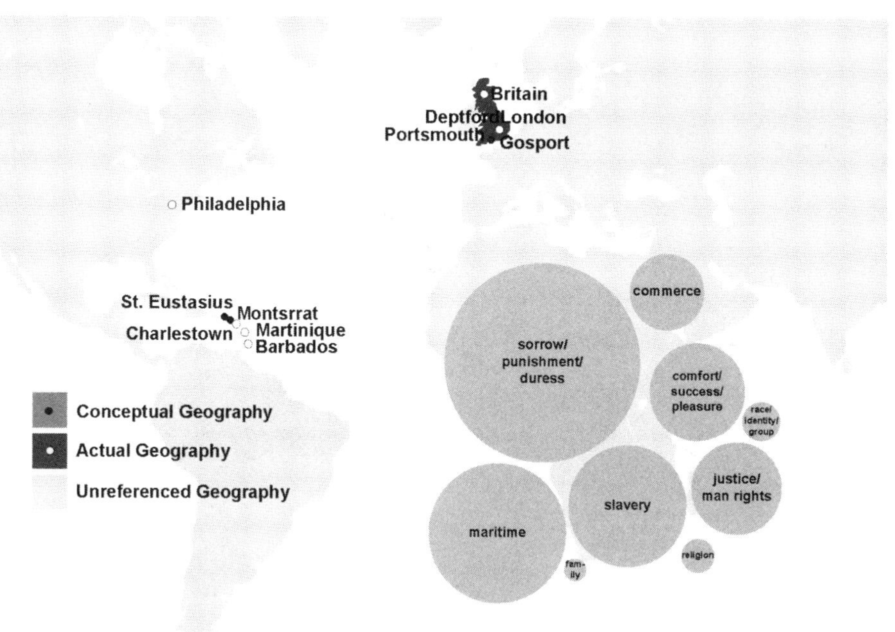

Fig. 6. Map of chapter 5: Equiano is kidnapped in England and forcibly taken to the West Indies to be sold as a slave.

by a shift into a new discursive register in the subsequent chapter and a notable decrease in mobility. In the first case, chapter 4 (fig. 1.5) reveals that Equiano's language is dominated by maritime discourse and that he mentions twelve sites he has visited (across Europe), together with the Levant, Turkey, and the West Indies—locations he mentions but does not visit. In this chapter, Equiano largely recounts his experience as a cabin boy in the Royal Navy: he is engaged on British ships that are fighting with the French in a European theater, and thus military language is the second most frequent notable discourse (behind maritime language) in the chapter. This surge in mobility, however, is followed by a marked decrease of movement in the next chapter, which narrates Equiano's forcible kidnapping and reenslavement in the West Indies following the discharge from active war duty of his owner from the Royal Navy at the close of the Seven Year's War in 1762. Notably, the depopulation of the map that occurs in chapter 5 is less extreme than that occurring in chapter 2, when Equiano first recounts the experience of the Middle Passage from Africa. This second "Middle Passage," which occurs in chapter 5, is not a voyage into the unknown for Equiano but a voyage to the known horrors of West Indian slavery. Nonetheless, the contrast between the maps that appear in chapters 4 (when Equiano is in active military duty)

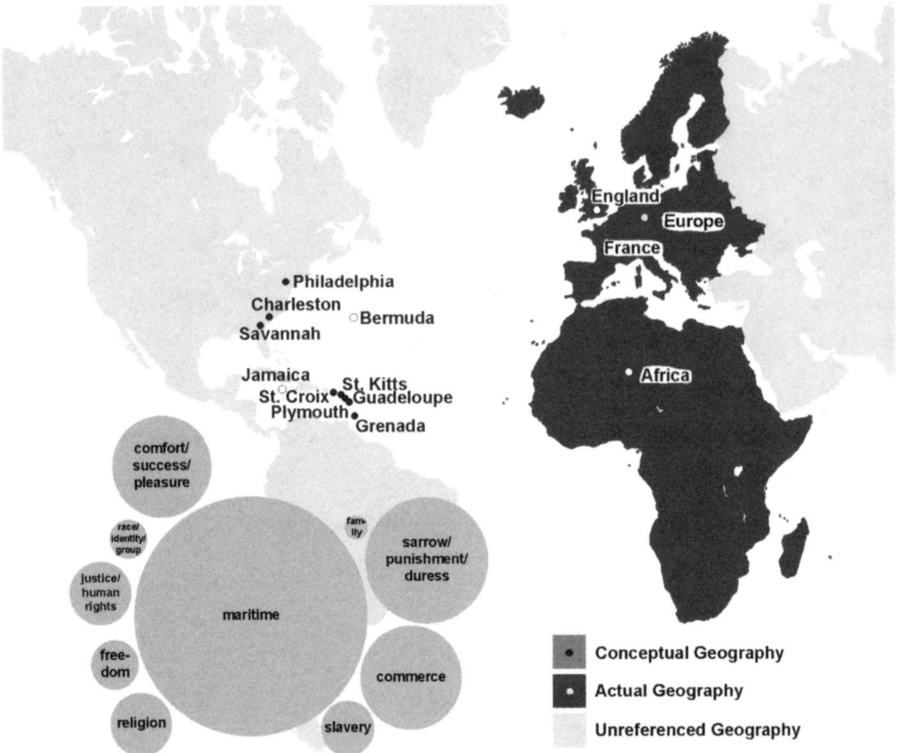

Fig. 7. Map of chapter 6: Equiano is employed as a slave on merchant ships trading between the North American colonies and the West Indies.

and 5 (when he is sold to the West Indies) remains striking; the map of reenslavement visible in chapter 5 is relatively bare of geographical and conceptual space. A significant shift in the dominant language of the two chapters occurs as well: whereas chapter 4 is dominated by maritime and military discourse, these terms recede in chapter 5. Unsurprisingly, given that the chapter describes the experience of a second Middle Passage and reenslavement in the West Indies, the language of sorrow predominates in the fifth chapter. However, two new conceptual fields emerge with force in this chapter—namely, the language of slavery and that of human rights and justice. The appearance of the latter discourse is particularly intriguing, given that this language was not present in the chapter narrating Equiano's first experience of the Middle Passage. As such, the emergence of a new conceptual field—that of human rights and justice—seems potentially to correlate more closely with the experience of geographical mobility that precedes this chapter than solely with the experience of enslavement itself.

A similar pattern is repeated as we move from chapter 6 to chapter 7: the high mobility of chapter 6 (fourteen place names) and the outsized dominance

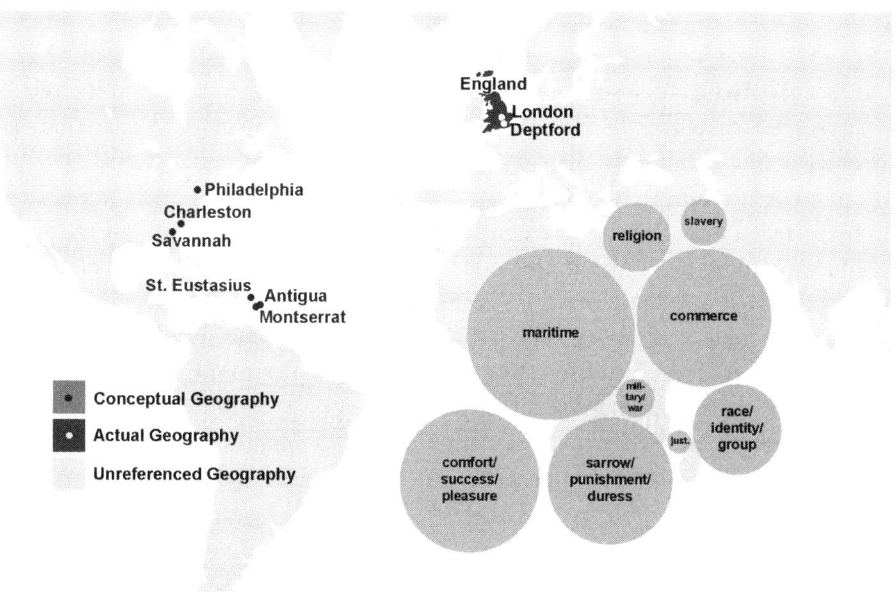

Fig. 8. Map of chapter 7: Equiano purchases his freedom; he remains employed as a wage earner on merchant ships trading between the North American colonies and the West Indies.

of maritime discourse is followed, in chapter 7, by a relatively depopulated map (nine place names), and an upsurge in the language of commerce that rivals maritime discourse for prominence in the chapter. What is intriguing, in this case, is that it is not the experience of enslavement that has generated a shift in spatial and conceptual registers (as in chapters 2 and 5) but precisely the opposite: namely, the experience of freedom. In chapter 6, Equiano describes being employed as an enslaved sailor and trader on board a ship that is plying goods between the North American colonies and the West Indies. In chapter 7, he purchases his freedom from his master and agrees to continue working as a wage earner on the same ship where he had previously labored as a slave. Accordingly, he continues to travel along largely the same routes that he sailed prior to becoming free; yet, the decrease of places named in the chapter indicates that Equiano may well have inhabited a different spatial world as a free man than he did as a slave. What exactly has changed in Equiano's spatial world? Does attaining freedom generate a process of "unworlding" comparable to the experience of being enslaved and subject to the Middle Passage? In some respects, it seems possible to answer this question in the affirmative, although a more apt term in this case might be "reworlding" or "reterritorialization" rather than unworlding.

The experience of reinhabiting the world—or inhabiting the world anew as a free man who was formerly enslaved—is, one might speculate, accompanied by an initial experience of destruction or deterritorialization that appears in the relative spatial barrenness of the map of the world that accompanies the narration of his legal manumission in chapter 7.

It is important to note, however, that coupled with the depopulating of the spatial terrain of the map in chapter 7, there is a discursive reconfiguration of Equiano's language—specifically, a notable increase in the language of commerce as well as of comfort and success. The marked increase in the language of commerce indicates that the physical mobility of the maritime world has the effect of catapulting Equiano into a new conceptual or ontological world—one that in this case is (perhaps surprisingly) characterized by the language of commerce more than the language of freedom itself. Equiano becomes a free man by transforming himself from a slave into a wage earner and trader—into *homo economicus*—and it is in this discursive register that he begins to remap the new space he inhabits as a free black man in the Atlantic world. In comparing the maps of chapters 6 and 7, one can thus see that spatial mobility seems to generate conceptual mobility, but the two occur less simultaneously than sequentially: an ontological reterritorialization of the map, one might conclude, thus also involves deterritorialization or a reconstruction of space itself. It seems clear, then, that the map of Equiano's world is not cumulative—that is, he does not simply add more places to the map as his experience of place is widened. Rather, the map of the world changes radically as the discursive terms in which his narrative unfolds shift. In this sense, Equiano's map corresponds to Massey's notion of space as a multiplicity of trajectories and "stories-so-far" that generate connections and disjunctions. "Current Western-type maps," wrote Massey, "give the impression that space is a surface—that it is the sphere of a completed horizontality. . . . What if space is the sphere not of a discrete multiplicity of inert *things*, even one which is thoroughly interrelated? What if, instead, it presents us with a heterogeneity of practices and *processes?* Then it will be not an already interconnected whole but an ongoing product of interconnections and not. Then it will be always unfinished and open. This arena of space is not firm ground on which to stand. In no way is it a surface."[14] As the ontology of Equiano's narrative shifts—from family, to commerce, to human rights, to religion—so too does the spatial world he inhabits undergo revision. And intriguingly, the reverse may be true as well: as the space Equiano inhabits shifts, so does the ontology of his story.

In a final iteration of the pattern we have seen above—one in which physical mobility seems to generate discursive and ontological mobility—an upsurge of mobility (twenty-one place names) and maritime discourse in chapter 9 is followed by a sharp decrease in mobility in chapter 10 (nine place names), together with the introduction of a new, strikingly dominant discourse—that of religion.

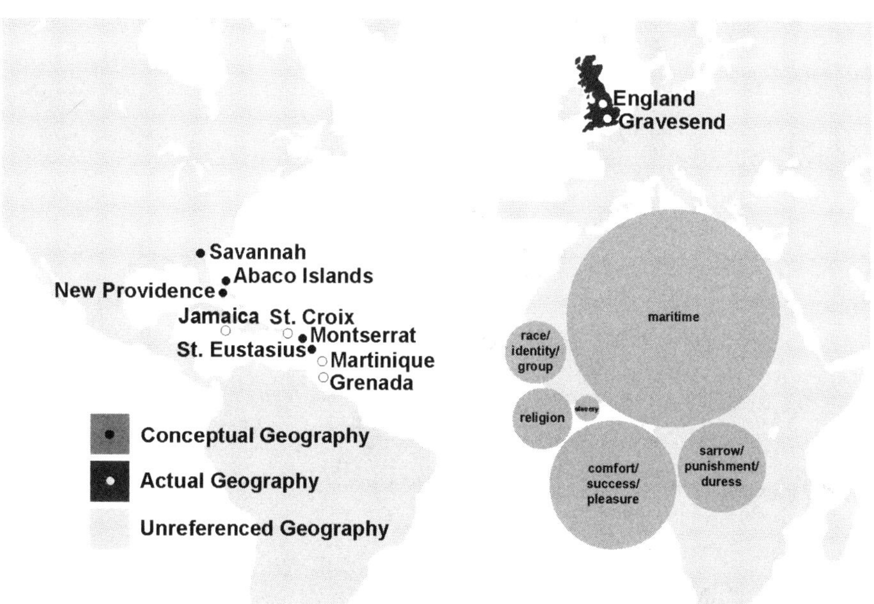

Fig. 9. Map of chapter 8: Equiano continues as a wage earner on ships trading between the North American colonies and the West Indies.

In chapter 9, Equiano is highly mobile, shipping out from England as a free man on an expedition to the North Pole as well as to a variety of locations in Europe, the Mediterranean, and the Americas. Finding that he is unable to make a living in England, he turns to the sea to find a livelihood and is extremely successful at making a life and living for himself as a sailor. In chapter 10 Equiano remains employed in these same activities—namely, working as a sailor. Indeed, during the course of chapter 10, he narrates his experience sailing to both Spain and Turkey. But scant spatial mapping of his journeys appears in this chapter because much of the chapter is devoted to religious ideation and the narrative of spiritual conversion Equiano undergoes. In spatial terms, the world disappears again—or rather, it appears in a sort of strange, far-flung way. Notably, the map of chapter 10 differs significantly from that of every other chapter in that it contains no Atlantic center of gravity. Rather, the geographical and conceptual maps are sparsely filled with spatially disparate sites, as if Equiano were untethered to any spatial geography—a condition that may reflect the dominance of the new spiritual geography introduced in this chapter. In chapter 10, then, one finds a spiritual map of Equiano's world that bears little resemblance to the map derived from chapter 11 (which might be characterized as Atlantic commercial) or the map derived from chapter 12 (which could arguably be called an abolitionist

Fig. 10. Map of chapter 9: Equiano relocates from the West Indies to London; he finds employment as a sailor and hairdresser on merchant ships and participates in an expedition to the North Pole.

Atlantic map). The analysis of the shifting maps of Equiano's *Narrative* reveals, at its most obvious, that the world is rarely the same from one chapter to the next for Equiano; Atlantic space is uneven, heterogeneous, and subject to revision, as are the ideas and ways of being that motivate Equiano's movements in this world.

The Uneven Atlantic

A static notion of Atlantic space—a sense of the Atlantic and its littoral as uniform, homogenous, and inert—is belied by the maps generated from Equiano's text. In Equiano's experience, the Atlantic is a space of competing and nonsynchronous ontologies, of deterritorialization and reterritorialization, of movement, fracture, and rupture. And indeed, as a number of critics have argued, the concept of static, homogenous space is one that coincides with a European, imperialist geopolitics rather than with the experience of Atlantic space of an individual such as Equiano or, more broadly, the experience of large numbers

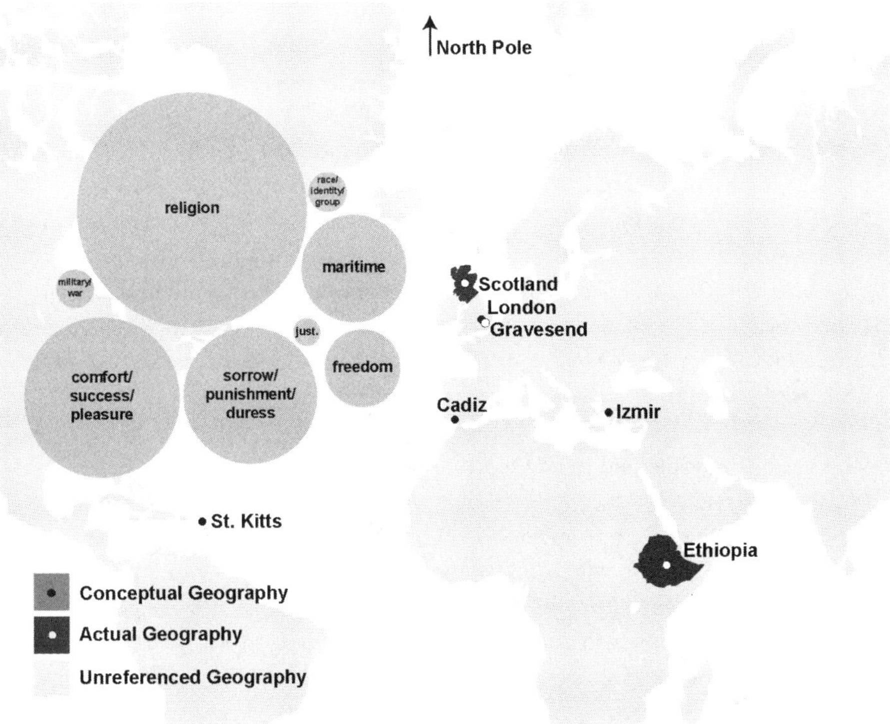

Figure 11. Map of chapter 10: Equiano experiences conversion to free grace and works in London and as a sailor.

of diasporic Africans and indigenous Americans who were key players in the formation of the eighteenth-century Atlantic world. For Massey, this "unthought cosmology" of imperialist space inheres, in particular, in the account of space as stable, apolitical, and closed. Massey thus proposed "a move away from that imagination of space as a continuous surface that the colonizer, as the only active agent, crosses to find the to-be-colonized simply 'there.' This would be space not as smooth surface but as the sphere or coexistence of a multiplicity of trajectories. . . . Spatializing that story [of European imperialism] enables an understanding of its positionality, its geographical embeddedness; an understanding of the spatiality of the production of knowledge itself."[15] This latter phrase—"the spatiality of the production of knowledge"—seems particularly germane to Equiano's *Narrative:* not only where one stands but how one conceives of space itself is at stake in constituting and legitimating the power relations that structure knowledge production in the Atlantic world. Thus, for example, the concept of the "Middle Passage" implies that crossing the Atlantic involves a movement between two geographical points—between two habitable worlds.[16] But for Equiano and presumably other enslaved Africans, the Atlantic crossing was not a movement between two places with equal geographical and ontological status but a movement from a known world into a nonworld. Moreover, it seems evident that, as Equiano gains experience in the uneven Atlantic world—experience of unworlding and reworlding accrued through maritime mobility—he becomes increasingly adept at employing the uneven spatiality of the production of knowledge to his own uses. For instance, in early portions of the *Narrative,* Equiano indicates his belief that the racialized oppression and inhumanity that he repeatedly suffers in the Americas will disappear when he "return[s] to Old England" (chapter 6). But this imperial geography of human rights—one in which civility and full humanity are located in the home/metropole and radiate outward with decreasing strength towards peripheral colonial sites—turns out to be only fitfully available to Equiano as a black man in London. Indeed, to aid a friend who has been kidnapped from London into West Indian slavery, Equiano finds himself donning white face in London as he attempts to take legal action against the friend's kidnapper. The appeal to English law is thus enacted together with a performance of English whiteness. In the event, neither serve Equiano well as he is able to accomplish neither his friend's release from slavery nor the punishment of his persecutor. Equiano's enslaved friend is tortured in the West Indies and soon dies; his kidnapping and death lay bare the politics of an imperial geography that promises a homogenous space of freedom to those in white face only in relation to the heterogeneous carving up of space such that those in black face inhabit sites of torture, forced labor, and death. This experience leads Equiano to abandon faith in an imperial geography and imperial knowledge production: he vows "to go to Turkey and . . . never more to return to England" and launches himself into the more habitable, fractured, and fungible space of the maritime world. As Edlie Wong argued, this incident also precipitates Equiano's spiritual crisis and subsequent conversion (mapped as a new discursive and spatial ontology in figure 11). In a sense, then, Equiano transforms the reality of his insistent deterritorialization into a resource: he uses the fracturing of space as a resource with which to inhabit other geographies and ontologies, including maritime and religious ones.[17] Maritime mobility thus becomes a primary means by which Equiano reestablishes the possibility of dwelling in the world when sites of dwelling become scenes of social death.

A second critique of the imperial nature of western cartography—that of Ricardo Padrón —gives further insight into the nature of the uneven Atlantic space that Equiano's *Narrative* maps. According to Padrón, "The modern West . . . naturalizes geometric, optical isotropic space as a fundamental epistemological category, and thereby gives undue authority to the abstractions of the mapmaker, the surveyor, the planner, the architect, and the like. Traditional 'representational spaces'—spaces as they are perceived—as the hearth or the geography of the sacred, are correspondingly stripped of their authority."[18] Padrón's account points to a different understanding of the heterogeneity of space than that found in Massey's work: spatial heterogeneity in this account is generated not simply by the multiple trajectories of those who inhabit space but by the fact that individuals have different (multiple) orders of spatial experience. Western modernity describes space as uniform, Cartesian, extensive, divisible, and homogenous. However, Equiano experiences Atlantic space in terms of the concatenation of multiple registers. For Equiano, domestic space—a local space of social belonging—makes possible the larger horizons of what we might call global space. The process of reworlding I have traced in Equiano's work thus involves an aspect of what Padrón calls "representational space" or what we might call domestic and/or intimate space, which in turn enables the unfolding or bodying forth of larger spatial imaginaries. In the Atlantic world of the eighteenth century, this insight seems particularly significant, given the importance of what I would characterize as relations of "intimate distance" in structuring the social, cultural, and economic dimensions of the Atlantic world. I use the term "intimate distance" to describe the intertwining of two kinds of spatial order within Atlantic communities: first, that of immediate, intimate relations that are often formed in nontraditional, contingent, and highly pragmatic terms (as, for example, aboard a ship, in a new colonial settlement, or among a diasporic or displaced group of persons), and second, that of distant and far-flung connections (as, for example, between white colonists and metropolitan Europeans, between enslaved African Americans and an African homeland, or between sites of the production of goods and sites of their consumption). The intimate space of the hearth—a "representational space," as Padrón describes it—thus remains integral to larger understandings of the structured relations of distance that crisscross Atlantic space. Thus, for instance, it is from within the intimacy of social relations that are established on the "little world" of the ship that Equiano is able to reconjecture the distal world of African, American, and European geographies. Both intimacy and distance—two forms of spatial relations—operate simultaneously but remain nonidentical. However, precisely the nonidentity of differential and entwined spatial registers disappears from sight in accounts of homogenous space.

Further, sites of Atlantic world intimacy and social belonging (which in turn co-constitute larger structures of spatial representation) may take any number of forms—including forms that are not easily captured by Western cartographic practices and vocabularies. Thus, for instance, as Alexander X. Byrd demonstrated, Equiano's use of terms such as "Igbo," "nation," and "country" vacillates over the course of the *Narrative,* a fact that Byrd argues is not indicative of a revisionary fictionalization of an African childhood on Equiano's part but of the noncoincidence of eighteenth-century African geographies of social, political, and cultural belonging with Western vocabularies and concepts of the same:

"Though he used the terms ['country' and 'nation'] in . . . relatively expansive ways . . . Vassa sometimes used the words to refer to more limited and ambiguously defined tracts"—tracts that had more geopolitical meaning in the Africa of his childhood than in the London metropole of his adulthood. Thus, "rather than indicating an unfamiliarity with being Igbo," wrote Byrd, "Vassa's apparently incomplete grasp and enigmatic expression of his Igboness actually suggests someone deeply familiar with and in some way affected by the social and political geography of the Biafran interior."[19] Byrd's analysis suggests that presumptions as to the homogeneity of space become ways of refusing to read or understand the disjunctive spatial imaginaries that structure the Atlantic world as a scene of forced encounter and incommensurability as well as a site in which intimacy and distance are constructed out of the debris of such collisions and convergences.

Given the task undertaken in this essay—that of mapping the heterogeneity of Atlantic space in Equiano's *Narrative* using GIS and text-mining tools— there is decided irony in relying upon GIS to do so, given that GIS might be described as the apogee of modern, Western cartographic practices. Indeed, within the field of geography, sustained debate has taken place over the question of the politics of knowledge production embedded in the technology of GIS itself. GIS, critics have argued, constitutes a "new imperial geography" central to a multibillion-dollar industry engaged in surveillance, militarization, and neo-imperialism.[20] More recently, however, efforts to critically engage GIS with anti-imperial spatial politics have also taken shape in the form, for instance, of work in "critical GIS," "GIS and society," and "participatory GIS," the last of which specifically attends to "the multiplicity of geographical realities rather than the disembodied, objective and technical 'solutions' which have tended to characterize many conventional GIS applications."[21] Work in the field of participatory GIS thus attempts to register competing spatial imaginaries and modes of spatial knowledge.

To my mind, the specific power of GIS lies not simply in its cartographic capacities but in its capacity to place multiple data sets in relation to one another by means of geospatial tags or anchors. And layering data sets in relation to one another may reveal as much in the way of discord and rupture as an increased fleshing out of stable, inert space. In its layered structure, GIS gives us precisely a model of space as relational and under construction, even if the terms of our construction remain largely encoded in traditionally Western geopolitical spatial terms. In the maps I have generated from Equiano's *Narrative,* it is clear, for instance, that conceptual space and geographical space are not always of the same order, and this creates moments of contradiction. Conceptual locations are often broadly defined in the language of the *Narrative* as, for instance, the "East Indies," whereas the geographical locations Equiano visits are typically more specifically delimited sites, such as port cities like Philadelphia or Bridgetown. Mapping these two related but nonetheless discrepant ontologies against

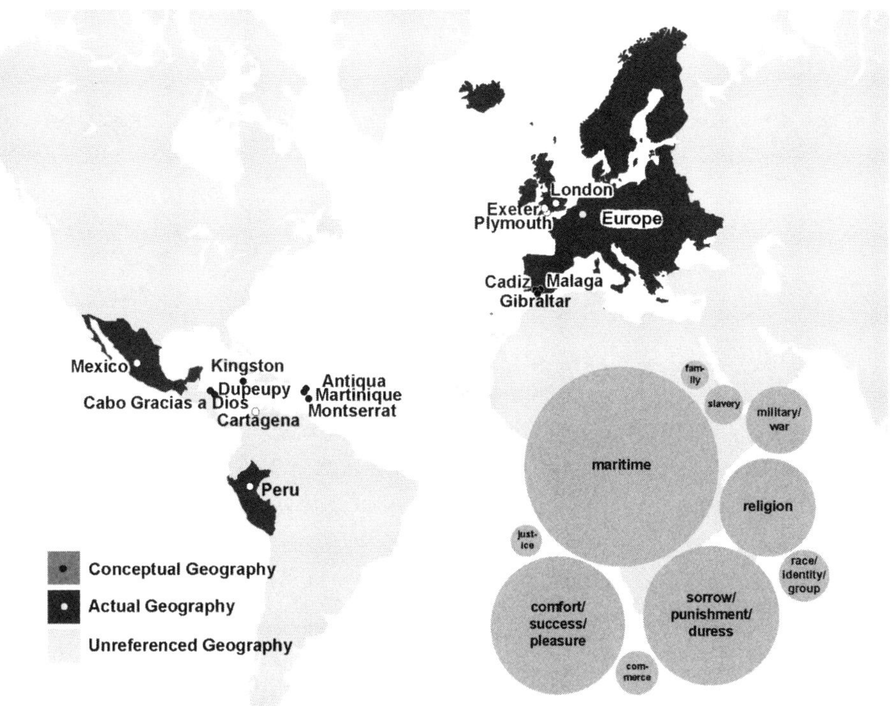

Fig. 12. Map of chapter 11: Equiano is employed as an overseer on a plantation on the Mosquito Coast (Honduras).

one another produces points of friction: as, for instance, in figure 2, where the whole continent of Africa is coded as black (a geographical space Equiano visited), save for the Gold Coast (which Equiano describes as extending from Senegal to Angola), which is coded as dark gray because it is described by Equiano as conceptual space that he has not visited. Clearly, Equiano has not visited *all* of Africa, and yet he describes the place he inhabits as a child as Africa, which I have, accordingly, encoded as black on the map. Two different vocabularies of space thus compete and contradict one another in figure 2, but this disjunction reveals that a shifting understanding of space (such as that discussed by Byrd) may be at stake in moving from an African to a European map of the world, or from a geographical to a conceptual map of the world. The layering capacity of GIS thus offers some possibility of reading this map's ruptures—the territorializations and deterritorializations—that emerge out of crises of interpretation and clashes of ontology, and from data fields that may speak to one another only in glancing terms.

Furthermore, the disruptive nature of the spatial—"its juxtaposition, its happenstance arrangement-in-relation-to-each-other, of previously unconnected

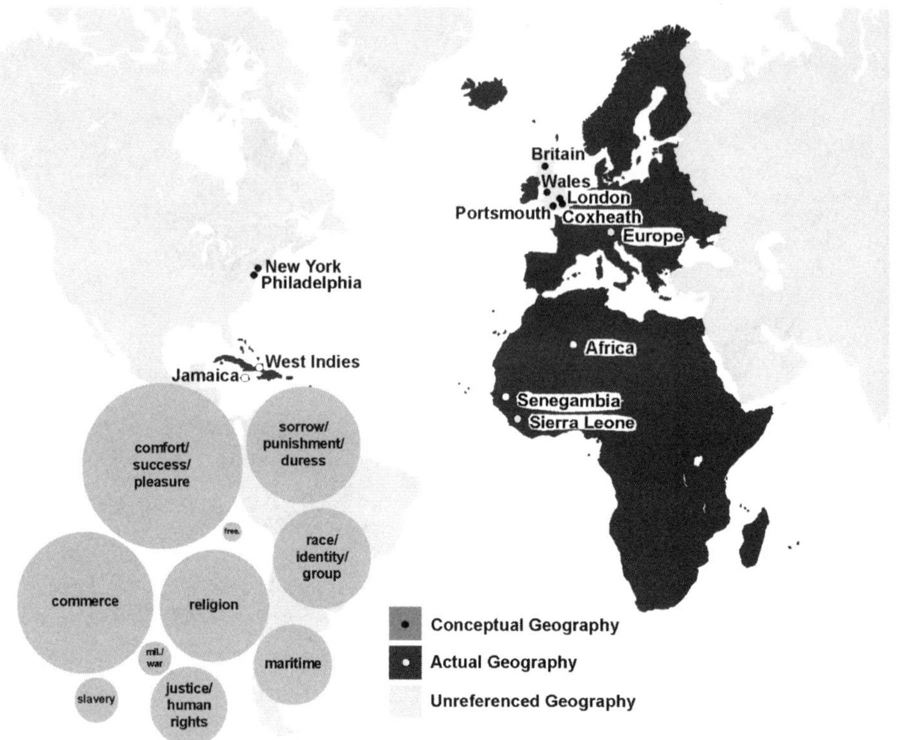

Fig. 13. Map of chapter 12: Equiano is briefly employed as commissary on a project to relocate poor black people from London to Sierra Leone.

narratives/temporalities; its openness and its condition of always being made," as Massey put it—defines its political possibility as well, namely its possibility of dislodging or offering an alternative perspective on a cartographic logic associated with Western imperialism.[22] And this political possibility seems borne out in mapping Equiano's *Narrative,* where disjunctions between spatial ontologies, and mobility among them, become a resource for Equiano to survive, thrive, and ultimately speak powerfully against slavery in the Atlantic world. In other words, spatial rupture becomes a means for Equiano to "change the joke and slip the yoke," in the words of Ralph Ellison—to elude the terms of geospatial ontologies that consign him to social death.

The promise of GIS in mapping a sea of eighteenth-century Atlantic texts is not, then, that of positivist revelation but that of opening new vectors of reading—not the elimination but the proliferation of modes of reading. In the field of literary studies, the activity of close reading has long served as the methodological soul of the discipline: teasing out meaning from language one sentence, one word, one phoneme at a time stands as the core labor of the critic whose attention is attuned to precisely the ways in which language generates meaning in "literary" ways—that is, in ways that are multireferential and which foreground language itself rather than use it as a transparent tool of reference. To transpose a text such as Equiano's *Narrative* into a map of his travels might appear to eradicate the literary itself: such a methodology would seem to involve abandoning altogether a concern with language as such, in favor of turning to that which language refers to beyond the text (such as place names or locations on a map). The method of translating literary texts into data points on maps and graphs has been most prominently propounded of late by Franco Moretti, who, with deliberate provocation, proposed that "distant reading" might profitably take the place of "close reading." Distant reading, Moretti argued, is necessary to understand literature as a system, as a historically defined whole, rather than as select pieces that define a theologically constructed canon: "A field this large cannot be understood by stitching together separate bits of knowledge about individual cases, because it *isn't* a sum of individual cases: it's a collective system, that should be grasped as such, as a whole."[23] Moretti is correct, to my mind, that large databases of text require new modes of reading, including "distant reading" such as that performed by digitally parsing, rather than reading, texts. Simply put, the large-scale dimensions of textual production in a field such as eighteenth-century Atlantic letters will not be accessible to us as individual readers, but fodder for analysis may appear by means of digital analysis. But Moretti's invocation of the totality of a literary system of texts strikes me as mistaken—in part because it is difficult to know how and where to trace the boundaries of such a totality but also because a totalizing impulse seems to look toward closed rather than open systems of knowledge production. Rather, distant reading should be added to a range of reading techniques (including close reading) that respond to the range of technologies we now use to materialize texts themselves. As Katherine Hayles has pointed out, "Literature in the twenty-first century is computational. . . . Almost all print books are digital files before they become books. . . . They should, then, properly be considered as electronic texts for which print is the output form."[24] This statement is now equally true with respect to the encoded digital files of eighteenth-century texts that form the corpus studied by students and researchers working in the field of Atlantic letters. Because these texts have been transcoded, we now have the capacity and the opportunity, if not responsibility, to engage in new modes of textual, visual, political, and theoretical analysis that are opened up by the materiality of code itself.

It is intriguing that the key scholarly debate today over Equiano's *Interesting Narrative* is, precisely, geographical. Was Equiano a native of Africa or America, and contingent upon that question, is his text fact or fiction? On the basis of the GIS analysis proposed here, it seems clear that the debate over the geography of Africa versus America also concerns how to represent multiple spatialities in a single text, given the shifting nature of space itself for an individual such as Equiano. Atlantic spatiality poses problems and resources because it is a space of colliding and competing spatial regimes—a space where the multiple registers of intimacy and distance structure forms of inhabiting the world. With respect to the Atlantic world, the nature of intersecting and mutually constituting trajectories emerges vividly from the sequential, visual mapping of the chapters of Equiano's *Narrative* that I have used GIS to perform. These maps, in turn, invite a closer reading of the way in which multiple spatialities were productive of the new relations that took shape within and defined the eighteenth-century Atlantic ocean and its littoral as an Atlantic world.

Clerics, Cartographers, and Kings

Mapping Power in the French Atlantic World, 1608–1752

George Edward Milne

In the spring of 1726, a Jesuit missionary and his escorts paddled up the Mississippi on their way to the Arkansas Post, a tiny settlement on the banks of the river. In the description of his voyage, the priest wrote, "I am not yet sufficiently acquainted with the Country and with the customs of the Savages to give you information of them; I shall only tell you that the Mississippi presents to the traveler nothing beautiful, nothing exceptional, save itself: nothing mars it but the continuous forest on both sides, and the frightful solitude in which a person is in during the whole voyage."[1]

This seemingly casual observation belies a significant shift in the manner in which French clerics, and those who employed information provided by them, envisioned the spaces of North America. Writing as a missionary, Father Paul du Poisson portrayed the region as empty—devoid of the reference points that marked his homeland. As bleak as his characterization might appear, it represented a departure from earlier missionaries' depictions of the interior of the continent as the realm of Satan, populated by his indigenous worshipers.[2] Over the course of the previous century, Catholic clergymen who ministered in the colonies had revised their descriptions of these unsubdued spaces. Their communiqués reveal a departure from tales of landscapes possessed by demonic forces to descriptions of rich unoccupied terrain in which France might build a Christian "civilization." At the heart of these depictions was emptiness—silences that came to dominate large sections of the texts that made up the emergent corpus of knowledge about the Atlantic World. Many of these texts were written items, like the letter penned by Father Poisson, but they also included geographic representations by cartographers such as Claude and Guillaume Delisle and Jean Baptist Bourguignon D'Anville.[3] It was precisely these silences that marked a search for authority, both political and "scientific," by clerics and cartographers who worked for the glory of their king. The first type was to be obtained through the erasure of native peoples who stood in the way of the French colonial project.

The second type was to be achieved by elimination of images and symbols that denigrated the credibility not only of the mapmakers but also of the priests who provided them with information. Thus the two groups joined together in an epistemic partnership in which missionaries donned the mantle of intellectual respectability when they provided reliable data to cartographers, from which the latter drafted their creations for a public that deferred to their expertise.

This partnership was a component of a larger convergence of interests of the French cartographic community with those of the state and church. At the beginning of the seventeenth century, mapmaking was the province of artisans. By gaining governmental and ecclesiastical approbation during the late 1600s, some cartographers entered the ranks of the scientific elite. At the start of the eighteenth century, Catholic clergymen sought similar respectability—that of refined intellectuals. They came closer to that goal when they began to provide accurate data for mapmakers. The French state benefited from yet another sort of authority. Maps acted as instruments of hegemony when they legitimated the Bourbon Dynasty's territorial claims. This convergence was marked by three characteristics. First was a general trend in missionaries' reports that moved away from portrayals of North America as a wilderness under the command of the Devil and his minions. These more benign accounts became prevalent as the second characteristic manifested itself during the early 1700s when priests in the colonies spent more time with French transplants than with the indigenes whom they had been sent to convert. Finally, this later wave of clerics based their depictions on empirically observed phenomena and thus painted far more "rational" pictures of France's overseas possessions. With the blessing of the state, cartographers incorporated their "rationality" into their maps and disseminated them to an eager and increasingly sophisticated public.

An important component in this shift was the growing attention that both groups paid to the networks of waterways that penetrated these realms. These riverine highways became central features in the maps produced with the aid of missionaries. They also became a part of the conceptual framework for imagining the spaces of New France and Louisiana. Eighteenth-century French missionaries and colonial officials sent home charts that signaled a change from portrayals of those "unknown" spaces that were replete with miniature drawings of animals, trees, and humans, to the river systems that wended through the blank portions ready for the mapmaker's quill. The abandonment of stylized images of inhabitants and other-than-human beings signaled more than a mere alteration in graphic design. Rather, it indicated a transformation in the manner in which these religious workers thought about such spaces, from areas controlled by dark unseen forces to receptive fields upon which a discourse of knowledge and power could be inscribed. In their later visualizations of the landscape, navigable rivers and streams functioned as the guides for this inscription, much like ruled lines guide a pen on an otherwise blank page. Their focus on hydrography helped propel this discourse and opened vast regions to military and civilian populations who could support missions to convert and control indigenous peoples.

These mapmakers' creations, although presented as analogues of reality, were selective representations that supported discrete regimes of power. Each one was a text, created to facilitate a particular reading and designed to reinforce political, scientific, or ecclesiastical authority. This required that those who produced them project a modicum of impartiality, that of enumerators rather than interpreters; otherwise they might have inadvertently revealed themselves as mere instruments of their patrons' quest for dominance.[4] This impartiality lent legitimacy to one of the primary cants of colonialism, one that justified the possession of that which formerly belonged to others. Cartographic practices offered the state a set of tools that sanitized an imperial process that Francis Xavier characterized as merely another way to "conjugate the verb 'to rob' in all of its moods and tenses."[5] Cooperation between Catholic priests and mapmakers scrubbed some of the profanity from the French grammar of conquest.

The communiqués from the mission fields furnished geographers who resided in the *métropole* with crucial evidence. Many of the prominent French cartographers of the seventeenth and eighteenth centuries were *géographes de cabinet,* men who did not conduct surveys themselves but instead worked from a variety of sources—visual, textual, and historic—to draft their maps. For these men who rarely worked outside their studios, Catholic priests made excellent informants for a number of reasons. The foremost among them were the social capital and moral prestige that the church possessed. Most Frenchmen relied upon these priests to guide them to eternal life; to trust their words on the location of geographic features was relatively easy. Another reason was that priests had access to the extensive networks maintained by their religious orders. Because of their uniform education and training, these men also possessed similar frames of reference and strong fraternal bonds. This permitted their members to travel and communicate over vast distances. Catholic orders, particularly the Jesuits, also operated a systems of schools and universities that acted as nexuses for their intellectual efforts. Clerics in these centers received and compiled information and then disseminated it among the learned circles of European society.[6] Moreover, priests were already part of a system of geographic reportage. During the seventeenth century French *curés* gathered data for diocesan and provincial maps for use by their bishops.[7] Finally, clergymen also garnered influence through their connections at the royal court or within other governmental or ecclesiastical institutions. Although the Jesuits gained a reputation for their relationships with those who held the reigns of power, they were by no means the only order to do so. The Fathers of the Foreign Missions also had well-placed operatives like Father Jean Bobé, a chaplain at Versailles, who often sent copies of his coreligionists' reports to cartographers such as Delisle and D'Anville.

Although the clerics naturally sought dominion over the spiritual affairs of the colonies, they desired a measure of scientific authority that was also the goal of France's preeminent cartographers. It was this desire for authority that helped generate the silence in the texts produced by both groups. For them, images of personal devils—indeed, images of indigenous peoples—worked against that purpose. This trend was manifest during the waning years of the seventeenth century as Catholics, both cleric and lay, mapped the interior of the continent. Their reports of these areas mentioned the beliefs of the American Indians. For instance, in 1673 Father Jacques Marquette wrote about the Indians' unfounded fears of a demon that lurked in the waters of the Mississippi, waiting for victims to devour.[8] Late seventeenth-century accounts such as his lacked the credulous tone related by previous missionaries. Marquette's dismissiveness stands in contrast to Jesuit Father Jean Pierron's characterization of Mohawk beliefs, "You think that the Master of life is a Demon, whom you call Agreskoue, and I, for my part, say that your Agreskoue is a slave whom God, who is the Master of our lives, keeps chained in Hell as a proud and wicked spirit." Rather, Marquette, like others in this second wave of proselytizers, cast Native American stories of evil spirits as the baseless products of superstitious imaginations instead of demonic manifestations that could be situated within Christian religious cosmology. For this later cohort of observers, the landscape was peopled by deluded sinners rather than populated by ravenous creatures from the nether world. By excluding supernatural beings in their descriptions, priest-informants gained intellectual capital with the scientifically minded intelligentsia, especially those interested in the field of geography.

This partnership between clerics and mapmakers had evolved during a cartographic revolution underway during the reigns of Louis XIV and his great-grandson Louis XV. The French monarchy had demonstrated an interest in maps long before the mid-seventeenth century, but many of these earlier charts depicted distance poorly. They often schematized crucial information such as the best routes through mountains for armies burdened with artillery trains or locations where generals could obtain lodging for their restive troops.[9] While such representations possessed a certain utility, they generally distorted physical space. Accurate renderings of such dimensions, however, were only part of the drafters' intentions.

The authors of these works also embellished their maps with iconic representations of the landscapes' features; they drew pictures of towns, castles, and inhabitants, both animal and human. These illustrations constituted crucial components of these maps' texts: they conveyed discrete bits of information about the terrain and its people. While these images reinforced social, political, and economic hierarchies through an emphasis on the property of the wealthy and powerful, they also reflected the goals of the mapmakers' patrons. For example, royal charts produced during the early years of the Bourbon dynasty glorified the king. The most obvious manifestations of this trend are evident in the decorative cartouches that featured images of the crown's subjugated enemies or the material benefits of the monarch's rule.[10] Aggrandizement was not the only agenda at work in the geography of Louis XIV's subjects; France's overseas possessions required material and spiritual support, and maps offered a means of attracting both.

Early-seventeenth-century communiqués from the missionaries in North America tended to portray the more forbidding aspects of Canada at the expense of geographic data. These depictions focused upon the daunting work that faced the clergy who sought to harvest the souls of the indigenous peoples. For many consumers of missionaries' correspondence, the obstacles of vast distances and harsh environments magnified the triumphs of those servants of the church who overcame them. Physical hindrances, as challenging as they might be to the imaginations of home-bound readers, paled in comparison to the dark forces that opposed the efforts of the priests and nuns who journeyed through the rugged landscape of New France.

One of the first clerics to attempt such a voyage, Father Gabriel Sagard, traveled up the Saint Lawrence and into the Great Lakes. To him, the very landscape appeared to have been cursed. In his memoir he wrote of dark forests incapable of producing wheat or wine, the components of the Eucharist. The swamps bred swarms of flies and mosquitoes, and the hot summers reminded the Franciscan of the fires of hell.[11] In spite of this infernal imagery, he conveyed the hope that he and his coreligionists would "transport to there our zeal and devotion . . . to conquer and erect monuments of our salvation where the Devil has resided in peace up until now."[12] Sagard repeated this *topos* when he characterized the rituals of the Amerindians as practices that "amuse the devil, maintaining and conserving these superstitious and extraordinary ties."[13] Nor was Sagard alone in his assessment of the New World as the domain of diabolical powers. Jesuit priests also sent back similar descriptions that portrayed the setbacks they encountered as examples of satanic machinations.[14] These clerics' writings helped construct a spiritual geography of France's Canadian possessions, replete with other-than-human inhabitants, that resonated with early modern believers who remained at home in Europe. Such accounts created a landscape that was as dangerous—stocked with demonic creatures similar to those that stalked the countryside of France—as it was strange.

Although such creatures catered to the sensibilities of many French readers, one seventeenth-century booster focused upon the more mundane features of the Saint Lawrence River Valley. Samuel de Champlain, a cartographer himself,

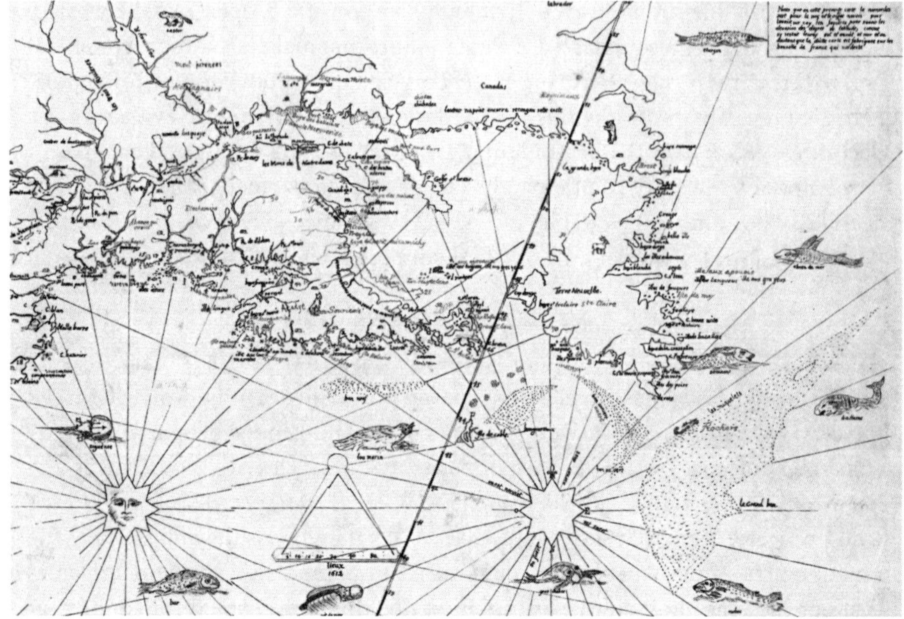

Fig. 1. Detail from Samuel de Champlain's map of the Gulf of Saint Lawrence (*Carte geographiqve de la novvelle Franse faictte par le sievr de Champlain Saint Tongois cappitaine ordinaire povr le roy en la marine faict len 1612.*) Courtesy of the Library of Congress. G3400 1612 .T5 Vault

spent enormous energy promoting his tiny settlement at the foot of Cap Diamond. His representations of Québec emphasized the opportunities afforded by an environment teeming with fish and deer—luxuries beyond the reach of the king's subjects in the mother country. He made certain to include drawings of such animals, along with the native peoples who hunted them. Although Champlain considered Catholic missionaries as allies in his vision of a viable colony, he believed that a key to its success was not to be found by merely attracting indigenous proselytes but also French immigrants. A landscape filled with game to appeal to the notoriously empty stomachs of France's peasantry painted a far more encouraging picture than one ruled by Satan's minions.

Champlain's representations notwithstanding, the needs of the French imperial project changed over the next half century. This was reflected in a shift away from the decorative geographical representations that were in vogue during the early years of Louis XIV's reign. When the king's chief minister, Jean Baptiste Colbert, took office in 1663, he ordered provincial officials to send their best maps to Paris as the first step in the compilation of a national atlas. In 1668 Colbert requested that the Royal Academy of Sciences, which had been founded two years earlier, devise a method to accurately map the territory of France. At the same time, the minister invited astronomer Jean-Dominique Cassini to complete the celestial observations that would enable the precise determination of longitude.[15] When employed in conjunction with newly developed surveying instruments, Cassini's tables facilitated calculations of distances and areas. A few months before his death in September 1683, Colbert commissioned the academy to undertake a complete survey of France. The first axis to be charted in this project began at Dieppe on the English Channel and ran through Paris to the Mediterranean coast.[16] The possibilities for establishing power over space through maps were not lost on other sectors of French officialdom. Bishops engaged cartographers to set the boundaries of their dioceses. Civilian functionaries did the same for their tax districts, while the army plotted invasion routes that led into the Dutch Republic.[17] The Ministry of Marine, which oversaw the navy and the colonies, instituted the *Société hydrographique* to chart the waterways of the *métropole* and France's overseas possessions.

The ensuing project quickly focused upon water routes for several reasons. First, the state stood to benefit from a comprehensive assessment of its coastlines and harbors, particularly as war with Holland loomed upon the horizon. At least some of the coming battles would have to be fought at sea. Cartographers and functionaries also had motives to focus upon rivers. In 1659 Louis XIV's government had signed a treaty with Spain on the Island of Pheasants in the Bidosoa River on the French border. More important than the location of its signing were the provisions that set the two nations' boundaries along the Pyrenees, whose peaks were to be determined by the locations of watersheds.[18] Another incentive for attention to rivers was somewhat more mundane. The royal surveyors computed distances by measuring the angles from either end of a predetermined baseline to a landmark such as a church steeple or other prominent feature. Forests and urban areas impeded their efforts, but rivers provided them with continuous and unobstructed sightlines. For example, Cassini's son led a mapping team that used the Loire as a corridor through the countryside during its expedition to chart the lands between the Rhine and the Bay of Biscay.[19]

These teams produced dozens of maps that underwrote the French state's power. These documents delineated ecclesiastical and legal jurisdictions, military assets, population centers, and tax districts. Equally important were the silences within these texts, the blank spaces that conveyed different aspects of the same discourse of governmental power: places that were of little importance, or peoples whose existence was inconsequential, who were minimized, or who disappeared entirely. As the Royal Academy assembled its grand atlas of France, those absences helped define the contours of political, economic, and church authority.

The cartographers were also on a quest to establish their professional authority. Up until the mid-seventeenth century, French mapmakers were not subject to

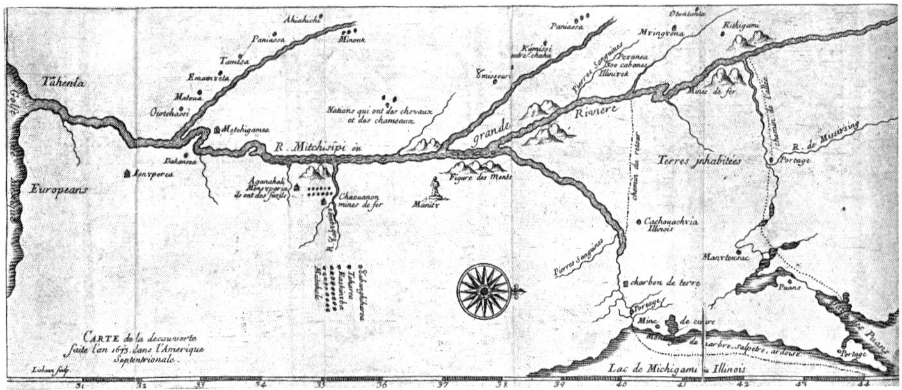

Fig. 2. Map based on Marquette's description of the Mississippi River. (*Carte de la découverte faite l'an 1673 dans l'Amérique septentrionale.* Liebaux, sculp.) Courtesy of the Library of Congress. G159 .T38, G4042.M5

laws that regulated printers and their guilds. Printers, however, looked jealously upon charting firms that used engraving technology that could be construed as competing with their trade. Louis XIV drew a border between the two professions when he decreed that engravers were limited to a single drum press. They could not own letter type, and they were forbidden to publish censored materials. These regulations did not extend to those who were not under guild supervision, such as members of the Royal Academy of Sculptors and Painters.[20] Thus, a way for cartographers to avoid the prying eyes of the printers' inspectors was to affiliate with one of the academies or the university.

This emerging discourse of cartography as a tool of statecraft became particularly important in France's New World possessions, but clerics remained crucial discussants within it. In the third quarter of the seventeenth century, while the great surveys of the French coastline were underway, Jesuit Father Jacques Marquette and layman Louis Jolliet journeyed south from the Great Lakes. They picked up the course of a grand river that Amerindians told them emptied into a vast sea to the South. Marquette's map of the Mississippi contained some elements of the older iconography of the first charts of Canada, but it also hinted at the adoption of new techniques.

On the east bank, in Illinois country, there is a small drawing of a figure labeled "Manitou," a general Algonquian term for other-than-human beings or impulses. The figure on the map was most likely a European's interpretation of a Native American monument on the banks of the Mississippi River. Marquette and Jolliet recorded in their journal that they had passed "high rocks with hideous monsters painted on them. . . . They are as large as a calf, with head and horns like a goat; their eyes are red; beard like a tiger's; and a face like a man's.

Their tails are so long that they pass over their heads and between their fore legs, under their belly, and ending like a fish tail. They are painted red, green, and black. They are so well drawn that I cannot believe they were drawn by Indians."[21] Francis Parkman wrote that Marquette drew the paintings on his manuscript map, but the original had disappeared by the mid-nineteenth century.[22]

When Melchisédec Thévenot published Marquette's journal in 1682, his printer appended the foldout map that is reproduced above.[23] Its engraver, a man named Liebaux, symbolized the "Manitou" as a human figure on a pedestal. He also listed himself as a "sculptor," a trade outside the supervision of the guilds by this time. When the priest's story made its way to the French reading public, the Native Americans' paintings had been transformed into an idol sporting an "eastern" appearance, complete with a turban and heavy coat. Thus a North American landmark had been converted into something that strongly resembled the quintessential "other": an "Oriental" "Moslem." The mapmaker had redrawn this indigenous site to personify Western Christendom's archenemy in a manner that had a double resonance for the book's purchaser. It evoked the latent fears of capture and suffering that require contextualization. After centuries of North African slave raids against the coasts of France, several Catholic religious orders had made ransoming imprisoned Christians from the "Turks" (the generic name for North Africans as well as those from the Levant) their primary vocation.[24] The text's message and format suggested to its readers that clerics like Marquette and his religious brethren possessed the means to obviate the dangers posed by the alterity of the Mississippi River Valley's inhabitants as well as non-Christian Mediterranean corsairs. Imbedded within that message was another: the expansion of the French state's power into the western Mediterranean and into the heart of the New World went hand in hand with the missions of the Catholic church.

The Marquette map also showed Native American communities and other landmarks that lined the banks of the river. It noted that certain peoples who lived there owned horses and muskets. At the same time, the chart also excluded a good number of indigenous populations or condensed them into undifferentiated groupings. Even at this early stage, the silences in his text communicated the relative importance of particular peoples and, more important, the diffuse nature of the region's political authority, which was exemplified by Marquette's reduction of Amerindian homelands to small dots surrounded by large swaths of empty space. Although it retained some of the schematic aspects of early charts, Marquette's map of the Mississippi also belied its author's intention to leave a record for others to follow.

The next recorded expedition to travel down the Mississippi was led by René-Robert Cavelier, sieur de La Salle. He embarked on a two-year trip that began in 1681. When he reached the mouth of the river at the Gulf of Mexico, he claimed all the lands it drained for the King of France. Thus the terms of La

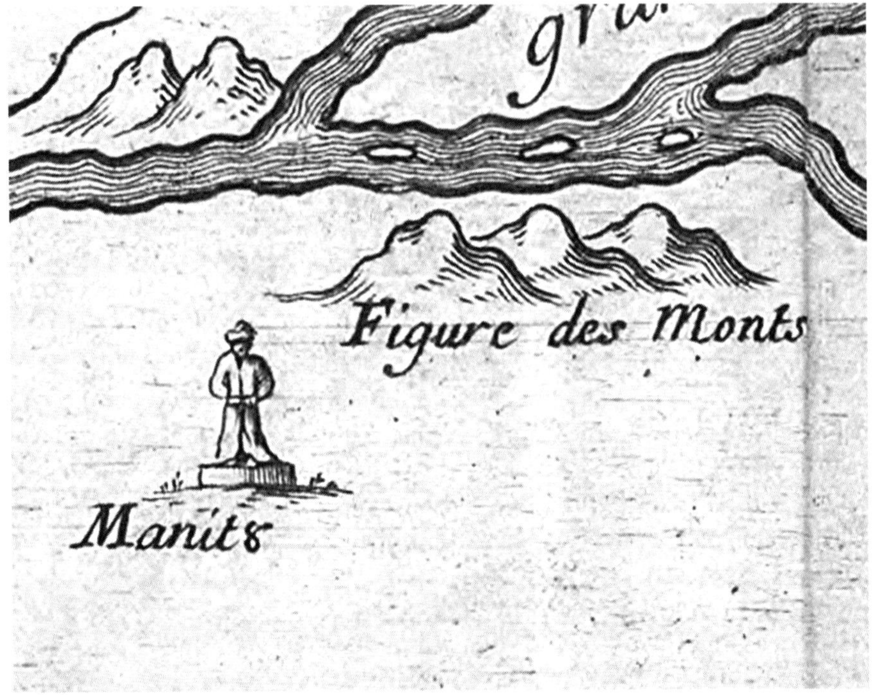

Fig. 3. Detail from the Marquette map showing the "manitou."
Courtesy of the Library of Congress.

Salle's declarations reproduced at least one of the practices that had been written into the Treaty of the Pyrenees. The river systems of North America, though yet unmapped, could be used to demarcate lands over which the French asserted hegemony. La Salle's company included Catholic priests Fathers Zénobe Membré and Douay Anastase, both Récollets. Another member of the same order, Father Louis Hennepin, had accompanied La Salle an earlier voyage. Hennepin was already attracting attention in Paris with tales of his imprisonment and subsequent adoption by a Sioux headman. He was soon to gain fame as the author of *Description de la Louisiane,* which reported on his experiences in the upper Mississippi River Valley.[25]

Although Hennepin's book was essentially a travel and captivity narrative, other clerics during the same era concentrated on gathering and disseminating empirical data rather than cataloging local curiosities. In 1685 a handful of priests from the Society of Jesus and the Fathers of the Foreign Missions left France for East Asia. The Jesuits brought with them sextants, compasses, and other surveying instruments to record the geographic data of their voyage.[26] By

Fig. 4. Delisle's 1703 map of Mexico, Florida, and English possessions. (*Carte du Mexique et de la Floride des Terres Angloises et des Isles Antilles : du cours et des environs de la Riviere de Mississipi* [sic], *dressée sur ungrand nombre de memoires principalemt. sur ceux de Mrs d'Iberville et le Sueur.*) Courtesy of the Library of Congress. G3300 1703 .L5 Vault

employing Cassini's astronomical tables, they accurately reckoned the longitude of the Cape of Good Hope. Father Thomas Gouye published his fellow Jesuits' findings in his 1688 book, *Recueil des observations physiques et mathématiques pour servir à la perfection de l'astronomie et de la géographie, envoyées de Siam par les jésuites missionnaires.* In it Gouye focused on meteorological and astronomical observations, complete with the calculations derived from them. In this manner he adhered more to the format of papers published by the Academy of Sciences than to the travelogue style of his predecessors.[27]

Such observations reinforced the value of the data that clerics provided for geographers. Guillaume Delisle's 1703 map of Louisiana exemplified the increasing collaboration between Catholic priests and cartographers. Among the contributors to Delisle's chart were the priests Douay Anastase, François de Montigny, and Jean-François Buisson de Saint-Cosme (the last two were priests of the Foreign Missions). He also employed the journal of Jesuit Paul Du Ru, who traveled with Pierre Le Moyne, sieur d'Iberville, on his voyage up the Mississippi in 1700.

Although their memoirs constituted only a fraction of the materials that Delisle used, his analysis of their writings demonstrated not only the cooperation between the French clergy and geographers but also the efforts of both groups to secure a measure of authority. Their communications made no mention of other-than-human inhabitants.

A chart of the Mississippi that Delisle had made the year before foreshadowed some of the impending shifts in French cartography. That previous rendering, based primarily on Jean-Baptiste Le Sueur's 1700–1701 journal, traced only the course of the river. It contained very few details beyond noting the mouths of the great river's tributaries. Nor did he indulge in graphic embellishments. His 1702 map was a functional navigational aid that laid bare the access to the interior of North America. Moreover, he listed his credentials as the geographer for the Academy of Sciences.

Delisle's continued quest for authority in the production of geographic knowledge is evident in his 1718 map of Louisiana. It also marked the continuity of collaboration between cartographers and clerics. For his *Carte de la Louisiane et du cours du Misssissipi,* he not only utilized material from Soupart's survey of the Gulf Coast but also included information contained in an extensive report by Father François Le Maire, a chaplain at Mobile who labored there under the auspices of the Foreign Missions. Father Bobé, who had extensive contacts with the order, had been forwarding missionaries' correspondence received at Versailles to Delisle's workshop as early as 1710.[28] Delisle, in turn, took special care to credit Le Maire's contributions in the map's header.

The new chart generated a good deal of ire in England, partly for Delisle's assertion that Carolina was named for the French king Charles IX. It reflected the kingdom's earlier geo-diplomatic practices, which used river drainage systems to designate France's territorial claims. Delisle thus extended Louis's dominion to the Appalachians, thereby hemming in Britain's colonies, at least on paper, to the Atlantic seaboard.[29] It also pushed Spanish borders back to the Pecos and Rio Grande Rivers. Regardless of the international controversy it stirred, the *Carte de la Louisiane* helped earn Delisle the title of *géographe du roi* (the king's geographer).[30]

Delisle's map is also notable for the manner in which it depicted Native communities. In his 1718 version of North America, the unbounded domains of Champlain's maps had shrunk to small pictorial representations of villages. The blank spaces of the Louisiana map, devoid of human inhabitants, seemed to offer ample room for immigrants. In this cartographic production, these silences served the interest of the state, which was then in the midst of a campaign to colonize the Gulf Coast as part of a larger scheme to finance the French national debt.[31] These smaller Amerindians' homelands presented fewer hindrances to European settlement than did Champlain's illustrated version. There was a

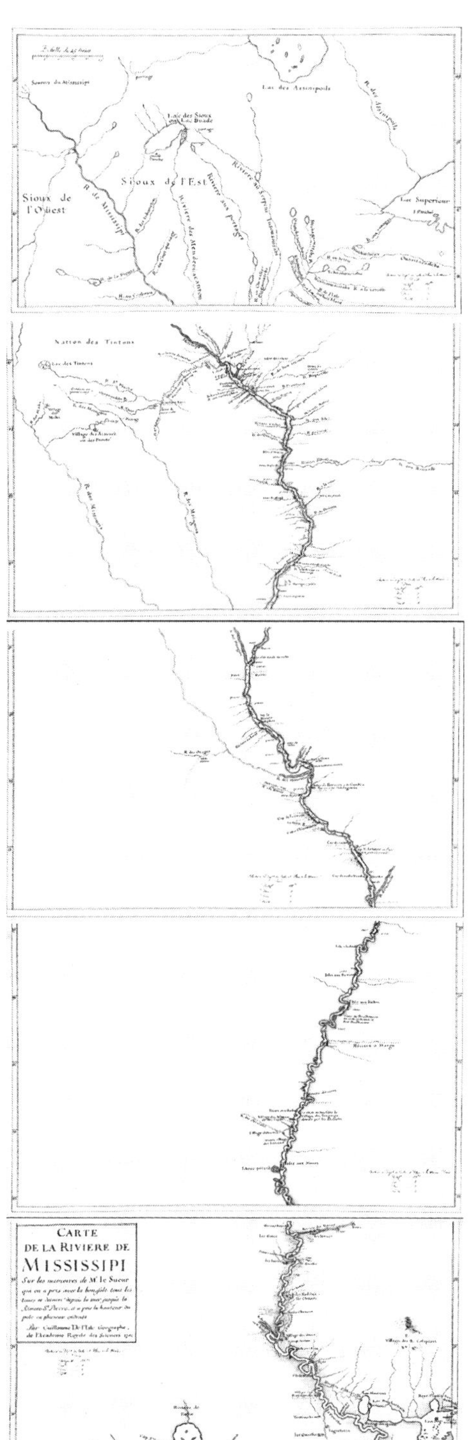

Fig. 5. Delisle's 1702 map of the Mississippi River. (*Carte de la rivière de Mississipi : sur les mémoires de Mr. Le Sueur qui en a pris avec la boussole tous les tours et detours depuis la mer jusqu'à la rivière St. Pierre, et a pris la hauteur du pole en plusieurs endroits / par Guillaume de L'Isle geographe de l'Academie des Sciences*) Courtesy of the Library of Congress. G4042.M5 1702 .L5 Vault

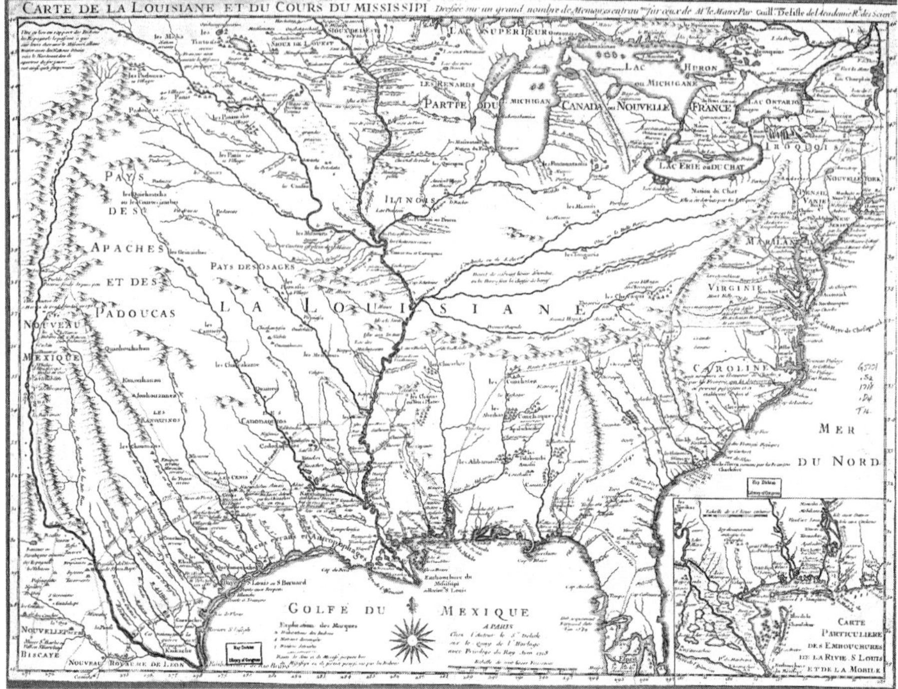

Fig. 6. Delisle's 1718 *Carte de la Louisiane et du cours du Mississippi.* Courtesy of the Library of Congress G3701.S2 1718 .D4 TIL

significant exception in Delisle's otherwise sparse production: along the Gulf Coast of Texas he inscribed the words *"Indiens errant et antropophages"* (wandering Indians and cannibals). This was the region that had swallowed up La Salle's ill-fated 1684 expedition to colonize the lower Mississippi River Valley. Like the Marquette map, Delisle's chart warned its viewers that dangerously "uncivilized" peoples who engaged in horrific practices lurked just beyond the pale.

By this time the French Empire and the Catholic Church had much experience working together to increase their overseas influences. A diminished indigenous presence benefited both since it was plain that the hordes of loyal Native converts envisioned by seventeenth-century imperialists had failed to materialize. Eighteenth-century bureaucrats instead focused upon exporting settlers to the New World rather than enlisting native peoples in its colonial project. This trend was reflected in the vocations of clergy who followed these newcomers. Unlike the earlier religious workers who sought proselytes among the First Nations of Canada, this latest wave of Catholic priests remained content to minister to European parishioners rather than venture into the forests and prairies of the new province. For instance, Father Le Maire had been sent by the Priests of the Foreign Missions to convert Amerindians, but he spent nearly all his time with Mobile's French transplants.

At the same time the clergy were devoting more of their efforts tending to the colonists' spiritual needs, the trend toward structuring Louisiana's spatial dimensions by means of its waterways was gaining momentum. Father Paul Du Ru's 1700 journal contains early examples of this development. He listed the Native American communities by the order in which he encountered them along the Mississippi. In a similar manner Father Le Maire organized his 1716 description of the Gulf Coast and Lower Mississippi Valley by dealing first with Mobile and its environs, then the shoreline west to the mouth of the great river, and then moving north as far as the mouth of the Arkansas. Jesuit Father Pierre-François Xavier de Charlevoix systematized his descriptions of the native peoples in a similar manner in his 1744 publication, *Histoire et description générale de la Nouvelle-France.*[32] He drew upon his 1721–22 voyage from Québec to New Orleans and ordered his descriptions from north to south along the Wabash, Ohio, and Mississippi Rivers. Mathurin Le Petit, also a Jesuit, reported on Native Americans who lived along the Mississippi in a south-to-north array as he had visited them in his travels from the Louisiana colonial capital.[33] This tendency to concentrate on waterways was echoed by secular authors. Marc-Antoine Calliot, a clerk who lived in New Orleans between 1729 and 1731, used a similar convention. In his unpublished "Relation du Mississippi," Calliot described each European and native community in a south-to-north sequence that "retraced" a journey he did not make.[34]

Many of these documents also found their way into the works of Jean Baptiste Bourguignon d'Anville, one of great cartographers of the eighteenth century, who also collaborated with Jesuit priests, especially Father Charlevoix. D'Anville's 1732 pencil draft of eastern Louisiana exemplified the transformation of the discourse from a decorative, celebratory style to an unadorned, "scientific" one.

Despite the decreased information regarding Native American communities, the cartographer saw fit to include Delisle's caveat about the inhabitants' cannibalistic tendencies. Along the western shores of the Gulf of Mexico, he wrote, "les Sauvages qui errant ces quartiers sont Ata-capa ou Mangeurs-d'Homes" (the Savages who wander these quarters are Ata-capa or Man-eaters). Like his predecessors, d'Anville drew upon a deep-seated repulsion for those who ate human flesh. He also included details of one of France's colonial rivals, Spain. He noted that "the Spanish are established [here] but in small numbers."

When d'Anville's draft was published in 1752, even more detail had been erased. It depicted the region between the Mississippi and Appalachians as essentially unoccupied lands dotted with a few native towns, easily accessed by a network of rivers and waterways. Gone even were the cannibals who had roamed the Texas coast; the dark powers that had ruled the continent had been redacted

Fig. 7. D'Anville's 1732 pencil draft of Louisiana. BnF Cartes et Plans, Ge.C. 9905. Used by permission of La Bibliothéque nationale de France.

by the engraver's stylus. Consumers of D'Anville's productions could see that the southeastern quadrant of North America lay open for domination by a colonial regime.

Another example of this shift away from references to Satanic control was the growing attention given to tracing the cultural practices of Amerindians to their supposed roots among the peoples of the ancient Mediterranean. Jesuit priest Joseph-François Lafitau published his study of the Old World "origins" of Native Americans in 1724, based in part on his own observations and those of his fellow religionists.[35] Antoine Le Page du Pratz, a plantation manager, detected apparent similarities in Natchez origin myths with the stories of Noah's flood.[36] Thus Roman Catholic clerics helped generate images of a "lost" people from Western Asia who inhabited the New World. They replaced previous images of a

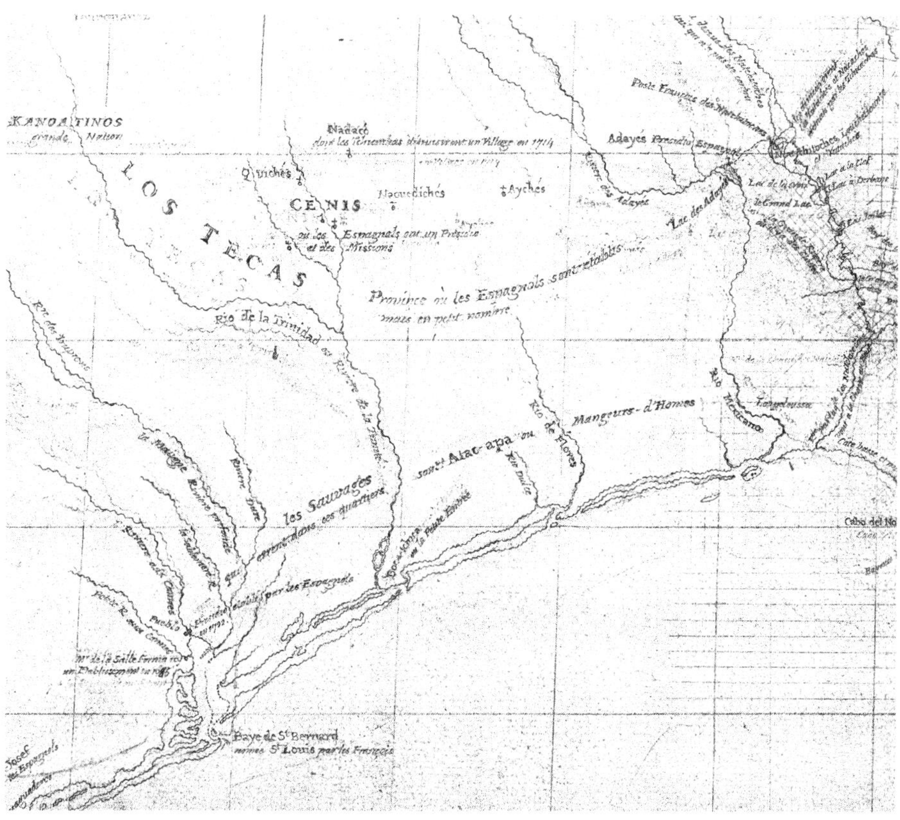

Fig. 8. D'Anville's 1732 rendering of the Texas coast and its man-eating inhabitants. Used by permission of La Bibliothéque nationale de France.

continent inhabited by devil worshippers with one peopled by redeemable populations that retained vestiges of Judaic and Classical religious practices. Moreover, these clerics had the teaching and publishing infrastructure to disseminate this new image. By their emphasis on "rational" depictions of North America, the priests who labored there gained a reputation as trustworthy sources of information for influential cartographic firms in Paris.

Cartographers also replicated the organization of space around the major rivers of French North America. After the 1730s they published charts of Louisiana based on surveys taken along the course of the colony's rivers and streams. Unlike maps of the early seventeenth century, these later examples contain little ornamentation. They often portray only the watercourses that had become Europeans' main routes into the interior. Gone were the fanciful depictions of natives and beasts, and in their place were increasingly detailed measurements of navigable waterways. Gone also were references to diabolic control of the

Fig. 9. The 1752 version taken from d'Anville's draft of 1732. (*Carte de la Louisiane par le Sr. d'Anville. Dressée en mai 1732.* [Gravée par] Guille. de la Haye). Courtesy of the Library of Congress. G3860 1732 .A5 Vault

landscape—the pen, ruler, and quadrant had exorcized the continent's demonic masters. A few mythological creatures remained, but the cartographers safely imprisoned them in decorative cartouches. These documents exemplify the evolution toward the demystification of North American space—one that lent itself to the extraction of resources and knowledge. Unlike Weber's Calvinist disenchantment of Europe that gave rise to Anglo-Dutch forms of capitalism, this Catholic version underwrote the projection of French military and economic power.[37]

Through the use of such methods, clerics and cartographers legitimized their status as guardians of their respective épistèmes. Together they reinforced each other's command over regimes of knowledge and power. The priests gained credibility as observers—reliable partners in scientific inquiry—who simultaneously reinforced their authority in other matters. The mapmakers, who drew upon ever-expanding sets of data to produce their charts and globes, gained status as creators of accurate analogues of the planet's surface. This symbiosis extended to the Old World as well as the New. At the same time that members of the Society of Jesus, the Récollets, and Congregation of the Foreign Missions took measurements of North America and Asia, their coreligionists gathered similar information at home. D'Anville sent his *Mémoire Instuctif* to clerics throughout France that furnished directions on noting the position of the sun as well as guidelines for describing key features of the local terrain. These were transformed into diocesan maps for use by tithe collectors and other ecclesiastical agents.[38]

Cartographers, by virtue of serving the church and state, gained prestige within the ranks of the intelligentsia. Some were welcomed into exclusive associations like the Royal Academy of the Sciences, while a select few earned further recognition as *géographes du roi.* Their conflicts with the printers' guilds over the production of illustrations and the possession of movable type faded into obscurity. Through their appeals to the rational and the presentation of the map as an empirical, neutral presentation of reality, they created spaces for cartographic practitioners among the officially recognized literati.

This social and political elevation of cartographers also came about because maps became increasingly valuable to the state as "a symbolic shorthand for a complex of nationalist ideas."[39] The work of Delisle and d'Anville, buttressed by the testimony of pious informants, constituted the foundations for France's claim over large sections of North America. A crucial element of this discourse of hegemony was its invocation of science—of dispassionate analyses and representations. It portrayed French colonialism as a natural condition that arose out of the absence of political and religious order in the hinterlands of Canada and Louisiana. This self-reflexive exercise was possible because of the apotheosis of technology in general, and cartographic technology in particular, assisted by the patronage of the church and state. Such homage concealed the dialogic quality of the texts: instead of being analogues of the "real," these maps were a form of communication that validated social, ecclesiastical, economic, and political hierarchies. The rhetoric of these texts generated an aura of objectivity that permeated these empirically charged productions. This impartiality was reinforced by appeals to mathematical certainty furnished by the latest computational tools. Thus, the syntax of eighteenth-century cartographic discourse obscured these maps' roles as instruments of the powerful and helped conceal the metaphoric nature of all maps.

Silence constituted an essential component of this discourse. For many who were beginning to believe that the universe was knowable, ignorance was becoming a temporary state of affairs. Indeed, the unknown offered a challenge. This is apparent in the cartographic productions of the mid-1700s. The crowded charts of the previous century gave way to maps that openly conceded that they were incomplete. D'Anville's 1752 depiction of the Birdfoot Delta of the Mississippi River informed the reader that *"Dans tout cet espace la Mer est basse et vazuese parsemée d'Isles dont le detail n'est pas connu suffisament."* (In all of this space the sea is shallow and muddy, dotted with islands, whose detail is not sufficiently known.) The map readily admitted its inadequacies. The vast portions of the continent of which Europeans knew little—the Great Plains, the Rocky Mountains, and the lands to the west of them—lay beyond the fringes of D'Anville's map like loose threads tucked under the hem of a garment. Its geographic rhetoric implied that although these regions were poorly surveyed, these shortcomings

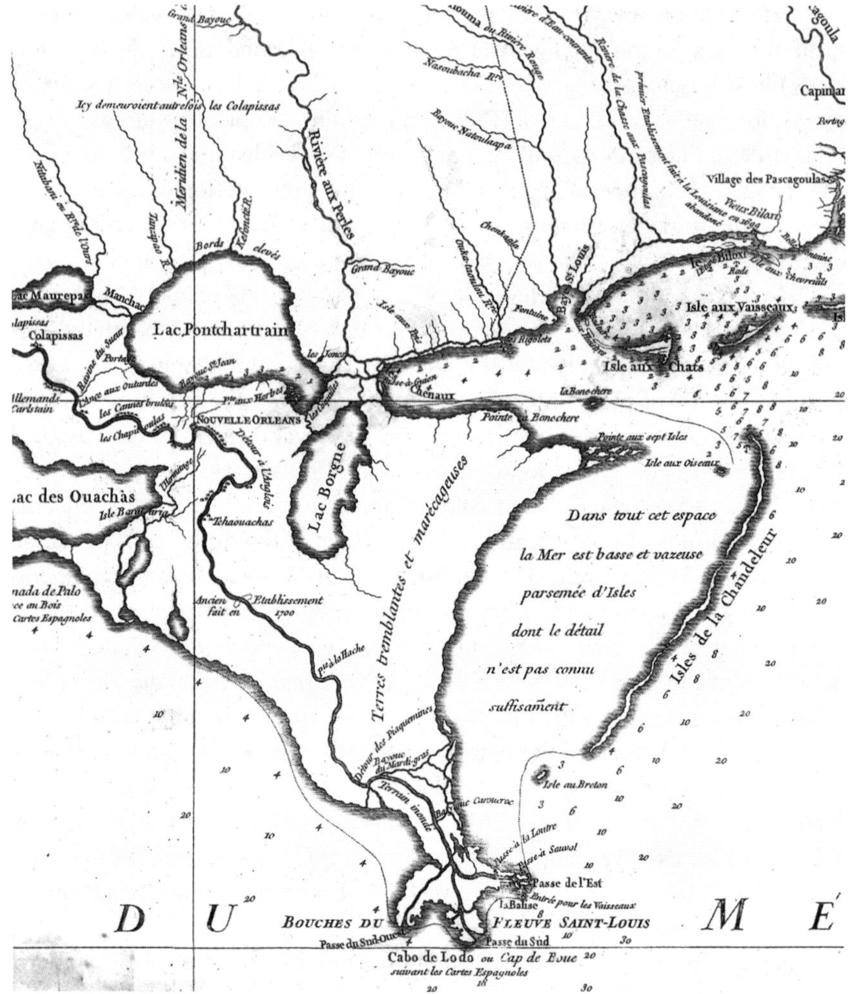

Fig. 10. Detail from the 1752 d'Anville map. Used by permission of La Bibliothéque nationale de France.

would soon be rectified. The unknown now had the potential to become known through empirical observation.

In a similar manner, Father Poisson's apprehension of the Mississippi River's "frightful solitude" hinted at a quiet optimism of the era. His ignorance of the immense landscape that he encountered was a temporary condition: "I am not *yet* sufficiently acquainted with the Country and with the customs of the Savages to give you information of them." Moreover, his description suggested that the region was empty, supine, and ripe for penetration. The river, whose contours were already committed to paper, led through this terrain. Perhaps the wonders of French technology would soon fill the silence with the sounds of colonists, busy in the nearby fields or at the tillers of their vessels.

The goals of the state, the clergy, and the cartographers thus converged in the French colonial project in the lower Mississippi Valley. The government endeavored to create settlements that exported tobacco and other commodities to the homeland. For this purpose they required depictions of a receptive landscape to encourage immigration and investment. The Catholic Church, particularly those orders with commitments to the mission fields of Louisiana and Illinois, wanted to establish authority over the region. Their supervision of the colonies' ecclesiastical affairs could now perhaps be reinforced by their newly won intellectual prestige. Communiqués that mentioned dark supernatural forces degraded the reliability of the priests' reports in the eyes of a reading public that was becoming increasingly sophisticated. In the state and church's search for power, Father Poisson's solitude had become far more useful than Father Sagard's devils.

Mapping Urban Religion in an Atlantic Port

Kyle B. Roberts

Upon first glance, the intersection of Ann and Nassau Streets in lower Manhattan, as reproduced in an 1830 issue of the *New-York Mirror*, looks like a typical early-nineteenth-century city block. In a view that could just as easily be seen in Dublin, Bristol, New Orleans, or a number of other Atlantic seaports, the commercial landscape appears to be advancing over the residential and religious landscape. Multistory brick storefronts overshadow and crowd out older wooden townhouses. A church spire provides the only ostensible religious element in an otherwise secular landscape, and even it looks consigned to the margin. If life imitates art, then Mammon appears to have banished God from the life and spaces of the growing city.

Such a read, while understandable given the way scholars have written about the modernizing city, glosses over a far more complex urban landscape. These seemingly secular structures housed people and institutions intimately connected to the spiritual currents of the Atlantic world. The congregation worshipping in the Presbyterian Church at the end of the block maintained personal and denominational ties to congregations around the city, throughout the region, and across the Atlantic. When they prayed for the expansion of Christ's kingdom, they imagined themselves as part of a circum-Atlantic community with a global reach. The men and women laboring two doors down at the headquarters of the American Bible Society, the three-story structure in the center of the block, had actually achieved that reach. They annually distributed hundreds of thousands of Bibles in various languages over national and international networks. Moral reform associations frequently met next door in Clinton Hall. Inspired by the 1833 British abolition of slavery, the American Anti-Slavery Society planned to gather here the following July to renew its call for abolition in the United States but switched at the last minute to Chatham Street Chapel to avoid detection. The spectacle of blacks and whites sitting side by side fanned embers of racial hatred already stoked by religious justifications for slavery. Before long, mobs ran rampant through the city, assaulting the bodies, homes, and churches

Fig. 1. "View of a Section of Ann and Nassau streets—taken from the south corner" from the *New York Mirror, and Ladies Literary Gazette* 8 (September 4, 1830): 65. Courtesy of the American Antiquarian Society.

of African Americans. The mob's violence cast a long shadow over the city's and nation's religious, social, and political life. Churches, publishing houses, rental halls, streets, and bodies were just a few of the diverse places in Atlantic ports where urban religion was formed, negotiated, and contested.

That New York provided nodes for local, national, and international religious networks and sites of interaction is not, in itself, surprising. For centuries, seaports stood as hubs for a vast array of networks—social, economic, political, and cultural—that crisscrossed the Atlantic. From around the Atlantic basin came much of the city's population, whether driven by ambition, necessity, bondage, or a desire for adventure. Men and women arrived on the same ships that transported commodities extracted from Atlantic hinterlands—furs in the seventeenth century, sugar in the eighteenth century, wheat and cotton in the nineteenth century—that formed the basis of the city's economy. Complex circum-Atlantic networks of production, distribution, and consumption reinforced political relationships, although those bonds were susceptible to challenge over time. In daily interactions in taverns, parlors, and meetinghouses, men and women debated topics—such as colonialism, revolution, and emancipation—of pressing concern in all corners of this world. The books they read, the goods they consumed, and the staged and impromptu performances they witnessed and participated in linked them to cultural and intellectual currents far beyond New York's wharfs. Characterization of the city's street life as "Babylonian confusion" in an 1850 guidebook aptly alludes to the pluralism of the city as much as to the interconnectedness of secular and spiritual conceptions within it.[1]

Given these connections, it is surprising the extent to which scholars have overlooked the place of urban religion in the development and experience of life in Atlantic world seaports. This essay seeks to reconcile this oversight by using

New York as a case study to explore urban religion from two different vantage points between the mid-seventeenth and mid-nineteenth centuries. Unique in what it achieved over its first two and a half centuries, New York is at the same time representative of the larger processes that shaped the evolution of seaports from colonial outposts into national and international commercial, political, and cultural centers. Technologies of mapping offer a fruitful way to approach urban religion, given the centrality of space to religious belief and practice. The advent of the spatial humanities, combining the humanist's concern with the experience and nuance of change over time and the geographer's technologies of mapping, provides scholars with a powerful means to visualize and analyze the influence of religion on the development of the city, the first part of this essay. But urban religion, like the city, is not constituted merely by the presence of material structures, as the second part of this essay explores. It is the product of innumerable movements and interactions in real and imagined spaces through which religious belief, practice, and understanding were constituted, negotiated, and contested by those who lived, moved, and had their being in Atlantic world cities.[2]

Mapping the Urban Landscape

Between 1620 and 1860, New York grew from an outpost of empire inhabited by several hundred Europeans, Africans, and Native Americans on the southern tip of Manhattan to an international commercial center with over eight hundred thousand residents scattered in neighborhoods all the way to the base of Central Park.[3] Urban historians have long acknowledged the dialogic nature of the city's development but rarely do they include religion as a participant in that conversation.[4] New York's reputation as Gotham has overshadowed serious consideration of the influence of the city's hundreds of churches, dozens of benevolent and reform associations, and thousands of believers on its physical development. Failing to account for their influence misses religion's crucial involvement in the life of Atlantic seaports, where the seeds of modernity—ethnic and religious pluralism, a complex market culture, large-scale participatory politics, and an emphasis on the liberal individual—first blossomed.[5] Every Atlantic port developed differently, but New York bears hallmarks common to many during this period.

Shortcomings of disciplinary training and technological complications have traditionally hampered scholars who wish to think spatially about urban religion in Atlantic world ports. Mapping on paper fails to capture the dynamism of spatial development over time, while written descriptions, even by the ablest hand, are rarely as evocative as visualizations. New thinking and technologies within the spatial humanities promise to make spatial analysis easier and to open up new avenues for research. Geographic Information Systems (GIS) software and web-based applications offer a means to combine the quantitative work of geographers with the qualitative work of humanists.[6]

Mapping New York's religious landscape reveals the extent to which it developed in dialogue with forces internal and external to the city. Decisions made by the city's religious communities—over where to build houses of worship, the proper relationship between church and state, the value and extent of religious toleration and freedom of conscience, and the obligations owed to the poor and downtrodden—reflected and in turn helped constitute the values of the larger urban spatial order. This can be seen in three distinct phases between the English conquest of New Amsterdam in 1664 and the outbreak of the American Civil War in 1861. The city's development needs to be understood not only as an internally generated phenomenon but also as part and parcel of a broader Atlantic process.

From its founding by the Dutch as a trading post in 1624, New Amsterdam resembled other colonial outposts throughout the Atlantic World. The physical layout of colonial settlements typically responded to multiple concerns. Order was first and foremost. The metropole relied upon the juxtaposition of places of political, economic, and religious authority to reinforce a landscape of symbolic power.[7] The physical concentration of these institutions buttressed the legitimacy of the local ruling body and, by extension, the Crown. Formal imperial dictates, such as the *Law of the Indies,* established guidelines for the creation of some settlements; the informal decision making of colonists influenced just as many others. Safety was another concern. Even where the production and trade of goods trumped the building of infrastructure, an effort was made to wall off colonial settlements out of fear of invasion by displaced indigenous peoples. For many European colonists, what it meant to be urbane, and by that civilized, was spatial. A sense of boundedness, reified through walls—real and imagined— that demarcated cities from the surrounding countryside, of density of settlement within those walls, and of ethnic and religious heterogeneity, permeated European cities and their colonial ports.[8] Most colonists wished to collapse the distance that separated them from their countries of origin, which they did by attempting to re-create the world they had left behind. The material environment fostered the illusion of familiarity amid alienating disorder. Churches, walls, and forts could function as an antidote to the disorder of a sprawling wilderness.[9]

The city's symbolic landscape survived the transition from Dutch to English rule in 1664—and back and forth again in 1673–74—except for a key difference. The Dutch had established the locus of their political authority, the center of their symbolic landscape, within the defensive walls of Fort Amsterdam at the southwestern tip of Manhattan Island. Here the Dutch Reformed Church stood next to the Governor's House and the Secretary's House, each reinforcing the authority of the other (although, as in many other colonial settlements, the scope of their authority often stood at odds).[10] Aware that the English would evict the Dutch and install their own officials and institutions, Pieter Stuyvesant insisted as a condition of capitulation upon "the liberty of their consciences in Divine Worship and church discipline," a right he had personally refused other dissenting religious groups.[11] James, Duke of York, patron and namesake of the new city, agreed to Dutch demands with the Duke's Laws of 1664, ensuring religious toleration for the open worship of different faiths, at least for Christians. Passage of the Act of Toleration further secured the conditions for a competitive religious landscape.

Mapping the city's religious landscape in the aftermath of the lifting of legal restrictions on public worship reveals the extent to which French Protestants, English Baptists and Quakers, Africans, and Portuguese Jews simultaneously reinforced and challenged the authority of the symbolic landscape. The British Atlantic had been awash in religious dissenters from the mid-seventeenth century onwards, unleashed by the Civil War in England, the Anglo-Dutch wars in the Caribbean, the ongoing work of Catholic missionary orders, and the African slave trade.[12] In an observation that might apply to Philadelphia, Dublin, or Port Royal, Thomas Dongan, royal governor of New York, reflected that in the city there were "not many of the Church of England; few Roman Catholics; abundance of Quakers . . . Singing Quakers; Ranting Quakers; Sabbatarians; Anti-Sabbatarians, some Anabaptists, some Independents, some Jews; in short, of all sorts of opinions there are some, and the most part of none at all."[13] By the end of the seventeenth century, the English moved out of the fort and reconfigured the symbolic landscape by creating an axis of power centered on the State House on Wall Street and Trinity Church at the corner of Broadway and Wall Street. In response, various national Protestant churches—Dutch, French, and Scottish—asserted their own authority by embedding themselves in the core of the city, adjacent to the colony's governmental structures and markets. Situation provided one means of asserting standing and place within the city; form, style, and size offered others.

National Protestant churches offered a significant challenge to the Anglican Church's authority as the colony's established church, but the real threat lay on the margins. Relegated to side streets and back lots in this symbolic landscape were Quakers, Methodists, and Baptists, who used their spatial location to craft an alternative order, as seen in figure 2. They grounded their authority not in their linkage to the power of the state but rather in the importance of the individual and congregation. They introduced new forms of sacred space by worshipping in workshops and barns, by using the banks of the Hudson and East Rivers to baptize converts, and by gathering in fields to hear itinerant preachers. In their meetinghouses, they crafted a powerful spiritual and visual aesthetic that stood in dialogue with trends and concerns within the city as much as around the Atlantic. In turn, those meetinghouses became the locus of new neighborhoods, further challenging the traditional linkage of religious, political, and economic

Fig. 2. Map of New York City churches, 1783. In the colonial city, the Anglican Church (marked with an "E") anchored the city's spiritual landscape. Other national Protestant churches—Dutch Reformed (D), Huguenot (H), and Presbyterian (P)—clustered nearby. Dissenting faiths—Baptists (B), Jews (J), Lutherans (L), Methodists (M), Moravians (F), and Quakers (Q) – emplaced themselves on side streets and back lots of the city, but within a generation would control the development of the city. Courtesy of the author.

power in the city's core. In their infancy on the eve of the American Revolution, dissenting faiths opened the way for a new spatial conceptualization after the war ended.

Revolutions throughout the Atlantic world at the end of the eighteenth century unleashed a liberating political ideology that inspired men and women to make the world anew. This new republican ethos of enterprise and self-reliance pervaded all aspects of urban social, political, economic, and religious life.[14] This new ethos quickly manifested itself as a challenge to one of the anchors of authority in the colonial spatial regime: the established church. On the eve of the American Revolution, the Anglican Church worshipped in the city's largest houses of worship, controlled the city's only college, owned a substantial amount of urban real estate, subsisted off public tax money, and retained discretion over the right of other faiths to incorporate, despite the Duke's Laws and the Act of Toleration. The Anglican Church's loyalist stance during the war did little to endear it to newly independent New Yorkers. In 1777 the New York State Legislature and seven years later the city's Common Council stripped the Anglican Church of its status and granted any religious body the right to incorporate.[15] The opening up of the spiritual marketplace coincided with a significant shift in how people decided where to worship. Voluntarism, which had long underlain the appeal of Atlantic world evangelicalism, replaced ethnicity as the primary determinant

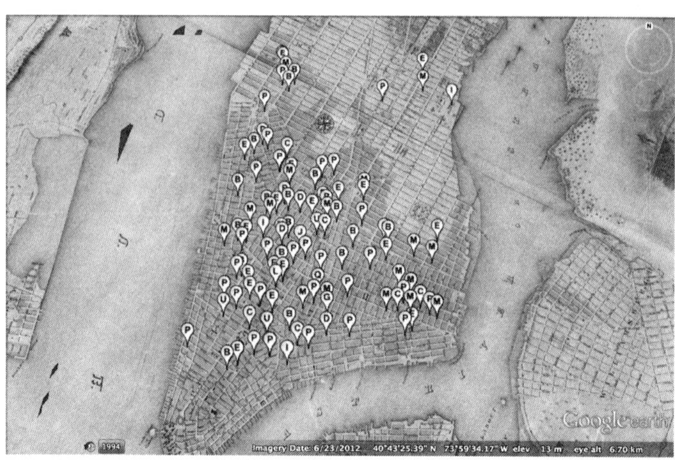

Fig. 3. "Map of New York City Churches, 1783." In the colonial city, the Anglican Church (marked with an "E") anchored the city's spiritual landscape. Other national Protestant churches—Dutch Reformed (D), Huguenot (H), and Presbyterian (P)—clustered nearby. Dissenting faiths—Baptists (B), Jews (J), Lutherans (L), Methodists (M), Moravians (F), and Quakers (Q)—emplaced themselves on side streets and back lots of the city, but within a generation would control the development of the city." Courtesy of the author.

of church membership. As the city began a century of unprecedented population growth after the Revolution, New Yorkers increasingly followed their hearts rather than their kin in deciding where to worship.

The spatial manifestation of this new ethos was the grid. In European cities a valuing of regularity and symmetry in urban organization dated back to the Renaissance. By the eighteenth century city planners had come to appreciate the ways in which the grid facilitated a disciplinary regime based on transparency and surveillance.[16] Grids appeared in Atlantic settlements as well, most notably in New Haven and Philadelphia, where their implementation reflected distinctly religious motivations. The grid unveiled in the Commissioner's Plan of 1811 responded ostensibly to the need to control the northward development of Manhattan Island, but it found supporters across all aspects of urban life. Instead of conforming to the preexistent Indian paths and makeshift roads that followed the topography of the land, the surveyors imposed a regular grid that refused to privilege particular places or parcels. Economic advocates of the grid, as Dell Upton has explained, had come to view commerce as "an all-encompassing, impersonal, systematic exchange of commodities" and saw the grid as facilitating maximum freedom of individual actions, with no preferential treatment for anyone.[17] Political advocates appreciated how transparent order, or the idea of it at least, opened the way for the smoother functioning of the city, whether in the placement and regulation of public markets or the city's inhabitants. For many of the city's denominations, the grid opened the way for the conversion of the city.

Faiths relegated to the margins of the colonial city, many of them evangelical, wholeheartedly embraced the potential of the grid's systematic landscape. Mapping makes clear that the centrifugal force of the early national systematic landscape replaced the centripetal force of the colonial symbolic landscape. Many national churches persisted in building in the core of the city, gambling on the traditional importance of their proximity to sacred and secular power. Yet the real growth, as figure 3 reveals, took place on the northern edge of settlement among evangelical New Yorkers. First carried throughout the Atlantic in the mid-eighteenth century by German Pietists and British itinerants, evangelicalism gained a second life at the end of the century with the launching of a global missionary movement. Evangelicalism appealed to men and women, black and white, rich and poor, but in New York it gained a particular foothold among artisans and mechanics who built new neighborhoods on the northern edge of settlement (with churches at the heart of them) after being pushed out of the old city by the rising cost of real estate. New York's emergence as an international commercial center, especially as the Erie Canal linked the internal United States with the broader Atlantic world, helped fund this expansion while innovations in local transportation, such as omnibus lines and railroads, facilitated it. From the end of the War of 1812 to the aftermath of the Panic of 1837, the city's population more than tripled and the number of churches kept pace.[18]

Seaman's Bethels, Houses of Refuge, Half-Orphan Asylums, charity schools, seminaries, and religious publishing houses represented just a few of the new institutions integrally situated in the sacred and secular landscapes of Atlantic ports in the early nineteenth century. Just as the systematic landscape transformed urban residents' understanding of power within the city, the founding of voluntary societies and associations emerged out of new transatlantic theories about the perfectibility of the individual and the obligation owed to one's neighbor. Where the state once assumed responsibility for the downtrodden, associations of private individuals, many of them inspired by evangelicalism's missionary call, began to provide relief, although in different ways than the state previously had done. An article in *Putnam's Magazine*'s "New-York Daguerreotyped" series provides a snapshot of just how extensive this landscape of benevolence had become at mid-century. In addition to institutions of relief and reform, the article also profiled Protestant organizations, such as the American Bible Society (ABS), the American Tract Society (ATS), and the American Seamen's Friend Society (ASFS), which had their national and international headquarters in New York and became the nexus for intellectual, commercial, and religious networks spanning the Atlantic. The ABS and ATS surpassed commercial publishers in their production and distribution of low-cost or free Bibles and books, while the ASFS sponsored a network of boarding houses, savings banks, and meetinghouses for sailors in all the major ports.

Protestant institutions with an Atlantic (and often a global) reach stood beside institutions that catered to the unprecedented numbers of non-Protestants circulating throughout the Atlantic by the second quarter of the nineteenth century. Famine in Ireland, political upheaval in the German states, and emancipation in the Caribbean touched off waves of immigration. Most only passed through New York en route to other destinations, but enough stayed behind that by 1860, one quarter of the city's population was Irish-born and one eighth German-born.[19] The way each group sought to situate itself within the city varied greatly. Irish immigrants lived in all corners of the city. Many Germans huddled on the Lower East Side in a neighborhood known as Kleindeutschland, conscientiously seeking to collapse the distance between their new homes and their homeland. The *Putnam's* article makes clear that each major immigrant community in the city had its own benevolent society. The names of these societies—the Friendly Sons of St. Patrick, the Hebrew Society for Widows and Orphans, the Italian Benevolent Society—spoke to the ongoing salience of real and imagined homelands as points of identification.[20] Many of their churches, cathedrals, and temples did the same.

Within this world, one faith's strategy for urban emplacement often shaped that of another, even if their theologies stood at odds. Taking his cue from the systematic evangelical Protestant landscape, Archbishop John Hughes created an institutional framework for the city's rapidly expanding Roman Catholic population. He built two dozen churches over twenty years, many of them impressive Gothic structures whose steeples competed with those of Protestant churches for prominence on the skyline. He also initiated an extensive system of parochial schools as an alternative to the Protestant-dominated public school system and invited different European orders to run benevolent organizations for the support of the city's Catholic population.[21] To a lesser extent, the city's Jewish community engaged in a similar process, increasing the number of synagogues six-fold and laying the groundwork for a range of schools and benevolent organizations.[22]

Immigration and commercial expansion in the second quarter of the nineteenth century ensured that Atlantic ports remained as connected as they had a century earlier, although the influx of new people and wealth had important consequences. The systematic landscape that provided the template for residential expansion to the north left older neighborhoods to commercial interests and immigrants who could not afford to live elsewhere. In New York, Bleecker Street, the hinge between the symbolic and systematic landscape, became a line of segmentation. North of Bleecker, developers initiated an unprecedented building boom between 1843 and the Panic of 1857. In a building frenzy, they rushed up the island from 14th to 50th Streets, laying out residential neighborhoods, complete with churches, for middle-class and elite families who earned their living from the city's bustling Atlantic economy. Developments in transportation technologies further aided this process of proto-suburbanization. South of Bleecker, older housing often became tenements for laboring families. The only new Protestant churches in this area tended to be mission chapels.

Beyond a simple functional segmentation, rapidly growing Atlantic cities came to be seen as morally segmented as well. Some referred to New York as two cities, while others, with decidedly ethnic and religious overtones, referred to it as two nations. "Sunshine and shadows" was a popular idiom among Protestant reformers for characterizing the city at mid-century.[23] If sunshine shone down on the middle-class Protestant neighborhoods to the north, then shadows disproportionately fell over Roman Catholic and Jewish neighborhoods in the old part of the city. Five Points became the spatial embodiment of this segmented landscape, a symbol of everything the systematic landscape was not.[24] Protestant optimism waned as Roman Catholic and Jewish communities thrived. Where the population nearly tripled between 1840 and 1860, the number of churches increased only by seventy percent, largely because Protestant church building failed to keep up.[25]

By the time of the American Civil War, new standards of cosmopolitanism had emerged that dictated what it meant to be a civilized city. Secular and religious planners embraced these new ideals and reshaped the city's landscape to fit them. Central Park, opened in 1859 but in the planning for over a decade previous, anchored this newly segmented landscape. To gain support for the park's passage, advocates relied upon arguments grounded in cosmopolitanism and moralism—to wit, that the truly great cities of the world should provide their residents with civic public spaces and that natural places could solve problems of class and ethic/racial strife increasingly endemic to the urban environment.[26] The city's dominant faiths did their part to foster settlement by laying claim to prime locations between 42nd and 60th Streets, the city's new frontier. The "Stranger's Guide" illustrated the most impressive of these structures, such as Temple Emmanu-El (1868), the nation's largest synagogue, and St. Patrick's (1858–73), a massive cathedral for the city's Catholic community and then the largest church in the city.[27] Pictured alongside these houses of worship were some of the benevolent institutions supported by the religious, such as St. Luke's Hospital, founded by an Episcopalian clergyman in 1846, and the Roman Catholic Orphan Asylum, which moved up from Mott and Prince Streets in 1851.

A little less than two hundred years after the English first took New Amsterdam from the Dutch, New York had grown from a colonial outpost into an international commercial center. Much of the fabric of the city over this period has been lost, but mapping in GIS allows us to reconstruct the urban landscape as it changed over time. The most striking aspect of this recovery is the role that the religious played in the growth of the city, a phenomenon common to cities throughout the Atlantic world.

Mapping Religion in the Streets

In 1842 Edward Burckhardt, a Swiss immigrant, climbed up into the steeple of the North Dutch church in the heart of southern Manhattan and sketched a 360-degree panorama of the city spread out beneath him. Congregations possessed some of the finest vantages for observing the contours of the expanding city, providing those fortunate enough to scale their heights with a God's-eye view. Church steeples and spires punctuate Burckhardt's panorama, celestial beacons providing familiar points of orientation and markers of religious achievement in an otherwise monotonous plain of rooftops. At such a height, Burckhardt took stock of the metropolis in its expansiveness, recording all that God—through his mortal intermediaries—had wrought over the preceding two centuries. Matching vision to representation, correlating spires with numbers and letters on a map, Burckhardt performed a sort of high-altitude wayfinding between the space of the page and the space of the city. The Swiss artist might have thought he had actually achieved a totalizing vision, the ability to see as God does, but the real city lay just beyond his view.

As Michel de Certeau has argued, the city cannot be understood from above; it exists down below. A city is constituted not by the soaring heights of man-made structures, but in the daily movements and interactions of men and women, the "ordinary practitioners of the city," on the ground. In their navigation of spaces visible and invisible, their adherence to predefined paths, and their willingness to transgress those routes, urban residents determined the meaning of the city every day.[28]

Urban religion similarly derives its meaning from the movements and interactions of men and women at the level of the street. From life-changing oceanic migrations to daily errands around the block, from meetinghouse rituals harking back to the primitive church to ongoing pilgrimages to the world to come, residents of Atlantic world seaports undertook a range of actual and imaginary movements across space and time. Thomas Tweed has used the spatial metaphors of crossing and dwelling to signal that religion is at its heart about moving across space and finding a place. Within a pluralistic urban context, crossing became all the more freighted with significance. Each walk along the wharfs, each Sunday worship service, each pass through the marketplace created the possibility of encountering someone new, someone whose beliefs, practices, and worldview might call one's own religious identity into question, whether intentionally or not. Dwelling might be seen as an antidote to crossing, granting urban residents the chance to situate themselves within specific spaces and places: body,

Fig. 4. Edward Burckhardt, "Panoramic View of New York City," 1842–45. Church steeples provided one of the best vantages for surveying the growing antebellum city, giving observers such as Edward Burckhardt a "God's eye view." Reprinted with permission of the New-York Historical Society.

household, congregation, city, nation, cosmos. But living in a city always meant defending the parameters of inclusion—of who did and did not belong. Each day urban residents faced challenges to who and what they were—a situation very different from what they faced in the small, homogenous communities from which many hailed.[29]

The appeal of religion lay in its ability to orient the residents of Atlantic world seaports in time and space, to provide an ever-changing map and compass for their lives. This was no small feat, given that they imagined themselves simultaneously existing within multiple and at times contradictory spatial and temporal realms. Each point of identification for urban Atlantic denizens—as a woman, as a domestic servant, as a New Yorker, as an African, as an evangelical Christian—was bound up in a specific spatial and temporal horizon. Their sense of belonging derived from the belief that they dwelled in spaces that ran the gamut from the actual to the imaginary and in temporalities as divergent as the primitive church (invoked through rituals), the present day, or the longed-for (or feared, depending on the perspective of the viewer) end of days. When thinking about the religious experience of Atlantic world residents, one must keep in mind the complex politics of spiritual emplacement.

Irreducible to simple points on a grid, the urban religion of Atlantic world ports requires a different kind of mapping, a careful excavation of the texts, images, and artifacts in which men and women documented the ordinary and extraordinary experiences of their lives. Spatiality existed as a distinct form of religious knowledge. It can be seen in the metaphors people use to describe their crossings and to situate themselves in the world, in the ways they represented in word and image the reality of everyday life on the streets, and in the conscious and unconscious decisions they made in moving through the city. Historical GIS can provide scholars with the big-picture contours—material, social, cultural, economic, and political—and a linear narrative of development, but meaning ultimately lies in the nonlinear ways women and men interacted with the city each day. Their world was densely metaphorical. Time and space frequently collapsed and expanded. One must keep an eye out for the fragmentary glimpses of their worldview and the processes that created it within the broad range of materials they left behind.

Narratives about the local, regional, and transnational migrations of those who crossed into seaports like New York provide a good starting point for reconstructing urban religion. In the metaphors men and women employed in telling their life stories, they revealed clues about how they envisioned their relationship to the city and its inhabitants. Many began life elsewhere, before being swept up in the currents that circulated around the Atlantic. Some arrived as refugees from communities in crisis—Dutch Sephardim in the mid-seventeenth century, French Protestants at the end of the seventeenth century, masters and slaves from St. Domingue at the end of the eighteenth century, Irish peasants in the mid-nineteenth century—who flooded the city's wharfs. Others arrived, against their will, as part of a centuries-long forced diaspora. For all, the experience of crossing into New York—whether on a coastal schooner, a transatlantic merchant vessel, or deep in the bowels of a slaver—profoundly shaped their sense of themselves and their relation to the world. Divie Bethune, a Scottish merchant, embraced New York as a city of deliverance after escaping the plantations of Tobago, a landscape of death he had experienced firsthand. He spent the rest of his life in New York, devoting himself to bettering the city through evangelical activism.[30] In contrast, Charles Lahatt, a German laborer, identified more with Christian in Bunyan's *The Pilgrim's Progress.* Lahatt approached New York as just another stop on a lifelong spiritual pilgrimage. Within a few years, he had moved on.[31]

Terrestrial crossings often intimately intertwined with corporeal and cosmic crossings. Guiding many throughout was their faith, their belief that a supernatural power watched over and gave meaning to their journey. George White, an evangelical, imagined his conversion experience as a corporeal crossing, as his heart hardened by sin melted under the influence of Christ's love. White offered a seemingly straightforward explanation for why he chose to move to New York after his conversion and subsequent manumission: "I felt anxious to become more acquainted with Christian people; and hearing that the Africans were treated with less severity and contempt in the northern, than in the southern states, I resolved to evade these scenes of brutal barbarity . . . and so set off for the city of New-York"[32] In so writing, White revealed how multiple motives and spatial conceptions of belonging often converged. White went to New York in search of a Christian community, but simultaneously revealed the other communities to which he wanted to belong: free (nonbarbarous), local (New York), regional (northern), and ethnic (Africa). Much of White's spiritual autobiography after arrival in New York is concerned with his frustrated efforts to find a spiritual home. He moved from one congregation to another, not finding the right fit until late in life. Yet throughout he remained motivated by his desire to help others make their own crossings. His description of his wife's deathbed experience paints a particularly vivid picture of crossing the ultimate horizon into the world to come.[33]

The urban religious dwelled within many *spaces*—the body, the household, the homeland, the cosmos—but the meetinghouse often provided the one *place* in which all came together. As John Corrigan notes in an essay on spatiality and religion, few places more effectively represent the manifold ways in which religion marks space than houses of worship.[34] Building a church, meetinghouse, or temple bound a congregation in the process of ordering a community and articulating an identity in brick and mortar. Decisions about form (whether to orient towards liturgy or preaching), style (whether to build in Gothic or Greek Revival), situation (whether to place it at the back of the lot, at the center of a major intersection, or somewhere in between), and name (whether to refer to it by a geographic or symbolic name) involved spatially informed decisions. Every choice reflected how the congregation chose to situate itself and to be perceived by the city at large.

Houses of worship often collapsed time and space by linking congregants to other communities of faith, past and present, near and far. Take, for example, the Methodist Episcopal meetinghouse on John Street. Built in 1768, the meetinghouse was the first Methodist meetinghouse in New York and North America. Methodists envisioned this meetinghouse as anchoring several different spatial imaginaries. Nineteenth-century congregants believed it had otherworldly origins. They lovingly attributed the meetinghouse's design to a vision seen by a founding member of the congregation. What the visionary saw, and Methodists ultimately built, however, bore an uncanny resemblance to Methodist meetinghouses then being constructed throughout the United Kingdom.[35] The form of the structure, unusual for the time, fell somewhere between vernacular domestic and traditional church architecture, a fact reinforced in its positioning in a mid-nineteenth-century illustration. The looming steeple of the Dutch church reminds the viewer of the standard form of national Protestant churches in colonial seaports, while the house in front of the meetinghouse suggests the domestic spaces in which evangelicalism often found a foothold. Finally, the figures populating the image reflect the congregation's diverse ties, from the formerly enslaved African American sexton to the British army captain and early Palatine

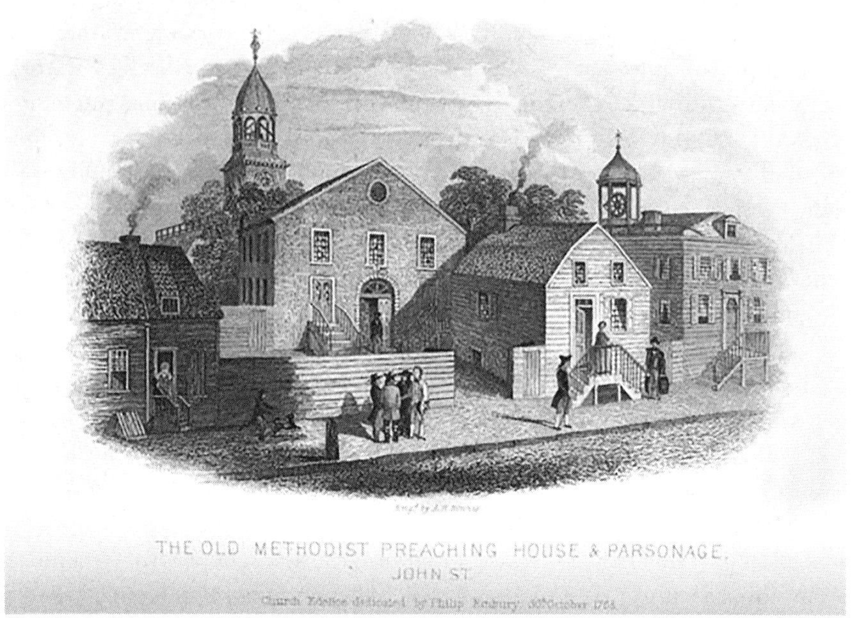

Fig. 5 . "The Old Methodist Preaching House & Parsonage, John St." Built in 1768, the John Street Methodist Episcopal meetinghouse located early worshippers to the city, the broader Atlantic World, and the world to come. Image by Joseph Beekman Smith in J. B. Wakeley, *Lost Chapters Recovered from the Early History of American Methodism* (New-York, 1858), facing p.108.

preacher.[36] In one place, the spaces of the local, the Atlantic, and the cosmic come together.

Inside the John Street meetinghouse, the Holy Spirit was believed to act upon the bodies of the unconverted. Ecstatic love feasts and fervent preaching encouraged unconverted listeners to ask God to melt hearts hardened by sin. Conversion could often be a communal experience rather than a solitary event. The interior arrangement of the meetinghouse charted a distinct social geography for this performance. Movable benches segregated by sex replaced family seating by pew, which, coupled with the equally radical decision not to segregate by race (at least initially), made the early Methodist church attractive to a broad range of congregants. Efforts by white worshippers at the end of the eighteenth century to reseat Africans and African Americans in specially designated seating shattered this community. George White, among others, walked out as a result. Methodists were by no means alone; the city's spiritual landscape grew increasingly fragmented as it grew more diverse over the nineteenth century.

Houses of worship could not contain the movement of the religious. Men and women flowed out of these structures and into the streets in ways that ran the gamut from the scripted and formal to the spontaneous and unofficial. These movements are recorded in a surprising array of sources, including newspaper articles, published and manuscript remembrances, and genre paintings. Within the colonial city, urban processions offered an important means of consolidating spiritual, political, and economic power, and often had their terminus at ecclesiastical structures. The African American celebration of Pinkster, an annual ritual of inversion with Dutch origins, represents only one of the best-known examples of the power of claiming space by processing through it in early New York.[37] Even greater competition to define urban space existed in the postcolonial spiritual marketplace. Mid-nineteenth-century Protestant Sunday school societies staged elaborate parades that channelled scholars from individual congregations over tributary streets to City Hall Park, the center of political power in the city. From there they marched en masse down Broadway to Castle Garden, one of the few spaces large enough to accommodate the assembled crowd. Organizers chose routes as important for the places they passed as the ones they avoided. Common to all was the experience of claiming ownership to the city through processing, effectively transforming a secular landscape into a sacred one, even if for just one day.

Not all movement though city streets was scripted. Impromptu actions reveal what the masses thought about the city's religious landscape and the proper place of different groups of people within it. The paths followed by mobs, for example, provide an alternative form of procession, manifested through very different rituals, but equally concerned with the actions of one group marking its place within the city—and denying the place of others. In the eighteenth century, mobs valued symbolic over actual violence, mostly aimed at property, to purge offending elements and restore consensus within the community. Democratic politics of the nineteenth century fractured those traditions. The mob that had been a safety valve now became a liability. Religion often lay at the heart of urban rioting, providing an impetus and justification for action, targets for aggression, and occasionally a body of participants. Radical preachers, evangelicals, and Irish Catholics all found themselves targets of other groups' aggression. But none bore the brunt more than African Americans. Four days after the Fourth of July in 1834, New York saw some of its worst racial rioting. The riots began in a confrontation at a church, of all places—the Chatham Street Chapel—between a group of blacks who gathered to celebrate the anniversary of the New York emancipation law and the white New York Sacred Music Society over the overbooking of the space. Violence broke out and was enacted upon the city's spiritual and secular landscapes over the next few days with unprecedented destruction. The mob's nighttime paths ran counter to the triumphant daytime processions of Sunday Schools and other groups. Rather than rushing into the symbolic core of the city, they moved out into residential neighborhoods, targeting the houses and churches of white ministers who supported abolition, before launching a full-scale assault on the black community, indiscriminately assaulting church, home, and body. Rituals, like the placing of candles in windows, arose among those who hoped the divine fury might pass them by. In the end, the militia suppressed the riot, but their actions left scars on the landscape that took a long time to heal.[38]

Planned or spontaneous, parades and riots proved infrequent phenomena. For many urban residents the daily experience of intermixing with people from a wide range of faiths in the city's streets came to define their beliefs, practices, and worldviews. A genre of children's books known as *City Cries* provides a useful, if unexpected, source for mapping the experience of the city's streets. A mid-nineteenth-century edition encapsulated on its cover page the "Babylonian confusion" of the city's streets. Inside, the genre introduced readers to the commercial, social, and physical geography of the city by focusing on the vendors (with their distinctive cries) who plied their wares on the city's streets. As such, the genre did several things. It documented the diversity of Atlantic world goods available in the city, such as oranges and pineapples from the West Indies; milk, meat, and vegetables from the hinterland; oysters from the coast; and hybrid cuisines like the Pepper Pot, which brought several Atlantic traditions together. As it mapped commodities, it also mapped the diversity of vendors—female and male, old and young, black and white, Protestant, Catholic, and Jewish—hawking these goods. Racial and ethno-religious markers distinguished vendors from one another and, in turn, defined the perception of entire communities of urban residents.

Even more important, the *City Cries* genre reveals how authors and publishers expected readers to think about the moral geography of the city's streets. Quaker publisher Samuel Wood used the first New York edition of *The Cries of New York* (1808) to put forward his own view of the pressing social and political issues of the time. Wood took pains to celebrate the industrious laboring classes in one passage and condemn slavery in another, two causes dear to the urban Quaker community.[39] A half century later, Aunt Jaunty's *The New York Cries* (1852) instructed readers to follow exterior appearance as a key to interior personality and worth, especially among new, unfamiliar immigrant populations. The "Image Seller," for example, was represented as an Italian, who acts as something of a buffoon, while the "Old Clothesman" is represented as a Jew looking to cheat the purchaser of his wares.[40] As Atlantic cities swelled in the mid–nineteenth century, accelerating a spatial process of social and economic segmentation, men and women increasingly questioned the people they saw around them. The transparency of the systematic city felt like an illusion. Innate goodness could no longer be assumed. Men and women increasingly looked to factors like religion to understand the strangers they met in the street and what their relation to them should be.[41]

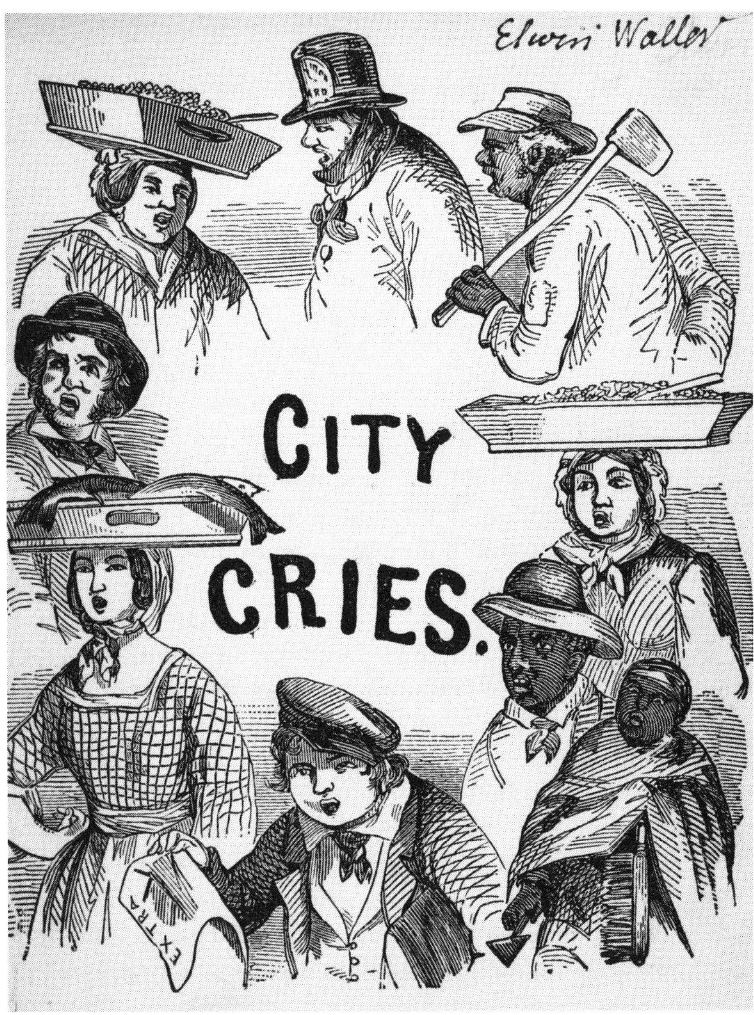

Fig. 6. The *City Cries* genre helped nineteenth-century Americans decipher the broad range of individuals they encountered on busy city streets. This image appeared on the cover of *City Cries: or, A Peep at Scenes in Town* (Philadelphia: George S. Appleton; New York: D. Appleton & Co., 1850). Reprinted with permission of the American Antiquarian Society.

Sources as diverse as spiritual autobiographies, newspaper accounts of riots, and mass-produced children's books remind us that urban religious beliefs, practices, and worldviews were formed, negotiated, and expressed in a range of spaces. Urban spaces generated possibilities for self-reflection and self-fashioning—in fact demanded them—for secular as well as religious identities in ways much different from in the hinterland. All men and women began from the point at which they located themselves within their bodies and their religious communities. All existed within an urban spiritual landscape in which belief was materially reified through rituals and daily practices determined by houses of worship, benevolent institutions, and other sacred spaces. Yet they also lived within a secular landscape that was contested and negotiated. Isolation was not an option in densely, ethnically, and religiously heterogeneous Atlantic world cities, regardless of how much one might have liked. Some became stricter in their orthodoxies in response to the daily reminder of others' failings, while others rejected religion entirely, freed from the surveillance of the local church. All modified their beliefs and practices, consciously and unconsciously, as a result of their urban experience.

Conclusion

Mapping urban religion in early New York City reveals not only the crucial and overlooked role religion played in the development of Atlantic world ports but also the ways in which beliefs, practices, and worldviews emerged from the experience of life within the city. Mapping the material manifestations of the city's spiritual landscape—its houses of worship, charitable institutions, and sites of ritual—through time and across space reveals the extent to which the principles organizing the urban landscape were reflected in, and constituted by, the spiritual landscape. A view from above can identify the ways in which this landscape was ideally to be ordered but not the ways in which the inhabitants of the city actually interacted with it. To do that, one must come down to the level of the street and employ different mapping tools. The experience of crossing and dwelling played an integral role in the experience of urban residents. In the midst of an Atlantic port, their faith might be reinforced or challenged as they came into contact with peoples of other faiths or of no discernable faith at all. New practices and rituals arose, and old ones were modified in response to their experience. For all, crossing through the space of the Atlantic and finding places in which to dwell within the city shaped their response to the city. In the end it is perhaps more useful not to debate whether New York and other Atlantic world seaports were Celestial Cities, Babylons, or Vanity Faires, but how they could be one, the other, or simultaneously all three. And to appreciate urban development and life, one needs to remember the role religion played in it all.

PART TWO

DISTANCE

Missionary Time and Space

The Atlantic World in the Early Modern Age

Luca Codignola

As all runners and mountaineers well know, distances run during daily sessions of training, accounting for any sort of slope and altitude variation, can now be calculated with extreme precision through a quick look at one's wrist computer. The only truly subjective element that remains is one's level of fitness, although that too can be computed with some precision. Commercial airplanes and missiles built for space exploration are able to calculate their air time down to the split second. Science fiction tells us that there is but one next step: "Beam me up, Scotty! There's no intelligent life down here." That was *Star Trek*'s Captain James T. Kirk ordering his chief engineer, Montgomery Scott, to disintegrate and transport him back to the starship *Enterprise* from some God-forsaken rotating piece of rock in a galaxy far, far away.[1] When they look at the past, historians are well aware that it has not always been like that. At least until the end of the eighteenth century, when scientific exploration really began, and at any rate not before the discovery of longitude, real distances between one's point of departure and arrival were difficult to calculate. Indeed, at best, traveling time could be guessed at. Much had to do with human expectations, and these changed significantly over time.[2] We now take for granted instant and personalized communication through telephone conversations, radio waves, television images, and computer connections. For centuries, however, the most one could do was to write a letter and hope for the best. For example, the arrival of the French fleet in Quebec City in the spring of each year, following a long winter of ice blockades, carried long-awaited personal letters as well as much-needed court orders. In 1633 the Jesuit Paul Le Jeune (1592–1664) remarked, "The letters that are sent to this country are like very rare and very fresh fruits; they are received with joy, are regarded with pleasure, and are relished as fruits of the terrestrial Paradise . . . like words from the other world."[3] If nothing arrived, one could do nothing but put up with another year of waiting.[4]

Historians routinely refer to the early nineteenth century as the period in which the first communication revolution took place, affecting human attitudes towards time and allowing a better estimate of distances. This revolution was marked by the invention of the telegraph (1837) and the commercial exploitation of steamship and train networks.[5] Other historians show similar developments in earlier times and do not necessarily link them to technological improvements. According to Gabriella Airaldi, it was during the tenth century that along the Mediterranean routes "time [became] shorter, transportation cheaper, and contacts easier." This quickened pace was mirrored in the notarial transactions of a dynamic port city such as Genoa, where not only the day but also the hour began to be noted.[6] But even when technological improvements were available, sometimes other considerations took precedence over time—that is, over the earlier arrival at the final destination. Consider the following episode. In July 1821 the bishop of New Orleans, the Sulpician Louis-Guillaume-Valentin Dubourg (1766–1833), asked his Québec colleague, Joseph-Octave Plessis (1763–1825), whether he could spare some of the Ursuline nuns living in the two convents of his diocese. Sixteen months later, in November 1822, a party consisting of six Ursulines, accompanied by a priest, Philippe Janvier (1792–1862), finally docked in the New Orleans harbor. Their trip could have been much quicker had they traveled by steamship. Yet a local prominent merchant, Lewis Willcocks (active 1816–1832), a trusted Catholic, had suggested that the group take advantage of a traditional brig, which not only was cheaper but also provided better accommodation and everything that was needed except wine and the use of a porter, both extras. In the end, Janvier chose comfort over speed for himself and his nuns. A few extra days or weeks would have not made much of a difference anyway.[7]

Whereas for more practical-oriented people, such as seamen and merchants, time and distance represented elements to be reckoned with in very down-to-earth terms (Will the water supply last until the next port? Will our sugar still be saleable when we arrive? Will we find icebergs along the route?), missionaries and churchmen in general tended to downplay such practical details—to which, as individuals, they were of course fully exposed—because in their mind the elements of time and distance took on a somewhat different meaning. In his ambitious book *Salvation and Globalization in the Early Jesuit Missions* (2008), Luke Clossey examines his subjects' particular psychological framework in a most perceptive chapter titled "Space, Time, and Truth in the Jesuit Psychology."[8] He starts off by stating that "understandings of distance are not uniform." He then explains why, when dealing with missionaries (the Jesuits being the main focus of his research), the practicalities involved in traveling to and from mission territories had little to do with their attitude towards time and space. Clossey shows, for example, how the arrival upon the global scene of Iberian America may have influenced the missionaries' psychological framework, especially with regard to the well-known mighty realities of Asia. There the painstaking labor of conversion had started off, at least in theory, centuries before Christopher

Columbus's discovery. Did these newly found American peoples awaiting conversion and salvation quicken or delay the arrival of Judgment Day—that is, the end of time? In 1631, Francesco Ingoli (1578–1649), the intelligent secretary of the Sacred Congregation de "Propaganda Fide," the Holy See's department in charge of non-Catholic countries, remarked that human beings had really no way to comprehend the reason of the late discovery of the New World. They could only presume a desire, on the part of God, to provide new opportunities for the salvation of humankind. These had been rendered necessary by the misbehavior of the people of Asia, Africa, and Europe, who, through faults of their own, had allowed Islamism and Protestantism to flourish. Indeed, in its infinite goodness, "that Most High Providence has determined that each thing has its time."[9] The debate on the philosophical significance of the New World on European thought has been, of course, amply studied, and so have the origins and the psychological framework of the members of the Society of Jesus. Neither needs be recounted here.[10] Clossey's conclusion, however, is original and relevant: "In the . . . missionaries' own motivations . . . distance played a role that was minimal."[11] Clossey's conclusion supports the view that the missionary urge to save heretics and infidels, together with their belief in being part of God's grand design, downplayed the significance of practical elements such as distance between one's home and destination and between members of the same religious community around the globe. In fact, missionary sources, including those of the Society of Jesus—a particularly well-studied community thanks to the abundance of written documents—also confirm the notion that the missionaries' concept of time did not really mean "traveling time" (say, two days from Catholic Paris to Protestant La Rochelle, or three years for a return voyage from Catholic Europe to the pagan East Indies) and that their concept of space was not limited to geographical distance in terms of ground or nautical miles separating two locations.

As for the Holy See (the pope and his bureaucracy), the time needed to accomplish a certain project might be calculated in terms of years, or decades, or even centuries. Rome's time was the time of eternity. For example, who knew how long it would take, in God's grand design, to save China? In fact, one could go as far as saying that the discovery of America represented, for Europe as well as for the Christian church, a relatively minor traumatic experience—one which, in any case, was rapidly absorbed. Indeed, new peoples needed to be brought into the mankind's genealogical tree; new lands had to be inscribed onto old maps; and the volume of trade and the number of ships involved increased dramatically. But mostly these were additional elements that did not tilt the balance of Christianity (a name that was then one and the same thing with humankind). For one thing, the Americas were closer than, say, Asia. European ships could make at least one and even two trips to America a year, whereas a voyage to

Dutch Batavia normally required eighteen months of travel, while a journey from Lisbon to Portuguese Goa entailed at least a year and a half.[12] For another, American peoples were certainly "different," but on the whole they were more distant and less threatening than, say, Arabs and black Africans. The southern shores of the Mediterranean Sea certainly remained more "foreign," in spite of the fact that some European nations, such as the Genoese, had always been in constant relationship with their inhabitants.[13] In fact, the northern and the southern shores of the Mediterranean Sea had little in common except their reciprocal hostility. Societal organization, languages, food, down to the color of the skin—everything was different.[14] The same cultural gap applied to the commercial posts established by the Portuguese along the western African coast since the fifteenth century. No conquests were ever made nor was there any form of cultural integration, except for the multiethnic communities of the Atlantic and Equatorial islands. In fact, these posts were mainly used by Europeans to deter other Europeans, and just as in Asia, they were tolerated by the Africans as long as they suited their needs.[15]

If one really wants to find a traumatic experience in the history of Christianity, then it is at the arrival of the Mongols on the global scene in 1221 that one must look. It is at that time that Christians suddenly discovered that the map of the world did not consist of a majority of Christians and Muslims at the center, with some barbarians living at its northern and eastern extremities. On the contrary, it then became very clear that Christianity was an island surrounded by pagans and that these must be considered the vast majority of the globe's population.[16] To be sure, as opposed to the Holy See and the Catholic church in general, a territorial bishop had more pressing concerns, as he was normally closer to the realities of everyday life (Will the missionary arrive this year or the next? Will I have the money to start building my cathedral and my seminary?). Even more so, the life of the missionary in the field was timed on a day-to-day basis (Will that infant be brought to me for baptism? Will I die during the next enemy raid? Has my application to meet with the court dignitary been granted? Will the promised native-language dictionary be available for the instruction of the aboriginal peoples this coming summer?). Within the Catholic Church itself, different approaches to time made for harsh epistolary exchanges between the man in the field and the distant authority, in which the former complained of the latter's scarce attention to his own pressing needs—a problem common to all bureaucratic structures to this day. In a parallel fashion, the concept of distance, like that of space, must be viewed not so much in terms of physical distance from one place to another, but of psychological distance from the mission fields.

Historians too are sometimes selective in applying the concepts of time and space to the historical characters they study. A telling example is John Carroll (1736–1815), the first bishop of Baltimore. He came from a Maryland Catholic family in which moderate Enlightenment ideas, including political tolerance, went along nicely with a personal adhesion to Catholicism and doctrinal firmness in religious matters. Usually depicting him as the quintessential American Catholic, historians tend to forget or to downplay that very early in his life, thirteen-year-old Carroll had been sent to the Flanders to study and that there he spent as many as twenty-four most formative years, in which he studied, taught, traveled extensively, witnessed the violent suppression of the Society of Jesus, and was himself arrested. After he returned to the United States in 1774, an accomplished thirty-nine-year-old man, Carroll not only remained in constant touch with the former friends and colleagues he had met in Europe but also established his Georgetown Academy (1789), later to become Georgetown University, where clerical students were to be admitted together with lay students without any religious bar on admittance, on the model of the Liège Academy he had attended.[17] In fact, Carroll's time abroad, before his return to America in 1774, was almost as long as the subsequent time he spent entirely in the United States.

Although in the early 1970s Atlantic historiography had yet to be invented as a school of thought,[18] I can date my earliest encounters with Atlantic history to two early seventeenth-century missionaries, the English Discalced Carmelite Simon Stock (born Thomas Doughty, 1574–1652) and the French Capuchin René de L'Escale (known in religion as Pacifique de Provins, 1588–1648). Stock spent all his adult life in the London-Canterbury region but for a rather long time took a major interest in the North American missions and feared the consequences of the earliest Puritan migrations. In 1625 he advocated the opening of a mission in Newfoundland because, he claimed, the newly arrived English of Massachusetts would otherwise "infest with heresy not only America, but also Japan, China, the Philippines and the East Indies, so near are they and of such easy journey and passage."[19] Stock's faulty knowledge of distances and travel times is not what is at stake here. Geographical misconceptions, of course, abounded in the early modern era. Columbus, for one, completely miscalculated the width of the Atlantic Ocean.[20] Misconceptions well survived the age of scientific exploration. For example, in 1817 another missionary, the Piedmontese Vincentian Felice De Andreis (1778–1820), described his station in St. Louis, Missouri, as "at the extremity of the Earth, on the banks of the Mississippi, with nothing between us and the Pacific Ocean, which separates us from China, but a few days of walking in a country that is only inhabited by beasts, or by savages who differ but little from these beasts."[21] In the same year, the bishop of Québec was echoing a similar image of the North American Great Plains when he suggested that the western nations, "nomadic and most ferocious peoples," were better left to the care of missionaries from Russia or California.[22] There again, the issue at stake is not whether these churchmen ignored the cartographical knowledge of their times but to what extent their flawed mental geography influenced their thoughts and actions. In Stock's case, the Atlantic Ocean stood before his eyes as an inviting large avenue towards North America and the rest of the known world, which should not be left in the hands of the competition.

Even more than Stock, Pacifique de Provins embodied the typical missionary energy of the early seventeenth century. During his long apostolate in Muslim lands, he preached in present-day Turkey, Syria, Lebanon, Jordan, Israel, Egypt, Iraq, and Iran (1621–1623, 1626–1629). Then he ran into problems with the upper echelons of his own order and switched his interests towards the Americas. In 1641 he ended up as superior of Acadia (present-day Nova Scotia and New Brunswick), a commission that one year later was made to encompass "all places in North America where French shall be, and in the whole of New France."[23] If interpreted literally, this commission would have given Pacifique de Provins power over Acadia, Canada, the Caribbean, and Brazil. Pacifique de Provins also lived in Guadeloupe in 1645–46, and visited Martinique, Dominica, and Marie-Galante. He eventually died on the Guiana coast in 1648, at sixty, "burdened with various climes oriental, southern, northern and western, in land and in sea."[24] As I read Pacifique de Provins's letters, the idea of an Atlantic world—hence the use of that very expression in my earliest article on him—grew naturally out of the realization of what kind of mental map inspired his activity and that of his Capuchin confrères.[25] This world map pictured them all as if they were one and the same thing—be it in the depths of poisonous Africa or on the promising coast of Dutch Brazil, in barren French Acadia or in the luscious West Indies. Jesuit missionary Jérôme Lalemant (1593–1673), for one, well caught the awe the missionary felt when facing the immense task God had entrusted to him: "We find ourselves here as if in the midst of a sea where a million persons are drowning."[26]

The visionary aspect of Pacifique de Provins's personality did not, however, prevent him from carefully assessing the pros and cons of his prospective destinations, including the ratio between the physical extension of his mission and the potential number of converts. Thus he refused to go personally to Acadia, a land of "woods and forests, so confused, that when the snow falls it does not melt for six full months" and where the aboriginal peoples were five hundred only, scattered in a two-to-three-hundred-league area.[27] Undoubtedly, Pacifique de Provins had a flawed approach to the geography of the Atlantic region, just as Stock did. Yet this is not very important. More significant is his systemic approach to distances in the Atlantic world. Clossey describes it as a "topological" approach—from "topology," the study of the nonquantitative properties of geometric space. He offers as the best known example of such an approach the iconic map of the London Underground, where what is important is the relationship between the various points, not their exact distance.[28] Pacifique de Provins also had a very subjective approach to time. This element was to be measured not in absolute and objective terms but rather by the urgency to accomplish the church's salvation project, of which he was one of God's instruments. His life quest had taken him to "northern America," a land where the propagation of the Gospel had "not been attempted for 500 years."[29] And yet aboriginal nations had to be selected carefully, because no time was to be wasted and he personally had no intention "to end his life in confessing 40 French Catholics." In his mind, "no hope is to be entertained for eternity to baptize twenty children in 20 years," Pacifique de Provins wrote of the Acadian aboriginal peoples.[30]

Slowly but steadily, my own early quest for "new" documents in the Roman archives had transformed itself into an attempt to understand how the Holy See's bureaucrats interpreted the world around them and tried to implement their Atlantic policies within a global strategy of expansion and eventual spiritual conquest. At the time, I felt no need for any overall theorethical framework or methodological novelties. The Roman documents with which I was then in almost daily contact were self-evident—or so they seemed. In 1985, when I first used the word "Atlantic" in the title of my article on Pacifique de Provins, I already was an Atlantic historian—but did not know it. Yet I was in good company. That very year, Tulio Halperín Donghi published *Reforma y disolución de los imperios ibérico,*[31] and John J. McCusker and Russell R. Menard published *The Economy of British America,* a book that for the first time described the economy of the British continental colonies together with the West Indies and New France.[32] A year later (1986) came Urs Bitterli's *Alte Welt Neue Welt,* a modelization of early contact in the Americas and around the globe;[33] the first volume of American historical geographer Donald W. Meinig's saga, *The Shaping of America,* another book whose paradigm was the Atlantic and continental dimension;[34] Alfred W. Crosby's environmentalist manifesto, *Ecological Imperialism,* a sort of second chapter of his revolutionary *The Columbian Exchange;*[35] Ian K. Steele's *English Atlantic,* which together with Karen O. Kupperman pioneered the idea of the subjective and indeed flexible dimension of the Atlantic Ocean;[36] and eventually the first two volumes of American historian Bernard Bailyn's magnum opus, collectively titled *The Peopling of British North America.*[37]

But what is, exactly, "Atlantic history," and what is the "Atlantic world" that it should help explain? A review in some depth of the development of this school of thought is needed before assessing whether it could make any difference in the evaluation of the topic of missionary time and space. Aside from Bailyn's version, which has somewhat imposed those two expressions into mainstream historiography, historians have provided very different answers to these two questions, starting from Nicholas P. Canny (1990) and ending with Federica Morelli (2013).[38] On geography there seems to be an overall agreement. All lands whose shores fall into the Atlantic Ocean belong to the Atlantic world—from Scandinavia to Portugal in Europe, from Morocco to South Africa in Africa, from Greenland to Patagonia in the Americas, including islands and archipelagos such as Iceland, Newfoundland, Bermuda, Haiti, the Azores, Fernando Poo, St. Helena, and South Georgia. Some maritime historians, however, actually disagree and point to the fact that Atlantic history forgets the Atlantic Ocean itself—that is, the perspective of those who look towards water and land from the bridge of a ship and do not simply use the ocean to move between two locations.[39] Some historical geographers have also tried to make sense of this enormous stretch of water and lands and to show to what extent the history of the Atlantic world has been determined, or at least influenced, by determinant and unavoidable elements such as sea currents, climates, waterways, and biological impacts. According to them, these elements were crucial in creating the variety of human settlements on both sides of the Atlantic Ocean and in defining migratory patterns.[40]

If there seems to be an overall agreement on the geography of the Atlantic world, there is much less agreement on the chronology of Atlantic history. As regards the *terminus a quo,* the contact between Norsemen, Inuit, and Beothuk is treated as a picturesque footnote, probably because it did not cause any major change on an international scale. (Because some "Atlantic" areas have received a disproportionate amount of attention and others none at all, this early contact might have helped bring in peripheral areas and peoples who are usually left outside of current historiography.) To be sure, even Columbus's landfall date has been abandoned as the commencement of Atlantic history. There are two reasons for this. The first is that, in spite of ethnohistory's own tenets, it does not seem proper that the lengthy history of America's aboriginal peoples be made to begin in conjunction with their earliest contact with the Europeans. The second reason is that, once Africans were made to enter Atlantic history as full subjects—after all, they were ten times more numerous than the Europeans in crossing the ocean—the *terminus a quo* must at least be brought back to the earliest Portuguese navigations of the early fifteenth century and to the exploitation of the Atlantic and Equatorial islands. In fact, it is now recognized that these islands provided a testing ground for social, political, economic, and demographic patterns later to be transferred to the Americas. Of this mighty process, then, Columbus's discovery was a most significant episode but certainly not a beginning.

The issue of the *terminus ad quem* is even more complicated. In spite of all best efforts, Atlantic history continues to be patterned along national chronologies. Traditionally, these follow teleological itineraries that identify a country's fault line in the date of its achieved independence. These ending moments then vary widely, from 1776 for the United States to 1898 for Cuba. This teleological and political vision of Atlantic history is, however, very unsatisfactory, because it leaves out countries such as Canada that never acquired independence through a revolution. Furthermore, it does not take into account certain dates that are most significant for the history of the slave trade, such as the abolition brought about by the French Revolution (1793), Haiti's independence (1804), British abolition (1834), the American Civil War (1865), and Brazilian abolition (1888). Finally, when one looks at the Atlantic world from the East, to select a *terminus ad quem* is even more difficult. In Africa elites always sided against the abolition of the slave trade, and there is no evident continental rupture of any sort.[41] In Europe, perhaps in 1815 with the end of the Napoleonic Wars and the beginning of mass migrations, one finds a common ground for agreement.[42]

How did the new Atlantic historiography come into being, and did it decide to shelve the fathers of the old Atlantic tradition? These were much revered historians such as France's Pierre Chaunu (1923–2009), Jacques Godechot (1907–1989), Charles de La Morandière, and Frédéric Mauro (1921–2001); Belgium's Charles Verlinden (1907–1996); America's Herbert E. Bolton (1870–1953), Robert R. Palmer (1909–2002), and John J. TePaske (1929–2007); Mexico's Pedro Armillas Garcia (1914–1984) and Silvio Zavala; Britain's James A. Williamson (1886–1964), John H. Parry (1914–1982), Charles R. Boxer (1904–2000), David B. Quinn (1909–2002), and John H. Elliott (born 1930); Ireland's Kenneth G. Davies (1924–1994); Switzerland's Max Silberschmidt; Portugal's Vitorino Barbosa de Magalhães Godinho (1918–2011); and Canada's William J. Eccles (1917–1998) and Marcel Trudel (1917–2011). Neo-Atlanticists had indeed come to the conclusion that these scholars had served their purpose and did not provide adequate answers to their new questions. They maintained that the old Atlantic historiography was born around World War II in an era of ethnic nationalism. At the time, the history of the Western world was interpreted at best through the nineteenth-century paradigm of the nation-state and at worst by nationalists who read history backward and searched for "the origins" of their country. An exceptionalist attitude, normally attributed to the United States only, was to be found in every country. Iberian-American countries showed it, whether they had attained political independence or not. British and Canadian historiographies in either language were no less affected, the former because of its imperial framework and the latter for the overwhelming importance of the identity debate.[43] Undoubtedly, the old Atlantic historiography had been strongly influenced by the overall idea of the creation of an international community based on Western values that were meant to be in opposition to the growing threat of worldwide communism.[44] Incidentally, in the same fashion as we now all agree on the fact that the threat of communism was not extraneous to the fortune of the idea of the "age of democratic revolutions," one could now surmise that the reaction to global Islamic fundamentalism is somewhat related to the attempt to interpret Atlantic history so as to make it into a positive element in the history of the world. Perhaps ironically, Cécile Vidal, one of the best representatives of the small but growing group of French Atlanticists, has pointed out that a "Muslim

Atlantic" has yet to be included in the ever-growing Atlantic container, in spite of the presence of so many Muslim slaves in Brazil, as briefly described also by Canny and Philip D. Morgan.[45] But the validity of this hypothesis can only be tested by a new generation of historians further removed from the political preoccupations of our present times.

Neo-Atlantic historians believe that the implicit nationalism of the previous generation of historians made it impossible for them to answer the new questions arising from the new values of polycentrism, diversity, multiethnicity, tolerance, and inclusion that were brought about by contemporary globalization.[46] In their view, we must wave good-bye to an old Atlantic world built on the idea of a common civilization and reaching its highest moment at the time of the democratic revolutions of the end of the eighteenth century. Instead, we must welcome a new Atlantic world that is "multicultural, multiethnic, and multiracial."[47] This new Atlantic world was, in Bailyn's words, "immensely complex," although it still constituted a "cohesive multicultural region."[48] It is this complexity that now makes possible the inclusion of the American aboriginal peoples and of the Africans on both sides of the ocean, together with special ethnic and social groups such as *castas,* the free African Americans, and the *petits blancs,* as pointed out by Dominique Rogers.[49] Here is John K. Thornton, an early Atlanticist, who in his latest book joins this neo-Atlanticist wave and sets himself aside from his old mentors—Fernand Braudel (1902–1985), Chaunu, and Mauro—to "include all the actors of the game, and on their own terms" ("full actors" is how Vidal describes them) and to write a history of the Atlantic world that is "inclusive, multicentric, and multiregional," one that may enable us to revise "our collective memory."[50] Several years ago, Greene, whose innovative approach helped open the door to the new Atlanticism, warned against interpreting the New England experience as the paradigm on which to assess the entire history of the United States.[51] More recently he has pointed out how this new multicultural approach has made it possible better to understand the "prenational" history of the United States. In Greene's view, this prenational history included places and communities that were "neither English nor exclusively indigenous" and must not be treated simply as a as a simple "*prehistory* of the United States."[52]

It is telling that this quest for inclusiveness has been more successful in countries, such as the United States, Canada, and Great Britain, where the reality of the new multiracial, multiethnic, and multicultural society have been first recognized and accepted. In Great Britain neo-Atlantic historians share the burden of doing away with British exceptionalism with the new imperial historiography. In the words of Kathleen Wilson, one of the latter's most important representatives, both schools must find "the genealogies and historiographies of national belonging and exclusion."[53] Conversely, a country such as France, which has not yet decided how to deal with the new values brought about by the new globalization, continues to nurture a historiography based on the idea of the nation-state and deals with its colonial past in the old imperial framework.[54] In France, for all purposes, Atlantic history remains in the margins of mainstream historiography,[55] and the few neo-Atlanticists it can boast belong more to the North American historiographical milieu than to the French one.[56] In fact, not only in France but elsewhere too, this ongoing battle against nationalism and exceptionalism is far from being won. Whereas in 2012 one of the best known representatives of the neo-Atlantic historiography, David Armitage, proclaimed that "the hegemony of national historiography is over,"[57] other historians are much less optimistic. In 2007 Jack P. Greene, one of the foremost revisionists of early American history, stated that "'the national idea' has ruled and continues to rule virtually without challenge."[58] Five years later, Jerry Bannister and Liam Riordan emphasized that in spite of globalization, "nationalism still shapes our understanding."[59] Alain Cabantous, a well-recognized specialist in maritime history, was no less critical of the neo-Atlantic school of history.[60]

Here we are then with a new reading of the past of the Atlantic world, one that is far from the limitations of national histories, the constraints of imperial history, and the teleological framework of European expansion. This new reading consists of two fundamental features. The first pertains to the moral and normative order. This feature implies that categories such as inclusion, diversity, and multiethnicity are intrinsically good. In their days, social history had preached the rewriting of history "from the bottom up" and had hoped for a new dignity for the inferior orders of society, while women's history had enlarged that view so as to include the other half of humankind. Neo-Atlanticists now believe that individuals or groups of individuals must be included in the narrative because they belong to ethnic or cultural communities. This is a process that in 2007 Greene described as a long-term movement meant to reverse the historiographical negligence towards "women, children, Indians, African Americans, people of mixed race, ethnic minorities, and socioeconomic subaltern groups in American history."[61] The second feature of this new reading of the Atlantic world pertains to the cognitive order. By studying these communities in their entirety and by using the Atlantic area as the overall reference framework, neo-Atlantic historians believe that not only are long-excluded actors brought back to light but also that the histories of the several communities that live on the Atlantic shores, now viewed as an "Atlantic world," become better known. Furthermore, reciprocal influences must now be read not only from east to west—that is, from Europe and Africa towards the Americas—but also from west to east, as returning influences. As a historian, I am not interested in the moral and normative features of the new Atlantic history. As W. J. Eccles, an Atlantic historian *ante litteram,* once wrote, though the present is always lurking about, "the historian is concerned with the past for its own sake, and only incidentally with what developed out of it."[62] I am, however, very much interested in the cognitive feature. To what extent have the promises made by the new Atlantic history been kept?

The experience of the so-called hemispheric or continental history—I see little difference between the two—as a new reading of the colonial history of the Americas makes one wonder about the distance that may intervene between enthusiastic initial hopes and rather modest final results. As is often recalled, as early as 1932 Herbert Bolton, then president of the American Historical Association, had exhorted his colleagues to abandon the narrow confinement of national histories and devote themselves to the grand history of the American continent. Those were the years of a nascent pan-Americanism in the political and cultural institutions of the American countries. Silvio Zavala, a Mexican historian, took up Bolton's challenge in his Pan American Institute of Geography and History. Zavala agreed with Bolton that the history of the Americas was not so much the result of the relations between colonies and their European mother countries but rather of the interactions among European, aboriginal peoples, and African Americans. However, results amounted to almost nothing. Bolton never completed the major synthesis he had planned, and the activities and publications promoted by Zavala produced no historiographical waves or even ripples. Ironically, during the last decade or so, the multicultural approach of the new Atlantic historiography has somewhat favored a rejuvenation of the hemispheric and continental history.[63] Amy Turner Bushnell and Greene, for example, like the opportunities for comparisons among the various colonial societies they provide.[64] Allan R. Greer is less enthusiastic about comparisons but believes that the hemispheric and continental approach may enlarge American and Canadian historians' angle of vision. In his view, this new angle would show the similarities of the biological, cultural, and colonizing features of all mother countries.[65] There too, however, there is little outside some well-meaning hopes and expectations. In practice, no one so far has been able to know, let alone manage, the vast historiographical production and transform it into an overall and balanced synthesis of hemispheric or continental history, if not for some special topics that are limited in time, space, and focus.[66]

Going back to the objectives of the new Atlantic historiography and the issue of their attainment, the apparently most significant feature of the past few years has been the passage from a static Atlantic world, geographically and chronologically contained, to a more abstract unit of analysis that requires a new methodological approach. The former belonged to the early Atlantic historians—although Bailyn too insists on considering the Atlantic world as a coherent space that is distinct from any other and, as such, exceptional.[67] Explaining the latter is more complicated. According to Morelli, the neo-Atlantic methodology "overlaps and at the same time includes other levels of analysis—the states, the empires, the continents," and, together with "post-colonial studies, subaltern studies, the new imperial history or the *histoire connectée,*" makes Africans and aboriginal peoples the protagonists of the early globalization on a par with the Europeans. In Morelli's view, neo-Atlantic historians must "study the individuals and the societies around the ocean following their connections . . . [and] place migrations, economic exchanges, commercial and religious networks in a single analytical context." Finally, Morelli hopes the study of European expansion be replaced by "that of the interactions among the three continents" in order finally to portray their inhabitants "with their ways of living, of working, of consuming, their cultural and religious practices, [and their] gender differences."[68] As if this were not enough, Vidal adds that the new Atlantic historiography "does not mean to impose itself to the detriment . . . of imperial history, of hemispheric history, of global history or of the *histoire connectée.*"[69] The implication is that whatever methodologies these schools of history use, they must be added to the baggage of the new Atlantic historiography. In sum, in about twenty years or so, neo-Atlantic history has moved from Bailyn's economic, migratory, and cultural networks to an Atlantic world of connections, interactions, and entanglements.[70] (Incidentally, the term *network,* so much in fashion in early American history until a few years ago, seems to have been one the earliest victims of the new Atlantic history.) Here we are, lastly, at the very final stage of the perhaps inevitable explosion of the neo-Atlantic history. If really one has to take into account everything and everyone, how could one avoid the fact that the history of the Atlantic world becomes quite simply one section of a vaster global history that takes into account all the connections, the interactions, and the entanglements caused by the early globalization?[71] This is what some early modern historians, such as Nicholas Canny,[72] Emma G. Rothschild,[73] Alison F. Games,[74] Peter A. Coclanis,[75] and Paul Cohen,[76] suggest. This is also the implication of a recent and most refined volume coedited by an international team of historians, two of whom, John G. Reid and Elizabeth A. Mancke, have always practiced Atlantic history.[77]

At this point, old Atlanticists have the right to feel at a loss and to wonder what is left out of this new historiographical school and, above all, what should *not* be done in the future, aside from not being Eurocentric and elitist —something that we have been repeating to ourselves for at least half a century. Everyone has found his or her own Atlantic world. Not only do we have British, French, Spanish, Portuguese, and Dutch Atlantics, but we also have a white (European), black (African), red (the ocean's proletarians), and green (Irish) Atlantic, let alone the religious (Catholic, Puritan, Anglican, Moravian, Quaker) and the thematic (revolutionary, exclusionary, repressive, Napoleonic, Loyalist) ones. To be sure, from the moral and normative viewpoint, we feel a certain degree of satisfaction that the new Atlantic gospel with its "good" values (inclusion, diversity, and multiethnicity) has defeated the nonbelievers. As

Greene has well described, in the United States "few early modern Americanists remain unconverted,"[78] and those who do so in Canada or in Europe are treated as stalwarts of reaction. Yet the overall feeling is that the increase in our knowledge stands only remotely in proportion to the theoretical efforts. For example, I was left rather cold when confronted by Hornsby's and Greer's attempts at modelizations, or before Armitage's three variants, or Greene's fifteen hypotheses, or American cultural historian Jorge Cañizares-Esguerra's typologies, just as I had been rather skeptical in the 1980s with regard to Bitterli's modelization of first contact or Denys Delâge's modelization of the relationship between periphery and center.[79] In fact, these scholars' best contribution to knowledge has come in the form of very traditional research monographs, whereas their methodological appeals have being immediately forgotten by their readers and the categories they suggested have, to my knowledge, never been used.

Furthermore, some elements of the new Atlantic history do not add up. First of all, the historiographical framework is basically American. This is not a negative element in itself, given the overpowering strength and organization of American research (universities, journals, libraries, archives, conferences, associations, subventions, and so on) and its conducive effects on the rest of the world. Yet this hegemony cannot go hand in hand with ignoring the results of research achieved in other countries. Whereas British, Canadian, Dutch, Iberian-American and—to a lesser extent—French historians follow the results of American research rather closely and have long internationalized their historiography, very few American historians have done so. Early North American history continues to be dominated by American scholars who, often for their uneasiness with foreign languages, rarely do look outside their borders. Even when, as Daniel K. Richter did, they make an effort to turn around the Eurocentric viewpoint and to rewrite history from the aboriginal point of view, it is rather evident that—as Greer has shown—the more the narrative moves forward, the more the continental perspective gets thinner. In the end, the aboriginal presence becomes little more than a contribution to the national history of the United States that ends with the revolutionary apotheosis.[80] In spite of its methodological proclamations, then, if one absent actor is to be found in the neo-Atlantic historiography, this is the aboriginal peoples.[81]

Second, in this new Atlantic world made of connections, interactions, and entanglements, but rejecting Eurocentrism in toto, another element that seems to have been lost along the way is Europe itself. And yet, as American historian Gayle K. Brunelle has pointed out, "Europe was as much a part of the Atlantic World as Africa or the Americas."[82] In fact, neo-Atlantic historians show little interest if any in the old continent and have reconsigned it to the traditional field of national histories. Is a history of the influence of the returning migrants on France being written? So far there has been some good work on the postdeportation Acadians, but unfortunately little else.[83] Is there any work being done on the personal connections between the Atlantic merchants and mariners and their families and friends back home? The mind goes to John F. Bosher's works mainly dating from the 1970s and the 1980s; but he is a historian of France, and neo-Atlantic historians never placed him in the pantheon of the early Atlanticists. A similar destiny befell, some years later, James S. Pritchard, Dale Miquelon, and Peter N. Moogk.[84] And what about the multiethnic military personnel sent to the Americas by the Spanish crown of French Emperor Napoleon I? Henry A. F. Kamen is hardly known to neo-Atlantic historians, perhaps because he is based in Spain, and only very recently have Napoleon I's Atlantic connections been the subject of inquiry, although there again the impulse came from Iberian-American historians, not neo-Atlanticists.[85] Finally, in spite of Annie R. M. Jourdan's 2004 book, the French Revolution seems to have lost its former centrality in the neo-Atlanticists' mind and has been somewhat replaced by the Haitian Revolution, except perhaps for American historian Laurent Dubois's 2009 article.[86] A number of articles on the international ramifications of the French Revolution do exist and are rather recent, but none of these seem to have made their way into the Atlantic discourse.[87]

Third, Canada, both as New France or British North America, remains a nonentity in neo-Atlantic historiography. At most, it appears as an appendix (together with the "other Americas") in some collections of essays that were published in the past few years. American scholars continue to show very little knowledge, if any, of what is published in French or in English north of the border. The only real exception is represented by Allan Greer, whose eclectic approach, smooth writing, sense for appealing topics, and familiarity with American research milieus have made him the Americans' primary conduit to the Canadian historical literature. The two historiographical syntheses that have appeared in the past decade or so in such learned journals as the *American Historical Review* (1999) and the *William and Mary Quarterly* (2010), the former written by Jeremy Adelman and Stephen Aron, the latter by Eric A. Hinderaker and Rebecca Horn, are most instructive, as they show a historiographical delay of about half a century.[88] To emphasize the backwardness of American historiography with regard to the so-called new topics of Atlantic history, a recent collective publication meant to answer the question of whether there was such a thing as a "Canadian Atlantic" started by saying that "a reasonable response would be to wonder what all the excitement is about," given the fact that Canadians, both in French and in English, had being practicing Atlantic history from time immemorial.[89] The ignorance of the Canadian reality is not a matter of minor concern. Historiographically, New France and British North America have always represented an alternative solution to the historical teleology of the Thirteen Colonies. As for the diffusion north of the Mexican border of the historiographical results produced in Iberian America or in the Iberian peninsula, all I can say is that whereas Iberian-American historiography seems to take into good account the important contributions of Lockhart and Schwartz, together with those of John H. Elliott,[90] American historiography of the age of revolutions does not seem to acknowledge either Halperín Donghi or François-Xavier Guerra (1942–2002), or the more recent works by Maria Teresa Calderón, Clément Thibaud, and José Maria Portillo Valdés.[91]

If so far I have mostly described the shortcomings of the new Atlantic history, it is because what is striking in it is the disproportion between what historians should be doing—or not be doing—and what has really been done, between the results that are already secured in the bank of historical knowledge and the magnitude of the objectives that should be attained. Such magnitude is indeed overwhelming. The possibility that an individual researcher can succeed in knowing, managing, and making sense even of a minimal portion of these connections, interactions, and entanglements is unrealistic. The enthusiasm that had dazzled the profession in the early 1970s at the beginning of the computer era, when some of its members came to believe that quantification of historical data and the unification of library catalogues would solve once and for all the problem of access to and management of sources, has long been gone.[92] When John Thornton wrote that he found and read documents and books that he could not even imagine before the arrival of the internet, he admitted to having been "overwhelm[ed]" by such an abundance.[93] For his part, Trevor Burnard conceded that any historian of America who tries to contextualize his knowledge by comparing it to the British experience in Asia would never be able to go beyond the level of an "amateur observer."[94] In a way, Philip D. Curtin was expressing a similar realization of the historian's limitations: "I know only a few of the more common languages. . . . With a good knowledge of Russian or Armenian or Chinese, this study [on the global character of the merchant communities] could have been considerably more authoritative. . . . On the other hand, to have taken the time necessary to learn all relevant languages would have meant that it [this study] would never have been written at all."[95]

It might as well be that all good books are now in the press and are made ready for the Christmas market, but so far the only overall topic that seems to have really profited from the impulse of the new Atlantic historiography is that of the new perception of Africa's role. On the one side, scholars such as David Eltis have used quantification to present us with new and accurate data on the volume and the places of the slave trade.[96] On the other side, Thornton, Linda M. Heywood, and Paul E. Lovejoy (with Herbert S. Klein before them)[97] have shown the active role played by African societies, the change that took place on the shores and interior of the African continent, and the cultural permanence of the African communities transported first to the Atlantic and Equatorial Islands and later to the Americas.[98] Although studies on Africa are, when taken together, the most relevant, a number of other books were published in the last decade or so that seem to be going in the right direction.[99] Aside from the authors mentioned so far, one should at least recall Evan Haefeli and Kevin Sweeney, *Captors and Captives* (2003); Peter E. Pope, *Fish into Wine* (2004); Philip P. Boucher, *France and the American Tropics* (2007); Daviken Studnicki-Gizbert, *A Nation Upon the Ocean Sea* (on Portuguese expansion, 2007); Matteo Sanfilippo, *Dalla Francia al Nuovo Mondo* (2008); Maurice Bric, *Ireland, Philadelphia and the Re-Invention of America* (2008); Carla Gardina Pestana, *Protestant Empire,* (2009), Aaron S. Fogleman, *Two Troubled Souls* (2013); and Audrey Horning, *Ireland in the Virginian Sea* (2013).[100] This impressive output, however, does not contradict the overall critical assessment on the usefulness of the new Atlantic historiography, in that one wonders whether these works owe more to the originality and perseverance of their authors than to the adherence to the dictates of the new Atlantic historiography.[101] More than a decade after Armitage's battle cry, "We are all Atlanticists now,"[102] one wonders whether the very down-to-earth suggestions for achieving new and original knowledge made by two other practitioners of Atlantic history, Greer and Greene, make more sense than ever. Greer invited scholars to continue "to look for ways to listen to the evidence of the primary sources and construct meaning." Greene, even more plainly, confirmed that "the tried and true method of producing new knowledge is through new research and the publication of monographs."[103]

At least up to a certain point, religion has entered the debate on the meaning and purpose of Atlantic history, mainly because of its role in providing an ideological justification to European conquest and expansion.[104] Yet Rome and the Holy See have been entirely left out, nor have they become part of the overall discussion of global history.[105] Still, just as much as Gardina Pestana has proven that "surveying religion from an Atlantic perspective offers a number of advantages,"[106] my own experience with early modern Roman documents had shown the usefulness of such a perspective for understanding the intellectual framework of the Roman Catholic churchmen who dealt with North America, whether missionaries in the field or bureaucrats working out of the Roman offices. It was this Atlantic perspective that made the French Crown abandon Canada and keep Saint-Pierre and Miquelon and the Caribbean sugar islands in 1763. It was a similar perspective that made the Holy See keen in providing assistance to the Capuchins who were active in the Orient, but almost deaf towards their confrères in French Acadia. Without such an overall perspective, it would be impossible to explain why thousands of Jesuits asked to be sent to Asia and only a few dozens to North America. Time and distance had nothing to do with those choices. Rather, these were the result of a careful assessment of their Atlantic and indeed global options.[107]

One has only to look at the way these Roman bureaucrats organized and coordinated their desks to detect the directions in which their interests went and what locations they considered close or distant. When the thirteen cardinals of the newly founded Propaganda Fide met for the first time in 1622, one of the items on their agenda was who was to take care of what geographical areas. The Italian peninsula and French-speaking France and Switzerland were assigned to desks no 1 and 2, Spain and Portugal to desks no 3 and 4. Northern Europe, from Belgium to Norway, including Ireland and Great Britain, were assigned to desk no 5. (Sea communication must have played a part in this assemblage.) The titulars of desks from no. 6 to 9 received the Germanic, Baltic, and Slav countries. The area from Venice to Constantinople was assigned to desks no. 10 and 11. There remained the Asian Middle East ("as far as India"), and Arabic Africa, which were assigned to desks no. 12 and 13. This geographical framework shows that well over a century after the discovery of the Americas, the universe was still centered on Europe and the Islamic world. Africa, as well as Asia—let alone America—were almost entirely left out of the picture, except for some cursory mentions of faraway colonies under the heading relating to Spain and Portugal.[108] A comparison with other "state of the world" documents that were compiled by Propaganda Fide bureaucrats later in the seventeenth and eighteenth centuries show that additions, such as the Far East (China, Japan, Korea, and the Southeast) and central Africa (the Congo), were slow in coming and could very easily be forgotten again. French and English North America, more often than not, were absent from such pictures, and, surely, there was not any hint of an Atlantic world.[109] In fact, if anything, the view from Rome arouses a global perspective rather than an Atlantic one. Documents on the United States and Canada are dispersed—indeed almost lost—among thousands of other documents or folders on Protestant Europe, Russia, northern and central Africa, China, Japan, India, and the East Indies. (As is to be expected, the role of North America, and especially of the United States, grew exponentially but not before the mid-nineteenth century.)[110]

The unpublished writings of the Roman bureaucrats, the well-known printed version of the so-called Jesuit relations, and concurrently the writings of priests and missionaries at various levels of the hierarchical ladder of dioceses such as London, Dublin, Baltimore, Paris, and Québec, strengthen the view that the main feature that really shaped the attitudes of all these churchmen was not so much the physical distance from any given place but rather their proximity to the action—that is, their experience in the field.[111] Their geographical location and the chronological brackets of their activity were of much lesser significance. For example, Apulia (a region in southern Italy), Huronia (in the North American Great Lakes region), or Brittany (in France) looked one and the same thing in the writings of their missionaries. The local inhabitants were described as savages;

the supposedly Catholic residents had not received the sacrament of confession for over thirty years; the Jesuit fathers were accused of causing illnesses, droughts, and other natural disasters; and local languages represented a major problem as sacred or regulatory texts had to be translated.[112]

In conclusion, one could well argue that those members of the Catholic church who were directly involved in the expansion of Catholicism shared a view of time and space that made for some overall coherence. This was especially true of the Atlantic world, which remained for them at least until well into the late eighteenth century a portion of the globe of lesser significance. Their concept of time and space, however, was only very partially determined by chronological time or physical distance. By focusing on a psychological understanding of time and space, one is more likely to interpret the "discovery" of 1492 and the consequent arrival of the Atlantic world onto the global scene, as significant as these moments may be in the history of humankind, as only a step in the overall process of European expansion. It has often been said that the conquest of Algeria's Ceuta in 1415 and the following conquest and use of the Atlantic and Equatorial Islands throughout the fifteenth century represented the real beginning of such expansion. Indeed, any master narrative of the Atlantic world that starts with Columbus's discovery would be somewhat flawed not because it is Eurocentric (which it is) but because it would not do justice to the complexity of the Europeans' concepts of time and space.

Religious Community and Cross-Religious Communication beyond the Atlantic World

The Lost Tribes in the Americas and Mecca

Brandon Marriott

In 1650 the Presbyterian minister Thomas Thorowgood published a treatise in London that claimed the indigenous peoples of the Americas were descendants of the Lost Tribes of Israel. Alongside references to scholarly writings and the New England missionary activities of the Puritan John Eliot, Thorowgood used the narrative of the Iberian Converso Antonio Montezinos, who declared to have found "the Children of Israel" in the jungles of South America.[1] Fifteen years later, the English *Gazette* reported: "It is now about three month since the *Jews* gave out that near 600000 men were arrived at *Mecha,* professing themselves to be of the lost Tribes."[2] These two stories of the Lost Tribes came to England, one from the Americas and the other from across the Mediterranean, in newspaper reports, treatises, stories, and personal correspondence that traveled across state, religious, and regional boundaries.

The movement and development of these narratives raise questions about the relationship between religion and space, both in terms of how religious and cross-religious communities were imagined in the early modern period and in terms of how the historian might most fruitfully approach such a study. More specifically, examining these Lost Tribes narratives brings into focus how religion affected perceptions of space, how people conceptualized space within religious frameworks, and how different spaces influenced religious beliefs and their transmission. Here, space is both real and imagined: something physical that takes time and effort to cross but also something that is imagined and understood in shifting ways that do not simply correlate with miles. In the increasingly dispersed religious communities in the early modern world, for example, the Atlantic space could be imagined as a barrier, a distance that divided, or it could be a pathway that could be crossed by people or information, offering a sense of continuity, community, and connection.

At the same time, the Lost Tribes narratives demand a critical consideration of the limits of an Atlantic world perspective when considering early modern religious networks and cross-religious communication. The movement of people, stories, and ideas associated with these case studies particularly raise questions about the relationship between the Atlantic and Mediterranean worlds. The concept of an Atlantic world developed largely out of the history of commerce, and its usage for historians of religion has primarily centered on Christian populations such as the Puritans, who can be neatly situated within this arena. Only recently have scholars of Jewish history started to engage with this concept; yet they have done so in a manner that focuses on how the Sephardic networks and communities fit into an Atlantic world perspective.[3]

This essay moves past such an approach by examining the Sephardic networks across both regions, suggesting that the Atlantic and Mediterranean worlds were deeply entwined. To do so, it explores the development of Puritan and Sephardic networks across the Atlantic before tracing the transmission of the two Lost Tribes narratives along, between, and beyond these paths to test the strength of connections across national, religious, and especially regional divides. It argues that religious communities and cross-religious communication produced, were produced by, and transcended ideas of space in the Atlantic world; by thinking of the Atlantic and the Mediterranean together, a more complex history of the movement of people, stories, and information emerges, illustrating the ways in which religious ideas shaped and were shaped by understandings and encounters with space.

The Creation of the Networks: The Puritans and the Sephardim

One of the great strengths offered by Atlantic history is its comparative nature, especially for often insular Jewish histories.[4] As such, this essay begins by comparing the creation of the Sephardic networks to their Puritan counterparts because both groups were involved in transmitting and changing the Lost Tribes narratives along transatlantic trade networks embedded in a shared religious identity.[5] To understand how and why these stories moved in and beyond these religious communities, it is important to explore the relationship between their creation, perceptions of space, and religious beliefs.

Migration established networks through which people, goods, and ideas moved, creating a sense of continuity and connection that linked distant places. Although great distances now sometimes separated members of religious communities, a sense of shared identity encouraged the shrinking of the perceived space of the early modern Atlantic. In the early modern period, this migration was often inspired by a combination of religious persecution and business opportunities. Puritan networks were formed in the 1620s and 1630s when Puritans resettled in North America and Bermuda en masse because they felt that religious life in England was no longer bearable. Sustained Puritan migration brought permanent merchants to New England who built a complex and profitable commercial structure that they integrated into the transatlantic trade. The interaction between economic and religious impetuses worked in mutually reinforcing ways. On the one hand, personal relationships, family connections, and correspondence among coreligionists aided in enlarging economic influence; the colonial merchant leadership was tied together through commercial and family relations. On the other, new merchants attracted to New England for economic reasons often became committed to the Puritan religio-political platform.[6]

The transatlantic Sephardic networks began over a century before their Puritan counterparts when Portugal forcefully converted its Jewish population to achieve religious uniformity in 1497. Many of these Conversos fled the Iberian Peninsula and sought new locations to form communities where, because of their conversions, they were accepted where Jews were not. Some Conversos fled westward, crossing the Atlantic and settling in Brazil, which established their earliest transatlantic ties as they maintained contacts with Conversos on the other side of the Atlantic.[7] Changing economic circumstances led to the addition of another layer in the Sephardic networks: when the Jews were readmitted into certain Western European states, such as the Dutch Republic, they followed the Conversos in migrating to both these states and their American colonies. This created intertwined Jewish-Converso networks that were reinforced by Conversos who returned to Judaism. Thus, religious persecution coupled with economic opportunities and a shared religious (or ethno-religious) identity created multilayered networks that bound Sephardic and Puritan communities together across the Atlantic world.

The Sephardim and the Puritans did not simply create their own networks but rather built them on established routes of movement for people, goods, and ideas. Their choices of settlement were influenced by existing trade routes, which shows the importance of previously established spaces—even of their persecutors—in influencing the decisions of the migrants. Most could not afford to, nor did they necessarily desire to, create new places for themselves that were entirely cut off from their former communities. Many Puritans followed the path of earlier English settlers to the northern hemisphere and settled in relatively close proximity to other colonies, while the Jews tended to follow their Converso brethren who had been guided to new places by Iberian trade routes. Considering the vast amount of "available" space in the Americas and the great distance these people put between themselves and their former homes, they did not isolate themselves but instead found locations at strategic points, utilizing previously established networks to further their activities and maintain connections to family, friends, and coreligionists.

The changing political and economic situation in Europe affected the places people chose to settle in the Americas. As the Sephardim became more integrated into the Dutch Republic, they began to employ Dutch networks to further their activities. The Sephardic nation's ability to use such connections led to early Jewish settlement in North America, while conflict among European states spurred frequent migration throughout the Atlantic world, which reinforced and expanded their networks.[8] Therefore, the migrants' heritage, combined with shifting circumstances in Europe, affected the spaces of movement and settlement in the Americas. These factors also encouraged further migration that solidified the sense of a transatlantic religious community, shrinking the perceived space of a region that three hundred years before had seemed monumental.

People situated in the Atlantic world transcended real space and constructed imaginary space in the conceptions of their religious communities that spanned states and oceans. The Sephardim saw themselves as a single demographic and social entity whose members belonged to one nation across vast expanses, while they differentiated themselves from other Jews who lived in their cities.[9] Indeed, two Sephardic Jews separated by the Atlantic in many contexts imagined less distance between them than between a Sephardic and an Ashkenazi Jew in Amsterdam. The Puritans similarly saw themselves as part of a religious community that transcended the Atlantic. Yet despite being part of a broader Protestant and Christian world, and sharing a history of persecution that drove them across the Atlantic, Puritans persecuted other sects such as the Quakers in their colonies. Both groups, in other words, imagined their religious communities in a manner that conceptually shrank the space between themselves and the people they perceived to be part of their community, while simultaneously creating space between themselves and other similarly oriented people who could be physically much closer.

The space of the Atlantic world itself was conceptualized within the religious frameworks of the migrants, highlighting another dimension in the interaction between religion and space. Puritans such as John Cotton and Thomas Hooker followed earlier Protestants and Catholics by imbuing their journey across the ocean away from Europe with religious meaning. Unlike the earlier Englishmen, however, the Puritans turned to the story of the Israelites fleeing Egypt instead of Abraham's journey to understand their migration. These connections were made explicit: the Puritans were the new Israelites, England was Egypt, New England was Canaan, and some, including John Winthrop, saw the Atlantic Ocean as the Red Sea. Their choice of story was significant because, unlike Abraham's peaceful migration, the story of the Exodus is apocalyptic in character: God's oppressed people escape from a sinful place to the Promised Land. Such eschatological views were rampant among the Puritans, who saw themselves as actually living out the end time's scenario.[10]

This conceptualization had two major implications for the interaction between religion and space. First, the specific correlation between the Atlantic

Ocean and the Red Sea shows the symbolic importance these people invested in the space of the Atlantic Ocean because it was in the Red Sea that the Israelites' Egyptian persecutors had perished. If God had used the Red Sea to protect the Israelites, and if the Puritans saw themselves as the new Israelites fleeing from bondage across the Red Sea, then how could God not use the new Red Sea as a barrier to protect them too? Yet while the Sephardim had a history of comparing their persecution to that of the Israelites, particularly when they were expelled from Spain, and while they had closer religious and historical connections to the ancient Jews, they did not frame the Atlantic in the same religious terms as the Puritans. Second, the Puritans' eschatological conceptualization of their transatlantic journey led them to conflate real time with end time. This created a sense of urgency because they believed they were living in the last days, which led to the increased transmission of these ideas. The transatlantic movement of their eschatological ideas produced shared understandings of time, thus developing a sense of continuity in Puritan life and further shrinking perceptions of space across the Atlantic world.

An Atlantic world perspective is often employed in studying the Puritans because their migration and imagined religious community were principally situated around and deeply invested in the Atlantic Ocean. Like the Puritans, the Sephardic nation employed transatlantic channels of movement and communication, and people on both sides of the ocean saw themselves as part of the same community. However, Sephardic conceptions of community were not confined to the Atlantic in the same ways. Unlike the Puritans, the Sephardic community forged strong ties from Brazil through Europe to the Ottoman Empire and beyond. Even before the establishment of their transatlantic connections, the Sephardim had built networks that stretched across the Mediterranean. The expulsion from Spain in 1492 led the Sephardim to migrate and settle around the Mediterranean in North Africa, Italy, and especially the Ottoman Empire (alongside Portugal, where they would be converted shortly thereafter). Religious persecution once again had spurred migration, producing connections between sites and forging a sense of community across physical distance; the Sephardim settling throughout the Mediterranean world maintained ties with their brethren who resettled in Western Europe, linking communities across both the Mediterranean and Atlantic worlds.

Amsterdam acted as a meeting point for Sephardic networks from both regions, with links to various points in the Americas, as well as to Livorno and Venice, which acted as hubs to the Levant. The Conversos also linked Amsterdam to communities in Iberia. Indeed, Amsterdam was so central for the seventeenth-century Jewry that Henry Mechoulan and Gerard Nahon go so far as to assert that in some respects even the Holy Land was a dependency of the Sephardic community there.[11] There were also ties between the Sephardim in the western hemisphere and those in Italy and other places in the Mediterranean, showing connections between the Atlantic and Mediterranean worlds independent of Amsterdam.[12]

The far-reaching ties reinforced by migration, common religious practices, business cooperation, and the circulation of ideas facilitated the Sephardic diaspora's conception of themselves as part of the same religious community. Although by the mid-seventeenth century Western Europe and transatlantic ties had taken on a central role for Sephardic communities, the earlier Mediterranean connections remained important. While they operated across the Atlantic world, this space was not as central or as bounded as it was for the Puritans. In other words, a consideration of religious communities and cross-religious communication involving Puritans and the Sephardim reveals that while the Atlantic framework may be useful for understanding one religious community, focusing exclusively on the Atlantic may obscure the experiences, wider connections, and self-conceptions of another.

Case Study 1: The Discovery of the Lost Tribes in the Americas

The movement of stories about the Lost Tribes in the Americas provides one lens through which to consider the ways religious communities and cross-religious communication operated both within and beyond the Atlantic world. Tracing the transmission of the well-known account of Antonio de Montezinos, for example, illustrates the ways in which networks both functioned across and produced particular understandings of space and religious community. In the mid-1640s Montezinos arrived in Amsterdam from the Americas, claiming to have discovered the home of his lost brethren in the jungles of modern-day Peru. He was told that God had brought them to this land, had done many great miracles for them, and "that the God of those Children of Israel is the true God, that all that which is engraven upon their stones is true; that about the end of the World they shall be Lords of the world . . . and those Children of Israel going forth out of their Country, shall subdue the whole World to them."[13] Montezinos's account not only furthered eschatological excitement, but it answered two questions that scholars in Europe had been pondering: what had happened to the Lost Tribes of Israel, and what were the origins of the American indigenous people?[14]

In Montezinos's story, the Lost Tribes accepted him as a brother and entrusted him with "a message of signal importance for the Jews of the global diaspora, namely, the proximate unfolding of the messianic redemption."[15] The acceptance of Montezinos's claims by Jews and Christians in Western Europe undermines the usefulness of a center-periphery model for understanding the movement of eschatological ideas. The relatively unexplored and unoccupied space on the very periphery of the "known" world served as an acceptable location for the emergence of a population that was expected to affect not only the entire Diaspora—whose heart was across the Atlantic and whose religious center was across both the Atlantic and the Mediterranean—but for the entire world as well.

At the same time, such a claim was perhaps possible for the very reason that it came from the periphery, separated from Europe by physical and imagined distances. The early modern period provided a fertile environment for the transmission of eschatological ideas, especially about the Lost Tribes. The combination of unexplored and being-explored space at this time meant that there were enough unknown areas where a hidden population could be dwelling, yet there were enough people going towards these places and communications coming from them to encourage the dissemination of such stories. At the same time, vast distances meant that such stories could not be readily verified or disproven.

The movement of Montezinos's narrative across the Atlantic and its subsequent dissemination provides insight into the cross-religious and transnational flow of ideas as they were developed, used, and transmitted for a range of reasons. From South America, Montezinos traveled to Amsterdam, where he shared the account with Sephardic leaders, including the rabbi Menasseh ben Israel. It was from Amsterdam that his story would travel to other parts of Europe and beyond. The path of Montezinos's travels reaffirms the importance of the Iberian legacy in that part of the Americas as well as Spanish imperial connections to the Dutch Republic in building an arena in which Sephardic migration would establish networks that further linked these places. It also reinforces the supremacy of Amsterdam as a central location for the seventeenth-century Sephardim.

The significance of the shared religious identity of the Sephardim is seen in ben Israel's endorsement and publishing of Montezinos's narrative. He described Montezinos as "our Montezinos, being a Portingal, and a Jew of our Order," and preferred Montzinos's account "before the opinion of all others, as most true."[16] He may not have previously known Montezinos, nor did he plan to travel to the Americas to confirm his claims, but he accepted Montezinos's testimony and encouraged others to do so based on a conception of shared identity and community.[17]

Ideas of space played a significant role in ben Israel's messianic platform, which he outlined using Montezinos's account in *The Hope of Israel* (1650). He wrote, "as Daniel saith, Dan. 12.7. And when the scattering of the holy people shall have an end, all those things shall be fulfilled. And this appeares now to be done, when as our Synagogues are found in America."[18] Because the Jews were now sufficiently scattered, they were ready to be brought back to the Holy Land by the messiah, and he repeated this expectation throughout his work.[19] Ben Israel even charted the major migrations of the Jews in the early modern period to show that the dispersion was becoming universal at a rapid rate.[20] This highlights another dimension of the relationship between eschatology and space because the movement of Jews across space was deeply entwined with ben Israel's perception of time, as Sephardic migration coupled with the transatlantic transmission of ideas relating to the Lost Tribes was interpreted to promote messianic excitement.

Wim Klooster has even argued that ben Israel encouraged the settlement of Jews in England and the Americas because he believed that such migration would accelerate their dispersal throughout the world, which was a precondition for the coming of the messiah.[21] As such, ben Israel not only interpreted migration in eschatological terms as the Puritans did, but he also took an active approach to it. In other words, he tried to push time ahead by moving people across more space.

While ben Israel accepted, interpreted, and promoted Montezinos's testimony within a Jewish messianic framework, the story did not stay in the Sephardic world; it was also spread to England, where its publishing was connected to Puritan narratives that were transmitted across the Atlantic. John Eliot was a Puritan missionary in New England who retained close ties to England, sending reports about his missionary endeavor to be published in London in an attempt to gain more support among a population that would most likely never travel across the Atlantic to witness his work.[22] Although Eliot's writings had nothing to do with the Lost Tribes, when the Presbyterian minister Thomas Thorowgood read them he became convinced that the indigenous people with whom Eliot was working could be of Jewish origins because centuries of "accumulated barbarianism" were removed and they were restored to Christianity so quickly.[23] This led him to begin his own investigation, and by 1648 Thorowgood concluded that they were indeed descendants of the Lost Tribes.

Eliot and Montezinos would never meet, but because of Thorowgood's interest, their narratives crafted in different parts of the Americas became woven insolubly together on the other side of the Atlantic. John Dury had heard of Montezinos's story when he was in the Dutch Republic, but it was not until 1648 when Thorowgood gave him a copy of his manuscript on the origins of the indigenous people of the Americas, titled *Iewes in America*, that Dury seriously considered Montezinos's story. Dury then requested a copy of it from ben Israel, which he shared with Thorowgood. Thorowgood was so taken with it that he added it to his treatise, incorporating Eliot's reports with arguments that indigenous people in the Americas were the descendants of the Lost Tribes. This differed from ben Israel's claim that the Lost Tribes existed as a distinct group; yet, according to Dury, Montezinos's narrative and Thorowgood's arguments were in "full agreement . . . concerning the Americans, that they are descended of the Hebrewes."[24] Here, Montezinos's account was understood and employed in contradictory ways by two people of different faiths over a testimony that connected them. This complicated, multistage process of transnational, cross-religious influence, occurring between the Dutch Republic and England, had implications for the publication of both the Dutch Jewish rabbi's and the English Presbyterian minister's texts: Thorowgood used Montezinos's testimony (from ben Israel via Dury) to further his argument, while Dury's questions to ben Israel (spurred by reading Thorowgood's text) prompted ben Israel to publish his own work on the subject.[25]

The scholarly works and information used to support these claims demonstrate the extent of transatlantic and cross-religious communication in this period, as well as its importance in shaping the beliefs of religious communities. In their texts ben Israel and Thorowgood cited a variety of scholarly works to support their claims. While sometimes they used the same evidence,[26] ben Israel tended to turn to reports from Catholic missionaries and even oral reports from Dutch mariners. Thorowgood, on the other hand, cited evidence from a range of sources all over the Americas, but his primary point of reference was John Eliot and the Puritans in New England. Although they undertook a similar research process, they developed and relied upon different transatlantic networks for developing their opinions about the Lost Tribes in the Americas.[27]

Montezinos's story was not just printed in one pamphlet in England; it was reprinted multiple times, mentioned in various works, and employed in a range of ways. Moreover, it was even transmitted back across the Atlantic to New England. After being reinterpreted next to Eliot's letters to promote a Christian millenarian platform, it was sent to John Eliot in *The Glorious Progress* and *Iewes in America*. As these stories crisscrossed the Atlantic, they shifted and thickened cross-religious communication, while producing links within religious communities that spanned the ocean and crossed state boundaries.

These ideas arriving from across the Atlantic reaffirmed Eliot's eschatological interest and led him to seek out corroborating evidence. In doing so, he found a secondhand report of circumcised indigenous populations in the south; this information came from a Mr. Dudley, who passed it on from Captain Cromwell, recently deceased in Boston. Stating that Cromwell's report was one of the most probable arguments he had heard, Eliot initiated a correspondence with Thorowgood on the topic. On Thorowgood's request, Eliot provided a statement of his views, which he published under the title "The Learned Conjectures of the Reverend John Eliot Touching the Americans" in the revised edition of *Jews in America* (1660).[28]

Thorowgood's eagerness to publish Eliot's firsthand report suggests how palpable the size of the Atlantic was for people in Europe, as he saw the gap between the two places as too large to cross in order to verify the information for himself; in this sense, the Atlantic was envisioned both as a space of connection through the movement of information and a barrier to his own movement. Yet, while the space of the Atlantic Ocean was perceived as vast from a European vantage point, these same Europeans did not see distances on the other side of the Atlantic as large at all because Eliot was seen as a reliable source of information on indigenous people who lived far away from him. Moreover, in their search to bolster their arguments, ben Israel and Thorowgood used examples of indigenous practices throughout the Americas, conflating different groups and the distances that separated them. The great distances between European communities in the Atlantic world also forced people who wanted to believe the stories to do so by relying primarily on hearsay, while such distances made it hard for those who did not to prove they were untrue. Ben Israel had to accept Montezinos's testimony on his word, and even Eliot, who lived in North America, had to rely on the claims of a dead man for corroborating evidence.

The movement of the Lost Tribes narratives highlights the fluidity of early modern transmission of information, interconnections among religious networks, and the importance of the differing arenas for each group. One report from South America to Amsterdam along Sephardic networks, alongside a stream of correspondence between New England and London along Puritan networks, led to a flurry of cross-religious activity between London and Amsterdam, followed by increased communication between London and New England regarding the information from South America. Therefore, different parts of the web of networks were employed at different times, and the movement of ideas in one part affected the rate of transmission in others. While the two transatlantic spheres had a cross-religious link through the Dutch Republic and England, there does not appear to be much other crossover. English Protestants rarely turned to Catholics in the Americas or other Jews aside from the Dutch Jewry, and ben Israel did not use New England Puritans, although he turned to Catholic missionaries. Montezinos's testimony may have reached Eliot in North America, but Eliot was not in contact with him, ben Israel, or other Jews despite being in correspondence with many English Protestants who were. Moreover, the Anglo-Dutch connection tended to move the narratives in only one direction, showing that network connections were not always employed in a reciprocal manner. Eliot's statements were neither published in the Dutch Republic nor used by ben Israel to further his argument, even though English Protestants directly connected Eliot's narratives to Montezinos's testimony and ben Israel could have used them to argue that the Lost Tribes were in North America, too.

Similarly, within the Dutch Republic, narratives about the Lost Tribes did not always travel as might be expected; rather, networks, senses of community, and the movement of information worked in complicated ways that challenge any assumptions about an easy relationship between physical proximity and increased communication. Ben Israel was part of a circle of Christian millenarians in Amsterdam, including Petrus Serrarius, who were expecting the conversion of the Jews and were closely linked to the English millenarians. However, there was greater transmission between the Dutch Jews and the English Protestants than between the Dutch Jews and Dutch Protestants or between the English Protestants and Dutch Protestants. Montezinos's account was translated and printed in full or at least discussed in over a half dozen pamphlets in England before 1655; yet the first Dutch version did not come out until 1666. This shows that sometimes what we might expect to be the weakest link—the one across both a religious and national divide—could be stronger than ties and paths of communication within the same religion or state.

Finally, the transmission of Montezinos's and Eliot's narratives shows how the real and imagined space of the Atlantic Ocean shaped these ideas. The debate over the Lost Tribes would probably never have reached the intensity it did if it were not for the vast size of the Atlantic world, which led to minimal reports and facilitated the spread of claims that could rarely be substantiated. In other words, the religious construct that transcended the Atlantic, connecting people and shrinking their perceptions of space, was more readily accepted because of the large distance across which it traveled. Thus, while shared information and ideas created a sense of continuity across the Atlantic, this occurred because many of the people viewed the Atlantic as too insurmountable a journey. Further, the eschatological value of the stories created a sense of urgency, which led to increased transmission that further perpetuated this cycle, creating stronger and more entwined connections across the Atlantic world.

The transmission of Montezinos's narrative not only shows how readily mental constructs moved across national and religious boundaries in the early modern Atlantic world, but it also highlights connections between the Atlantic and Mediterranean worlds in two manners. Indeed, thinking about stories of the Lost Tribes in the Americas within a Mediterranean context complicates an already complicated narrative of cross-religious and cross-state communication, serving as a reminder that such historical patterns were not confined or given meaning solely by the Atlantic world. First, six months before Dury heard of Montezinos's account in the Dutch Republic, a "godly man" in the Hague told him that a Jew there (whom Dury knew) had received letters from Istanbul informing him that a messenger had arrived from the Lost Tribes.[29] Dury shared both this and Montezinos's story with Thorowgood. Thus, two stories about the Lost Tribes transmitted along Sephardic networks to the Dutch Republic from opposite directions were shared with English Protestants. One wonders what would have happened if Thorowgood had been able to get a copy of the letter from Istanbul about the Lost Tribes instead of, or alongside, Montezinos's. The fact that he managed to get the one from South America but not from the Ottoman Empire may provide clues about the nature of these far-flung networks. In this case, there was a more direct path in the transmission of knowledge across the Atlantic. In addition, the fact that the story about the Lost Tribes from the

Mediterranean world came together with its counterpart from the Atlantic world in Western Europe challenges a sense of isolation and uniqueness about the place of the Atlantic and the Americas in cross-religious communication about the Lost Tribes; instead, it pushes us to think about conceptions of the Americas in relation to religious ideas alongside those of other places.

Second, the influence of *The Hope of Israel* can be seen across both the Atlantic and the Mediterranean worlds. In the Atlantic, Joao de Yllan, who was born in Portugal but worked in Brazil, became a founder of the first Jewish congregation in the Caribbean, which he and the other Sephardic leaders named "the Hope of Israel" a year after ben Israel published his book.[30] In the Mediterranean world in 1659, *The Hope of Israel* was published in Spanish in the Ottoman Empire at Abraham Gabbai's Smyrna printing house. This edition contained four poems—one of which may have been written by a key figure in Sabbatai Sevi's circle, suggesting links between Sabbatai Sevi and the printing of ben Israel's *The Hope of Israel* in the Ottoman Empire.[31] Mechoulan and Nahon even suggest that the arrival of Montezinos in Amsterdam probably initiated a new phase of interest in messianic ideas among the Jews there that would culminate in the Sabbatian movement. After all, it was in the peak year of Sevi's messianic movement that ben Israel's text was published in Dutch, which was clearly designed to enlighten the Dutch public about Jewish messianism.[32] Moreover, these Atlantic and Mediterranean influences became further entangled when Joao de Yllan moved to Amsterdam and became an enthusiastic Sabbatian; from here he wrote to the English king for a free pass during one of the Anglo-Dutch Wars for a ship to take him and his brethren home to the Holy Land, believing their restoration had come.[33] Thus, considering the transmission and development of narratives of the Lost Tribes in the Americas—from Montezinos to ben Israel, from Eliot to Thorowgood and beyond—can demonstrate complicated connections between and among religious communities around the Atlantic and Mediterranean worlds, as religious ideas, perceptions of space, and the movement of people and beliefs became entwined in and built upon one another.

Case Study 2: The Lost Tribes and the Sack of Mecca

Montezinos's testimony in ben Israel's *The Hope of Israel* may have been, as suggested, connected with the rise of Sabbatai Sevi and the Sabbatian movement. A second case study—this time concerned with narratives of the Lost Tribes in Mecca, which traveled along Sephardic networks from the Mediterranean world and across the Atlantic—further demonstrates the ways in which perceptions of space, senses of religious community, and communication across religious and state boundaries shaped and were shaped by one another. In the mid-1660s Sabbatai Sevi emerged as a messianic claimant in the Ottoman Empire and amassed a large number of Jewish followers throughout the world before he converted to

Islam under the threat of death.[34] Sabbatai was supported by the Prophet Nathan in Gaza, who was said to have begun preaching around the late spring of 1665 that the Lost Tribes would conquer Palestine. Various legends then emerged in which Nathan was said to have met messengers from the Lost Tribes during excursions in the wilderness of Gaza who told him that his brethren would reemerge shortly. These stories were spread throughout the Jewish world along a variety of paths; familial networks were particularly vital in their early movement as Raphael Joseph, the head of the Jewish community in Egypt, had sent his brother Hayyim Joseph as an emissary to report on Nathan's activities. Hayyim reported the stories of the Lost Tribes to Raphael, who forwarded them to his other brother Solomon Joseph in Livorno.[35] In these ways, rumors of the Lost Tribes spawned by the Sabbatian movement began to circulate among the European Jewries.

One such rumor that spread throughout Europe was of an army of the Lost Tribes sacking Mecca. Gershom Scholem has argued that at the base of the rumors was most likely an original report about the new prophet or messiah; the stories of the Lost Tribes could have been a translation of the actual messianic movement into the imaginative language of popular legend because of the vague nature of the early ideas. However, he consistently claimed that there is no evidence to show that the legends of the army of the Lost Tribes originated in Gaza.[36] So where did this story come from? Examining Italian newspapers recently unearthed from archives in Italy provides insights into the origins of this story and shows how the spaces through which it traveled and the influence of developing religious movements contributed to its evolution.

On April 25, 1665, an *avvisi,* or early newspaper, in Venice published the story of an army of Arabs who went to Mecca, robbed it, and carried away the corpse of Muhammad with the treasury.[37] This story apparently came to Venice from Smyrna via Livorno, and it failed to mention the Lost Tribes or even any Jews at all. Moreover, it was transmitted in the spring of 1665 before news of Nathan's prophecies or the Sabbatian movement reached Italy. This suggests that at the base of the Lost Tribes rumor was a story of an Arab sack of Mecca.

The story resurfaced in the Venetian newspaper four months later, in the summer of 1665, with a significant addition. The Venetian newspaper of August 8 reported that there was still constant talk of the Arab attack on Mecca, but the Arabs were now joined by a great number of Jewish inhabitants, who had appointed a chief and given him the title of king.[38] Then, on August 29, it reported that the Arabs and Jews who had stripped, robbed, and burned Mecca had now returned to their country with their rich booty.[39] This time, the "*numero grandissimo*" (great number) of Jews had become "*numero infinito*" (an infinite number of Jews), which shows another change that resonates with an image of the Lost Tribes. These two stories did not list their sources; instead they stated, "*viene ancora replicato*" (it is still repeated) and "*parla costantamente dell'invasione fatta*" (the invasion is constantly spoken about), which suggests that this version originated from rumors circulating around Venice and not from a particular place or source, unlike the stories that only included an Arab force and specifically listed their origins. In the later reports, then, the original report of the Arab sack of Mecca appears to have been coming together with rumors about the Lost Tribes just as Nathan's early prophecies and rumors of the Lost Tribes were beginning to circulate. These narratives converged and entwined to create a new story that linked the sack of Mecca with the Lost Tribes, showing how the spaces that the story traveled across affected its content.

By the time the story was published in England, it was the Lost Tribes who were sacking Mecca. Thus, the space of the Mediterranean played a role in shaping the story because ideas from different places were added to an original report, changing its content as it moved across state boundaries: a report of an Arab army from the Ottoman Empire was mixed with rumors in Italy that were coming from another part of the Levant relating to a Jewish messianic movement. These two narratives combined to become, first, an Arab army together with an infinite amount of Jews, and, by the time it reached England, as the Lost Tribes themselves.

The story, however, did not end there because a week later the English *Gazette* noted that the story of the Lost Tribes was based on a political rebellion by the Bassa of Bissery. Despite this admission, on January 25, 1666, it reported that the Jews and Arabs had united under the Jewish leader Gioraban (Jeroboam) from Aden, took Medina and Mecca, destroyed Mohammad's tomb, and were heading towards the Holy Land.[40] The *Gazette* did not seem to make the connection between the earlier story of the Lost Tribes sacking Mecca and this story. Moreover, there were some significant additions in this report: now their leader had a name, and they were heading towards the Holy Land instead of returning home, which shows an added eschatological element that was not in the Venetian newspapers but rather was included as the story moved farther away from its origin. This story continued to appear in the *Gazette*, and the February 22 issue relayed a report from Istanbul via Venice that provided a fuller account of the Arab-Jewish army led by Gioraban—who was now, in these renditions, their prophet.[41] In fact, the story was so widespread in Europe that the *Gazette* even printed a report from Vienna that claimed, "The Jews in this City made a publick Jubile, with great expressions of joy, upon the news they have brought them of the success of their Brethren in *Asia* against the Turk, which continues to be confirmed from several parts, though with some differences of circumstances."[42]

The story was transmitted from Italy to the Dutch Republic along Sephardic networks through the Mediterranean in a manner similar to that of the Sabbatian movement. It appears to have reached England from the Dutch Republic three months before the *Gazette* printed its first story (which was the period that the *Gazette* claimed the Jews of the Dutch Republic were spreading it, as well as just after the time that the Venetian newspaper printed it). Specifically, the story surfaces in the correspondence of Henry Oldenburg, the secretary of the Royal Society, who also worked on the *Gazette,* which may explain how it ended up being printed in the newspaper. Oldenburg most likely heard of it from Peter Serrarius, who was in close contact with Menasseh ben Israel and other members of the Dutch Jewry, because in Oldenburg's letters to Robert Boyle, the discussion of the attack on Mecca is followed by a reference to Serrarius.[43] The movement of this story further highlights the Sephardic connection to the Dutch Republic from the Mediterranean as well as the importance of Amsterdam as an Anglo-Dutch cross-religious hub. Unlike with the previous case study, this story came to English Protestants via a Dutch Protestant, showing an extra intermediary in the process. Regardless, the networks that brought both stories about the Lost Tribes to England fifteen years apart from opposite sides of the world overlapped in their entrance through the Dutch Republic, situated as a critical site for the transmission of eschatological ideas in, through, and from both the Atlantic and the Mediterranean worlds.

There was not just overlap in Western Europe, though. Rumors of the Lost Tribes from the Sabbatian movement as well as the Sabbatian movement itself were spread along Sephardic Jewish networks across the Atlantic, and their acceptance in diversely located communities further demonstrates the maintenance of Jewish connections across both regions. Further, Sabbatian rumors of the Lost Tribes reached Puritan communities in the Americas and actually reinvigorated John Eliot's interest in the Lost Tribes, which had waned in the late 1650s.[44] Therefore, not only were the Sephardim connected with one another across the Mediterranean and Atlantic worlds, but there were also cross-religious connections that linked them to the Protestants in England and the Americas in the 1650s and the 1660s, as rumors that resulted from the emergence of a Jewish messiah in the Ottoman Empire affected the beliefs of a Puritan in North America. It was also the earlier transatlantic movement of ideas relating to the Lost Tribes in the Americas that set the foundation for greater interest in the later rumors and the Sabbatian movement a decade later. In these ways, both the Sephardic nation and the English Puritans in the Atlantic world were part of larger, more complicated networks, suggesting the need to place the Atlantic world within a broader, and even global, context when examining the movement of religious ideas that connected people across both space and time.

Conclusion

In the mid-seventeenth century, stories about the Lost Tribes traveled around and across the Atlantic and Mediterranean worlds, crossing state and religious boundaries as they moved and developed. These narratives provide a lens through which to consider the complex relationship between religion and space in the early modern world. Religion played a significant, if sometimes indirect, role in shrinking the perceived space of both the Atlantic and Mediterranean worlds as religious persecution spurred migration, which in turn created networks of communication and movement. These networks produced and maintained shared religious identities that solidified communities, and encouraged the transmission of religious ideas that promoted a sense of continuity across space. The movement of eschatological ideas also shifted perceptions of time that then affected ideas of space.

Physical and imagined space also had a primary role in the shaping of self-conceptualizations and beliefs of religious communities. Each group simultaneously transcended physical distances and created imaginary space in their constructions of religious community that spanned states and oceans, as members migrated to new locations. Religious ideas were also affected by the spaces and distances through which they traveled, as the story of the sack of Mecca demonstrated, while the vast and distant spaces from which Montezinos's narrative emerged and across which it traveled had implications for its acceptance. Space was even interpreted to promote eschatological tension (in the case of the Puritans) and was actively transcended to advance eschatological hopes (in the case of ben Israel).

While perceptions of space, religious beliefs, and senses of community were present and inextricably linked in the transmission of eschatological stories about the Lost Tribes, the movement and development of these narratives also have important implications for regional approaches to the study of religion and space. Kagan and Morgan noted in the preface to *Atlantic Diasporas* that regional perspectives—especially that of the Atlantic world—emerged as a challenge to parochial national narratives, seeking to expand horizons and encourage broader thinking in historical analyses. As this chapter has shown, such a view illuminates important trends. An Atlantic world framework has highlighted transnational connections and cross-religious influences between Western Europe and the Americas, while analyzing the Mediterranean demonstrates how a story developed across similar divides between the Ottoman Empire, Italy, the Dutch Republic, and England. Yet, ultimately, both regional perspectives are limiting. An Atlantic world framework may be useful for understanding one religious community that fits into its boundaries (the Puritans), but it obscures the wider connections and self-conceptions of another (the Sephardim). It also neglects to account for the broader ties between the two groups in relation to the cross-religious networks that spanned the divide between the Atlantic and Mediterranean worlds. In other words, it neglects the impact of ideas that emerged among the Sephardim in the Mediterranean region on the Puritans in the Atlantic world. In this sense, an approach that only considers one or the other fails to take into account long-range, cross-religious influence and communication. While each story primarily moved within the region in which it originated, both found their way deep into the other region: Montezinos's account from South America ended up being printed in the Ottoman Empire, while the rumors of the Lost Tribes from the Ottoman Empire ended up in the Americas. These connections suggest that, like the regional perspective's challenge to the national framework, a wider lens and maybe even a global one can illuminate new trends, expand horizons, and encourage broader views about historical phenomena.

This has significant historiographical implications because, as Adam Sutcliffe has had the foresight to acknowledge, if only in passing, early modern ties between Christian Europe and the Ottoman Empire tend to be overshadowed by a focus on conflict. Instead of considering Jewish links between the two places, he maintains, Western Jews tend to suppress these connections in favor of drawing a stark separation between the orientalized romance of medieval Iberia and a decisively Western Jewish modernity. According to Sutcliffe, "Atlantic Jewish history, if not placed within a global context, risks further reinforcing this misleading and unhelpful division."[45] This essay suggests that the possibilities and importance of placing the Atlantic world within a broader context is important for more than just Jewish history. Such a regional focus promotes a view that separates Western Europe and its westward expansion from the rest of the world—a world that was not only connected to it but played an important role in shaping it as well.

The Religious Spaces of American Whaling

Richard J. Callahan, Jr.

There is no place that is not haunted by many different spirits hidden there in silence, spirits one can "invoke" or not. Haunted places are the only ones people can live in.

Michel de Certeau, *The Practice of Everyday Life* (1984)

The ship *Morrison,* under the command of Captain Samuel Green, Jr., set out from New London, Connecticut, on September 16, 1844, bound for the North Pacific on a whaling voyage. The ship headed east across the Atlantic, planning to round the southern tip of Africa into the Indian Ocean and the Pacific. By October 17 the ship was approximately two days' sail north-northwest of the Cape Verde Islands. The prospect of a potential stop at Cape Verde for supplies put the Reverend Thomas Douglass into a contemplative mood. Douglass was not a whaling man himself; he was catching a ride aboard the *Morrison* to the Sandwich Islands (known today as Hawai'i), where he was to work as a missionary. Shipboard life was new to him. He had spent the first week or so aboard seasick. But now, more than about the weather, he was concerned about the night watch's ability to stay awake. He was anxious about running into close-passing ships. They had encountered six vessels over the past month, one coming quite near.[1]

Cape Verde was a familiar port to New England whalers. Douglass knew that he might be able to send some letters back home from there, prompting him to think about the people and activities he was missing while traveling about the ocean. "Of everything interesting in the progress of science, Literature, Commerce, & Religion, both in our own country & in the whole civilized world we must be content to remain ignorant for a long time," he wrote in his journal. "We are now separated from home by a distance of more than three thousand miles & we are increasing that distance at the rate of nearly two hundred miles per day." Yet, he wrote, neither the vast expanse of the open ocean nor "even infinite space itself can in the least retard or obstruct the delightful mental communion of mutual friends. By imagination we can thus instantly annihilate distance." Considering the problem of distance and connection, of the relationship between the spaces of memory, desire, and geography, Douglass—a well-educated Protestant minister—surprisingly turned his mind to the popular practice of mesmerism: "could we but transfer our bodily senses with our thoughts, as the advocates of mesmerism pretend to do, our intercourse consisting no longer of mere visions of fancy, would assume the character of actual reality."

Just a few months earlier, in April 1844, a whaling man in the north Pacific also felt the tug of his New England home pulling at his heart and mind. And, in response, he also reached for mesmerism. About two hundred miles from the Sandwich Islands and four months into his voyage, Daniel Kimball Ritchie, second mate on the ship *Israel* of New Bedford, dreamed that he put a crewmate into a mesmeric sleep and "sent him to a certain house in Boston where he could a tale unfold."[2]

A little over a year and a half later, Ritchie took mesmerism a step further. Now on the ship *Herald* of New Bedford, having shipped aboard in the Sandwich Islands after he was released from jail (where he had been locked up over a dispute with the captain of the *Israel*), Ritchie wrote the following entry, dated January 22, 1846, in his journal:

> This evening at 8 o clock I put a young man into Mesmeric sleep & went with him to N Bedford to his fathers house. he described the rooms & told me that his mother oldest sister & Aunt were in it. he then went home with me & described our house told me that there was an elderly lady settling by the fire reading or sewing. described the room and furniture. he then went into the kitchen told me there was a young woman cooking something in a pot. he then went into the Front yard said there was snow on the ground. I then took him to Boston to no 12 Carver Street he said there was two young ladies in the room one was reading out of a gilt edged book. we then went to Newton, to Mr Collins house & went into the sitting room. he said their was an old lady setting in a chair by the Fire. I asked if there was any one else in the room he said he could see a young lady putting a stick of wood on the fire. he said the old lady was crooked. we then went to Boston to the same house we was at before in Carver Street he said he saw the young ladies one had got up and was looking in glass the other one stood by the fire he said they were very pretty.

Two days later he again wrote that he "put young Bryant into a Mesmeric Sleep & magnatized his organs. all of which experiments were satisfactory."

Several days after that, he tried again, this time without success. But in response to the terrible luck the ship was having at capturing whales, he also wished that he could "magnatize a whale and get him."

Douglass and Ritchie were very different men, traveling the space of the oceans for different purposes; yet for both of them mesmerism—a partly scientific, partly religious practice growing in popularity in the United States during the 1840s—provided a language for thinking about space and the annihilation of distance.[3] Connected through the language of mesmerism, they were also linked by their presence aboard whaling ships plying the world's oceans. With their references to the play of proximity and distance between themselves and their "home" on New England's North Atlantic coast, Douglass and Ritchie hinted at the connections between antebellum New England (an Atlantic world formation) and global networks of trade, labor, and religious activity. The space of the ocean itself, merging the Atlantic into the Pacific, connecting New England, the Sandwich Islands, and Cape Verde, the setting for both whale hunting and soul saving, has remained largely invisible to historians of religion despite its importance as a site of religious engagement and production in the modern world.

Growing up on the coast of Massachusetts, I spent a lot of time in the ocean, on the ocean, and dreaming about the ocean. The New Bedford Whaling Museum, the Essex Institute and the Peabody Museum of Salem (now combined as the Peabody Essex Museum), and Mystic Seaport in Mystic, Connecticut, were familiar sites of family and school trips. They brought to life, through images, objects, and stories, the history of seafaring in the area where I grew up. That history included, in no small part, voyages in and through the Pacific Ocean. From the very beginnings of the young republic, merchant ships connected Salem and Boston with China, India, and, later, Japan. Whalers headed out from New Bedford, New London, and other New England ports to spend an average of two to four years roaming the Atlantic and, especially, the Pacific in search of whale oil. Images of the Pacific Islands and their inhabitants competed in my imagination with those of whales being harpooned and cut up shipside, black smoke rising above the ocean as the whales were "tried out" and their oil barreled. Material artifacts from the islands and from Asia populated these museums—whale teeth, baskets, jewelry, wooden carvings, masks, shields, headdresses, tools, furniture—enough to shape my sense of eighteenth- and nineteenth-century American seafaring as a global enterprise that traversed and inhabited the spaces of the Atlantic and the Pacific. Though, of course, Americans exchanged goods and bodies regularly with European countries and with Africa—a history that is being extensively revisited in studies of the Atlantic world—it was Pacific spaces, places, peoples, objects, and stories that stuck in my mind. Perhaps the European connections were too obvious, too often told, and not "exotic" enough to catch my attention.

Perhaps the stories of the African connections overemphasized the slave trade to a point where I didn't notice anything else. And certainly, the Pacific held a romantic aura; it was a curiosity produced and encouraged by the museums and by literature of sailors on the South Seas and in the South Pacific Islands. Regardless, what is important is that my heritage, my identity, my sense of the history of my place, was heavily informed by an image of seafaring that connected the New England coast—Massachusetts, in particular—to the Pacific Ocean.

The sea was, of course, not the only history shaping the identity of Massachusetts's shores. Another strong influence was a historical narrative that included the Pilgrims, the American Revolution, and a storyline that wrapped the religious and the political closely together around those two foci. That narrative was not only a local one; it might be called a version of the "official" American history, the basic outline of the American origin myth familiar to schoolchildren across the nation and celebrated during Thanksgiving and the Fourth of July. But it also *was* a local story for those who grew up where I did, where those events were never *just* descriptions contained in books. They happened right here, down the street, across town, in houses and buildings and fields and churches that could be visited and played around and passed every day on the way to the store or school. American history, the stories of our national origins, was part of the *place* and thereby part of the identity of those of us growing up there. And that place, and identity, also included a historical awareness, if hazy, of connections between the Atlantic and Pacific Oceans.

Later in life, as I began to study American religious history and the broader field of religious studies in graduate school, I began to notice a bifurcation that was not at first clear, but that has come increasingly into focus and grown unsettling. On the one hand, the foundational and influential narratives of American religious history that have shaped not only the nation's sense of the past but also the questions of its present, have not included the Pacific or the people who lived in or worked the Pacific.[4] In fact, they tended not to include the ocean at all. This did not fit with my self-understanding of the place that, nonetheless, formed a central role in the typical narratives of American religious history. Many of the elements were there: Pilgrims, Puritans, coastal Massachusetts, port towns, and immigrants—but where was the sea that was so centrally a part of that world? The recent influence of the Atlantic world paradigm on the study of early American religious history has offered a potential fix to this absence, but the Atlantic world perspective, despite its name, tends to neglect the space of the ocean as a place of experiential and historical significance. And Atlantic world models do not account for Pacific connections that were present from the start of the young republic.

On the other hand, and extending the sense of bifurcation, many of the theoretical perspectives that have informed the modern academic study of religion—from E. B. Tylor to Emile Durkheim, from Sigmund Freud to Mircea Eliade—were constructed from materials largely collected from the South Pacific islands in the very waters where New England whaling men spent most of their time during the nineteenth century.[5] But just as those islands and the experiences of Americans working and exchanging among them have been absent from American religious history, neither did the presence of Americans or other Atlantic world actors who were involved in networks of exchange with Pacific islanders appear anywhere in relation to theories of religion produced from Pacific island evidence. These two bodies of disciplinary knowledge—American religious history and theorizing about religion—were in fact spatially intertwined. They connected through the space of the ocean. The very possibility of each of them was linked to processes of global travel and exchange that tied the Atlantic world to the Pacific, New England to South Pacific Islands, the labor of the ocean to social, cultural, and industrial transformations in the United States, and, in emerging languages of cultural comparison, "West" to "East," "civilized" to "primitive," and "religion" to "superstition." And the American whaling industry, based in New England, was a crucial part of this process that extended Atlantic formations into the Pacific and transformed them both.

The Atlantic world, as a system and a paradigm for historical scholarship, begins with the idea of the interconnectedness of various peoples, economies, and nations. As soon as networks of exchange of goods, bodies, and ideas began to connect Europe, Africa, and the Americas in the fifteenth century, the histories and developments of each of these entities could no longer fully be understood in isolation from one another. Atlantic history, as a field of study since the 1990s, has challenged traditional histories that were written with the point of view of the nation as the basic unit of analysis. Atlantic history connected the dots, so to speak, between emerging nations and an emerging modern world connected by the waters of the Atlantic, making visible interactions and influences that were previously unseen or neglected.

Historian David Armitage has usefully identified three main organizing practices of Atlantic history, which he names circum-Atlantic, trans-Atlantic, and cis-Atlantic. Each is differentiated by its perspective and basic units of analysis. "Circum-Atlantic history" is "the transnational history of the Atlantic world," focused on the Atlantic as "a particular zone of exchange and interchange, circulation and transmission."[6] This form of Atlantic history most clearly examines the Atlantic world as a system in which each piece, each place, is connected to others. The connections matter here, and the system through which places are connected is understood to be a critical element in the development of those places and the world they constitute. In the study of religion, Jon F. Sensbach's *Rebecca's Revival: Creating Black Christianity in the Atlantic World* is a strong example of the circum-Atlantic concept.[7] At its center is one West Indies–born woman, Rebecca Protten, who began life as a slave but, after converting to Christianity, acquired her freedom. Sensbach reconstructs her life as a Moravian missionary circulating through the Atlantic world from the Caribbean to Europe and to Africa. Her story unsettles common historical assumptions about race, gender, mobility, and authority, and illuminates the ways in which local places were intimately connected through maritime transportation to places seemingly too far away to matter. From the perspective of American religious history, Sensbach's story also challenges the boundaries of nation-based narration, since Protten's world was clearly wider than national or colonial borders.

"Trans-Atlantic history" is international in scope, and comparative in perspective. "Unlike the 'symbiotic, but asymmetric' relations of land and sea traced by Atlantic history as an oceanic history," Armitage explains, "trans-Atlantic history concentrates on the shores of the ocean, and assumes the existence of nations and states, as well as societies and economic formations (like plantations or cities), around the Atlantic rim."[8] A good example from religious history is Jorge Cañizares-Esguerra's *Puritan Conquistadors: Iberianizing the Atlantic, 1500–1700.*[9] Cañizares-Esguerra took two examples of European colonization of the Americas—the Spanish in South America and the Puritans in North America—which usually are treated quite distinctly. He found a shared colonial discourse that figured colonization as a form of "exorcism" and cultivation, and argued that his comparison reveals that Puritan and Iberian colonization were tied more closely together than historians had previously imagined. Rather than being two distinct projects, they were part of the same religious world that was dominantly shaped by Iberian Atlantic practices. Cañizares-Esguerra thus reframed common historical perspectives and challenged ideas of "American exceptionalism" on new grounds.

Finally, "cis-Atlantic history" treats the history of a particular place within the context of Atlantic world connections. Immigration, economics, intellectual influences, and so forth, which flow from the wider Atlantic to American places and vice versa, help make sense of the United States as a place connected to the wider world rather than as a place of self-becoming. April Lee Hatfield's *Atlantic Virginia: Intercolonial Relations in the Seventeenth Century,* for instance, situates Virginia as part of a network of geographic relations that included Europe, Africa, and the Caribbean.[10] Placing colonial Virginia in connection with other English colonies in the Caribbean raises new questions and illuminates historical formations that otherwise remained unremarkable.

For all of the power of the Atlantic world paradigm—and it has shown great power in transforming the contexts, players, and influences that historians pay attention to and the questions that they ask—American seafaring, especially the whaling industry, highlights two of its limitations. First, although Atlantic history is defined by the Atlantic Ocean, the space of the ocean itself as ocean has typically been neglected.[11] It appears as a medium, a space of connectivity, by which disparate land-based places are linked or through which objects, bodies, or ideas circulate. But the materiality of the ocean itself, the time and space of the water, is missing. Yet the ocean has been a place of work, a place of sustenance, a place of hope and fear, and a place of desire and desperation for many people. Whalers who went to sea for anywhere from two to five years, no less than merchant mariners and other seafarers, were often as familiar with life on a ship at sea as they were with life on land. And part of that familiarity was knowledge of the weather, the winds, the currents, and the creatures that lived in the sea. Historian Jeffrey Bolster has pushed this idea further, making the point that the *living sea* has been absent in Atlantic world studies, despite its importance (materially and symbolically) to the human actors who lived around it, moved through it, and fed from it. "The interactions of human maritime communities with the marine biological communities on which they depend seem to have remained largely uninvestigated," he noted, "because of the enduring assumption that the ocean exists outside of history."[12] Whaling brings into sharp focus both the space of the ocean as a place of human experience, labor, culture, and interaction that is historically situated, and the interaction between human actors and the natural life of the sea. Whaling crews, sailing the oceans for years at a time, navigated currents and winds to hunt the sea's creatures. The space of the ocean was not simply a conduit of transportation for whaling men; it was the space of life, death, work, and sociality, tying human to natural history.

Whaling (and seafaring more generally) also problematizes the geographic and temporal boundaries of the Atlantic world, which scholars often define as beginning around 1500 and ending around 1800. The presumption behind these boundary points is that the Atlantic world ceases to meaningfully designate a discrete system beyond the formation of the United States (severing some of the colonial ties between Europe and the Americas) and the African slave trade. What this presumption neglects to examine sufficiently, however, is the fluidity of the boundaries between the Atlantic and the Pacific and the continuity of activities across these boundaries. Atlantic world players began to have a presence in the Pacific in connection with the Asian trade during the seventeenth and eighteenth centuries. The Euro-American involvement in trade, fishing, and colonizing in the Pacific that began in the late eighteenth century and increased throughout the nineteenth century was tied, very directly, to Atlantic world actors and institutions. It might be more accurate to understand what might be called the "Euro-American Pacific" as an extension of the Atlantic world, increasing in significance over the course of the nineteenth century.[13] The expansion of the Atlantic world into the Pacific, creating an Atlantic Pacific within the wider Pacific, was due to interconnected relationships between the intersections of human and natural history, between natural, technological, political, and religious factors. In the context of American whaling, it was the pursuit of sperm whales, valued for their oil, that led Atlantic world actors into the Pacific. The Pacific was on the other side of the earth from Massachusetts, but these two places were intimately linked and part of the same world. New Englanders plied the Pacific waters, anchored off Pacific Islands, worked with and against Pacific Island residents, and came to know Pacific spaces. With whalers (and other seafarers) came missionaries and other Atlantic world social forces and cultural formations. And, with whalers, the Pacific came back to the Atlantic world, especially through New Bedford, Massachusetts. Unlike many other seafaring trades in which ships and mariners passed through Pacific waters on their way to Asian destinations, whaling men became intimately connected to the islands, peoples, and spaces of the Pacific because of the time they spent pursuing their Pacific prey.

Despite the widespread popularity of Melville's *Moby-Dick,* it is difficult today to appreciate the reach and importance of whaling in nineteenth-century America. By its zenith in the mid-nineteenth century, whaling was one of the largest industries in the United States, the third largest in New England and New York. New Bedford, the global center of the whaling industry, was the richest American port. The products of whaling—from oil to bone—were used in lighting, industrial lubrication, carriage making, clothing, perfume, and many other products. In this sense, whaling had an impact far inland (in the United States and internationally) and throughout the emerging industrial factory economy.[14]

Whaling was part of New England life from the beginning of the colonial period.[15] A quick sketch of American whaling would note its beginnings as a coastal activity in which whales were captured just offshore and brought back to the beach for processing into oil. It was also an activity that was shot through with mythological and legendary significance from the beginning. For instance, the development of whaling on the island of Nantucket was said to have been aided in 1690 by a man from Cape Cod named Ichabod Paddock who, according to legend, had once been swallowed by a whale. In the whale's belly a mermaid and the Devil played cards for his soul. Sperm whales were said to have been "discovered" in the Atlantic initially in 1712 when a Nantucket captain, hunting for right whales, was blown off course out to deep waters in a storm. There he spied and killed a sperm whale. From that point on, it is said, Nantucketers sailed farther and farther out from shore in pursuit of sperm.[16] Whale oil was in high demand from early on in the colonial history of the northeast coast of what would become the United States, even to the point of creating the need for laws governing ownership and distribution in the case of beached whales or carcasses that washed ashore. By 1717 Cotton Mather called whale oil "a staple commodity of the [Massachusetts Bay] colony" and praised American whaling men in prayer and thanksgiving.[17]

Competition for control of the whale fisheries of the North Atlantic off the American coast was an undernoted driver of the political tensions between England and France in the seventeenth and eighteenth centuries.[18] By the mid-eighteenth century Quaker-dominated Nantucket had emerged as the center of colonial American whaling, sending ships first to the North and later to the South Atlantic in pursuit of right and sperm whales in response to the noticeable decline of whales along the coast beginning around 1720. By 1763 Nantucket ships were whaling off the coast of Guinea; by 1765 they were off the West Indies and the Caribbean; by 1774 they were voyaging as far as the coast of Brazil in pursuit of their prey. Ships grew larger to travel farther distances for longer periods of time and to accommodate the equipment needed for "trying out" (processing) whale oil at sea. The market for whale products also grew, extending to both sides of the Atlantic and including the American colonies, England, France, and Germany. In 1774 the colonial whaling fleet included 360 vessels from fifteen New England and New York ports. The event that finally halted the steady growth of the whaling industry was the Revolutionary War. Nantucket, for reasons in part economic and in part religious (the Quakers who dominated the island were pacifists), remained neutral during the war, which ironically put them at odds with the Massachusetts authorities who placed them under embargo. In any case, the market for whale products shrank during wartime, and whaling vessels were at risk of being captured and commissioned as privateers for either side if they did venture out. After the war the British set a high tariff on imported whale oil, determined to create their own whaling fleet, and President Thomas Jefferson forbade American vessels from embarking on foreign voyages. Some Nantucket whalers left for Nova Scotia. Others moved to Dunkirk to whale for France. The War of 1812 further hindered the industry.

When whaling finally recovered, New Bedford rose to prominence over Nantucket as the premiere American whaling port, due as much to the natural life of the ocean as to the economic savvy of people such as Quaker businessman William Rotch, Jr.[19] American whaling literally outgrew the capabilities of Nantucket Harbor as a result of sperm whales growing scarcer in the Atlantic. The same pursuit of spermaceti that led whalers to expand the reach of their voyages to all corners of the Atlantic drove them eventually into the Pacific. A British whaler first rounded Cape Horn in 1790, and when the American fleet began to build back its strength, it did so by following that Pacific path.[20] Voyages of such a distance required yet larger vessels—larger than could easily navigate Nantucket's shallow harbor. Ships returning from the Pacific also carried such large amounts of oil that it proved more practical to deliver their barrels straight to the mainland in New Bedford's port.

The classic whaling ship of the nineteenth century weighed three hundred tons. It was manned by thirty to thirty-five men, carried four boats that were lowered to pursue whales, and could carry up to four thousand barrels of oil. The ship was in a real sense a mobile factory and a social and cultural world unto itself. Its crew consisted of a captain and his officers (usually two or three mates), a cook, a cooper, and four "boatsteerers" (harpooners); the rest were ordinary seamen, sharing space in the forecastle and duties throughout the vessel. Ordinary seamen hauled sails, washed and maintained the boat, and rowed the whaleboats when they were lowered whenever a whale was spied. They cut up the whale alongside the ship once they had killed it, boiled its blubber into oil, and stored the oil away into barrels below. They gathered wood, water, and food on Pacific islands over the course of their three- to four-year voyages and often interacted with islanders in benevolent and malevolent ways. They traded with islanders for goods and for sex, and some men chose to abandon their ships in favor of short- or, sometimes, long-term island life. When whaling ships returned to their home ports, they often carried a different crew than they had set out with, as some men had deserted, others had died, and new men had shipped on board. Many of these men were from the Pacific Islands, Cape Verde, and the Azores. New Bedford, by the 1830s, was a thoroughly cosmopolitan city, described by one historian as follows:

> New Bedford knew bearded and tattooed harpooners who sea-legged their way into brothels and grog-shops; timid and unsophisticated green hands from the farms of the interior; veteran tars who knew the price of a harlot in Zanzibar and the cost of ale in London; mutineers and masters who should have been slave-drivers; sperm oil from the Seychelles Islands and whalebone from Kamchatka; barnacles acquired in every one of the seven seas; scrimshaw work and Chinese tea, Oriental silk and souvenirs from the Fiji Islands; bonanza voyages and penniless hands; log-books telling of stove boats and account-books telling of exorbitant charges; rope-walks and sail-lofts, outfitters and ship-chandlers; Quaker and Cape Verde half-breed, Puritan and Kanaka; pure sperm oil which had been baled out of the head of a cachalot and black and stinking whale oil which had been four years at sea; stories of murder and of rape in the South Seas; yarns of cheap love in Paita and of frozen noses in the Sea of Okhotsk; Seamen's Bethel and dens of drunken vice; counting-houses with high stools and lays of 1/200 of the net proceeds; toggle harpoons and tubs filled with coiled whaleline; nauseating forecastles and the spacious lawns of the leading whaling merchants; "lobscouse" and "duff," ship's bread filled with worms and salt-horse which had thrice crossed the equator![21]

Clearly, New Bedford was globally connected. It was not just a town in Massachusetts or New England. It was a node on a global network, owing as much to the Pacific as much as it did to the Atlantic. And this network of mobility and exchange was charged with religious activity and significance.

The Seamen's Bethel stands directly across the street from the New Bedford Whaling Museum on Johnny Cake Hill. It is one of those places in New Bedford where the present connects to the past both through an "actual" human history and through a history conjured by Melville's *Moby-Dick*. In the novel the bethel figures prominently as the site where Ishmael witnesses an extraordinary sermon by Father Mapple, a chaplain whose ocean-oriented world reads scripture and life through the experiences of the sea. All around the inside of the bethel—the present, physical, geographic space, not the novel's space—are plaques in memory of mariners who have died at sea. Their dates run from the heyday of whaling to the present. The bethel is still in use, standing next door to the Mariner's Home, also still in use, providing spiritual and material aid to seamen and their families. Both were founded by the New Bedford Port Society in the mid-nineteenth century. Like the American Seamen's Friend Society, founded in 1826, the New Bedford Port Society was a missionary organization dedicated to the reform of seamen. "The object of this Society," the A.S.F.S. constitution read, "shall be to ameliorate the condition, and improve the moral and religious character of seamen, by the establishment of well-regulated boarding houses, and suitable libraries and reading-rooms, when practicable."[22]

The Seamen's Bethel is a reminder that the history of whaling is intertwined with religious history. Another way to put it is that whaling was not something that went on apart from religion. The work of whaling, the distant, dangerous spaces into which it brought people, the activities and behaviors in which whaling men took part—all evoked, invoked, and provoked religious discourses and practices. Families and friends in New Bedford and surrounding towns have spent generations praying for and memorializing men (and sometimes women) at sea. And yet the very existence of the American Seamen's Friend Society and the New Bedford Port Society illustrate that nineteenth-century religious reformers saw an absence of religion among sailors—and among whaling men in particular. They also call attention to the importance of class as a variable that needs to be considered in the recovery of the religious worlds of seafaring. It was not uncommon for middle-class nineteenth-century observers to report a neglect of religion and moral behavior among the working class. In the case of seafaring, the peculiarities of life aboard a ship at sea and lengthy absences from the norms of landed social activity created an even greater barrier, both real and perceived, between sailors and the increasingly manners-and-image-conscious emerging American middle class. Religious reform organizations targeted particular communities as being in need of material aid and moral guidance; in the case of Port Societies and Seamen's Friend Societies, the object of benevolence was the sailor whose very mobility, according to missionaries and reformers, made him the target of malicious individuals and groups who sought to take advantage of his need for companionship, entertainment, and a place to stay while between voyages. Reformers' publications, such as the *Sailor's Magazine,* were replete with stories of dance halls, drinking establishments, and brothels in busy ports that preyed upon newly arrived sailors. Boardinghouses, too, lured sailors with promises of food, drink, and shelter, then charged exorbitant rates and otherwise relieved men of their cash.[23] The lack of a settled *place* made sailors vulnerable and also made them morally unsettled. Part of the efforts at reform, therefore, entailed attempts to overcome the spatial distancing of sailors from mainstream society. If they were to be brought into the social order morally and embraced (rather than marginalized) by "good" society in an effort to improve their lot, then they also had to be reached in their global mobility. The A.S.F.S. operated in twenty-eight ports in North America, nine in Central and South America, twenty-five in Europe, nine in Asia, and nine "on islands on the high seas." One historian has noted that "a distinctive feature of these foreign missions was that each Chaplain or Superintendent spoke the English language, and sought to provide his guests with a homelike, Christian-hearth atmosphere that encouraged camaraderie and clean living."[24] In other words, they attempted to overcome distance by making outposts of "home" throughout the world in places where sailors landed.

Seamen's bethels and missionary outposts on Pacific islands were a regular feature in whaling men's lives, serving for some, at times, as a welcome touchstone to home: familiar language and customs, a settled, domestic space that served as a temporary respite from years-long voyaging across the waters, and news from home (and a resource for sending news back home) meant that the islands could be nodes in a global reach of the Atlantic world beyond the Atlantic. At the same time, though, the Pacific islands were not home at all. They were inhabited by peoples who were decidedly not European, or even Atlantic, in the eyes of those whose home was in or around the Atlantic world. In the European imagination, some Pacific Islands were the dwelling place of cannibals—a perception strong enough that when the Nantucket whale ship *Essex* was stove by a whale in 1820 (a real-life source for the climax of Melville's *Moby-Dick*), the survivors chose to risk heading for the Galapagos Islands and South America, a distance of over two thousand miles and against the wind, rather than the closer Marquesas or Society Islands because these were said to be home to cannibals. "There were, in all of us, twenty [survivors]; six of whom were blacks, and we had three boats," according to Owen Chase, first mate of the *Essex* and one of eight who ultimately survived the disaster. "We examined our navigators, to ascertain the nearest land, and found it was the Marquesas Islands. The Society Islands were next; these islands we were entirely ignorant of; if inhabited, we presumed they were by savages, from whom we had as much to fear, as from the elements, or even death itself."[25] Life for whaling men in the Pacific required navigating moral mappings of unknown space.

If cannibals were one imagined threat, missionaries more commonly policed a different moral danger on the Pacific islands: sex and drink. Whalers, in particular, had a reputation for sexual encounters with Pacific women and a general lack of moral discipline when ashore on liberty while their ships restocked wood, water, and food on the islands. Bethels and missionaries stationed on Pacific islands aimed their efforts at whaling men at least as much (if not more so) as they did at converting natives. For this reason, though some sailors found missionaries to be a welcome connection to home in the midst of watery chaos, others had a more antagonistic view of those whom they saw as impeding their freedoms, even out there in the midst of the ocean on the other side of the world from their place of origin.[26] Nevertheless, American- or British-based Christian outposts throughout the oceans served as touchstones for whaling men that extended the Atlantic world into the Pacific, while also highlighting the distance and difference between these two watery spaces. Pacific islands were both "other" and nodes connecting to home.

Another way that Seamen's Friends Societies and Port Societies connected "home" to ship in the nineteenth century, when voyages increasingly left the familiar Atlantic behind, was by means of portable libraries that included religious tracts and other literature deemed to be both interesting to whaling men and conducive to character building. The work of whaling involved long periods of boredom, and if whaling men's journals are to be believed, then reading materials were a highly valued source of entertainment and discussion among crewmembers. Sailors' reform societies took advantage of this fact by providing reading material that also coincided with evangelical emphasis on the importance of reading and education for moral development. By encouraging reading and supplying reading material that did not encourage immoral behavior, reformers again sought to overcome the potential for chaos and degradation that accompanied the mobility and out-of-placeness inherent in the seafaring life. Portable libraries, like seamen's bethels and missionaries, were innovative responses to particular spatial dilemmas produced by the unsettled, ungrounded realities of extended maritime labor.[27]

If missionaries and reformers were intent on reaching out to the margins, bringing "home" to the peripheries of the traveled world, whaling men navigated their disorientation through religious idioms that worked to provide touchstones of meaning and significance in the midst of the vast oceanic expanses that they traversed.[28] Whaling ships were in one sense extremely mobile, plying the world's waters with no particular destination in mind, hunting whales wherever they might be found. Yet, in another sense, they were also extremely static: small worlds of men working together in a confined space in which they not only labored for a living but also contemplated their place in the natural world that surrounded them and the social worlds that they were both a part of (on the ship) and peripheral to (back home).

The journals and logbooks of whaling ships provide an intriguing glimpse into the religious aspects of the world of whaling that reveals different concerns than those of the American Seamen's Friend Society and other missionary and reform organizations, offering the point of view of the seamen themselves engaged in their work and lives at sea. Logbooks primarily recorded basic information. Sometimes there was more to say, but that depended upon the writer. Journals often offered more personal reflections, desires, and despairs. Bit by bit, over the course of reading many logs and journals, one begins to form a picture of some of the ways that religion appeared aboard ships. For instance, sometimes, though not regularly, ships had worship services on the Sabbath.[29] Sometimes these were led by the captain or sometimes by a crew member. Sometimes these services were skipped in favor of catching whales, though the issue of whether or not it was proper to catch whales on the Sabbath was subject to heated debate.[30] Whaling men read books on religious topics, such as Jacob Abbott's *The Young Christian,* Henry Milman's *History of the Jews,* Adam Clark's commentaries on the Bible, and publications of the American Tract Society. They also sometimes discussed matters of doctrine or religious history with crewmates.[31] In some cases journal writers condemned the hypocrisy of captains who professed Christianity but did not treat their crews in a Christian way.[32] Whaling men detailed the unfamiliar "superstitions" and ritual practices of natives they encountered and worked alongside, and they described their own rituals of the sea, like the visit of King Neptune on crossing of the equator.[33] In short, religion (the activities and behaviors typically associated with that term) was far from absent in the experience of whaling men. Whether or not whaling men were themselves "religious" begs the question of what one means by the terms "religion" or "religious." But they certainly were engaged with religion.

Every whaling ship kept a logbook, and the logbooks of whaling ships all have one thing in common: every day, regardless of whatever other events or information they might document, logbooks recorded the ship's latitude, longitude, and heading, the wind and weather conditions, and the number of whales sighted or killed. When one reads through ships' logs, this information becomes a repetitive mantra illuminating the central importance of these three elements to world of whalers. First, orientation was paramount. A daily reckoning of location, read from the stars, abstract as it was, gave a sense of place to men who spent most of their time away from stationary landmarks. Second, the wind and weather determined their relationship to the world around them and their possibilities and limitations each day. Despite the skills of the sailors and the technologies of their vessels, sailors' lives were in a fundamental sense dependent upon the whims of the natural environment. Where (and whether) they could move, their comfort and labor requirements, as well as their basic safety, were at stake. Finally, recording the sightings or captures of whales—or their absence—was a daily reminder of why the ship and its crew were there in the first place, far from home and living on the water. Each of these very practical, even mundane facts, however, in their insistence and regularity, posed significant existential, social, and even transcendent problems in the context of the spatial realities of life aboard a ship at sea for years at a time, removed from the historical structures of the Atlantic world networks closer to home.

Atlantic world actors —alongside Pacific crewmates and residents—constantly undertook the work of orientation to make the Pacific Ocean an inhabitable *place* as part of religious labor of the sea. The ocean itself, where men on ships lived and worked in intimate relationship with the water, the wind, the sun, and the rain, was inhabited through material, ritual, and mythical means. Recording longitude and latitude was one geographical means of orientation, but Pacific whaling men practiced more symbolic orienting practices as well. The elaborate and pervasive ceremony of initiation into the maritime community upon "crossing the line" (crossing the equator) for the first time is a useful example. Typically, on approaching the equator, the "greenhands" (new sailors) were told that a ship was approaching, and they were ordered to go below decks. There they were blindfolded and brought up on deck one by one, where they would be asked a number of questions, lathered with tar, and "shaved." They were then unexpectedly dunked into a barrel of water and congratulated by someone dressed as "King Neptune." Historian Margaret Creighton noted that "published accounts of the ceremony suggest that seamen had to swear to social laws that contradicted bourgeois etiquette and claimed sailors' right to material well-being."[34] Thus earth dwellers became sea dwellers, separating themselves and their community from the expectations of the mainland and making the sea their own. As a product of the Atlantic world, the King Neptune ceremony marked the initiation of long-distance sailors, those who had traveled far enough to cross the equator. It was possible to journey back and forth between Europe and the Americas, as so many people did, without becoming a being of the sea. But it is important to note that New England whalers could not reach the Pacific without crossing the equator: to be a Pacific whaling man meant, by necessity, that one had to give oneself over to this new oceanic identity oriented to the wind and the waves instead of the land.

Investigating another example of religiously significant orienting practices deriving from the particular spatial problems of Pacific whaling, maritime literary scholar Hester Blum has explored the importance, and ambivalent nature, of death and burial at sea for both sailors and for sea narratives representing them.[35] Grave markers erected on remote Pacific islands provided a haunting trace of those who had been there before, while at the same time they called attention to the great distance between the bodies of the deceased and the loved ones who would mourn them. Whaling logbooks and journals recorded sightings of such memorials and the complicated sense of place they provoked in both their lonely isolation and their comfortable recognition:

> Sat Sept. 13, 1834
> . . . along shore we observed a grave stone it proved to be a humble stone raised to commemorate the memory of Robert Lovett the young man who lost his life where we were here the first time it was in good preservation though I perceived some sacrilegious hand had been cutting on one side of it there was a small space inclosed around the grave by a dich which was tabooed I should think if ships visiting here would paint it it would be preserved for a number of years and thus the grave of this unfortunate young man would be visited by strangers and impress upon their minds the uncertainty of life and that although he had no kind relative to sooth his last moments though he died far from home and its kind sympathies and his eyes were closed by the rough hands of sailors and borne by them to his lonely grave in a foreign land yet he shal wake from his leaden slumbers when the voice of God and the trumpet of the arch angel shall summons the world to judgment when sorrow and pain shall be no more and death shall be swallowed up in victory.[36]

Memorial plaques back home, as in the Seamen's Bethel in New Bedford, were distant markers of the connection between the New England mainland and the lost souls on the other side of the world. Stories, memories, and markers of deaths and burials on or about various oceanic locations—on islands or simply at particular latitudes or longitudes—made the ocean a place with a human history, oftentimes a place with specific Atlantic world resonances and Christian cultural referents.

If the work of whaling and the long Pacific voyages of the industry made Atlantic world sailors into citizens of the sea, subjects of King Neptune who lived and worked side by side with Pacific islanders, it also became the occasion for many whaling men's consideration of the significance and meaning of a human life that would require such work. Especially as the whaling industry grew larger and whales became more scarce and harder to capture, whaling journals documented the daily, growing despair of individual seamen who saw their labor and their time amounting to nothing. Many men who joined whaling crews did so with the hope of returning home in a few years with a profit that would give them a leg up in their lives. They were often recently married or planning to marry. Wanting to care for their families financially, they made a gamble: give their lives to the sea for a time, and make some money. Lisa Norling's *Captain Ahab Had a Wife: New England Women and the Whalefishery, 1720–1870* details the effect that such decisions had on the lives of women left behind and notes that these women must be included as part of the real history of the work of whaling.[37] Ironically, as the journeys became longer in the nineteenth century with the opening of the Pacific whaling grounds, the drive for a husband to go off to sea as the breadwinner for his family grew with the rise of romantic evangelical ideals of domesticity. Being at sea for a year or more on a ship that was not catching many whales often forced men to confront the significance of their lives in clearly religious terms. For instance, Lorenzo Pierce, captain of the ship *Minnesota* out of New York, recorded the following series of entries in his log in 1868:

> Lorenzo Peirce [the ship's owner] is certainly an Unfortunate Man in whaling his ships do not get Oil: oh. Could this poor unfortunate Minnesota get one whale this season how thankfull I should be I would gladly give it all for charatable and holy purposes. I earnestly pray that we may yet befavoured; grant in mercy heavenly parent that though unworthy that heavens divine blessings may once more attend us—
>
> July 16
> Heavenly parent grant in mercy that heavens blessings may once more attend me; I pray. If I am or can be blessed to get one whale this season, I will try to become a better man and strive to be a Christian in the future
>
> July 18
> Heavenly father grant in mercy. I pray that heavenly favours and blessings may attend this poor and unfortunate vessel with favour
>
> July 18
> Oh lord in mercy I pray that this poor bark may be favoured to get one whale is my earnest prayer! Heavenly father if we are but favoured I will try to be a humble and devoted Christian
>
> July 26
> Lorenzo Peirce is certainly a ruined man! My damnation is certain this voyage I have previously been favoured but now ruined: the hand of devine providence is against this unfortunate vessel it is impossible to get one whale we have seen whales twice and got nothing. I do not expect to get a whale it seems utterly impossible for us to get one.

> Aug 1
> I know that I have reached the greatest height of my prosperity and means: I am now in the decline of life my limited means in regard money is now leaving me; I shall yet be without money or friends in consequence of this unfortunate voyage; I shall yet be reduced to want and beggary I know the very hand of providence is against us on this voyage in consequence of my sins and ingratitude to my parents and brother the lord will not suffer me to prosper any more—his mercy is clean gone forever; all blessings are withheald from this poor unfortunate vessel.[38]

Pierce's desperation is deep, but the general feeling that somehow one's life is worthless and that God has a hand in that worthlessness is a recurrent theme among unlucky whalers. I use the term "unlucky" intentionally, for in thinking about the relationship between one's labor and one's success at hunting whales, whaling men toyed with a variety of causal models. Here, Pierce saw "the hand of devine providence is against this unfortunate vessel." But other logkeepers also used the terms "luck," "fate," and "fortune" to describe their success. Each of these was a way of exploring notions of theodicy and causality in relation to available idioms and tropes from religious and "secular" history. The work of whaling provoked such experimentation, such "trying out" of various meanings of the significance of the success or failure of labor that depended so immensely on nonhuman forces like the weather and what Jeffrey Bolster referred to as the "living sea." This intermixing of religious purpose with economic success, or the interdependence of a sense of human value and a particular sort of economic activity that was highly embedded within the nonhuman forces of the natural world, produced a deeply religious problematic that was certainly not new to the American (or Atlantic world) experience. But to engage in such labor at the far reaches of the Earth, enveloped by the living sea and far from the land-based lives that typically make up narratives of religious history, entailed an important spatial dimension that would become increasingly important in the rapidly globalizing world. As the Atlantic world gave way to the global spaces of the ocean that reached into the Euro-Pacific, new concerns about the meanings of self and other, about the relationship between human subjects and economic labor, and about meaningful orientation in the world grew apace.

Returning to the scenes that opened this essay, one sees that the religious space of the whaling ship upon the open ocean was intimately tied to orienting concerns. For both the Reverend Thomas Douglass and Daniel Kimball Ritchie, the popular religious practice of mesmerism became a trope through which to voice the desire to overcome the vast spaces between self and home that were part of the everyday life of Pacific whaling. And it is revealing that, at the same time, Ritchie's contemplation of the power of mesmerism also led him to desire harnessing its power for attracting whales, thus ensuring the success and purpose of the labor that was the reason behind the seafaring life. The vast space of the oceans, particularly the Pacific, haunts the Atlantic world. This is a religious history that has been neglected, leaving a yawning gap in representations of the spaces and concerns of religious life in New England and the Atlantic in the nineteenth century.

PART THREE

DESIGN

Spatial Hegemony and Evangelization

A Network-Based View of an Early Franciscan Doctrinal Settlement in Highland Peru

Steven A. Wernke and Lauren E. Kohut

How were the spaces of early Catholic evangelization in the Andean region organized? By what manipulations of the built environment were new rhythms of daily life and religious practice among the former subjects of the Inka to be inculcated? Such questions are as important as they have been obscure. In the early years following the Spanish invasion of the Americas, religious proselytization was part of a larger colonial social engineering program that linked urbanism, social order, and domestic and religious propriety.[1] The establishment of early *doctrinas* (doctrinal settlements), usually composed of a chapel and atrium, friary, and associated village, was central to that project. Prior to a massive colonial resettlement project conducted in the 1570s—the *reducción* (literally, "reduction") of the Viceroy Francisco de Toledo—most doctrinas were established at extant Andean villages. Yet how the actual built spaces of early evangelization variously articulated with antecedent cultic and ceremonial spaces of these settlements remains almost entirely undocumented, either archaeologically or in written sources.

In general, very little is known about the material and spatial dimensions of the period of the "first evangelization" in Peru—the era prior to the reforms of the decrees of the Third Ecclesiastical Council of Lima (1582–83), when church institutions and provincial infrastructure were weak and a formal parish structure had not yet arrived in many highland areas of the viceroyalty. Compared to New Spain, the earliest stratum of ecclesiastical documentation is exceedingly thin in the Peruvian Viceroyalty: no printed breviaries or other catechetical guides *(cartillas)* from the period exist, and correspondence and reports are extremely rare.[2] The documentary corpus is largely limited to high-level prescriptive texts, such as the first two ecclesiastical councils of Lima. Ecclesiastical memorials recount the period of the first evangelization but are framed by triumphalist narratives of spiritual conquest and mass conversion. Such documents shed light on the institutional and ideological context of the early church in Peru but say little about how evangelization was actually put into practice or the myriad indigenous responses to it.

Archaeological research of early mission settlements in the Andes, though still in its infancy, is thus the key means for illuminating how domestic and ritual practices were transformed during early evangelization. Far from simply "filling the gaps" of the documentary record, analysis of the physical spaces of evangelization provides the only means for exploring the role of the material world in those transformations. Reshaping the built environment of the peoples of the Indies was considered of paramount importance from the earliest years following the Spanish invasion. The Spanish Crown and colonial policymakers considered the replacement or restructuring of indigenous settlements as the key to creating a new social order. Just as *urbs* was to produce *civitas*—urban community—so too was civitas to produce *policia*—social order.[3] As Tom Cummins has written, "Bestowing Christian order on the New World was a royal obligation. Its fulfillment was first a philosophical and then a pragmatic problem. It meant, philosophically, the formation of a civilized community of men, the *consortium hominium*. This was to be achieved, as Anthony Pagden has described, by creating a *civilis societas* of which the *civitas* (the city) was the most natural and perfect community; where the practice of virtue and pursuit of happiness were possible and man could achieve his purpose, his *telos*."[4]

Spanish theologians of the sixteenth century, moreover, saw the city as an instrument of God implanted in nature. Beyond logistical or administrative efficiencies, the establishment of cities was necessary to fulfill the spiritual obligations of the Crown.[5] In 1549 Charles I first decreed the necessity of settlement consolidation in Peru, largely in response to the prelates of several orders who wrote to him of their difficulties in evangelization among the dispersed hamlets of the rural Andean countryside.[6] During the tumultuous times of plunder, Inka revolt, and civil war among the Spanish in the 1550s and 1560s, the colonial church and administrative apparatus in Peru were neither sufficiently developed nor staffed to carry out anything remotely on the scale of a viceroyalty-wide resettlement campaign, but some settlement consolidation had occurred in rural doctrinas. Given the transformative role ascribed to the built environment by the Spanish, understanding how existing settlements were converted to doctrinas in the decades prior to the reducciónes is of critical importance. The first ecclesiastical council of Lima mentions that doctrinas were to be built in the principal settlements where the primary *kurakas* (Andean native lords) resided,[7] but little beyond that is known about how chapels, friaries, or other buildings were fitted to these settlements, or how they were otherwise modified with incipient settlement consolidation.

Even before the Toledan reducciones, policy thinkers had begun proposing specific ways to reconfigure settlements to maximize surveillance by representatives of the church and state. The policy recommendations for overhauling the viceregal state forwarded by jurist Juan de Matienzo in his treatise *Gobierno del Perú* included specific prescriptions and a sketch map for the ideal organization of planned colonial towns.[8] Matienzo's proposals formed the basis of the Toledan reforms, the centerpiece of which was a viceroyalty-wide general tour and inspection *(visita general),* during which a complete census, cadastral survey, and the resettlement program itself, were implemented. Toledo's instructions regarding the emplacement of reducciónes in local landscapes were rather vague and left considerable leeway to the *visitadores* (census magistrates), and the processes of resettlement and the actual construction of the reducciónes is poorly documented.[9] But his prescriptions for the internal organization of the reducciónes were quite detailed and explicit in their emphasis on discipline and surveillance:

> . . . leaving an open space for the plaza and a site for the church . . . and a large space for the council houses and the offices of justice for mayors, and jail with different rooms for men and women, and a room for the jailer.
>
> Item: You shall lay out the Indians houses with doors opening onto the streets, so that no house opens into the house of another Indian, but that each have a separate house.[10]

The spatial structure of the reducciónes was to produce an unmediated relationship between households and the monitoring institutions of the church and state—embodied by the priest, town council, and visiting magistrate. Thomas Abercrombie likens the panopticism evident in the designs of Toledo (and, by extension, those of Phillip II) to the colonial policies enacted much later in nineteenth-century Egypt,[11] as discussed by Timothy Mitchell.[12] Mitchell was in part concerned with tracing the colonial history and colonizing effects of surveillance and disciplinary mechanisms—a well-founded point not considered in Foucault's analyses (centered as they were in Western Europe).[13] Building on the work of Bourdieu[14] and de Certeau[15]—particularly on the relationships between habitus, domestic space, and the constitution of subjectivity in the novel spatial and temporal regimentations introduced by colonial powers—Mitchell sees the panoptic technologies of power in modern Europe as colonial in origin. For Abercrombie, the Toledan project represents an independent and much earlier attempt to construct a finely attuned monitoring and disciplinary regime: "Nineteenth-century Egypt seems an echo, not of nineteenth-century epistemology, but of sixteenth-century Spanish empire."[16] But Peter Gose cautions against an overly totalizing view of surveillance in the reducciónes: "The temptation to invoke Foucault here is understandable, but risks mistaking the will to inspect

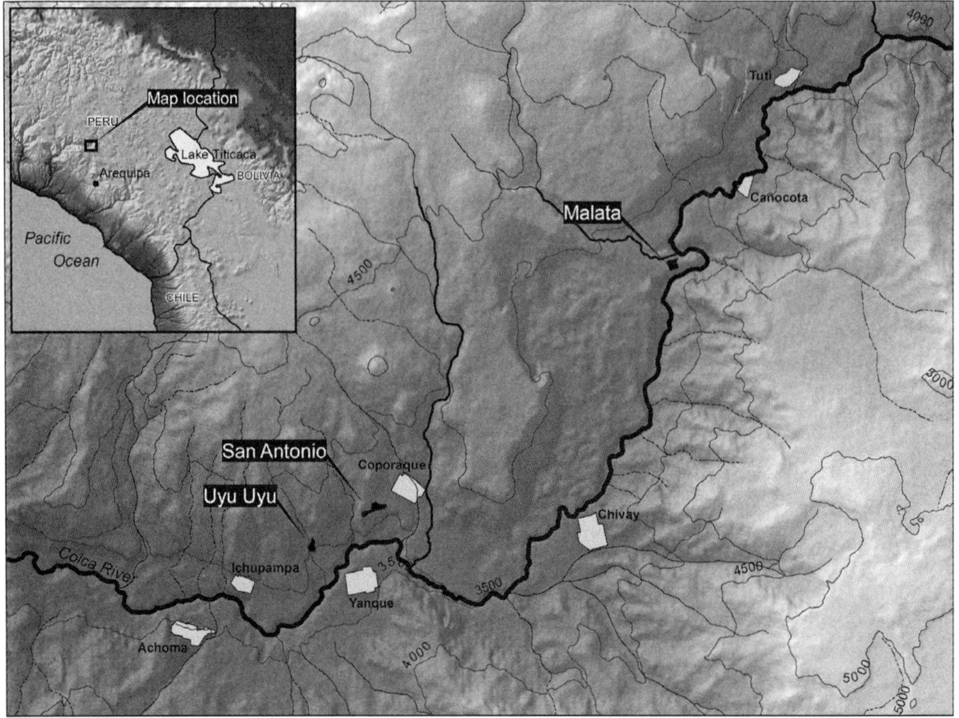

Fig. 1. The upper Colca Valley, showing the location of Malata and other settlements discussed in the text.

and correct, which is amply evident in Toledo's writings, for their actual achievement on the ground, which was at best episodic."[17]

Shedding light on this topic, then, requires analysis of the actual built spaces of reducciónes and their precursors. A handful of important projects have conducted site-level mapping and excavations at reducciónes,[18] but their antecedents—that is, highland settlements dating to the first four decades of colonial rule prior to reducción—remain almost entirely undocumented. In this essay, we offer a sounding in such a transitional context by exploring evidence for the restructuring of space at a direct precursor to the reducciónes—a small Inka outpost that became a Franciscan doctrina between the 1540s and 1560s in the Colca Valley of southern highland Peru (fig. 1). We find evidence for the installation of surveillance features related to the funneling of traffic through the doctrina to its plaza and chapel, likely enacted during processionals that were central to the liturgical practices of the early colonial era, and infer colonialist intent to monitor and regulate ritual practice through such reshaping of the built environment. But the effectiveness of these changes is less clear and surely not as total as intended, since they must have depended at least in part on their congruence and resonance with cognate prehispanic spaces and practices, which were present in the settlement.

Early Colonial Religious Eradication and Accommodation in the Colca Valley

Following the Spanish invasion of Peru, the Colca Valley, the largest valley in the western range of the southern Peruvian cordillera, was one of the earliest locales of evangelization in the highlands by the Franciscan order. This early intervention likely owes to the regional economic and political importance of the valley. The *encomiendas*[19] of the Colca Valley were among the richest in the viceroyalty. The valley, with an estimated terminal prehispanic population of around seventy thousand,[20] was divided between two major ethnic groups: the Quechua-speaking Cabanas of the lower reaches of the valley, and the Aymara-speaking Collaguas of the central and upper parts of the valley. The Collaguas were divided into two ranked, subethnic groups: the lower-ranking Laricollaguas, with their capital of Lari in the central part of the valley, and the higher-ranking Yanquecollaguas of the upper and middle reaches of the valley. All three—Cabanaconde, Yanquecollaguas, and Laricollaguas—were further subdivided into ranked moieties or *sayas* (higher-ranking Hanansaya, lower-ranking Hurinsaya), each of which was in turn constituted by a number of *ayllus*—named, ancestor-focused kindreds.[21] As part of the first major round of grants of encomienda by Francisco Pizarro (January 22, 1540), all of Yanquecollaguas was granted to his half-brother Gonzalo, while Laricollaguas was divided by moiety and granted to Marcos Retamoso (Hanansaya) and Alonso Rodríguez Picado (Hurinsaya).[22] The friars were most likely sent to the province at the request of one or more of these highly prominent *encomenderos*.[23] Though coeval documentation of their initial entry are lacking, a Franciscan memorial written around 1585 recounted the arrival of a small group of friars headed by one Fray Juan de Monzón, along with Fray Juan de Chaves, about forty years earlier—that is, sometime around 1545.[24]

Little beyond this bare characterization is known with any certainty. The Franciscan memorial portrays Monzón as a zealous itinerant preacher who conducted mass baptisms and embarked on a vigorous anti-idolatry campaign, destroying the shrines of the ancient *huacas* (Andean landscape deities and associated shrines) and erecting crosses in their place throughout the province. Such extirpation campaigns were typical of initial evangelization,[25] but so too is the hagiographic tenor of their description in the memorial. In any case, Monzón was evidently much preferred over their notoriously abusive encomendero Gonzalo Pizarro, since in 1547 the Collaguas provided safe haven for the commissary general of the order, Jerónimo de Villacarrillo, from Pizarro, who was then leading his revolt against the first viceroy, Blasco Nuñez Vela, and the institution of the New Laws, which advocated indigenous rights and sharply curtailed the privileges and heritability of *encomiendas.* Villacarrillo, an outspoken critic of the Pizarrist revolt, had fled Lima under threat by Pizarro's infamous coconspirator, Francisco de Carvajal, and secreted away in the Colca Valley before moving south to the province of Charcas.[26]

With the support of the second acting Viceroy Pedro de La Gasca and the new encomendero Francisco Noguerol de Ulloa, the Franciscans expanded and formalized their mission in the Colca Valley in the years following the defeat of the Pizarrist rebellion in 1548. By the 1560s—the height of the Counter-Reformation in Europe—church institutions throughout the Peruvian viceroyalty were similarly moving toward more uniform doctrine and methods of proselytization.[27] These changes following the experimentations of the first evangelization were in line with the aggressive Counter-Reformation decrees of the Council of Trent, which called for greater doctrinal rigidity and uniformity, complete catechetical guidance, and full sacramentation for all Christians.[28] More proximately, they were also a reaction to a flood of reports of continued idolatry and the spread of a millenarian cult in the central highlands (the *taki onqoy*) that prophesized the overthrow of the Christian deity by Andean huacas.[29]

In 1560 Villacarrillo assigned four new friars to the valley, who established the convent of the Immaculate Conception in Yanque, and another was built at Callalli in the upper reaches of the valley.[30] By the mid-1560s, around the time Lima received the first decrees of the Council of Trent, a more formal system of doctrinas seems to have been in place locally,[31] most likely one of primary and *visita* (visitation) doctrinas. In this system, Malata likely functioned as a visita doctrina under the jurisdiction of the convent in Callalli. It was also during the 1560s that the friars evidently began to congregate households from surrounding settlements to the doctrinas. At the doctrina of San Antonio near Coporaque, the friars resettled members of several ayllus from surrounding hamlets.[32] This was likely part of a general pattern at the time, and Malata shows evidence for growth and remodeling over its brief use life as a doctrina. By the 1570s, all these doctrinas were superseded by the reducciónes in the wake of Toledo's visita general, when the population of this and nearly all other highland valleys of the viceroyalty was forcibly resettled from their ancestral villages and hamlets to gridded reducción villages built around a central plaza and church.[33]

Prior archaeological survey in the central section of the Colca Valley has documented chapels at four settlements with major Inka period (Late Horizon; A.D. 1450–1532) occupations, which almost certainly constitute four of the early doctrinas described in the ecclesiastical sources.[34] It is unclear whether they originated in the initial incursion in the 1540s or the subsequent expansion of the Franciscan mission in the 1560s. Two of them are located at the largest pre-Inkaic settlements that became secondary administrative centers under Inka rule: Uyu

Fig. 2. Panorama of Malata from the north. The chapel is at the far right.

Uyu and San Antonio. Those settlements were forcibly abandoned with the establishment of the reducciónes, so their chapels must predate the 1570s. The other two are situated within the Toledan reducciónes of Coporaque and Yanque (the colonial provincial capital). The chapel of San Sebastian in Coporaque predates the surrounding reducción by about a decade, circa 1565.[35] In Yanque—the former primary Inka administrative center of the valley—the relict chapel remains undated but shares a number of architectural traits with the other three. The original Franciscan convent of Yanque was built over by the current church and rectory, which was substantially rebuilt, along with most of the other churches in the valley, following a major earthquake in 1688.[36]

The continuity between Inka administrative centers and early centers of Franciscan evangelization reflects how the friars grafted onto Inka-era centers of power.[37] Within Uyu Uyu and San Antonio, close associations between the chapels and Inkaic ceremonial spaces are evident. At Uyu Uyu, a large 4.5-hectare town with 159 domestic structures, the chapel is situated directly on the former Inkaic ceremonial plaza, opposite an Inka *kallanka* (great hall) structure—a long and narrow (29.0 x 6.8 meters) building with seven trapezoidal doorways that open onto the plaza. At San Antonio, a similarly sized settlement, the chapel occupies a promontory hilltop visible from the residential area of the town and adjacent to a kallanka and plaza, which occupy the ridge between them.

Such open plaza spaces and associated kallankas were central features in Inka settlements throughout the empire.[38] They were used as staging grounds for elaborate processionals and commensal rituals in which imperial representatives reified an imperial ideology of state beneficence through the conspicuous redistribution of staple and prestige goods in reciprocity for subjects' loyalty and labor services. The performance of staged commensal ritual was a primary idiom of state-subject relations, as the Inka was presented as a living ancestor-deity, cosmological center, and father-provider to his subject "children."[39] Though the material and labor embodied in the redistributed goods paled by comparison to the labor services provided to the state, such rituals engaged archetypical constructs of Andean personhood and community, defined by varied conceptions of reciprocity among people and among the living, the ancestors, and the animating forces of the landscape.

The close associations between the Franciscan chapels and Inka administrative architecture suggest that the friars' early pastoral efforts, in contrast to the view of eradication and replacement evident in the documentary record, mobilized spatial analogies that referenced such practices and archetypes in the process of inculcating new Catholic rites.[40] Consistent with early evangelization elsewhere in the Andes,[41] as well as Mesoamerica,[42] the earliest evangelical strategies in the Colca Valley seem to have resonated with prehispanic analogs by focusing on outdoor catechesis and pageantry in a participatory and performative pastoral approach. Such practices are evident at the site of Malata.

Malata: An Inka Provincial Outpost and Early Franciscan Doctrina

Malata is located high in the Colca Valley at 3850 meters above sea level in a transitional ecozone between the agricultural core of the valley and the high-altitude puna grasslands, where pastoralism is practiced. A mixed agro-pastoralist economy continues to be practiced by residents who live near the site today. The village, composed of eighty standing fieldstone structures in a 1.6-hectare core habitational area, occupies a shallow draw in a broad alluvial terrace above the deep gorge of the Colca river.

Similar to the other doctrinas in the valley, Malata features Inkaic and Catholic public and ritual spaces in close spatial association: at the western end of the site, a small, great-hall Inka structure and its associated plaza is situated to the adjacent south of a rustic chapel and atrium fronting a plaza with a large building in the center of its south edge. A few domestic compounds are situated between them, while the main residential sector of domestic structures stretches downslope to the east, and a handful of domestic buildings are situated apart from the rest of the settlement on the high slopes to the west. Archaeological investigations directed by Wernke at the site included mapping, surface survey, and test-pit excavations in 2006, excavation of the chapel and surrounding atrium in 2007, and excavation of a variety of domestic structures, as well as the Inka structure and the large building on the plaza in 2008 (fig. 3). To date, it is the only such early doctrina to have been extensively excavated in the Andean highlands.

The Inka and Spanish colonial presence at Malata likely owes to its location near the main Inka road through the upper valley toward the Inka capital of Cuzco. Malata and other sites like it engaged the emerging Spanish Pacific and Atlantic trade systems by means of this road as well, which likely functioned as one of the main "feeder lines"[43] linking Cuzco and Arequipa. Encounters with traffic on this road, along with the periodic presence of the friars and encomenderos,

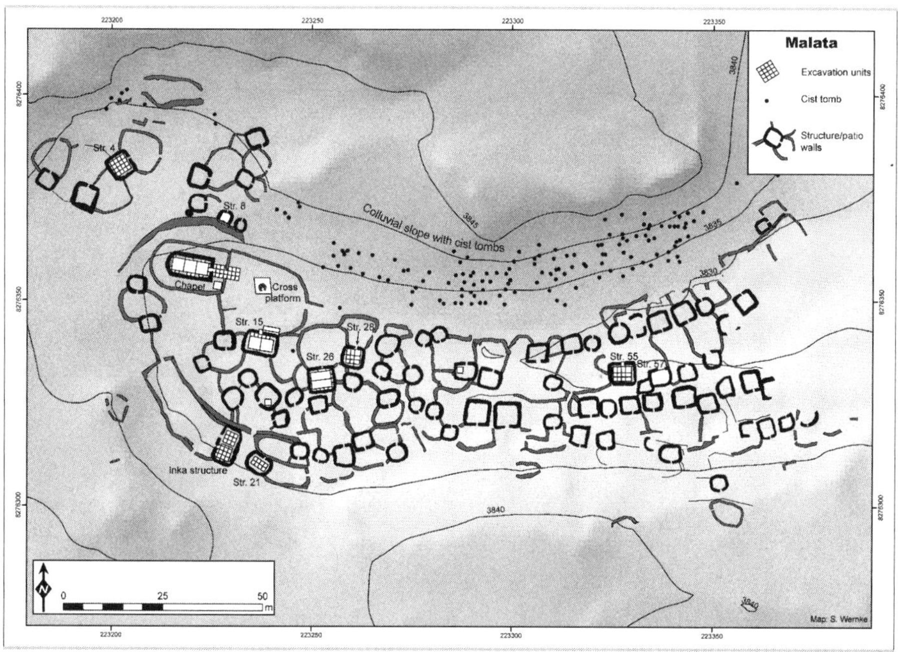

Fig. 3. Architectural map of Malata, showing excavation units.

would have constituted the main modes of articulation between the people of the Colca Valley and the broader flows of goods and people of the burgeoning Spanish global colonial network. Though highland colonial exchange networks were still nascent in the mid-sixteenth century, some easily transportable trade goods did make their way to local households. Small glass beads of the Nueva Cádiz style—a drawn, sometimes twisted, blue bead of square cross section produced during the first half of the sixteenth century[44]—were present in secure living surfaces of several domestic structures at Malata (fig. 4).[45] Caret-head iron nails, also diagnostic of the first half of the sixteenth century,[46] were recovered from several house floors and in a fill layer below the floor of the Inka structure (indicating its continued modification and use during colonial times.[47] The ceramic assemblage from the site is dominated by local variants of Inka imperial styles, which make up 89 percent of the diagnostics (n = 5948 of 6659). Consistent with a short, early colonial occupation, just 9 percent (n = 580) of the diagnostics were of colonial wares. Of these, the vast majority were undecorated colonial earthenwares; only two fragments from a single vessel of a green glazed ware was recovered. Overall, the low quantities of colonial artifacts, the presence of artifacts diagnostic of manufacture prior to the mid–sixteenth century, and the total absence of those postdating that time, point unequivocally to an early

Fig. 4. Panorama of plaza area. Note the alignment of the plaza entry, the doorway of structure 15, and the chapel entry with central cross platform (oval outline).

and brief colonial use-life from the early to mid-sixteenth century, all consistent with documentary descriptions of the early Franciscan doctrinas in the valley and their replacement with the establishment of the Toledan reducciónes in the 1570s.

Malata under Inka Rule

Prior to becoming a doctrina, Malata appears to have functioned as a secondary- or tertiary-level outpost during the Inka occupation of the valley. Unlike other such sites in the valley with Inka architecture, however, there are no indices for a significant occupation of Malata during the preceding Late Intermediate Period (A.D. 1000–1450). Of the fourteen structures excavated, none have produced Late Intermediate Period ceramics in primary contexts. The site thus appears to have originated as a prerogative of Inka administration, but it clearly would have been a relatively minor outpost, judging by its small size and expedient architecture.

However minor a role the site played in overall imperial administration in the valley, it retains elements of Inka settlement planning found in larger scale at other administrative sites within the valley and on a monumental scale at large regional administrative centers spaced over the main highways of the highlands and coast. In addition to the Inka great halls and plazas documented at Uyu Uyu and San Antonio discussed above, similar arrangements have been identified at sites such as Kallimarka in the lower valley, Lari, Tunsa, and Kitaplaza in the central valley, and Laiqa Laiqa and Auquimarka in the upper valley.[48] In most of those cases, the great halls range in size from 20 to 30 meters long and 7 to 10 meters wide, with three to seven trapezoidal doorways. At Malata, the pattern is reproduced on a smaller scale proportional to the size of the village. A small great hall structure measuring 9.6 x 6.0 meters with two trapezoidal doorways that open westward to a long (24.0 x 8.5 meters) plaza is situated atop a terrace on the higher, western end of the site. Though of a different scale, the same coupling between a large (relative to domestic structures), long, multidoor structure facing a plaza space suggests similar ceremonial functions to those hypothesized for the other examples in the valley. And indeed this is the most parsimonious interpretation for this structure. Our excavations in the Inka structure at Malata recovered significantly higher proportions of finely crafted Collagua Inka-style serving vessels in floor-level contexts than in those of domestic structures.[49] The great hall and its associated plaza thus appear to have been the focal public ceremonial space during the Inka occupation.

Spatial Transformations: Malata Becomes a Doctrina

Our excavations have also revealed that the site both grew considerably and was significantly remodeled according to distinct urban design principles during the site's short occupation as a Franciscan doctrina. As discussed elsewhere,[50] excavations in front of the chapel show that it was originally built on the natural hill slope and fronted by four entry steps, without the enclosing atrium or fronting plaza. The stratigraphic sequence clearly shows that all but one of these chapel entry steps were later buried by the fill and leveled surface of the terraced atrium around the chapel. Significantly, the eastern wall of the atrium, which functions as a retaining wall for the atrium fill, also forms the western wall of the plaza in front of the chapel. Once this retaining wall was in place, steps were built from the plaza up to the entry of the atrium. So the atrium, plaza, and steps leading to the atrium from the plaza were added after the initial construction and some period of use of the chapel.[51]

The plaza itself, which measures 20 x 16 meters, was not extensively leveled but instead is irregularly shaped to fit the sloping landscape. Nonetheless, its layout and features reveal a clear sense of planning. In the center of the plaza stands the remains of a three-tiered circular fieldstone feature (2 meters in diameter) that almost certainly served as a platform for a central cross. This platform aligns roughly with the single entry to the plaza to the east and the steps up to the chapel atrium to the west, such that one entering the plaza would have seen the cross straight ahead with the chapel entry directly beyond. The cross platform also aligns with the doorway of the large colonial structure (structure 15) fronting the south side of the plaza (fig. 4). Excavations of the interior of this structure produced none of the features found in domestic structures at the site (in fact, no discrete features were identified in its clean, silty, hard-packed floor surface), clearly establishing that it was not a domestic structure and likely served as a public or administrative building.[52]

The basic features of what became standard elements of Spanish urban planning are thus present at Malata: church, atrium, plaza, cross, and civic building. In this earliest period of evangelization, they were not built at once but fitted to an existing settlement, first with the construction of the chapel on the natural hill slope, and then at some later date the atrium and plaza elements were retrofitted, perhaps during the 1560s as the Franciscan mission in the valley expanded.

Evidence from the residential area also points to significant growth and the addition of newly configured domestic compounds during Malata's mission occupation.[53] There are two main forms of domestic structures at Malata: circular (n = 24) and rectilinear (n = 41) in floor plan. Both forms are found in the Colca Valley and are generally linked to differences in economic focus: rectilinear houses dominate agriculturalist settlements below about 3800 meters, while circular houses predominate among high-altitude pastoralist sites, with herding settlements above 4000 meters composed exclusively of circular houses.[54] At Malata, located in the transitional suni ecozone and its associated mixed-agro-pastoralist economy, the presence of both could therefore conceivably reflect a mixed population of agriculturalist and pastoralist households. There are even a small number (n = 4) of seemingly "transitional" ovoid houses of an intermediate form between the circular and rectilinear floor plans.

The presence of distinct house forms set side by side at Malata, however, appears to be a product of different periods of construction rather than differences in the occupational foci of their dwellers. The spatial organization of the domestic compounds of circular and rectilinear buildings, as well as their place in the overall site plan is quite distinct. Rectilinear domestic buildings, with few exceptions, are located on the eastern and western ends of the site, suggesting that they were later additions to an older residential core of circular house compounds (see fig. 3 above). The patio compounds of rectilinear structures are also organized distinctly from those of circular houses. While circular buildings are generally arranged in groups of at least two small buildings that open to a shared patio space, rectilinear houses tend to be situated singly within enclosing patio walls. These differences, combined with the presence of diagnostic colonial architectural features among some of the rectilinear buildings and prehispanic design features in the circular buildings, point to distinct periods of construction, with rectilinear houses dating to the colonial occupation and the circular buildings dating primarily to the Inka era.

The excavation results support the colonial-origin hypothesis for the rectilinear buildings.[55] Among the rectilinear domestic structures of the western extreme of the site, one structure in particular—structure 4—was identified as the possible lodging for the visiting friar. This hypothesis was based on its location, arrangement, and form: it is situated to the adjacent northwest of the chapel, along the high end of the site and separated from the main residential area as a single structure enclosed in a large patio area. Though not ostentatious by any measure, it is the fourth-largest domestic structures at the site. The presence of an arched niche at the base of the wall near its northwest corner is also a diagnostic colonial feature. Excavation of nearly the entire interior of this structure revealed a number of distinctive attributes not found in other domestic structures at the site. Most notably, the interior was internally divided by a fieldstone wall forming a second small room in its southwest corner—the only such example of a domestic structure with a divided interior space among the structures excavated. Its ceramic assemblage was composed of a significantly higher proportion of colonial wares (27 percent, n = 90 of 337) than other domestic structures. It was also the only structure from which a green glazed ware was recovered—likely a Morisco Green–style bowl (diagnostic of the first half of the sixteenth century). Iron artifacts recovered in its northeast corner, just inside the doorway—including a caret-head nail and large fragments of hardware (likely door fittings)—also point to the distinctive identity of its inhabitant. Analysis of botanical collections from the structure also indicates unusual patterns of consumption: fully 29 percent of the overall site assemblage of maize was recovered from this structure—by far the largest collection from any structure—and no quinoa was recovered.[56] Given that the site is located above the effective altitudinal limit of maize cultivation, the prevalence of maize signals privileged access to this highly valued crop, either through exchange relations or, most likely, through tribute (as friars were owed tribute in staples under the tribute system of the Viceroy Marqués de Cañete [1556–61]).[57] In sum, the unique characteristics and contents of this domestic structure indeed point to inhabitants of distinctive domestic practices and consumption habits. The combined lines of evidence make it the most likely building to have served as lodging for the visiting friar, who probably came for short stays during pastoral rounds.

Most important for this discussion, however, is the organization of domestic compounds in the eastern third of the settlement, composing a separate neighborhood where mostly rectilinear houses are arranged as rows facing one another across more or less straight streets.[58] This neighborhood of linearly aligned rectilinear houses appears to have been added to the settlement during the short period when it was used as a doctrina. Given that other doctrinas are documented to have expanded with the resettlement of households from neighboring settlements, this seems the most likely scenario here as well. A large terminal prehispanic settlement (Auquimarka) is located less than a kilometer to the north of Malata and is the most likely origin place for these resettled households.

In sum, this evidence, combined with excavation data and the reconstructed remodeling sequence of the chapel atrium and central plaza, indicates that Malata grew and was increasingly formalized according to a distinct urban model during its short use life as a doctrina. The relationship between the establishment of a new neighborhood at the eastern end of the site and the construction and formalization of the plaza area is unclear, but given the short span of the colonial occupation, the two are probably related—that is, as settlement consolidation proceeded and as ecclesiastical edicts trended to increasing sacramentation and doctrinal purity through the mid-sixteenth century, the more formal atrium and plaza were constructed.

The one notable exception to the distribution of rectilinear housing to the far ends of the site is a large rectilinear domestic structure (structure 26) and associated ovoid building (structure 28) to the adjacent east of the colonial plaza, situated along the main path immediately before entering the plaza. The compound is clearly laid out to regulate access to the larger structure 26 and its large patio. Access to the compound is restricted to a single entrance, requiring the visitor to pass by the entrance of the smaller structure 28 before reaching the larger patio and entrance of structure 26. The much smaller, rustic, ovoid structure 28 thus appears to play a monitoring or reception role for structure 26 and its patio area. In fact, structure 26 is the largest house at the site, with an interior floor area of 29 square meters. It is also impressive for the quality of masonry, including dressed cornerstone and doorway coursings, as well as for its mass and volume as compared to other domestic structures, with 80-centimeters-thick walls and high gables. Both prehispanic and colonial features are evident in the building. Notably, its doorway, which measures just 60 centimeters wide at its base, is consistent with the dimensions of the distinctively narrow doorways that are a diagnostic feature of the local prehispanic architectural style of the Collaguas.[59] But a distinct angle change at the gable shoulder is also readily apparent—a detail not found among Collagua domestic structures. The smaller structure 28 is an irregularly shaped ovoid structure without gables. Structures of this form with hipped roofs have not been documented at prehispanic settlements in the valley. Because of these attributes and the location of this compound, it was hypothesized to be an elite indigenous household built during the early colonial era—most likely that of the ranking village kuraka.

The results of excavations in these structures are consistent with this interpretation. The smaller structure 28 was full of domestic refuse, indicative of food preparation, weaving, and food serving. Artifact densities in this building were among the highest of any context at Malata. Ceramics recovered from structure 28 ranged from utilitarian cooking vessels to the finest Inka polychromes recovered from the site. A circular flagstone platform—common to all excavated domestic structures at the site—was situated in its southwest corner, associated with large fragments of several serving and cooking vessels, as well as a *wichuña* (a loom pick made of a camelid metatarsal). This structure was clearly used during the colonial occupation for a range of household production activities. Structure 26, by contrast, was much cleaner, with a more regular, hard-packed silty floor with lower artifact densities. A hearth feature was situated in its northeast corner, inside the doorway to the left, below a vent hole in the eastern gable. A circular flagstone platform was also present in this structure, located in the center of the rear wall, directly in front of the doorway. A wichuña was also recovered next to this feature, along with a concentration of sherds. A Nueva Cádiz bead was recovered from the lowest floor-level contexts in this structure, indicating colonial period occupation.

The contextual, architectural, and artifactual evidence are all consistent with the interpretation of this compound as the dwelling of the ranking indigenous household of the doctrina. Its intrusive position among the agglutinated circular structure compounds adjacent to the plaza signals indirect administration of the doctrina through indigenous elites—a scenario consistent with descriptions of the early evangelization of the valley in ecclesiastical memorials. Its location and organization must have associated the authority of the kuraka with the public, administrative, and sacred colonial spaces in the doctrina: the plaza and chapel. As we explore below, its position in the network of pathways through the doctrina also clearly enabled its inhabitants to monitor the rest of the populace of the doctrina as they filed past in processional to the plaza and chapel.

Tracking Movement and Surveillance: Spatial Network Analysis Methods

Though modest in scale, Malata presents a rare opportunity for detailed in situ analysis of the restructuring of space—and movement through it—at an early Andean doctrina. A significant portion of our research at the site therefore was focused on documenting its standing architecture and the horizontal stratigraphy of walls and wall joins that separate areas of the site, to track the flow of movement as individuals would have walked from their houses to the Inka and colonial plazas (and chapel beyond). Many of the same walls that delineate domestic patio groups at Malata also form the borders of pathways through the site. After extensive brush clearing, a precise map of all these walls, including data on wall joins, heights, and other data, was completed.[60] Most of these walls are not tall enough to physically block ingress/egress, but their construction apparently delineates the preferred or sanctioned routing; deviations were probably considered transgressions.

Perhaps the most striking feature of this ideal routing plan is the presence of a single entrance to the colonial plaza, accessed via a single path leading along the north edge of the residential area to the east, past the elite domestic compound of structures 26 and 28, and through the entrance to the plaza. All paths thus converged and would have literally created a processional to the plaza.[61] The elite indigenous compound of structures 26 and 28 was adjacent to the very center of this directed network of paths. The rows of rectilinear buildings in the "new neighborhood" at the east end of the site also appear to have more ready access to the colonial plaza than the circular houses, which are more concentrated around the Inka great hall structure and its plaza.

Our experiences and observations moving through the site over the course of three excavation seasons informed the kind of analysis presented below, which simulates movement through the site and patterns of visibility between households. The model is conceptually straightforward, but its execution is somewhat involved and requires explication. In outline, we model two aspects of movement and surveillance at the site: (1) the movement of walkers, using the shortest route from the doorway of each domestic structure to each of the two plazas (in separate simulation iterations), and (2) the visibility of each respective walker relative to each of the other domestic structures—that is, a measure of the domestic structures from which each respective walker was visible. Creating the model involved first constructing a network dataset in the GIS, using the Network Analyst extension of ESRI ArcMap. Network Analyst is designed primarily for modern applications such as road or multimodal transportation networks, but many of its functions can be easily adapted to archaeological applications. Network data sets are composed of origin and terminal point features (called junctions) and pathways represented by polyline features, (called edges). In this case the junctions represented the doorways of each domestic structure (n = 73) and the center point of each plaza, and the edges represented the network of paths through the site (fig. 5). Determining the shortest routes between each structure and each of the two plazas was accomplished using the "closest facility" function in Network Analyst. Determining the visibility of a given walker relative to the inhabitants of each of the other structures required a set of standardized rules and extensive ground truthing (that is, actually walking the route at the site and checking for visibility). The visibility of a walker from a given structure was recorded as "yes" (code = 1) if that walker had to pass directly in front of it; or if one intervening path was present, it would be recorded as "yes" if there was an unobscured view from the doorway to the path in question.

The resulting network data matrices follow standard binary conventions for social network analysis. Two matrices were generated: one in which the Inka plaza is the network destination point and one in which the colonial plaza is the network destination point. Each is composed of a 73 x 73 matrix, each axis composed of structure numbers in ascending order. The rows in this matrix represent "walkers"—that is, a given row codes data for a person leaving from the doorway of that structure and taking the shortest route to the Inkaic or colonial plaza endpoint. The columns represent "observers"—individuals standing in the doorway of each respective structure. The matrix encodes whether a given walker is visible to a given observer standing in her respective doorway. For example, if the walker from structure 1 making her way along the shortest path to the Inka plaza (row 1 in the matrix) was visible to the observer standing in the doorway of structure 2 (column 2 in the matrix), that cell (row 1, column 2) would be coded "1"; if not, it would be coded "0," likewise for structures 3, 4, 5, and so on, until

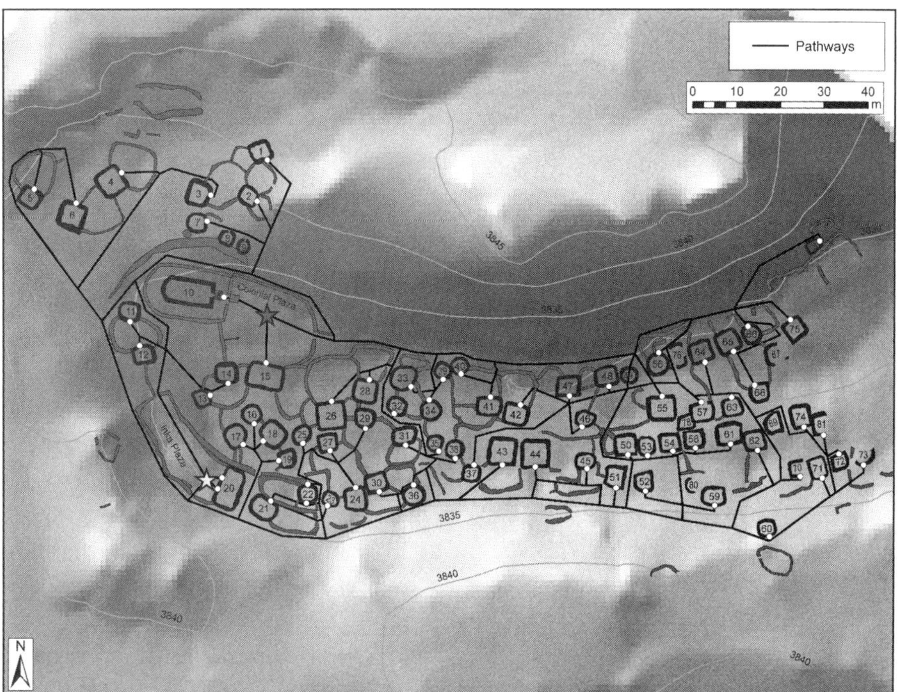

Fig. 5. Basemap of the Malata network data set.

all 73 cells of that row were completed (cases of "self-observation"—for example, row 1, column 1—were coded as "1"). Each column thus encodes the surveillance data for a given structure. The sum of the values in each column, by extension, provides a heuristic measure of its aggregate "surveillance power." These aggregate surveillance power values were then joined to the attribute table of point features representing the origin points (the doorways of each structure) in the GIS. Proportional point size symbology was then generated using this aggregate surveillance power attribute.

This analysis thus combines off-the-shelf GIS analytical capabilities with a case-specific application of surveillance modeling. As a heuristic model, it is not strictly falsifiable and relies on simplified assumptions of movement and visibility, but it provides a plausible, systematic means for simulating changes in the organization. There are, of course, several other ways of profitably modeling movement and access patterns. For example, space syntax analysis, as developed by Hillier and Hanson,[62] has been employed at the site to illustrate distinct patterns of access within and between domestic compounds.[63] But the method employed here provides a robust and visually intuitive means of tracking movement and surveillance through the site. The following analyses track the changes in traffic patterning through the site as the spatial organization of the site was modified with the construction of the atrium and colonial plaza, shifting the focus of the site from the Inka to colonial plaza (and chapel beyond). These shifts in spatial organization, focus, and movement were also related systematically to patterns of surveillance power.

Proceeding through Malata: Contrasting Inka- and Colonial-Era Pathways

The resulting network data set permits a variety of measures for characterizing the spatial organization of the site. In the results that follow, each walking simulation was run twice using the doorways of domestic structures as starting points: once using the Inka plaza as the destination and once using the colonial plaza as the destination. Though many of the colonial-era rectilinear domestic structures were not yet built when the Inka great hall and its adjoining plaza were used under Inka rule, modeling movement to it is still useful on two grounds: (1) as learned from excavations, the great hall continued to be used during the colonial occupation, and (2) modeling movement to the Inka plaza provides a point of contrast to the colonial plaza network, thereby providing insights into the changes effected during the growth and formalization of the doctrina through time.

As a first step, a map displaying the routes used by households to each of the plazas illustrates aggregate movement through the site and how it changed after colonial era remodeling. The resulting maps in figure 6 display these aggregate routes by varying the line thickness of each path segment used in proportion to the number of walkers (modeling one walker per domestic structure). The networks to each of the two plazas are obviously very different, essentially presenting mirror images of each other. Traffic to the plaza in front of the Inka great hall structure converged on the main path running east-west along the southern edge of the main residential area and entered the plaza through the side entrance (where steps are still preserved today) near the southeastern corner of the plaza. Other traffic was routed through the second entrance to the plaza at the western end of the plaza. Two entrances were thus used to access the Inka plaza. Given clear evidence for the predominance of serving vessels in the great hall itself, the plaza was almost certainly used for the kinds of public commensal ceremonies that enacted and reified state-subject relations, as discussed above.

Figure 6B shows traffic patterns after the colonial plaza was constructed and became the focal point of public assembly. Here, the path running east-west along the northern edge of the main residential area was the main thoroughfare, funneling traffic to it and through the single entrance to the plaza, forming a processional. Of note also are the two transverse paths—one near the eastern

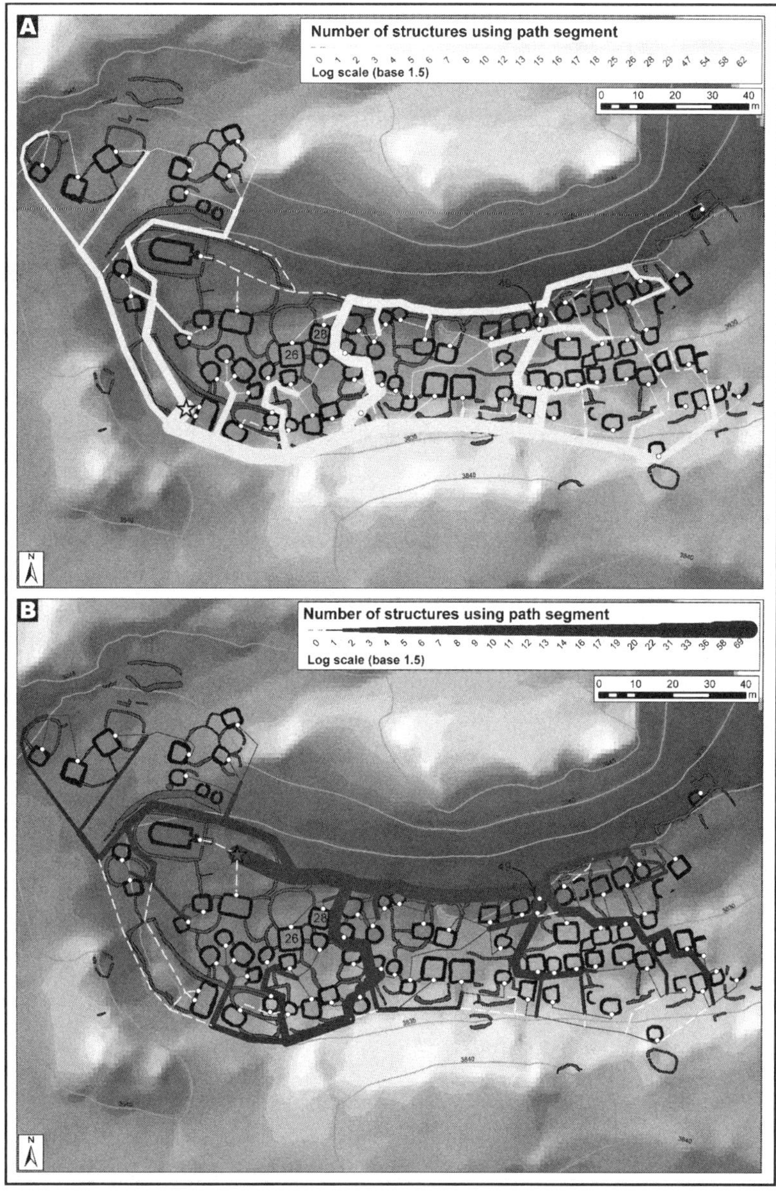

Fig. 6. Simulated foot traffic patterns through the Malata pathway network, with the Inka plaza (A) and colonial plaza (B) as destinations. Path thickness is proportional to amount of traffic.

end of the residential area and one near the western end—which routed traffic from the southern side of the residential area to the main path along its northern edge. Two remarkable surveillance features are evident in these transverse paths. The transverse path to the east literally routes through a small circular structure (structure 49) with two doorways—forcing walkers to pass through this building at the junction of the transverse and main paths. Clearly, this structure played some kind of monitoring role. The junction of the western transverse path and main northern path into the plaza is equally notable, since it is located to the adjacent east of the elite compound of structures 26 and 28, forcing all walkers to file in front of that compound just before they entered the plaza.

Equally important for understanding the spatial restructuring of the site are the pathways that were not used in each of the aggregate path network maps. When the Inka plaza is modeled as the destination, the last segment of the main northern path—the most-trafficked path segment when the colonial plaza is the focus—was not even used, nor was the double-door "monitoring" structure 49. Conversely, when the colonial plaza is the destination, the paths in and around the Inka plaza were not used. Clearly, the two networks were not integrated or complementary but were instead counterpoised and in tension with one another: going to one plaza from one's house required a very different set of pathways than for the other plaza. By extension, domestic compounds must have been positioned distinctly in terms of their network centrality relative to each of two plazas. As explored elsewhere,[64] during Inkaic times the compounds of circular structures to the adjacent north of the great hall and plaza were the most central but were among the most distal in the network relative to the colonial plaza, despite their proximity in absolute distance. Conversely, the rows of rectilinear houses of the eastern "new neighborhood" were disproportionately distal in the relative space of the network to the Inka plaza, while they were more central (that is, better connected) relative to the colonial plaza than their absolute distance from it would suggest.

Surveillance and Indirect Rule

These simulated patterns of movement through the site thus point to significant remapping of the spatial organization of the site, as traffic was diverted away from the former focus of ceremonialism during Inka times and funneled past an elite compound into the colonial plaza and chapel beyond. Though this refocusing and funneling implies changes in who could observe whom as people moved through the doctrina, our model of surveillance patterns provides a means for systematizing what would otherwise be left to impressionistic interpretation. As discussed above, our model takes into account the orientation of domestic structures relative to the paths by simulating an observer in the doorway of each building and tallies the number of walkers from other houses as they made their way (along their respective least-distance pathways) to the colonial plaza and chapel.

The results of the simulation show differences in surveillance patterns relative to the two plazas (fig. 7). The shift in surveillance from the southern to northern sides of the residential area of the village is evident, reflecting the Inka and colonial plaza destinations, respectively (compare figs. 7A and 7B). The network directed to the colonial plaza shows a more centralized surveillance pattern, in which the structures of the indigenous elite compound (structure 26 and 28) would have had a view of the members of every other household as they filed past the compound before entering the plaza. Only the public building in the plaza and chapel itself have higher surveillance values. The "monitoring" structure (structure 49) in the eastern neighborhood also stands out: in that case, traffic from all households in that part of the site (which was likely predominantly composed of recently resettled households during Malata's use life as a doctrina) would not only be visible to anyone in that structure, but also would literally have to pass through the structure to access the main path to the plaza. These patterns seem hardly fortuitous, given the strategic, nodal locations of these structures and the historically documented preoccupation with surveillance at doctrinas.

As were areas of low traffic, the patterns of structures with low surveillance power relative to the foot traffic to the colonial plaza are also inferentially useful. For example, the circular structures of the old core residential area have generally very low surveillance values. Even in cases of circular structures adjacent to the main path into the colonial plaza, such as structures 39 and 40, because they are oriented away from the path, they have no surveillance power, while the neighboring rectilinear structures 41 and 42 are roughly aligned with each other side by side facing the path with high surveillance potentials (surveillance values of 30 and 28, respectively). The probable friar's quarters—structure 4—has markedly low surveillance values, largely as a result of being separated from the rest of the residential area. Though this compound, located on the higher western end of the site, affords a vista over the nearby chapel and plaza, as well as a portion of the residential area, it was apparently not situated to provide daily monitoring of movement through the site. Instead, the friar would have been dependent on the indigenous elite for day-to-day monitoring.

Finally, a map of the differences between the surveillance power for each structure relative to the traffic patterns to the Inka plaza and the colonial plaza provides a view of which domestic structures gained and lost potential for monitoring. Figure 8, which presents these results, was calculated by subtracting the surveillance power of each structure relative to the Inka plaza from its surveillance power relative to the colonial plaza. Gray circles thus represent losses in surveillance power, while white dots indicate gains in surveillance power as individuals traveled to the colonial plaza. The size of the circle is proportional to the

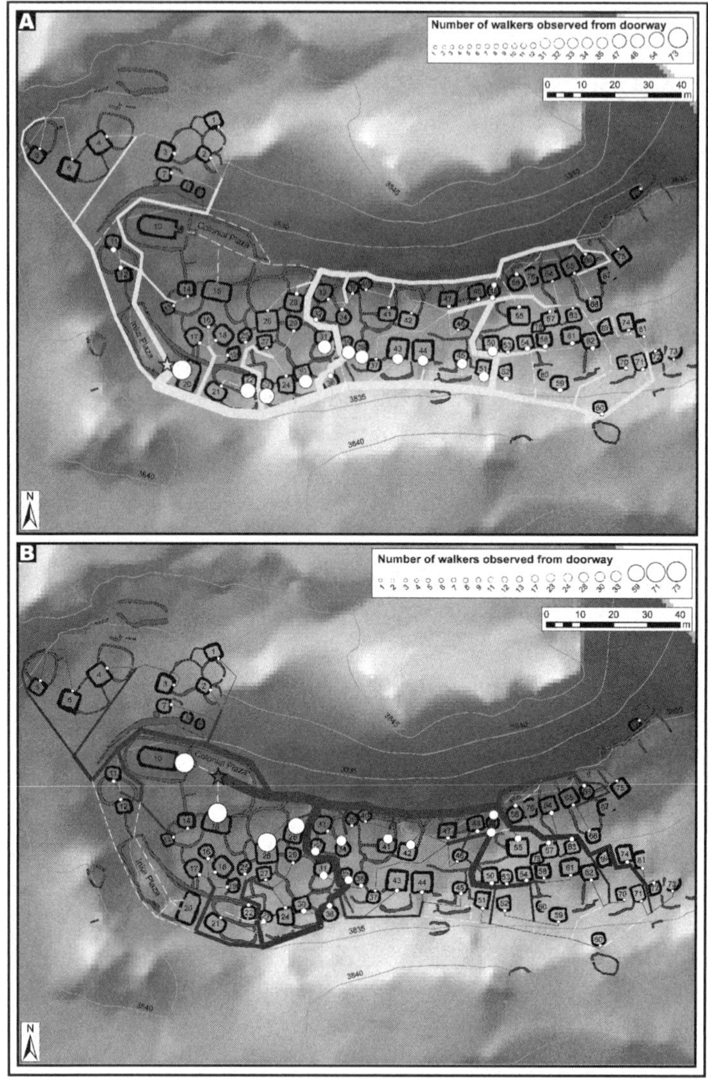

Fig. 7. Surveillance simulation maps relative to the Inka plaza (A) and colonial plaza (B) as the destinations. The size of the circle in the structure doorway is proportional to the number of walkers observed.

loss or gain. This map shows clearly that the chapel and public structure in the plaza, followed by the structures of the indigenous elite compound (structure 26 and 28) were the clear "gainers" in the spatial reorientation, while the Inka great hall structure, which saw literally no traffic past it in (again, under the least-distance assumptions of the model), was the biggest "loser" of surveillance power

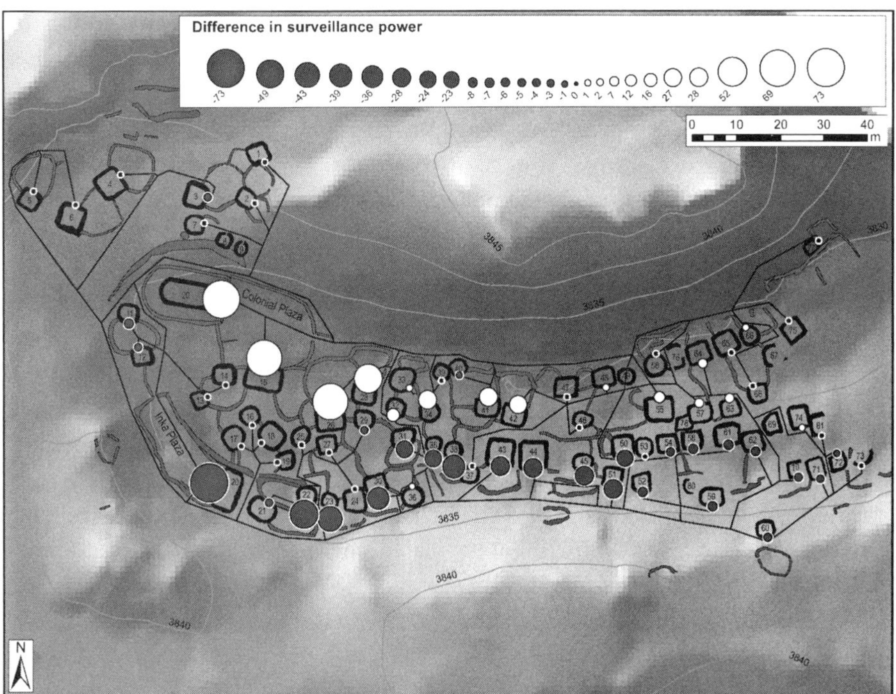

Fig. 8. Map of differences in surveillance power relative to the two plazas. Gray circles represent losses in surveillance power, and white circles represent gains in surveillance power (see text).

as the site was reoriented to the colonial plaza and chapel. This map clearly shows how the site had isolated and turned its back on the former Inka-era ceremonial focus of the settlement.

Discussion and Conclusion

Malata thus provides the first detailed view of how the built environment—and movement through it—was transformed at a first-generation postconquest doctrina in the highland Andes. The evidence clearly points to the introduction of new kinds of domestic spaces and a remapping of the connections between domestic and ritual spaces during the brief use period of the site as a doctrina, which had the double effect of isolating the former Inkaic ceremonial precinct while refocusing the ceremonial and ritual center of the site to the colonial plaza and chapel. The peripheral position of the compound identified as the friar's quarters and central position and surveillance power of the indigenous elite domestic compound next to the colonial plaza suggest continued dependence on the authority of indigenous elites. We have suggested that the physical reconfiguration of the site funneled foot traffic to create processionals into (and likely, around) the plaza and into the chapel. To a surprising degree, then, the rather deterministic view of the built environment and its role in the production of Christian subjects evident in the writings of clerics, policy thinkers, and the Crown during the early to mid-sixteenth century are seen manifested even in this early postconquest setting. Surveillance and the social pressures of "seeing" and "being seen" while participating in certain public ceremonials were apparently considered important means for enforcing and ensuring the inculcation of the new order.

But to return to the discussion that opened this essay, these simulations throw more light on the intentions than the effectiveness of the new spatial order. Effectiveness would require more diachronic analysis, but one must keep in mind that over the *longue durée,* Catholic evangelization in the Andes did not in fact produce anything approaching a homogeneous set of practices and beliefs, but instead the myriad local Andean Catholicisms seen today.[65] Reconsideration of how habitus and architecture might be related can open up discussion into how such hybrid practices first emerged in places like Malata. In an important sense, Bourdieu's original conception of this relationship is not far from that expressed by Matienzo, Toledo, and other Spanish colonial policy thinkers, since he saw the habitus as prediscursive, subconscious schemata, inculcated in the habitual practices of daily life (which were in turn structured by the spaces of the house), to the point that its classificatory and structural properties are "beyond the reach of introspective scrutiny or control by the will."[66] While this inscrutable aspect of the habitus concept has been problematized from a number of angles, the observations of Antonius Robben in his ethnographic analysis of the relationship between habitus and house form in modern northeastern Brazil are particularly apt. As Robben pointed out, "Although the habitus may not become subject to discursive scrutiny, its reproduction in practice is always a contextual interpretation and therefore open to interactional diversity."[67] Such would appear to be especially the case in the context of a first postconquest generation doctrina, where even the ontological status of buildings, let alone their uses or meanings, would not necessarily be shared by colonizer and colonized. Indeed, one might expect that restructuring of space and the attendant changes of daily and ritual practice would have the effect of throwing into relief—and thus opening up formerly prediscursive, routinized ways of dwelling and doing to (now-discursive) scrutiny. Thus, formerly (in this case, prehispanic) hegemonic forms and practices—and colonialist attempts to replace them with new ones—could become destabilized and politicized.

In this sense, Robben's concept of "spatial hegemony" can clarify the relationship between hegemonic architectural spaces and the varied forms of practice that can develop within them. Robben shows how the spaces of a single, routinized house form came to be used and conceived of differently according to the different class affiliations and labor relations of their inhabitants and the varied relationship between concepts of public and private spheres that derive from and reinforce those relations: "The spatial structure itself is hegemonic—in the sense that it reflects a dominant and pervasive ideological conception of family relations—but its appropriation and social definition in domestic practice are not." Similarly, in the case of Malata, the implantation of a new hegemonic model for the proper structuring of the built forms of a settlement can be appreciated, but their apperception, use, and significance must have depended on their resonance with cognate forms that were readily at hand. Those preexisting forms and the practices associated with them must have been opened up for scrutiny in light of the catechetical complex and its associated practices instituted at the site. Thus, the taken-for-grantedness of "what we do and the way we do things in this kind of space" (for example, in a plaza with an associated ceremonial structure) could become grist for commentary and revalorization in light of an alternative model (for example, a plaza with a public building and adjacent chapel and atrium). The construction of a space of indoctrination could thus produce a new kind of local place of ambiguous and contested significance. In no small measure, it was such persistent heterodoxy that provoked the radical dislocations of the reducción program of the following decade. Though only one example, the changes in spatial configuration of Malata provide otherwise inaccessible microscale insights into how new kinds of colonial Andean communities emerged despite the imposition of an increasingly uniform and disciplinary regime of proselytization in the early Spanish colonial era.

Stone Walls Do Not a Prison Make

French America's Cosmopolitan Cloisters

Jan Noel

Sister Juchereau Saint-Ignace, daughter of a prominent bourgeois family, sat down and recorded an improbable incident in the annals of her convent, the Québec Hôtel-Dieu, in 1703. English forces attacking the port of Cadiz had deliberately dragged an image of the blessed Virgin through the mud in the filthiest parts of town. Longing to repair the insult, Sister Juchereau and the other nuns in her convent "resolved to make honourable amends, and in the refectory each Religious took a day according to her rank in the order. The chosen one . . . fasted that day, took discipline, dined on the ground at the feet of the most blessed Virgin exposed on the Superior's table, approaching barefoot, with a rope around her neck and a taper in her hand, kneeling and praying aloud: 'Holy Virgin, we know not how to express the sorrow which seized us when we learned the evil treatment the English heretics gave to one of your images at . . . Cadiz . . . offer you the best reparation we can for the outrage.'"[1] War was again raging in Europe when Brother Albert Jamet published an edition of the Hôtel-Dieu annals in 1939, and the sisters were still making their ritual atonement for the Cadiz travesty 236 years later.

The incident illustrates the peculiar way in which French transatlantic convents situated themselves in the cosmos, an alignment that might be seen as the triumph of imagination over distance. The far reaches of eternity, which seem distant to many and nonexistent to others, were quite near for them. Vandalizing an image of God's Mother represented a deep injury to a bosom companion that required reparation. The little cells and choirs where "brides of Christ" prayed and meditated at night were in a sense roofless, for they opened directly onto that place where their prayers could salve Mary's pain. Traversing the distance required a leap of faith but no physical travel. This imaginative life and the material basis on which it rested characterized what Teresa of Avila called the "Interior Castle,"[2] the cloister.

The distances covered were not entirely spiritual or imaginative ones. There was a triumph over physical distance too. One scholar characterized French overseas missions as "floating" cloisters.[3] They maintained ties with institutions in France, with neighboring colonies, and with the continental interior. They interacted with indigenous people as well as with migrants from Latin America and Africa. They recruited sisters from diverse places and forged trade links across great distances. All this meant that a nun could spend her life behind the grille and yet reach thousands. She did not need to go out into the world because the world came to her. These connections allowed cloisters to maintain their distinctive way of life when they faced loss of the mother country and Protestant takeover. In short, cloistered nuns surmounted those stone walls in many and astonishing ways—spiritual, social, economic, and political.

This study encompasses five colonial convents in Canada and Louisiana. The Ursulines (who schooled girls in both Québec and New Orleans) and the Augustinian nuns (who administered Québec's Hôtel-Dieu and its General Hospice) were cloistered when they came to the new world, while the Sisters of Saint Joseph, who staffed Montreal's Hôtel-Dieu hospital, embraced cloister not long after their arrival.[4] Cloister required nuns to take permanent vows of poverty, chastity, and obedience. They were, in the general course of things, required to remain in the convent behind barred windows and locked gates and—apart from carefully defined hours and spaces for teaching and nursing—to interact with the public through grilles.[5] Those committed to this way of life arrived in the tiny embattled outposts of Québec and Montreal in the seventeenth century. As the colony grew, they encountered both support and opposition from French authorities. The strength of their foundation was tried when Canada was conquered by a Protestant power in 1759–60. In a similar vein, the Ursulines who arrived in New Orleans in 1727 faced initial growing pains and successes, then underwent regime changes to Spanish rule in 1767 and American rule in 1803. They later weathered a militant wave of evangelical Protestantism (and subsequent secularizing forces). All five convents remain in existence today. Their buoyancy distinguishes them from their motherhouses across the Atlantic, which were forcibly dissolved during the French Revolution, scattering sisters to the winds. The survival of their colonial counterparts invites us to analyze their notable spatial achievements. First was their triumph of imagination over distance when they became the first females to conduct foreign missions, turning their enclosures into towers of strength and self-affirmation. Their second accomplishment was to connect with clients and protectors across great distances.

Traveling to Territories of Grace

Enclosure did not seem to match New World needs. Aware of cloister's restrictions, Jesuits in Canada and colonial administrators in Louisiana had solicited French laywomen or uncloistered hospital sisters to assist their operations.[6] With some dismay they received instead small bands of zealots who wore veils and passed most of their days behind a grille, who had won ecclesiastical permission to make the unprecedented trip. They perceived the new land as a "territory of grace"[7] rife with miraculous happenings. Yet this vanguard was conservative, operating with profound respect for their Rules. They rapidly reproduced the three-story, walled stone architecture and tiny individual cells of French provincial convents in fledgling settlements surrounded by wilderness.

In the first half of the seventeenth century, when the Canadian missionaries set out, they benefited directly from unusual religious fervor in the highest circles of France. Early in that century, Louis XIV's mother, Anne of Austria, herself sponsored missionary enterprises, as did a number of aristocrats. The Québec Hôtel-Dieu was a philanthropic project of the Duchess of Aiguillon, niece of Cardinal Richelieu, while the Ursulines benefited from the sponsorship of Madame de la Peltrie and the Montreal Hôtel-Dieu from the riches of Madame de Buillon, widow of a French Finance Minister. The age still had one foot in medieval Christianity, and in early years Marie de l'Incarnation and other nuns in France and Canada showed their ardor with self-flagellation, burning, eating disgusting substances, or other tortures that fell out of ecclesiastical favor as the century wore on. Equally prominent was a commitment to spread the gospel, be the recipients superstitious French peasants or *"sauvages"* (people of the woods) in faraway North America. The first goal was to imbue them with Christianity, but it was acknowledged that addressing health and education was also part of the mission.[8]

An aura of divine dispensation attended the journey. A vision of Mary beckoned Marie de l'Incarnation to a fog-covered land with steep precipices, which her confessor identified as Canada. A seemingly miraculous encounter with a Jesuit "whom she did not know and who did not know her"[9] inspired one of the Louisiana sisters to travel, while another experienced a vision of New Orleans ten years before the mission was conceived. There were heart-rending departures from distraught or disapproving relatives. The archbishop of Paris stopped one sister on the brink of departure, declaring he would not expose her to the perils of the sea and the barbarians. The ship that transported the Ursuline and Hôtel-Dieu sisters to Québec in 1639 was severely battered by storms and saved at the last minute from hitting an iceberg. A dozen Ursulines who headed to New Orleans in 1727 were encircled by pirates. When their ship later ran aground, the nuns volunteered to let the captain hurl their possessions overboard, underlining their pilgrim status. They were pilgrims very far from home; entering the Mississippi Delta, they camped in a jungle full of serpents, snakes, scorpions, crocodiles, vipers, ticks, and frogs, where "our sailors put cane in the form of a cradle around a mattress and enclosed us two by two in our tents where we lay down all fully dressed. Then they covered the cradle with a big cloth" against the mosquitoes.[10] Farther north the Augustinian sisters who had only tree branches to sleep on when they landed at Québec in August 1639 awoke to find themselves covered with caterpillars. In both settlements the new arrivals were also harassed by naysayers who declared their projects' folly.[11]

The literature of heroic travel was brought to bear. Sisters found classical or biblical images to describe the divinely inspired odyssey. Just as God's chosen people nearly perished in the sea, so did they. The Sisters of St. Joseph annalist compared the male and female founders of Montreal to "Israelites of old."[12] An Ursuline sister bound for New Orleans was thrilled when the ship neared "the blessed country for which I long as if it were the Promised Land."[13] The epic continued when the chosen stepped ashore. There were years when it seemed likely the missions would be abandoned because of attacks by the Iroquois; several sisters found things so trying that they did return to France. In 1659, when the Sisters of St. Joseph arrived to help the Montreal hospital's lay founder Jeanne Mance, they found an outpost still under siege, "a barbarous place where nations have fought us from that day to this," with the Iroquois sometimes hiding at night in the courtyard to capture and torture any sister who ventured outside. Mance, along with nun-pharmacist Judith Bresoles, who rang the tocsin to warn of attack, were "Christian Amazons," Bresoles being also "a true Judith in courage and fidelity."[14]

Saints trod the new land. Sister Macé was in her lifetime regarded as a saint and Sister Bresoles's cures were considered miraculous.[15] Marie de l'Incarnation, compared to Theresa of Avila in her own lifetime, was singled out for praise by preachers such as Fenelon and Bossuet. Five years after her death, *La Vie de Marie de l'incarnation* appeared, the first of many biographies of this famous mystic, followed by her correspondence and spiritual writings. A biography of the saintly Mother St. Catherine Augustin at the Québec Hôtel-Dieu was published three years after her 1668 death.

The times themselves seemed miraculous. The nuns recorded numerous instances of stilled storms and averted catastrophes, divine pageants that sometimes included the populace. For example, the annalist of the Hôtel-Dieu recorded the scene when Anglo-American invaders sailed up the St. Lawrence in 1711. The sisters redoubled their penances and devotions to appease a God "strongly irate against this poor country where, in effect, sinfulness mounted every day." The frightened colonists followed suit: "The Ladies became more modest. . . . they took a vow to stop wearing ribbons and lace, to cover up cleavage and faithfully perform several holy practices they imposed on themselves for a year," even promising to build a victory chapel in Mary's honor. When the invaders perished in a shipwreck, "all the world avowed that the hand of God was responsible."[16] The Canadian mission was portrayed in convents in France as "removal from all satisfactions of the senses, the continual death of all that is human" or "being nailed to the Cross."[17] Colonial sisters, though, felt the hand of God supporting them in the New World.

Fig. 1. This painting of the Montreal Hotel-Dieu circa 1700 is a conventional rendering of an ancien régime hospital. To modern eyes it presents an odd spatial juxtaposition of an everyday scene and a celestial figure. For the sisters Christ was not distant or abstract but a looming presence in the wards. In laborious tribute to him, they washed the feet of each new patient to reenact his humble service to his disciples the night before he died. Their "permeable cloister" allowed them to work in the wards while prayer, chanting, and meditation through the day and night kept the Other World constantly in view. Permission of the Collection of the Religious Hospitallers of Saint-Joseph in Montreal.

Closing In

Despite their venturesome crossing (a route that never attracted extensive emigration from France), the sisters clung ardently to their cloistered way of life. It seemed to serve as shelter amid the Atlantic storms, as fortress in alien territory. Wearing their habits and traveling with other nuns constituted a form of portable cloister, reinforced by chanting divine office and holding religious processions on deck. Those bound for Louisiana convened daily to pray at 4:00 and 8:00 A.M. and 5:00 and 8:00 P.M. and to attend mass and recite the Angelus.[18] They professed joy when a 5:00 A.M. arrival in New Orleans allowed them to proceed to their dwelling without embarrassment. That group expressed relief that a priest was willing to trek to their convent at the edge of town: "We observe cloister here with as much regularity as the convents of France. If we had the misfortune of Reverend Beaubois getting sick and being unable to say Mass, we would be without it on Easter Day and even for six months, rather than go out of our convent to attend Mass at the parish church."[19]

The obituary of their superior, Marie Tranchepain, captured a similar proclivity, declaring that the "sweetest pleasure that she savoured was to be alone for conversation with God, whose presence she never lost, even in the middle of the most dissipated occupations."[20] The "dissipation" presumably consisted not of mardi gras revelry but of the cares of school and hospital. They seem to have been a distraction from the true delight, solitary conversation with God. Here, in a distant setting, was timeless refuge. It could also be a buffer against secular demands. This happened in New Orleans when the Ursulines refused to walk across town to do medical work until the authorities kept their promise to build a convent adjoining the hospital.[21]

The Rule that Marie de l'Incarnation and Father Jerome Lalemant composed for the Québec Ursulines in 1647 gives a sense of the cloistered lifestyle and its interiority, which buffered the intrusions of a foreign world. Nuns received communion through an eight-inch wicket locked at other times; they received outsiders in their locked parlor peering out between a double grille covered by a curtain except when the sister's veil was lowered (with exceptions made for visiting spiritual advisors, close relatives, and Indians). In the parlor they were, the Rule said, "out of their element and subject to ambush by the enemy of our happiness," where they should not venture except under orders and with another sister. Large reminders of SILENCE were to be placed on doors connecting parlor to cloister, and no unedifying news was to be repeated. The sisters were to keep deep silence from after evening recreation until after morning mass. They were to cultivate cheerful equanimity, a measured voice, and modest gaze, "especially in the parlour and above all in the presence of men." What were simple sins against the sixth commandment became "sacrilege" for brides of Christ. In an "entire perfect holocaust," the vow of chastity might extend to all other bodily comforts. Nuns were to avoid touching one another, even playfully, though they were allowed passing salutations and affectionate conversation, "especially with native seminarians who must be the delight of their hearts."[22] Citing the "holy Council of Trent" on cloister, the 1647 Rule commended the "holy and happy prison . . . the fortress enclosing the principal riches and treasures of the blood of Jesus Christ and the happiness of their condition."

The Rule also described the spartan cells the nuns were to occupy. The cupboard-style beds in which the first sisters fended off frostbite yielded to a small room with plain curtains and coverlets, a wooden chair, a little table convertible into a *pre-dieu,* a simple crucifix, and a picture of Mary, a few other images or a modest reliquary, the book of Rules and Constitutions, the New Testament, *Imitation of Christ,* and one or two spiritual books on the advice of the superior.

Each cell should have a little candelabra and "all that is necessary to write conveniently," a sign that written reflection was part of the calling. They could also have "instruments of mortification to the extent that devotion and obedience permitted their use."[23] So attached was the superior to this Rule that she vehemently resisted attempts by her ecclesiastical superior François Laval to change it (reducing liturgical chanting, for example), vowing to oppose him "to the very limits of obedience."[24]

Another aspect of these enclosed institutions was self-government. Nuns would meet to elect their chief officers, rotating some offices yearly. The Rule of the Québec Augustinians, for example, stipulated that those who had been choir sisters for at least six years were to select the major officers (about a dozen) by secret ballot. A mother superior could not be elected for more than two successive three-year terms, which helped prevent the position from becoming the fiefdom of a powerful individual; an elected council to advise her helped democratize decision making.[25] The class system remained in evidence, excluding the lay sisters as well as the newer choir nuns from voting. Still, the degree of self-determination contrasts with the pictures often painted of patriarchal families and institutions of the day.

Montreal's Sisters of St. Joseph had a Rule of their own, to which they too were quite committed. For the first dozen years after their arrival, they resisted attempts by various ecclesiastics to place the Montreal Hôtel-Dieu under the Québec Augustinian order. They were, on the other hand, happy to accept cloister, identifying (as some scholars have done)[26] its value in securing recruits and respectability. Permanent vows and fixed dowries promised a certain institutional solidity and security. That surely appealed to them as the most impoverished of the three orders discussed here.

Marie Morin, annalist of the Sisters of St. Joseph (an early Canadian recruit who joined at age fourteen and lived for sixty-nine years a nun) described rigorous adherence to cloister under daunting conditions. The order spent its first three decades in a log dwelling. This was so flimsy that snow had to be swept out on winter mornings, while bread got rock hard and glasses of water froze in fifteen minutes. The sisters hastened to erect wooden stakes around that little shack, forerunner of the stone wall. They received confession and communion through the grille of a cramped wooden cabinet adjoining the chapel. They descended a few steps to reach their choir, a "hole" six feet by nine without light or air, stifling enough for daily hours of chant but mortifying during eight-day retreats.[27] Their quarters were of the same quality: four cells separated by a board, wooden blocks for chairs. Young Sister Morin watched spellbound the self-inflicted sufferings of Judith Bresoles, who shunned coverlets in winter and sat up in bed most of the night praying, chanting, and performing penances. With naïve candor, Morin confided to posterity, "You may be astonished, my dear sisters, that I could know these details, but . . . there was just a simple board separating her cell from mine and without her knowledge I made a little hole to more easily watch and listen as I was her neighbor for about fifteen or sixteen years."[28]

These *dévotes* kept their Rule "with great fervour and exactitude." Their convent suffered three devastating fires in the space of forty years, forcing them to spend some weeks in private dwellings or other convents. Even while living with others they made every effort to perform Divine Office. When necessity required a door-to-door foray to raise money, far from being curious to see the town, they expressed great relief to return to the rebuilt convent, exhausted and "firmly resolved to close up together and reject propositions to go out again."[29] Candle in hand, they "all followed our Lord . . . as our divine spouse, hearts full of joy and consolation to enclose ourselves with Him in the cloister of love that we have guarded to please Him and where He has also guarded us. . . . It was our rampart day and night."[30] Though various internal locked doors slowed their escape during a fire in 1721, these were carefully reinstalled.

Shadows flicker across the annals that remind us that the world outside the convent gates was not necessarily a friendly one. Marie Morin and her sisters were mortified by the looting of their pharmacy and convent during the 1695 fire.[31] When two sisters of an uncloistered order, the Congregation of Notre Dame, traveled to Québec, they were accused of being on the prowl to find husbands. One of the sisters in New Orleans supervising a procession of students in honor of St. Ursula worried that the armed soldiers who participated were doing so insincerely.[32] Marie de l'Incarnation was chastised more than once by priests for overstepping her womanly station.[33] Though convents did have their supporters, these were not necessarily the majority. That is consistent with early modern attitudes towards women who lacked the protection of a husband or father. Historians have illuminated frequently uncomfortable situations of unmarried women[34] ("calamitous creatures" short on income and respect, dependent on the whims of relatives or employers), of superannuated domestics turned out into the cold, of widows commonly living in penury. Legal documents relating to dowries and convent investments, personally signed by numbers of nuns, imbue them with the dignity of adults who had decisions to make, assets to manage.[35] The material conditions and the *caritas* of cloisters were not always ideal, and only some would have experienced a "perfect holocaust" of love. But there were four walls, three meals, elected leaders, and at least a chance of meaningful community. For what was doubtless a variety of reasons, those inside seemed to be attached to cloister. The cabins of the early years soon grew to three-story stone buildings, and Canadian recruits began to outnumber those from France. By 1700 the Canadian hospitals and the Ursulines each had several dozen choir nuns as well as a few lay sisters.

As one considers the divine odyssey that brought cloisters to French America, one can only acknowledge the centrality of the spirit world in this improbable and imaginative transplantation. It was very unusual for a new and tenuous colony to receive an injection of educated female immigrants; in Canada this happened more than two decades before Crown government and troops arrived to protect the place. As scholars have observed, religion has its own epistemologies and metaphysics. It involves internalization of a particular idea of moral calling and particular relationships to secular and religious laws, causing it to operate for many believers as "a foundational mode of self-identity and spatial behaviors."[36] In this case faith handed a passport to parties who did not ordinarily travel. Portents received in cells transported the cloistered to New France and kept them cloistered after arrival.

Still, the form seems somewhat ill-suited to a transatlantic mission to "go teach all nations." Cells inside convent fortresses were perhaps suitable for crowded medieval towns, but what sense did they make in the vast open spaces of Canada and Louisiana? Did the form mutate in response to the mission and the environment? Apart from the spiritual dimensions of sisterly life and travels, what were the more practical survival mechanisms developed for a life so far from home?

Extending Outward

Ursulines came to Canada with the idea of bringing the gospel to female natives and schooling them in French ways, while hospital sisters aimed to combine religious edification with healthcare for natives of both sexes. In Québec and particularly in Montreal, they claimed a number of converts, especially among Wyandot and Montagnais allies of the French. However, the Ursulines had difficulty retaining seminarians who tended to "climb like squirrels over our palisade"[37] to rejoin their parents in native encampments. Soon enough the would-be converts proved largely uninterested in the Franco-Christian way of life, and plans for intermarriages of Christianized Indians with colonial men foundered. Their ranks in any case were dramatically thinned as thousands fell victim to European diseases or fur trade warfare. After many years of vigorous effort, including mastering several native languages, Marie de l'Incarnation in 1668 made the rueful admission that "we have more experience than anyone else, and have observed that of a hundred who have passed through our hands we have scarcely civilized one."[38] Though a handful of native students and patients remained, the focus in the late seventeenth century changed to serving French colonists.

In the eighteenth century, the business the nuns had with First Nations shifted to points in the continental interior. Convent workshops began to manufacture articles for the western trade. These included medicines made in convent pharmacies and shipped to forts. A hospice that opened in Montreal in the 1740s began manufacturing shirts and sending them west in fur trade canoes.[39] Sisters also sewed and embroidered vestments for hinterland services probably attended by French traders and their native wives. The New Orleans ministry to the First Nations, undertaken in the less fervid climate of the eighteenth century, did not last very long, nor was it embraced with the ardor seen in early Canada. Only a year after arrival, Sister St. Stanislaus wrote off Indian women as creatures who "under a modest air, hide the passions of beasts" (and she was scarcely more enthusiastic about the "vain" French women). Altogether, she declared, "the devil has a great empire here."[40] In both colonies the sisters directed their gaze away from aboriginal people towards other groups.

We should note how distance enhanced the value of colonial convents, making their establishment an event of vastly greater significance than it was in France. By 1764 France had some two hundred communities running about 1,730 hospitals, with particularly dense coverage in Paris and northwest France, the birthplace of most colonial migrants.[41] Schools were also thick upon the ground. The Ursulines, just one of many teaching orders, had 350 schools after their rapid seventeenth-century spread. To colonists the arrival of even one such institution was a heartening injection of badly needed services. The New Orleans sisters were flocked by parents "carried away with joy to see us, saying they no longer worry that they will return to France since they have here what they need to educate their daughters."[42] There and in Québec, sisters found that female settlers lacked even the most rudimentary education.

Cloisters reached out to the colonial poor. The ports of Québec and New Orleans presented newcomers of all kinds at the convent gates. The Crown subsidized the Hotels-Dieu to care for soldiers who became ill on the trip over, and a number of sisters died from the contagions.[43] Sisters also took care of female immigrants arriving in port. The Ursulines housed some of the brides sent over by the Crown to marry Canadian colonists in the period from 1663 to 1673. Convents also took in a number of captives whom Indian allies brought to Canada after raids on New England frontiers, including Haverhill in Massachusetts and Wells in today's Maine. Some of the captives became Catholics and married Canadian men, while a handful of others became nuns.[44]

In New Orleans the "devil's empire" remained in evidence, since it was a destination for French sex-trade workers. Sister St. Stanislaus reported in 1727 that that there were enough bad girls there to "fill a reformatory," whom the authorities ordered placed on a wooden horse and whipped, while thieves faced quick execution.[45] Some of these unfortunates, or their children, doubtless became part of the large religion classes opened by the Ursulines. The sisters also developed classes, almost from the start, for the African slaves, another group often shipped into the port. The creole daughter of a wealthy planter who took the veil in 1773 carried out that ministry, which apparently included some literacy training, for four decades.[46]

Convents offered a number of other services to the urban poor. While those who could afford it paid daily fees at the Hôtel-Dieu, the many who could not were treated for free. The authorities noted in 1731 that the Québec Hôtel-Dieu patients included soldiers and *habitants* "who are nearly all without distinction transported to the hospitals when they are ill."[47] Officials that same decade reported some forty patients were regularly treated at the Montreal Hôtel-Dieu, mostly for free. The outreach seems to have touched hearts. Having "a special affection for that community," Montreal's populace came forward to help when it burned down in 1734. Country dwellers sent wood and wheat, town workers donated labor, and donors contributed three thousand *livres* towards rebuilding.[48] The New Orleans Ursulines overcame their initial reluctance and developed hospital services there as well.

In addition to care of the sick, cloisters opened their doors to custodial care. The General Hospice (Hôpital-Général) of Québec was founded in 1692 and staffed by the Augustinians. As with a number of Hôpitaux Généraux in France in the seventeenth century, the purpose was to take charge of a growing number of beggars, prostitutes, petty criminals, and vagabonds—the great *renfermement des pauvres* that has been variously analyzed by historians as calculated social control or helpful social service.[49] It had aspects of both. A hospice combined the functions of correction of a workhouse with custodial care of the disabled, orphaned, and other needy or homeless people. There was also industrial training for boys and girls. The Québec hospice housed about forty inmates in 1730, double that number by 1748. When the regular hospital (the Hôtel-Dieu) was full or incapacitated in times of epidemic or war, the Hospice also received the ill. An intendant reported general praise for the hospice, noting that the meals served there did even more than the medicines. The New Orleans sisters likewise sheltered the homeless, and their orphanage was the most praised part of their work. They answered a dramatic need in taking in the thirty orphans after a 1729 Natchez raid a hundred miles north of the city. The convent also gave refuge to battered and destitute women.[50]

The Ursulines, though better known for elite education, also instructed some townspeople who had little money for fees. Following French tradition, their schools in New Orleans and Québec featured classes for day students *(externes)*. These girls were often of a lower class than the boarders. In New Orleans, Sister St. Stanislaus reported after landing that "the inhabitants, seeing that we do not want to take any money for instructing the day students, are filled with gratitude and help us in every way they can."[51]

The network extended to the upper reaches of society as well. Even in the early days when space was tight, they all took in paying pensioners. Providing rooms for elite widows and boarding schools for elite daughters promoted revenues, legacies, and fresh recruits. It was reported at one point, for example, that the young boarders with the New Orleans Ursulines all wanted to be nuns. Converts also functioned as hostels for lady travelers and those concerned about safety when their officer-husbands were away.[52] The hospitals followed *ancien régime* custom in setting aside special quarters for officers so that they need not mingle with the other patients.

The propertied townspeople supplied the cloisters with a lifeline to protectors beyond the gate, reinforced by ties of kin. Unlike priests, most Canadian nuns by the eighteenth century were born in the colony. With many relatives in the local shops, warehouses, regiments, council seats, and government posts, supplies were purchased, requests met, donations received. Loans were extended or forgiven, lands swapped for services. Officials contributed to dowries for needy noble postulants.[53] Convents educated officials' daughters and cared for their widows. Nuns taught their own nieces (many of whom took the veil) and boarded their own elderly relatives.

Convents gradually built clientage systems that extended their connections beyond the towns. While some of the early noble nuns were pious recluses, in the more secular climate of the eighteenth century they tended to act more strategically. Part of the charmed circle constituting the king's "family," some had grown up in ruling cliques. In the convent they continued to cultivate those ties, which extended from their kinsmen in the officer class to colonial governors and intendants, who in turn represented their interests to the minister of marine and the king at Versailles. No cloister had fewer than 19 percent noblewomen in its ranks. At times at the Québec Hospice, the most aristocratic of such institutions, nearly half the choir nuns were daughters of noble officers and officials—heavy overrepresentation in a population that was about 4 percent noble.[54] As if recognizing the value of such connections, convents often elected noblewomen to their highest administrative offices,[55] where they supervised general operations, the novices, the spiritual life of sisters, finances, schooling, and hospital wards. Mother St. Claude de Ramezay, daughter of a Montreal governor, spent thirty-two years as either the hospice's financial director or its superior and spearheaded an addition to the convent that helped make its grounds a fashionable place of resort for the town's upper classes.[56] For their part, bourgeois sisters could contribute business skills and connections.

Cloister rules could bend to permit face-to-face contact with the mighty. The New Orleans sisters reported visits from officials such as the governor, Monsieur Perier, and his wife who "do us the honour of coming to see us often. The Lieutenant of the King is also a perfect gentleman. . . . They overwhelm us with all kinds of presents."[57] It was not unknown for Québec sisters to attend a dinner party at the governor's mansion. Early eighteenth-century Canadian governor Pierre Rigaud de Vaudreuil and his wife (an Ursuline alumna) broke cloister by dropping into convents with their entourages of officers or of ladies and girls, raising the ire of successive bishops.[58] Yet such friends were invaluable to convents.

In other ways, too, the cloisters extended their reach. The aristocratic Bishop St. Vallier, former chaplain in the French court, established the Québec Hospice in 1692 and got Augustinians to serve there. He secured hefty donations from French elites including Madame de Maintenon herself.[59] Some years later an intendant wrote to Versailles to confirm his impression that the court wished him to treat that convent better than the others. The transatlantic network clearly affected fortunes in the cloisters.

In this chess game, having a bishop was not necessarily an advantage. The fact that colonial prelates were frequently absentees encouraged sisterly liberties. A battle for control at the Québec Hospice illustrates how secular forces might be better guardians of convent mandates to elect their own superior. When the sisters took a different side in the course of some ecclesiastical infighting, the bishop's office attempted to deprive them of their chaplain and replace the aristocratic Mother Duchesnay as superior.[60] The nuns appealed directly to Versailles with their version of events. Mother Duchesnay tactfully heaped praise on colonial governor Beauharnois[61] but also endorsed as "simple and truthful" an accompanying memoir from Sister Agnes, the convent secretary. The latter's note "on behalf of the whole community" claimed that the governor in trying to resolve matters had intimidated and misled some of the younger or more timid nuns. (The governor was evidently a frequent visitor, only convincing some of the more impressionable sisters "after a thousand entreaties.") But Sister Agnes reiterated the general desire to retain their chaplain and choice of superior.[62] This was all done with such finesse that the governor in the end sided with them against the bishop's office.

It was not appreciated when the cloistered reached out and recruited powerful allies to thwart bishops. The latter continued their efforts to weaken convents' self-government. In 1730 Bishop Dosquet accused the hospice of an abusive "spirit of independence and liberty" and asked the minister to reduce the sisters' numbers.[63] Hoping to break the rule of proud noblewomen,[64] he arbitrarily appointed a non-noble nun as superior after Mother Duchesnay died. Eight members of the noble faction retired to their cells during this illegal procedure, taking care first to disable the convent bell (apparently rung to signal a decision).[65] After inspecting the convent's constitution, the governor and the intendant supported the nuns and asked the minister to call for a new election.[66] Nearby at the Hôtel-Dieu, Mother Juchereau de Saint-Ignace also endured election manipulations by a bishop, but she appealed to Versailles through another powerful ecclesiastic and won support for her position.[67] The New Orleans sisters threatened to decamp for Saint Domingue when there was an attempt to interfere with their self-governance.[68]

The nuns incurred resentment because they were making financial decisions ordinarily made by committees of laymen in many hospices and hospitals in France. Convents fended off successive efforts to saddle them with lay administrators for decades after Intendant Dupuy's charge in the 1720s that the Québec Hôtel-Dieu was entirely out of line with French practice in overseeing their own budget.They were known even to refuse to hand over their accounts for official perusal. The sisters' "open resistance to order and justice" were symptomatic, asserted Dupuy, "of a country in which one inhaled Independence." Other officials also declared the sisters less submissive than French ones. It was suggested that their autonomy might be due to their arrival in the foundational period—that odyssey that brought them to the colony decades before there were any bishops or intendants on the scene.[69]

The evidence seems to support historian Micheline D'Allaire's assessment of convent skill in securing the protection of the powerful.[70] Their diverse services to rich and poor certainly strengthened their hand; there was no substitute for what officials deemed their "indispensable services." But when rulers had to make choices between conflicting claims, the carefully cultivated networks of kin, caste, and clientage that connected the cloistered nuns with the outside world could tip the balance in their favor.

There were also supportive Catholic networks that stretched from behind the grille all the way across the sea. These were reinforced by the continuing arrival of nuns from France for a generation or two after their establishment. By the mid-seventeenth century, for example, the Québec Ursulines had welcomed new arrivals from Tours, Dieppe, Ploermel, Magny-en-Vexin, and Paris, while various parts of France supplied the Québec Hôtel-Dieu with fifteen new members during the course of the century. Seventeen reinforcements joined the original dozen in Louisiana during the first century of establishment there.[71] Along with the personnel, a steady stream of transatlantic religious objects, correspondence, and parcels bound them to the French church. The Ursulines in particular at their early eighteenth-century height had a remarkable network consisting of 350 convents and ten thousand nuns. The obituaries of members who migrated to the colonies were printed and circulated around the network, keeping attachments alive. There was curricular continuity, too, with Québec pupils using textbooks sent from France.[72] Precious pharmaceutical ingredients also crossed the sea. Convents had clerical procurers in France who lobbied for them and secured supplies, including an assortment of much-appreciated fabrics. This was a two-way street. Ursulines in France took inspiration from missions in Canada,[73] and French émigré priests later sought refuge after the revolution. Some performed chaplaincy and other services in convents, where they doubtless electrified the nuns with horror stories of the smashed convents and martyred clergy in godless France.

Convents on Streetscapes and Landscapes

In certain ways New World cloisters differentiated themselves from French models and became "naturalized" in the wider but less developed colonial landscapes. Because of their early arrival and a dearth of other colonial institutions, convents always occupied a large proportion of colonial streetscapes at the heart of town. Street-level shops that the Montréal Hôtel-Dieu opened in the late eighteenth century exemplified another aspect of all the cloisters: they produced a wide variety of goods for sale to the public. Convents were also in possession of some half-dozen of the huge rural tracts known as *seigneuries,* supplying marketable hay and firewood, as well as wheat, corn, meat, and provisions for their institutions. They benefited from colonial conditions that historical geographers have identified: abundant land, scarce labor, and the gravitational pull of the fur trade. The convents were able to engage in artisanal production without much worry about competition or opposition, given the dearth of manufacturing in Canada and Louisiana and the absence of guilds. All this production fed and financed nuns, patients, and pupils, and made its way through the economy to townspeople, regiments, country parishes, and distant fur trade posts.

In line with tradition, convents carved out productive space, much of it within their walls (see fig. 8.2). This included sizeable gardens and orchards. Besides selling preserves, produce, and baked goods locally,[74] convent gardens also served markets hundreds of miles away. Sisters with pharmaceutical training made remedies not just for their patients but also for sale outside the hospitals; these were shipped as far away as Forts Chambly, Frontenac, Niagara, and Detroit. They sent others to country priests for distribution.[75] Sisters also acquired, as dowry offerings or through donation or purchase, a number of urban properties that produced food, wood, or rental income. By the mid-eighteenth century political and military officials in Québec complained bitterly that the large enclosure of the Hôtel-Dieu monopolized increasingly scarce urban lots and hindered access to the fortifications needed for protection against a growing English threat. Their observance of their rules from the earliest days may have bolstered their claims when convents insisted on the integrity of their space. The New Orleans Ursulines also had productive urban plots housing dairy cattle and other livestock.[76]

Convent property was prominent on the rural landscape, too. In Canada this was because of royal grants of seigneuries to colonial convents at a time when land seemed boundless. Indeed, about a quarter of all seigneurial lands in Canada were in church hands. At Québec the Hôtel-Dieu possessed a seigneurie at Ile aux Oyes. The Ursulines also held a seigneurie, while the Hospice had full or part possession of three, including the particularly valuable St. Vallier seigneurie. Hundreds of *habitant* farmers paid dues to convent seigneuresses. Valuable supplies of grain, hay, and wood came from these tracts, and some were sold to the army and other institutions. In Louisiana the Ursulines had two Mississippi River plantations that supplied them with food and placed them among the major landholders in the region.

Landholdings were supplemented with manufactures. In Montréal, for example, the Sisters of St. Joseph built a portfolio consisting of land revenues, investments locally and in France, and a range of manufactures. They also profited from *congés* (fur-trading licenses they could sell to others) and from

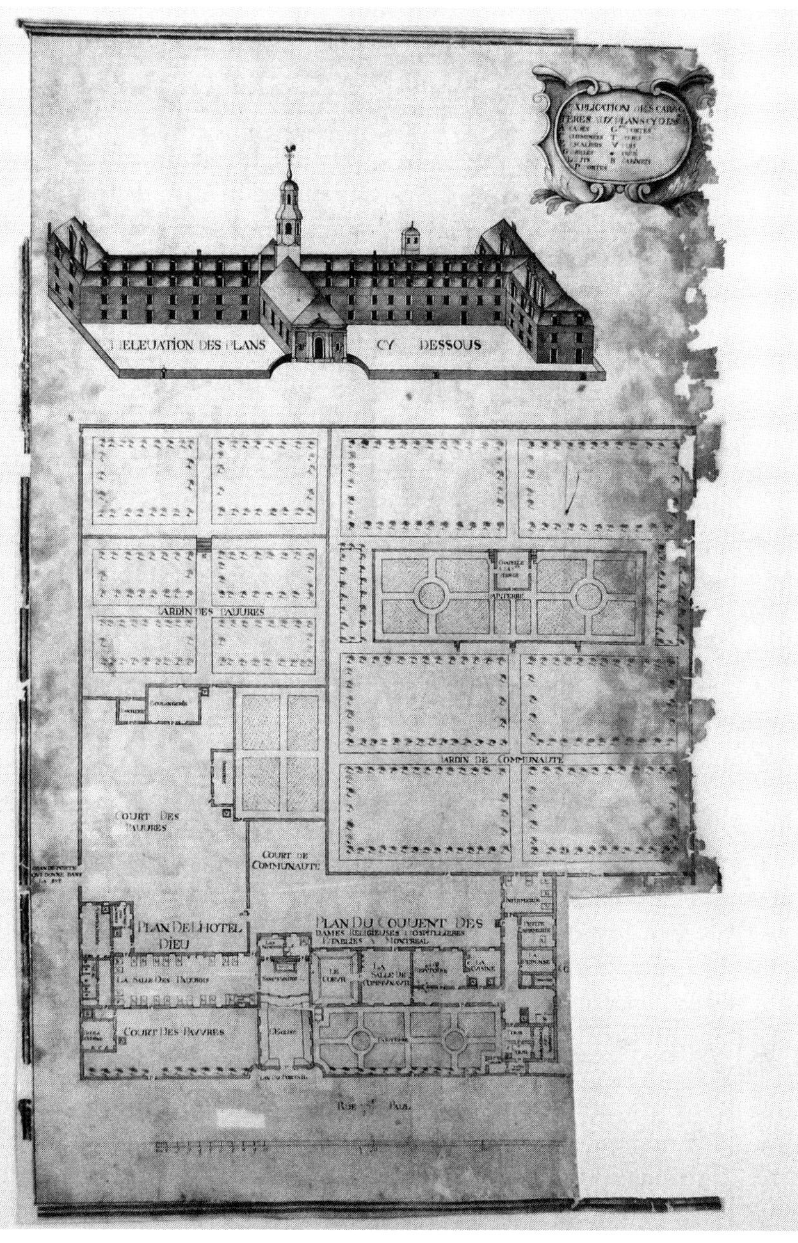

Fig. 2. Plan of L'Hôtel-Dieu de Montreal. Convents enclosed substantial areas of urban land, and those within produced a surplus of foodstuffs and other items for sale. The Montreal Hotel-Dieu was typical in having an on-site stable and chicken coop, laundry, and bakery. A shoemaking operation generated revenue, and herb gardens provided ingredients for pharmaceuticals that were made on-site and shipped throughout the colony, even to distant fur-trade posts. The duplications of chapels, courtyards, gardens, kitchens and other facilities allowed the sisters to combine social service with intensely private community life. Permission of the Collection of the Religious Hospitallers of Saint-Joseph in Montreal.

baking, sewing, preparing pharmaceuticals, weaving fabric, making rope, and even cutting window panes for Montréalers. Their shoemaking workshop was a sizable operation, as shown by the loss of six hundred pairs and many tools in a 1734 fire.[77] In fact, 82 percent of their revenues came from their own assets and labors.[78] After losing their French subsidies in the late eighteenth century, they stepped up production of boxes, fine gilt work, and bread and candles, even making soap from cast-off army butter.[79] In New Orleans the sisters ran carpentry and shoemaking operations.[80]

While convents in France also profited from their lands and labors, the range and extent of convent activities expanded in the colonial setting. A scholar of *ancien régime* French hospitals observed that those in Canada relied on a considerably wider range of production than was common in the mother country.[81] She offered no reasons for the difference, but one can surmise that enterprise, driven by economic need, found an opening because of French America's labor shortages and weak industrial development. Emily Clark found that the New Orleans sisters also relied more heavily on their own lands and labors than did their counterparts in northwestern France. She believes that convents in France may have been in line with other *ancien régime* charitable institutions, which received an estimated 57 to 100 percent of revenues from *rentes* (passive investments), yielding modest fixed returns.[82]

In the colonies opportunity knocked more aggressively. In a setting where officials frequently lamented the impoverished elite and the lack of enterprise, convents were one of the few institutions that could scrape together a certain amount of working capital by drawing on dowries and revenues. They had a pool of labor and the organizational skills to manage it. As noted, they had strong connections with local and institutional buyers, including kin, other convents, fur traders, the army, and government shipyards. All these factors helped them develop a wide range of revenue sources and lengthy trade lines, regardless of cloister walls.

It is clear that being spatially enclosed did not bar convents from extending their control over sizeable properties and a significant labor force. Their assets positioned them on the avenues of trade and communication connecting colonial towns with western trade posts, transatlantic ports, clerical networks, and the court in France. Under "friendly fire" during French rule, they learned how to resist incursions by ecclesiastical and secular overlords, and how to develop and manage a complex economic portfolio—all of which would serve them well in crisis times ahead.

Withstanding Regime Changes

How did cloisters respond when events jeopardized their very existence? The eighteenth century brought successive shock waves. Metropolitan and colonial institutions lost funds in the French bankruptcy induced by the John Law scheme in the 1720s in which the French government had forced convents to invest. Colonial losses were cushioned by their many other sources of income, and in contrast to their French counterparts, none were forced to close. Like France, where dissolution of Catholic male and female orders attended the great upheaval of 1789, Canada suffered a violent regime change. The colony was captured by British forces in 1759–60 and permanently transferred to the Protestant power in 1763. The conquest era caused a considerable drop in the ranks of male clergy. Yet Canadian convents not only safeguarded themselves but helped the larger society make the transition to British rule. While serving as medical and refugee centers during the invasion, they won the goodwill of the British authorities through care of British wounded and diplomacy with the new regime.

In Canada the populace endured years of warfare between French and British imperial forces, leaving the poorly supplied colony hungry and exhausted. During General James Wolfe's bombardment of Québec in 1759, townspeople came pouring into the suburban hospice with their belongings. Ursuline and Hôtel-Dieu nuns also fled their bombed-out convents and came streaming over the fields, carrying their bedding. Eight hundred refugees crammed into the hospice.[83] On the fateful night of September 12, 1759, Wolfe's troops slipped past French sentries and occupied the heights above the town. The sisters, who customarily rose at 4:00 A.M., were among the first to learn of the surprise landing. The French commander Louis-Joseph Montcalm rushed into action without waiting for nearby reinforcements and lost the fatal encounter.

That night, hospice nuns carrying soup to patients were frightened by the loud knock of a British officer at the door. But the nuns had already woven the victors into their network, and he promised they would suffer no harm. From the time General James Wolfe sailed up the river, the nuns had cared not only for their own side but for wounded British captives. Before his death General Wolfe promised to spare the convent.[84] Wolfe's successor, General James Murray, donated flour and lard to the hospice and paid the expenses of the British patients. (Could he have been touched by the wool stockings the Ursulines knit to protect his kilted regiments during the Québec winter?) After the war, he lobbied both the French and English governments to aid the convents.

Each order made its peace with the new regime. The Québec Hôtel-Dieu had its wards taken over for a quarter century to serve as a British military hospital, but the sisters maintained cordial relations with the new rulers. In Montréal the Hôtel-Dieu's care of British troops won General Amherst's favor. In the 1760s and for many years to come, the British government stepped into the role formerly occupied by France, reimbursing convents for their care of the ill and the handicapped.[85]

The change of empires in the 1760s led to an influx of new peoples into what was now English Québec. Convents adapted. In Québec one of the New England captives who had taken the Ursuline veil, Esther Wheelwright, was elected superior, her knowledge of English an asset as the convent gradually developed English classes. In the nineteenth century it attracted boarders from as far away as Nova Scotia and the United States. When an influx of emigrants from the British Isles after 1815 placed a heavy strain on social services, the government contributed thousands to rebuild the Québec Hôtel-Dieu.

In Louisiana the change of rule was not violent. It was through negotiations that New Orleans and its convent came under markedly conservative Spanish rule in 1767. They changed hands a second time as the result of the Louisiana Purchase by the United States in 1803. The latter transfer brought particular challenges. There was democratic opposition to *ancien régime* social outlooks. Soon a wave of anti-Catholicism welled up, all the more threatening because it was attended by a gender ideology hostile to unmarried women in positions of authority.

Louisiana under Spanish rule saw major immigration from the Spanish Americas, with New Orleans's population surging from about ten thousand in 1767 to fifty thousand in 1800. The Ursulines made some timely property acquisitions, and the resulting assets helped them maintain their own policies about dowries rather than those sought by their new bishop in Havana. There was a change in convent personnel as a steady stream of postulants arrived from Cuba. The sisters made friends among creole planters, accepting their daughters into the same classes as the daughters of Spanish officials and Anglo-American merchants. There was some mixing, too, with "free girls of colour" in the Ursuline classrooms, a phenomenon historian Emily Clark believes contrasted with the growing racial bar beyond the convent walls. The sisters also continued their ministry to the city's black population. The convent did make some concessions to local prejudice around the turn of the century, though, allowing more distinctions in the boarding school based on color.[86]

Even as they struggled to uphold their own versions of Catholic universalism, the New Orleans sisters came face to face with an alien credo: Republicanism. When the United States acquired Louisiana in 1803, there was an influx of American settlers. The *ancien régime* outlook of the nuns began to seem archaic and elitist. At the same time, the nuns were surprisingly successful and aggressive players on the booming local real estate market to an extent that dismayed even their own lawyer, and they had several run-ins with the town council on various issues. Soon fresh waves of thought from the Republic created further tensions. In the 1820s and 1830s, a hardening "separate spheres" dogmatism marched in tandem with an increasingly militant evangelical Protestantism. Persuaded that a more moral society would ensue if mothers of all classes stayed home and devoted their existence to the young, adherents showed little patience for those they perceived as haughty and authoritarian women running large civic institutions. After an Ursuline convent in Charleston, Massachusetts, was burned to the ground by a mob in 1834, the New Orleans Ursuline orphanage came under criticism for alleged mistreatments of barefoot children in its wards, a campaign fanned by Protestants and others who were attempting to establish a rival institution. In particular, the *ancien régime* practice of having white orphans serve meals to the boarders (including some creole boarders) sat well neither with ideals of democracy nor with a hardening racial ideology imported from the plantation South. As Clark has shown, the sisters did lose a battle when the town council voted to suspend support. However, they ultimately won the war when their sounder finances (and inexpensive long-term staff, a perennial convent advantage) allowed them to surpass the competing institution.[87]

Convent captivity tales enjoyed great success. In Montréal the Hôtel-Dieu gained international notoriety through Maria Monk's sensational 1836 account of priests slipping into the cloister at night and impregnating compliant nuns, who then murdered the offspring. This exciting book sold over 300,000 copies in the next three decades.[88] Leaders from both French and English communities in Montréal refused to countenance the scurrilous (and soon discredited) defamation of the Hôtel-Dieu, which continued to serve patients from both groups as it had done since the conquest. As women outside the cloisters faced increasing constraints, convents continued to provide a range of occupations and administrative positions for talented and strong-minded individuals.

Scholars debate whether Tridentine insistence on cloistering hampered the mission of religious women, and these colonial findings support the view that cloister was probably more a help than a hindrance. Having examined the divine odyssey and terrestrial connections of colonial convents, one begins to appreciate how it was that they stood their ground during upheavals. They drew strength, spiritual and communal, from their cloistered existence. From within that box they extended their reach. Supplying services that were scarcer than in France, they benefited from New World land and economic opportunities. They developed contacts of all kinds across seas and continents. As one scholar noted of European cloisters, a spiritual vocation did not render them "silent and removed."[89] They forged ties across a four-thousand-mile span from Detroit to Versailles, fanning out to bring new people and practices from English and Spanish colonies into their orbit, too. Their story confirms that while walls and grilles were permeable, they were real entities, closely guarded by the inmates themselves. And why not? Such constraints proved quite compatible with transatlantic emigration, with clientage networks, with economic innovation, and with retention of contested rights. Cloisters thousands of miles from their motherland could survive military conquest and regime change. Theirs were spaces hemmed in by European tradition. Yet, as their miracle-strewn odyssey and annals suggest, their own concept of the space open to them was as boundless as the seven seas, as high as the heavens showering whatever mix of grace and snow fell on those first log convents.

The improbable transatlantic transplantation of the boxed-in ascetic came about because of heavenly portents and devout delusions of converting a continent. When the clouds parted and reality set in, the customary spatial form showed its resilience. As Old World convents dissolved, those planted on exotic and militarily vulnerable settings in French America adapted and flourished—with quite a lot of help from far-flung friends. While it was no utopia, the French North American convent offered autonomy and community that contrasts with the options for middle-class widows, maiden aunts, or governesses living on sufferance in the homes of others. The old-age security and medical care that even the humblest lay sisters enjoyed contrasts with the fate of many superannuated servants. This well-constructed box *was* a box, and few living in circumstances of security and freedom would choose to inhabit it today. God, if more distant, is considered more benign, no longer requiring the sacrifice of self-immolating vestals. But the life had merit. While even a privileged laywoman might still seek a "Room of One's Own" in the twentieth century, colonial nuns constructed such a room (and sisterly workshop, garden, refectory, and place of worship) hundreds of years earlier than that. This spatial accomplishment transformed the lives of thousands of nuns, and it touched the populations they served across the centuries.

Configuring and Reconfiguring Cathedral Space in the Spanish Atlantic

From Cathedral-Mosque to Baroque Machine

Sing D'Arcy

When in the early 1520s Luis de Moya and his team began the construction of the Cathedral of Santa María de la Encarnación in Santo Domingo, the architectural links that would unite the American and European shores of the Atlantic were cemented into place. This act of spiritual and temporal confidence was a declamation in stone that the Christian and Spanish presence in the Americas would not only be permanent but also one sanctioned by Heaven itself. The emigration of Moya, the team of builders, and the very designs themselves from Seville, *puerto y puerta de las Indias,* reflect the formal and symbolic influence this city was to have on the development of ecclesiastical architecture not only within Spain but in the Hispanic world as a whole. While much scholarship has been directed at the formal evolution of the architecture of the Ibero-American Atlantic, the role in which this architectural development was shaped by and came to configure notions of religion and space within a transatlantic context has been less well explored.

To investigate the wealth of ideas and challenges that this theme implies, this essay charts a course that symbolically replicates that of Moya—one that begins in Seville and continues into the New World. This course is one of an analysis of spatial morphology and typology, while simultaneously being one mapped by the distinct religious and cultural contexts unique to the expanse of the Hispanic realm. It is these contexts, I believe, that shaped the development of ecclesiastical space in Spain and the Americas and not, as conventional historiography paints, an evolution based on teleologically ingrained deviations or misinterpretations of continental European models and styles, in particular those of the French Gothic and later the Roman Baroque.

The contexts in question are those of reconquest and conquest, which like the construction of the cathedrals of Seville and Santo Domingo, were both spiritual (religious) and temporal (spatial). The moments of greatest symbolic weight during the Spanish reconquest were marked by the reappropriation, reconfiguration, and eventual rebuilding of mosques into churches. While the initial act of reconfiguring Islamic space to Christian space was a symbol of victory, the ongoing evangelization of the heterodox population was realized through the construction of new spaces that incorporated the planimetric characteristics of the mosque while implementing a distinctly Christian volumetric and spatial configuration. This is best represented in the translation of the morphology of the cathedral-mosque into the *iglesia-salón*—hall church. It is this model that Moya brought with him from Seville in the 1520s and with it the same spiritual and spatial tactics that charged it with such potent symbolic force.

The morphology of the *iglesia-salón* and its configuration of the liturgical nucleus *"al español"* was adopted almost universally as the basis for all cathedral constructions in the cities of reconquest Spain and those in the Americas. As had been demonstrated in Spain, the long time frame of cathedral-scale constructions meant that the interior configuration of the ecclesiastical space could not be fully realized until the fabric of the structure had been completed. This implied a lag of generations between the benediction of the foundation stone and the consecration of the high altar. While the *iglesia-salón* had been the expression of the absolute triumph of the reconquest, it was the seventeenth- and eighteenth-century interior that manifested the apogee of the utopian vision of the conquest and its program of spiritual control and ecclesiastical power.

Extant spaces, in the case of the Peninsula, or recently completed ones, in the case of the Americas, were equipped with suites of Baroque machines—*máquinas*—which transformed the *iglesia-salón* into a "magic garden," configured by glittering altarpieces, organ cases, and devotional chapels.[1] Each of these *máquinas,* like their theatrical counterparts, were designed to exaggerate the emotive and dramatic experience of a particular scene.

The spatial and emotional experience is choreographed on the play of tension between the isotropic volume of the *iglesia-salón* and the discrete spatial entities of the *máquinas,* designed to illicit sensations of shock and wonder, leaving the experiensor vulnerable to spiritual affectation. While this characteristic of affect is to be found in all aspects of Baroque culture, it could be argued that its most extreme spatial manifestations were in the ecclesiastical interiors of the Hispanic realm. While the Counter-Reformation church in Continental Europe had to validate its position and contend with maintaining its congregations in the face of Protestantism, its mission in the Atlantic was considerably more complex: it had to gain *and* maintain. This was a continuation of the religious and spatial program of reconquest Spain. It was a program that was manifested spatially from the thirteenth through to the eighteenth centuries—first, through the *iglesia–salón* and, second, through its transformation during the Baroque.

As a means of synthesis in a large thematic ocean, the evolution and reconfiguration of the transatlantic *iglesia-salón* and Hispanic model of the liturgical nucleus is used as a chronological and spatial anchor. Within this framework the interventions of the seventeenth and eighteenth centuries will be contextualized through an analysis of the "suite of *máquinas*" as a religious, spatial, and cultural phenomenon unique to the Ibero-American Baroque. In addition to the varied examples cited, two spaces in particular will be the focus of attention owing to their gravitational weight: Seville Cathedral, as the archetype of the cathedral-mosque turned *iglesia-salón* will form the point of reference on the Peninsula, while Mexico City Cathedral will be used to illustrate the development and transformation of this typology during the Baroque. While the interiors of Ibero-American cathedrals may be characterized by the penumbra encountered within, it is hoped that this discussion will provide a means of dispelling the misconception that the legacy between religion and space in the Hispanic Atlantic produced little of serious interest or lasting importance, instead shifting attention away from the historically ingrained "series of negative topoi"[2] towards a more profound understanding of the complexities and richness offered upon closer analysis.

The *Iglesia-Salón*

An *iglesia-salón,* or hall church, also known as *hallenkirche* in German, can be defined as a church in which the vaults of the nave and lateral aisles are similar or almost similar in height. The resultant external form of the building and configuration of the internal space is parallelepipedon in nature, notably lacking transepts. The configuration of space is far more isotropic when compared to the strong monoaxiality of the typical stepped basilical section, which is the basis for nearly all Western-European Christian construction. Directionality is modulated within the internal space through the positioning of the piers and the proportional relationship between height and plan. Further subtleties are derived from the relationship of lateral aisle width, column spacing, and the patterning of the central nave vaulting.

The *iglesia-salón escalonada* is similar in morphological structure, being differentiated by the fact that the vaulting in the lateral naves is lower in height than the central nave. Often the small difference in height between the central nave vaults allows for minimal penetrations or none at all, leading to the distinctive internal illumination conditions found in many Iberian churches. This model was the most prevalent model for large cathedrals, starting with Toledo and followed by the highly influential design of Seville, which inspired a host of other projects both within the Peninsula and the Americas.

The presence of foreign ideas imported into the Iberian Peninsula from north of the Pyrenees has been a constant feature of the development of Iberian culture for centuries. The implantation of the Gothic tradition in Spain owes a great deal to the French, Flemish, and German master builders. The early Gothic

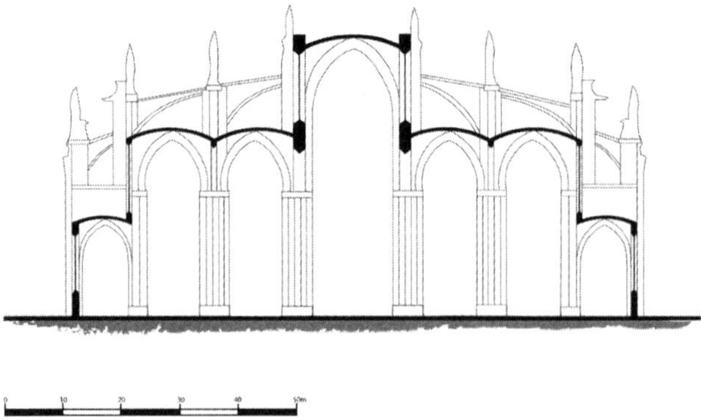

Fig. 1. Seville Cathedral: The cross section cuts across the nave and lateral aisles. It shows the stepped *escalonada* form of the cathedral. This was an innovative design response that allowed the large floor areas of the former mosques to be subsumed by the new structure.

cathedrals such as those of Avila, Toledo, Leon, Burgos, Cuenca, and Seville are all thought to have been conceived by foreign masters.[3] While foreign systems and knowledge formed much of the basis of the designs, the realization of these imported models was changed radically to adapt to the new cultural, religious, social, and aesthetic needs of the kingdoms of the Peninsula.

The Cathedral of Seville, commenced in 1402, has been cited by scholars as the most influential of the model of the *iglesia-salón* in Spain. Attributed to the northern French masters Carlín and Ysambert,[4] the design of Seville's hybrid hall-and-stepped section was followed closely by the project for the Cathedral of Astorga around 1470, attributed to the German immigrant Juan de Colonia, or another member of the family. Colonia's never-realized design for Astorga was the first true *iglesia-salón* with a complete absence of transepts and all vaulting at the same height. This fact has led some to consider it a direct import of a German model *hallenkirche*.[5] As master masons moved around from job to job, either as consultants on particular design issues, or to undertake large-scale projects, the model of the *iglesia-salón* became distributed throughout central Spain, reaching its greatest level of sophistication in the sixteenth century. However, the acceptance of the *hallenkirche* transplant hypothesis into Spain was questioned by the scholar Norbert Nussbaum who believed that attempts to connect the German models directly to the Spanish ones had harvested "doubtful results"; he preferred to see the hybrid Spanish model as a result of a variety of influences.[6]

In addition to the two previously discussed theories regarding the emergence of the *iglesia-salón* in Spain, there is a third that traces its influences back from Seville through to the earlier Cathedral of Toledo, commenced in 1226. It has traditionally been thought that Toledo Cathedral's structural model especially that of the chevet, was based on the French model of Bourges Cathedral.Recent scholarship has put forward the idea that the real impulse for the implantation of French models into Spain may not have been from a structural or purely architectonic prerogative but from a sociopolitical one.[7]

The promoter of Toledo's "new" cathedral (to be built in the French manner) was Archbishop Rodrigo Ximénez de Rada (1170–1247). Ximénez de Rada was an important cleric, statesman, and writer and close ally of King Alfonso VIII of Castile (1155–1214). He had studied at the University of the Sorbonne and would have undoubtedly visited the much-lauded chevet of the Basilica of Saint Denis, recently completed in 1144. Just as Suger had utilized a new architectural language for his symbolic program, so too the use of a similar aestheto-political tactic would have clearly symbolized Ximénez de Rada's personal triumph in securing the primacy for Toledo, the consolidation of the Castilian monarchy with its capital (also in Toledo), as well as the victorious and unstoppable progress of the Christian reconquest of the Peninsula.

The Cathedral-Mosques of the Reconquest

Regardless of the extent to which Ximénez de Rada may have been inspired by Suger's act of transforming a Carolingian basilica into a New Jerusalem on Earth,[8] the Toledan archbishop and his master builder Martín had a very different context in which to work. The new Saint Denis was constructed on the site of an existing Christian basilica, whose dedication and function were more or less transferable to the new structure. The town of Saint Denis, just outside of Paris, was not a densely developed urban nucleus, having as its primary function a royal burial site and monastery, and there was no urban issue as such to deal with. Toledo, however, was no mere village: it was an important city with a dense urban fabric that had been developing for centuries.[9] As was the case in the majority of the conquered Islamic cities—Toledo, Seville, Cordoba, Granada, Malaga, Guadix, Jaen—the main mosque, along with the majority of the extant urban fabric, was not destroyed but occupied and transformed into the cathedral or primary church.

The occupation and conversion of the principal mosque into a cathedral had on the one hand an economic rationale, especially in times of war when finances were limited, and on the other an important symbolic one. The cost of erecting a new building to house large numbers of people was a costly act even in prosperous times; because of that, when the victorious authorities found well-built spaces, designed to house large congregations and located strategically in the center of the city, there seemed little sense in demolishing and rebuilding. A few readjustments would be adequate, at least in the short to medium term. The occupation of the most important building in a city and its subsequent conversion into a temple of the victorious faith had very strong symbolic significance for the authorities as well as for the vanquished inhabitants. The scholar Antonio Almagro Gorbea stated, "There can be no doubt that the appropriation of these sites was one of the greatest signs of the appropriation of conquered territory, and greater when the building, for its history or quality or its visibility, contained clear symbolic significance for the defeated. It was in a way a form of depriving them of part of their identity."[10]

After the fall of Toledo to the Christian forces of Alfonso VI in 1085, the great mosque was purified and consecrated according to rite in the Pontifical Ceremonial for such transformations, and dedicated under the avocation of the Virgin Mary.[11] As was practice at the time, one of the primary acts of transforming the space into one suitable for Christian liturgy was the reorientation of the internal space. The orientation of the internal space according to Islamic practice was that the focus of worship, the *mihrab,* was placed in the *quiblah* wall. This meant that the focus of worship was on the long-axis wall. The internal configuration was subsequently changed to east-west with the presbytery—*capilla mayor*—located at the east, which meant that the focus of worship was reoriented to the short-axis wall. Despite the appearance to a contemporary viewer on plan, this did not necessarily impart the feeling of a stepped basilical section, as all the ceiling heights within the mosque space would have generally been the same. The internal space, with its hypostyle columnated configuration would have also been isotropic. The task of converting this type of space, inherently alien to Christian worship, into one that would, first, function for the Christian liturgy and, second, convey some symbolic sense of a Christian space, would have been a challenge for the eleventh-century Chapter of Toledo. This same challenge, repeated on the Peninsula and later in the Americas, can be seen as the underlying theme that shaped the development of cathedral space in the Spanish Atlantic.

One manner in which to delineate space in an otherwise isotropic configuration is to construct visual barriers, either solid, as in the form of walls, or with some degree of visual permeability, such as screens. The construction of a segregated presbytery that contained the main altar in the eastern half of the space as well as a segregated choir in the western half of the space not only took advantage of the ample available floor space but also allowed the spaces near the perimeter walls to be dedicated to private chapels and the space between the liturgical nucleus and the ring of outer chapels to be used for general circulation and processions. What was configured was in many respects a prototypical spatial distribution for all Hispanic cathedrals and collegiate churches to be built until the nineteenth century.

While the cathedral-mosque was by its very hybrid nature a unique spatial typology, it did pose major inconveniences for the developing liturgy of the Roman Catholic rite. One major problem that the hypostyle structure of mosques bequeathed on new Christianized spaces was the narrowness of the naves and aisles and the density of the columnation that was wholly unsuited to liturgical needs. The interior spaces were generally very dark, as a result of the uniform roof height and deep plan. Almagro Gorbea described the possible environment of the Cathedral-mosque of Seville as "dark and cluttered," which no doubt formed the basis for the eventual rebuilding of cathedral-mosques into Gothic structures.[12]

Some 140 years had passed between Ximénez de Rada's decision to rebuild Toledo Cathedral and his predecessor de Sedirac's controversial act of seizing the mosque in the name of Christianity.[13] Inspired by the new Gothic vision and its symbolic associations, Ximénez de Rada engaged the French master Martín for the task. This task was highly charged in a political and religious sense: Ximénez de Rada was constructing the cathedral primate, which would be flooded with the "light of God" as in Suger's model and not be the "dark and cluttered" space of the previous religious legacy. The construction in stone would be in marked contrast to the previous construction in brick and plaster. Even though Toledo had returned to Christian control for over a century, the reconquest was still in progress. Seville was still under Islamic control when the foundation stone of Toledo Cathedral was laid in 1226 by King Fernando III, who twenty-two years later would conquer that Atlantic city for Christian and Castilian rule. It would have been completely unacceptable if a new cathedral were lesser in size or scale to that of the mosque structure it was going to replace.[14]

The great mosque of Seville completed in 1197 was similarly converted into a cathedral in 1248 with the fall of the city to the Castilian forces of King Fernando III. With the conversion of the mosque to cathedral, the ceremonial rite and internal configuration of the space was modeled directly on that of Toledo.[15] The mosque of Seville, like that of Cordoba, was considerably larger than Toledo's. There had been much discussion, since 1388, of demolishing the cathedral-mosque owing to earthquake damage and its poor condition, though the decision to rebuild did not take place until 1401.[16] While the seventeenth-century chronicler Diego Ortiz de Zúñiga reports of the events over 250 years later, it is possible to see that, despite the earthquake damage suffered to the fabric, there was a pressing desire by the chapter to possess a building similar, or greater than those of rival cities. Recorded in Ortiz de Zúñiga's entry for the year 1401 is the famous unsubstantiated line stating, "Let us build a church so large that those who see it will take us for madmen."[17] It had long been seen that the cathedral-mosque was no longer suitable nor sufficiently dignified for the ceremonial and liturgical uses of a burgeoning city like Seville. Ortiz de Zúñiga claimed that there was not enough room in the cathedral; curiously, he stated that while it was not "small," the clergy could not fit in the "cramped" building. When Ortiz de Zúñiga referred to the "cramped" building, it is possible that he

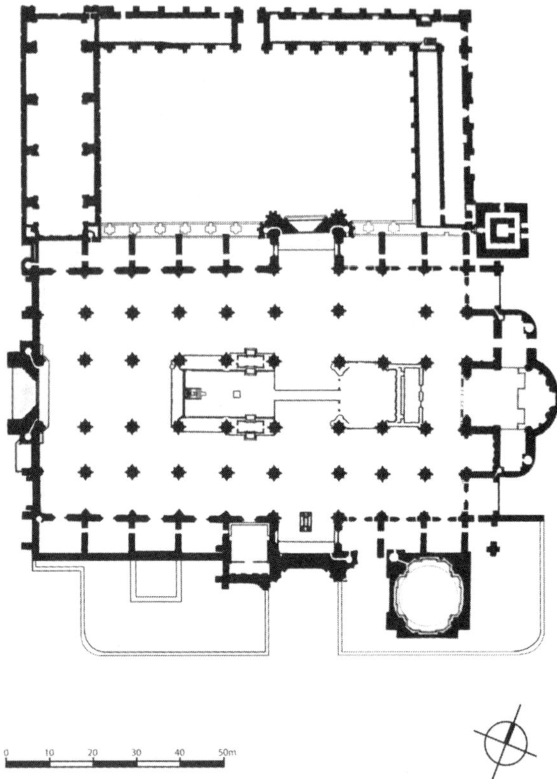

Fig. 2. Plan of Seville Cathedral: In the center of the Cathedral are the two screened clerical reserves—the canons' choir to the west (*coro*) and the presbytery (*capilla mayor*) to the east. These are linked by a narrow balustraded passage (*via sacra*). Image by author after Almagro Gorbea 2007.

was referring to the cramped conditions of the canons' choir—*coro*—and not the large cathedral-mosque as a whole. This reading is further validated by an additional comment stating that the celebration of the liturgy could not be enacted with "majestic dignity."[18] This could be read as arising from the configuration of the *coro* of the cathedral-mosque.

Considering that the mosque had a column spacing of 4.5 meters and a general internal arch height of 5.46 meters, except the central north-south nave which had a height of 7 meters, it is understandable that the chapter considered it unsuitable and undesirable to preserve the building.[19] The scholar Antonio Collantes de Téran questioned the motives behind the chapter's decision to undertake such an enormous project. While Seville was an important city, the discovery of the Americas for Spain was not to occur for another ninety-one years. It was not, therefore, the world powerhouse it would become when the last stone was laid in 1506. He speculated that the chapter was in many ways obliged to at least match or surpass the civic presence of the mosque, as failure to do so may have been read as a sign of weakness or incapability. In many ways the building of the cathedral was a speculative venture between city and God, an act of "confidence in the future," which in Seville's case paid off in 1492.[20] The Cathedral of Santo Domingo can also be seen in these terms: some thirty years since the first Spanish contact with the Americas, a stone cathedral in the model of Seville was erected, a physical wager with heaven and a symbol of a new future in a new world.

The architectural historian Fernando Chueca Goita argued that there was in essence a transferal of spatial concepts from the old structure to the new one. He suggested that Toledo broke the neutrality of the Islamic spatial configuration by the incorporation of the chevet, while Seville's orthogonal plan signified that the transfer of spatial model from Islam to Christianity was total.[21] If this was the case, it could be posited that the destruction of Amerindian temples, rather than their reconfiguration, implied a desire by the Spanish to negate the possibility of any form of spatial transfer, instead implanting one they saw as clearly Christian. The association of religious spaces stemming from an Abrahamic religious framework may have been an acceptable concession for the preservation or reconfiguration of mosques and synagogues as Christian spaces until such time as a new structure could be built; yet the immediate destruction of Amerindian temples implies that the criteria for assessing the appropriateness of the indigenous spatial models was distinct from the debate that was current within the Peninsula.

The issue of cultural and architectural transfer in the case of Seville Cathedral, and its flow-on effects, is an open-ended question. What is undeniable is the impact that the new cathedral model had on Castilian architecture and that of the Americas.

Seville Cathedral and Its Legacy

The uniform height of the lateral aisles, the regularity of bays and vaulting, and the rectangular plan challenged the traditional basilical model. Seville Cathedral can be seen as one of the first large structures to break with the Gothic idea of spatial compartmentalization.[22] Isotropic in nature, spatial definition is provided by the *capilla mayor* and the *coro.* While the designers of the Cathedral forged a new spatial model, the liturgical configuration was a direct inheritance from Toledo Cathedral. Seville Cathedral was used as a basis for numerous cathedrals both within the Peninsula as well as in the Americas. The *Catedral Nueva* of Salamanca, begun 1512, follows the plan of Seville, though scaled down to a three-aisled version.[23] The resolution of the section was a subject of much debate, with numerous propositions being put forward. The most radical, though never realized, was that by Juan de Rasines (1490–1542) and Vasco de Zarza (died 1524), which proposed an *iglesia-salón*-style section, with the nave and adjacent aisles

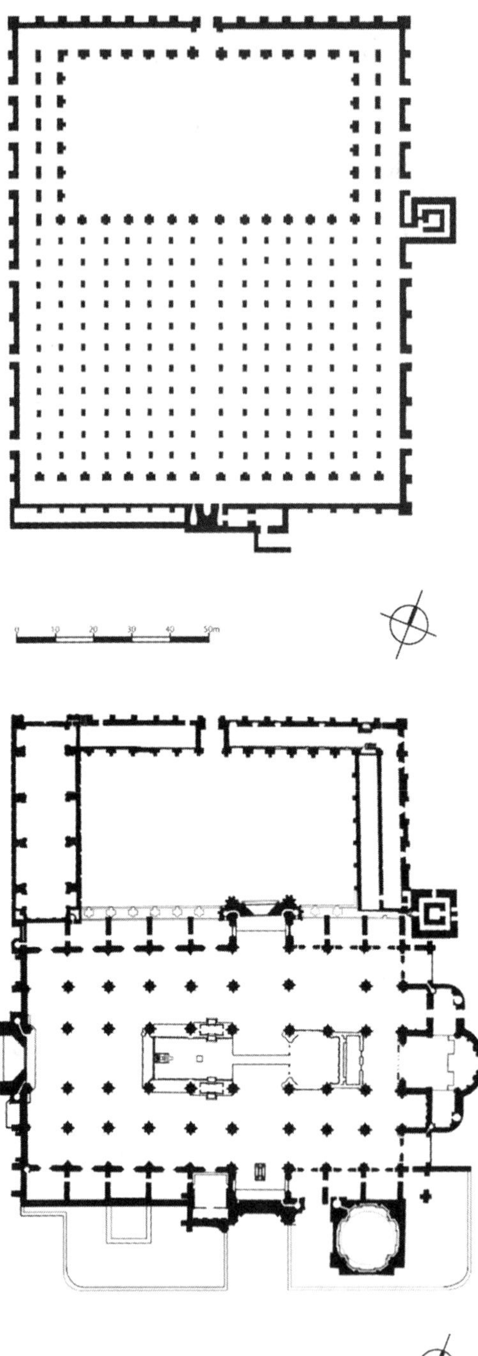

Fig. 3 . The new cathedral occupies in its entirety the footprint of the former mosque. The original courtyard of the mosque, the *Patio de los naranjos* (at the top of the plan) was preserved, together with the base of the minaret. Images by author after Almagro Gorbea 2007.

at the same height, only having the outer aisles with Seville-style cellular chapels at a lower height.

The Cathedral of Santo Domingo, Dominican Republic, was the first cathedral constructed in the Americas. The current building, begun in the 1520s and consecrated in 1541, is a purely Sevillian venture. Not only was the design sent from the Andalusian city but also the architect, Luis de Moya, and the labor used. The design of the cathedral is a three-aisled rectangular plan with the central vault only slightly higher than the aisles.

The original intent of the 1554 design for Mexico City Cathedral was to be as grand as Seville, but owing to scarcity of resources, Archbishop Montúfar contented himself with a cathedral similar in scale to Salamanca or Segovia.[24] The design was by Claudio de Arziniega (ca. 1525–1593), who prior to his departure for the Americas had spent some time in Seville, so he would have been intimately familiar with the recently completed *Magna Hispalensis.*[25] Work started in 1573 on a three-aisled *iglesia-salón* design. This was changed around 1612, when the designs for the completion of the vaults were sent to Madrid for royal approval. The Royal Architect, Juan Gómez de Mora (1586–1648), revised the project to a traditional stepped model—*escalonada*—to save time, as there was much pressure to terminate the works.[26] While the legacy of the cathedral has been traced to models of Jaen and Valladolid, the various changes in architects, as well as styles, would better define the building as an eclectic solution drawing on diverse models from the Peninsula. Nonetheless, the interior space of the cathedral retains its monumentality and openness.

Puebla Cathedral follows the three-aisled rectangular plan with cellular chapels and also was commenced with the section of an *iglesia-salón,* having its vaults at the same height. Work began in 1557 under the Extremaduran architect Francisco Becerra (ca. 1545–1605) yet, as in Mexico City, interventions in the middle of the seventeenth century changed the section to a stepped one, again for reasons of cost and time. Interestingly, the revising architect Gómez de Trasmonte (died ca. 1647) thought that the stepped section was more "modern" and less "clumsy."[27] This model is found repeatedly throughout the Americas. The cathedrals of Guadalajara and Mérida, while smaller in scale, were completed in the *iglesia-salón* model.

The development of the *iglesia-salón* as primary spatial typology of ecclesiastical architecture within Spain and the Americas was a result of a particular cultural legacy of conquest and colonization, consolidation, and evangelization. The urban and symbolic need expressed through the reappropriation of mosque and Amerindian sites and their subsequent transformation into Christian cathedrals generated a response unique to these conditions. The classical *a lo romano* assimilation of Gothic forms in the sixteenth century and their exportation to the Americas gave rise to a transcontinental model of religious space, which owing

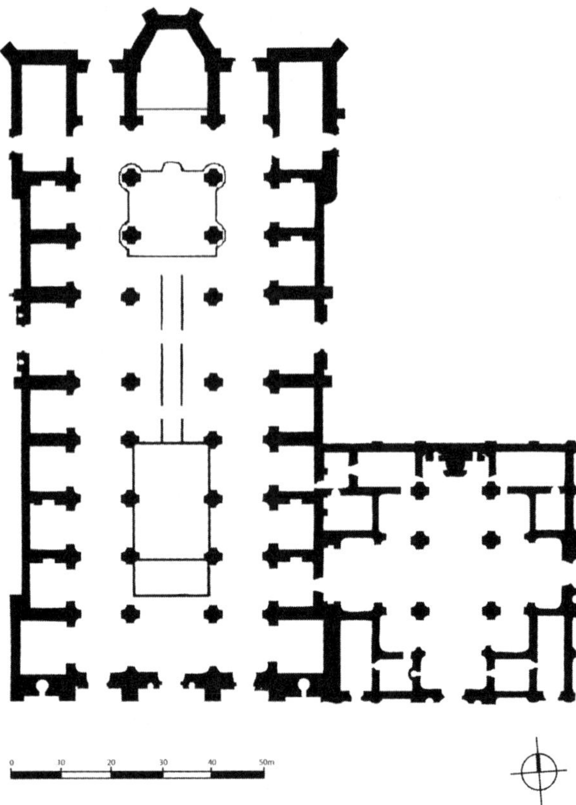

Fig. 4. Plan of Mexico City Cathedral. The interior configuration follows the Peninsula model of a "church within a church." What can be seen as an innovation here is the elongation of the *via sacra* allowing for a greater number of congregation members to be accommodated between the *coro* and *capilla mayor.* This also brings the *trascoro* much closer to the urban realm of the great Zócalo outside.

to its hybrid nature was readily transformed and reinterpreted according to need and context. Despite the numerous variations and adaptations that occurred over the centuries, one aspect of the morphology did not vary, that of the sacred reserves of the clergy—the *capilla mayor* and the *coro.* These two sites, which in essence form the liturgical nucleus of the Hispanic cathedral, were to undergo radical transformation during the seventeenth and eighteenth centuries. Accompanied by a new array of spatial typologies developed in response to the new cultural contexts of an Atlantic Baroque, the interior of Ibero-American cathedrals was to continue the symbolic and evangelical program of the previous centuries.

It could be argued that the symbolic intensity of the reconquest was manifest in the construction of the cathedrals of the Peninsula and later, by political

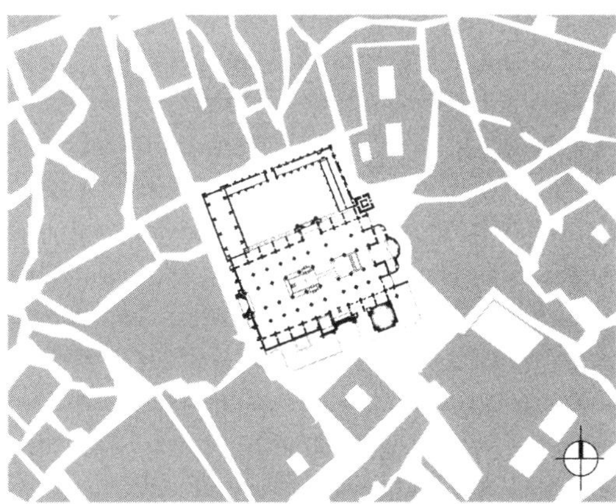

Fig. 5. This image shows the complex network of streets and squares of Seville in the eighteenth century. The urban morphology that had been implanted by the Almoravids was still the paradigm.

and religious extension, the Americas. The process of the conceptualization and actualization of religious space in the Hispanic Atlantic—seizure, conversion, reconfiguration, destruction, reconstruction, and reconfiguration—was realized as a series of synchronous ventures defined by the physical and symbolic links that united Spain with its Atlantic realms. One only needs to consider the differing cultural contexts at the end of the fifteenth century between the papal and city states of Italy and the multicultural, multifaith, transcontinental conglomeration that was "Spain" at the exact same moment. Apart from the exceptional projects of the new Saint Peter's Basilica in Rome, or that of Saint Paul's London, the cathedral age within Italy and the rest of Europe was more or less over. Their resources and invention were focused on equipping existing ancient churches with new façades, altarpieces, frescoes, and additions. Architectural experimentation and theorization was occurring on a macro-level urban exploration of individual churches and squares, and at the micro-level of the spatial configuration of chapels, all of which was occurring in completely Christianized cultures. Whereas the developments in ecclesiastical architecture and religious space in late-Medieval and Renaissance Europe followed on as part of a natural progression parallel to the shifts in philosophical and material culture, religious space in the Hispanic realm was operating in a completely different and, to some extent, completely new context.

The simultaneous "completion" and "commencement" of the reconquest and conquest at the end of the fifteenth century saw the initiation of the construction of five new cathedrals in Andalusia alone and scores commenced in the viceroyalties during the following three centuries. The venture of converting and constructing new Christianopolises in the recently converted areas of southern Spain and in alien cultural contexts of the Americas necessitated a conceptualization of religious space that would, as an inherent necessity, depart from the European paradigms. Tying into the earlier argument of the Hispanic configuration of the liturgical nucleus—that is, of a separated presbytery and choir—it could be put forward that one reason for its adoption, replication, and perseverance was, above the symbolic occupation and colonization of the Islamic plan, its suitability to the evangelical program of the reconquest and conquest.

By separating the presbytery from the choir by one or more bays, visual access to the high altar was realized. Whereas the configuration of religious space in cultures with a long tradition of Christian practice minimize, or highly control, visual permeability to the altar by means of choir screens, the need for an immediate, accessible, and popular visualization of the tenants of Christianity—the Mass and, at its climax, the Transubstantiation—in post-reconquest Spain and the Americas was of utmost priority. It could be inferred that the religious spaces of those cultures with long traditions of Christianity, or those stemming from the early church, had been conditioned to the mediation, and perhaps integral role, of the choir screen in the laity's participation in the Mass. It has even been argued that these screens and the pictographic representations on them became substitutes for the miraculous acts taking place within, which the excluded laity might only glimpse.[28] This can be seen in the configuration and demarcation of the interior space in the double-choir configuration of Visigothic Spanish churches, the *jubé* in France, *lettner* in Germany, *tramezzo* in Italy, or rood screen in England.

The symbolic and physical role of an impermeable screen was, in the Spanish configuration, displaced westward to form the rear wall of the choir or, as it is known, the *trascoro.* The physical barrier demarcates the profane world of the urban exterior as well as the sacred clerical reserve of the choir. It is similarly walled to the north and south. Ironwork grilles—*rejas*—close off the spaces that front the crossing, allowing the laity close physical proximity and complete visual permeability into the liturgical nucleus. This act of visual engagement and physical proximity to the ceremony of the Mass, instigated as a norm in Spanish cathedrals some three hundred years before the Council of Trent, would have no doubt been beneficial in the evangelical mission of the Spanish church grappling with the task of converting and maintaining the converted Muslim and Jewish Spaniards and the Amerindian population.

In a feature common to many New World cathedrals, the distance between the *capilla mayor* and *coro* is extended to a maximum, generally at least three or more bays, allowing for a larger congregation to be incorporated into the principal space. The *via sacra,* the narrow balustraded passage that links the two clerical reserves, is transformed into an elongated processional path, which would have provided for an opportunity to elaborate an even more sumptuous and pompous celebration of the Divine Offices. The greater number of laity accommodated with closer physical and visual proximity to the ceremonial enactment can be read as a spatial and programmatic response to the need for an immediate and impressive form of sensorial evangelization.

Given that many of the great cathedrals in Spain and the Americas were not begun until the sixteenth century, it was inevitable that the construction process would drag on well into the succeeding centuries owing to the sheer scale and ambition of the projects, economic crises—which acutely affected building in the early seventeenth century—war and rebellion, or natural disaster. The completion of the fabric of the structure, especially the closing of the nave vaults, was the main determining factor that influenced the configuration of ecclesiastical space. With the completion of the vaults, work could begin on equipping the interior with the necessary spaces appropriate for a building of cathedral rank. The time lag between ideation and realization meant that the church authorities inheriting the completed spaces had to contend with what was, in essence, an outmoded model of conceiving religious space. While it must be acknowledged that ecclesiastical practice and hierarchy were characterized by inertia, the cultural contexts of the seventeenth and eighteenth centuries were markedly different from those of the fifteenth and sixteenth centuries and thus demanded a spatial response adequate for the times.

The Ecclesiastical Interior and the Culture of the Atlantic Baroque

The architecture of the Hispanic Baroque is fundamentally an architecture of the interior. The contained and controllable environments of the interior were conducive to the theatrical elaboration of artifice—an artifice not contrary to nature but rather an improved version of it. The Baroque mindset conceived of nature as a work of ingenious divinity and the world as a *máquina* designed according to plan and doctrine.[29] Through artifice man imitated God and emulated nature, creating new worlds, and as the seventeenth-century painter Federico Zuccari stated, "with the aid of painting and sculpture, one can produce new paradises on earth."[30] This idea of creating a new Christian world was fundamental to the ideology of the American conquest and the resultant material culture. Baroque space was a revolt against classicist concerns, displacing decorum with wonder, marvel, and novelty or, as the eminent historian José Antonio Maravall noted, "the Spanish mentality of the Baroque epoch had the general quality of deriving satisfaction from all artifice, from whatever ingenious invention of human art that appeared, in terms of the novelty it offered."[31]

It is important not to trivialize the Baroque by assuming that all wonder was created with the same means for the same ends. Within the Baroque there were varying degrees of wonder, "some glittering and cheap, others more subtle and rare,"[32] and any type of wonder requires the experiensor to be ignorant to some degree of the causes of the experience. Without ignorance there can be no curiosity. The mechanisms of the Baroque failed against those so erudite or skeptical to see through the show, nor was it effective against those so ignorant or uninformed that they displayed no natural curiosity. Set squarely as its target were the urban masses of the New and Old Worlds, hungry for novelty, distraction, and diversion.

The predominant spatial typologies developed during the Ibero-American Baroque can all be considered as artifices of wonder; each operating via different means to create different effects, for different targets and different experiences. The term that may best describe these constructions is *máquina*—machine. This term can be used to describe anything from a large and sumptuous building, a speculative or fantastical design, a theater machine, something assembled from many parts to form a whole, and on a literal and symbolic level a device that takes advantage of, directs, or regulates the action of a force.[33] Consider the notion raised by the last section of the possible uses attributed to *máquinas*. If it is a device that "takes advantage of, directs, or regulates the action of a force," these spaces are, in the context of Maravall's analysis of Baroque culture, true machines of hierarchical power: "the culture of the baroque is an instrument to achieve effects whose object is to act upon human beings. . . . In sum, the baroque is nothing but a complex of cultural media *[medios]* of a very diverse sort that are assembled and articulated to work adequately with human beings . . . so as to succeed practically in directing them and keeping them integrated in the social system."[34]

The social system in question was the church and Crown, each using architecture as a *medio* for its own ends. The Crown and the entailing aristocracy and municipal authorities were the promoters of palaces, gardens, squares, city gates, fountains, bull rings, and ephemera constructed for celebrations. Whereas the legacy of the Crown was exterior, urbanistic, and façade-based, that of the church was an interiorized continuation of that ribbon—ecclesiastical space was an extension of the civic space, governed by liminal conditions, yet still completely integrated. These ecclesiastical spaces, like the town square, were assembled from multiple façades housed under vaults instead of open to the sky, and inversely during great festivities exterior urban spaces would be transformed into interior spaces by means of ephemeral altars, and temporary hoardings painted to simulate rich church interiors.[35]

These interior spaces of churches and cathedrals, like the palaces, fountains, and bull rings, were a *medio* for the church. The integration in this context was, on the one hand, the Counter-Reformation and on the other, the evangelization of the New World. In an attempt to stem the influences of Protestantism, and in the larger Atlantic context, suppress Islamic, Jewish and Amerindian beliefs, the promulgation, repackaging, and revamping of church dogma through an emphasis on popular devotion combined with a reformed liturgy to have an enormous effect on ecclesiastical art and architecture on both sides of the Atlantic. This new modality resulted in subsequent metamorphosis of the arts. The scholar María Teresa Sánchez Albarracín saw the shift in artistic production determined by an intrinsic change in the reasons for production, stating: "If we accept that previously religious art had a spiritual goal, aimed at pure and simple religious exaltation; it now had to strive to have a social intervention, one which modified determined behaviour of the population."[36]

The modified religious behavior of the population within the context of ecclesiastical space in the Atlantic had as its roots the reforms of the Council of Trent and by extension a continuance of the evangelical program of the early conquest. Fundamental to the way in which people were to experience the liturgy within the space was a number of key factors related to dogma. First, the importance of the Eucharist was primary: the council reaffirmed the real presence of Christ through the Transubstantiation, and validated the worship, exposition, and veneration of the Eucharist. Visual accessibility to the Eucharist was now of primary importance in the configuration of the interior space. Second, the Mass was not to be a mere reminder of the Paschal gathering but an act of continual renovation of Christ's sacrifice, to be participated in frequently and as the consummate act of Christian practice. Greater congregational participation at Mass would therefore require that the interior space, especially in front of the main altar, be capacitated to accommodate increased numbers. Finally, the validation of the invocation of saints, their relics and sacred imagery, would not only result in the proliferation of specific devotional spaces dedicated to these practices but also ensure that the threat of iconoclasm would remain far from the centers of Catholic artistic production.

While the decrees of Trent did not specifically rule on architectural issues, they did, however, urge a general reform of the arts, music, and architecture, noting that their primary purpose was for sacred, pious, and didactic purposes and not a case of *ars gratia artis*—an accusation that had been leveled at much of the artistic production in the decades prior to and during the council. The immediate changes in ecclesiastical space that occurred in Spain and the Americas directly as a result of the council are not as tangible as might first be thought. The responsibility of instigating and administrating the reforms was at a diocesan level; thus, despite the council's desire to reduce the instances of heterodox practices, it was, in effect, very difficult to enforce. This was the case in the Spanish realm, where the tradition of positioning the *coro* in the middle of the nave, *al español,* was challenged in light of the reforms mentioned above. It is interesting to note that, although opinion was divided over the location of the *coro,* a number of views held that the traditional disposition *al español* of presbytery, congregation, and *coro* allowed the congregation much greater visible access to the altar and kept the area clear for the clergy.[37] A petition in 1605 to the Sacra Rituum Congregatio (the body of the Roman Curia that regulates liturgical practice) by a number of Spanish cathedral chapters pleading an exemption under a case of traditional usage was successful.[38] The success of the 1605 petition of exemption essentially curtailed any radical reform of ecclesiastical space in the Hispanic world, at least in regard to cathedrals, where institutional hierarchy and its physical manifestations were of the utmost importance.

The few examples of Tridentine reform that had a direct impact on the trajectory of Spanish-Atlantic architecture are both by Juan de Herrera (1530–1597): the Basilica of El Escorial and the incomplete Cathedral of Valladolid. The Basilica of the Escorial was the centerpiece of Felipe II's program for the palace/monastery complex, where art, architecture, and music were mimetic conceptions of Counter-Reformation and Tridentine ideals. The Cathedral of Valladolid, designed around 1580, is not only of great importance in terms of Herrera's production but also in terms of the configuration of the interior space. In Herrera's plans for the cathedral, what immediately draws attention is the configuration of the presbytery and the *coro*. Embodying to the letter the reforms of Trent, the altar is placed in clear view of the congregation in the nave. The *retablo* is not present, allowing the altar to regain its symbolism of a place of sacrifice.[39] The nave is kept clear to accommodate the masses, and the *coro* is placed behind the altar—what is in essence a retrochoir. Perhaps owing to the nonrealization of the project, as designed by Herrera, this configuration was never really adopted in Spain, though it did find more acceptance in neighboring Portugal.

The spatial configuration conferred through interior reconfiguration was not typically unified or legible in a conventional sense. Once again I return to the idea of the ecclesiastical space of the Ibero-American Baroque conceived not as exterior form containing interior—an interior housing furniture and ornament—but instead propose the model of an enclosed space, a form of "sacred black box" in which multiple *máquinas* operate much like a theater of machines. Florian Nelle wrote in relation to the ideation of instruments and theater during the Baroque: "Instruments have a double function in the seventeenth century. They are a source of wonder and at the same time are intended to aid orientation in the new reality they reveal. . . . it applies especially to instruments of political culture, which reveal new forms of society. In particular this includes the theatre of machines, which not only visualizes that transformation of literary myths into the world of the absolutist state, but also performs it on stage. . . . This accessible utopia can become the scene for stagings of faith, power, and science."[40]

Using Nelle's analysis as a lens, one can read the above statement in the context of Ibero-American architecture, where through new spatial typologies that operate in the same manner as instruments and machines, the utopia of salvation

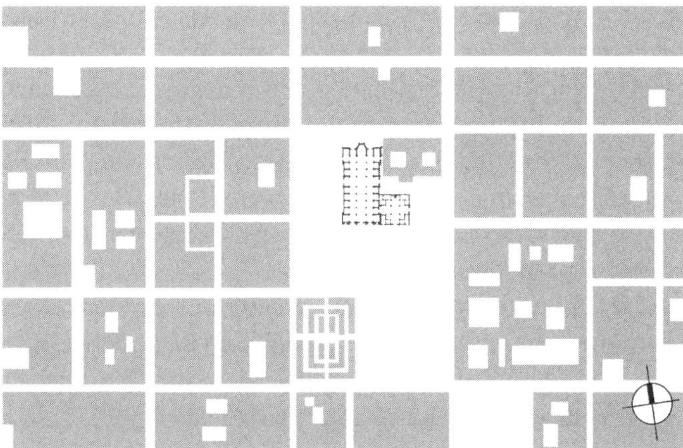

Fig. 6. This image shows the relationship between the cathedral interior and the urban environment in the eighteenth century. The Augustinian model of a gridded Christianopolis replaces the Peninsula labyrinthine model. At the heart of the city is the cathedral, and by extension, its heart is the *coro* and *capilla mayor.*

becomes accessible to the masses faithful to church and Crown and, perhaps of particular pertinence to the Americas, the condition of Spanish rule and the Christian faith.

The conception and construction of a Christian—and Spanish—utopia in the Americas conscripted architectural and urban space from its very inception. The imposition of a gridded city plan, at its center church and Crown, was diametrically opposed to the Islamic legacy of the Peninsula with its labyrinthine urbanism. This move clearly stated the desire for a new, ordered, humanistic society current with philosophy and architectural theory of the time. The spatial manifestation of this utopia did not dissolve as the realization of its impossibility became evident in the seventeenth century; instead it adapted and transformed itself to a modified "accessible utopia" of the Baroque. The *iglesia-salón* which had been the Spanish model of utopic Christian space, in essence an act of colonial imposition, became in the seventeenth and eighteenth centuries the site of transformation through which the "new reality" and "new form" of the post-utopian colonial society was revealed. Fueled by the decadence of the programs of the reconquest and conquest, the Hispanic Baroque burned the reserves of remaining vigor in a brilliant and spectacular manner. Even if utopia was never to be realized on Earth, the soul could, however, be temporarily transported in a moment of sensorial ecstasy.

As such, for the designers of Ibero-American Baroque, it could be argued that it was not so much the contemporary concerns of an abstract space that was a primary design parameter but rather the resurfacing—*revistimiento*—of space, whether extant or new, equipping it with and for the correct and efficacious operation of these *máquinas, retablos, camarines,* sacramental chapels, organ cases, and ephemera. As Jan Lazardzig stated, "a performance aimed at an audience is essential to the idea of the machine in the seventeenth century. Relating to the audience is necessary in bridging the gap between illusion and reality, and allows the machine to become an object of admiration and therefore be guaranteed to 'function.' Accordingly, the machine denotes a technique of persuasion, defining perspectives and actions."[41]

These *máquinas* populate and define the interior spaces of churches, cathedrals, and convents, each a distinct *medio* employed for different purposes with distinct techniques of persuasion. Those aspects of popular religious fervor—Marianism, the cult of the Eucharist, saints, and relics—were the grounds that these new spatial types exploited to maximum effect. The spaces were relatively intimate in comparison to the larger volume of the church or cathedral, intensifying the personal experience and aiding the communion with the sacred. The subjective (personal devotion) is paired with the collective (the liturgy, the saints, processions) in typically Baroque fashion. Contrast is effected to its maximum in the manner in which the intense focal points set up by the *máquinas* are played off against the main volume of the space, which is generally quite simple, especially if it is a Gothic or classical space. It is this suite of machines that could be seen to best define the conception of architectural space in the context of seventeenth- and eighteenth-century Spain and the Americas.

The *Máquina* and the Configuration of Baroque Ecclesiastical Space

To demonstrate the manner in which ecclesiastical space was conceived as a rhetorical device, I return to the idea of the machine and its role in the configuration of the Baroque interior. The multivalent nature and application of the term *máquina* can be seen from its entry in the 1780 edition of the dictionary of the Real Academia Española. The definitions it is accorded are these: an artifice of wood, or other material to realize something; a great deal of something; a grand and sumptuous building; a fantasy, or design from one which realizes something; a designed combination of many heterogeneous parts, with some that move; a suite of things arranged in an order that represents something.[42] The scholar Javier Aparicio Maydeu, in his study on the work of the great Baroque playwright Pedro Calderón de la Barca, insightfully noted that the hagiographic plays of Calderón were "instruments" of ideological control, a "weapon for the inspiration and control of religious sentiment, a machine *[máquina]* of the Counter-reformation."[43] I would like to put forward the idea that the configuration of ecclesiastical space can be defined in both the physical, mechanical terms of the dictionary definition and in the ideological context as espoused by Aparicio

Maydeu. On the one hand, it is possible to see the individual elements that formed part of the interior configuration as independent autonomous machines; a *retablo* was, after all, a timber structure, which through its formal elements of design affected the experiensor and which, reaching its greatest proliferation during the Baroque, was one of the most commonly deployed weapons of mass conversion. When these individual elements are combined into a cohesive unit, a "suite of things arranged in an order which represents something," the reading of Baroque ecclesiastical space becomes far more legible, beyond the initial sensorial shock or, as in many contemporary instances, incomprehension and repulsion.

Initially I stated my intent to use Moya's journey as a symbolic structure to organize my argument. In the previous sections it was seen how the *iglesia-salón* evolved from the cathedral-mosque in the contexts of reconquest Spain. In its subsummation of the mosque, the visible trace of the vanquished was explicitly left manifest. This is best exemplified in the Cathedral of Seville, where form, space, and trace are melded into a new morphology. It is this manner of conceiving cathedral space that was implanted in the Americas. While modest in comparison to its Betic counterpart, the Cathedral of Santo Domingo is significant, as it was the first cathedral primate in the Americas and serves as the tangible link between the spatial and spiritual models of the Peninsula and the Americas. It is not here, however, that I focus my attention, but rather on the Cathedral of Mexico City, which can be considered to best demonstrates the idea of cathedral space in the Spanish Atlantic.

The Cathedral of Mexico City, built atop the former sacred precinct of the Aztec capital of Tenochtitlan, was instigated in response to the independence of the archdiocese in 1547 from its suffrage to Seville. Archbishop Montúfar (1489–1572), promoter of the project, did not want the new structure to be a mere imitation but rather a rival.[44] The tactic of reappropriation may have been adequate for the Peninsular condition but not for the utopia of New Spain. The creation of a new society necessitated the creation of new spatial and urban models. Whereas the reconfiguration and reconstruction of sacred space in reconquest Spain had been a prolonged process, the immediate destruction of *Huey Teocalli,* the Great Temple of Tenochtitlan, signaled that the program had shifted intensity. Despite the shift in intensity, the labor of constructing a great cathedral was an obstacle that could not be avoided. However, when considered in terms of cathedral-building time scale, the some one hundred years it took from the laying of the foundation stone to the closing of the nave vaults in 1667 was remarkably fast. With the fabric complete, the task of configuring the interior ecclesiastical space could begin.

In the ideation and realization of Mexico City Cathedral, both as a structure and as a space, it is possible to see how religious space was conceived and configured in the Spanish Atlantic. Whereas the cathedrals of the Peninsula were inserted into existing urban fabric and hence had their overall scale and dimensions fixed, as did the relation and interface between the interior ecclesiastical space and the exterior civic space, the cathedrals of the New World were centered in a newly configured urban model. The cathedral was located in the heart of the gridded Christianopolis; the nexus of civic and sacred is mediated by the facade, which is conceived as a retable façade—*retablo fachada*—which in the American Atlantic assumes a greater symbolic role than in the Peninsula. This idea of space, and its nexus, is repeated within the interior; the liturgical nucleus of presbytery and choir is the ecclesiastical mirror of the civic space formed outside. The Cathedral of Mexico City mirrors in the configuration of its liturgical nucleus the civic nature of the interior cathedral space.

Within the large expanse of the interior, a covered replication of the open square in front, the space is configured rhythmically by the piers and vaults. Under this stone canopy is a series of discrete spaces defined not by the structure itself but rather by the objects that inhabit it. Just as the freedom to create a new model of urban fabric resulted in new modes of organizing space, Mexico City Cathedral displays in the most salient manner the interaction between structure and interior. In a rare instance of a cathedral interior, unity of authorship allows one to experience a cohesive realization of the baroque idea of cathedral space. Each *máquina* was specifically designed to form part of the great interior suite. The series of altarpieces designed by Jerónimo Balbás (died 1748) configure the interior spaces of sacrifice from east to west, while the choir stalls and organ cases configure the clerical space north to south. Except for the lost element of Balbás's baldachin-like high altar, *el Ciprés,* destroyed in 1844, the liturgical nucleus is almost completely intact.[45] This is in contrast to other Spanish ecclesiastical interiors that were typically assemblages of different stylistic elements from differing epochs. In other cases, as has occurred in the Americas and the Peninsula, reformers and restorers have removed or destroyed key spatial elements, rendering their baroque configurations illegible.

Balbás's role as a key figure in the Ibero-American baroque has been acknowledged as far back as the late eighteenth century, though not always in a positive light. His works and those of his contemporaries were common targets for the academy critics of the Enlightenment. Agustín Ceán Bermúdez (1749–1829)—an important Spanish scholar and art historian—labeled Balbás the "heresiarch of architecture in Andalusia."[46] Despite having his reputation tarnished for nearly two hundred years, he was at the time considered the greatest designer in the realm. After the spectacular success of his *retablo mayor* of the Church of the Sagrario of Seville Cathedral, he was awarded the three commissions for Mexico City Cathedral. Whereas his magnum opus in Seville was destroyed in 1824 following pressure on the Cathedral Chapter from Ceán Bermúdez,[47] the *retablo* of the *Capilla de los Reyes* remains as testimony to the relationship between the two sides of the Spanish Atlantic during the baroque as the *iglesia-salón* had done during the previous century.

The *Capilla de los Reyes* and the *trascoro* (1725–1732), the latter reconstructed after almost being destroyed by fire in 1967, together form the key defining elements of the interior space of the Cathedral. The spatial depth of the *trascoro* is planar; the shallow spatial depth is created by the use of *estípites* that stand proud of the principal face, a common compositional technique used in both *retablos* and *trascoros* of the eighteenth century.[48] Balbás was instrumental in the introduction of the *estípite* to the *retablos* of the Seville school and later, upon his transatlantic relocation, the Americas.[49] It is not the spatial qualities of the Altar del Perdón that are of interest here but rather its use as an element within the spatial sequencing of the cathedral. Balbás's design for the *trascoro* takes the form of a triumphal arch whose composition shows great innovation of the *retablo* typology, where the arched attic story competes for attention with the main body. The emphasis of this design is the vertical, whose expression is reinforced by the two lateral aisles of the *trascoro.* With the construction of this gigantic golden screen at the rear of the *coro* that faces the great western portals opening onto the Zócalo square of the city, this space becomes a transitional space between the civic and the sacred. This altar can be defined as an interior facade to the *coro,* a true *retablo-fachada.* The relationship between horizontal gathering spaces and vertical sacred space, part of the indigenous Mesoamerican tradition, was utilized by the friars in the early evangelical period of colonization in the configuration of the open chapels of the sixteenth century, reconciling "different traditions and the unique demands of the new context."[50] It could be argued that this spatial relationship was transferred to the sacred/urban nexus of the cathedral facade and within the interior to the *trascoro.*

The "church within a church" created by the Altar del Perdón reiterates the "building within a building" configuration of the *coro*—a distinct, compartmentalized space defined by architectonic screens. The relationship between vertical planes (sacred) and horizontal planes (profane) are repeated exterior and interior, and are motives repeated throughout the configuration of ecclesiastical space of the Ibero-American baroque and its mediation with the civic space of the exterior: cathedral façade (vertical and sacred) and Zócalo (horizontal and profane) are a pairing that is repeated in the relationship between the Altar del Perdón, the vertical façade of the ecclesiastical realm of the *coro,* and the horizontal nave area in front, which is used for popular devotion. The *trascoro* is eponymous with the principal door behind which it stands, the Puerta del Perdón, mirroring the symbolic link between the two vertical planes. Whereas in the development of cathedral space in the Peninsula cultural transference had taken place within the volumetric configuration, in the American Atlantic the transference occurred in the relationship between open spaces and sacred planes.

As such, the double-façade mirror organ cases form the side walls to the *coro* and present the lateral aisles with their respective music-producing screens. These vertical walls of sight and sound are similarly used to demarcate the sacred from the profane. Ecclesiastical space was not restricted to a purely spatial configuration. The liminal configuration of space through the participation of music defined ceremony and worked together with the architecture to affect the experiensor. The double-façade mirror organ, a conception peculiar to the Ibero-American baroque cathedral, directed its potential not only inwards towards the clerical reserve but in the seventeenth and eighteenth centuries, via the rear facade, outwards towards the laity congregating in the aisles. In the 1690s Mexico City Cathedral was the first in the Spanish realm to equip itself with a new baroque model of the double-facade organ, later to be completed by its mirror twin in 1734.

The scholar Juan Anaya Duarte stated that sacred space possesses as one of its characteristics the ability to simultaneously attract and repel. It could be argued that the *trascoro* and the organ cases of Mexico City Cathedral embody this duality perhaps better than any other feature of ecclesiastical space.[51] Their elaborate and populist motifs attract visually and spiritually, sonically, and physically. The gilt lure and enchanting sounds attract the faithful and the curious deeper into the sacred space; yet, at the same moment, they repel the exterior and its associated contaminating influences of the profane world, be they physical elements such as wind, dust, and noise or other, more abstract concerns such as the preservation of the realm of the clergy and their execution of Praise and Sacrifice.

On important feast days the main portals of cathedrals were opened, allowing for the ecclesiastical and civic spaces to merge. This merging was mediated by the space in front of the *trascoro*. The *trascoro* not only performed the function of screening the sacred space of the presbytery but simultaneously provided a visual, physical, and populist presence of the church. Standing in the Zócalo looking towards and into the interior of the cathedral, the presence of the sacred is not distant but present, immediate, and accessible. This visual, spatial, and symbolic linking was a key element developed through the positioning of cathedrals on axis to the main square in the new gridded city. The architecture of the Ibero-American baroque strove for the visual attraction, sonic astonishment, and emotional affectation of the faithful through the novel, the ingenious, and the amazing, while simultaneously repelling them and reinforcing the status quos of dogma, institution, separation, and prohibition.[52]

It can be argued that the interior space of Hispanic baroque cathedrals were conceived as an integrated sum of individual architectonic elements which formed a "sacred scenography," whose narrative was the relative position of each of these individual elements within the "compositional argument" of the space as a whole.[53] This conception of space, both physically and symbolically, should be read as a fundamentally rhetorical one in which each section, while autonomous, has an integrated and sequenced role to play in the overall argument.

This particularly baroque way of perceiving and structuring the world—a world based on rhetorical structures—ingeniously argued and employing every means possible to convince and affect—permeated all aspects of material culture. An analysis of architectural space in the seventeenth and eighteenth centuries—the inheritance of compartmentalized spaces, architectonic screens, a tendency for relief detailing, and intense ornamentation—only gains force of meaning when read as tools in the architectural rhetoric of the baroque and not as means to their own ends.

These new ways of configuring space are a new spatial paradigm; as the scholar Allen Weiss stated, "the possibilities of theological symbolization unveil novel paradigms, ones in accord with the new sciences and mathematical systems being developed contemporaneously."[54] Thus, rather than being a pure throwback to some form of national architectural coding, the developments of the Ibero-American baroque were a response to the new religious, political, scientific, and artistic conditions of the times.

Conclusion

The cathedrals constructed in the viceroyalties of the Americas should not be considered as mere imitations or direct transplantations from the Peninsula. Apart from the obvious stylistic differences in their realization, the conception of religious space within these structures goes far beyond the mimicry of distant sources. Ecclesiastical space in the Americas, as can be seen in the case of Mexico City Cathedral, demonstrates a synthesis and development of the Hispanic model. Propelled by a continuing need for the ongoing evangelization of the population, the models of space developed on the Peninsula were extended to their limits, first in the *iglesia-salón,* and second in the transformation of these models during the Baroque.

The development of the *iglesia-salón* as the primary typology for cathedral-space in the Spanish Atlantic was the result of a synchronous program of building in the Peninsula and the Americas. The conditions of the conquest and reconquest provided the religious, political, philosophical, and spatial framework that enabled the universal adoption of the particular mode of ecclesiastical space that originated with the occupation, reconfiguration, and rebuilding of mosque spaces, and was later reinterpreted and redeployed for the new contexts of the American Atlantic. Fundamental to this is the role that the liturgical nucleus *al español* played within the internal configuration of the cathedral space and, in the American context, that of the extended urban space. While the extent of this role varied in each particular city and structure, the embedding of the clerical reserve in the very heart of the cathedral—the most important enclosed space in the imagining of the Hispanic culture—provides insight into the way in which religious space was conceived and configured in the Atlantic world of the early modern age. This conception at its most sophisticated responded to and embodied the complex, heterodox, and conflicting nature of the cultures and faiths it simultaneously oppressed, symbolized, and celebrated.

PART FOUR

IDENTITIES

Emigration, Transatlantic Communication, and Methodist Identity in Nineteenth-Century Ontario and Québec

Todd Webb

On March 20, 1855, readers of the *Watchman,* one of the leading newspapers of the Wesleyan Methodist Church in Britain, had the chance to peruse a report from "Theophilus," identified as "our correspondent" in the British North American colonies of Lower and Upper Canada—present-day Québec and Ontario. At first glance, the article appeared to be a celebration of the present and future connections between the Methodists in the two Canadas and Britain. Theophilus described the efforts of his fellow Canadian Methodists to raise £10,000 that year for the Wesleyan Methodist Missionary Society (WMMS) in London, England. The leading Canadian laity had mastered the lessons taught by their metropolitan counterparts—"the Farmers, Healds, Smiths, Woods, and Chappels" of British Wesleyanism, whose "zeal hath provoked many here for the fame of their doings long ago reached us." Theophilus also wrote—thirty years before the fact, as it turned out—about the completion of a transcontinental railway linking eastern British North America with the colony of British Columbia. "When that takes place," he stated, the Canadian Methodists could expect visits from "Wesleyan Missionaries" on their way from Britain to "China or Australasia, or somewhere else on the other side of the globe, where they can find . . . souls without salvation. I am sure such visitations will be welcome." Having already learned from the British Wesleyan example, Canadian Methodism was set to become the great conduit of communication between the church in Britain and its missions in the East. The transatlantic links between the British Wesleyan and Canadian Methodist communities seemed to be on the high road to perfection.

And yet, while applauding the current and future connections between Canadian Methodism and British Wesleyanism, Theophilus also raised some troubling points about the overall relationship between the colonies and the metropole. He pointed out, rather tartly, that "many of the people of Britain, and professing intelligence too, blunder sadly when they speak of us." He wondered, "Does Canada know more of England than England does of Canada?"[1] In other words, how exactly did colonies such as Lower and Upper Canada fit into the British Empire? And, more specifically, to what extent had settler groups, such as the Methodists, managed to overcome the various challenges to political and cultural integration posed by geographical distance? In one form or another, these questions exercised the minds of British colonists throughout the nineteenth century.[2]

Strange to say, finding answers to those questions has not been a pressing concern among historians of religion in nineteenth-century Canada. We know something about the links, at both the clerical and lay level, between British Wesleyanism and American Methodism and between the Methodists in Britain and the Canadas during the 1800s.[3] On the whole, however, scholars have been more interested in examining what they describe as the growing cultural exceptionalism of Canadian Methodism. The narrative they have constructed goes something like this: between 1791 and 1814 both the Methodist Episcopal Church in the United States and the Wesleyan Methodist Church in Britain began to send missionaries to Lower and Upper Canada. In 1820, in an effort to avoid denominational conflict, the two churches split the gospel work in the colonies, with the British Wesleyans taking Lower Canada and the American Methodists Upper Canada. Attempting to demonstrate their loyalty to Britain, the Upper Canadian Methodist Episcopals distanced themselves from the American church during the 1820s. In 1828 they formed the independent Methodist Episcopal Church in Canada, or, more simply, the Canadian Methodist Church. Five years later, in 1833, the Canadian Methodists agreed to unite with the British Wesleyans, forming the Wesleyan Methodist Church in Canada. That partnership did not go well. The liberal Canadian Methodists clashed with the conservative British Wesleyans, and the union collapsed in 1840. There followed seven years of conflict between the British Wesleyans and the Canadian Methodists. In 1847, thanks to the impact of a number of internal and external forces, the British Wesleyans and the Canadian Methodists reunited. In 1854 the British Wesleyan community in Lower Canada was folded into the larger Canadian Methodist Church. That arrangement persisted well beyond 1874, when the British Wesleyans and Canadian Methodists finally agreed to go their separate ways. By the time the Canadian Methodists became independent in 1874, they were, we are told, a culturally unique group within North Atlantic Methodism, poised between the radicalism of American evangelical Protestantism and the conservatism of British Wesleyanism. In this account, the British Wesleyans were an other against whom the Canadian Methodists defined their sense of self.[4]

This essay takes a different tack, arguing that during the nineteenth century the Methodists in Lower and Upper Canada did not become a distinct cultural group; instead, they were increasingly integrated into a larger transatlantic world and culture. This was true of both the British Wesleyan community in the Canadas and the Canadian Methodists, despite the denominational upheavals of the 1830s, 1840s, and 1850s. A powerful missionary impulse within British Wesleyanism and mass migration from Britain to Lower and Upper Canada helped forge a sense of belonging to what David Armitage and others call the Atlantic World—an area of cultural exchange and contestation, in which a variety of interconnected societies took shape in Europe, the Americas, and Africa after 1492. But where Armitage argues that the history of that region came to an end "with the age of revolutions in the late eighteenth and early nineteenth centuries," the Methodist case demonstrates that the analytical possibilities of Atlantic history extend well into the nineteenth century.[5] To situate the Methodists of Britain and the Canadas within that paradigm, however, the insights of J. G. A. Pocock are essential. As Pocock points out, any form of national or local exceptionalism, whether political, social, or cultural, was a rarity rather than a norm, particularly in Britain's Atlantic world. Colonies of settlement, like Lower and Upper Canada, were part "of an expanding zone of cultural conflict and creation" emanating from the British Isles. That is not to say that the process of cultural formation among the Methodists and other groups in the Canadas was a "simple one-way imperial success story." It was full of ambivalences, leading to the creation of a "diversity of interacting and varyingly autonomous cultures" within the larger framework of British identity.[6]

But how exactly did those transplanted British cultures take shape? To answer that question, one must look to the spatial turn in the humanities. Drawing on advances in GIS mapping, scholars have become increasingly aware of the "influence of physical or geographical space on human behavior and cultural development." That is not to say that historians have had an easy job of it. As Edward Ayers argued, "trying to comprehend space, place, and time in concert has always proven difficult." A growing awareness of the close link between space and time has, nevertheless, opened up new ways to understand cultural development within the Atlantic World. The idea of "deep contingency" is a case in point. As Ayers notes, by fusing a sense of both place and time, "deep contingency tries to suggest how societies can change their self-understanding quickly and profoundly."[7] Just such a rapid and far-reaching cultural change occurred among the British Wesleyans and Canadian Methodists of Lower and Upper Canada during the nineteenth century. It was driven forward by the bureaucratic failures of the WMMS and the difficulty of conquering geographic distance in an era before reliable transoceanic communication. Both of those factors created a highly important but hitherto overlooked spatial and temporal division between Methodism in Britain and the Canadas. That divide frequently left the Methodists in the two colonies feeling ignored or abandoned by the Wesleyan church on the other side of the Atlantic. In response, the ministers and laity of Lower and Upper Canada, whether they were British or North American by birth, began to insist on their equality with, if not superiority to, their coreligionists in Britain. As a result, by the mid-1800s a new but recognizably British culture had taken root among the Methodists in the Canadas. They had become near-perfect examples of British loyalists: a group that asserted "a British identity for reasons not always apparent or agreeable to the makers of policy and opinion in the United Kingdom."[8]

I

The roots of that cultural change lay deep in the Methodist past. Thanks to the frequently conflicting aims of its founder, John Wesley, Methodism was built on a series of contradictions. It was centralized but flexible; it was autocratic, in terms of its government, but also populist and expansive. These contrasting forces powered the growth of Methodism on both sides of the Atlantic in the eighteenth and early nineteenth centuries.

John Wesley was notoriously dictatorial when it came to denominational government. He jealously guarded the prerogative of determining which laity could or could not become Methodists; he alone had the power to appoint, ordain, dismiss, and station ministers; and he controlled the money raised among the laity to support the ministry and to fund both chapel building and overseas missions. When Wesley died in 1791, all his power passed to the conference—a gathering of all the ministers in the church that took place every summer. The vast majority of the laity had no direct voice in the central governing body of their own church. As Wesley himself said in 1790, "we are no republicans, and never intend to be. It would be better for those that are so minded to go quietly away." Most members of the conference agreed. Each year that assembly struck different committees to station the preachers, to determine if any of them needed to be disciplined, and to decide who might make a valuable addition to the ministerial ranks. If the rules of the church needed revising, only the conference could make the changes; if the church was racked by doctrinal dispute, only the conference could settle it. When critics of the conference argued that it had all the makings of a vast engine of ministerial despotism, they were not far off the truth.[9]

Yet the denominational structure that Wesley bequeathed to his followers allowed the Wesleyan Methodist Church to exploit any opening that appeared among Britain's sinful multitudes. Wherever groups of men and women were attracted by the Methodist promise of eternal salvation, Wesley or one of his preachers organized them into societies. The laity who made up these societies met once a week in smaller groups, known as classes or class meetings, to monitor one another's spiritual progress. Methodist ministers visited every society and its classes regularly, traveling from one group to another on a set circuit, preaching and making new converts as they went. In 1791 the conference grouped the circuits into larger administrative units—the districts—each overseen by a chairman selected from among the church's senior ministers.[10]

Since few itinerant preachers could cover every part of a circuit in a week, Wesley and his successors also appointed a number of laymen to help the ministry carry the load. Unordained and unpaid lay or local preachers conducted services for each society when the regular minister was unavailable; trustees made sure that any chapels the church built or bought were only used by Methodist preachers; stewards drew up the financial accounts for every chapel, society, and circuit; and class leaders supervised the weekly class meetings. Every three months the itinerant preachers held a meeting with all the lay officials on each circuit to deal with the spiritual and secular concerns of their specific part of the church. These Quarterly Meetings were, however, subordinate to the conference and, after 1791, to the annual all-ministerial district meetings as well. Still, expansion was relatively easy under this regime: when new societies were formed, a minister divided them into classes, while the conference created a new circuit, assigned a minister to make the rounds, and permitted him to call as many laymen into the field as the work might require. There were 7 circuits in Britain in 1746; there were 114 forty-five years later.[11]

Wesley never had any intention, however, of confining his redeeming mission to the British Isles. In March 1739, less than a year after he experienced his own conversion, Wesley began to conceive his efforts to spread scriptural holiness throughout the land in broader terms. "I look upon *all the world* as *my parish,*" he stated. "This is the work I know God has called me to." Nine years later, Wesley was more convinced than ever of his divinely ordained purpose. Writing from Dublin, he noted that "whenever I see one or a thousand men running into hell, be it in England, Ireland or France, yea, in Europe, Asia, Africa or America, I will stop them if I can; as a minister of Christ, I will beseech them in His name to turn back and be reconciled to God."[12] Wesley made little distinction between the gospel work at home and abroad. His preachers would go anywhere, among any people who might benefit from the Methodist brand of evangelical Protestantism, whether the strictly heathen or fellow Britons who were settling the colonies of the Empire.

Thanks to Wesley's flexible approach to denominational growth, Wesleyan Methodism spread quickly throughout the North Atlantic region. From the 1760s on, Wesley directed the activities of Methodist ministers in the Thirteen Colonies, Nova Scotia, Newfoundland, Prince Edward Island, and the West Indies. Reacting to millennial expectations produced by the French Revolution, a headstrong minister, Thomas Coke, traveled to Paris in 1791 to establish a new mission. That episode ended badly—revolutionaries threatened to hang Coke and two other missionaries from the nearest lamppost—but the ongoing mission to what had become the United States of America scored spectacular successes.[13] In the mid-1780s the political forces unleashed by the American Revolution and rapid denominational growth among the Methodists in the former colonies combined to create the independent Methodist Episcopal Church in the United States. Two hundred fifty-two itinerant preachers were overseeing 129 circuits by 1791.[14] That same year, the American Methodists also began to establish circuits among the settlers in the British North American colonies of Lower and Upper Canada.

II

A Methodist Episcopal mission to Lower and Upper Canada made sense as long as the English-speaking population of those colonies was 80 percent American by birth or descent. The American Methodist preachers certainly saw the Canadas as an extension of their gospel field in New England and upstate New York.[15] But the forces of demographic change unleashed by the ending of the Napoleonic Wars and the politics of loyalty in the British North American colonies altered that situation.

More than a million people from the United Kingdom crossed the Atlantic and settled in Britain's North American colonies between 1815 and 1874. From 1815 to 1837 alone, more settlers from England, Ireland, and Scotland made their way to British North America than to the United States or the other colonies of the Empire. These numbers dropped in the 1840s, but remained sizeable through the 1850s and 1860s.[16] In the early period of mass migration, between 1815 and 1835, the majority of immigrants were Scots or Irish Protestants. Methodists probably constituted a small percentage of the Lowlanders who left Scotland for the Canadas; a much more significant number of Irish Protestant settlers were Methodists. By 1871 Methodists made up 34 percent of the Irish Protestant families in Ontario. Most of these were Wesleyans, with only a small number belonging to various British Wesleyan splinter groups, such as the Primitive Methodists and the Bible Christians.[17] The flood tide of English emigration began in the 1830s, and it persisted until the closing of the Upper Canadian frontier in the 1850s and 1860s. Until boom times returned in the early 1870s, yearly immigration from England was measured in thousands rather than tens of thousands. As was the case among the Irish Protestants, many of these English emigrants were Wesleyan Methodists.[18] The fact that the early stages of English migration to the Canadas were dominated by movement out of Yorkshire and the northern counties made this almost inevitable: that region was the heartland of Wesleyan Methodism in nineteenth-century Britain.[19]

Wesleyan ministers in Britain might very well complain, then, about emigration reducing the church membership in some parts of England and Ireland, but at the same time the Methodist population of Lower and Upper Canada was becoming more British and Wesleyan by the year.[20] As their letters and journals attest, both the British Wesleyan missionaries stationed in the Canadas and their American Methodist counterparts were keenly aware of this demographic shift. Everywhere these ministers went, they found settlers with close ties to the Wesleyan church in Britain. While traveling through the Eastern Townships of Lower Canada in 1822, for instance, the British missionary John DePutron lodged "with a kind and affectionate family who emigrated from Holderness [in Yorkshire] about 2 years ago." He added, "I refer to Mr. Tho[ma]s Hewson, who is well known in that part of England to many of our preachers." Two years later, in the vicinity of Peterborough, Upper Canada, the American Methodist preacher Anson Green came across "a godly old Yorkshire woman," an Irish Methodist lay preacher "by the name of Blackstock," and "a sterling family, who were Wesleyans in England," all in the space of a week.[21]

The British Wesleyan missionaries and American Methodist ministers in Lower and Upper Canada responded to this influx in the same way: rather than building up their numbers through conversions alone, they turned a considerable portion of their energies to incorporating as many of the immigrants as possible into their respective churches. The British missionaries, for instance, attempted to reach out to any of their recently arrived coreligionists who came through the towns and cities of the Canadas, sometimes giving them money raised among pioneers who had already established themselves.[22] More often, however, they formed such settlers into societies and classes on the established Wesleyan pattern.[23] The missionaries also made efforts to keep in close contact with "fellow countrymen" who were "obliged to [go] into the wilderness, where there is no Temple, no Priest, [n]or place of public worship, to which they have access." In the early 1830s, in a characteristic move, the missionaries formed a new society among the "Methodists from Ireland" near Wesleyville on the eastern bank of the Ottawa River. The American Methodist preachers also followed the Wesleyan immigrants from Britain as they moved into areas like South Monaghan and Cavan townships in Upper Canada. They formed new societies around the town of York during the 1820s, primarily serving the English, Irish, and Scottish arrivals, who "generally expressed a desire to have the Gospel preached among them." Traveling through New Ireland, Lower Canada, in 1837, the British missionary John Borland described the outcome of this effort. Through the "instrumentality" of dedicated ministers like himself, many settlers had been "reclaimed from their . . . wanderings in apostasy, who, were previously to their coming to this country united in church fellowship with our people in Europe."[24]

In the process, the Methodists in Lower and Upper Canada began to conceptualize those colonies as extensions of the British Wesleyan gospel field, no less deserving of attention and support than Ireland or the dark corners of Lancashire. Within a year of arriving in Lower Canada, the British Wesleyan missionaries wrote to their superiors in London, England, arguing that "the great and continual emigration" from the United Kingdom, "among whom there are many Methodists," called for the dispatch of more preachers to the province and the town of Kingston in Upper Canada. The missionaries saw the rest of Upper Canada in the same light. At the very least, the town of York required a British Wesleyan minister: "vast numbers of emigrants from the United Kingdom of Great Britain are resorting there every year," James Booth noted, "and many of them are the fruit of your labours at home, and many of them children of praying parents[;] how desirable should it be to have a British Missionary here, to direct them in a strange land, to the stranger's friend." Similarly, at L'Achigan, Lower Canada, James Knowlan found "settlers . . . from Ireland & Scotland; but chiefly from the former; and they are in great want of spiritual instruction." They were, he made sure to point out, "most anxious to have a Missionary among them."[25] From the missionaries' point of view, migration to the Canadas was creating both opportunities and obligations for the British Wesleyan church.

British Wesleyan settlers, particularly in Upper Canada, tended to situate themselves in the same transatlantic context. In January 1820 the laity around Newcastle, Upper Canada, pointed out that seven townships in their district were "newly settled and now settling upon by European emigrants, many of whom belonged to the Methodist Society at home" and who were "anxious to have continuation of those enjoyments with which they were blessed in their highly favoured country." Eight months later another group of settlers in Upper Canada asked a missionary who passed through whether the Wesleyan hierarchy in Britain would send them a minister. "If our preachers in Ireland only knew our state," they said, "we are sure they would send one." In 1841 the laity in Kingston, Upper Canada, wrote that while "your Memorialists beg leave to state that . . . we are favoured with the labours and pastoral care of the British Wesleyan Missionaries[,] there are hundreds of our fellow men residing in the surrounding Country who are destitute of the instructions of those Ministers whom they regard and love." "Most of those persons have emigrated from Great Britain within the last twenty years," they added, "and were brought to a knowledge of the truth under the . . . ministry of the Wesleyan Ministers at home and on this account . . . they feel warmly attached to that Body." The Kingston settlers also pointed out that preparations were being made for the reception of "a great influx of emigrants from England, Ireland & Scotland," many of whom would be Wesleyans with "a claim" on the "attentions and pastoral care" of the church in the old country.[26]

In addition to demographic change, there was a political dimension to this lay demand for British missionaries. In the aftermath of the Loyalist exodus and the War of 1812, loyalty to Britain defined the political culture of Anglo-American settler society in Lower and Upper Canada. In that context it is not surprising to find the leading laity of Montréal complaining in 1815 that their association with Methodist Episcopal preachers from the United States had led others to see them as "a *nest of sedition.*" "This," the Montréalers stated, "is an odium which as British Subjects we cannot endure; we are willing to bear all the indignity and reproach which wicked men may cast upon us for the Cross of Christ, but to have our fidelity as Britons suspected we cannot [abide] with." Five years later, laymen near Newcastle, Upper Canada, argued that the labors of an "American Methodist Preacher . . . were they sufficient, are for many reasons, unacceptable to the inhabitants of Canada." The political opinions of the Methodist Episcopal ministers were repugnant to the colonial authorities, and this had "much limited their usefulness to His Majesty's subjects, many of whom, though not opposed to Methodism, never hear them."[27] American Methodists in the Canadas, both preachers and laity, struck back during the 1810s and early 1820s, making strident claims to their own loyalist credentials. Despite those efforts, British Wesleyan laity continued to level charges of republicanism and possible treason against the Canadian Methodists into the 1830s.[28] Such accusations were given added weight during the rebellions against the colonial governments of Lower and Upper Canada in 1837 and 1838, in which some Methodists played a role.[29]

So, it only made sense that by the 1830s the leaders of both the British Wesleyan church and the recently independent Methodist Episcopal Church in Canada were happy to see Lower and Upper Canada as an integral part of a greater Britain. When the two churches agreed to unite in 1833, one of the most influential of the Wesleyans in Britain, Jabez Bunting, noted that "*patriotic duty* . . . recommend[s] this union. Numerous emigrants from Britain and Ireland are going every year to Canada, many of them were once part of our own flocks. They have a claim upon our sympathy and attention." Another of the British Wesleyan church's leading men, Robert Alder, reiterated Bunting's point in more sweeping terms, arguing that despite "all that has been stated by a certain class of political economists," the Canadas were entitled to "the protection and encouragements of the parent state." After all, "there are many families in the United Kingdom who have near and dear relatives settled in various parts of America, and are looking towards it as their future abode."[30] Where Britons went, British institutions, whether in church or state, must surely follow.

The Methodist Episcopal Church in Canada, or Canadian Methodists, could not agree more; and, by way of proof, they also directed their "most anxious attention" to "the many emigrants from the mother country, and especially to the professors and families of Wesleyan Methodism." It was an effort that their brethren among the British Wesleyan ministry found particularly gratifying and which they repeatedly encouraged, observing that it was "an interesting part" of Canadian Methodism's "great work to follow these sheep into the wilderness, and bring them into the fold of Christ." The Canadian Methodists responded in turn, pointing out to the lay members of their church that "among the numerous emigrants from the Mother Country . . . there are many who have been members or hearers in the Wesleyan Church at home." "They are our brethren," the Canadian Methodist ministers added, "and we should receive, and welcome, and help them as such." As the British Wesleyans proudly declared in 1862, the Methodists of the Canadas and Britain were "united by the ties of race and kindred."[31]

III

Well before the British Wesleyans and Canadian Methodists reached that happy level of unity, however, the church in Britain had to grapple with a pressing problem: how best to control its expanding overseas missions. Almost instinctively, the British ministry turned to the Wesleyan tradition of centralization. Sometimes the British Conference oversaw the mission field, but more often it delegated its authority in that area to the Wesleyan Methodist Missionary Society (WMMS). That decision had serious implications for Methodism in Lower and Upper Canada.

Organized between 1813 and 1818, the WMMS was one of the most important administrative bodies in the Wesleyan church. It was responsible for "the superintendence of the Collection and Disbursement of all Monies raised for Foreign Missions . . . and also the *General Management*" of the missions during the interval between the annual meetings of the conference. It consisted of the president and secretary of the conference, twenty-four ministers, and, in a rare departure from Wesleyan practice, twenty-four wealthy laymen. That mixed membership was also divided along regional lines. Sixteen lay and clerical members came from the English provinces, while the rest were drawn from the greater London area. In theory the entire WMMS met once a month in the capital, but in reality most of the day-to-day work of the missions was in the hands of three secretaries, each a minister appointed by the conference. At first, only one of these preachers lived in the main offices of the WMMS—the Mission House at 77 Hatton Garden, London—and "devote[d] himself on the Week-Days . . . to the service of the Missions exclusively." Eventually all three were released from regular preaching duties. The conference added a fourth secretary in 1834; they divided the mission field among them, each concentrating on a different geographical area.[32]

The WMMS aimed to keep the tightest possible control over the missions, but it was plagued by bureaucratic difficulties. At the most basic level, three or four secretaries still proved insufficient to oversee the church's increasingly far-flung missions. The sheer crush of work often seemed to be on the verge of overwhelming them. In 1820, for instance, one of the secretaries, Joseph Taylor, wrote to a missionary stationed in the Canadas explaining that "your minutes have been duly received but owing to the press of business we have not yet been able to take up the several points contained in them & when we shall be able I cannot say."[33]

In the short term the situation might improve marginally, but any unexpected development tended to throw the Mission House off kilter. In 1834 Secretary John Beecham explained the WMMS's delay in sending important information to the missionaries in Upper Canada by noting that "we were pressed . . . by the death of two of the Secretaries, and had all our Missions throughout the world to attend to, as well as the concerns of Canada." Four years later, another secretary, Robert Alder, described receiving forty-five letters from "Caffraria, & other parts of S. Africa; from St. Mary's & Macarthy's Island on the Western Coast; from Van Dieman's land & New Zealand, from Jamaica, the Bahamas, North America, Sweden & France," all in one day. He did not indicate that this was an unusually heavy load for the Mission House. The secretaries' frequent inability to master this constant influx of correspondence was "calculated to awaken some degree of anxiety," one of them, Elijah Hoole, admitted in 1847. "An increasing attention to the several departments of our home system, and our Foreign Correspondence is absolutely necessary," he added. The WMMS was not exactly a well-oiled bureaucratic machine.[34]

In its efforts to impose some sort of order on the British Wesleyan missions, the WMMS also had to contend with forces beyond its control. The weakness of the North American postal system put limits on the secretaries' ability to keep in close contact with the various Methodist groups in Lower and Upper Canada, especially during the first half of the nineteenth century. Letters could easily go astray once they reached the colonies. In June 1820 the British missionary Richard Williams wrote to Joseph Taylor, pointing out that "your letter dated 8th of January 1820 came to hand last Monday after having remained a long time in one of the country Post offices, which is not an infrequent thing and by means of which some of our letters from you are lost altogether."[35] The rudimentary nature of the transatlantic mails did not help this situation. Until 1815 private ships and a packet operating between Falmouth, Québec, Montréal, and New York were the only postal links between Britain and British North America. After the Treaty of Ghent, sailing companies began to provide regularly scheduled voyages between New York and Liverpool and between Boston and London. These vessels were faster and their rates cheaper than the Falmouth packet. As a result, by the 1820s and 1830s most letters to and from Lower and Upper Canada were carried by American ships and passed through New York.[36]

That did not solve all of the WMMS's problems: there were still numerous places along the way where communications could and did break down. In 1823 the WMMS complained about missionaries who entrusted the minutes of their district meetings "to persons who do not forward them." Sixteen years later, however, one of the secretaries made the exact same mistake while traveling to the Canadas. Robert Alder gave an important letter to a "Mr. Sands" of New York to be sent on to his colleagues in Britain. For whatever reason, Sands decided to put the letter on "the Sailing Packet on the 8th of July so that I am not now surprised," Alder explained to his fellow secretary, Jabez Bunting, "that you had not received it on the 1st of August" in time for the British Conference.[37] The WMMS was still learning how to work the North Atlantic postal system to its advantage by the 1840s.

In the meantime, the production and distribution of denominational literature created another area of difficulty for the secretaries. The slowness and general unreliability of the transatlantic post tended to undermine the whole purpose of the WMMS's publications: to keep the various parts of the British Wesleyan mission field in close contact and to foster a sense of common purpose. The *Wesleyan Missionary Notices*—distributed to all the missionaries and to any laity who collected at least one shilling a month to support the WMMS—were sometimes "printed at so early a period in the month, that we have not been able to give any interesting information, which we might receive after the 13th of the month" from faraway places such as Lower and Upper Canada. This, Secretary John Beecham lamented, "has often been very mortifying to ourselves, and our friends have often been disappointed to find no allusion in the notice when they have received it of something highly interesting . . . an imperfect report of which they had heard during the month."[38] Instead of creating unity, the *Notices* threatened to produce discontent among both laity and missionaries.

Even if the secretaries could solve this problem with relative ease, the denominational magazines, newspapers, and pamphlets that the WMMS regularly sent overseas could only do some good if they arrived in decent time. Often they did not. In 1821 John DePutron complained that, "no information" from Britain had reached the Wesleyan missionaries in the Canadas, "for my magazines etc. are not yet arrived though it is in season." Similarly, in 1837 one of the leading British ministers in the Canadas, William Martin Harvard, could not understand why he had to wait so long to receive the official journal of the British Conference, the *Wesleyan Methodist Magazine.* "The Sept[ember] number," he wrote, "did not come to hand till June; though we are but six weeks from England." This sort of thing shocked even the usually stoic secretaries. In March 1844 Robert Alder wrote to one of the British Wesleyans in the Canadas, pointing out how surprised the WMMS was that the missionaries had yet to receive several important publications from home, even though "we sent a supply out for Eastern and Western Canada the last Spring."[39]

The flaws in the WMMS bureaucracy, combined with the complex nature of transatlantic communication, quickly translated into tensions between the denominational core and periphery. Even as they developed a vision of Lower and Upper Canada as provinces of a greater Britain, the various Methodist groups in those colonies were also left with a sometimes profound sense of isolation from their brethren on the other side of the Atlantic. "No kind Brother seems to think us worthy of his notice, or a few lines of church news from home," one of the British missionaries told Secretary Joseph Taylor in 1820. "What can be the reason my dear Brother? You have been a Missionary. . . . You know what a Missionary must feel under such circumstances that has the work at heart. My mind is *pained*. Do write me tho[ugh] I am a stranger to you. Do, I beg, be familiar and write me as often as you can." At once desperate and demanding, this tone predominated in many missionaries' letters and reports. They wrote about how "anxious" they were "to hear" from the church authorities in Britain and how "painful & discouraging" it was not to know exactly how the WMMS wanted them to conduct their mission work.[40] At other times, the missionaries let their superiors in London know, in no uncertain terms, that they were "grieved, at the *apparent* neglect" with which their communications seemed to be treated. Since, the future secretary Robert Alder declared, his letters "referred to matters, not only of importance to myself personally, but to the cause of God," he had expected to hear from the Mission House in short order. Into the 1830s and 1840s, the missionaries continued to convey this image of a people abandoned, receiving no news from their homeland and facing the prospect of having to act alone, without the "counsel and direction" of their fathers and brethren in Britain.[41]

The same language appeared in the correspondence of both the British Wesleyan laity in the Canadas and the Canadian Methodists. Whether asking for denominational news and publications from Britain or requesting money for their mission, the leading laymen in the Canadas were often either dismayed or angry when answers did not come from the WMMS. Writing to Britain in 1834, the Montréal businessman William Lunn was entirely convinced that it was "useless to make any representations, public or private, respecting" his part of the British Wesleyan mission field to the secretaries. Two years later, that frustration had become full-blown paranoia. "As you have not written to me for [a] very long time," Lunn stated to Robert Alder, "of course you must have taken offense at something I do not know." According to another Montréal merchant, John Mathewson, Lunn eventually vowed not to write to the WMMS again until he received a reply to his previous letters.[42] The Canadian Methodists were equally put out on the rarer occasions when their "communications to the Mission House" were "treated with entire neglect." The British Wesleyan Conference could be just as lax as the WMMS at times: its pronouncements to the Canadian Methodist Conference sometimes failed to arrive at their intended destination, even during times of transatlantic denominational crisis.[43]

This feeling of isolation from the Wesleyan church in Britain complicated any notion of Lower and Upper Canada as simple extensions of the home country. In an attempt to garner more consistent attention from the WMMS, the British Wesleyan missionaries and their lay supporters, in particular, claimed that the colonies were actually greater than Great Britain. In 1824 William Lunn wrote to Secretary Richard Watson expressing the fear that the British Conference had "an erroneous idea of Canada[;] either you have received very imperfect accounts of it, or none at all." In response, he described the colony as a "fine interesting Country," whose "prosperity advances with the rapid increase of its settlements." Lunn also suggested that the Canadas were an improvement on the old country, in terms of its climate at any rate—"the weather in Upper Canada is as fine as in England," he stated, "and the soil quite as good, certainly the winters are finer and more healthy." The missionaries took a somewhat different tack, countering perceived neglect by declaring their own superiority to the secretaries and the WMMS. Serving in Upper Canada in 1834, William Lord told Robert Alder that while he (Alder) may have "seen something of Methodism in this Province," he could not possibly "understand it, nor can any one without *residing* here & mixing with the people & attending the various meetings," which, of course, Lord himself had been doing. Benjamin Slight took up a similar line fourteen years later, noting that "what Canada is, and what its wants are, is a subject but little known, & but little thought of" outside the colonies. "It can only properly be appreciated," he added, "by those who travel through the land in the discharge of ministerial duties."[44] As these comments suggest, despite the influx of British and Wesleyan immigrants, some of the missionaries and laity in the Canadas were prepared to define their sense of self against the home country and their denominational leadership.

IV

It would nevertheless be wrong to suggest that the WMMS was a bureaucratic disaster from beginning to end or that the Atlantic remained an insurmountable barrier to effective communication throughout the nineteenth century. After the mid-1840s neither of those statements held true. Over the following thirty years, the transoceanic connections that had taken shape since 1814 drew the Wesleyans in Britain and the Methodists in Lower and Upper Canada ever more tightly together in a greater Britain. Even with all that improvement, however, tension between the denominational center and periphery remained unavoidable, and the process of cultural formation among the Methodists in the colonies continued apace.

Beginning in the mid-1840s, the secretaries started to implement new policies that indicated a growing trust in the efficiency of transatlantic communications. In 1844 Robert Alder stated that while some publications might continue to go astray, it was no longer necessary or even desirable, given the continued expansion of the British Wesleyan mission field, for missionaries stationed in Lower and Upper Canada to write to the WMMS once every three months, as had been the norm since 1818. "Instead of writing four times a year to us," each missionary in the colonies would now send a report, "relating to everything connected with the spiritual and secular state and prospects of the work under his care," to a minister selected by the WMMS. It was that minister's responsibility to "prepare and forward to the Secretaries a clear and comprehensive quarterly statement, founded upon these reports." Alder was sure that this plan would "place the work as a whole more fully and constantly before us, and through the medium of the *[Wesleyan Missionary] Notices* before our friends generally."[45] Thanks to technological change, that usually proved to be the case. In 1848 the Cunard shipping company introduced a Liverpool-Halifax-New York steam packet service. This resulted in a weekly mail run during the summer and a fortnightly service the rest of the year. The shipping magnate Hugh Allan went one better in 1856, establishing a biweekly postal run between Liverpool and Québec City. In 1859 this service became weekly.[46] Transatlantic space was becoming smaller by the year.

On the surface, then, the Methodists in the Canadas and Britain were less and less troubled by problems posed by the Atlantic crossing. The British missionaries, laity, and their Canadian Methodist brethren certainly voiced far fewer complaints about not receiving letters and publications from Britain than they had over the previous thirty years. And there is other evidence of growing transatlantic closeness, beyond the strictly negative. The British missionary Matthew Richey wrote to Robert Alder from Montréal in 1846, noting with some pride that the "Wesleyan community" on both sides of the Atlantic had "received through the columns of the *Watchman,* such ample information concerning the dimensions, architectural beauty, and auspicious dedication of our new sanctuary in St. James' Street" that he deemed it "superfluous to do more than simply advert to that memorable occasion" in his letter. In the 1850s the British missionaries in Lower Canada regularly received news about the deaths of the leading figures in the home church and, on at least one occasion, passed a suitably laudatory resolution at their district meeting. The Canada Conference of 1865 resolved that its thanks should be presented to the WMMS "for the donation of a copy of the London *Watchman* to each of the Ministers of this Conference . . . and, as well, for the liberal supply of the Missionary publications sent for circulation among our people."[47] The Methodists in the Canadas seemed to be well and truly plugged into a larger British world by the mid-nineteenth century.

Despite that growing connection, transatlantic distance continued to be a source of tension during the second half of the nineteenth century, a point demonstrated by the Methodist practice of sending deputations of ministers back and forth across the ocean. When the British Wesleyan and Canadian Methodists agreed to reunite in 1847, a section of their Articles of Union stated that "the Canada Conference should have the same power" as other affiliated churches to send "Representatives" to the British Conference. The Canadian Methodists took advantage of this provision, dispatching eleven deputations to Britain over the next twenty-seven years. The Canadian Methodists expected the British Wesleyans to reciprocate. In 1856 the British ministers John Hannah and Frederick Jobson did pass through the Canadas. The British missionary Enoch Wood noted that "this transient call from two such distinguished men, ministers of the Parent Body, was very much appreciated." Jobson himself recorded large numbers of "British emigrants" in Toronto pressing them for news about the home church. "In the small vestry of Richmond Street Chapel," he wrote, "I must have counted not less than twenty Methodists who had emigrated from our own county of Lincoln" alone. Two years later, a former president of the British Conference, Francis West, was rumored to be coming to Lower and Upper Canada; Enoch Wood advised one of the secretaries not to lay too much of a burden on him. West should be free to see the gospel work in the Canadas and to preach in some of the principal churches of Canadian Methodism. That was the only way, Wood wrote, to make "our people . . . feel there is in reality a bond of Union between us and you."[48]

Sometimes the British Wesleyan church did not deliver, leading the Methodists in the Canadas to stress, once again, the unique importance of their field of labor within John Wesley's world parish. When Francis West failed to put in an appearance in 1859, for example, the British missionary Joseph Stinson was disappointed. "I have no doubt," he noted, "but his ministerial labours and his counsels would have done us good. I think with you, that the growing importance of our great work on this vast continent is such, as demands and will amply justify & repay the trouble & expense of a pretty frequent visit from the Father Land of one or two of our beloved Fathers and Brethren." Stinson added, "Our Conference is young & ardent, we have a glorious field before us, and we shall be better prepared to meet the necessities of the times and accomplish our work by the maintenance of a close connection with the Parent Conference." Other ministers in Lower and Upper Canada felt the same way. Enoch Wood urged the British Conference to send one of the WMMS secretaries in West's place. "Let us have a delegation to ourselves," he wrote, "whose eyes and ears, whose heart and pen will do us justice, and the great country we are taking a leading part in evangelizing." In 1863 Wood sent another letter to the WMMS, explaining that "we heartily desire to maintain our Union with you," but the Methodists in the Canadas had cause "to complain that so few of the Representatives of the Parent Body" had appeared before a conference "which in sixteen years has increased from One hundred and seventy to more than Six hundred Ministers and Preachers now receiving appointments."[49] There was a sense of grievance behind those words. Even with more reliable transatlantic communication, distance continued to be a source of tension and cultural change among the Methodists in Lower and Upper Canada.

V

The British Wesleyan missionaries, their lay supporters, and the Canadian Methodists became increasingly integrated into an Atlantic world during the nineteenth century. In cultural terms, an influx of British and Wesleyan immigrants during the forty-odd years after 1815 and the politics of loyalty in Lower and Upper Canada manifested themselves in a growing sense among missionaries, settlers, and Canadian Methodists alike that those colonies were extensions of the British Wesleyan gospel field and that they needed to be treated as such by the British Conference and the WMMS. The denominational authorities in the home country and the colonies heartily agreed. By the 1860s the Methodists in the Canadas were plugged into a transatlantic British Wesleyan church. That does not mean, however, that Wesleyan Methodism was the perfect vehicle for transferring British identity from one side of the ocean to the other. In actuality, a spatial and temporal division, created by the difficulty of transoceanic communication and the bureaucratic failures of the WMMS and, to a lesser extent, of the British Conference, triggered a rapid cultural change among the colonial Methodists. Feeling isolated and overlooked, the Methodist clergy and laity in Lower and Upper Canada repositioned themselves within the Atlantic World. They forged a new self-image as loyal Britons—a people whose British identity was contingent, shaped by the constantly shifting contours of their relationship with the metropolitan church.

Situating Lower and Upper Canadian Methodism in the dual context of the Atlantic World and the spatial turn necessarily affects the way one views its overall development. Its history can no longer be presented as a story of growing Canadian Methodist exceptionalism. Instead, Methodism in nineteenth-century Québec and Ontario should be seen as part of wider cultural trends in British North America. As Richard W. Vaudry noted, for instance, the men and women who made up the Church of England in the Canadas also "operated within transatlantic networks of politics, diplomacy, commerce, the church, and the military." These networks, however, were never seamless in their operation; as a result, they left colonial Anglicans with a "sense of exile and abandonment" that would have been all too familiar to the Methodists in Lower and Upper Canada.[50] One can see that same combination of space, time, and identity repeated all across the British Empire. Groups as diverse as nineteenth-century Ulster Protestants and white Rhodesian farmers in the mid-twentieth century shared the contingent identity that took shape among the Methodists in the Canadas. They were Britons abroad, but they were also inhabitants of a new and different country that required new and different modes of thought and existence. The cultural transformation that occurred within the Methodist community in Lower and Upper Canada was certainly "fraught with ambivalences"—but it was not unique.[51]

Confessional Spaces and Religious Places

Lutherans in America, 1698–1748

Elizabeth Lewis Pardoe

European confessionalization culminated in the 1648 Treaty of Westphalia, which codified the premise that geographical space required uniformity of political and religious practice to achieve peace. Although Puritan New England enforced uniformity, Dutch New York, Swedish Delaware, and Quaker Pennsylvania did not. As a result, a group of Lutheran ministers accustomed to the goal of religious uniformity across space and within individual places of religious practice arrived in the British North American colonies to discover a diversity of practice across space and within places of worship. Exactly one century after the Westphalian settlement drew religious violence in continental Europe to a close, these colonial Lutherans imposed order on perceived confessional chaos. In the half-century preceding 1748, they negotiated the decision to share confessional space across ethnic, political, and geographic boundaries. This agreement came with the simultaneous demand that individual places of worship not share their physical structures with Calvinists, Moravians, or others. Lutherans thus achieved American confessionalization by extricating it from a geographically based political process. In short, they overturned The Treaty of Westphalia one century after its creation and forty years before the Constitution.

Cuius regio eius religio tidied European maps and insured that within a given political border, only one religion could merit recognition. However, Atlantic waves carried Lutheran migrants from confessional constraint to colonial chaos. Missionary ministers from across northern Europe followed fretfully behind in an attempt to connect souls scattered from the Mohawk Valley of upstate New York to the Susquehannah Valley of western Pennsylvania back across the ocean to synods ensconced on European soil. This distance in space and culture complicated missionaries' ability to transmit and translate their experience, as they had been charged by the synod, to those whose wellbeing they had in mind. The differences among Anglicans, Calvinists, and Lutherans—let alone among Dutch, Prussian, Swabian, and Swedish Lutheranism—meant little to families for whom a pastor came as a passing luxury. No prince had the power to enforce

Fig. 1. "Lutheran Europe 1698–1748," courtesy of the author. Background: Fredericko de Ewit, *Nova et Accurata Toutius Europu Descriptio.* [S.I., 1700?]. Library of Congress, Map Collections.

sectarian strictures in this region. Parents had their children baptized by whoever claimed to have the power to do so. Their standards and those of synods across the sea differed in the extreme.

Most Atlantic world scholarship stresses the commonalities of political economy established upon racial and gender hierarchies that connected Bristol, Bermuda, and Boston, as well as Cadiz and Cancun. However, Protestant religious practice ruptured en route across the Atlantic. Where the descendants of Thomas Muentzer's adherents made their transatlantic homes, the right of local choice, which Luther revoked following the Peasant's Revolt of 1525, thrived in 1725.[1] Lutherans lived throughout the mid-Atlantic colonies, and their preachers moved among them with little concern for political distinctions. The distances between shepherds and their scattered spiritual flocks meant long periods when no pastor was present. In between visits from ordained ministers, Lutherans happily had well-spoken tailors or preachers from other denominations baptize their babies and soothe their souls. German Lutherans might reluctantly join forces with Swedes in the new world, but omitting ordination passed beyond the pale for those sent to shepherd Lutheran flocks back into the confessional fold.

In the "new" world, defining "church" as a single confessional physical structure for "outward" worship became a central clerical task.[2] Clergy had to reshape colonists' spatial assumptions about religious practice from something done near home—when a cleric happened along—to a set of rites worth riding cross-country to complete. While Frederick the Great cleared Prussia's woods in search of civility and the British strove to build Jerusalem on deforested fields, their transatlantic cousins lingered among Penn's Woods and eluded European ministers' attempts to confessionalize these later-day barbarians.[3]

These ministers had to tackle a shift in spatial and temporal frames not unlike those that John Gaddis has argued are endemic to the practice of history.[4] For success in this larger confessional context, individual souls needed saving. This task could not wait for churches to rise and congregants to come. Ministers had to ride out, find languishing souls, and save them fast before a confessional competitor got there first. For the purpose of this analysis, "space" constitutes the distance between "places," and "places" mean constructs created by people, whether residential groups with set boundaries or buildings.[5] The Lutheran ministers who braved Atlantic waves spent much of their energy assessing how to deal simultaneously with each.

When confessional authorities arrived in a given "place," they found themselves confronted by another issue of "space." The politics of reputation strained to cross geographic space. Conducting confessional rites of baptism, confirmation, marriage, and burial proved phenomenally difficult when confessional records existed across colonial borders, the Atlantic, and very possibly not at all. The man or woman standing in front of the pastor ready to take marriage vows could easily have a spouse awaiting money for passage. Distance could work in an individual pastor's favor. Just as ministers had difficulty tracking down marriages across the Atlantic, a Lutheran farmer in rural New York was unlikely to know of a newly arrived preacher's scandalous exploits in Pennsylvania, let alone the Palatinate.

Although American historians have ascribed different labels to these issues over time, seductive frontiers, barbaric backcountries, mediated middle grounds, and neglected peripheries existed simultaneously and coterminously.[6] What the farmer saw as a seductive frontier of free land, the pastor gazed upon in horror as a neglected periphery of lost souls. One man's Eden made another's purgatory. The process of reformulation or reformation negotiated across national variants of confessional practice[7] took the half century between the 1698 construction of the first Lutheran-American place, Wilmington's Old Swede's Church, and the consecration of St. Michael's Lutheran Church of Philadelphia in 1748 by the first Lutheran-American organization to claim authority over geographical space.

As the eighteenth century dawned under English rule, Lutherans performed their first independent act as an American institution. The first minister to take Lutheran orders in North America embodied the multinational character of his church in the ostensibly English colonies. In 1703 Delaware Swedes ordained Justus Falckner, a German, allowing him to accept a call and preach to the Dutch in New York and East Jersey. Lutherans first came to North America in the mid-seventeenth century as the Dutch and Swedes established permanent settlements on the Hudson and Delaware Rivers, respectively. These communities enveloped a myriad of ethnicities and religions. However, all the earliest Lutherans were dependent upon European consistories to supply them with preachers and prayer books.[8]

Only so far from confessional order could a pietist place himself in a position of power. Falckner's position as the first Lutheran pastor ordained in America reflected more than the diversity of the population to whom he would preach; it underscored the placement of Lutheran pietists, ostracized as radicals within Europe, at the geographical and spiritual heart of American Lutheranism. Falckner's family exemplified the hereditary Lutheran clergy that emerged in the first century and a half following the Reformation.[9] Falckner was the son, grandson, and brother of Lutheran ministers; his position as a Lutheran cleric seemed inevitable. However, the pietism flourishing at the Prussian University of Halle influenced both Justus and his scandal-ridden brother, Daniel. They came to the new world as sons who had strayed from the orthodox fold. Before he knelt in Gloria Dei Church to receive ordination from Swedish pastors, Justus Falckner retreated to a cabin along the Wissahickon Creek as a mystical hermit among the theosophical pietists gathered there under the leadership of Johannes Kelpius.[10]

The eclectic mix of souls who gathered to watch Justus take his vows and accept the burdens of an American congregation included his theosophical brethren, orthodox Swedish ministers, Englishmen of various sects, and perhaps a few Indians.[11] Earlier, Falckner had written "concerning the condition of the churches in these parts" that they were "still pretty bad." First, "The Aborigines or Indians" remained "in their blindness and barbarity" because of a "lack of sufficient good instruction." The Indians were "angered at the bad living of the Christians, especially at the system of trading which is driven with them," causing the Indians to "only learn vices which they did not have formerly, such as drunkenness, stealing & c." The Europeans who taught such vices to their native neighbors constituted the "local Christian minority," who were "divided into almost innumerable sects, which pre-eminently may be called sects and hordes." The diverse lot included "Quakers, Anabaptists, Naturalists, Rationalists, Independents, Sabbatarians and many others, especially secret insinuating sects, whom one does not know what to make of." Such sects, both overt and hidden, "all united in these beautiful principles, if it please the Gods *(si Dis placet):* Do away with all good order, and live for yourself as it please you!"[12]

Falckner blamed the "hordes" of "sects" on the faith of the proprietors who made his presence in the "new" world possible. Pennsylvania served as "a dissecting-room of the Quakers." Though "our theologians" might try to "dissect this carcase [*sic*] and discover its interiors, they could not do it so well as the Quakers here in this country are now doing themselves." Falckner concluded that "by transgressing their own principles," the Quakers "shew in plain daylight the kind of spirit that moves them." The Friends had "become Ishmaels of all well regulated church-institutions."[13]

Within this chaotic constellation, Falckner counted "three confessions and nations" of "The Protestant Church." Only Lutherans, Calvinists, and Presbyterians fell under Falckner's definition of Protestant "confessions." The Protestant "nations" included "an English Protestant Church and a Swedish Protestant Lutheran Church; and also persons of the German nation of the Evangelical Lutheran and Reformed churches." From an overlapping nexus of "confessions and nations," Falckner selected the Swedes and Germans for particular scrutiny. The Swedes had established two congregations led by "two devout, learned and conscientious preachers," including the Swedish pastor Andreas Rudman. Falckner credited the Swedes with trying "to instil the true fear and knowledge of God into his hearers, who previously, from a lack of good instruction and church discipline, had become rather unruly." Using a good pietist's distinction between inner and outer faith, Falckner remarked, "The outward worship of God is held in the Swedish language, and partly according to the Swedish liturgy, as far as church ceremonies are concerned."[14]

Germans had not fared so well as Swedes in their attempt to launch Lutheranism in a new confessional space across the Atlantic. Falckner stressed that "merely several Evangelical Lutheran Germans, and not the German Evangelical Lutheran Church" found a home in the new province. Without institutional guidance, "those who are destitute of altar and priest forsooth roam about in this desert a deplorable condition indeed." Perhaps more frightening to the Lutheran were the "large number of Germans who, however, have partly crawled among the different sects who use the English tongue, which is first learned by all who come here."

Geographically and spiritually adrift among Quakers, Anabaptists, and Freethinkers, these Germans "assimilate with no one" and "allow their children to grow up in the same manner." Falckner surmised "the spirit of errors and sects has here erected for itself an asylum" and blamed such untamed toleration for "the lack of establishment of an outward and visible church assembly."

When newcomers arrived on American shores, finding "no better outward divine service, they rather select one than none at all[,] although they are already *Libertini.*"[15]

Lost among the libertines, Justus Falckner and his brother Daniel found a place to worship in "the Swedish church, although we understand little or nothing of their language," and were "the means of influencing divers Germans by our example." Like the Falckner brothers, these Germans "now and then come to the assemblies, even though they do not know the language." Despite the language barrier, Falckner considered their mere attendance as evidence that "they are gradually being redeemed from barbarism, and becoming accustomed to an orderly outward service." In a cross-cultural attempt to preserve Lutheranism on American shores, Reverend Rudman, the Swede, "offered, regardless of the difficulty to assume the German dialect" and "to go to this trouble and now and then to deliver a German address in the Swedish church, until the Germans can have a church of their own, together with the necessary establishment."[16]

The successful creation of a new Lutheran confessional space necessitated flexibility over the ethnic/linguistic identities of religious places. Falckner reported that "the Germans[,] who still love the evangelical truth and an outward church order, much prefer to attend the Swedish churches here until they can also have their divine worship in their own language as a people." Through their efforts, the Swedes and their German parishioners provided limited means "to spread the Gospel truth in these wilds, whereby many of their brethren and fellow-countrymen may be brought from wrong to right, from darkness to light, and from the whirlpool of sectaries to the peace and quiet of the true church."[17]

The souls of Indians and Quakers required equal attention if Lutherans were to establish confessional hegemony in the New World. Falckner thought if only he had an organ in his place of worship, sinful souls would pour out of the woods, across the miles, and into his pews, where they would hear the "Word." He predicted that "music would contribute much towards a good Christian service" and "not only attract and civilize the wild Indian" but also "do much good in spreading the Gospel truths among the sects and others by attracting them."[18] The German predicted "that the Indians would come running from far and near to listen to such [the organ's] unknown melody, and upon that account might become willing to accept our language and teaching." Falckner hoped the organ would induce Indians "to remain with people who had such agreeable things; for they are said to come ever so far to listen to one who plays even upon a reed-pipe," possessing "an extraordinary love . . . for any melodious and ringing sound." The power of the organ lay exclusively in Lutheran hands, since "the melancholy, Saturnine stingy Quaker spirit has abolished all such music." The organ's "novelty" would "tend to attract many of the young people away from the Quakers and sects to attend services where such music was found, even against the wishes of their parents," allowing the Lutherans "to show them [the youth and through them their parents] the truth and their error."[19]

The Swedish church could also employ the organ to attract their own settlers across North America's open spaces into places of worship. According to Falckner, "the majority of the Swedes are young people, and mostly live scattered in the forest, far from the churches." Believing that "we by nature are all inclined to good, and above all to what may serve our souls, such as the Word of God which is dead and gone, so are especially the youth." Falckner understood that Swedish youths "would sooner rest on a Sunday and seek some pleasure" after "they have performed heavy labor for the whole week, as is customary here" before choosing to travel "several miles to listen to a sermon." However, with the addition of an organ, young Swedes "would consider church-going as a recreation for their senses." Falckner accurately recalled that "Luther of blessed memory" encouraged "the use of the organ and sacred music for this very reason, that it is serviceable, and induces the young and simple and, says he foolish folk, to listen unto and receive God's Word." Falckner stressed that "even a small organ-instrument and music" in America's "solitude and wilderness" would "prove far more useful than many hundreds in Europe, where there is already a superfluity of such things; and the more common they are, the more they are misused."[20]

A transatlantic virus, yellow fever, which struck New York in 1702, forced the first transatlantic Lutheran ordination. Andreas Rudman, a Swede, had accepted the call to minister to the diverse Lutherans of Manhattan, Long Island, and East Jersey. However, the preacher and his family were brought down under the yellow fever. Having already lost one son to the scourge, Reverend Rudman decided to flee the city and return to Pennsylvania. Rather than "desert his little flock," Rudman pleaded with Falckner to accept the call to New York. Although the pietist had chosen not to follow the ministry in "greater and more lucrative churches" in Europe because he disdained "the abandoned life of courtiers and others," Rudman assured Falckner, "Here matters are very different," and he promised a congregation of "guile less scattered sheep, few, docile obedient—thirsty and famished." After being assured that the Swedish ministers had received permission to perform an ordination so distant from the locus of ecclesiastical power, on November 24, 1703, the Reverends Andreas Rudman, Erick Bioerck, and Andrew Sandel ordained Justus Falckner, and he went to accept his calling as shepherd to New York's "scattered sheep."[21]

Finding virtually no administrative or physical church structure in New York or Albany, Falckner sent out pleas to the Delaware Swedes, Pennsylvania Germans, and Dutch of St. Thomas, asking for assistance in organizing the New York Lutherans. The St. Thomas contingent replied with a pledge of funds to be used exclusively for a new church building. Falckner preferred to refurbish the current dilapidated structure and placed the St. Thomas funds in trust for future use.

Searching for further support, Falckner wrote the Amsterdam Consistory in 1705 and begged for their continued "zeal and care for the true Evangelical Protestant Church." For their part, the New York Lutherans vowed that they would "arduously apply ourselves to inculcate the same in our children and descendants."[22]

The description sent to Amsterdam employed the language of confessional competition, and stressed the loss of physical and spiritual Lutheran space to the Reformed majority under the official tolerance of British law. Citing "many years without a Pastor," the congregation reported that it had become "dispersed" and "the young people and many of the older ones have gone over to the so-called Reformed Sect." Those who remained in the congregation were "poor and many, especially the young people, ignorant on account of the lack of Bibles, Catechisms, Psalm and Hymn books." Despite their self-proclaimed misery, the New Amsterdam Lutherans stood alone as "the only Dutch Lutheran Congregations in America that is yet all right" and begged assistance so that "this single little spark" would not "be extinguished by those owls who hate the light."[23]

While Justus Falckner served his New York ministry, a dispute over European authority in American geographic space broke out that would rock the Lutheran Church in America for decades to come. A tailor named Johann Bernhard Van Dieren attempted to assume the pulpit in some of Falckner's more distant congregations. Van Dieren claimed that the Lutheran preacher at London's St. James's Palace had sent him to the colonies. However, he lacked any evidence of such a calling. The Swedish minister Andreas Hesselius wrote from Delaware that despite Van Dieren's "zeal," a true Lutheran preacher would wait to be called by a specific congregation. "Only he, is worthy of the ministry who is ordained unwillingly," Hesselius concluded.[24]

With Falckner far away, Van Dieren made a grab for his pulpit and straggling spiritual sheep. Van Dieren emerged from a long German tradition of tailors who found their way into the Lutheran clergy by performing the tasks of schoolmasters in rural villages.[25] Lutheran tradition of congregants selecting their own clerics strengthened Van Dieren's claims. The South German Peasants' War of the 1520s caused Luther to regret his initial liberalism in this regard, because the selection of uneducated lay preachers posed an ongoing problem during the early Reformation. The problem reappeared in the unstructured churches of the American colonies.[26] Justus Falckner's pietist leanings made him somewhat sympathetic to the claims of the pious but uneducated preacher, and he died in 1723, leaving the New York Lutherans without a pastor and without the funds to support one.[27]

The Amsterdam Consistory received a letter from New York in December 1723 asking for financial help with the "large expenditures" needed "to secure another pastor." The New Yorkers could neither offer a new pastor "a proper yearly salary" nor maintain their churches, "of which the one in New York City in particular is in a dilapidated condition for want of necessary repairs." The bearer of the letter, Johannes Sybrant, visited "congregations adhering to the Lutheran and Unaltered Augsburg Confession in Amsterdam and other places" to ask "for a gift of love and mercy" towards paying a future pastor's salary.[28] In March, Sybrant arrived in Hamburg carrying a letter from the Amsterdam Consistory, promising a salary of fifty pounds in New York currency as well as 200 guilders for his comfortable passage, collected among the New York, Albany, and Hackensack congregations for an unmarried pastor able to preach in Dutch. The spurious origins of Sybrant's promise plagued Wilhelm Berkenmeyer when he answered the call to defend "the Lord's vineyard" against the persistent danger of "little foxes."[29] Berkenmeyer left his post catechizing prisoners and traveled with Sybrant to Amsterdam, where he was ordained before departing for the Lutherans' confessional frontier.[30]

The Orthodox Wilhelm Christoph Berkenmeyer quickly assumed authority over Lutheran space in America. He shifted the focus of Lutheran life from the Swedish consistory to his own Hamburg Ministerium. In 1726 Berkenmeyer sent petitions on behalf of the Germans and Dutch living around Albany and the Mohawk Valley to Hamburg, requesting the services of another minister. The petition claimed that if New York City Lutherans suffered from lack of religious attention, Hudson and Schoharie Valley Lutherans fared far worse. As Berkenmeyer later described "the complete confusion" he found in Schoharie, "The Lutherans were against the Reformed, and the German-speaking against the Dutch." The German Lutheran church was "in ruins," because the Germans had broken confessional ranks in favor of ethnic ties. They refused to attend the Dutch Lutheran church and instead met in a barn with "a Calvinistic reader."[31]

Berkenmeyer described the Albany Lutherans as oppressed by fines from the Dutch government as they "planted the Evangelical Lutheran religion in the midst of the savages of this country." British toleration brought relief, but the Lutherans were nonetheless "left for about twenty years as sheep without a shepherd." In an unguarded condition, many in the Lutheran flock "did not shy away from embracing a strange religion." In the competitive religious environment of the New World, Berkenmeyer noted with mixed emotions that "our very neighbors have been moved to pity by our miserable condition, and have offered to assist us." The Lutherans' status at the bottom of the confessional heap at least allowed them the opportunity "to gather a collection within the government of [the province of] New York. Without an improved church in Albany, Berkenmeyer foresaw "that our religion would be bound to die out completely," since the "young people have no grounding of religion in their hearts, while the aged, who are still somewhat versed in it, are drawing nearer to the grave."[32]

Berkenmeyer's and the Swedes' ability to replace Justus Falckner's surviving, scandal-ridden brother, Daniel, depended on whether clerics in Sweden would accept the New York Lutherans' desire to unite officially with those on the Delaware in a conjoined confessional space. Shortly after Berkenmeyer sent the call for a pastor for the Hudson and Schoharie Valleys, the Dutch Lutherans living around Raritan, New Jersey, sent their own call to Amsterdam requesting a replacement. Hackensack Lutherans contemplated joining Raritan but refused when some in Raritan decided to keep Daniel Falckner in the pulpit. Instead, the Hackensack group turned to "a vagabond preacher," Caspar Stoever, whom the Swedish Lutherans had refused to ordain. By Berkenmeyer's account, the Swedes offered to call a minister from Sweden to take the Raritan pulpit, but Daniel Falckner managed to stop the call.[33]

When Hamburg supplied Reverend Michael Knoll in response to the Albany petition, Berkenmeyer left Knoll to care for the New York City and New Jersey Lutherans and took it upon himself to attempt the salvation of Albany.[34] Berkenmeyer spent the years between 1731 and his death in 1750 struggling to bring his parishioners and the American Lutheran pastorate into step with his orthodox ideas of confessional organization and devotion.

The *Albany Protocol* documents Berkenmeyer's trials as a man of order surrounded by confessional chaos. Things began badly when he learned the Hackensack Lutherans had accepted Johann Van Dieren.[35] The Raritan Lutherans allowed the "vagabond" Johann Caspar Stoever to preach, and Berkenmeyer promptly involved himself in encouraging Daniel Falckner's retirement. Falckner and Berkenmeyer could not agree whether the new pastor should be called through Falckner's choice, London, the political capital of the empire, or Berkenmeyer's preference, Germany, the cultural center of the faith. Nor could the parishioners issuing the call decide whether to offer the new pastor payment in New York or New Jersey currency. Even the pastor's port of entry led to dispute. Though the congregants wished the pastor to arrive in New York, Berkenmeyer convinced them to offer the choice of arriving in Philadelphia should it prove the speedier option. The final order stated that the minister would have to preach in German when in "The Mountains, Rachgeway (Rockaway), and Hanover." Worship would turn away from Falckner's pietist leanings and follow the orthodox Amsterdam order of service and the Unaltered Augsburg Confession.[36]

Johannes Spahler arrived in New York in 1733 and answered the call from Rhinebeck and East Camp of his own accord. Spahler performed Pastor Knoll's marriage and thereby won himself some legitimacy.[37] When Berkenmeyer began to make a public issue of his unpaid salary, members of the Newton congregation began attending Spahler's services in East Camp rather than pay for Berkenmeyer's services. Not only were Berkenmeyer's parishioners turning to Spahler, but Spahler also snubbed Berkenmeyer by failing to visit him when their paths crossed.[38] Meanwhile, Spahler continued to increase his circle of influence. Berkenmeyer noted that "the malcontents" took Spahler to Klaverack, Justus

Falckner's home town. The malcontents' leader was Falckner's brother-in-law, who was now married to Falckner's niece, which surely magnified the insult.[39]

Pastor Knoll later denied that he had provided Spahler with the signed credentials that Berkenmeyer's "malcontents" used in persuading other parishioners to accept Spahler. Berkenmeyer declared that he "would rather throw Spahler right out the door than acknowledge him as a lawful pastor." However, when asked to intervene in the congregation's dispute over whether to keep Spahler, Berkenmeyer blamed both "the friends and the enemies" of the supposed pastor for the situation: "They might do what they liked and have a good time with their Magister."[40] Nevertheless, when Hannes Kurtz wanted Berkenmeyer to baptize his child at his father's house "for those people who would have nothing to do with Spa[h]ler," Berkenmeyer intervened and made a failed attempt at a truce.[41]

Berkenmeyer subsequently sent a letter to the East Camp church council, bemoaned the lack of "collegial confidence" with Spahler, and objected to his "unusual" baptisms and ministry of "the Lord's Supper in a manner unheard of among all the Lutherans the world over." Above all, Berkenmeyer, through his Loonenburg church council, protested Spahler's rejection of the Amsterdam Constitution, which "was in common use at the founding of the Lutheran Church here in America." The Loonenburg council argued that the Amsterdam constitution "most carefully avoids, in agreement with other Evangelical Lutheran churches, giving any opportunity for scorn and slander to our neighbors who are outside our church."[42] Instead of interpreting the letter as a plea for peace and tolerance, Spahler absorbed the underlying implication and declared, "Do you not see that B[erkenmeyer] wants to be my superintendant?" Spahler also rejected a similar letter from Knoll, ending the first attempt at institutional uniformity across Lutherans' confessional space in New York and New Jersey.[43]

The Lutheran clergy found the regulation of marital relationships particularly difficult an ocean away from the paperwork and people who first sanctified their parishioners' unions. Pastor Knoll was warned of one such case before leaving Germany. Erich Hoyer, the Norwegian cousin of one of Knoll's colleagues, had run off with another man's wife, a woman named Catharina, and fled Europe to live in sin in Hackensack.[44] Knoll forced his friend to send a letter to his wayward cousin begging him to reform his life.[45] To Knoll's horror, he discovered upon his arrival in Hackensack that Hoyer was considered an upstanding member of his new community and had been asked to house the new pastor.

Hoyer's Norway and Knoll's Denmark were under the same crown and thus Hoyer was Knoll's "countryman."[46] Their shared European space created expectations of a shared colonial place. Regardless, Knoll informed the church council of Hoyer's crime and asked them to rush the completion of the parsonage to extricate him from a house of sin. When Knoll left Hoyer's ahead of schedule, Catharina was incensed.

Although they changed kingdoms, the couple had not changed confessions by crossing the Atlantic. Knoll expected Catharina to return to her legal husband in Norway, if he still would have her. Hoyer proposed that Knoll marry them instead. The pastor would not consider such a solution, proclaiming "one cannot run away from God and his Word, even when one has moved from Norway to Hackensack."[47]

Without Westphalia's clarity of sectarian and secular authority to guide them, the case continued to bounce among those who laid claim to power in British America's messy freedom. Erich refused to leave Catharina on the grounds that he had vowed to her that he would not. Hoyer had every reason to expect that the private vows between lovers would be given legal status. German ecclesiastical courts respected the vows between fiancées as binding, and women could successfully take to court any man who had promised them marriage and then balked.[48] At the heart of secular marriage controls lay the relegation of property from the couple's parents.[49] In Erich and Catharina's minds, they were no doubt married in the eyes of God, and having declined their inheritances, nothing else mattered. Unfortunately for them, they were still not married in the eyes of Michael Knoll so long as Catharina's husband lived and sought reconciliation. Knoll considered their private vows perjury.[50]

Knoll wrote to Berkenmeyer for advice and offered to travel with Hoyer to meet with Berkenmeyer for a personal mediation. Berkenmeyer had previously admitted Hoyer to communion. When Knoll let it be known that Hoyer was an adulterer, banned from the Norwegian church, the followers of Johann Van Dieren delighted in the revelation as evidence of Berkenmeyer's unworthiness. Knoll claimed to have told them that Berkenmeyer had not known of Hoyer's fall from grace but added, "Should they hear of it that your reverence is taking Hoyer's part so strongly, they would have reason to rejoice and to slander you, and I would not know what to say." Probably for this very reason, Berkenmeyer had pleaded with Knoll to keep the matter quiet.

Berkenmeyer and Knoll each assessed the case from a spatial perspective but drew opposite conclusions. Berkenmeyer considered Hoyer's banishment from Norway sufficient punishment for his sins.[51] Knoll was determined to make it known that the ban of the Lutheran Church was inescapable and that "fleeing to another country" would not "destroy its force."[52] Whereas Berkenmeyer was concerned "that the years after which an adulteress is to return to her husband have passed by at least four times," Knoll found civil law irrelevant, proclaiming that "adultery is adultery and remains adultery, even if it were continued for a thousand years."

Berkenmeyer accepted the separation of his confession from governmental authority. In colonial New York and New Jersey, the clergy lacked "worldly power and force." Hoyer's separation from his common law wife "must be obtained through civil authority." As for Hoyer's desire to wed the mother of his children, Berkenmeyer pointed out, "The priestly solemnization of marriage can be neither granted nor refused without the approval of the honorable civil authorities of the land."[53] The absence of a confessional state failed to persuade Knoll, who insisted that he wished merely the power to uphold the Norwegian church ban keeping Hoyer from Lutheran services so long as he continued to commit adultery in the church's eyes.[54]

Fortunately for Erich and Catharina, a skipper arrived in Hackensack who knew everyone in their home village and could testify that Catharina had spoken the truth when she claimed that her sister had forced her into her first marriage. The skipper added that Catharina's husband, Boy Simensen, had "out of jealousy treated her with harsh words and blows." Not only had Catharina saved herself and her first daughter from an abusive husband and father, but the skipper also informed them that Simensen had divorced Catharina two years before in court and then promptly died, leaving his estate to Catharina's sister.[55] Since Simensen had divorced Catharina in 1731, she had been legally free to marry Erich Hoyer for the entire time Knoll harassed them in Hackensack.

If Berkenmeyer's main concern was that the couple would turn to the likes of Van Dieren, Knoll now feared they would choose a different religious place, an "Anglican or Calvinistic church," should he not agree to marry them. Knoll admitted that "the laws of this country permit such people to marry." Knoll disapproved of such laws, and he asked, "Whether the pastor where they live, if he himself is hesitant to marry them, can leave the public repentance and the marriage to his colleague in the vicinity?" Knoll wondered if the couple should still be required to separate, since "Danish, Swedish and Saxon laws prohibit the adulterer from marrying the adulteress or abducted woman, even when the latter's husband has died."[56] The Hamburg ministerium wrote Knoll to marry the couple and legitimize their children. American law permitted such marriages as had "Luther in his treatise on *The Babylonian Captivity of the Church,* which permits such marriages, provided no attempts were made on the life of the husband."[57] In a private letter the ministerium scolded Knoll—as had Berkenmeyer—for revealing the Hoyers' sins to the church council without speaking to them in private first.[58]

Two years later, Berkenmeyer dealt with an adulterous marriage that crisscrossed confessional spaces and religious places: an English bride, a German groom, and a Dutch Reformed minister in a British colony. In February 1735 at the Newton church council, "Johann Dewald Lucas, a German weaver, appeared and was asked if he admitted that Betty, the English woman, had been his wife before he married Christyne [*sic*], Plank's widow." When Lucas could provide "only trifling excuses," he "was declared to be an adulterer by living thus with Christijne and deserved death according to the law of the country." Lucas was not a member of Berkenmeyer's congregation, and the church council sent him to the secular Court at Esopus. Christijne, however, was a Lutheran, and the council decided to report on the matter to the Lutherans in New York and Hackensack to see "what action should be brought against her according to our church constitution."[59]

Unlike Catharina Hoyer's first husband, Johann Lucas's first wife had agreed to a separation. Lucas and the English woman, Betty, had been married by the Reformed minister Gualterus Dubois in New York City. However, Lucas claimed that Betty had "reproached him that she had not been married according to the English rite with the exchange of rings" and "had often deserted him for two weeks periods." These excursions led to "fighting between themselves, and she had once kicked him in a sensitive spot"—an event witnessed by a soldier. Having agreed to separate, Johann gave Betty "a pair of shoes, some dresses, and three shillings for traveling" and "escorted her on a boat to New Jersey." After his move to Newton, Johann had even written Betty to ascertain "if she had any claims on him," because he wished to take communion with a clear conscience. Much to his regret, Johann never "thought of" getting a court order legalizing his separation from Betty. "Otherwise he would have insisted on a court order" and eliminated the possibility that Betty could change her mind and ruin Johann's new life with his new, Lutheran wife and child.[60]

Berkenmeyer had to unravel the ecclesiastical and civil jurisdictions under which the supposed crime had been committed when Betty showed up in Newton claiming to be the victim of adultery and asking his assistance in reclaiming her husband.[61] When brought before the church council to explain the matter, Johann Lucas, like Erich Hoyer, insisted that he could not leave his current wife and children. After the council "represented to him with fitting severity, that he had above all to fear God," Johann "wanted to know what advice to follow in the matter." Berkenmeyer dispatched Johann to the civil courts and to his own Reformed Church for punishment. However, Christina fell clearly under Berkenmeyer's guiding hand, and she "was to be subject to the church censure of our Lutheran consistory until she separates herself from him [Johann] of her own accord and judgement to the satisfaction of the consistory and its judicial opinion." Nevertheless, the council would reconsider its decision should "the civil authorities find and give a different remedy in the matter."[62]

The council thought it possible that the "civil authorities" would consider Johann's grounds for separation from Betty valid and pardon his behavior, but Johann made the mistake of becoming obstreperous and antagonizing the council. Johann claimed to be unable to afford court expenses and then added more complaints of Betty's "evil" doings. Attempting and failing to use a biblical passage as his defense, Johann concluded "that the people were to blame, for they had not restrained him when he consorted with Christina." Although Berkenmeyer did not record the outburst in the minutes, he thought they showed "so much more clearly the evil nature of the case and the person."[63]

Berkenmeyer suspected that Lucas was not as much attracted to Christina herself as to the inheritance Christina and her child from her first marriage had received upon her husband's death. While Christina "was not very intelligent" in Berkenmeyer's opinion, she was "known to us to be of irreproachable conduct."[64] The council concluded that Christina, "though not quite ignorant, was still trapped by cunning," whereas Lucas was a "malicious deserter" and guilty of adultery. This left Betty categorized as Johann's victim and free to remarry, while Johann, the "malicious deserter," could "never be granted freedom to enter into a second marriage." Because Berkenmeyer considered Christina under "the statement that whoever married a separated person also destroys the marriage," she was also guilty of adultery despite the mitigating circumstances of her limited intellect and Johann's manipulations.[65]

Berkenmeyer wrote his colleagues in New York, Hackensack, and Raritan to inquire about how Christina's punishment should be handled. Although he wished to delay and avoid Christina's excommunication if possible, Berkenmeyer laid out the right of the American pastors to excommunicate her in the absence of a formal consistory.[66] Soon Berkenmeyer would try to create an American consistory to give his ministry the institutional formality and force he so desired.

The dissatisfied congregation in Raritan, New Jersey, gave Berkenmeyer the opportunity to formalize his loose association of Lutheran church councils. Pastor Johann August Wolf accepted the call to the Lutheran pulpit in Raritan, New Jersey, in 1734 and promptly alienated his parishioners. The Hamburg Ministerium had found it difficult to fill the call and turned to Wolf, the cousin of a senior minister. Wolf quickly proved himself totally unfit for a rural colonial ministry. He was unable to preach from memory and unwilling to associate with his parishioners, and Henry Muhlenberg, the patriarch of American Lutheranism, punned that he was "a wolf, destroyer of the flock."[67]

Berkenmeyer called a "Classical Assembly" to arbitrate between the Raritan lay leaders and Reverend Wolf, who had resorted to calling one of his protesting parishioners a "boor" and informing him from the pulpit that his letters had found their use "as toilet paper."[68] Pastor Knoll recognized that Wolf was an alcoholic and a generally obnoxious character, and he gave his approval to another pastoral candidate coming from Philadelphia to visit the Raritan parish. Berkenmeyer, however, disapproved strongly of the "half-Quakerish" candidate and insisted that a called minister could never be dismissed by his parishioners. The Raritan leaders were willing to pay Wolf to leave, but Berkenmeyer's assembly negotiated a settlement in which Wolf promised to master preaching by memory—a skill he claimed to have lost during his Atlantic crossing—if the parish would begin to provide his salary.

Although Berkenmeyer thought he had managed to negotiate a happy conclusion to the Raritan crisis in 1735, it raged until 1745 when Henry Muhlenberg was brought in as part of a court arbitration to settle the dispute.[69] Berkenmeyer's refusal to remove Wolf left Raritan destabilized for a full decade, so that when Muhlenberg arrived, many had not received communion "for many years." Muhlenberg instructed and confirmed twenty-four "older young people," prompting their parents to declare, "It is enough if only our children, who have been wandering like lost sheep, are found and brought back again." The year 1735 proved a bad one for Lutherans in America. Shortly after Berkenmeyer condemned Raritan to a Lutheran version of purgatory, he announced that Lutheranism "was brought completely to the grave" in Newton, New York, when "the banns were published for the daughter of Mr. Andries Elig with a Dutchman of the Reformed [faith]."[70]

In his ill-fated attempts to establish confessional order within colonial chaos, Berkenmeyer grappled unsuccessfully with the diversity of secular and sectarian authorities vying for influence in the eighteenth-century mid-Atlantic and longed for the comparative order of post-Westphalian Europe. While piecing together the marital status of yet another would-be bridegroom, Berkenmeyer wrote, "It may be assumed that the law of the country may be too feeble to protect us or even to promote Christianity among us and to avert evil." The minister claimed that "the freedom of our country, the law of toleration, *the liberty of conscience,*" could not be "blamed" for the "misuse" people made of them: "To this, however, belongs [the fact] that everyone takes the freedom to live according to his own religion, that is, according to his conscience, or really according to his personal judgement." Americans, "by adhering to the worldly laws and in treading under foot the divine and most of all the ecclesiastical laws," thought "themselves to have more justice and security than the greatest monarch in Christianity assumes to himself." The monarch, Berkenmeyer trusted, "submits his own conscience and sovereignty to consistorial decisions."[71]

By contrast, Henry Muhlenberg had a specific enemy upon whom he set his sights and against whom he defined himself and his confession. Without his battle against and victory over the Moravian Church, Muhlenberg might have suffered Berkenmeyer's fate. When Muhlenberg arrived in Philadelphia, he discovered that Count Nicholas von Zinzendorf, the leading sponsor of the Moravians, presented himself as a Lutheran. The basis of Zinzendorf's claim rested with the Moravians' ecumenical theology. The Moravians claimed to adhere to the Augsburg Confession, but they also insisted that the confession had no meaning and that anyone could worship with them so long as they accepted Christ.[72]

In Pennsylvania as in New York, Lutheran congregations scattered in the absence of officially sanctioned pastors. When Muhlenberg first visited the New Hanover congregation to which he was called, some members had accepted a "quacksalver" named Schmid as their preacher, while "others had separated themselves because of Schmid's scandalous life." Another segment "would have no more to do with churches or parsons because conditions had for a long time been so wretched and slovenly," and "still others had joined with the Moravian Brethren." Muhlenberg's litany concluded, "Many believed nothing and some had been drawn into numerous sects." As Berkenmeyer and Knoll had found, "Some had married and begotten children and had never been baptized, nor ever been to the Lord's Supper."[73]

A Mr. Valentin Kraft served the Lutherans of Philadelphia and Germantown when Muhlenberg arrived. Muhlenberg heard of Kraft while staying in Charleston and learned that he had been "deposed" in his home duchy of Zweibruecken. In Pennsylvania, "Mr. Kraft had traveled through the whole province," appointing "deacons and elders here and there." This assemblage of lay leaders "established a general presbytery in the whole country and a special presbytery, as he [Kraft] called it in Philadelphia." Kraft also "organized a consistory of which he was the president and Mr. Stoever the *assessor.*" Muhlenberg described Stoever, who was discounted as a "vagabond" by Berkenmeyer and denied ordination by the Swedes, as a "bookbinder whom the scoundrelly collector, Schultze, appointed, *salva venia,* a so-called Lutheran preacher here in a barn." This act "conferred the dignity of ordination upon his [Stoever's] disreputable behavior." Muhlenberg thought just as little of the "few more lazy and drunken schoolmasters" whom Kraft single-handedly ordained in order to "place them as preachers in vacant places."[74]

Kraft wished to control Muhlenberg's entry into the German Lutheran congregations. However, Muhlenberg turned to Swedish Lutherans and their pastor Peter Tranberg, who recognized Muhlenberg's papers certifying him as a university-educated, ordained, and called pastor, endorsed by the British court through the Reverend Court Preacher Frederick Ziegenhagen.[75] The Germans denied they had ever accepted Kraft, and because Kraft lacked any European documentation, he was promptly eliminated from competition. The following day, Muhlenberg visited the governor, showed his documents, and received the governor's offer of "every kind office." That afternoon Muhlenberg went to "the English minister of the Episcopal Church who is also the commissary of the churches." The English cleric attested to his "very friendly relations with our Lutheran brethren, the Swedish *ministers,*" and stated his desire "to continue the same" with Muhlenberg. Thus Muhlenberg won his first battle by gaining the critical Philadelphia pulpit, ingratiating himself to British authorities, and delegitimizing Kraft's ad hoc consistory.[76]

The summer before Muhlenberg arrived in Philadelphia, the Moravians, Lutherans, and Reformed came to blows over the house the Lutherans and Reformed rented together for their services. Zinzendorf claimed to be "a

Lutheran pastor and won the confidence of the people to such an extent that they had given him a written call." As he preached, "a few buttons of the sheep's clothing flew open and the other side of his face was revealed, which made the sheep suspicious and scattered them." Lutherans took what they could from their place of worship—the church record book, the alms bag, the alms chest, the chalice, and the key to the building—and then locked the Moravians out. When the Moravians broke the lock in order to preach, Lutherans and Reformed intervened with "rough work on a Sunday," as "they trampled, pushed, and knocked each other about, and the women began to scream; in short there was a tumult."[77]

When Muhlenberg took over the Philadelphia congregation, a Lutheran-turned-Moravian elder still held the church book. When Lutheran deacons requested that he return the book, the man informed them that it was now in Zinzendorf's possession. Muhlenberg agreed to speak with the count but on his arrival discovered "a large gathering of his generals and corporals" with "the Count presiding at a small table." Zinzendorf proceeded to interrogate Muhlenberg and berate him for attempting to steal what Zinzendorf claimed as his congregation. Indeed, Zinzendorf had also created a consistory. The count informed Muhlenberg that he was "inspector of all the Lutheran churches in Pennsylvania and Lutheran pastor in Philadelphia." Zinzendorf had "held synods in the country and here" and had "also installed pastors in several places and even deposed a pastor named Stoever."[78]

Muhlenberg again turned to the Swedes as the true Lutherans able to prove who among the German speakers claiming to be Lutherans were confessionally sound. "If you are such a genuine Lutheran," Muhlenberg asked Zinzendorf, "why would they not let you preach in the Swedish church?" In those places where Zinzendorf had won a following among Lutherans, Muhlenberg blamed "the young people," who had "been neglected and have, for the most part, grown up without any knowledge or reading of the Word of God." In Muhlenberg's eyes, the congregations in New Hannover and Providence never accepted Zinzendorf because of their stronger confessional background. The count happily allowed the newcomer to take over those rural congregations. Even after promising to do so at the mayor's request, however, he refused to return the Philadelphia congregation's Church Book. Muhlenberg, having convinced the mayor that he was the true Lutheran pastor and that Zinzendorf was a liar, claimed another victory in his quest to establish himself as the true father of the Lutheran faith in Pennsylvania.[79]

Upset that the English, Swedes, Quakers, Moravians, and Catholics all had places of worship in Philadelphia while "the Germans alone have nothing," Muhlenberg set his sights on erecting a German Lutheran church. Quickly dispatching his deacons to find an appropriate piece of land, Muhlenberg then faced the challenge of raising the funds to erect the structure. Four of Muhlenberg's deacons took on personal debt to build the church. Muhlenberg reported to his superiors at the University of Halle his incorrect belief that Pennsylvania law permitted only Anglicans and Lutherans to build churches. Mixed with apology for the extra cost, Muhlenberg boasted that the Lutherans "must also erect a steeple for bells, and this will reach an elevation of eighty-five feet." Although Muhlenberg's "opponents" anticipated that the four deacons would land in debtors' prison and cast a shadow on the project, Muhlenberg's congregation worshipped proudly in the structure for the first time on October 20, 1743. Thrilled with his success, Muhlenberg wrote Halle, "Oh, God, what a blessing this is in this strange, wild country!"[80]

In 1745 Muhlenberg experienced two windfalls that assured his ascendancy as leader of the colonial Lutherans. First, the Halle Ministerium sent three additional men to serve with Muhlenberg in the Pennsylvania mission. One, Peter Brunnholtz, was a pastor. The other two, Johann Nicholas Kurtz and J. H. Schaum, were to serve as catechists. Second, Muhlenberg made a critical alliance and married Conrad Weiser's daughter, Anna. The marriage spared Muhlenberg from the gossip he was subject to as a bachelor and linked him with one of the most influential Germans in Pennsylvania—one whom the Moravians had desperately wished to bring into their own fold.[81] Lutherans considered Muhlenberg's marriage a triumph for their confession.[82] Muhlenberg's travels to the Weiser homestead in Tulpehocken also concluded with the Lutheran congregation placing themselves under his care until Halle could send another pastor to take the Tulpehocken pulpit. Tulpehocken experienced an ongoing Lutheran-Moravian scuffle much like that Muhlenberg first discovered in Philadelphia. Capturing the Tulpehocken pulpit, as well as its most esteemed resident's daughter, secured a double victory.[83]

Muhlenberg then traveled triumphantly to Raritan and settled the dispute between the parishioners and Pastor Wolf. Muhlenberg recognized the potential to make inroads into Berkenmeyer's sphere of influence. The Raritan congregations asked Muhlenberg to send them a pastor, and Muhlenberg wrote Halle, "If we once have the door opened to us here, we can extend our operations in the surrounding regions." Without action from Halle, Muhlenberg feared the New Jersey congregations would fall into the Moravian flock. As an interim solution, Muhlenberg dispatched Nicholas Kurtz "for the early winter months to hold services and conduct school."[84]

Muhlenberg's struggles with Moravians never ceased. In Lancaster a Swedish Moravian, Peter Nyberg, divided the Lutheran parish with his claim that Moravians and Lutherans adhered to the same principles. Pietists, he claimed, were heretics who could not reconcile themselves with Moravians. Muhlenberg wrote to Halle and asked that the neutral University of Tübingen as well as the Swedish Consistory discuss the matter. While he awaited the inevitable denial

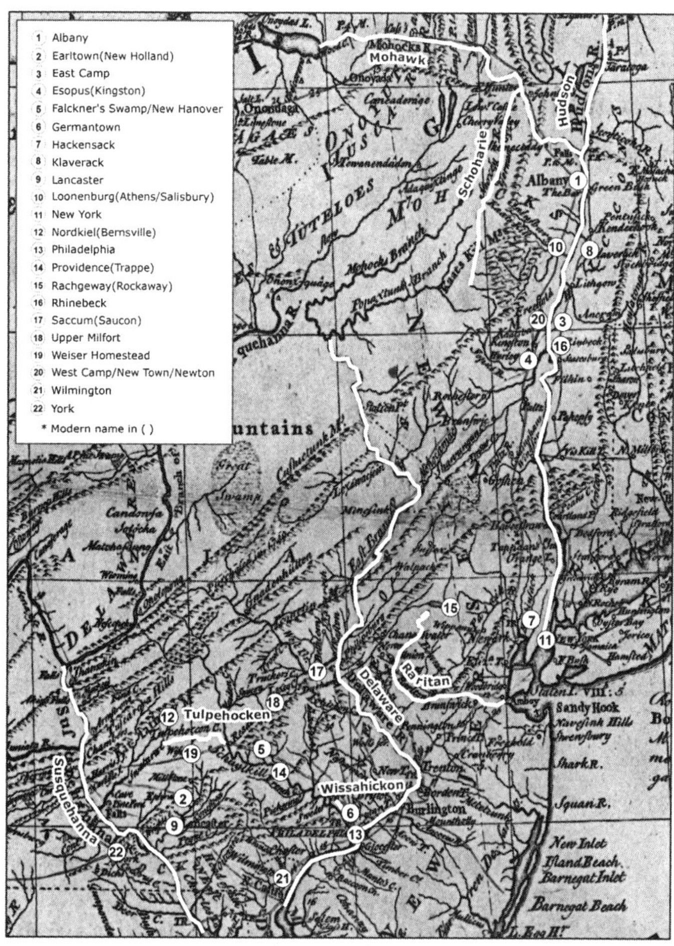

Fig. 2. "Lutheran America 1698–1748," courtesy of the author. Background: Lewis Evans, *A General Map of the Middle British Colonies, in America* (Philadelphia, 1755). Library of Congress, Map Collections.

of any Lutheran-Moravian affinity, Moravians and Lutherans in Lancaster proceeded to lock one another out of churches and sue one another in the fashion well established in Philadelphia and Tulpehocken. Conrad Weiser tried and failed to negotiate a conclusion to the Lancaster crisis, but it simmered even after Nyberg left the Lutheran church and built his own.[85]

Muhlenberg rode throughout Pennsylvania and to Maryland and New Jersey attempting to win souls for Lutherans and to end Moravian influence in America.[86] Further trials came in the form of Caspar Stoever, "who drank himself drunk in an inn and vomited in the presence of all sorts of sectarian people, which is charged upto our account because he is called a Lutheran preacher." Another man called himself "Carl Rudolf, Prince of Wuerttemberg," claimed to be a Lutheran pastor, and disparaged Muhlenberg's growing circle "as horrible Pietists."[87] Upon meeting an Indian chief in the company of Conrad Weiser, Muhlenberg mused, "When one looks at these poor people, one deplores their blindness and darkness," but Christian hypocrisy surpassed Indian heathenism in its horrors. When Indians observed European settlers, Muhlenberg surmised that "they think we are to be deplored, which is true, in so far as we have the light and for the most part do not walk in the light, but love darkness more than the light!"[88]

In April 1748 Pastor Johann Friedrich Handshuh arrived from Germany to join the Halle missionaries in Philadelphia. With a quorum of three, the pastors could ordain more of their own kind on American soil for the first time since Justus Falckner. The three men first wrote a liturgy especially adapted for the German Lutherans from the Rhineland who populated their congregations. The South-Germans would have judged the more orthodox Swedish liturgy "papistical." The pastors chose the liturgy used by the Savoy Church in London as their starting point. Handshuh took over the troublesome Lancaster parish, Kurtz served in Tulpehocken, and Schaum traveled to the westernmost outpost, York, while Muhlenberg and Brunnholtz shared the responsibility for Philadelphia, Germantown, and the surrounding congregations.

In August 1748 three Hallensian ministers, Swedish Provost Sandin, Pastor Johann Christoph Hartwick (who had come to New York at the behest of the Hamburg Consistory), and three Reformed ministers serving as witnesses processed through the streets of Philadelphia before consecrating St. Michael's Lutheran Church and ordaining Nicholas Kurtz. English, Swedish, and German echoed through the structure as delegates from New Hannover (Falckner's Swamp), Providence (Trappe), Upper Milfort, Saccum (Saucon), Philadelphia, Germantown, Lancaster, Earltown, Tulpehocken, and Nordkiel (Bernsville) listened. The newly formed synod remembered "with what distress, temptations, trials, and fisticuffs the building had been begun," and the Philadelphia church council pledged "to keep the church unto their children and children's children."[89] The Evangelical Lutheran Ministerium of Pennsylvania and the Adjacent States united Lutherans from across Europe in America and set a precedent for the possibility that *eius religio* could exist regardless of *cuius regio.*

Confessional Spatiality in the Puritan Atlantic

Heather Miyano Kopelson

In some ways the puritan minister Michael Wigglesworth is an obvious starting place for a spatially inclined investigation of religion and the Atlantic World.[1] He is familiar to many students of early American religion, literature, and history as the author of *The Day of Doom,* a verse meditation on Judgment Day, which lays out the theological tenets of predestination in which individuals can but struggle to accept their fates in the face of the decrees of an all-powerful and demanding God. Almost as well known are his personal and epistolary transatlantic crossings between England and New England, movements and connections that could be readily linked to specific people and even latitudinal and longitudinal coordinates.[2]

But Wigglesworth's life also offers a glimmer of a more expansive puritan Atlantic, a puritan-influenced world that included—but extended beyond—Wigglesworth and his clerical compatriots. His Atlantic travels suggest a conception of religiously bounded space that encompassed many other locales along with New England, one perceived and created through religious affiliation and practice. Shortly after the publication of *Day of Doom* in 1662, Wigglesworth traveled to Bermuda and found the religious environment to be entirely unremarkable.[3] As he was not a man who saw religion in some parts of his life and not in others, his failure to comment on religious life in Bermuda was significant. Had the spiritual environment been abhorrent to him, there would have been no reason for him to refrain from commenting to that effect.[4]

The apparent familiarity of Bermuda's atmosphere to one puritan minister is a hint that puritanism existed in a wider context than England and eastern Massachusetts. In the middle of the seventeenth century, a spectrum of colonies shared a distinct culture of English religious dissent that extended beyond the sermonizing and lecturing of the puritan meetinghouse to shape a larger sense of community. This spectrum also included places such as Rhode Island and Providence Plantations, founded by Massachusetts exiles but still in the same religious world as the Bay Colony. Individuals disagreed over the boundaries of that community and how to determine who might belong to it. They turned to the critical factors of race and religion to define those boundaries and to make them appear inevitable and unchangeable rather than malleable and contingent on context. These struggles over community definition revealed differing maps of the puritan Atlantic and competing organizational schemes for its resources.

Studies of religion and the Atlantic World face a difficult question of how one measures the subject of investigation. What counts as religion or religious influence? How does one quantify faith? Including actions as well as texts, in addition to expanding the definition of texts, is a way to get at those sometimes intangible aspects, the ephemeral movement of body and mind.[5] In addition, framing the conversation around questions about spatiality and its relational qualities might also offer a way to approach the problem of quantification, which was part of the very development of the Atlantic World system in the early modern era, without reproducing the census concerns of early modern imperial administrators. While this essay does not employ the technical tools of geographical information science as do others in this volume, it ends by suggesting how such GIScience could enable the multilevel mapping of religious practice in the Atlantic World. By developing ways to map different kinds of data simultaneously, allowing for some flow and flux between them, scholars would be closer to the dynamic quality of religion and the Atlantic World.

Bounding the Late-Seventeenth-Century Puritan Atlantic

"Puritan Atlantic" looks at those parts of the Atlantic world where Puritans exerted substantial influence on the institutions and practices of society. In addition to Rhode Island and Bermuda, several colonies and locales outside the New England colonies of Massachusetts, Plymouth, New Haven, and Connecticut were part of the puritan Atlantic, an idea that does not depend as heavily on self-identification as does the "Protestant International," a confessional network that understood itself to be fighting against a worldwide Catholic threat.[6] While specific and articulated connections among dissenting Protestants did exist in the puritan Atlantic, they did not fill the entire space.[7]

The phrase "puritan Atlantic" highlights common aspects of the shared religious culture in places where "hot" Protestants, those seeking reform beyond that instituted by the Church of England, played a major role.[8] In addition to Rhode Island and Bermuda, several colonies and locales outside the orthodox New England colonies of Massachusetts, Plymouth, New Haven, and Connecticut were part of the puritan Atlantic, including Providence Island, the Bahamas, Antigua, Barbados, and parts of the Chesapeake, Long Island, and New Jersey. The label points to the connections among and between these places, as well as their relationships with England. That shared culture changed dissenting Protestants' perception of space by creating intimate links between physically far-flung places and by making geographical neighbors into strangers.[9] These locations have separately received scholarly attention, but considering them as part of a shared confessional spatiality would allow for more attention to the fluctuations of dissenting English culture in the Atlantic World more broadly.[10]

The puritan Atlantic helps push one's understanding of the interplay between the physical and mental worlds of Atlantic actors, between intense local knowledge and a strongly crafted perception of confessional spatiality. Seventeenth-century English Protestants understood their religious communities through the metaphor of the body of Christ, so that both visible congregations of the faithful and the invisible community of the saved throughout the world were part of a body of which Christ was the head. They described churches and groups of individuals as specific members of that body: limbs, sinew, or blood. Communities in far-flung locales considered each other to be members of the same body. This body of Christ was linked to, but not the same as, the body politic. The points of overlap and disjuncture between these two bodies reveal the contours of how people determined the boundary between themselves and others, between insider and outsider. Although generally perceived to be rigid and restrictive, the puritan body of Christ proved more permeable to racial differences than the body politic because of the emphasis on voluntary membership. Relative distances did not always match the geography of the physical world in the cognitive space of the puritan Atlantic. The conceptual space of the body of Christ changed the mental maps of those who inhabited it, even as the inhabitants' actions created that space and changed the relationships between themselves and others. It was a way of organizing society on the local level and simultaneously of understanding the vast amounts of physical space of the Atlantic.

As the puritan English in southern New England and Bermuda tried to create new societies, they brought a particular kind of order to their communities—godly order was meant to be paramount. Although a full investigation is outside the scope of this essay, English puritans were not the only ones in the colonies who had a sense of order inspired by belief in divine power. Africans who had been enslaved and forcibly transported across the Atlantic and by way of the Caribbean came from societies with beliefs about how humans ought to interact with one another and with the divine. Indigenous peoples whose homelands had been appropriated for colonial settlement also had worldviews with specific visions of how social relationships should be organized. An investigation of a confessional spatiality emphasizes relationships between and among individuals, communities, and the divine and thus supports a parallel comparison between Christianity and religions without extensive written theologies.[11] Considering English puritans, Africans, and indigenous peoples of the Americas from the same academic platform makes it easier to catch the swirling currents of belief and practice among groups of people and to see how their respective maps overlay each other.

While Rhode Island, Massachusetts, and Bermuda differed from each other in significant ways, they more closely resembled each other in key aspects than they did other English colonies. As a group of dissenting colonies, they were definably separate from the British plantation colonies, whether southern mainland or Caribbean, as well as the mid-Atlantic colonies; they were colonized by the "hotter" sorts of Protestants seeking reform beyond that instituted by the Church of England. These (loosely defined) puritans influenced social structures and cultural order in all three colonies, but they did not control social institutions in all three places in equal measure.[12] While these separate colonies shared a dissenting ethos, each location had a particular trajectory. For instance, puritans and Baptists visited and even preached to each other's congregations in London during the seventeenth century, including John Bunyan, author of the allegory for Christian conversion *A Pilgrim's Progress*. At the same time in Massachusetts Bay, ruling puritans persecuted Baptists as religious outlaws for their insistence on adult baptism.[13] Without an established church in Rhode Island and Providence Plantations, Baptists there did not face the same persecution and exclusion from town government. But they did have to contend with internal schisms.[14] Conflicts over the appropriate life stage for baptism do not appear in Bermuda's records. Similarly, much early American scholarship takes the public conversion narrative required in most of New England's puritan churches relating an individual's spiritual and physical struggles to discern the working of God's grace upon and in them as the marker of a "truly" puritan church. However, these public displays were not a common practice in English congregations, although they considered themselves to be every bit as committed to purifying the Church of England if not more so because they had stayed in England.[15] A capacious definition of puritan religiosity that includes a wide spectrum of behavior encompasses such regional variations.

Massachusetts, Rhode Island, and Bermuda shared a key spatial characteristic: all faced early and intense difficulties with their topographical and geographical boundedness. The ocean constrained the physical expansion of the mainland colonies along one border (east for Massachusetts, south for Rhode Island), while other polities, Native and European, impeded them on the others. Massachusetts had to contend with Nipmucs, the Pocumtucks, and other tribes in the Connecticut River Valley area, Massachusetts and Wampanoags along the coast, as well as Pennacooks, Pequots, and Mahicans. To the north and east, Abenakis and Haudenosaunees (Iroquois), as well as the French, undercut the Bay Colony's ambitions of geographical growth in what is now Maine and at times seemed to threaten its survival. Rhode Island faced Wampanoags in the northeastern part of the colony, Narragansetts, Niantics along the south shore, and the Pequot survivors of the 1637 Pequot War with the English, who joined Mohegan communities based primarily in Connecticut but whose territory also included the southwest corner of Rhode Island.[16] Rhode Island and Massachusetts could only encompass more territory in direct conflict with the charter claims of Connecticut, New York, and Plymouth.[17] The charter granted to Rhode Island and Providence Plantations by Charles II in 1663 overlapped with Connecticut's new 1662 charter to the west and Plymouth and Massachusetts' borders to the east.[18] The lands granted in these charters were often more imaginative exercises than an indication of what the English could actually control of Algonquian homelands, but they still gesture towards the multiple levels of contestation over place even within the English space of New England.

As an uninhabited archipelago, a mere twenty-one square miles of land that lies in the Atlantic nearly six hundred miles from the nearest land (what is now Cape Hatteras on the coast of North Carolina), Bermuda differed from the mainland colonies. A preexisting topography separated New England from Bermuda, which had no established human sense of place. All inhabitants of the island colony were newcomers who simultaneously established its conceptual and physical landscapes. The island-born constituted a majority of the inhabitants by the mid-seventeenth century, an unusual demographic situation that offered an earlier hospitable environment for combinations of indigenous, English, and African beliefs and practices than in other colonies, where the constant influx of African-born people and established indigenous communities renewed knowledge about cultural and religious practices. Bermudians of color were mostly insiders rather than outsiders to Christianity, a familiarity that white Bermudians largely recognized because they had grown up alongside one another and lived together in the same households. A similar shift away from African-born individuals did not happen in British mainland North American colonies until the beginning of the nineteenth century.[19]

The late seventeenth century was a difficult time in the puritan Atlantic. In the years after the failure of the Protectorate and through the reign of George I, the aim of a pure Protestant community seemed under attack from every direction. The period after 1660 saw the increasingly strict enforcement of the decrees and practices of the Church of England on the eastern side of the Atlantic and, on the western side, the revocation of the Massachusetts Bay charter, the institution and downfall of the Dominion of New England, and heightened warfare with Algonquian peoples, including the extremely bloody King Philip's War. With the Revocation of the Edict of Nantes in 1685, it appeared that Protestantism might be in danger of being wiped from the face of the earth. In 1688 and 1689, royal officials' attempts to hide the news that the Protestant William of Orange had taken over the English throne from the Catholic James II seemed to point to a Catholic conspiracy, a conspiracy formed to put the colonies under the control of France and—by extension—the Pope.[20] For those who were convinced or hopeful that Protestant countries, especially England, were to take part in bringing about the new Jerusalem, the prospect of their apostatizing to Catholicism was seen as a sign of the end of this world and Satan's triumph.[21]

The late seventeenth century was a pivotal period for Native peoples in southern New England, with King Philip's War, shifting intertribal alliances, and ever-expanding land encroachment by the English. Economic relationships also shifted after New England colonial governments disestablished wampum as a legal currency.[22] While King Philip's War and later conflicts were devastating to many southeastern Algonquian peoples, they did not disappear from southern New England after 1676.[23] However, after that point they could not marshal direct military opposition to the English, and it became increasingly difficult for individual Natives and Africans to win recognition or space from the English for their competing worldviews. Natives were much more than pawns on a European chessboard; the English and other Europeans often only dimly perceived the complex political calculations of which they were only one part.

The puritan Atlantic becomes a less useful organizing concept once England tightened its control of its American colonies and brought them into closer order. The year 1723 marks a point at which the law and social practice increasingly codified hierarchies of race and servitude, as well as New England merchants' sharply increased participation in carrying the human cargo of the slave trade. New England was economically dependent on the slave trade long before New England ship captains carried enslaved Africans in large numbers. After the English Civil War cut off the flood of migrants to New England in the 1640s—and with them their money and support of the local staples market—a large portion of New England's economy rested on the demand of British slave colonies in the Caribbean for those staples.[24] Bermuda's turn to maritime activity and shipbuilding, which began after the dissolution of the governing Somers Islands Company in 1684, was fully established by the early 1720s, a shift whose success depended on the labor of enslaved Bermudians at sea and on shore.[25] In Rhode Island, planters in the Narragansett region turned to enslaved African labor even as they institutionalized their exploitation of Narragansetts' labor through hereditary pauperdom, in which children inherited the debt obligations and indentured servitude of their parents.[26] However, economic considerations were not the only cause of change. Relations among the colonies shifted as England tried to strengthen each colony's connection to the metropole, while changes within puritanism meant that ministers no longer dictated specific behaviors to be enforced or punished by magistrates.

England's closer attention to its empire meant that legal structures in the colonies moved closer to common law practices, a move that marked a shift towards more uneven power relations between men and women. While the puritan vision of godly rules meted out harsh punishments to women who stepped outside the bounds of proper behavior, it also punished men for sexual and moral lapses and reduced their power over their wives, thus coming close to a single standard for sexual and moral conduct. However, between 1690 and 1723, most puritan ministers' view of the proper relationship between godly order and civil authority shifted so that ministers were no longer directing the civil authorities about which behaviors to punish. Legal reforms of the 1690s, which brought common law and specifically trained lawyers more forcefully into colonial courts, also weakened the influence of a distinct ethos on governmental and legal structures.[27] These reforms were an outgrowth of Charles II's earlier push towards greater centralization, which, although it succeeded to varying extents from place to place, had been aimed at all the English colonies.[28]

In New England, even when the puritan Atlantic was at its strongest, it was a thin overlay on what remained fundamentally Native space. That preexisting topography separated New England from Bermuda, which had no indigenous inhabitants and no established human spatial organization. The northeastern coast was contested space, not only in terms of competition over land and other resources, but also in how Europeans and Natives thought of resources and how they defined what it meant to share space. Although southern Algonquians varied in particular burial rituals, preferred family forms, governmental structures, and dialects and languages, they shared an idea of the space of the Northeast as a "common pot" on which all depended for sustenance and in which those who could take control of more owed assistance to those who were weaker and so had less. The common pot was not a conflict-free paradise: those who had less owed allegiance and acquiescence to a lower place in the social hierarchy to those who had more. The English had a more exclusionary view in which the privilege of the powerful was to bound off space and to exclude others from it and its resources. puritans attempted to mold the northeastern coast to their experiences and expectations in order to make their own place. But Natives often turned colonial institutions to their own use to subvert attempted European control and reshaping of space, for instance by using writing to assert their own understanding of proper land use. Southern Algonquians perceived their multiple communities as strongly linked to homelands, to connections along waterways, and through kin relationships.[29]

Natives in northeastern America cultivated relationships with kin and allied tribes, as well as made their own appeals to European monarchs, based on their understandings of connection between peoples and places. Native political topographies functioned quite differently and took little notice of differences among the English like those between Baptist and puritan. While their homelands did not match up with English-drawn colonial boundaries, Algonquians contending with southern New England demonstrated an astute understanding of the rivalries among English colonies as well as those among European empires.[30]

Race, Religion, and Identity

In the seventeenth-century puritan Atlantic, religion, along with other categories of difference such as race and gender, provided a vocabulary and structure to describe and maintain boundaries between insider and outsider. Categories of inclusion and exclusion were dynamic, so that no one was always an insider or an outsider. In many cases the internal divisions within a given group did not matter to others, so that Massachusetts Bay puritans might lump all English in Rhode Island together even as they struggled among themselves; or the Narragansetts might consider all English in the colonies as one as against their efforts to take advantage of their alliance with the English king, even as Rhode Island and Massachusetts Bay fought over control of land. After the outbreak of King Philip's War, the English were largely inclined to make fewer distinctions among tribes and tended to see all Indians as enemies, actual or potential, at the same time that the New England colonies differed sharply over the war. Narragansetts, who stayed out of the first stages of the war, suffered the effects of this generalizing mentality when English militia surrounded a winter camp near South Kingstown, Rhode Island, and killed hundreds of people, including noncombatants, in the Great Swamp Massacre.[31]

Individuals' and groups' senses of themselves in place and their ordered perception of their relationship to the rest of the world did not always line up exactly with their location in geographic space. The indeterminacy and tension among different categories of belonging and affinity (race, region, gender, and religion) are what makes attention to identity a useful means for unraveling the complexities of seventeenth-century social structures. Identity emphasizes the significance of religious affiliation as a means to determine insider/outsider status, as determined primarily through practice in addition to any explicit, articulated theological stance. In this context, the term points to the ways in which people related to each other and created categories of difference. Individuals and groups took what was soft, malleable, and contested and described it as if it were hard, intrinsic, and nonnegotiable, even as they maintained multiple allegiances.[32]

Techniques of differentiation based on skin color, religion, and gender were not new to the seventeenth century, nor did Europeans have a monopoly on them.[33] Neither the seventeenth century, nor the eighteenth century, nor the sixteenth century is the origin point for a calcified notion of biological race. Indeed, the search for that origin point distracts our attention from the ways in which categories of difference have functioned at specific times and places.[34] However, European intellectuals did spend many pages trying to figure out the cause and meaning of human difference during the sixteenth and seventeenth centuries as their societies came into contact with peoples in Africa and the Americas. In the seventeenth century, English Christians believed that an individual's body could reveal her or his spiritual state. Like other Europeans, they searched for a universal language of bodies in their encounters—real or imagined—with Africans and indigenous people of the Americas.[35] Abstract ideas about the body affected notions of how people were supposed to live together and interact with one another, of how people were meant to exist in relative space. Disputes over people's physical bodies had religious resonance, just as religious concepts of the body affected people's perceptions of their own and others' bodies.[36] While English colonists certainly used skin color and freedom status to categorize people in the middle of the seventeenth century, those specific markers were not the only ones to which they turned.[37]

The religious and racial currents of categorization ebbed and flowed across each other in more than one place. European theologians wrote treatises on the origins of Africans and Indians according to biblical accounts.[38] Puritan divines and enthusiasts in Old and New England picked up on some of those themes of the origins of all people. Some put forth the idea that Natives were one of the Lost Tribes and the eastern coast of North America the new Israel, as support for their decision to leave England. This theory of Indians' Israelite origins also encouraged metropolitan support for the colonies. By supporting the colonies, the English in Old England would be supporting Indian conversion, which would help bring about the second coming of Christ and the millennium. For others, Indians were Gentiles and could only experience mass conversion after the conversion of the Jews. A few might be eligible for conversion before the millennium, but their origins precluded their attainment of Christianity before that series of events.[39] The discussion hinged on the issue of America's relative place in Europe's sense of space and whether America was a long-separated part of the same whole or an entirely different entity whose full incorporation into the European Christian world required the end of this world.

Disconnect between religious affiliation and political boundaries intensified anxiety about the fate of countries and empires. Church and state, while not always harmonious in practice, were meant to work together. Once England became Protestant, high-level and popular rhetoric about the imperial powers of Portugal, Spain, and France often couched rationale for fears of, and wars with, these polities as a religious battle between Protestant and Catholic.[40] But that distinction was not always the case. The existence of English Catholics and French Huguenots disrupted the supposed correspondence between English and Protestant, or French and Catholic.[41] The commercial rivalry between the two Protestant powers of England and the Netherlands intensified into war three times during the seventeenth century, testimony that religious affiliation was not the only concern driving foreign policy. Ireland remained a potent Catholic force at the geographic core of an English empire. Many English Protestants asked themselves what it meant to be a professor of the faith and a member of a community, commonwealth, nation, and empire, an uncertainty only amplified by their interactions with each other and with Natives and Africans.

Between the second half of the seventeenth century and the first two decades of the eighteenth, the primary tools of definition shifted from those of religious affiliation to racialist ones. English and other European descriptions of Jews used rhetoric about their existence as a visually different race and linked supposed character traits to physiognomy. The English likened Spanish and French Catholics to the indigenous people with whom they interacted. Thus framed, the separation between Protestants and Catholics frequently overshadowed variations among particular strains of English dissenters. That evolution of difference drew on elements of a transatlantic intellectual culture but was also rooted in local circumstances.

Developing ideas of race depended upon shifting notions of religious identity. The calcification of racial categories of "white," "black," and "Indian" developed in tandem with the hardening of religious boundaries between "Christian" and "heathen," and between "Catholic" and "Protestant," even as the separation between what scholars identify as different branches of Protestants lessened in the face of a perceived Catholic threat. The experience of Catholic Irish in southern New England and Bermuda during this period underscores the strength of anti-Catholic sentiment and its complication of any simple separation between Europeans and non-Europeans in the creation of categories of social hierarchy. Protestants discovered similarities among themselves as a result of finding a common enemy in Catholics, although anti-Catholicism created division among Protestants as well: "papist" remained a common, yet still powerful epithet against one's theological enemies no matter who they were.[42] The conversion of Africans and Natives, and thus their membership in the body of Christ, had the potential to unsettle social hierarchies of slavery, race, and gender through connection to the body politic. By 1723 racially defined social hierarchies had emerged that contained the ambiguities created by religious practice and biblical discourse.

Defining the Body of Christ

The body of Christ is a central metaphor and entity that organizes Christian belief and practice. For Christians generally, Jesus Christ, the son of God, was and is simultaneously fully divine and fully human. Christ's body as a historical human body was significant because it meant that he was fully human and truly suffered pain and death for the sins of all humanity. The body of Christ has also referred to the church, so that Christians are members of one body, the church.

Not only have people interpreted the body of Christ in various ways at different times and places, but they have also had conflicting interpretations in the same time and place. The process of discerning these meanings is complex and does not end in neatly packaged answers, as the meanings themselves are often ambiguous. However, following these crisscrossing branches—much like following the path of neurons in the brain—can lead to unexpected synapses, moments of connection between seemingly disparate elements. A more apt analogy for the seventeenth century is one concerning veins and the circulation of blood; following all the interpretations of the body of Christ moves one through all aspects of religious culture in the dissenting Atlantic, a motion that itself is vital to the functioning of the whole body.

Interpretations of the body of Christ among religious thinkers in seventeenth-century Europe and the puritan Atlantic reveal how people thought about community in a way that intrinsically involved religion as well as cultural readings of the body. Sectarian allegiances shared a common trait with developing ideas about racial or ethnic difference in that both provided ways for people to define who belonged in their community and who had to be kept outside it. Separate strains of Christianity held differing views about what the ideal community should look like, how it should work, and who should be in it. Understanding how the body of Christ structured English communities highlights the points at which sectarian and racial differences categorized people similarly and the points at which those definitions diverged and ceased to overlap.[43]

As a religious concept and as a body onto which individuals projected physical qualities, the body of Christ could simultaneously serve both means of defining community. It was a conceptual space that could be infinitely expansive or intimately focused on the inner workings of an individual soul. And yet, the idea was not malleable *ad infinitum,* because individuals' physical and bodily understanding constrained their understanding of how the body of Christ organized itself. Moreover, while embodied experience provided a common origin point for human interpretation of the world, specific explanations varied over time and among cultures. The four planes of the human body (front, back, and two sides) and the movement of the sun meant that many peoples have divided the world into four directions, but they varied in which one they designated as the principal direction.[44]

Christians of all kinds perceived their churches as the body of Christ. The metaphor affected the social organization of religious life for the people (mostly Europeans) who brought the idea into the complex new Atlantic communities of the English colonies. Ideas around the body of Christ existed in a context in which many kinds of bodies held power. The control of bodily intimacy was an essential part of social and familial hierarchies.[45] Christians used the body of Christ, which included their own tangible bodies, to help them understand their relationship to the divine and to each other. Individually and collectively, they were members of that body, while Christ was the head. Puritans, Baptists, and Quakers all sought to act from scripture, although they often did not recognize the similarity of their efforts. It is significant that the texts they studied, whether in formal university studies in preparation to become ministers, in neighborhood or familial gatherings, or in meetings for worship, contained embodied images to which they could relate from their own experience of how their limbs and organs worked in concert. Although doctrinal differences proliferated, Baptists believed that the body of Christ ought to be composed solely of active believers, so that baptism, the mark of admission into that body, should not be administered to any but an adult. The Society of Friends defined the body of Christ somewhat differently in that each person had the potential to find the indwelling Light of Christ within her- or himself and thus be saved from sin. That individual sharing of the one Light was fostered in regular meetings for worship and business and in communication among meetings.[46] Quakers' array of bodily metaphors focused less on individual body parts working in concert than did those of Baptists or puritans, but they did not altogether abandon Christ's body as a metaphor for their communities. That body of the church may have been less hierarchical than Calvinist ones, but it was still a whole entity and not merely a chance conglomeration of individuals.

The relation of one body part to another helped ministers articulate their vision of a proper visible church in which members were bound to one another with indissoluble bonds. In this language of physical or "natural" bodies and body parts, they struggled to balance an understanding of a hierarchy of importance among those parts against the transformative nature of Christ and the divine gift of salvation. The parts of the body were all necessary to the whole because they had varying forms and functions, but their contributions were not all of the same significance. In a letter of instruction to their younger coreligionists, dissenting ministers exhorted them to "let every one Design and Aim to be serviceable in his Place and Relation" because "every little Member of our natural Body profits the whole; the Eye is the light of all the Body; the Tongue pleads for the whole, or for any part; the Hand receives and labours as much as for the Foot, or the Head, as for it self." The phrase "serviceable in his Place and Relation" is important here because it signaled the hierarchy among body parts. While "every part must be useful to the Whole," some were "little" ones that played a lesser role. The head relied on the other body parts, but its authority was meant to reign supreme.[47]

This bodily understood hierarchy existed among Quakers as well. When Mary Penington wrote in support of the creation of a separate women's meeting, she sought to reassure critics of the plan by comparing women to lesser parts of the body: "The men need not grudge us this place in the body, wherein we are meet helps, and usurp not authority over them, and act as the inferior parts of the body, being members, though but a finger or toe."[48] Men and women Friends might all be members of Christ's body, but membership meant neither equality nor commensurate authority—women acted as "the inferior parts" and were "a finger or toe" while men were the unspecified superior parts of the body.[49]

The religious leaders and thinkers John Calvin, George Fox, and John Winthrop explored the problem of connecting the parts of the body through a discussion of the function of sinews or ligaments. Each saw a different aspect of religious life as the binding matter of the body, but the imagery remained the same. Calvin described church discipline as the "sinews, through which the members of the body hold together, each in its own place." Without the sinews of discipline, including the power to excommunicate members and declare them as outside of the body, the church would dissolve because there would be nothing to hold it together.[50] In puritan theology, broadly defined, the unity of the invisible church in, and as, the body of Christ bound separate congregations together without an analogous bureaucratic structure to express that binding. Individuals who had been saved through God's grace were members of the invisible church; ideally, the membership of the visible church would match up with the invisible church of the elect.[51] All were held together, but all were not equal because "each" was "in its own place." In terms of salvation, however, members of the elect were equal to one another.

Winthrop's "A Modell of Christian Charity," an address written in 1630 that aimed to serve as a guide for the community to be founded in New England, labeled Christ's love as the sinews knitting members together in one church. Winthrop reminded his audience, "Christ and his church make one body," a body whose "ligaments hereof being Christ or his love." Only with "propper ligamentes" could a body be perfect, "a glorious body without spot or wrinckle." The spotless physical state mirrored the perfect spiritual condition.[52] Winthrop further detailed how Christ's love brings bodily changes: the assemblage of parts that formed a "disproportionate" body become "the most perfect and best proportioned body in the world."[53] After Christ transforms them, all the parts exist in such a "contiguous . . . speciall relation as they must needes partake of each others strength and infirmity, joy, and sorrowe, weale and woe." The members of the body can no longer fully separate from one another because of those changes. They will "necessarily" experience a "Sympathy," which creates a "native desire and endeavour, to strengthen defend preserve and comfort the other."[54] He concluded, "That love is as absolutely necessary to the being of the body of Christ, as the sinewes and other ligaments of a naturall body are to the being of that body."[55] Winthrop emphasized the binding nature of the "naturall" body, finishing with a reiteration of the connection between the one body of the church and the physical body.

George Fox also took up the metaphor of a substantial, physical body bound together by sinews. He reminded his readers, "the Head Christ Jesus, from which all the Body by Joynts and Bands, having Nourishment ministred from Christ their Head, and knot together, increaseth with the Increase of God." Ephesians 4:16 describes Christ as the head "From whom the whole body fitly joyned together, and compacted by that which every joynt supplyeth, according to the effectuall working in the measure of every part, maketh increase of the body." Fox's addition of "bands" strengthened the bodily imagery of the passage and made it more anatomically specific.[56] This body was not an inchoate mass but one whose members were connected to each other, indeed were knotted to each other and to Christ.Fox's bands or sinews were spiritual nourishment rather than Calvin's sinews of discipline or Winthrop's sinews of love, but all envisioned the ideal religious community as one in which individuals related to each other in the same way that the parts of a human body worked together. The spatial contours of such linkages for a given group could be tracked and those pathways traced through mapping visits, exchanges of letters, or remembrances on community occasions, to list only a few examples.

The Body Politic

Because bodily metaphors were based in the universal experience of having a physical body, the English and other Europeans found them to be useful in the explication of other types of group organization. The corporate entity of the body politic shared some characteristics with the body of Christ—most obviously the significance of bodily metaphor as a way to understand relationships between human beings in a given community—but the two were not identical in function or in composition. The body politic explained and justified a hierarchical, static society, while the body of Christ was meant to change its members and offer a new model for social organization that did not depend on established worldly sources of power such as wealth or bloodline. Different interpretations of these bodies existed, but the broad contrast between static and transformative remained.

Political bodies had appeared in English literature at least since the twelfth century, but bodily metaphors became more popular beginning in the sixteenth century as a means to lend a sense of natural and inherent authority to the English government. Political theorists and the Crown attempted to make the body of Christ and the body politic appear as connected as possible to claim divine authority for the monarch.[57] The concept of the king's two bodies—one natural and subject to decay, the other divine and eternal—came out of the belief in Christ's dual nature of human and divine and demonstrates the intertwined nature of political and religious thought in Europe from the medieval through the early modern period. Transposed onto the body of the monarch, Christ's dual nature provided a model in which the authority of the monarchy continued and passed on even when a particular monarch succumbed to mortality and died. The concept of the body politic did not inherently contain a connection to the divine. By making that connection between the body of Christ and the monarch, political writers described a body politic with a divinely ordained king or queen as the head.[58]

When Oliver Cromwell, the leaders of the army, and the Parliament beheaded Charles I in 1649, they removed what they believed to be a diseased member of the body politic. Charles II's restoration to the throne of England in 1660 reinstated the link between the monarch's body and Christ's.[59] The Glorious Revolution of 1688–89 challenged hereditary divine kingship by ousting James II in favor of the Dutch William of Orange and Mary, James II's daughter. William's supporters envisioned a tight overlap between the body of Christ and the body politic in which Protestant monarchs ruled over a Protestant country by virtue of their religious affiliation. Belonging to a particular body of Christ trumped aristocratic bloodlines.[60]

Some strongly anti-Catholic colonists took advantage of the chaos in England following the change in royal leadership to push for a decentralized empire that followed the lineaments of a Protestant body of Christ rather than those of a body politic headed by a monarch. New England agitators created a perception that Edmund Andros, the governor of the Dominion of New England, was a secret Catholic whose policies were geared towards strengthening New England's enemies, Native Catholics and their French allies in New France. Crown officials in New England misjudged how easily colonists might associate royal administration with the supposed tyranny of popery and were beaten back by a conflagration that threatened to consume the part of the imperial framework that was their bailiwick and in 1689 ended the Dominion of New England. However, royal officials in the English Caribbean saw the need to direct the conflation of the body of Christ and body politic into one. Even though many of the same rumors about the papist sympathies of imperial administration that circulated in New England existed and may even have originated in the Caribbean, in the 1690s officials in the island colonies were able to fan ordinary colonists' fear of Catholics into a contained fire that drew English colonists together as subjects of a newly centralized Protestant empire under the control of a powerful monarch. King William's War, which included conflicts from northern New England to the Caribbean between 1689 and 1697, assisted colonists in defining the body politic of the empire as one that was contiguous with a Protestant body of Christ. Exactly whom that definition excluded besides French Catholics depended on the specifics of local contests, but they all linked their part of the conflict to the fate of the imperial and Protestant whole.[61]

Applied to the political organization of English society overall, bodily metaphor expressed and encouraged a static hierarchy of family and state. Just as physical bodies performed best when each part fulfilled its function, social bodies were most healthful when their members accepted their places and performed their natural and ordained roles. With the body politic, individuals had particular roles to fill that gave them more or less power in relation to those around them. English authors elaborated the metaphor in great detail, so that husbandmen and laborers were usually the feet, the monarch was the head, and other occupations filled in the territory between—lawyers might be the lungs, for instance. Even when English representations of the body politic moved from the monarchical or aristocratic body to the common body, writers and thinkers assigned body parallels to a multitude of societal positions.[62]

Among English puritans, the body politic was related to the body of Christ, but the two entities did not entirely coincide in membership or in structure. The body of Christ was composed of the elect who would receive salvation at Judgment Day. The body politic—though it was meant to be coequal with the perfected form of the body of Christ—of necessity contained nonelect inhabitants of this world, those whom Christ had not saved. One could be part of the body politic without having full liberties since the body was made up of subordinate parts as well as the head. For the church as the body of Christ, Christ was the head, and its members existed in hierarchical arrangements. But the purpose of the body of Christ, the common characteristic among all its members, was salvation; all members of the elect received salvation in equal measure. The body politic, on the other hand, was primarily based on hierarchy.

When puritan communities tried to bring the two bodily metaphors into close concordance so that human government followed divine order, Africans and Natives sometimes found precarious places in English communities through becoming members of the body of Christ, or they formed a body of Christ that strengthened their own bodies politic.[63] Their conversion and resulting presence in the body of Christ had the potential to unsettle social hierarchies of slavery, race, and gender because of the overlap between the body of Christ and the body politic, a congruence whose exact measure was itself in dispute. Even if the potential to upset hierarchy was not always realized, the possibility always threatened as groups disagreed on the appropriate relationship between parts of the body.[64]

The idea that Christ wrought bodily transformation in the members of his church was a powerful one with potentially troubling implications for a world based on hierarchical labor relationships. If those who were different in kind and characteristic shared in one body through baptism, that transformation wrought a disruptive similarity among the members of the body. In seventeenth-century slave-owning societies, the emancipatory potential of baptism led some enslaved and baptized individuals to claim freedom. Many European officials had to contend with enslaved African Christians who demanded the fulfillment of the promises that all were one under Christ, despite centuries of a Christian intellectual tradition that distinguished between spiritual freedom through conversion and physical slavery and held the two states to be compatible.[65] Enslaved individuals continued to press for freedom based on their membership in the body of Christ. English colonial governments responded by passing acts specifying that baptism did not grant freedom, especially after seeing their partial success in New Netherland.[66] In addition to Bermuda, six colonies passed such legislation between 1664 and 1706. The New England colonies were not among them, although in 1694 a group of clergy requested that Massachusetts have such an act so that owners would be more willing to encourage their slaves to be baptized.[67]

The push to equate baptism and freedom did not exist in the same way in southern New England Native communities. While many Natives were in long-term indentured servitude and multigenerational debt relationships with English creditors, the English assumption was generally still that they were free in the sense of not being chattel slaves. Even after African men married into Native villages in the late seventeenth and early eighteenth centuries, making the children of Native mothers and African fathers prone to English classification as "mulatto" or "mustee" and therefore eligible for heritable slavery, those children worked to prove their mothers' Native status as the means to avoid being enslaved rather than turning to arguments based on baptism.[68] English governments, both imperial and local, gradually came to define Natives of the Americas and Africans as foreign substances in the body politic. This process of definition was irregular from place to place and fluctuated over time but by the beginning of the eighteenth century had solidified into standard practice and codified law.

Mapping Multiple Religious Topographies

Using GIScience to visualize how these conceptual maps of the body of Christ and the body politic differed, where their outlines merged and diverged, would offer a deeper perspective on the complex process of defining difference through religion and race in the seventeenth-century puritan Atlantic. The capability to display multiple layers would also make manifest the many competing human practices that defined overlapping cultural places in a single space, some of which made use of the body of Christ, while others did not. For instance, instead of a simple line to display the epistolary links of English puritans or the itineraries of traveling Quakers, GIScience could be used to convey the perceived shape of a community and distance between geographic spaces by showing places as closer together the more times people in one place mentioned those in another, or when they used similar vessels and distribution practices for the ritual meal of the Lord's Supper. If community members denigrated other places or individuals, that would push their locations further apart.

Some of this work has already been done for Native communities in southern New England, and scholars and community members continue to incorporate even more features of GIS technology. There is a rich concentration of such work on the Connecticut River Valley. Lisa Brooks has produced visual representations of these Native conceptualizations of space in northeastern America using ArcGIS, mapping conceptual organizations of space onto the waterways and forests of the Northeast.[69] The team involved in the Pocumtuck Valley Memorial Association's online exhibit about the 1704 raid on Deerfield has put together a layered map titled "Settlement Patterns in the Connecticut River Valley" that displays the interactions between Native homelands and English settlements.[70] While the Deerfield maps are not particularly concerned with religious practice, a similar layering technique could be used to show the development in frequency or in geographic spread of a given practice.

An example of where GIScience could enhance the understanding of complex and shifting communities comes from the work of Kathleen Bragdon. Bragdon has mapped the regional networks of Quabaugs, Pennacooks, and Cowesets to demonstrate the frequency of linkages from a single community across geographical space. She did so to emphasize that a typical Native community in the late seventeenth and eighteenth centuries included members from several different places and that the "composite" membership of "praying towns" of Christian Indians and other Natives was not an English creation. Those networks are printed as static, separate figures of circles connected by lines. Bragdon's discussion emphasized the fluidity of the groupings over time, even during an individual's lifetime.[71] An interactive map of the networks that showed how the connections changed over time would immediately convey the core of her argument that many Native communities had members with links to multiple places and that the membership of those communities fluctuated. GIScience could be helpful in mapping out these overlapping categories and contingent affiliations, either for an individual or a community, and could add in more variables such as participation in puritan practices. If one molds the visual representation of physical space so that it expresses the perceived cultural distance between the subject and other individuals or groups depending on which affiliation is dominant at any given point, one could see how particular groupings affect a given topography. More dynamic visual representations of the networks would also help make sense of how these parts were connected into a whole and show more clearly that the connection among the parts created multiple wholes that were greater than the sum of the parts.

Drawing the bounds of confessional spatiality with the tools of GIScience focuses on the relational aspects of religion in the Atlantic world. Dynamic ways of mapping enable the consideration of people's competing definitions of themselves and others, and permit scholars to adapt the categories according to the ways in which Atlantic World actors who were not officials and category-makers might have seen them. Thinking about how the different Atlantics map onto each other could reveal more about each individual Atlantic.

NOTES

Introduction

1. Cicero, *De oratore,* trans. E. W. Sutton, with an introduction by H. Rackham (Cambridge, Mass: Harvard University Press, 1942), 2:lxxxvi, 351–54.

2. Eleanor A. Maguire, "Spatial Navigation," in *Neuroergonomics: The Brain at Work,* ed. Raja Parasuranam and Matthew Rizzo (New York: Oxford University Press, 2007), 137. See also D. W. Lee, L. E. Miyasato, and N. S. Clayton, "Neurobiological Bases of Spatial Learning in the Natural Environment," *Neuroreport* 9 (1998): R15–R27, in which the authors explore this in the avian and mammalian hippocampus.

3. Yadin Dudai and Mary Carruthers, "The Janus Face of Mnemosyne" *Nature* 434 (March 31, 2005): 567.

4. David J. Bodenhamer, John Corrigan, and Trevor M. Harris, *The Spatial Humanities: GIS and the Future of Humanities Scholarship* (Bloomington: Indiana University Press, 2010). See also Bodenhamer, Corrigan, and Harris, eds., *Deep Maps and Spatial Narratives* (Bloomington: Indiana University Press, 2015); Ian Gregory and Alistair Geddes, eds., *Towards Spatial Humanities: Historical GIS and Spatial History* (Bloomington: Indiana University Press, 2014); Ian N. Gregory, Niall A. Cunningham, C. D. Lloyd, Ian G. Shuttleworth, and Paul S. Ell, *Troubled Geographies: A Spatial History of Religion and Society in Ireland* (Bloomington: Indiana University Press, 2013).

5. I do not mean here "bilocal" in the anthropological sense of place of residence based on kinship patterning. I refer instead to theories about "experiences" of bilocality that some scholars have described as taking place in one geographic location.

6. See, for example, Jared Diamond, *Guns, Germs, and Steel: The Fates of Human Societies* (New York: Norton, 1997).

7. Bernard Bailyn, *Atlantic History: Concept and Contours* (Cambridge, Mass.: Harvard University Press, 2005); Alan Taylor, *American Colonies* (New York: Viking, 2001); John Thornton, *Africa and Africans in the Making of the Atlantic World, 1400–1680* (Cambridge, U.K.: Cambridge University Press, 1998); Douglas Egerton, Alison Games, Jane G. Landers, Kris Lane, and Donald R. Wright, *The Atlantic World: A History, 1400–1888* (Wheeling, Ill.: Harlan Davidson, 2007); David Armitage and Michael J. Braddick, *The British Atlantic World, 1500–1800* (New York: Palgrave Macmillan, 2002).

8. See the essays in *The Creation of the British Atlantic World,* ed. Elizabeth Mancke and Carole Shammas (Baltimore: Johns Hopkins University Press, 2005). On the British Atlantic as part of a broader approach to colonization that was manifest in Australasia as well, see these essays specifically: William M. Offutt, "The Atlantic Rules: The Legalistic Turn in Colonial British America"; Elizabeth Mancke, "Chartered Enterprises and the

Evolution of the British Atlantic World"; and John E. Crowley, "A Visual Empire: Seeing the British Atlantic World From a Global British Perspective."

9. The recent literature on this and the debates that they prompt have been well discussed. For a sampling of criticisms, see Alison Games, Philip J. Stern, Paul W. Mapp, and Peter A. Coclanis, "Forum: Beyond the Atlantic," *William and Mary Quarterly,* 3rd ser., 63, no. 4 (2006): 675–742; Peter A. Coclanis, "Drang Nach Osten: Bernard Bailyn, the World-Island, and the Idea of Atlantic History," *Journal of World History* 13, no. 2 (2002): 169–82; and Coclanis, "Atlantic World or Atlantic/World?" *William and Mary Quarterly,* 3rd ser., 63, no. 4 (2006): 725–42; Jack P. Green and Philip D. Morgan, *Atlantic History: A Critical Appraisal,* Reinterpreting History series (Oxford, U.K.: Oxford University Press, 2009). Other recent discussions of the Atlantic world that support its utility as an organizing tool include Thomas Benjamin, *The Atlantic World: Europeans, Africans, Indians, and Their Shared History, 1400–1900* (Cambridge, UK: Cambridge University Press, 2009); Egerton, Games, Landers, Lane, and Wright, *Atlantic World;* Wim Klooster and Alfred Padula, eds., *The Atlantic World: Essays on Slavery, Migration, and Imagination* (Upper Saddle River, N.J.: Prentice Hall, 2004); Bailyn, *Atlantic History;* Bernard Bailyn and Patricia L. Denault, eds. *Soundings in Atlantic History: Latent Structures and Intellectual Currents, 1500–1830* (Cambridge, Mass.: Harvard University Press, 2009); David Brion Davis, *Inhuman Bondage: The Rise and Fall of Slavery in the New World* (New York: Oxford University Press, 2006); Felipe Fernández-Armesto, "The Origins of the European Atlantic," *Itinerario* 24 (2000): 111–28; Armitage and Braddick, *British Atlantic World.*

10. J. H. Elliott, "Afterword: Atlantic History, a Circumnavigation," in Armitage and Braddick, *British Atlantic World,* 239.

11. Recent work by Benjamin Schmidt, among a few others, has begun to establish some beachheads for exploring that issue. See Schmidt, "The Dutch Atlantic: From Provincialism to Globalism," in *Atlantic History: A Critical Reappraisal,* ed. Jack P. Greene and Philip D. Morgan (New York: Oxford University Press, 2009), 163–90.

12. Peter A. Coclanis, "Drang Nach Osten, 169–82; and Coclanis, "Atlantic World or Atlantic/World?" 725–42.

13. Camilla Agostini, *Objetos da Escravidão: Abordagens sobre a cultura material da escravidão e seu legado* (Rio de Janeiro: 7Letras, 2013). I am grateful to the author for providing me with English language sections of her additional work in progress.

14. Ian N. Gregory, Niall A. Cunningham, C. D. Lloyd, Ian G. Shuttleworth, and Paul S. Ell, eds., *Troubled Geographies: A Spatial History of Religion and Society in Ireland* (Bloomington: Indiana University Press, 2013); Anne Kelly Knowles, Tim Cole, and Alberto Giordano, eds., *Geographies of the Holocaust* (Bloomington: Indiana University Press, 2014).

15. For an early, informed proposal by scholars and historians in religious studies to work across several fields of spatial scholarship in interdisciplinary fashion, see David Chidester and Edward T. Linenthal, introduction, in *American Sacred Space,* ed. Chidester and Linenthal (Bloomington: Indiana University Press, 1995), 1–42. Geographers also made efforts to find common ground in talking about religion and space. One example is the work of Anne Buttimer, salient aspects of which are summarized in her "Afterword: Reflections on Geography, Religion, and Belief Systems," *Annals of the Association of American Geographers* 96, no. 1 (2006): 197–202. See also "Forum," *Annals of the Association of American Geographers* 96, no. 1 (2006): 165–202, including James Proctor, "Introduction: Theorizing and Studying Religion," 165–68.

16. George Lakoff and Mark Johnson, *Metaphors We Live By* (Chicago: University of Chicago Press, 1980); Anne Buttimer and David Seamon, eds., *The Human Experience of Space and Place* (New York: St. Martin's, 1980); Henri Lefebvre, *La Production de l'Espace* (Paris: Anthropos, 1974).

17. Yi-Fu Tuan, *Topophilia: A Study of Environmental Perception, Attitudes, and Values* (Englewood Cliffs, N.J.: Prentice Hall, 1974); Edward Relph, *Place and Placelessness* (London: Pion, 1976).

18. Jared Diamond, *Guns, Germs, and Steel: The Fates of Human Societies* (New York: Norton, 1997). See also Barry Cunliffe, *Europe between the Oceans: 9000 BC–AD 1000* (New Haven, Conn.: Yale University Press, 2008), and the review of that book by Benjamin Schwarz, "Geography is Destiny," in the *Atlantic,* December 2008, 105.

19. Franco Moretti, *Atlas of the European Novel, 1800–1900* (New York: Verso, 1998).

20. Linenthal and Chidester, introduction.

21. Kliever proposed that "those interested in story and religion should take spatiality more seriously—even more seriously than time. Whether we speak of biography, history or ontology, the places we were and the places we will be concern us most intimately and urgently. . . . A comprehensive survey of the latest scientific and philosophical studies of spatiality shows that human spatiality is not the qualityless continuum of the physical sciences or of geometric space. Lived space is always territorial (divided into privileged habitats), hodological (woven into complex networks) and kinesthetic (traversed by intentional activity). Lived movement is always a matter of place (centers of personal and possible meaning), direction (orientations toward actual and symbolic situations), and distance (intervals of existing and envisioned relationships). In human spatiality, quantity and quality, the public and the private, memory and anticipation, freedom and limits, body and consciousness are insolubly bound together." See Lonnie D. Kliever, "Story and Space: the Forgotten Dimension," *Journal of the American Academy of Religion,* supp. 45 (1977): 221. Kliever explicitly repeated some of the core ideas presented in an earlier article by Larry E. Shiner, particularly Shiner's emphasis on "lived space": this was Shiner's claim that space was hodological (an idea Shiner had credited to Kurt Lewin) and his observation that movement from one space to another (that is, space as kinesthetic) was crucial to understanding lived space and religion (Shiner, "Sacred Space, Profane Space, Human Space," *Journal of the American Academy of Religion* 40, no. 4 [1972]: 425, 428–29). Shiner criticized the "artificiality" of sacred/profane distinctions of space and proposed a joining of "metric space" and cultural representations of space. His claim that movement through space is an important part of understanding religion was subsequently taken up by writers such as David Carrasco, "The Sacrifice of Tezcatlipaca: To Change Place," in *To Change Place: Aztec Ceremonial Landscapes,* ed. Carrasco (Niwot: University Press of Colorado, 1991), 31–57, and most recently by Thomas A. Tweed, *Crossing and Dwelling: A Theory of Religion* (Cambridge, Mass.: Harvard University Press, 2006).

22. Shiner, "Sacred Space, Profane Space, Human Space," 425–36. Shiner's work retains certain affinities for the traditional phenomenological approach, however. See Michel de Certeau, *The Practice of Everyday Life,* trans. Steven Rendall (Berkeley: University of California Press, 1984); Bruno Latour, *Reassembling the Social: An Introduction to Actor-Network-Theory* (Oxford, U.K.: Oxford University Press, 2005); and Latour, *The Pasteurization of France,* trans. Alan Sheridan and John Law (Cambridge, Mass.: Harvard University Press, 1988).

23. Jonathan Z. Smith, *To Take Place: Toward Theory in Ritual* (Chicago: University of Chicago Press, 1987), 28.

24. Smith, who is not always clear on this point, has nevertheless noted, "Absolute difference is not a category of thought but one that denies the possibility of thought" (Smith, *To Take Place,* 34–35).

25. Ronald L. Grimes, "Jonathan Z. Smith's Theory of Ritual Space," *Religion* 29, no. 3 (1999): 266, 267. A fuller criticism of Smith's thinking about ritual and emplacement is in Grimes, *Rite Out of Place: Ritual, Media, and the Arts* (New York: Oxford University Press, 2006).

26. Translations have rendered the French *lieu* as "place." "Location" is also a fair translation and perhaps a better one to avoid confusion.

27. See John Corrigan, "Genealogies of Emplacement," in Bodenhamer, Corrigan, and Harris, *Spatial Humanities,* 127–47.

28. Michel Foucault, *Discipline and Punish: The Birth of the Prison,* trans. Alan Sheridan (New York: Vintage, 1995). For Foucault, bodies are disciplined to maximize their docility under the surveillance of a panoptic power, and discipline is constituted as a "unitary technique by which the body is reduced as a 'political' force at the least cost and maximized as a useful force" (221).

29. Certeau, *Practice of Everyday Life,* 117. Certeau's "space," then, is not the stable home/dwelling of Heidegger but something like Henri Lefebvre's "social space" or Edward Soja's "thirdspace." See Henri Lefebvre, *The Production of Space,* trans. Donald Nicholson-Smith (Oxford: Blackwell, 1991); and Edward Soja, *Thirdspace: Journeys to Los Angeles and Other Real-and-Imagined Places* (Cambridge, Mass.: Blackwell, 1996).

30. Christine M. Thomas has remarked on Smith's preoccupation with the origins of sacred space in "Place and Memory: Response to Jonathan Z. Smith on *To Take Place,* on the Occasion of its Twentieth Anniversary," *Journal of the American Academy of Religion* 76, no. 3 (2008): 777. Geographic theory in general, including Certeau's, has not evidenced much interest in that question, and it appears in Smith's writing as another holdover from a way of thinking about space more closely allied to an Eliadean approach. Kim Knott has proposed a useful understanding of religion and space that stresses human embodiment in *The Location of Religion: A Spatial Analysis* (London: Equinox, 2005).

31. Veikko Anttonen, "Rethinking the Sacred: The Notions of 'Human Body' and 'Territory' in Conceptualizing Religion," in *The Sacred and Its Scholars: Comparative Religious Methodologies for the Study of Primary Religious Data,* ed. Thomas A. Idinopolous and E. A. Yonan (Leiden, Netherlands: Brill, 1996), 36–64; Veikko Anttonen, "Sacred," in *Guide to the Study of Religion,* ed. Russell T. McCutcheon and Willi Braun (London: Cassell, 2000), 271–82; W. Richard Comstock, "A Behavioral Approach to the Sacred: Category Formation in Religious Studies," *Journal of the American Academy of Religion* 49, no. 4 (1981): 625–43; Mary Douglas, *Purity and Danger: An Analysis of Concepts of Pollution and Taboo* (London: Routledge and Kegan Paul, 1978); Douglas, *Natural Symbols: Explorations in Cosmology* (New York: Pantheon, 1970).

32. Tweed, *Crossings and Dwellings,* 79.

33. Knott, *The Location of Religion;* Kim Knott, "Spatial Theory and Spatial Methodology, Their Relationship and Application: A Transatlantic Engagement," *Journal of the American Academy of Religion* 77 (2009): 413–24.

34. Michel Foucault, "Of Other Spaces," *Diacritics* 16 (Spring 1986): 22.

A Sea of Texts

1. David Armitage, "Three Concepts of Atlantic History," in *The British Atlantic World, 1500–1800*, ed. David Armitage and Michael J. Braddick (Basingstoke, U.K.: Palgrave, 2002), 11–27.

2. Matthew Sparkes, "Acknowledging Responsibility for Space," *Progress in Human Geography* 31, no. 3 (2007): 396.

3. Doreen Massey, *For Space* (London: Sage, 2005), 9.

4. John Corrigan, "Qualitative GIS and Emergent Semantics," in *The Spatial Humanities: GIS and the Future of Humanities Scholarship*, ed. David J. Bodenhamer, John Corrigan, and Trevor M. Harris (Bloomington: Indiana University Press, 2010), 76.

5. In my own experience, students are eager to switch to electronic texts over printed ones, primarily because of the cost savings on the price of books; thus, even when one assigns a print edition of a book and asks students to purchase it, many students will ferret out electronic editions and use them instead of the print editions.

6. All references to Equiano's *Narrative* (including text-mining and GIS analyses below) are to the Project Gutenberg electronic edition available here: http://www.gutenberg.org/files/15399/15399-h/15399-h.htm (accessed Jan. 7, 2017). Because this text does not have page numbers, I have referenced citations according to chapter numbers.

7. I am extremely grateful to Glen Aronson for his assistance and expertise in creating these maps.

8. The tool used for this process is available at *Compleat Lexical Tutor*, http://www.lextutor.ca/key/ (accessed Jan. 7, 2017). The lextutor keyword extractor uses what is known as the "Brown corpus" (Brown University Standard Corpus of Present-Day American English) as the baseline against which to identify statistically unusual words. The Brown corpus was compiled by Henry Kucera and W. Nelson Francis and published in 1967 in *Computational Analysis of Present-Day American English* (Providence, R.I.: Brown University Press). The corpus is based on a sample of roughly one million words derived from fifteen separate genres of writing available in English in 1961. The obvious limitation of this corpus for an analysis of Equiano's text lies in the fact that the corpus is derived from texts in circulation some one hundred years later than the date at which Equiano wrote. A large-scale analysis of eighteenth-century Atlantic texts would require the use and/or creation of an alternative corpus—a project beyond the scope of the current analysis. The results derived from using the Brown corpus to analyze Equiano's text do not, however, seem to indicate large-scale shifts in linguistic usage. In other words, the statistically unusual words that the keyword extractor identified do not seem to include many words that might be defined as archaic today; rather, the words are generally ones that remain in common use. Accordingly, the use of the Brown corpus for this analysis does not seem likely to have significantly skewed the findings as compared to the use of a corpus keyed to eighteenth-century texts.

9. This step in the mapping process I devised is the most interpretive insofar as it involved the generation of categories on the basis of my sense of the topics around which words on the list clustered. In some cases this was more than obvious—particularly, for instance, with respect to language regarding maritime matters, which dominates in many of the chapters. In other cases, words were more difficult to categorize because of their capacity to signify within multiple conceptual fields. (I did not include all words on the

lists in categories, given that some did not seem to belong to any of the key groupings I discerned.) Given that my aim in this effort was to imagine how large-scale databases might be categorized on the basis of a small-scale experiment with Equiano's text, I generally regarded my categorizing efforts in this case as a blunt instrument—one not intended to eradicate interpretation of the text but to enable further interpretation of it. It seems clear that refinements in the categorizing work would be possible and desirable for the analysis of large-scale textual databases; indeed, tools for such categorization may already exist and might be modified for use in analyzing eighteenth-century texts. For a recent example of such categorization, see the study, "Pulse of the Nation: U.S. Mood Throughout the Day inferred from Twitter." http://www.ccs.neu.edu/home/amislove/twittermood/, which analyzes twitter messages for their mood content on the basis of a corpus titled ANEW (Affective Norms for English Words) developed by the NIMH Center for Emotion and Attention (CSEA) at the University of Florida.

10. The latter argument has been put forth by Vincent Caretta, most recently in his biography of Equiano, *Equiano the African: Biography of a Self-Made Man* (Athens: University of Georgia Press, 2005). For critical responses to this argument, see the essays collected in *Olaudah Equiano and the Igbo World: History, Society and Atlantic Diaspora Connections,* ed. Chima J. Korieh (Trenton, N.J.: Eritrea: 2009), as well as Cathy Davidson, "Olaudah Equiano, Written by Himself," *Novel* 40, nos. 1–2 (2006): 18–51.

11. Édouard Glissant, *Poetics of Relation,* trans. Betsy Wing (Ann Arbor: University of Michigan Press, 1997), 6–7.

12. Stephanie E. Smallwood, *Saltwater Slavery: A Middle Passage from Africa to American Diaspora* (Cambridge, Mass.: Harvard University Press, 2007), 122, 207.

13. Philip D. Morgan, "Maritime Slavery," *Slavery and Abolition* 31, no. 3 (2010): 311. The most influential work on eighteenth-century black mariners is W. Jeffrey Bolster, *Black Jacks: African American Seamen in the Age of Sail* (Cambridge, Mass.: Harvard University Press, 1997). Bolster noted the connection between black sailors and early African American print narratives in particular: "Whereas white seamen were among the most marginalized men in white society, black seamen found access to privileges, worldliness, and wealth denied to most slaves. Nothing conveys this more strikingly than the fact that sailors wrote the first six autobiographies of blacks published in English before 1800. . . . Seafaring men were in the vanguard of defining a new black ethnicity for the many African peoples dispersed by Atlantic slavery" (36).

14. Massey, *For Space,* 107.

15. Massey, *For Space,* 63.

16. See Smallwood, *Saltwater Slavery,* 207.

17. Edlie Wong, *Neither Fugitive nor Free: Atlantic Slavery, Freedom Suits, and the Legal Culture of Travel* (New York: New York University Press, 2009), 31–33.

18. Ricardo Padrón, "Mapping Plus Ultra: Cartography, Space, and Hispanic Modernity," *Representations* 79 (Summer 2002): 28.

19. Alexander X. Byrd, "Eboe, Country, Nation, and Gustavus Vassa's *Interesting Narrative,*" *William and Mary Quarterly,* 3rd ser., 63, no. 1 (2006): 128, 124. In related terms, Elizabeth Mancke has argued, "Some of our most significant spatial and temporal categories—in particular, 'colonies' and 'colonial'—are products of the historiography of the rise of the nation-state and reflect those concerns and assumptions. The shift to Atlantic history, trans-imperial histories, and the ethnic histories of non-European peoples in the

Americas, both indigenous and Africans, obliges us to scrutinize these categories, recognize their specificity and descriptive power, and use spatial and temporal descriptors that reflect the continent's historical complexity and the historiographic achievements of the past thirty years." See Mancke, "Time, Space, and the History of Early Modern North America," *History Compass* 2 (2004): 1–11.

20. For critiques of GIS, see the essays collected in *Ground Truth: The Social Implications of Geographic Information Systems,* ed. John Pickles (New York: Guilford, 1995), as well as Pickles's reflections on the debates and developments that ensued in the decade following the publication of this volume in "*Ground Truth* 1995–2005," *Transactions in GIS* 10 (2006): 763–72. For a history of debates between GIS practitioners and its critics in the field of geography, see Nadine Schuurman, "Trouble in the Heartland: GIS and its Critics in the 1990s," *Progress in Human Geography* 24 (2000): 569–90.

21. Christine E. Dunn, "Participatory GIS—A People's GIS?" *Progress in Human Geography* 31 (October 2007): 616.

22. Massey, *For Space,* 39.

23. Franco Moretti, *Graphs, Maps, Trees: Abstract Models for Literary History* (London: Verso, 2005), 4. More provocatively, Moretti recommends distant reading in a *New Left Review* piece as a strategy of "less is more": "And if you want to look beyond the canon (and of course, world literature will do so: it would be absurd if it didn't!) close reading will not do it. It's not designed to do it, it's designed to do the opposite. At bottom, it's a theological exercise—very solemn treatment of very few texts taken very seriously—whereas what we really need is a little pact with the devil: we know how to read texts, now let's learn how *not* to read them. Distant reading: where distance, let me repeat it, *is a condition of knowledge:* it allows you to focus on units that are much smaller or much larger than the text: devices, themes, tropes—or genres and systems. And if, between the very small and the very large, the text itself disappears, well, it is one of those cases when one can justifiably say, less is more. If we want to understand the system in its entirety, we must accept losing something. We always pay a price for theoretical knowledge: reality is infinitely rich; concepts are abstract, are poor. But it's precisely this 'poverty' that makes it possible to handle them, and therefore to know. This is why less is actually more." See Moretti, "Conjectures on World Literature," *New Left Review* 1 (January/February 2000): 57.

24. N. Katherine Hayles, *Electronic Literature: New Horizons for the Literary* (Notre Dame, Ind.: University of Notre Dame Press, 2010), 43.

Clerics, Cartographers, and Kings

1. Father Paul du Poisson to Father Patouillet, 1726, in *The Jesuit Relations and Allied Documents: Travels and Explorations of the Jesuit Missionaries in North America (1610–1791)* vol. 67, eds. Reuben Gold Thwaites and Edna Kenton (New York: A. & C. Boni, 1925), 249. Subsequent references to this multivolume source will be abbreviated *JR,* followed by volume number and page number.

2. Hiersome Lalemant, September 4, 1663, in *JR* 48:61.

3. For a discussion of the textuality of maps, see J. B. Harley, "Silences and Secrecy: The Hidden Agenda of Cartography in Early Modern Europe," *Imago Mundi* 40 (1988): 57–76. For a more recent treatment of maps as texts, see Martin Brückner, *The Geographic Revolution in Early America: Maps, Literacy, and National Identity* (Chapel Hill: University of North Carolina Press, 2006), 13–44.

4. J. B. Harley's work on the deconstruction of maps forms the theoretical foundation of my argument. See "Texts and Contexts in the Interpretations of Early Maps" and "Maps, Knowledge, and Power," chaps. 1 and 2 in Harley, *The New Nature of Maps: Essays in the History of Cartography,* ed. Paul Laxton (Baltimore: Johns Hopkins University Press, 2001. See also Christine Marie Petto, *When France Was King of Cartography: The Patronage and Production of Maps in Early Modern France,* Toposophia: Sustainability, Dwelling, Design (Lanham, Md.: Lexington Books, 2007), 9–14.

5. Quoted in N. A. M. Rodger, *The Safeguard of the Sea: A Naval History of Britain, 660–1649* (New York: Norton, 1998), 293.

6. Steven J. Harris, "Mapping Jesuit Science: The Role of Travel in the Geography of Knowledge," in *The Jesuits: Cultures, Sciences, and the Arts, 1540–1773,* ed. John W. O'Malley, Gauvin Alexander Bailey, Steven J. Harris, and T. Frank Kennedy (Toronto: University of Toronto Press, 1999), 212–40.

7. Petto, *When France Was King,* 36–40.

8. Father Jacques Marquette to Claude Dablon, 1673, *JR* 59:97.

9. David Buisseret, ed. *Monarchs, Ministers, and Maps: The Emergence of Cartography as a Tool of Government in Early Modern Europe* (Chicago: University of Chicago Press, 1992), 101–3.

10. Petto, *When France Was King,* 21–30.

11. Cornelius J. Jaenen, "Gabriel Sagard: A Franciscan among the Hurons," in *The Human Tradition in Colonial America,* ed. Ian K. Steele and Nancy L. Roden (Wilmington, Del.: Scholarly Resources, 1999), 40–42.

12. Gabriel Sagard, *Le grand voyage du pays des Hurons* (1632; reprint, Québec: Bibliothèque Québécoise, 2007), 80.

13. Ibid., 259.

14. Father Charles L'Allemant to Father Jerome l'Allemant, August 1, 1626, *JR* 4:221.

15. Josef W. Konvitz, *Cartography in France, 1660–1848: Science, Engineering, and Statecraft* (Chicago: University of Chicago Press, 1987), 4.

16. Ibid., 6.

17. Petto, *When France Was King,* 28–30. See also Paul W. Mapp, *The Elusive West and the Contest for Empire 1713–1763* (Chapel Hill: University of North Carolina Press, 2011), 172–76.

18. William James Roosen, *The Age of Louis XIV: The Rise of Modern Diplomacy* (Cambridge, Mass.: Schenkman, 1976), 17–18.

19. Konvitz, *Cartography in France,* 17.

20. Petto, *When France Was King,* 146–53.

21. Pere Marquette and Sieur Joliet, "An Account of the Discovery of Some New Countries and Nations in North America" in *Historical Collections of Louisiana Embracing Many Rare and Valuable Documents,* trans. and ed. Benjamin Franklin French (Philadelphia: Daniels and Smith, 1850), 291.

22. Francis Parkman, *La Salle and the Discovery of the Great West in France and England in North America,* vol. 1 (1869; reprint, New York: Penguin, 1983), 767n1.

23. Jacques Marquette, "Decouverte de quelques pays et nations de L'amerique septentrionale," in *Recueil de voyages de Mr. Thevenot,* ed. Mr. Thevenot (Paris: Estienne Michallet, 1682), 1–43.

24. Brett Rushforth, *Bonds of Alliance: Indigenous and Atlantic Slaveries in New France* (Chapel Hill: University of North Carolina Press, 2012), 82–85.

25. Jean-Roch Rioux, "Louis Hennepin," *Dictionary of Canadian Biography Online* (2000), http://www.biographi.ca/009004-119.01-e.php?&id_nbr=841&interval=20&&PHPSESSID=2e27pvlebuqtfam5iaktse4eu2 (accessed November 2, 2010).

26. Florence Hsia, "Jesuits, Jupiter's Satellites, and the Académie Royale Des Sciences," in O'Malley, Bailey, Harris, and Kennedy, *The Jesuits,* 242; Mapp, *The Elusive West,* 198, 228–29.

27. Ibid., 247–48.

28. Petto, *When France Was King,* 100–106.

29. Delisle's assertion about the name of Carolina took place soon after the Treaty of Utrecht had been signed. According to its terms, France ceded Acadia (present-day Nova Scotia) to Britain. Anglo-French disputes over the boundaries of that province continued for fifty years. See Dale Miquelon, "Envisioning the French Empire: Utrecht, 1711–1713," *French Historical Studies* 24, no. 4 (2001): 653–77; and Miquelon, "Ambiguous Concession: What Diplomatic Archives Reveal about Article 15 of the Treaty of Utrecht and France's North American Policy," *William and Mary Quarterly* 67, no. 3 (2010): 459–80.

30. Petto, *When France Was King,* 106.

31. Glenn R. Conrad, "*Emigration Forcée:* A French Attempt to Populate Louisiana 1716–1720," in *The French Experience in Louisiana,* ed. Glenn R. Conrad (Lafayette: Center for Louisiana Studies, 1995), 125–35; Marcel Giraud, "La Compagnie D'occident, 1717–1718," *Revue Historique* 226, fasc. 1 (1961): 23–56.

32. Pierre-François-Xavier de Charlevoix, *Histoire et description générale de la Nouvelle-France avec le Journal historique d'un voyage fait par ordre du roi dans l'Amerique septentrionnale,* vol. I (Paris: Chez Nyon Fils, 1744).

33. His letter was first published in *Lettres edifiantes et curieuses ecrites des missions étrangeres par quelques Missionaires de la Compagnie de Jesus,* vol. 20 (Paris: N. Le Clerc, 1731). See also Le Petit, *JR* 68: 175–83

34. Marc Antoine Caillot, "Relation du Mississippi," ca. 1731–1758, Miss. 2005.001, Historic New Orleans Collection, 102–18.

35. Joseph-François Lafitau, *Mœurs des sauvages ameriquains, comparées aux mœurs des premiers temps,* 2 vols. (Paris: Saugrain l'aîne, 1724).

36. Antoine Le Page du Pratz, *Histoire de la Louisiane, Contenant la Découverte de ce vaste Pays; sa Description géographique; un Voyage dans les Terres,* vol. 2 (Paris: Lambert, 1758), 27.

37. Max Weber, *The Protestant Ethic and the Spirit of Capitalism, with Other Writings on the Rise of the West,* trans. Stephen Kalbeg (New York: Oxford University Press, 2009), 107.

38. Petto, *When France Was King,* 61–62.

39. Harley, "Maps, Knowledge, and Power," 62.

Mapping Urban Religion in an Atlantic Port

1. Introduction, *City Cries: or, A Peep at Scenes in Town* (Philadelphia, 1850), [iii]. For a discussion of the fluidity of Atlantic world cultures, see James Sidbury and Jorge Cañizares-Esguerra, "Mapping Ethnogenesis in the Early Modern Atlantic," *William and Mary Quarterly* 68, no. 2 (2011): 181–208.

2. By urban religion I mean not simply religious beliefs and practices that happen to take place in the city and could take place anywhere, but the distinct beliefs, practices, and worldviews that emerge from the intersection of the religion and the city. Robert A. Orsi, introduction, *Gods of the City: Religion and the American Urban Landscape,* ed. Orsi (Bloomington: Indiana University Press, 1999), 44.

3. Ira Rosenwaike, *Population History of New York City* (Syracuse, N.Y.: Syracuse University Press, 1972), 3, 36.

4. The essential overview for New York is Edwin G. Burrows and Mike Wallace, *Gotham: A History of New York City to 1898* (New York: Oxford University Press, 1999). For works that argue for specific factors shaping the development of the city, see Robert G. Albion, *The Rise of New York Port, 1815–1860* (Hamden, Conn.: Archon Books, 1961); Elizabeth Blackmar, *Manhattan for Rent, 1785–1850* (Ithaca, N.Y.: Cornell University Press, 1989); Mona Domosh, *Invented Cities: The Creation of Landscape in Nineteenth-Century New York and Boston* (New Haven, Conn.: Yale University Press, 1996); David M. Scobey, *Empire City: The Making and Meaning of the New York City Landscape* (Philadelphia: Temple University Press, 2002). For an important exception in considering religion as a factor, albeit as secondary to population growth and the rise of commercial capitalism, see Nan A. Rothschild, *New York City Neighborhoods: The 18th Century* (San Diego: Academic Press, 1990).

5. See Jon Butler, introduction, *Becoming America: The Revolution before 1776* (Cambridge, Mass.: Harvard University Press, 2000). For a provocative argument linking modernization and urban space, see Miles Ogborn, *Spaces of Modernity: London's Geographies 1680–1780* (New York: Guilford Press, 1998).

6. David Bodenhamer, "The Potential of Spatial Humanities," in *The Spatial Humanities: GIS and the Future of Humanities Scholarship,* ed. Bodenhamer, John Corrigan, and Trevor M. Harris, (Bloomington: Indiana University Press, 2010), 14–30.

7. Sometimes this happened quite literally, as with the Laws of the Indies (1542), which spelled out the placement of streets, the location of institutions, and other details for Spanish American cities. See Jay Kinsbruner, *The Colonial Spanish-American City: Urban Life in the Age of Atlantic Capitalism* (Austin: University of Texas Press, 2005).

8. For a helpful overview of early modern notions of the city, see Peter Arnade, Martha C. Howell, and Walter Simons, "Fertile Spaces: The Productivity of Urban Space in Northern Europe," *Journal of Interdisciplinary History* 32 (Spring 2002): 515–48.

9. The desire to replicate the Old World in the New proved such a desperate impulse that it led to moments of absurdity, as seen in a map purportedly of "Nowel Amsterdam en L'Amerique" in 1672 (during the period when the Dutch had temporarily won it back from the English). The French engraver Jollain, in fact, simply modeled it on a view of Lisbon, Portugal, issued many years earlier. Nothing about the view actually matched anything New York had to offer at that time. Reprinted in John A. Kouwenhoven, *The Columbia Historical Portrait of New York: An Essay in Graphic History* (1953; reprint, New York: Harper and Row, 1972), 43.

10. Doreen Grieg, *The Reluctant Colonists: Netherlanders Abroad in the Seventeenth and Eighteenth Centuries* (Assen/Maastricht, Netherlands: Van Gorcum, 1987), 102–5. For a good example of the disastrous consequences of competing bodies of authority, see Andrew L. Knaut, *The Pueblo Revolt of 1680: Conquest and Resistance in Seventeenth-Century New Mexico* (Norman: University of Oklahoma Press, 1995).

11. Enforcement of religious conformity increased in the 1650s as Stuyvesant and the Dominies of the Dutch Church sought to curtail the practice of other religious faiths brought on by an increasing number of settlers in this growing Atlantic world port. So fanatical had Pieter Stuyvesant become in trying to enforce worship that the West India

Company ordered him to back off in 1653 and allow other faiths to worship privately. Randall H. Balmer, *A Perfect Babel of Confusion: Dutch Religion and English Culture in the Middle Colonies* (New York: Oxford University Press, 1989), 3–5; Burrows and Wallace, *Gotham,* 59–61.

12. Carla Gardina Pestana, *The English Atlantic in an Age of Revolution, 1640–1661* (Cambridge, Mass.: Harvard University Press, 2004).

13. The presence of such diversity, despite the fact that in 1695 only four faiths had consecrated houses of worship (plus a Jewish burial ground), would have been especially apparent to Dongan, a Roman Catholic in a city without a Catholic church. Quoted in Burrows and Wallace, *Gotham,* 94.

14. For the clearest explanation of New York's systematic landscape, see Dell Upton, "Inventing the Metropolis: Civilization and Urbanity in Antebellum New York," in *Art and the Empire City, New York, 1825–1861,* ed. Catherine Hoover Voorsanger and John K. Howat (New Haven, Conn.: Yale University Press, 2000), 3–45; Upton, *Another City: Urban Life and Urban Spaces in the New American Republic* (New Haven, Conn.: Yale University Press, 2008). For a good explanation of the context of this period, see Joyce Appleby, *Inheriting the Revolution: The First Generation of Americans* (Cambridge, Mass.: Belknap Press of Harvard University Press, 2000).

15. See Richard Pointer, *Protestant Pluralism and the New York Experience: A Study of Eighteenth-Century Religious Diversity* (Bloomington: Indiana University Press, 1998), 104–5.

16. For a good overview of the relationship between grids and cities, see John Bender, "The City and the Rise of the Penitentiary: *A Journal of the Plague Year,*" chap. 3 in *Imagining the Penitentiary: Fiction and the Architecture of the Mind in Eighteenth-Century England* (Chicago: University of Chicago Press, 1987).

17. The grid would facilitate higher ordering forces, they believed, in insuring that self-interest would be restrained by the self-regulation of the market. Upton, "Inventing the Metropolis," 8.

18. The number of churches grew from 54 to 165 while the city's population rose from 100,233 in 1815 to 311,660 in 1840, an increase of 3.34 percent. Thus, while the population increased by nearly 210 percent, the number of churches kept steady at 200 percent. Kyle B. Roberts, *Evangelical Gotham: Religion and the Making of New York City, 1783–1860* (Chicago: University of Chicago Press, 2016), Table A.3, 267.
p.408, line 5. 1994).See Rosenwaike, *Population History,* 18, 35.

19. Rosenwaike, *Population History of New York City,* 41, 43.

20. "The Benevolent Institutions of New York," *Putnam's Monthly Magazine of American Literature, Science, and Art* 1 (June 1853): 673–86.

21. Roman Catholics built twenty-two churches between 1840 and 1860, increasing from ten to thirty-two. The standard history of New York's Catholic population is Jay P. Dolan, *The Immigrant Church: New York's Irish and German Catholics, 1815–1865* (Baltimore: Johns Hopkins University Press, 1975).

22. Jews founded congregations at a faster rate, expanding the number of synagogues from three to seventeen during the same period.

23. Eric Homberger, introduction, *Scenes from the Life of a City: Corruption and Conscience in Old New York* (New Haven, Conn.: Yale University Press, 1994).

24. See Tyler Anbinder, "The Making of Five Points," chap. 1 in *Five Points: The Nineteenth Century Neighborhood That Invented Tap Dance, Stole Elections, and Became the World's Most Notorious Slum* (New York: Free Press, 2001).

25. The population of the city rose from 311,660 in 1840 to 813,669 in 1860. Meanwhile the number of churches increased from 165 to 281. Roberts, *Evangelical Gotham,* 267.

26. *Bartlett's Illustrated Map of New York City* from 1870 illustrates the extent to which New York was in dialogue as much with cities across the Atlantic as across America; see G. H. Bartlett, *Bartlett's Illustrated Map of New York City* (New York: Major and Knapp, 1870). On the history of Central Park, see Eric Homberger, "New York Demands a Park and Will Have It, Be the Cost What It May," chap. 4 in *Scenes from the Life of a City: Corruption and Conscience in Old New York* (New Haven, Conn.: Yale University Press, 1994); Roy Rosenzweig and Elizabeth Blackmar, *The Park and the People: A History of Central Park* (Ithaca, N.Y.: Cornell University Press, 1992). On the new urban cosmopolitanism, see David Schuyler, *The New Urban Landscape: The Redefinition of City Form in Nineteenth-Century America* (Baltimore: Johns Hopkins University Press, 1986).

27. David W. Dunlap, *From Abyssinian to Zion: A Guide to Manhattan's Houses of Worship* (New York: Columbia University Press, 2004).

28. Michel de Certeau, "Walking in the City," chap. 7 in *The Practice of Everyday Life* (Berkeley: University of California Press, 1984), 93.

29. Thomas A. Tweed, *Crossing and Dwelling: A Theory of Religion* (Cambridge, Mass.: Harvard University Press, 2006).

30. Of the other young men who shipped out with Bethune from Scotland to Tobago, all but one died of malaria. Bethune retold this narrative, refining it as he went, in response to different crises he faced. It served as a reminder of the confidence he knew he should have in the Lord at moments when he stood most in need of it, when "hope had almost died." When life went smoothly, Bethune did not write about it, a possible insight into the writing habits of other spiritual autobiographers. See Divie Bethune, Diary (February 21, 1796—February 5, 1797), Collection of the William Clements Library, University of Michigan, Ann Arbor.

31. Charles Lahatt, "Personal Account," in "Misc. Mss. Lahatt, Charles," New York Historical Society.

32. In turn, his change of heart provided the necessary conditions for the crossing of his body from enslavement into legal freedom, as he orchestrated his master's conversion. *A Brief Account of the Life, Experience, Travels, and Gospel Labours of George White, an African; Written by Himself and Revised by a Friend* (New York, 1810), reprinted in *Black Itinerants of the Gospel: The Narratives of John Jea and George White,* ed. Graham Russell Hodges (Madison, Wis.: Madison House, 1993), 53.

33. White's efforts to find a spiritual community included joining the Methodist Church, then leaving it with others to found the African Society, trying several times to gain a teaching license, and then finally finding a home in Richard Allen's AME church. For White's account of his wife Mary's final crossing, see *A Brief Account,* 74–76.

34. John Corrigan, "Spatiality and Religion," in *The Spatial Turn: Interdisciplinary Perspectives,* ed. Barney Wharf and Santa Arias (London: Routledge, 2009), 168–69.

35. She had firsthand familiarity with these structures from her migration from Ireland to New York. Bangs in his 1818 dedication sermon for the second John Street seemed to have originated the story. Nathan Bangs, *The Substance of a Sermon Preached on the*

Opening of the Methodist Church in John-Street, in the City of New York, On the Morning of the 4th of January, 1818 (New York, 1818). See also J. B. Wakeley, *Lost Chapters Recovered from the Early History of American Methodism* (New York, 1858), 65–66.

36. During the life of Methodism's founder John Wesley (1703–1791), Methodist meetinghouses functioned as auxiliaries to the Established Church. In form and style, the meetinghouse on John Street stood in direct dialogue with Trinity and St. Paul's, the Anglican churches around the corner on Broadway, and in direct conversation with pre- and post-Reformation Christian churches.

37. Paul Gilje, *The Road to Mobocracy: Popular Disorder in New York City, 1763–1834* (Chapel Hill: University of North Carolina Press, 1987), 19–20.

38. Gilje, *Road to Mobocracy,* 162–69; Manisha Sinha, "Black Abolitionism: The Assault on Southern Slavery and the Struggle for Racial Equality," in *Slavery in New York,* ed. Ira Berlin and Leslie M. Harris (New York: New Press, 2005), 246–47.

39. Wood, for example, used a a young girl selling radishes—"doing good, by being engaged in some useful employment"—to rebuke "the gentleman-hog" who "only live[s] to eat, drink, and sleep." A year after the banning of the Atlantic slave trade, Wood used the example of a young boy selling gingerbread to ask how "good and sweet" the snack would taste if the slave-plantation-produced molasses had been made "by the sweat of a dear father, or tender mother, a beloved brother, or affectionate sister, an only son, or innocent daughter, torn from us, and from all that is near and dear, in this world." *The Cries of New York* (New York, 1808), 17, 31.

40. *Aunt Jaunty's Tales: The New York Cries* (New York, ca. 1852). "We can make an excuse for your bad English, on account of your coming from a foreign country," the text explains about the Italian image seller, "for your fortunes and complexion declare that you are an Italian who has visited America in hopes of making a fortune, which I fear you will not do at your present trade." The practice of the Old Clothesman, the author explains, "is to buy all his goods as cheaply as he can, though he afterwards sells them at an immense profit."

41. On this phenomenon, see Karen Halttunen, *Confidence Men and Painted Women: A Study of Middle-Class Culture in America, 1830–70* (New Haven, Conn.: Yale University Press, 1982).

Missionary Time and Space

Portions of this essay dealing with Atlantic historiography were also published, in a revised form, in Luca Codignola, "Ma che cosa è questo Atlantico? Un modernista di fronte alla storiografia delle buone intenzioni," *Eunomia: Rivista semestrale di Storia e Politica Internazionali,* n.s. 5, no. 2 (2016), special issue in honor of Prof. Antonio Donno, ed. by Giuliana Iurlano (online publication in Italian).

1. Whether the sentence was actually uttered in any of the *Star Trek* episodes (1966–) is a controversial issue. The "far away galaxy" piece is, of course, from *Star Wars,* Episode IV: *A New Hope.*

2. In *Stranded in the Present: Modern Time and the Melancholy of History* (Cambridge, Mass.: Harvard University Press, 2004), Peter Fritzsche describes with finesse and originality the subjectivity of time and the significance of the French Revolution for making people aware for the first time that things could change or had indeed changed in their own lifetime. In a forum that appeared in 2005, John G. Reid and I shared a reflection

on the psychological extent of the Atlantic Ocean. See Luca Codignola, "How Wide Is the Atlantic Ocean? Larger and Larger" and John G. Reid, "How Wide is the Ocean? Not Wide Enough!" in *Acadiensis* 34, no. 2 (2005): 74–80 and 81–87, respectively. Thomas Wien, "Quelle est la largeur de l'Atlantique? Le 'François Canadien' entre proximité et distance, 1660–1760," in *Français? La nation en débat entre colonies et métropole (XVIe–XIXe)*, ed. Cécile Vidal (Paris: Éditions de l'École des Hautes Études en Sciences Sociales, 2014), 55–75, is more interested in the shifting of cultural and national identity, another way to assess distance.

3. Paul Le Jeune, *Relation de ce qui s'est passe en la Nouvelle France en l'année* 1633 (Paris: Sébastien Cramoisy, 1634), 3; reprinted in *Monumenta Novae Franciae*, ed. Lucien Campeau, vol. 2, *Établissement à Québec* (1616–1634) (Rome: Monumenta Hist. Soc. Iesu and Institutum Historicum Societatis Iesu; Québec: Les Presses de l'Université Laval; Montréal: Les Éditions Bellarmin, 1979), and translated in *The Jesuit Relations and Allied Documents: Travels and Explorations of the Jesuit Missionaries in New France 1610–1791*, ed. Reuben G. Thwaites, vol. 5, *Québec: 1632–1633* (Cleveland: Burrow Brothers, 1897), 83.

4. See Ian K. Steele, *The English Atlantic 1675–1740: An Exploration of Communication and Community* (New York: Oxford University Press, 1986); Kenneth J. Banks, *Chasing Empire across the Sea: Communications and the State in the French Atlantic, 1713–1763* (Montréal: McGill-Queen's University Press, 2002). Both are pioneer studies in the field of transatlantic communication.

5. John J. McCusker, "The Demise of Distance: The Business Press and the Origins of the Information Revolution in the Early Modern Atlantic World," *American Historical Review* 110, no. 2 (2005): 295–321, emphasizes the significance of the spread of commercial and financial newspapers between 1500 and 1800. See also Fritzsche, *Stranded in the Present*, 48, on misconceptions and commonplaces regarding the timing of this technological revolution.

6. Gabriella Airaldi, *Storia della Liguria*, vol. 2, *Dal 643 al 1492* (Genoa, Italy: Marietti, 2009), 133–35, quotation at p. 133.

7. Louis-Guillaume-Valentin Dubourg to Joseph-Octave Plessis, St. Louis, July 27, 1821, Archives de l'Archidiocèse de Québec (hereafter AAQ), 7 CM, I, 104, ff. 1rv–2rv; Philippe Janvier to [Plessis], Albany, September 21, 1822, AAQ, 7 CM, I, 116, f. 1rv; Lewis Willcocks to Janvier, New York, September 11, 1822, AAQ, 7 CM, 1, 113, f. 1rv; Bertrand Martial to Plessis, New Orleans, November 13, 1822, AAQ, 7 CM, I, 119, ff. 1rv–2rv.

8. Luke Clossey, *Salvation and Globalization in the Early Jesuit Missions* (Cambridge, U.K.: Cambridge University Press, 2008), 90–113.

9. Francesco Ingoli, *Relazione delle Quattro Parti del Mondo*, ed. Fabio Tosi (Vatican City: Urbaniana University Press, 1999), 231 (original in Italian).

10. For a classic philosophical treatment, see Giuliano Gliozzi, *Adamo e il Nuovo Mondo. La nascita dell'antropologia come ideologia coloniale: dalle genealogie bibliche alle teorie razziali (1500–1700)* (Florence: La Nuova Italia, 1977). For the latest overviews on the Jesuits, see John W. O'Malley, SJ, Gauvin Alexander Bailey, Steven J. Fontijn Harris, and T. Frank Kennedy, SJ, eds., *The Jesuits: Culture, Sciences, and the Arts, 1540–1773* (Toronto: University of Toronto Press, 1999); O'Malley, Bailey, Harris, and Kennedy, eds., *The Jesuits II: Cultures, Sciences, and the Arts 1540–1773* (Toronto: University of Toronto Press, 2006); Nicholas P. Cushner, *Why Have You Come Here? The Jesuits and the First Evangelization of Native America* (Oxford, U.K.: Oxford University Press, 2006); Michela Catto, Guido Mongini, and Silvia Mostaccio, eds., *Evangelizzazione e globalizzazione:*

Le missioni gesuitiche nell'età moderna tra storia e storiografia, ([Rome]: Società Editrice Dante Alighieri, 2010).

11. Clossey, *Salvation and Globalization,* 113. For a short but illuminating essay on the evolving notion of foreign missions within the framework of a Catholic universalism aiming "at the rationalization of action through the mastering of time and space," see Claude Prudhomme, "Gestion du temps, gestion de l'espace et modernité dans le catholicisme," in *Temps, espace et modernités: Mélanges offertes à Serge Courville et Normand Séguin,* ed. Brigitte Caulier and Yvan Rousseau (Québec: Les Presses de l'Université Laval, 2009), 387–99, quotation at p. 387 (original in French).

12. In the mid-fourteenth century, Venice sent one ship a year on average to the Middle East; a century later, Genoa had a fleet of some thirty ships. Yet in the 1520s more than a hundred ships went back and forth between Spain and its American colonies, and in the seventeenth century there were some sixty to ninety ships a year going from Portugal to Brazil. See Jacques Heers, *Gênes au XVe siècle. Activité économique et problèmes sociaux* (Paris: SEVPEN, 1961), 280–82; Carla Rahn Phillips, "The Growth and Composition of Trade in the Iberian Empires, 1450–1750," in *The Rise of Merchant Empires: Long-Distance Trade in the Early Modern World,* ed. James D. Tracy (New York: Cambridge University Press, 1990), 37–38, 49, 52, 78, 82, 100–101; Paul Butel, "France, the Antilles, and Europe in the Seventeenth and Eighteenth Centuries: Renewals of Foreign Trade," in Tracy, *Rise of Merchant Empires,* 171; Japp R. Bruijn, "Productivity, Profitability, and Costs of Private and Corporate Dutch Ship Owing in the Seventeenth and Eighteenth Centuries," in Tracy, *Rise of Merchant Empires,* 190.

13. Airaldi, *Genova e la Liguria nel Medioevo* (Turin: UTET, 1986); Steven A. Epstein, *Genoa and the Genoese 958–1528* (Chapel Hill: University of North Carolina Press, 1996).

14. For an interpretation, see Bernard Lewis, *Cultures in Conflict: Christians, Muslims, and Jews in the Age of Discovery* (New York: Oxford University Press, 1995). For more recent, different perspectives, see Juan Cole, "Playing Muslim: Bonaparte's Army of the Orient and Euro-Muslim Creolization," in *The Age of Revolutions in Global Context, c. 1760–1840,* ed. David Armitage and Sanjay Subrahmanyam (Basingstoke, U.K.: Palgrave Macmillan, 2010), 125–43; Brian A. Catlos, *Muslims of Medieval Latin Christendom, ca. 1050–1614* (Cambridge, U.K.: Cambridge University Press, 2014). For the last outpouring of Western anti-Islamic sentiments before the twenty-first century, see Lawrence A. Peskin, *Captives and Countrymen: Barbary Slaves and the American Public* (Baltimore: Johns Hopkins University Press, 2009).

15. John W. Blake, *European Beginnings in West Africa 1454–1578: A Survey of the First Century of White Enterprise in West Africa, with Special Emphasis upon the Rivalry of the Great Powers* (London, 1937), republished with a new preface as *West Africa: Quest for God and Gold 1454–1578: A Survey . . .* (London: Rowman and Kittlefield, 1977); John K. Thornton, *Africa and Africans in the Making of the Atlantic World, 1400–1680* (Cambridge, U.K.: Cambridge University Press, 1992); George E. Brooks, *Eurafricans in Western Africa: Commerce, Social Status, Gender, and Religious Observance from the Sixteenth to the Eighteenth Century* (Athens: Ohio University Press, 2003); John K. Thornton, "The Portuguese in Africa," in *Portuguese Oceanic Expansion, 1400–1800,* ed. Francisco Bethencourt and Diogo Ramada Curto (Cambridge, U.K.: Cambridge University Press, 2007), 138–60.

16. Jean Richard, *La Papauté et les missions d'Orient au Moyen Age (XIIIe–XVe siècles)* (Rome: École Française de Rome, 1977), 7, 66–68, 292. This point is discussed in

Codignola and Giovanni Pizzorusso, "Les lieux, les méthodes et les sources de l'expansion missionnaire du Moyen Age au XVIIe siècle: Rome sur la voie de la centralisation," in *Transferts culturels et métissages Amérique/Europe XVIe–XXe siècle,* ed. Laurier Turgeon, Denys Delâge, and Réal Ouellet (Québec: Les Presses de l'Université Laval, 1996), 489–512.

17. Maurice Whitehead, *English Jesuit Education: Expulsion, Suppression, Survival and Restoration, 1762–1803* (Farnham, U.K.: Ashgate, 2013), 105, 163–64, 192–93. On Carroll's early years, see Annabelle M. Melville, *John Carroll of Baltimore: Founder of the American Catholic Hierarchy* (New York: Charles Scribner's Sons, 1955), 11–37; Luca Codignola, "Roman Catholic Conservatism in a New North Atlantic World, 1760–1829," *William and Mary Quarterly,* 3rd ser., 64, no. 4 (2007): 717–56.

18. At the time, microhistory was reaching its peak and beginning its way out. Notice the dates of three milestone publications: John Demos, *A Little Commonwealth: Family Life in Plymouth Colony* (New York: Oxford University Press, 1970); Emmanuel Le Roy Ladurie, *Montaillou, village occitan de 1294 à 1324* (Paris: Gallimard, 1975); Carlo Ginzburg, *Il formaggio e i vermi: Il cosmo di un mugnaio del '500* (Turin: Einaudi, 1976). See also Sigurður Gylfi Magnússon, "The Singularization of History: Social History and Microhistory within the Postmodern State of Knowledge," *Journal of Social History* 36, no. 3 (2003): 701–35; and Lara Putnam, "To Study the Fragments/Whole: Microhistory and the Atlantic World," *Journal of Social History* 39, no. 3 (2006): 615–30.

19. Simon Stock to [Propaganda Fide], London, May 31, 1625, Archives of the Sacred Congregation "de Propaganda Fide," Rome (hereafter APF), SOCG, vol. 347, ff. 227rv, 234rv; printed in Luca Codignola, *The Coldest Harbour of the Land: Simon Stock and Lord Baltimore's Colony in Newfoundland, 1621–1649* (Montréal: McGill-Queen's University Press, 1988), 84 (original in Italian).

20. See Luca Codignola, preface to *Relation du premier voyage entrepris par Christophe Colomb pour la découverte du Nouveau-Monde en 1492* by Christopher Columbus (Montréal: Boréal, 2005), 9–24.

21. Felice De Andreis, CM, to Carlo Domenico Sicardi, CM, St. Louis, Mo., [February 24, 1817], APF, Congressi, America Centrale, vol. 8, ff. 32rv–37rv (original in Italian).

22. [Plessis] to Francesco Fontana, Rome, November 17, 1819, AAQ, 10 CM, III, 152, ff. 1rv–2rv (original in Latin).

23. General Congregation, [Rome], February 14, 1642, APF, Acta, vol. 15, ff. 29v–30r (original in Latin).

24. Pacifique de Provins to Propaganda Fide, Paris, June 26, 1647, APF, SOCG, vol. 145, ff. 103rv, 106rv (original in Italian).

25. Luca Codignola, "A World Yet to Be Conquered: Pacifique de Provins and the Atlantic World, 1629–1648," in *Canada ieri e oggi. Atti del 6° Convegno Internazionale di Studi Canadesi. Selva di Fasano, 27–31 marzo 1985,* vol. 3, *Sezione storica,* ed. Codignola and Raimondo Luraghi (Fasano, Italy: Schena, 1986), 59–84. At the time the expression "Atlantic world" was not the commonplace formula it later became. Note that when this article was revised and republished—as "Pacifique de Provins and the Capuchin Network in Africa and America," in *Proceedings of the Fifteenth Meeting of the French Colonial Historical Society. Martinique and Guadeloupe, May 1989,* ed. Patricia Galloway and Philip P. Boucher (Lanham, Md.: University Press of America, 1992), 46–60—the editors dropped "Atlantic World" from its original title. On Pacifique de Provins, see also Matteo Binasco,

Viaggiatori e missionari nel Seicento: Pacifique de Provins fra Levante, Acadia e Guyana (1622–1648) (Novi Ligure, Italy: Città del Silenzio, 2006).

26. Jérôme Lalemant, "Relation de l'employ des Pères de la Compagnie de Jésus qui sont aux Hurons, païs de la Nouvelle-France, depuis le mois de juin 1638 jusques au mois de juin 1639: Adressée au révérend Père Paul Le Jeune, supérieur des missions de la Compagnie de Jésus en la Nouvelle-France," in Le Jeune, *Relation de ce qui s'est passé en la Nouvelle-France en l'année 1639* (Paris: Sébastien Cramoisy, 1639), 34; reprinted in Campeau, *Monumenta Novae Franciae,* IV, *Les grandes épreuves (1638–1640)* (1989), 371, and translated in Thwaites, *Jesuit Relations,* vol. 17, *Hurons and Three Rivers: 1639–1640* (1898), 21 (original in French).

27. Pacifique de Provins to Ingoli, Paris, December 12, 1641, APF, SOCG, vol. 141, ff. 107rv, 114rv (original in Italian).

28. Clossey, *Salvation and Globalization,* 90. One may add that the fragmented universe of the "Net Generation" is similarly topological—bits and pieces of knowledge that are completely unconnected and need not refer to any authorial or authoritative source. See, on this point, Luca Codignola, "Too Much of a Good Thing? Or, A Historian Swamped by the Web," in *Exploring the Paradigm Shift: New Publication Cultures in the Humanities,* ed. Péter Dávidházi (Amsterdam: Amsterdam University Press, 2014), 63–87.

29. Pacifique de Provins to [Ingoli], March 9, 1644, APF, SOCG, vol. 259, ff. 205rv–206rv (original in Italian).

30. Pacifique de Provins to Ingoli, Paris, December 12, 1641, APF, SOCG, vol.141, ff. 107rv, 114rv (original in Italian); Pacifique de Provins to Ingoli, Paris, June 24, 1644, APF, SOCG, vol. 199, ff. 399rv, 406rv.

31. Tulio Halperín Donghi, *Reforma y disolución de los imperios ibéricos, 1750–1850* (Madrid: Alianza, 1985).

32. John J. McCusker and Russell R. Menard, *The Economy of British America, 1607–1789* (Chapel Hill: University of North Carolina Press, 1985). See also McCusker, *Essays in the Economic History of the Atlantic World* (London: Routledge, 1997); McCusker and Kenneth Morgan, eds., *The Early Modern Atlantic Economy* (Cambridge, New York: Cambridge University Press, 2000); and McCusker, introduction to "Trade in the Atlantic World," special section of *Business History Review* 74, no. 4 (2005), 697–844. For the early interest of Jack P. Greene in the West Indies, see "Society and Economy in the British Caribbean during the Seventeenth and Eighteenth Centuries: A Review Essay," *American Historical Review* 79, no. 5 (1974): 1499–1517.

33. Urs Bitterli, *Alte Welt Neue Welt: Formen des europäisch-uberseeischen Kulturkontakts vom 15. bis 18. Jarhundert* (München [Munich]: C. H. Beck'sche Verlagsbuchhandlung, Oscar Beck, 1986), translated as *Cultures in Conflict: Encounters between European and Non-European Cultures, 1492–1800* (Stanford, Calif.: Stanford University Press, 1989).

34. Donald W. Meinig, *The Shaping of America: A Geographical Perspective on 500 Years of History,* 4 vols. (New Haven, Conn.: Yale University Press, 1986–2005). Note the newly conceptualized maps that depict psychological as well as spatial distances.

35. Alfred W. Crosby, Jr., *Ecological Imperialism: The Biological Expansion of Europe 900–1900* (Cambridge, U.K.: Cambridge University Press, 1986). Also by Crosby: *The Columbian Exchange: Biological and Cultural Consequences of 1492* (Westport, Conn.: Greenwood Press, 1972); *Germs, Seeds, and Animals: Studies in Ecological History* (Armonk, N.Y.: M. E. Sharpe, 1994); "Ecological Imperialism: The Overseas Migration of

Western Europeans as a Biological Phenomenon," in *American Encounters: Natives and Newcomers from European Contact to Indian Removal, 1500–1850,* ed. Peter C. Mancall and James H. Merrell (New York: Routledge, 2000), 53–67.

36. Steele, *English Atlantic,* 5; Ian K. Steele, "The Empire and the Provincial Elites: An Interpretation of Some Recent Writings on the English Atlantic, 1675–1740," in *The British Atlantic before the American Revolution,* ed. Peter J. Marshall and Glyndwr A. Williams (London: Frank Cass, 1980), 2–32; Karen O. Kupperman, ed., *America in European Consciousness, 1493–1750* (Chapel Hill: University of North Carolina Press, 1995) ("Thus the Atlantic seemed to shrink, its American shore brought closer by the establishment of Euro-American societies. But this new familiarity also hid a greater distance" [22]); Kupperman, "The Love-Hate Relationship with Experts in the Early Modern Atlantic," *Early American Studies* 9, no. 2 (2011): 248–67; Kupperman, *The Atlantic in World History* (Oxford, U.K.: Oxford University Press, 2012).

37. Bernard Bailyn, *The Peopling of British North America: An Introduction* (New York: Knopf, 1986); Bailyn, with the assistance of Barbara DeWolfe, *Voyagers to the West: A Passage in the Peopling of America on the Eve of the Revolution* (New York: Alfred A Knopf, 1986). Bailyn, of course, was most instrumental in theorizing and promoting the idea of Atlantic history through his books and his leadership in Harvard University's program titled "The International Seminar on the History of the Atlantic World." Over fifteen years (1995–2010), Bailyn's Harvard seminar invited 366 young scholars, of whom 164 were non-Americans, and managed to establish an international network of Atlantic historians.

38. Nicholas P. Canny, "The British Atlantic World: Working Toward a Definition," *Historical Journal* 33, no. 2 (1990): 479–97; Federica Morelli, *Il mondo atlantico. Una storia senza confini (secoli XV-XIX)* (Rome: Carocci editore, 2013).

39. On this perspective, see, for example, Bernhard Klein and Gesa Mackenthun, eds., *Sea Changes: Historicizing the Ocean* (Abingdon, U.K.: Routledge, 2004).

40. Meinig, *Shaping of America;* Stephen J. Hornsby, Victor A. Konrad, and James J. Herlan, eds., *The Northeastern Borderlands: Four Centuries of Interaction* (Orono: University of Maine, 1989); Hornsby, *British Atlantic, American Frontier: Spaces of Power in Early Modern British America* (Hanover, N.H.: University Press of New England, 2005); Hornsby, "Early Modern Canada as Maritime Space," in "Is There a 'Canadian' Atlantic World?," special forum, ed. John G. Reid, Huw V. Bowen, and Elizabeth A. Mancke, *International Journal of Maritime History* 21, no. 1 (2009): 287–90; Hornsby, "Geographies of the British Atlantic World," in *Britain's Oceanic Empire: Atlantic and Indian Ocean Worlds, c.1550–1850,* ed. H. V. Bowen, Elizabeth Mancke, and John G. Reid (Cambridge, U.K.: Cambridge University Press, 2012), 15–44. See also Cécile Vidal, introduction, "Atlantique français," ed. Vidal, special issue of *Outre-Mers: Revue d'histoire* 362–63 (1er semestre 2009): 7–37, esp. 12–13.

41. Nicholas P. Canny and Philip D. Morgan, eds., *The Oxford Handbook of the Atlantic World 1450–1850* (Oxford, U.K.: Oxford University Press, 2011), 16.

42. With regard to general histories of the Atlantic world, both R. Douglas Egerton, Alison F. Games, Jane G. Landers, Kris Lane, and Donald R. Wright, *The Atlantic World: A History, 1400–1888* (Wheeling, Ill.: Harlan Davidson, Inc., 2007), and Thomas Benjamin, Timothy D. Hall, and David E. Rutheford, eds., *The Atlantic World in the Age of Empire* (Boston: Houghton Mifflin Company, 2001), start with 1400 and end in 1888 and 1900,

respectively. Morelli, *Mondo atlantico,* is less clear-cut but tends to end with the beginning of Iberian-American independences.

43. Rahn Phillips, "The Iberian Atlantic," *Itinerario* 23 (1999): 84–106; Joyce E. Chaplin, "Expansion and Exceptionalism in Early American History," *Journal of American History* 89, no. 4 (2003): 1430–55; Donna R. Gabaccia, "A Long Atlantic in a Wider World," *Atlantic Studies* 1, no. 1 (2004): 1–27; Christopher A. Bayly, Sven Beckert, Matthew Connelly, Isabel Hofmeyr, Wendy Kozol, and Patricia Seed, "AHR Conversation: On Transnational History," *American Historical Review* 111, no. 5 (2006): 1440–64; Michael W. Zuckerman, "Exceptionalism after All; Or, The Perils of Postcolonialism," *William and Mary Quarterly,* 3rd ser., 64, no. 2 (April 2007): 259–62; Joyce E. Chaplin, "The Atlantic Ocean and Its Contemporary Meanings, 1492–1808," in *Atlantic History: A Critical Appraisal,* ed. Jack P. Greene and P. D. Morgan (New York: Oxford University Press, 2009), 35–55; Anthony J. R. Russell-Wood, "The Portuguese Atlantic, 1415–1808," in Greene and Morgan, *Atlantic History,* 81–109; Klooster, "The Northern European Atlantic World," in Greene and Morgan, *Atlantic History,* 165–80; Ida Altman, "The Spanish Atlantic, 1650–1780," in Greene and Morgan, *Atlantic History,* 183–200; Joyce E. Chaplin, "The British Atlantic," in Greene and Morgan, *Atlantic History,* 219–34; Christopher Hodson and Brett Rushforth, "Absolutely Atlantic: Colonialism and the Early Modern French State in Recent Historiography," *History Compass* 8, no. 1 (2010): 101–17; Allan R. Greer, "National, Transnational, and Hypernational Historiographies: New France Meets Early American History," *Canadian Historical Review* 91, no. 4 (2010): 695–724; Clément Thibaud, Gabriel Entin, Alejandro Gómez and Morelli, eds., *L'Atlantique révolutionnaire: Une perspective ibéro-américaine* (Bécherel, France: Les Perséides Éditions, 2013), 11–23.

44. See these works by Bernard Bailyn: "The Challenge of Modern Historiography," *American Historical Review* 87, no. 1 (1982): 1–24; *Strangers within the Realm: Cultural Margins of the First British Empire,* ed. with P. D. Morgan (Chapel Hill: University of North Carolina Press, 1991); "The Idea of Atlantic History," *Itinerario* 20, no. 1 (1996): 19–44; *Atlantic History: Concept and Contours* (Cambridge, Mass.: Harvard University Press, 2005); *Soundings in Atlantic History: Latent Structures and Intellectual Currents, 1500–1830,* ed. with Patricia L. Denault (Cambridge, Mass.: Harvard University Press, 2009). See also Peter A. Coclanis, "*Drang Nach Osten:* Bernard Bailyn, the World-Island, and the Idea of Atlantic History," *Journal of World History* 13, no. 1 (2002): 169–82; Ian K. Steele, "Bernard Bailyn's American Atlantic," *History and Theory* 46, no. 1 (February 2007), 48–58; Eric A. Hinderaker and Rebecca Horn, "Territorial Crossings: Histories and Historiographies of the Early Americas," *William and Mary Quarterly,* 3rd ser., 62, no. 3 (2010): 395–432; and Manuel Covo, "La Révolution haïtienne entre études révolutionnaires et *Atlantic History,*" in Thibaud, Entin, Gómez and Morelli, eds., *Atlantique révolutionnaire,* 259–88.

45. Vidal, introduction, "Atlantique français," 21 (original in French); Canny and Morgan, *Oxford Handbook of Atlantic World,* 16. Cécile Vidal's production in the field of Atlantic history is remarkable; see also *Histoire de l'Amérique française,* ed. with Gilles Havard (Paris: Flammarion, 2003); "The Reluctance of French Historians to Address Atlantic History," *Southern Quarterly* 43, no. 4 (2006): 153–89; *De Québec à l'Amérique française: Histoire et mémoire,* ed. with Thomas Wien and Yves Frenette (Québec: Les Presses de l'Université Laval, 2007), 95–124; "Making New France New Again," (with Gilles Havard), *Common-Place* 7 (July 2007), http://www.common-place.org/vol-07/no-04/harvard/

(accessed Jan. 8, 2017); "L'histoire atlantique de part et d'autre de l'Atlantique" (ed.), special issue of *Nuevo Mundo, Mundos Nuevos* (2008) http://nuevomundo.revues.org/index10233.html (accessed Jan. 8, 2017); *Atlantique français* (ed.), 7–139; *Sociétés, colonisations et esclavages dans le monde atlantique: Historiographie des sociétés américaines des XVI*ᵉ*-XIX*ᵉ *siècles,* ed. with François-Joseph Ruggiu (Bécherel: Les Perséides, 2009); "Pour une histoire globale du monde atlantique ou des histoires connectées dans et au-délà du monde atlantique?" *Annales: Histoire, Sciences Sociales* 57, no. 2 (April–June 2012), 391–413; *Louisiana: Crossroads of the Atlantic World* (ed.), (Philadelphia: University of Pennsylvania Press, 2013); *Français? La nation en débat entre colonies et métropole XVIe-XIXe* (ed.) and "Location and the Conceptualization of Historical Frameworks: Early American History and Its Multiple Reconfigurations in the United States and in Europe" (with Trevor Burnard), in *Historians across Borders: Writing American History in a Global Age,* ed. Nicolas Barreyre, Michael Heale, Stephen Tuck, and Vidal (Berkeley: University of California Press, 2014), 141–62.

46. Vidal, introduction, "Atlantique français"; Hornsby, "Early Modern Canada" (2009); Greer, "National, Transnational"; Jack P. Greene, ed., *Exclusionary Empire: English Liberty Overseas, 1600–1900* (New York: Cambridge University Press, 2010); Vidal, "Pour une histoire globale."

47. Vidal, introduction, "Atlantique français," 8 (original in French).

48. Bailyn and Denault, *Soundings in Atlantic History,* 3.

49. Dominique Rogers, "Fécondité et limites du concept d'histoire atlantique pour la connaissance des villes et des sociétés urbaines antillauses modernes (XVIIᵉ–XVIIIᵉ siècles)," *Outre-Mers: Revue d'histoire* 378–79 (1er semestre 2013): 119–36.

50. John K. Thornton, *A Cultural History of the Atlantic World, 1250–1820* (Cambridge, U.K.: Cambridge University Press, 2012), 3; Vidal, "Pour une histoire globale," 392 (the French original is "acteurs à part entière"). See also Thornton, "The African Background to American Colonization," in *The Cambridge Economic History of the United States,* ed. Stanley L. Engerman and Robert E. Gallman, vol. 1, *The Colonial Era* (New York: Cambridge University Press, 1996), 53–94.

51. Jack P. Greene and J. R. Pole, eds., *Colonial British America: Essays in the New History of the Early Modern Era* (Baltimore: Johns Hopkins University Press, 1984); Greene, *Pursuit of Happiness: The Social Development of Early Modern British Colonies and the Formation of American Culture* (Chapel Hill: University of North Carolina Press, 1988). On Greene's warning, see Jerry Bannister, *The Rule of the Admirals: Law, Custom, and Naval Government in Newfoundland, 1699–1832* (Toronto: University of Toronto Press, 2003), 5–6; and Bannister and Liam Riordan, eds., *The Loyal Atlantic: Remaking the British Atlantic in the Revolutionary Era* (Toronto: University of Toronto Press, 2012), 159.

52. Jack P. Greene, "Comparing Early Modern American Worlds: Some Reflections on the Promise of a Hemispheric Perspective," *History Compass* 1 (May 2002): 1–10, reprinted in Greene and Morgan, *Atlantic History,* and retitled "Hemispheric History and Atlantic History," 299–315, quotation at 4 (Greene's emphasis); Greene, "Reformulating Englishness: Cultural Adaptation and Provinciality in the Construction of Corporate Identity in Colonial British America," chap. 2 in *Creating the British Atlantic: Essays on Transplantation, Adaptation, and Continuity* (Charlottesville: University of Virginia Press, 2013), 19–32, quotation at 21. Also by Greene: *Colonial British America,* ed. with J. R. Pole; *The Intellectual Construction of America: Exceptionalism and Identity from 1492 to 1800* (Chapel Hill:

University of North Carolina Press, 1993); *Interpreting Early America: Historiographical Essays* (Charlottesville: University of Virginia Press, 1996); "Peripheries, Centers, and the Construction of Early Modern American Empires" (with Amy Turner Bushnell), in *Negotiated Empires: Centers and Peripheries in the Americas, 1500–1820,* ed. Christine Daniels and Michael V. Kennedy (New York: Routledge, 2002), 1–14; "Transatlantic Colonization and the Redefinition of Empire in the Early Modern Era: The British-American Experience," in Daniels and Kennedy, *Negotiated Empires,* 267–82; "Comparing Early Modern American Worlds: Some Reflections on the Promise of a Hemispheric Perspective," *History Compass* 1 (May 2002), 1–10; "La primera revolución atlántica: resistencia, rebelión y construcción de nación en los Estados Unidos," in *Las revoluciones en el mundo atlántico,* ed. María Teresa Calderón and Thibaud (Bogotá: Taurus, 2006), 19–38; "Colonial History and National History: Reflections on a Continuing Problem," *William and Mary Quarterly,* 3rd ser., 64, no. 2 (2007): 235–50.

53. Kathleen Wilson, ed., *A New Imperial History: Culture, Identity and Modernity in Britain and the Empire, 1660–1840* (Cambridge, U.K.: Cambridge University Press, 2004), 3. See also Ned C. Landsman, "Nation, Migration, and the Province in the First British Empire: Scotland and the Americas, 1600–1800," in "The New British History in Atlantic Perspective," ed. David Armitage, special section of *American Historical Review* 104, no. 2 (1999): 463–75; Jane H. Ohlmeyer, "Seventeenth-Century Ireland and the New British and Atlantic Histories," in Armitage, "New British History," 446–62; John G. A. Pocock, "The New British History in Atlantic Perspective: An Antipodean Commentary," in Armitage, "New British History," 490–500; Marco Mariano and Federica Morelli, eds., "European Perspectives on a Longer Atlantic World," special issue of *Nuevo Mundo Mundos Nuevos* (2012), http://nuevomundo.revues.org/63476 (accessed Jan. 8, 2017); and Nial Whelehan, *Ireland beyond the Nation-State: Antecedents of Transnational History in Irish Historiography,* Working Paper Series (Edinburgh: University of Edinburgh, School of History, Classics and Archaeology, 2013).

54. Hodson and Rushforth, "Absolutely Atlantic"; Trevor Burnard and Allan Potofsky, eds., "The French Atlantic and the Caribbean, 1600–1800," special issue of *French History* 25, no. 1 (2011): 1–107; Alain Cabantous, "Résistance de principe ou lucidité intellectuelle? Les historiens français et l'histoire atlantique," *Revue historique* 114, fasc. 3, no. 663 (2012): 705–26.

55. Vidal, introduction, "Atlantique français"; Christophe Belaubre, Jordana Dym, and John Savage, eds., *Napoléon et les Amériques: Histoire atlantique and empire napoléonien* (Toulouse, France: Presses de l'Université de Toulouse Le Mirail, 2009), 1–20; Covo, "Révolution haïtienne."

56. Aside from the publications of Vidal and Havard already mentioned, see Mickael Augeron, Didier Poton, and Bertrand Van Ruymbeke, eds., *Les Huguenots et l'Atlantique* (Paris: Presses Universitaires de Paris-Sorbonne/Les Indes Savantes, 2009); Nathalie Dessens, "Napoleon and Louisiana: New Atlantic Perspectives," in *Napoleon's Atlantic: The Impact of Napoleonic Empire in the Atlantic World,* ed. Christophe Belaubre, Jordana Dym, and John Savage (Leiden, Netherlands: Brill, 2010), 63–77; Marcel Dorigny, ed., "L'Atlantique," special issue of *Dix-Huitième Siècle* 33 (2001): 5–316; Dorigny and Fabrice Le Goff, *Atlas des premières colonisations: XVe–début XIXe siècle; des conquistadores aux libérateurs* (Paris: Éditions Autrement, 2013); Pierre Gervais, "Neither Imperial, nor Atlantic. A Merchant Perspective on International Trade in the Eighteenth Century," in

"New Perspectives on the Atlantic," ed. Allan Potofsky, special issue of *History of European Ideas* 34, no. 4 (2008): 465–72; Pierre Gervais, "A Merchant or a French Atlantic? Eighteenth-century Account Books as Narratives of a Transnational Merchant Political Economy," in Burnard and Potofsky, "French Atlantic and the Caribbean," 28–47; Gilles Havard, "L'historiographie de la Nouvelle-France en France au cours du XXe siècle: nostalgie, oubli et renouveau," in Wien, Vidal, and Frenette, *De Québec à l'Amérique française,* 95–124; Havard, "Les Indiens et l'histoire coloniale nord-américaine: les défis de l'ethnohistoire," in Vidal and Ruggiu, eds., *Sociétés, colonisations et esclavages dans le monde atlantique. Historiographie des sociétés américaines des XVIe-XIXe siècles* (Bécherel: Les Perséides, 2009), pp. 95–142; Havard and Mickaël Augeron, eds., *Un continent en partage: Cinq siècles de rencontres entre Amérindiens et Français* (Paris: Les Indes Savantes, 2013); Silvia Marzagalli, "The French Atlantic," *Itinerario* 23 (1999) : 70–83; Silvia Marzagalli, "Sur les origines de l'"Atlantic History': Paradigme interprétatif de l'histoire des espaces atlantiques à l'époque moderne," in Dorigny, *Atlantique,* 17–31; Silvia Marzagalli, "L'histoire atlantique en Europe," in Vidal, ed., *Histoire atlantique de part et d'autre* (2008); Marzagalli, "The French Atlantic World in the Seventeenth and Eighteenth Centuries," in Canny and Morgan, *Oxford Handbook of the Atlantic World,* 235–51; Allan Potofsky, "La révolution transatlantique des émigrés, Des réseaux aux institutions," in Marcel Dorigny, ed., *Atlantique* (2001), 247–63; Potofsky, "The Political Economy of the French-American Debate: The Ideological Uses of Atlantic Commerce, 1787 to 1800," *William and Mary Quarterly,* 3rd ser., 63, no. 3 (July 2006), 488–516; Potofsky, "New Perspectives on the Atlantic," 383–473; Potofsky, "The One and the Many: The Two Revolutions Question and the 'Consumer-Commercial' Atlantic, 1789," in *Rethinking the Atlantic World: Europe and America in the Age of Democratic Revolution,* ed. Manuela Albertone and Antonino de Francesco (Basingstoke, U.K.: Palgrave Macmillan, 2009), 17–45; Potofsky, "Paris-on-the-Atlantic from the Old Regime to the Revolution," in Burnard and Potofsky, "French Atlantic and the Caribbean," 89–107; François-Joseph Ruggiu, "Extraction, Wealth and Industry: The Ideas of Noblesse and of Gentility in the English and French Atlantics (17th-18th Centuries)," in Potofsky, *New Perspectives,* 444–55; Ruggiu, "Le destin de la noblesse du Canada, de l'Empire français à l'Empire britannique," *Revue d'histoire de l'Amérique française* 66, no. 1 (2012): 37–63; Bertrand Van Ruymbeke and Randy J. Sparks, eds., *Memory and Identity: The Huguenots in France and the Atlantic Diaspora* (Columbia: University of South Carolina Press, 2003); Van Ruymbeke, *From New Babylon to Eden: The Huguenots and Their Migration to Colonial South Carolina* (Columbia: University of South Carolina Press, 2006); Van Ruymbeke, "Refugiés or Émigrés? Early Modern French Migrations to British North America and the United States (c.1680–c.1820)," *Itinerario* 30, no. 2 (2006), 12–32; Van Ruymbeke, "'A Dominion of True Believers Not a Republic for Heretics': French Colonial Religious Policy and Settlement of Early Louisiana, 1699–1739," in *French Colonial Louisiana and the Atlantic World,* ed. Bradley G. Bond (Baton Rouge: Louisiana State University Press, 2005), 83–94; and Van Ruymbeke, "L'histoire atlantique aux États-Unis: la périphérie au centre," in Vidal, *Histoire atlantique de part et d'autre.*

57. David Armitage, "*Itinerario* to host on-line discussion with Prof. David Armitage," http://blog.journals.cambridge.org/2012/11/itinerario-to-host-on-line-discussion-with-prof-david-armitage/ (accessed Jan. 8, 2017). Also by Armitage: "The New World and British Historical Thought: From Richard Hakluyt to William Robertson," in Kupperman, *America in European Consciousness* (1995), 52–75; *Theories of Empire, 1450–1800*

(ed.), (Aldershot, U.K.: Ashgate Variorum, 1998); "New British History," 426–500; *The Ideological Origins of the British Empire* (Cambridge, U.K.: Cambridge University Press, 2000); "The Red Atlantic," *Reviews in American History* 29, no. 4 (2001), 479–86; *The British Atlantic World, 1500–1800,* ed. with Michael J. Braddick (Basingstoke, U.K.: Palgrave Macmillan, 2002); *Greater Britain 1516–1776: Essays in Atlantic History* (Aldershot, U.K.: Ashgate Variorum, 2004); "From Colonial History to Postcolonial History: A Turn Too Far?" *William and Mary Quarterly,* 3rd ser., 64, no. 2 (2007): 251–54; *Age of Revolutions,* ed. with Sanjay Subrahmanyam; "The American Revolution in Atlantic Perspective," in Canny and Morgan, *Oxford Handbook of the Atlantic World,* 516–32.

58. Greene, "Colonial History and National History," reprinted in Greene, *Creating the British Atlantic,* 78.

59. Bannister and Riordan, *Loyal Atlantic,* 23. See also Jerry Bannister, "Citizen of the Atlantic. Benjamin Lester's Social World in England, 1768–69," *Newfoundland Quarterly* 96, no. 3 (2003): 32–37; Bannister, *Rule of the Admirals;* Bannister, "The Loyal Atlantic," in Reid, Bowen, and Mancke, "Is There a 'Canadian' Atlantic World?," 290–95; Bannister, "The Oriental Atlantic: Governance and Regulatory Frameworks in the British Atlantic World," in Bowen, Mancke, and Reid, *Britain's Oceanic Empire,* 151–76. On the "loyal Atlantic," see also Elizabeth J. Errington, "Loyalists and Loyalism in the American Revolution and Beyond," *Acadiensis* 41, no. 2 (2012): 164–73; Maya Jasanoff, "The Other Side of Revolution: Loyalists in the British Empire," *William and Mary Quarterly,* 3rd ser., 65, no. 2 (2008): 205–32; Jasanoff, "Revolutionary Exiles: The American Loyalist and French Émigré Diasporas," in Armitage and Subrahmanyam, *Age of Revolutions,* 37–58; and Jasanoff, *Liberty's Exiles: American Loyalists in the Revolutionary World* (New York: Knopf, 2011).

60. Alain Cabantous, "Résistance de principe ou lucidité intellectuelle? Les historiens français et l'histoire atlantique," *Revue historique* 315, fasc. 3, no. 663 (2012): 705–26, esp. 709. Also by Cabantous: *Foi chrétienne et milieux maritimes (XVe-XXe siècles): Actes du Colloque; Paris, Collège de France, 23–25 septembre 1987,* ed. with Françoise Hildesheimer (Paris: Éditions Publisud, 1987); *Le ciel dans la mer: Christianisme et civilisation maritime (XVe-XIXe siècle)* (Paris: Librairie Arthème Fayard, 1990); "On the Writing of the Religious History of Seafarers," *International Journal of Maritime History* 3, no. 1 (1991): 213–18; "Les finistères de la catholicité. Missions littorales et construction identitaire en France aux XVIIe et XVIIIe siècles," in "Les frontières de la mission," ed. Catherine Brice and Luca Codignola, special section of *Mélanges de l'École Française de Rome* 109, no. 2 (1997): 653–69.

61. Jack P. Greene, "Colonial History and National History" (2007), reprinted in Greene, *Creating the British Atlantic,* 77.

62. W. J. Eccles, *France in America* (New York: Harper and Row, 1972), ii.

63. Jack P. Greene, "Hemispheric History and Atlantic History," reprinted in Greene, *Creating the British Atlantic,* 5, 13–14; Greene, "Comparing Early Modern American Worlds: Some Reflections on the Promise of a Hemispheric Perspective," *History Compass* 1 (May 2002), 1–10; Felipe Fernández-Armesto, *The Americas: A Hemispheric History* (New York: Modern Library, 2003); April L. Hatfield, *Atlantic Virginia: Intercolonial Relations in the Seventeenth Century* (Philadelphia: University of Pennsylvania Press, 2004); Caroline F. Levander and Robert S. Levine, eds., *Hemispheric American Studies* (New Brunswick, N.J.: Rutgers University Press, 2008). See also Hinderaker and Horn, "Territorial Crossings"; and Vidal, "Pour une histoire globale."

64. Bushnell and Greene, "Peripheries, Centers"; Greene and Morgan, *Atlantic History.* See also Amy Turner Bushnell, ed., *Establishing Exceptionalism: Historiography and the Colonial Americas* (Aldershot, U.K.: Variorum, 1995); Bushnell, "Indigenous America and the Limits of the Atlantic World, 1493–1825," in Greene and Morgan, *Atlantic History,* 191–221. See also Eliga H. Gould, "Comparing Atlantic Histories," *Reviews in American History* 38, no. 1 (2010): 8–16; and Hinderaker and Horn, "Territorial Crossing."

65. Greer, "National, Transnational." Also by Allan Greer: "La Nouvelle France / Les Nouvelles Frances," in "Roundtable on Peter Moogk's *La Nouvelle France,*" special section of *French Colonial History* 4 (2003): 15–18; "Comparisons: New France," in *A Companion to Colonial America,* ed. Daniel Vickers (Malden, U.K.: Blackwell, 2003), 469–88; "La Nouvelle-France dans le contexte de l'histoire des Amériques," in Philippe Joutard, Wien, and Poton, eds., *Mémoires de Nouvelle-France. De France en Nouvelle-France* (Rennes: Presses Universitaires de Rennes, 2005), 155–66; "A Catholic Atlantic" (with Kenneth Mills) *The Atlantic in Global History 1500–2000,* ed. Jorge Cañizares-Esguerra and Erik R. Seeman (Upper Saddle River, N.J.: Pearson–Prentice Hall, 2007), 3–19; "Towards a Comparative Study of Jesuit Missions and Indigenous Peoples in Seventeenth-Century Canada and Paraguay," in *Native Christians: Modes and Effects of Christianity among Indigenous Peoples of the Americas,* ed. Robin M. Wright and Aparecida Vilaca (Aldershot, U.K.: Ashgate, 2009), 21–32.

66. For a successful example, see James Lockhart and Stuart B. Schwartz, *Early Latin America: A History of Colonial Spanish America and Brazil* (Cambridge, U.K.: Cambridge University Press, 1983). For a less successful one, see Lester D. Langley, *The Americas in the Age of Revolution, 1750–1850* (New Haven, Conn.: Yale University Press, 1996). See also Greene and Morgan, *Atlantic History;* Hinderaker and Horn, "Territorial Crossings"; Hodson and Rushforth, "Absolutely Atlantic"; Emma G. Rothschild, "Late Atlantic History," in Canny and Morgan, *Oxford Handbook of the Atlantic World,* 634–48; and Covo, "Révolution haïtienne."

67. Gould, "Comparing Atlantic Histories." See also Alan L. Karras, "The Atlantic World as a Unit of Study," in *Atlantic American Societies: From Columbus through Abolition 1492–1888,* ed. Karras and John R. McNeill (London: Routledge, 1992), 1–15.

68. Morelli, *Mondo atlantico,* 10–11 (original in Italian). See also Morelli, Thibaud, and Geneviève Verdo, eds., *Les empires atlantiques des Lumières au libéralisme (1763–1865)* (Rennes: Presses Universitaires de Rennes, 2009); Federica Morelli and Alajandro E. Gómez, "La nueva Historia Atlántica: un asunto de escalas," *Nuevo Mundo Mundos Nuevos* (2006), http://nuevomundo.revues.org/2102 (accessed Jan. 8, 2017).

69. Vidal, introduction, "Atlantique français," 8–9 (original in French).

70. Gould, "Comparing Atlantic Histories." Also by Eliga H. Gould: "A Virtual Nation: Greater Britain and the Imperial Legacy of the American Revolution," in Armitage, "New British History in Atlantic Perspective," 476–89; *The Persistence of Empire: British Political Culture in the Age of the American Revolution* (Chapel Hill: University of North Carolina Press, 2000); "Revolution and Counter-Revolution," in Armitage and Braddick, *British Atlantic World,* 196–213; "Zones of Law, Zones of Violence: The Legal Geography of the British Atlantic, circa 1772," *William and Mary Quarterly,* 3rd ser., 60, no. 3 (2003): 471–510; *Empire and Nation: The American Revolution in the Atlantic World,* ed. with Peter S. Onuf (Baltimore: Johns Hopkins University Press, 2005); "Entangled Histories, Entangled Worlds: The English-Speaking Atlantic as a Spanish Periphery," *American Historical*

Review 112, no. 3 (2007): 764–86; "Entangled Atlantic Histories: A Response from the Anglo-American Periphery," *American Historical Review* 112, no. 5 (2007): 1414–22; "Atlantic History and the Literary Turn," *William and Mary Quarterly*, 3rd ser., 65, no. 1 (2008): 175–80; *Among the Powers of the Earth: The American Revolution and the Making of a New World Empire* (Cambridge, Mass.: Harvard University Press, 2012).

71. On global history and its implications for Atlantic history, see Ian K. Steele, "Exploding Colonial American History: Amerindian, Atlantic, and Global Perspectives," *Reviews in American History* 26, no. 1 (1998): 70–95; Bruce Mazlish, "Comparing Global History to World History," *Journal of Interdisciplinary History* 28, no. 3 (1998): 385–93; David Eltis, "Atlantic History in Global Perspective," *Itinerario* 23, no. 2 (1999): 141–61; Frederick Cooper, "Le concept de mondialisation sert-il à quelque chose? Un point de vue d'historien," *Critique internationale* 10, no. 1 (2001): 101–24; Olivier Pétré-Grénouilleau, *Les traites négrières: Essai d'histoire globale* (Paris: NRF, 2004); Bruce Mazlish, *The New Global History* (New York: Routledge, 2006); Philip J. Stern, "British Asia and British Atlantic: Comparisons and Connections," *William and Mary Quarterly*, 3rd ser., 63, no. 4 (2006): 693–712; Paul W. Mapp, "Atlantic History from Imperial, Continental, and Pacific Perspectives," *William and Mary Quarterly,* 3rd ser., 63, no. 4 (2006), 713–24; Cañizares-Esguerra and Seeman, *Atlantic in Global History;* David Cannadine, ed., *Empire, the Sea, and Global History. Britain's Maritime World, c.1760–c.1840* (New York: Palgrave Macmillan, 2007); Caroline Douki and Philippe Minard, eds., "Histoire globale, histoires connectées: un changement d'échelle historiographique?," special section of *Revue d'histoire moderne et contemporaine* 54, no. 4-bis (2007): 7–103; Sanjay Subrahmanyam, "Holding the World in Balance: The Connected Histories of the Iberian Overseas Empires, 1500–1640," *American Historical Review* 112, no. 5 (2007): 1359–85; Simon P. Newman, "Making Sense of Atlantic World Histories: A British Perspective," in Vidal, *Histoire atlantique de part et d'autre;* Nicholas Canny, "Atlantic History and Global History," in Greene and Morgan, *Atlantic History,* 317–36; Armitage and Subrahmanyam, *Age of Revolutions;* C. A. Bayly, "The Age of Revolutions in Global Context: An Afterword," in Armitage and Subrahmanyam, *Age of Revolutions,* 209–17; Jan De Vries, "Reflections on Doing Global History," in Armitage and Subrahmanyam, *Age of Revolutions,* 32–47; Jean-Frédéric Schaub, "Notes on Some Discontents in the Historical Narrative," in Armitage and Subrahmanyam, *Age of Revolutions,* 48–65; John Darwin, "Reflections on Doing Global History," in Armitage and Subrahmanyam, *Age of Revolutions,* 196–99; Vidal, "Pour une histoire globale du monde atlantique"; Maxine Berg, ed., *Writing the History of the Global: Challenges for the 21st Century* (Oxford, U.K.: Oxford University Press, 2013).

72. Nicholas Canny's work includes: *Colonial Identity in the Atlantic World, 1500–1800,* ed. with Anthony Pagden (Princeton, N.J.: Princeton University Press, 1987); *Kingdom and Colony: Ireland in the Atlantic World, 1560–1800* (Baltimore: Johns Hopkins University Press, 1988); *Europeans on the Move: Studies on European Migration, 1500–1800* (Oxford, U.K.: Clarendon Press, 1994); *The Origins of Empire: British Overseas Enterprise to the Close of the Seventeenth Century,* ed. with Alaine M. Low (Oxford, U.K.: Oxford University Press, 1998); "Writing Atlantic History; or, Reconfiguring the History of Colonial British America," *Journal of American History* 86, no. 3 (1999): 1093–1114; "Atlantic History: What and Why?" *European Review* 9, no. 4 (2001): 399–411; "Atlantic History, 1492–1700: Scope, Sources and Methods," in Horst Pietschmann, ed., *Atlantic History. History of the Atlantic System 1580–1830: Papers presented at an International Conference, held*

28 August–1 September, 1999, in Hamburg, organized by the Department of History, University of Hamburg, in cooperation with Joachim Jungius-Gesellschaft der Wissenschaft, Hamburg, supported by Deutsche Forschungsgemeineschaft (Göttingen, Germany: Vandenhoek and Ruprecht, 2002), 55–64; "Atlantic History and Global History," in Greene and Morgan, *Atlantic History,* 317–36; *Oxford Handbook of Atlantic World,* ed. with P. D. Morgan.

73. Rothschild, "Late Atlantic History."

74. Alison F. Games's work includes: "The English Atlantic World: A View from London," in "Empire, Society, and Labor: Essays in Honor of Richard S. Dunn," ed. Nicholas Canny, Joseph E. Illick, Gary B. Nash, and William Pencak, special supplemental issue of *Pennsylvania History* 64 (Spring 1997): 46–72; "Teaching Atlantic History," *Itinerario* 23, no. 2 (1999): 162–74; "Migration," in Armitage and Braddick, *British Atlantic World* (2002), 31–50; "Atlantic Constraints and Global Opportunities," *History Compass* 1, no. 1 (2003): 1–4; "Atlantic History: Definitions, Challenges, and Opportunities," *American Historical Review* 111, no. 3 (June 2006): 741–57; "Beyond the Atlantic: English Globetrotters and Transoceanic Connections," *William and Mary Quarterly,* 3rd ser., 63, no. 4 (2006): 675–92; *The Web of Empire: English Cosmopolitans in an Age of Expansion 1560–1660* (Oxford, U.K.: Oxford University Press, 2008); "Atlantic History and Interdisciplinary Approaches," *William and Mary Quarterly,* 3rd ser., 65, no. 1 (2008): 167–70; "Migrations and Frontiers," in *The Atlantic World 1450–2000,* ed. Toyin Falola and Kevin David Roberts (Bloomington: Indiana University Press, 2008), 48–65.

75. For Peter A. Coclanis, see esp. "Atlantic World or Atlantic/World?" *William and Mary Quarterly,* 3rd ser., 63, no. 4 (2006): 725–42; and "Beyond Atlantic History," in Greene and Morgan, *Atlantic History,* 337–56. See also "In Retrospective: McCusker and Menard's *Economy of British America,*" *Reviews in American History* 30, no. 2 (2002): 183–97; and *The Atlantic Economy during the Seventeenth and Eighteenth Century: Organization, Operation, Practice, and Personnel* (ed.), (Columbia: University of South Carolina Press, 2005).

76. Paul Cohen, "Was There an Amerindian Atlantic? Reflections on the Limits of a Historiographical Concept," in Potofsky, *New Perspectives,* 388–410.

77. Bowen, Mancke, and Reid, *Britain's Oceanic Empire,* For Elizabeth A. Mancke, see also "Another British America: A Canadian Model for the Early Modern British Empire," *The Journal of Imperial and Commonwealth History* 25, no. 1 (1997): 1–36; "Negotiating an Empire. Britain and Its Overseas Peripheries, c. 1550–1780," in Daniels and Kennedy, *Negotiated Empires,* 235–65; "Empire and State," in Armitage and Braddick, *British Atlantic World,* 175–95, 280–84; "Elites, States, and the Imperial Contest for Acadia," with John G. Reid, in *The "Conquest" of Acadia, 1710: Imperial, Colonial, and Aboriginal Constructions,* with other contributions by Reid, Maurice Basque, Barry Moody, Geoffrey G. Plank, and William C. Wicken (Toronto: University of Toronto Press, 2004), 25–47; "Imperial Transitions," also in *The "Conquest" of Acadia,* 178–202; *The Creation of the British Atlantic World,* ed. with Carole Shammas (Baltimore: Johns Hopkins University Press, 2005); and "Polity Formation and Atlantic Political Narratives," in Canny and Morgan, *Oxford Handbook of the Atlantic World,* 382–400. For John G. Reid, see *Acadia, Maine, and New Scotland: Marginal Colonies in the Seventeenth Century* (Toronto: University of Toronto Press, 1981); "Imperialism, Diplomacies, and the conquest of Acadia," in *The "Conquest" of Acadia,* 101–23; "*Pax Britannica* or *Pax Indigena?* Planter Nova Scotia (1760–1782) and Competing Strategies of Pacification," *Canadian Historical Review* 85, no. 4 (2004):

669–92; "How Wide is the Ocean" (2005), 81–87; *Essays on Northeastern North America: Seventeenth and Eighteenth Centuries* (Toronto: University of Toronto Press, 2008); "From Global Processes to Continental Strategies: The Emergence of British North America to 1783" (with Mancke), in *Canada and the British Empire,* ed. Phillip A. Buckner (Oxford: Oxford University Press, 2008), 22–42; "Empire, the Maritime Colonies, and the Supplanting of Mi'kma'ki/Wulstukwik, 1780–1820," *Acadiensis* 38, no. 2 (2009): 78–97; and "Imperial-Aboriginal Friendship in Eighteenth-Century Mi'kma'ki/Wulstukwik," in Bannister and Riordan, *Loyal Atlantic,* 75–102.

78. Jack P. Greene, "Hemispheric History and Atlantic History," reprinted in Greene, *Creating the British Atlantic,* 3–4.

79. Hornsby, *British Atlantic, American Frontier;* Jorge Cañizares-Esguerra, "Whose Centers and Whose Peripheries? Eighteenth-Century Intellectual History in Atlantic Perspective," in Klooster and Padula, *Atlantic World,* 148–59; Cañizares-Esguerra, "Typology in the Atlantic World: Early Modern Readings of Colonization," in Bailyn and Denault, *Soundings in Atlantic History,* 237–64; Bitterli, *Alte Welt Neue Welt;* Denys Delâge, *Le pays renversé: Amérindiens et européens en Amérique du nord-est 1600–1664* (Montréal: Boréal Express, 1985). In later years, Delâge abandoned his constraining models in favor of more in-depth ethnohistorical publications. See also Jorge Cañizares-Esguerra, "Some Caveats about the 'Atlantic' Paradigm," *History Compass* 1, no. 1 (2003): 1–4; and Cañizares-Esguerra, *Puritan Conquistadors: Iberianizing the Atlantic, 1500–1700* (Stanford, Calif.: Stanford University Press, 2006).

80. Daniel K. Richter, *Facing East from Indian Country: A Native History of Early America* (Cambridge, Mass.: Harvard University Press, 2001). See Greer, "National, Transnational."

81. Reid, whose Atlantic publications are listed above, is one major exception in this regard.

82. Gayle K. Brunelle, review of Banks, *Chasing Empire,* for *H-Atlantic* (2003), http://www.h-net.org/reviews/showrev.php?id = 8415 (accessed January 8, 2017).

83. John A. Dickinson, "Les chemins migratoires et l'établissement des Acadiens à Saint-Denis au XVIIIe siècle," La Société Historique Acadienne, *Les Cahiers* 24, nos. 1–2 (1998): 57–69; Jean-François Mouhot, *Les Réfugiés acadiens en France 1758–1785. L'impossible réintégration?* (Québec: Septentrion, 2009).

84. John F. Bosher, *The Canada Merchants 1713–1763* (Oxford, U.K.: Clarendon Press, 1987); Bosher, *Business and Religion in the Age of New France, 1600–1760. Twenty-Two Studies* (Toronto: Canadian Scholars' Press, 1994); Bosher, "Huguenot Merchants and the Protestant International in the Seventeenth Century," *William and Mary Quarterly,* 3rd ser., 52, 2 (1995): 77–102; James S. Pritchard, *In Search of Empire: The French in the Americas, 1670–1730* (Cambridge, U.K.: Cambridge University Press, 2004); Pritchard, David Eltis, and David Richardson, "The Significance of the French Slave Trade to the Evolution of the French Atlantic World before 1716," in *Extending the Frontiers: Essays on the New Transatlantic Slave Trade Database,* ed. Eltis and Richardson (New Haven, Conn.: Yale University Press, 2008), 205–27; Pritchard, "France: Maritime Empire, Continental Commitment," in *China Goes to Sea: Maritime Transformation in Comparative Historical Perspective,* ed. Andrew S. Erikson, Lyle J. Goldstein, and Carnes Lord (Annapolis, Md.: Naval Institute Press, 2009), 123–43; Dale Miquelon, "Les Pontchartrains se penchent sur leurs cartes de l'Amérique: les cartes et l'impérialisme, 1690–1712," *Revue d'histoire de*

l'Amérique française 59, nos. 1–2 (2005): 7–52; Miquelon, "After Ryswick: The Five Nations Iroquois in French Diplomacy," *Native Studies Review* 18, no. 1 (2009), 5–24; Miquelon, "Ambiguous Concession: What Diplomatic Archives Reveal about Article 15 of the Treaty of Utrecht and France's North American Policy," *William and Mary Quarterly,* 3rd ser., 67, no. 3 (2010): 459–86; Peter Moogk, "Reluctant Exiles: Emigrants from France in Canada before 1760," *William and Mary Quarterly,* 3rd ser., 46, no. 3 (1989): 463–505; Moogk, *La Nouvelle France: The Making of French Canada—A Cultural History* (East Lansing: Michigan State University Press, 2000); Moogk, "Writing the Cultural History of Pre-1760 European Colonists," in "Roundtable on Peter Moogk's *La Nouvelle France,*" 1–14.

85. Henry A. F. Kamen, *Spain's Road to Empire: The Making of a World Power, 1492–1763* (London: Allen Lane, Penguin, 2002), published in the United States as *Empire: How Spain Became a World Power, 1492–1763* (New York: HarperCollins, 2003); Christophe Belaubre, Jordana Dym, and John Savage, eds., *Napoléon et les Amériques: Histoire atlantique et empire napoléonien* (Toulouse, France: Presses de l'Université de Toulouse Le Mirail, 2009). See also Annie R. M. Jourdan's review of the English edition of the latter book, *Napoleon's Atlantic: The Impact of Napoleonic Empire in the Atlantic World* (Leiden, Netherlands: Brill, 2010), in *H-France Review* 11, no. 223 (2011), which is in agreement with my opinion; and Jourdan, "The Napoleonic Empire in the Age of Revolutions: The Contrast of Two National Representations," in *The Napoleonic Empire and the New European Political Culture,* ed. Michael Broers, Peter Hicks, and Agustín Guimerá (Basingstoke, U.K.: Palgrave Macmillan, 2012), 313–26.

86. David P. Geggus, ed., *The Impact of the Haitian Revolution in the Atlantic World* (Columbia: University of South Carolina Press, 2001); Annie R. M. Jourdan, *La Révolution, une exception française?* (Paris: Flammarion, 2004); Laurent Dubois, *Avengers of the New World: The Story of the Haitian Revolution* (Cambridge, Mass.: Belknap Press of Harvard University Press, 2004); Dubois, *A Colony of Citizens: Revolution and Slave Emancipation in the French Caribbean, 1787–1804* (Chapel Hill: University of North Carolina Press, 2004); Anne Pérotin-Dumon, "Aux Antilles: bilan et perspectives préliminaires sur l'étude d'un passé violent," in *La Révolution à l'oeuvre. Perspectives actuelles dans l'histoire de la Révolution française,* ed. Jean-Clément Martin (Rennes, France: Presses Universitaires de Rennes, 2005), 241–53; David P. Geggus and Norman S. Fiering, eds., *The World of the Haitian Revolution* (Bloomington: Indiana University Press, 2009); Dubois, "An Atlantic Revolution," in "The French Revolution Twenty Years After the Bicentennial," special section of *French Historical Studies* 32, no. 4 (2009): 655–61; David P. Geggus, "The Caribbean in the Age of Revolution," in Armitage and Subrahmanyam, *Age of Revolutions,* 83–100; Jeremy D. Popkin, *A Concise History of the Haitian Revolution* (Hoboken, N.J.: Blackwell/John Wiley, 2011).

87. Jourdan, *La Révolution;* Lynn Hunt, "The French Revolution in Global Context," in Armitage and Subrahmanyam, *Age of Revolutions,* 125–43; Thomas E. Kaiser, "A Tale of Two Narratives: The French Revolution in International Context, 1787–93," in *A Companion to the French Revolution,* ed. Peter McPhee (Oxford, U.K.: Wiley-Blackwell, 2012), 161–77; Mike Rapport, "The International Repercussions of the French Revolution," in McPhee, *Companion to the French Revolution,* 381–96; Suzanne M. Desan, Lynn Hunt, and William M. Nelson, eds., *The French Revolution in Global Perspective* (Ithaca, N.Y.: Cornell University Press, 2013).

88. Jeremy Adelman and Stephen Aron, "From Borderlands to Borders: Empires, Nation-States, and the Peoples in Between in North American History," *American Historical Review* 109, no. 3 (1999): 814–41; Adelman and Aron, "Of Lively Exchanges and Larger Perspectives," *American Historical Review* 109, no. 4 (October 1999): 1235–39 (a rejoinder to commentaries by Evan Haefeli, Pekka Hämäläinen, Christopher Ebert Schmidt-Nowara, and John R. Wunder); Hinderaker and Horn, "Territorial Crossings." See also Jeremy Adelman, *Sovereignty and Revolution in the Iberian Atlantic* (Princeton, N.J.: Princeton University Press, 2006); Adelman, "An Age of Imperial Revolutions," *American Historical Review* 113, no. 2 (2008): 319–40; Adelman, "Iberian Passages: Continuity and Change in the South Atlantic," in Armitage and Subrahmanyam, *Age of Revolutions,* 59–82; Eric A. Hinderaker, "Diplomacy between Britons and Native Americans, c.1600–1830," in *Britain's Oceanic Empire,* ed. Bowen, Mancke, and Reid, 218–48.

89. Reid, Bowen, and Mancke, "Is There a 'Canadian' Atlantic World?," 263.

90. See, for example, James Lockhart, *Of Things of the Indies: Essays Old and New in Early Latin American History* (Stanford, Calif.: Stanford University Press, 2000); Stuart B. Schwartz, ed., *Implicit Understandings: Observing, Reporting, and Reflecting on the Encounter between Europeans and Other Peoples in the Early Modern Era* (Cambridge, U.K.: Cambridge University Press, 1994); Schwartz, ed., *Tropical Babylons: Sugar and the Making of the Atlantic World, 1450–1680* (Chapel Hill: University of North Carolina Press, 2004); Schwartz, "Virginia and the Atlantic World," in *The Atlantic World and Virginia, 1550–1624,* ed. Peter C. Mancall (Chapel Hill: University of North Carolina Press, 2007), 558–70; Schwartz, *All Can Be Saved: Religious Tolerance and Salvation in the Iberian Atlantic World* (New Haven, Conn.: Yale University Press, 2008) (on which see the forum in *William and Quarterly,* 3rd ser., 66, no. 2 [2009]: 409–33, with contributions by David D. Hall, Lu Ann Homza, Andrew R. Murphy, and Marcy Norton and a rejoinder by Schwartz); Schwartz, "The Iberian Atlantic to 1650," in Canny and Morgan, *Oxford Handbook of the Atlantic World,* 147–64; John H. Elliott, "The Old World and the New Revisited," in Kupperman, *America in European Consciousness,* 391–408; Elliott, "Comparative History," in Carlos Barros, *Historia a debate / Histoire à débat / History under Debate,* vol. 3, *Otros enfoques* (Santiago de Compostela, Spain: HAD, 1995), 9–19; Elliott, "Atlantic History: A Circumnavigation," in Armitage and Braddick, *British Atlantic World,* 233–49; Elliott, *Empires of the Atlantic World: Britain and Spain in America 1492–1830* (New Haven, Conn.: Yale University Press, 2006); Elliott, "The Iberian Atlantic and Virginia," in Mancall, *Atlantic World and Virginia,* 541–57.

91. François-Xavier Guerra, *Modernidad y independencias. Ensayos sobre las revoluciones hispánicas* (Madrid: Mapfre, 1992); Calderón and Thibaud, *Revoluciones en el mundo atlantico;* José Maria Portillo Valdés, *Crisis atlántica: Autonomía y independencia en la crisis de la monarquía hispana* (Madrid: Marcial Pons, 2006); Portillo Valdés, "Imperial Spain," in *The Napoleonic Empire and the New European Political Culture,* ed. Michael Broers, Peter Hicks, and Agustín Guimerá (Houndmills, U.K.: Palgrave Macmillan, 2012), 282–92.

92. Codignola, "Too Much of a Good Thing?"

93. Thornton, *Cultural History,* xiv.

94. Trevor Burnard, "Placing British Settlement in the Americas in Comparative Perspective," in Bowen, Mancke, and Reid, *Britain's Oceanic Empire,* 407–32, quotation at 408.

Also by Burnard: "'The Dog That Did Not Bark'? Periodization in Early American History," *Uncommon Sense: A Newsletter Published by the Omohundro Institute of Early American History and Culture* 119 (Fall 2004): 24–30; "Only Connect: The Rise (and Fall?) of Atlantic History," *Historically Speaking* 7, no. 6 (2006): 19–21; "Empire Matters? The Historiography of Imperialism in Early America, 1492–1830," *History of European Ideas* 33, no. 1 (2007): 87–101; "The British Atlantic," in Greene and Morgan, *Atlantic History*, 111–36.

95. Philip D. A. Curtin, *Cross-Cultural Trade in World History* (Cambridge, U.K.: Cambridge University Press, 1984), x. Also by Curtin: *The Image of Africa: British Ideas and Actions, 1780–1850* (Madison: University of Wisconsin Press, 1964); *The Atlantic Slave Trade: A Census* (Madison: University of Wisconsin Press, 1969); "Africa and the Wider Monetary World, 1250–1850," in *Precious Metals in the Later Medieval and Early Modern Worlds*, ed. J. F. Richards (Durham, N.C.: Carolina Academic Press, 1983), 231–68.

96. David Eltis and David Richardson, *Atlas of the Transatlantic Slave Trade* (New Haven, Conn.: Yale University Press, 2010). See also Eltis, *The Rise of African Slavery in the Americas* (Cambridge, U.K.: Cambridge University Press, 2000); Eltis, "Free and Coerced Migrations from the Old World to the New," in *Coerced and Free Migrations: Global Perspectives*, ed. Eltis (Stanford, Calif.: Stanford University Press, 2002), 33–75; Eltis and Richardson, *Extending the Frontiers;* Eltis, "Africa, Slavery, and the Slave Trade, Mid-Seventeenth to Mid-Eighteenth Century," in Canny and Morgan, *Oxford Handbook of the Atlantic World*, 271–86.

97. Herbert S. Klein, *The Atlantic Slave Trade* (Cambridge, New York: Cambridge University Press, 1999); Klein, Stanley L. Engerman, Robin Haines, and Ralph Shlomowitz, "Transoceanic Mortality: The Slave Trade in Comparative Perspective," *William and Mary Quarterly*, 3rd ser., 58, no. 1 (2001): 93–117; Klein, "The Structure of the Atlantic Slave Trade in the 19th Century: An Assessment," *Outre-Mers. Revue d'histoire* 89, nos. 336–337 (2002): 63–77; Klein, "The Atlantic Slave Trade: Recent Research and Findings," in Pietschmann, *Atlantic History*, 301–20; Paul E. Lovejoy, "Islam, Slavery, and Political Transformation in West Africa: Constraints on the Trans-Atlantic Slave Trade," *Outre-Mers: Revue d'histoire* 89, nos. 336–337 (2002): 247–82; Lovejoy, "The Black Atlantic in the Construction of the 'Western' World: Alternative Approaches to the 'Europeanization' of the Americas," in *The Historical Practice of Diversity: Transcultural Interactions from the Early Modern Mediterranean to the Postcolonial World*, ed. Dirk Hoerder, Christiane Harzig, and Adrian Shubert (New York: Berghahn Books, 2003), 109–33; Lovejoy, "Trans-Atlantic Transformations: The Origins and Identity of Africans in the Americas," in Klooster and Padula, *Atlantic World* (2005), 126–46; John K. Thornton, "Cannibals, Witches, and Slave Traders in the Atlantic World," *William and Mary Quarterly*, 3rd ser., 60, no. 2 (2003): 273–94; Thornton, *Africa and Africans;* Thornton, "African Background"; Thornton, *Cultural History of the Atlantic World;* Linda M. Heywood and Thornton, "Central African Leadership and the Appropriation of European Culture," in Mancall, *Atlantic World and Virginia*, 194–224; Heywood and Thornton, *Central Africans, Atlantic Creoles, and the Foundation of the Americas, 1585–1660* (New York: Cambridge University Press, 2007); Heywood and Thornton, "Kongo and Dahomey, 1660–1815: African Political Leadership in the Era of the Slave Trade and Its Impact on the Formation of African Identity in Brazil," in Bailyn and Denault, *Soundings in Atlantic History*, 86–111.

98. See also Barbara L. Solow, ed., *Slavery and the Rise of the Atlantic System* (Cambridge, U.K.: Cambridge University Press, 1991); P. D. Morgan, ed., "African and American

Atlantic Worlds," special issue of *William and Mary Quarterly* 56, no. 2 (April 1999): 241–414; Darlene C. Hill and Jacqueline McLeod, eds., *Crossing Boundaries: Comparative History of Black People in Diaspora* (Bloomington: Indiana University Press, 2001); Jason Ward, "The Other Atlantic World," *History Compass* 1, no. 1 (2003), 1–6; Klooster and Padula, *Atlantic World;* James P. P. Horn and P. D. Morgan, "Settlers and Slaves: European and African Migrations to Early Modern British America," in Mancke and Shammas, *Creation of the British Atlantic World,* 19–44; Jon F. Sensbach, *Rebecca's Revival: Creating Black Christianity in the Atlantic World* (Cambridge, Mass.: Harvard University Press, 2006); James H. Sweet, "African Identity and Slave Resistance in the Portuguese Atlantic," in Mancall, *Atlantic World and Virginia,* 225–47; Gunvor Simonsen, "Moving in Circles: African and Black History in the Atlantic World," in Vidal, ed., *Histoire atlantique de part et d'autre,* http://nuevomundo.revues.org/index10233.html (accessed January 8, 2017); Falola and Roberts, *Atlantic World;* Randy J. Sparks, *The Two Princes of Calabar: An Eighteenth-Century Atlantic Odyssey* (Cambridge, Mass.: Harvard University Press, 2009); James H. Sweet, "Mistaken Identities? Olaudah Equiano, Domingo Álvares, and the Methodological Challenges of Studying the African Diaspora," *American Historical Review* 114, no. 2 (2009): 279–306; Joseph C. Miller, "The Dynamics of History in Africa and the Atlantic 'Age of Revolutions,'" in Armitage and Subrahmanyam, *Age of Revolutions,* 101–24; William A. Pettigrew, *Freedom's Debt: The Royal African Company and the Politics of the Atlantic Slave Trade, 1672–1752* (Chapel Hill: University of North Carolina Press, 2013), a timely reminder that more that half a century have passed since K. G. Davies, *The Royal African Company* (London: Longmans, Green, 1957); and Lisa A. Lindsay and John Wood Sweet, *Biography and the Black Atlantic* (Philadelphia: University of Pennsylvania Press, 2014).

99. One field of study that has been waning for quite some time is political history, which is where, in the 1950s, Atlantic history got started. See Jacques Godechot, *Histoire de l'Atlantique* (Paris: Presses Universitaires de France, 1947); Godechot and R. R. Palmer, "Le problème de l'Atlantique du XVIIIe au XXe siècle," in *Relazioni del X congresso internazionale di scienze storiche,* vol. 5, *Storia contemporanea* (Florence: G. C. Sansoni, 1955), 175–239; Godechot, *Les Révolutions (1770–1799)* (Paris: Presses Universitaires de France, 1963); and R. R. Palmer, *The Age of the Democratic Revolution: A Political History of Europe and America,* 2 vols. (Princeton, N.J.: Princeton University Press, 1959–64). See, however, Klooster, *Revolutions in the Atlantic World: A Comparative History* (New York: New York University Press, 2009); Albertone and de Francesco, *Rethinking the Atlantic World;* Michel Ducharme, *Le concept de liberté au Canada à l'époque des révolutions atlantiques (1776–1838)* (Montréal: McGill-Queen's University Press, 2010); Matteo Battistini, "Un mondo in disordine: le diverse storie dell'Atlantico," *Ricerche di storia politica* 2 (2012): 1–16; and Joanna Innes and Mark Philip, eds., *Re-Imagining Democracy in the Age of Revolutions: America, France, Britain, Ireland, 1750–1850* (Oxford, U.K.: Oxford University Press, 2013). Conversely, economic history is still well represented. See David J. Hancock, *Citizens of the World: London Merchants and the Integration of the British Atlantic Community, 1735–1785* (Cambridge, U.K.: Cambridge University Press, 1995); Hancock, "The British Atlantic History, World Co-ordination, Complexity and Emergence of an Atlantic Market Economy 1651–1815," *Itinerario* 23, no. 2 (1999): 107–27; Hancock, "Rethinking *The Economy of British America,*" in *The Economy of Early America: Historical Perspectives and New Directions,* ed. Cathy Matson (University Park: Pennsylvania State

University Press, 2006), 71–106; Hancock, "Atlantic Trade and Commodities, 1402–1815," in Canny and P. D. Morgan, *Oxford Handbook to the Atlantic World,* 324–40; Pieter C. Emmer and Klooster, "The Dutch Atlantic, 1600–1800. Expansion without Empire," *Itinerario* 23, no. 2 (1999): 48–69; Emmer, "The Myth of Early Globalisation: The Atlantic Economy, 1500–1800," in Vidal, ed., *Histoire atlantique de part et d'autre,* special issue of *Nuevo Mundo Mundos Nuevos* (2008) ; Cathy Matson, ed., "The Atlantic Economy in an Era of Revolutions," special issue of *William and Mary Quarterly,* 3rd ser., 62, no. 3 (2005): 357–526; Matson, *Economy of Early America;* and Matson, "Imperial Political Economy: An Ideological Debate and Shifting Practices," *William and Mary Quarterly,* 3rd ser., 69, no. 1 (2012): 35–40.

100. Evan Haefeli and Kevin Sweeney, *Captors and Captives: The 1704 French and Indian Raid on Deerfield* (Amherst: University of Massachusetts Press, 2003); Peter E. Pope, *Fish into Wine: The Newfoundland Plantation in the Seventeenth Century* (Chapel Hill: University of North Carolina Press, 2004); Philip P. Boucher, *France and the American Tropics to 1700: Tropics of Discontent?* (Baltimore: Johns Hopkins University Press, 2007); Daviken Studnicki-Gizbert, *A Nation Upon the Ocean Sea: Portugal's Atlantic Diaspora and the Crisis of the Spanish Empire, 1492–1640* (Oxford, U.K.: Oxford University Press, 2007); Matteo Sanfilippo, *Dalla Francia al Nuovo Mondo: feudi e signorie nella valle del San Lorenzo* (Viterbo, Italy: Sette Città, 2008); Maurice Bric, *Ireland, Philadelphia and the Re-Invention of America 1760–1800* (Dublin: Four Courts Press, 2008); Carla Gardina Pestana, *Protestant Empire: Religion and the Making of the British Atlantic World* (Philadelphia: University of Pennsylvania Press, 2009); Aaron S. Fogleman, *Two Troubled Souls: An Eighteenth-Century Couple's Spiritual Journey in the Atlantic World* (Chapel Hill: University of North Carolina Press, 2013); Audrey Horning, *Ireland in the Virginian Sea: Colonialism and the British Atlantic* (Chapel Hill: University of North Carolina Press, 2013).

101. See also Evan Haefeli, "A Note on the Use of North American Borderlands," *American Historical Review* 104, no. 4 (1999): 1222–25; Peter Pope, "Comparisons: Atlantic Canada," in Vickers, *Companion to Colonial America,* 489–507; Pope and Shannon Lewis-Simpson, eds., *Exploring Atlantic Transitions: Archaeologies of Transience and Permanence in New Found Lands* (Suffolk, U.K.: Boydell Press, 2013); Philip P. Boucher, "The 'Frontier Era' of the French Caribbean, 1620s–1690s," in Daniels and Kennedy, *Negotiated Empires,* 207–34; Boucher, "Revisioning the 'French Atlantic': Or, How to Think about the French Presence in the Atlantic, 1550–1625," in Mancall, *Atlantic World and Virginia,* 274–306; Boucher, "French Proprietary Colonies in the Greater Caribbean, 1620s-1670s," in *Constructing Early Modern Empires: Proprietary Ventures in the Atlantic World, 1500–1750,* ed. Lou H. Roper and Van Ruymbeke (Leiden, Netherlands: Brill, 2007), 163–88; Daviken Studnicki-Gizbert, "La 'nation' portugaise: Réseaux marchands dans l'espace atlantique à l'époque moderne," in "Les réseaux marchands à l'époque moderne," ed. Anthony Molho and Ramada Curto, special section of *Annales: Histoire, Sciences sociales* 58, no. 3 (2003): 627–48; Bric, "The American Revolution and Ireland," in Greene and Pole, *Companion to the American Revolution* (2000), 511–14; Carla Gardina Pestana, *The English Atlantic in an Age of Revolution, 1640–1661* (Cambridge, Mass.: Harvard University Press, 2004); Gardina Pestana, "Religion," in Armitage and Braddick, *British Atlantic World,* 69–89; Michel Ducharme, "Canada in the Age of Revolutions: Rethinking Canadian Intellectual History in an Atlantic Perspective," in *Contesting Clio's Craft: New Directions and Debates in Canadian History,* ed. Chris Dummitt and Michael Dawson (London: University of London,

School of Advanced Study, Institute for the Study of the Americas, 2009), 162–86; and Audrey Horning, "*Leim am Mhadaigh:* Exploring Unwanted Histories of the Atlantic World," in Pope and Lewis-Simpson, *Exploring Atlantic Transitions,* 93–102.

102. David Armitage, "Three Concepts of Atlantic History," in Armitage and Braddick, *British Atlantic World,*11–27, quotation at 11. At the time, Armitage stated that Atlantic history had emerged as a distinct subfield "only in the last decade or so" (12).

103. Greer, "National, Transnational," 716; Jack P. Greene, "Hemispheric History and Atlantic History," reprinted in Greene, *Creating the British Atlantic,* 17.

104. For the Protestant world, see, for example, Gardina Pestana, "Religion," (2002); Gardina Pestana, *Protestant Empire;* Greer and Mills, "Catholic Atlantic"; Kenneth Mills, "Religion in the Atlantic World," in Canny and Morgan, *Oxford Handbook of the Atlantic World,* 433–48; and Carla Gardina Pestana, "The Missionary Impulse in the Atlantic World, 1500–1800: Or How Protestants Learned to be Missionaries," *Social Sciences and Missions* 36, no. 1 (2013): 9–39. For the Catholic World, see Morelli, *Mondo Atlantico,* 154–167 (limited to Iberian America). See also Emily J. Clark and Mary Laven, eds., *Women and Religion in the Atlantic Age, 1550–1900* (Farnham, U.K.: Ashgate, 2013).

105. There have been, of course, significant works on religious transplantation, but they pertain more to the domain of traditional bilateral relations rather than to that of Atlantic history proper. Two recent innovative works on French ecclesiastical communities, for example, fall straight in this category. See Dominique Deslandres, John A. Dickinson, and Ollivier Hubert, eds., *Les Sulpiciens de Montréal: Une histoire de pouvoir et de discrétion 1657–2007* (Montréal: Fides, 2007); and Caroline Galland, *Pour la gloire de Dieu et du Roi. Les récollets en Nouvelle-France aux XVII*[e] *et XVIII*[e] *siècles* (Paris: Les Éditions du Cerf, 2012).

106. Gardina Pestana, *Protestant Empire,* 258.

107. Luca Codignola, "Competing Networks: Roman Catholic Ecclesiastics in French North America, 1610–58," *Canadian Historical Review* 80, no. 4 (1999): 539–84.

108. [Giovanni Battista Agucchi], "Diuisio Prouinciarum totius Orbis Terrarum in tredecim partes pro Illustrissimis et Reuerendissimis DD. Cardinalibus S. Congregationis de propaganda fide. facta a Reuerendissimo D. Agucchio iuxta decretum eiusdem Congregationis," [Rome, shortly before March 8, 1622], APF, Miscellanee Diverse, vol. 22, ff. 290rv–294rv, 299rv; General Congregation, [Rome], March 1622, APF, Acta, vol. 3, ff. 3rv–5rv, published in *Sacrae Congregationis de Propaganda Fide Memoria Rerum,* ed. Josef Metzler, OMI, vol. III/2, *1622–1972* (Rome: Herder, 1976), 659–61.

109. General Congregation, [Rome], July 12, 1655, APF, Acta, vol. 24, ff. 37rv–38r; "Nomina Regnorum, et Prouincium," [Rome, June 1657], APF, Congressi, Missioni, vol. 1, ff. 25rv–26rv; General Congregation, [Rome], June 14, 1657, APF, Acta, vol. 26, 125–29. The Far East disappeared again from a subsequent 1698 state of the world document. See also Special Congregation, [Rome], October 3, 1698, APF, Congregazioni Particolari, vol. 105, ff. 12rv, 17rv; and *Libellvs divisionis provinciarum Orbis Terrarum. Pro Eminentiss. & Reuerendiss. Dominis Cardinalibvs Sacrae Congr. de Propaganda Fide* (Romae: Typis eiusd. Sac. Congr., [1698]), APF, Miscellanea Varia, vol. XIV/A, 642[a]rv-642[k]rv. For a detailed discussion of these documents, see Giovanni Pizzorusso and Matteo Sanfilippo, "La Santa Sede e la geografia del Nuovo Mondo, 1492–1908," in *Genova, Colombo, il mare e l'emigrazione italiana nelle Americhe. Atti del XXVI Congresso Geografico Italiano (Genova, 4–9 maggio 1992): Contributi scientifici,* ed. Claudio Cerreti (Rome: Istituto della Enciclopedia Italiana, 1996), 607–32; and Luca Codignola, "L'area nord-atlantica secondo

la curia pontificia. I funzionari di Propaganda Fide, 1622–1816," in *Giovanni Caboto e le vie dell'Atlantico Settentrionale. Atti del Convegno Internazionale di Studi. Roma, 29 settembre-1 ottobre 1997,* ed. Marcella Arca Petrucci and Simonetta Conti (Genoa, Italy: Brigati, 1999), 201–12.

110. For the latest assessment of the availability and usefulness of Roman sources, see Pierre Hurtubise, Luca Codignola, and Fernand Harvey, eds., *L'Amérique du Nord française dans les archives religieuses de Rome 1600–1922: Guide de recherche* (Québec: Éditions de l'IQRS and Les Presses de l'Université Laval, 1999); and Martin Pâquet, Matteo Sanfilippo, and Jean-Philippe Warren, eds., *Le Saint-Siège, le Québec et l'Amérique française: Les archives vaticanes, pistes et défis* (Québec: Presses de l'Université Laval, 2013). Both are also useful for English-speaking North America.

111. This is the conclusion reached in Luca Codignola, "The Holy See and the Conversion of the Indians in French and British North America, 1486–1760," in Kupperman, *America in European Consciousness,* 195–242; Codignola, "The Holy See and the Conversion of the Aboriginal Peoples in North America, 1760–1830," in *Ethnographies and Exchanges: Native Americans, Moravians, and Catholics in Early North America,* ed. Anthony G. Roeber (University Park: Pennsylvania State University Press, 2008), 77–95; and Codignola, "Roman Catholic Conservatism."

112. The "variety of the situations . . . both from the chronological and the spatial point of view . . . from the end of the seventeenth through the early nineteenth century . . . what was really striking in the relationship between missionaries and the subjects of their missions was of the similarity of the situations and its overall continuity" (Luca Codignola, "Les frontières de la mission: Efficacité missionnaire, acculturation réciproque et centralisation romaine," in Brice and Codignola, "Les frontières de la mission," 785–92, quotations at 785 (original in French). For a more substantive examination, see Codignola and Giovanni Pizzorusso, "Les lieux, les méthodes et les sources" (1996); Chantal Gauthier, "Activité missionnaire en frontière de catholicité. L'exemple du Valais et de l'ancienne Rhétie (1550–1650)" (doctoral thesis, University of Montréal, 2002); and Dominique Deslandres, *Croire et faire croire: Les missions françaises au XVIIe siècle (1600–1650)* (Paris: Fayard, 2003).

Religious Community and Cross-Religious Communication beyond the Atlantic World

1. See "The Relation of Master Antonie Monterinos, translated out of the French Copie sent by Manaseh ben Israel" in Thomas Thorowgood, *Iewes in America, or, Probabilities that the Americans are of that race . . .* (1650).

2. *Oxford Gazette,* December 11, 1665.

3. For example, see Richard Kagan and Philip Morgan, eds., *Atlantic Diasporas: Jews, Conversos, and Crypto-Jews in the Age of Mercantilism, 1500–1800* (Baltimore: John Hopkins University Press, 2009); Paolo Bernardini and Norman Fiering, eds., *The Jews and the Expansion of Europe to the West, 1450–1850* (New York: Berghahn, 2001); and "Port Jews of the Atlantic," special issue, *Jewish History* 20, no. 2 (2006).

4. Adam Sutcliffe, "Jewish History in an Age of Atlanticism," in Kagan and Morgan, *Atlantic Diasporas,* 30.

5. Defining "Sephardim" is particularly difficult because it can encompass a wide array of people of different nationalities, ethnicities, and religious practices. While

Jonathan Israel has argued that the Sephardim and the Iberian crypto-Jews (who would have been part of the Conversos or New Christians) constituted two distinct, yet connected networks, this chapter employs a very broad definition of the Sephardim because it was their diversity that allowed them to function so effectively in cutting across so many boundaries. To oversimplify, the Sephardim included Jews and Conversos (including crypto-Jews) who originated in Iberia and a Sephardic family often consisted of both Jews and Conversos in Europe and the Americas. For more, see Jonathan Israel, *Diasporas within a Diaspora: Jews, Crypto-Jews and the World Maritime Empires* (Leiden, Netherlands: E. J. Brill, 2002).

6. For more on the Puritan migration, see Alan Taylor, *American Colonies: The Settling of North America* (New York: Penguin Press, 2002); Allen French, *Charles I and the Puritan Upheaval: A Study of the Causes of the Great Migration* (London: George Allen and Unwin, 1955); Robert Brenner, *Merchants and Revolution: Commercial Change, Political Conflict, and London's Overseas Traders, 1550–1653* (Cambridge, U.K.: Cambridge University Press, 1993); and Bernard Bailyn, *New England Merchants in the Seventeenth Century* (Cambridge, Mass.: Harvard University Press, 1955).

7. In particular, the advent of the Brazilian sugar trade after 1560 led to a large Converso transatlantic trading community and forged connections among the Sephardic Diaspora. The growth of the Inquisition in the Americas led crypto-Jewish networks to diminish, while Jewish networks grew as they settled in northeastern Brazil and then in the Caribbean and Guiana. There were wide connections among the Sephardim across the Atlantic world. The Amsterdam Jewry utilized their ties to their brethren in the American colonies to expand the Dutch West India Company's economic influence, while other Conversos and Jews used the Sephardic networks to distinguish themselves in the precious metals trade from Mexico and Peru to Seville. There were even connections to West Africa after the Sephardic community of Amsterdam sent a Portuguese-born Jew to serve as a rabbi to the Senegalese Jews as part of a trade mission (which further highlights the intersection of religion and trade). For more on the creation and expansion of Sephardic networks across the Atlantic world, see, alongside Kagan and Morgan's *Atlantic Diasporas,* Benjamin Gampel, ed., *Crisis and Creativity in the Sephardic World 1391–1648* (New York: Columbia University Press, 1997); and Jonathan Israel, *European Jewry in the Age of Mercantilism 1550–1750* (Oxford, U.K.: Littman Library of Jewish Civilization, 1998).

8. When twenty-three Jewish refugees fled from Brazil to New Amsterdam after the Portuguese recaptured the colonies, the director of New Amsterdam wanted them to leave. The Jews in New Amsterdam, however, contacted the Dutch Jewry, whose intercession led the Dutch West India Company to grant the Jews permission to stay despite protests from the director. Moreover, the Brazilian revolt led to the migration of two hundred Jewish families to Amsterdam between 1645 and 1655. Those who left Brazil were vital in establishing new congregations throughout the Americas. Indeed, the majority of seventeenth-century Jewish congregations in the Americas were founded by Jews who had left Recife. See Paul Mendes-Flohr and Jehuda Reinharz, eds., *The Jews in the Modern World* (Oxford, U.K.: Oxford University Press, 1995); Bruno Feitler, "Jews and New Christians in Dutch Brazil, 1630–1654," in Kagan and Morgan, *Atlantic Diasporas,* 123–51; and Wim Klooster, "Networks of Colonial Entrepreneurs: The Founders of the Jewish Settlements in Dutch America, 1650s and 1660s," in Kagan and Morgan, *Atlantic Diasporas,* 33–49.

9. Francesca Trivellato (44) stated that they appropriated the term "nation" to distinguish themselves from Ashkenazi, Romaniote, and Italian Jews, and the "men of the nation" did not hide their feelings of superiority and pride. The Sephardim may have sent money to help other Jewish communities, but they did not always welcome them in their cities. In Amsterdam, they actually used their resources to transfer the Ashkenazi Jewish refugees from the Thirty Year's War as well as the Eastern European Jewish refugees in 1648 and 1649 out of their city. Ben Israel even arguably developed closer relationships with Protestants in England than he did with the Ashkenazi Jews in his own city, and when he had problems in London, it was the English Protestants he turned to for help. Moreover, as Richard Popkin notes, it is significant that when ben Israel came to believe that the coming of the messiah was imminent, he went to the home of the Protestant millenarian, Petrus Serrarius, rather than the Sephardic synagogue. It is, however, important to remember that the manner in which these people envisioned their community was fluid and subject to change based on circumstance and surrounding. For more, see Francesca Trivellato, *The Familiarity of Strangers: The Sephardic Diaspora, Livorno, and Cross-cultural Trade in the Early Modern Period* (New Haven, Conn.: Yale University Press, 2009); Yosef Kaplan, "The Self-Definition of the Sephardic Jews of Western Europe and Their Relation to the Alien and the Stranger," in *Crisis and Creativity in the Sephardic World 1391–1648,* ed. Benjamin Gampel (New York: Columbia University Press, 1997), 59–76; Miriam Bodian, *Hebrews of the Portuguese Nation: Conversos and Community in Early Modern Amsterdam* (Bloomington: Indiana University Press, 1997); and Miriam Bodian, "'Men of the Nation': The Shaping of Converso Identity in Early Modern Europe," *Past and Present* 143 (1994): 48–76.

10. The Puritans themselves made this connection. John Cotton used this story when he delineated the apocalyptic elements of the Puritan journey to America. He also placed Elizabeth's reign in the time of the seventh trumpet, furthering the view that the end was near. Some Puritans saw New England as a refuge designed by God for his chosen people to escape the imminent judgment, while others saw themselves as the true church fleeing into the wilderness that was foretold in Revelation. For a more thorough discussion on the ways the English understood their migration, see Avihu Zakai, *Exile and Kingdom: History and Apocalypse in the Puritan Migration to America* (Cambridge, U.K.: Cambridge University Press, 1992).

11. Henry Mechoulan and Gerard Nahon, *Menasseh ben Israel, The Hope of Israel: The English Translation by Moses Wall, 1652,* trans. Richenda George (Oxford, U.K.: Oxford University Press, 1987), 17. For more on the importance of the Sephardic networks in Italy, see Trivellato, *Familiarity of Strangers.*

12. For instance, sixteenth-century Conversos in Portugal and Brazil worked with the Sephardic Jews in Venice and Pisa to import Brazilian sugar to Italy. Moreover, as Klooster points out, the refugees who arrived on a ship in Livorno in 1654 most likely came from Dutch Brazil, and many of them did not stay there but instead returned to Dutch Guiana, where they settled with immigrants from the Dutch Republic. Benyamin Bueno de Mequita, for example, was part of the Dutch Brazilian Diaspora who ended up in Livorno before leaving the Mediterranean to return to the far side of the Atlantic, where he settled in Jamaica and then New York. See Klooster, "Networks of Colonial Entrepreneurs"; and Jonathan Israel, "Jews and Crypto-Jews in the Atlantic World Systems, 1500–1800," in Kagan and Morgan, *Atlantic Diasporas,* 3–17.

13. Menasseh ben Israel, *The Hope of Israel* (1650), 4–5.

14. Edward Winslow made the connection between these two ideas explicit before he turned to ben Israel for expertise, noting that the rabbi believed the Lost Tribes were "certainly transported into America." See "The Epistle Dedicatory," in Edward Winslow, *The Glorious Progress Amongst the Indians in New England* (1649).

15. Ronnie Perelis, "'These Indians Are Jews!': Lost Tribes, Crypto-Jews, and Jewish Self-Fashioning in Antonio de Montezinos's Relacion of 1644," in Kagan and Morgan, *Atlantic Diasporas*, 195–211.

16. He also wrote that he found "no opinion more probable, nor agreeable to reason, then that of our Montezinos, who saith, that the first inhabitants of America, were the ten Tribes of the Israelites." Ben Israel, *The Hope of Israel*, 17–18.

17. He goes on to discuss how he spent six months with Montezinos, during which time Montezinos not only took an oath in his presence testifying to his story, but also repeated the same oath on his deathbed two years later. Ben Israel himself had Iberian heritage, had planned to migrate to South America at one point, and had relatives and business ventures there, showing the importance of transatlantic connections. For more on ben Israel, see the classic text by Cecil Roth, *A Life of Menasseh ben Israel: Rabbi, Printer, and Diplomat* (Philadelphia: Jewish Publication Society of America, 1945), and the newer one by Yosef Kaplan, Henry Mechoulan, and Richard Popkin, eds., *Menasseh ben Israel and His World* (Leiden, Netherlands: E. J. Brill, 1989).

18. Ben Israel, *Hope of Israel*, 42.

19. Ben Israel, *Hope of Israel*, 33: Unlike his Puritan contemporaries, ben Israel refused to speculate when this would happen; however, he believed that although he could not "exactly shew the time of our redemption, yet we judge it to be near." See ben Israel, *Hope of Israel*, 36.

20. Richard W. Cogley, "'Some Other Kinde of Being and Condition': The Controversy in Mid-Seventeenth-Century England over the Peopling of Ancient America," *Journal of the History of Ideas* 68, no. 1 (2007): 47, 37–38.

21. Klooster, "Networks of Colonial Entrepreneurs," 42.

22. The importance of this transatlantic channel was even noted by Thorowgood when he stated, "This worke would be much prospered by a stocke of wise and constant correspondence mutually betwixt Old and New England in regard of this businesse, what progresse is made in the worke, what meet to bee done for its furtherance, &c. Such communication of counsells would marvelously encourage and quicken the Americans conversion." Thorowgood, *Iewes in America*, 94.

23. Cogley, "Some Other Kinde of Being and Condition," 53. Thorowgood himself said, "When the glad tidings of the Gospels sounding in America by the preaching of the English arrived hither, my soule also rejoyced within me, and I remembred certaine papers that had been laid aside a long time, upon review of them, and some additions to them, they were privately communicated unto such as perswaded earnestly they might behold further light." See Thorowgood, *Iewes in America*.

24. See "An Epistolicall Discourse of Mr. Iohn Dury," in Thorowgood, *Iewes in America*.

25. Ben Israel responded to Dury "in two Letters, telling me that by the occasion of the Questions which I proposed unto him concerning this adjoyned Narrative of Mr. *Antonie Monterinos*, hee to give me satisfaction, had written insteed of a Letter, a Treatise, which hee shortly would publish, and whereof I should receive so many Copies as I

should desire." See "An Epistolicall Discourse of Mr. Iohn Dury," in Thorowgood, *Iewes in America.*

26. For instance, ben Israel and Thorowgood cited the example of sepulchers on Azores that apparently had ancient Hebrew letters on it. This similarity could have been a result of more cross-religious fertilization, but it was most likely just part of their parallel investigations, which occurred since neither Thorowgood nor ben Israel ever visited the Americas.

27. For instance, ben Israel (17) claimed a Dutch Mariner told him that when he was in America, he met a group of well-bred, clothed, and bearded white men who had no commerce with the Spanish. Ben Israel added, "I heard that story by accident from that Dutch Master of the Ship; whence some of us guessing them to be Israelites, had purposed to send him againe to enquire more fully. But he dyed suddenly the last yeare, whence it seemes that God doth not permit that those purposes should take any effect till the end of dayes." Thorowgood (5–6) used New Englanders, writing that Master R. Williams in New England "was desired to observe if hee found any thing Judaicall among them, &c. He kindly answers to those Letters from *Salem* in New England, 20th of the 10th moneth, more than ten yeers since, in *hac verba.* Three things make me yet suspect that the poore natives came from the southward, and are Jewes or Jewish *quodammodo,* and not from the Northern barbarous as some imagine."

28. Cogley, "John Eliot and the Origins of the American Indians," *Early American Literature* 21, no. 3 (1986/1987): 210–25. 217. This letter by Eliot was the longest statement by someone in North America on the origins of the indigenous people there.

29. See "An Epistolicall Discourse of Mr. Iohn Dury," in Thorowgood, *Iewes in America.* The Lost Tribes living in both Asia and the Americas were not seen as problematic because some people, like ben Israel, believed that the Lost Tribes were living in hiding throughout the world, which—to some extent—paralleled the widespread dispersion of the Jewish Diaspora.

30. Klooster, "Networks of Colonial Entrepreneurs," 41. Other major communities in the Americas took this name as well.

31. Jacob Barnai, "Christian Messianism and the Portuguese Marranos: The Emergence of Sabbateanism in Smyrna," *Jewish History* 7, no. 2 (1993): 121.

32. Mechoulan and Nahon, *Menasseh ben Israel,* 81, 91.

33. Klooster, "Networks of Colonial Entrepreneurs," 41.

34. For more on the Sabbatian movement, see Gershom Scholem, *Sabbatai Sevi: The Mystical Messiah, 1626–1676,* trans. R. J. Zwi Werblowsky (Princeton, N.J.: Princeton University Press, 1973).

35. Scholem, *Sabbatai Sevi,* 353, 353n.

36. Scholem, *Sabbatai Sevi,* 332, 342–43, 350.

37. The Biblioteca Centrale in Florence has a large collection of Venetian avvisi, including this one, *Codd Magliabechiani, XXV, 743,* 81 : Venezia, Aprile 25, 1665. This is confirmed in a later printing of the newspaper on September 5 that tells the same story in which corps of an Arab army went to Mecca, sacked, and burned the city, taking away Muhammad's body with the city's treasure. Like the first report, this one had only an Arab force, actually listed the source of its information (letters from the Levant via Marseilles), and mentioned the rebellion in Babylon as well, which further demonstrates that the story of the Arab army was coming from letters from the Levant. See *Codd Magliabechiani, XXV, 743,* 94: Venezia, Settembre 5, 1665.

38. BCF, *Codd Magliabechiani, XXV, 743,* 84: Venezia, Agosto 8, 1665.

39. BCF, *Codd Magliabechiani, XXV, 743,* 93: Venezia, Agosto 29, 1665.

40. *Oxford Gazette,* January 25, 1666.

41. *London Gazette,* February 22, 1666.

42. *London Gazette,* March 5, 1666. For a more thorough discussion on the manners in which these rumors were connected to the Sabbatian movement, see Brandon Marriott, "The Birth Pangs of the Messiah: Transnational Networks and Cross-Religious Exchange in the Age of Sabbatai Sevi" (D.Phil. diss., University of Oxford, 2012), or a revised version of the thesis forthcoming with Ashgate Press.

43. For example, he wrote, "" ust, as I was going to send away these letters, came some both of France and Holland to my hands, wch are all considerable; but I have not time, to adde ym now: only this I shall touch. Yt ye French letters assure ye death of the K. of Spain; and ye Dutch ye Meccha-news. M. Serrarius tells me, yt ye transcribing of Mr. Borrels manuscript goes on a pace." And a week later, "I cannot adde any more, yn to intimate in a word, yt the Meccha-news grows stronger. . . . I know not, Sr, whether I mentioned to you in my last Mr. Serrarius, his desire, about the disbursing of some mony for the transcribing of Mr. Borrels papers." A. Hall and M. Hall, eds., *The Correspondence of Henry Oldenburg,* vol. 2, *1663–1665* (Madison: University of Wisconsin Press, 1966), 534, 545.

44. Cogley, "John Eliot and the Origins of the American Indians," 221–22.

45. Sutcliffe, "Jewish History in an Age of Atlanticism," 25.

The Religious Spaces of American Whaling

1. Thomas Douglass, journal kept aboard ship *Morrison* of New London, Samuel Green, Jr., master, September 1844–May 1848, Mystic Seaport Log #343, W. Blunt White Library, Mystic Seaport Museum, Inc.

2. Daniel Kimball Ritchie, logbook of the ship *Israel* of New Bedford, James Finch, master, December 5, 1843–February 20, 1845, KWM #478. All logs listed as KWM (originally Kendall Whaling Museum logs) are housed at the New Bedford Whaling Museum Research Library.

3. On mesmerism as popular religious practice, see Catherine L. Albanese, *Nature Religion: From the Algonkian Indians to the New Age* (Chicago: University of Chicago Press, 1991); and Robert Fuller, *Mesmerism and the American Cure of Souls* (Philadelphia: University of Pennsylvania Press, 1982).

4. Laurie Maffly-Kipp's "Eastward Ho! American Religion from the Perspective of the Pacific Rim," in *Retelling U.S. Religious History,* ed. Thomas A. Tweed (Berkeley: University of California Press, 1997), 127–48, is an excellent overview of American religious historians' neglect of the Pacific and an intriguing glimpse at a number of ways that a Pacific perspective might reframe our understanding of our religious past and present. More broadly, the Pacific has been visible in literature of the sea, such as novels by Melville, Dana, and London. But despite the fact that these particular authors actually worked on ships sailing through the Atlantic and the Pacific, their writing is recognized more for their literary importance than for their historical notice of the actual American presence in the Pacific as working people in a globalizing economy. The American public seems to be more familiar with a literary Pacific than a dynamic, physical Pacific filled with American, European, Asian, African, and Pacific actors during the nineteenth century.

5. For instance, Emile Durkheim, *Elementary Forms of Religious Life* (1912), based its analysis of society and religion on the Arunta (or Arrernte) of central Australia, drawing from studies and descriptions by missionaries and travelers as well as early anthropologists. Sam Gill, *Storytracking: Texts, Stories, and Histories in Central Australia* (Oxford, U.K.: Oxford University Press, 1998), tracks back through the sources on Australian indigenous life used by Mircea Eliade in his theorizing on religion. While New England whaling men did not have extensive contact with the Arrernte, they were in contact with Australian indigenous peoples from early on. The American whaling vessel *Union* spent the winter of 1804 on Kangaroo Island off southern Australia, thirty-two years before that area was settled by Europeans, and hundreds of American whaling ships operated off the coast of western Australia in the mid-nineteenth century, landing for supplies. Edward B. Tylor's *Primitive Culture* (1872) drew on evidence from indigenous populations around the world, many of them in the South Pacific. The sources he referenced, written in many cases by English missionaries, often mentioned the presence of American whaling men on the islands, though this information does not play a part in Tylor's analysis. See, for instance, George Turner's 1861 book *Nineteen Years in Polynesia: Missionary Life, Travels, and Researches in the Islands of the Pacific* or Thomas Williams's 1858 *Fiji and the Fijians: The Islands and Their Inhabitants.* Sigmund Freud's *Totem and Taboo* (1913) built a theory of religion from the Polynesian concept and practice of *tabu.* See also David Chidester, *Savage Systems: Colonialism and Comparative Religion in South Africa* (Charlottesville: University of Virginia Press, 1996), for a study of the relationship between European colonial presence among indigenous peoples and the use of those peoples as data for the theorizing of religion.

6. David Armitage, "Three Concepts of Atlantic History," in *The British Atlantic World, 1500–1800,* ed. Armitage and Michael J. Braddick (New York: Palgrave Macmillan, 2002), 15–16.

7. Jon F. Sensbach, *Rebecca's Revival: Creating Black Christianity in the Atlantic World* (Cambridge, Mass.: Harvard University Press, 2006). Another example is Randy Sparks, *The Two Princes of Calabar: An Eighteenth-Century Atlantic Odyssey* (Cambridge, Mass.: Harvard University Press, 2009).

8. Armitage, "Three Concepts of Atlantic History," 18–19.

9. Jorge Cañizares-Esguerra, *Puritan Conquistadors: Iberianizing the Atlantic, 1500–1700* (Stanford, Calif.: Stanford University Press, 2006).

10. April Lee Hatfield, *Atlantic Virginia: Intercolonial Relations in the Seventeenth Century* (Philadelphia: University of Pennsylvania Press, 2004).

11. Exceptions that prove the rule include maritime historians such as Marcus Rediker, whose books *Between the Devil and the Deep Blue Sea: Merchant Seamen, Pirates, and the Anglo-American Maritime World, 1700–1750* (Cambridge, U.K.: Cambridge University Press, 1987) and *The Many-Headed Hydra: Sailors, Slaves, Commoners, and the Hidden History of the Revolutionary Atlantic* (Boston: Beacon Press, 2000) explore maritime labor.

12. W. Jeffrey Bolster, "Putting the Ocean in Atlantic History: Maritime Communities and Marine Ecology in the Northwest Atlantic, 1500–1800," *American Historical Review* 113, no. 1 (2008): 23. See also Steven Mentz, "Toward a Blue Cultural Studies: The Sea, Maritime Culture, and Early Modern English Literature," *Literature Compass* 6, no. 5 (2009): 997–1013. One attempt to combat the idea that the "ocean exists outside

of history" is Bernhard Klein and Gesa Mackenthun, eds., *Sea Changes: Historicizing the Ocean* (New York: Routledge, 2004).

13. For insightful articles on the limits and extensions of the Atlantic world, see Peter A. Coclanis, "Atlantic World or Atlantic/World?" *William and Mary Quarterly*, 3rd ser., 63, no. 4 (2006): 725–42; Dona Gabaccia, "A Long Atlantic in a Wider World," *Atlantic Studies* 1, no. 1 (2004): 1–27; Alison Games, "Beyond the Atlantic: English Globetrotters and Transoceanic Connections," *William and Mary Quarterly*, 3rd ser., 63, no. 4 (2006): 675–92; Games, "Atlantic History: Definitions, Challenges, and Opportunities," *American Historical Review* 111, no. 3 (2006): 741–57; Paul W. Mapp, "Atlantic History from Imperial, Continental, and Pacific Perspectives," *William and Mary Quarterly*, 3rd ser., 63, no. 4 (2006): 713–24; Matt K. Matsuda, "The Pacific," *American Historical Review* 111, no. 3 (2006): 758–80; Philip J. Stern, "British Asia and British Atlantic: Comparisons and Connections," *William and Mary Quarterly*, 3rd ser. 63, no. 4 (2006): 693–712; and Reed Ueda, "Pushing the Atlantic Envelope: Interoceanic Perspectives on Atlantic History," in *The Atlantic in Global History, 1500–2000*, ed. Jorge Cañizares-Esguerra and Erik R. Seeman (Upper Saddle River, N.J.: Pearson Prentice Hall, 2007), 163–75. See also Matt Matsuda, *Pacific Worlds: A History of Seas, People, and Cultures* (Cambridge, U.K.: Cambridge University Press, 2012), on the complexity and diversity within and around the Pacific Ocean. There is not one Pacific world, Matsuda has asserted, but many: "Pacific worlds are not synonymous with just one declared and defined 'Pacific,' but with multiple seas, cultures, and peoples, and especially the overlapping transits between them" (2).

14. For a thorough study of the economics of the U.S. whaling industry in the nineteenth century, see Lance E. Davis, Robert E. Gallman, and Karin Gleiter, *In Pursuit of Leviathan: Technology, Institutions, Productivity, and Profits in American Whaling, 1816–1906* (Chicago: University of Chicago Press, 1997.

15. It is unclear whether Native Americans in that area actively hunted whales. See Eric Jay Dolin, *Leviathan: The History of Whaling in America* (New York: Norton, 2007), 36–38.

16. Both of these stories can be found in Dolin, *Leviathan.*

17. Mather is quoted in Glover M. Allen, "The Whalebone Whales of New England," *Memoirs of the Boston Society of Natural History* 8, no. 2 (1916): 154. He also published a sermon in 1717 titled "The Thankful Christian," addressed "especially unto them, who after the good successes of a whaling season, would express their gratitude unto God their Saviour" (Boston: B. Green for Samuel Garrish, 1717). See also Nancy Shoemaker, "Oil and Bone," *Common-Place* 8, no. 2 (2008), online journal, http://www.common-place.org/article/oil-and-bone/. Accessed December 21, 2016.

18. On the international politics of North Atlantic whaling and its role in Colonial American political history, see Alexander Starbuck, *History of the American Whale Fishery from Its Earliest Inception to the Year 1876* (Waltham, Mass., 1878).

19. Rotch, a prominent Nantucket whaling leader, was a key figure in the post-Revolution rise of New Bedford's whaling industry.

20. Europeans had been traveling around Cape Horn since the fifteenth century but typically in an easterly direction returning from the Arabian Sea or the East Indies to Europe.

21. Elmo Paul Hohman, *The American Whaleman: A Study of Life and Labor in the Whaling Industry* (New York: Longmans, Green, 1920), 46.

22. Quoted in Roald Kverndal, *Seamen's Missions: Their Origin and Early Growth* (Pasadena, Calif.: William Carey Library, 1986), 457.

23. Glenn S. Gordinier, "Evangelists, Land Sharks, and the Character of Seamen's Benevolence in 19th Century America," *Log of Mystic Seaport* 43, no. 2 (1991): 31–37.

24. Stuart M. Frank, "The Seamen's Friend," *Log of Mystic Seaport* 29, no. 2 (1977): 55.

25. Thomas Farel Heffernan, *Stove by a Whale: Owen Chase and the* Essex (Hanover, N.H.: University Press of New England), 35. Ironically, the *Essex* crewmembers ended up resorting to cannibalism themselves, eating dead crewmates and drawing lots to select who among themselves would sacrifice his life so that the others might eat his body.

26. Briton Cooper Busch, *Whaling Will Never Do for Me: The American Whaleman in the Nineteenth Century* (Lexington: University Press of Kentucky, 1994). 105–34.

27. David H. Stam, "The Lord's Librarians: The American Seamen's Friend Society and Their Loan Libraries, 1837–1967; An Historical Excursion with Some Unanswered Questions," *Coriolis* 3, no. 1 (2012): 45–59.

28. On religion as orientation, see Thomas A. Tweed, *Crossing and Dwelling: A Theory of Religion* (Cambridge, Mass.: Harvard University Press, 2006).

29. See, for instance, the following logs in the collection of the Kendall Library at the New Bedford Whaling Museum: John R. Sturgis, logbook of ship *Robert Edwards* of New Bedford, John R. Sturgis, master, September 6, 1853–July 25, 1857, KWM #340; Jared S. Crandall, logbook of the bark *Prudent* of Stonington, W. Ellery Nash, master, June 6, 1848–June 3, 1850, KWM #541; unidentified keeper, logbook of bark *Arab* of Fairhaven, Samuel Bunker, master, September 24, 1831-December 18, 1834, KWM #592; Thomas Jefferson Barritt, logbook of the bark *Vermont* of Mystic, Jonathan Nash Jr., master, November 13, 1843–February 2, 1845, KWM #808. See also Stephen R. Berry, "Early American Ships' Logs as Theological Texts: Divining the Sacred amidst the Mundane (and Maritime)," *Coriolis* 4, no. 2 (2013): 1–18.

30. Busch, *Whaling Will Never Do for Me*, 121–23. The question of Sunday labor was raised in industrial America throughout the nineteenth century (and earlier), but it had a particular resonance aboard whaling ships because it was difficult for some to pass up their much-sought-after prey if it happened to appear on a Sunday.

31. George Bliss, journal kept aboard the brig *Chase* of Rochester, Massachusetts, Matthew Mayhew, master, August 1839–October 1840, PEM #1205, Peabody Essex Museum.

32. William Silver, journal kept aboard ship *Bengal* of Salem, George S. Russell, master, March 1832–February 1835, PEM #1832B3, Peabody Essex Museum.

33. Harriet Allen, journal kept aboard bark *Merlin* of New Bedford, David E. Allen, master, June 23, 1868–April 12, 1872, KWM #401; Holden S. Wilcox, journal kept aboard ship *Columbus* of Fairhaven, Benjamin Ellis, master, July 30, 1837–February 21, 1839, KWM #52; Thomas R. Bryant, Jr., journal kept aboard ship *Elizabeth* of New Bedford, Michael Baker, master, October 26, 1847–June 22, 1851, KWM #77; Jared S. Crandall, journal kept aboard bark *Prudent* of Stonington, W. Ellery Nash, master, June 6, 1848–June 3, 1850, KWM #541; David Wordell, journal kept aboard ship *Canton* of New Bedford, Abraham Gardner, master, October 25, 1834–May 20, 1838, KWM #252; Frederick Howland Smith, journal kept aboard ship *Lydia* of Fairhaven, John Wood Leonard, master, January 5, 1855–March 4, 1857, KWM #101; Samuel Tripp Braley, log of ship *Arab* of Fairhaven, Samuel Tripp Braley, master, November 22, 1845–June 2, 1849, KWM #259; Frederic P. Tabor, journal kept aboard schooner *Petrel* of New Bedford, John S. Howland, master,

October 22, 1865-July 23, 1866, KWM #268; George R. Coggeshall, journal kept aboard ship *Samuel Robertson* of Fairhaven, William Washburn, master, August 25, 1849–April 22, 1852, KWM #330; Joseph Bogart Hersey, journal kept aboard brig *Phoenix* of Provincetown, Nathan Small, master, March 22, 1845–May 6, 1846, KWM #366; Gilbert Pendleton, Jr., journal kept aboard ship *Thomas Williams* of Stonington, John Manwaring, master, August 29, 1840–March 20, 1842, KWM #367.

34. This general description draws from Margaret S. Creighton, *Rites and Passages: The Experience of American Whaling, 1830–1870* (Cambridge, U.K.: Cambridge University Press, 1995), 117–21.

35. Hester Blum, *The View from the Masthead: Maritime Imagination and Antebellum American Sea Narratives* (Chapel Hill: University of North Carolina Press, 2008), 158–92.

36. William Silver, journal kept aboard ship *Bengal,* George S. Russell, master, March 1832–February 1835, PEM #1832B3, Peabody Essex Museum.

37. Lisa Norling, *Captain Ahab Had a Wife: New England Women and the Whalefishery, 1720–1870* (Chapel Hill: University of North Carolina Press, 2000).

38. Clothier Pierce, Jr., journal kept aboard bark *Minnesota,* Clothier Pierce, Jr., master, June 25, 1868–June 17, 1872, ODHS #0098, New Bedford Whaling Museum Research Library. Spellings as in the original.

Spatial Hegemony and Evangelization

1. See Juan Carlos Estenssoro, "El simio de Dios: los indígenas y la Iglesia frente a la evangelización del Perú, siglos XVI–XVII," *Bulletin de l'Institut Francais d'*Études Andines 30, no. 3 (2001): 455–74. Also Estenssoro, *Del paganismo a la santidad: la incorporación de los indios del Perú al catolicismo, 1532–1750,* 1ra ed, Travaux de l'Institut français d'études andines, t. 156 (Lima: IFEA, Pontificia Universidad Católica del Perú, Instituto Riva-Agüero, 2003).

2. For a comprehensive discussion of early liturgical texts in Peru, see Alan Durston, *Pastoral Quechua: The History of Christian Translation in Colonial Peru, 1550–1650* (Notre Dame, Ind.: University of Notre Dame Press, 2007). Also Estenssoro, *Del paganismo a la santidad.*

3. See Richard L. Kagan, *Urban Images of the Hispanic World, 1493–1793* (New Haven, Conn.: Yale University Press, 2000), 1–39.

4. See Tom Cummins, "Forms of Andean Colonial Towns, Free Will, and Marriage," in *The Archaeology of Colonialism,* ed. C. L. Lyons and J. K. Papadopoulos (Los Angeles: Getty Research Institute, 2002), 200.

5. Kagan, *Urban Images.*

6. Alejandro Málaga Medina, "Las reducciones en el Perú (1532–1600)," *Historia y cultura* 8 (1974): 150.

7. Rubén Vargas Ugarte, "Primer Concilio Limense," in *Concilios Limenses (1551–1772),* ed. R. Vargas Ugarte (1551–1552; reprint, Lima: Tipografía Peruana, 1952).

8. Juan de Matienzo, *Gobierno del Perú* (1567; reprint, Buenos Aires: Compañía sud-americana de billetes de banco, 1910).

9. See, however, Catherine J. Julien, *Condesuyo: The Political Division of Territory under Inca and Spanish Rule* (Bonn, Germany: Bonner Amerikanistische Studien, 1991). Also see Gary Urton, "Arquitectura pública como texto social: la historia de un muro de adobe en Pacariqtambo, Peru (1915–1985)," *Revista Andina* 6, no. 1 (1988): 225–61. Also

Steven A. Wernke, *Negotiated Settlements: Andean Communities and Landscapes under Inka and Spanish Colonialism* (Gainesville: University Press of Florida).

10. Francisco de Toledo, María Justina Sarabia Viejo, and Guillermo Lohmann Villena. *Francisco de Toledo: disposiciones gubernativas para el Virreinato del Perú,* 2 vols., Publicaciones de la Escuela de Estudios Hispano-Americanos de Sevilla 320 (no. general), 347 (Sevilla [Seville, Spain]: Escuela de Estudios Hispano-Americanos; Consejo Superior de Investigaciones Científicas; Monte de Piedad y Caja de Ahorros de Sevilla, 1986), 3435.

11. Thomas A. Abercrombie, *Pathways of Memory and Power: Ethnography and History among an Andean People* (Madison: University of Wisconsin Press, 1998): 246–48.

12. Timothy Mitchell, *Colonising Egypt* (Berkeley: University of California Press, 1988).

13. For example, see Michel Foucault, *Discipline and Punish: The Birth of the Prison* (New York: Pantheon, 1977); and Foucault *The History of Sexuality* (New York: Pantheon, 1978).

14. Pierre Bourdieu, *Outline of a Theory of Practice,* trans. R. Nice (Cambridge, U.K.: Cambridge University Press, 1977).

15. Michel de Certeau, *The Practice of Everyday Life* (Berkeley: University of California Press, 1984).

16. Abercrombie, *Pathways of Memory and Power,* 247–48.

17. Peter Gose, "Converting the Ancestors: Indirect Rule, Settlement Consolidation, and the Struggle over Burial in Colonial Peru, 1532–1614," in *Conversion: Old Worlds and New,* ed. Kenneth Mills and Anthony Grafton (Rochester, N.Y.: University of Rochester Press, 2003), 149.

18. See Jeffrey Quilter et al., "Traces of a Lost Language and Number System Discovered on the North Coast of Peru," *American Anthropologist* 112, no. 3 (2010): 357–69. Also Mary Van Buren, Peter T. Bürgi, and Prudence M. Rice, "Torata Alta: a Late Highland Settlement in the Osmore Drainage," in *Domestic Architecture, Ethnicity, and Complementarity in the South-Central Andes*, ed. M. S. Aldenderfer (Iowa City: University of Iowa Press, 1993).

19. An *encomienda* was a trusteeship granted to Spaniards for rights to Indian labor and tribute in exchange for duties of taxation and religious indoctrination.

20. Noble David Cook, *The People of the Colca Valley: A Population Study* (Boulder, Colo.: Westview Press, 1982).

21. Juan de Ulloa Mogollón, "Relación de la provincia de los Collaguas para la descripción de las Indias que su magestad manda hacer," in *Relaciones Geográficas de Indias,* ed. M. Jimenez de la Espada (1586; reprint, Madrid: Ediciones Atlas, 1965).

22. Alejandro Málaga Medina, "Los Collagua en la historia de Arequipa en el siglo XVI," in *Collaguas I,* ed. F. Pease (Lima: Pontificia Universidad Católica del Perú, 1977).

23. Antonine Tibesar, *Franciscan Beginnings in Early Colonial Peru* (Washington, D.C.: Academy of American Franciscan History, 1953), 65.

24. ACSFL (Archivo del Convento de San Francisco de Lima), registro 15, parte 5.

25. Sabine MacCormack, "The Heart Has Its Reasons: Predicaments of Missionary Christianity in Early Colonial Peru," *Hispanic American Historical Review* 65, no. 3 (1985): 443–66.

26. Tibesar, *Franciscan Beginnings in Early Colonial Peru,* 65.

27. Alan Durston, *Pastoral Quechua,* 71. See also Estenssoro, *Del paganismo a la santidad,* 139–45.

28. Estenssoro, "El simio de Dios" and *Del paganismo a la santidad.*

29. See, for example, Luis Millones, ed., *El Retorno de las huacas: estudios y documentos sobre el Taki Onqoy, siglo XVI,* 1ra. ed., *Fuentes e investigaciones para la historia del Perú* (Lima: Instituto de Estudios Peruanos, 1990). Also Steve Stern, "El Taki Onqoy y la sociedad andina (Huamanga, siglo XVI)," *Allpanchis* 16, no. 19 (1982): 49–77.

30. Diego de Córdoba y Salinas, *Chrónica franciscana de las provincias del Perú* (1651; reprint, Washington, D.C.: Academy of American Franciscan History, 1957), 151–57.

31. Noble David Cook, "'Tomando posesión' Luis Gerónimo de Oré y el retorno de los franciscanos a las doctrinas del valle del Colca," in *El hombre y los Andes: homenaje a Franklin Pease G.Y.,* ed. J. Flores Espinoza and R. Varón Gabai (Lima: Pontificia Universidad Católica del Perú, 2002).

32. Francisco Xavier Echeverría y Morales, *Memoria de la santa iglesia de Arequipa* (1804; reprint, Arequipa: Imprenta Portugal, 1952).

33. See. for example. Noble David Cook, *People of the Volcano: Andean Counterpoint in the Colca Valley of Peru* (Durham, N.C.: Duke University Press, 2007), 91–104; Cummins, "Forms of Andean Colonial Towns"; Jeremy R. Mumford, *Vertical Empire: The General Resettlement of Indians in the Colonial Andes* (Durham, N.C.: Duke University Press, 2012); and Wernke, *Negotiated Settlements.*

34. Wernke, *Negotiated Settlements.*

35. Málaga Medina, "Los Collaguaen la historia de Arequia en el siglo XVI," 101. See also Luis Enrique Tord, *Templos coloniales del Colca—Arequipa* (Lima: Atlas, 1983), 87.

36. Maria A. Benavides, "The Franciscan Church of Yanque (Arequipa) and Andean Culture," *The Americas* 50, no. 3 (1994): 419–36.

37. Wernke, *Negotiated Settlements.*

38. John Hyslop, *Inka Settlement Planning* (Austin: University of Texas Press, 1990).

39. See, for example, Tamara Bray, "Inca Pottery as Culinary Equipment: Food, Feasting, and Gender in Imperial State Design," *Latin American Antiquity* 14, no. 1 (2003): 1–22; Lawrence S. Coben, "Other Cuzcos: Replicated Theaters of Inka Power," in *Archaeology of Performance: Theaters of Power, Community, and Politics,* ed. Takeshi Inomata and Lawrence S. Coben (Berkeley: Altamira Press, 2006); Tom D. Dillehay, "El colonialismo inka, el consumo de chicha y los festines desde una perspectiva de banquetes políticos," *Boletín de Arqueología PUCP* 7 (2003): 355–63; and Susan E. Ramírez, *To Feed and Be Fed: The Cosmological Bases of Authority and Identity in the Andes* (Stanford, Calif.: Stanford University Press, 2005).

40. Wernke, *Negotiated Settlements.*

41. Estenssoro, "El simio de Dios"; MacCormack, "The Heart Has Its Reasons."

42. Louise M. Burkhart, "Pious Performances: Christian Pageantry and Native Identity in Early Colonial Mexico," in *Native Traditions in the Postconquest World,* ed. Elizabeth Hill Boone and Tom Cummins (Washington, D.C.: Dumbarton Oaks, 1998); Samuel Y. Edgerton and Jorge Pérez de Lara, *Theaters of Conversion: Religious Architecture and Indian Artisans In Colonial Mexico* (Albuquerque: University of New Mexico Press, 2001); Craig A. Hanson, "The Hispanic Horizon in Yucatan: A Model of Franciscan Missionization," *Ancient Mesoamerica* 6, no. 1 (1995): 15–28; Jaime Lara, *City, Temple, Stage: Eschatological Architecture and Liturgical Theatrics in New Spain* (Notre Dame, Ind.: University of Notre Dame, 2004).

43. See James Lockhart, "Trunk Lines and Feeder Lines: The Spanish Reaction to American Resources," in *Transatlantic Encounters: Europeans and Andeans in the Sixteenth*

Century, ed. Kenneth J. Andrien and Rolena Adorno (Los Angeles: University of California Press, 1991).

44. Marvin T. Smith and Mary Elizabeth Good, *Early Sixteenth Century Glass Beads in the Spanish Colonial Trade* (Greenwood, Miss.: Cottonlandia Museum Publications, 1982).

45. Steven A. Wernke, "Households in Transition: Reconstructing Domestic Organization at an Early Colonial Mission in the Andean Highlands," in *Decolonizing Indigenous Histories: Exploring Prehistoric/Colonial Transitions in Archaeology,* ed. Maxine Oland, Stobhan M. Hart, and Liam Frink (Tucson: University of Arizona Press, 2013).

46. Richard Flint and Shirley Cushing Flint, *The Coronado Expedition: From the Distance of 460 Years* (Albuquerque: University of New Mexico Press, 2003).

47. Wernke, "Households in Transition."

48. Miriam Doutriaux, "Imperial Conquest in a Multiethnic Setting: The Inka Occupation of the Colca Valley, Peru" (Ph.D. diss. Department of Anthropology, University of California, Berkeley, 2004); Wernke, *Negotiated Settlements;* Wernke, "The Politics of Community and Inka Statecraft in the Colca Valley, Peru," *Latin American Antiquity* 17, no. 2 (2006): 177–208; Wernke, 2007. [AU: There's no previous citation of Wernke from 2007; please provide full citation.

49. Wernke, 2010 ; Travis M. Williams, "The Restructuring of Social Spaces and Practices in a Trans-Conquest Andean Settlement" (B.A. honors thesis, Department of Anthropology, Vanderbilt University, 2009); Ronald Yim and Steven A. Wernke, "From Pots to Practices: Investigating Ceremonial and Domestic Practices in the Terminal Prehispanic and Early Colonial Andes through Ceramic Analysis," in *Vanderbilt Undergraduate Summer Research Program Conference* (Nashville, 2009).

50. Steven A. Wernke, "Convergences: Producing Colonial Hybridity at an Early Doctrina in Highland Peru," in *Enduring Conquests: Rethinking the Archaeology of Resistance to Spanish Colonialism in the Americas* (Santa Fe: School for Advanced Research Press, 2011).

51. Wernke, "Convergences."

52. Wernke, "Convergences"; Steven A. Wernke, Teddy Abel Traslaviña, and Ericka M. Guerra Santander, "La transformación del espacio arquitectónico en una doctrina temprana en el Valle del Colca," in *Arquitectura prehispánica tardía: construcción y poder en los Andes centrales,* ed. K. Lane and M. Luján Dávila (Lima: Universidad Católica Sedes Sapientiae, 2010).

53. Wernke, "Households in Transition."

54. Wernke, "Households in Transition."

55. Wernke, "Households in Transition."

56. Lizette Muñoz and David Goldstein, "Paleoethnobotanical Studies in the Collesuyo Region: The Case of Malata," in *75th Annual Meeting of the Society for American Archaeology* (St. Louis, 2010).

57. Cook, *People of the Volcano.*

58. Wernke, Traslaviña, and Guerra Santander, "La transformación del espacio arquitectónico."

59. Wernke, *Negotiated Settlements.* Also Wernke, "The Politics of Community."

60. Wernke, Traslaviña, and Guerra Santander, "La transformación del espacio arquitectónico."

61. Steven A. Wernke, "Spatial Network Analysis of a Terminal Prehispanic and Early Colonial Settlement in Highland Peru," *Journal of Archaeological Science* 39, no. 4 (2012): 1111–22.

62. Julienne Hanson, *Decoding Homes and Houses* (Cambridge, U.K.: Cambridge University Press, 1998; Bill Hillier, *Space Is the Machine: A Configurational Theory of Architecture* (New York: Cambridge University Press, 1996); Bill Hillier and Julienne Hanson, *The Social Logic of Space* (New York: Cambridge University Press, 1984).

63. Teddy Abel Traslaviña Arias, "La materialización del discurso evangelizador y su repercusión en el ámbito doméstico: El caso de Malata, una doctrina colonial temprana en el Valle del Colca," in *Simposio Internacional de Arqueología Histórica* (Lima, 2010).

64. Wernke, "Spatial Network Analysis."

65. See Peter Gose, *Invaders as Ancestors: On The Intercultural Making and Unmaking of Spanish Colonialism in the Andes* (Toronto: University of Toronto Press, 2008).

66. Bourdieu, *Outline of a Theory of Practice,* 466.

67. Antonius C. G. M. Robben, "Habits of the Home: Spatial Hegemony and the Structuration of House and Society in Brazil," *American Anthropologist* 91, no. 3 (1989): 571.

Stone Walls Do Not a Prison Make

1. Jeanne-Francoise Juchereau de St-Ignace et Marie Andrée Duplessis de Ste Hélène, *Les Annales de l'Hôtel-Dieu de Québec 1636–1716,* ed. Albert Jamet (Québec: Hotel Dieu, 1939), 314–15.

2. This point is developed in Barbara Wolshinsky, "Spatial Ambiguities and Conventual Openings," in *Classical Unities: Place, Time, Action,* ed. Erec Koch (Tubingen, Germany: Narr, 2002), 113–20.

3. Heidi Keller-Lapp, "Floating Cloisters and *Femmes Fortes:* Ursuline Missionaries in Ancien Régime France and Its Colonies" (Ph.D. diss., University of California San Diego, 2005).

4. Although uncloistered sisters also arrived in these settings, we concentrate on the cloistered orders, because of the contrast of their enclosure and the expansive mission they undertook.

5. For discussion of cloister in France see Elizabeth Rapley, *A Social History of the Cloister: Daily Life in the Teaching Monasteries of the Old Regime* (Montréal: McGill-Queen's University Press, 2001), 111–18. Mother Superiors and other officers sometimes went outside to conduct convent business, and there were some formal occasions on which convents sent representatives to government banquets, religious processions, and other events.

6. Emily Clark, *Masterless Mistresses: The New Orleans Ursulines and the Development of a New World Society, 1727–1834* (Chapel Hill: University of North Carolina Press, 2007), 41; Guy-Marie Oury, *Les Ursulines de Québec 1639–1953* (Sillery, Québec: Septention, 1999), 18, 40.

7. "Territory of grace" is Keith Luria's phrase, cited in introduction, *Women, Religion and the Atlantic World,* ed. Daniella Kostroun and Lisa Vollendorf (Toronto: University of Toronto Press, 2009) , 7. Emily Clark, ed., *Voices from an Early American Convent* (Baton Rouge: Louisiana State University Press, 2007), 20, notes the special permission required.

8. Oury, *Ursulines de Québec,* 61, notes that before leaving France they pledged to teach their native boarders literacy as well as Christianity. The Société de Notre Dame, which founded Montréal in 1641, named founding a hospital and converting the natives as its two central aims. On the primary mission to catechize rather than educate in French Ursuline convents, see Laurence Lux-Sterritt, "Between the Cloister and the World: The Successful Compromise of the Ursulines of Toulouse," *French History* 16, no. 3 (2002): 253.

9. Clark, *Masterless Mistresses,* 51.

10. Clark, *Voices from an Early American Convent,* 68.

11. Clark, *Masterless Mistresses,* 55, discusses New Orleans, as does Clark, *Voices from an Early American Convent,* 53, 59–60, 68–69. The founding of Montréal astride Iroquois trade routes was deemed in Québec "la folle enterprise." The caterpillars are mentioned in Juchereau, *Annales de l'Hôtel-Dieu,* 20.

12. Marie Morin, *Histoire simple et veritable: Les annals de L'Hôtel-Dieu de Montréal, 1659–1725,* ed. Ghislaine Legendre (Montréal: Presses de l'université de Montréal, 1979), 52–54.

13. Clark, *Voices from an Early American Convent,* 22.

14. Morin, *Histoire simple et veritable,* 134–35, 162–63, 174–75. The Jesuits also described the women in these heroic terms.

15. Morin, *Histoire simple et veritable,* 33, 163, 175.

16. Juchereau, *Annales de l'Hôtel-Dieu,* 361–65.

17. Cited in Marie-Claude Dinet-Lecomte, *Les soeurs hospitalières en France aux XVIIe et XVIIIe siècles* (Paris: Honoré Champion, 2005), 420–21, drawn from correspondence between the Montréal and Québec hospitals and their sisterly colleagues and relatives in Bayeux and Beaufort.

18. Clark, *Voices from an Early American Convent,* 55.

19. Clark, *Voices from an Early American Convent,* 43; see also 77.

20. Clark, *Voices from an Early American Convent,* 109.

21. Heidi Keller-Lapp, "Floating Cloisters and Heroic Women: French Ursuline Missionaries, 1639–1744," *World History Connected,* http://worldhistoryconnected.press.illinois.edu/4.3/lapp.html. Accessed October 1, 2010.

22. Soeur Gabrielle Lapointe, *Constitution et Reglements des Premières Ursulines de Québec par le Père Jérome Lalemant S.J. 1647* (Québec: Monastére des Ursulines, 1974), xvii. Other excerpts cited here are found on 8–10, 13, 49, 101.

23. Lapointe, *Constitution et Reglements,* 121–23.

24. The result was something of a stalemate. Laval made the changes he sought after the death of the renowned founder. For a detailed discussion, see Oury, *Ursulines de Québec,* 68–69, 98–101, 148.

25. Chapter 9 of Francois Rousseau, *La Croix et Le Scalpel: Histoire des Augustines de l'Hôtel-Dieu de Québec I: 1639–1892* (Sillery, Québec: Septentrion, 1989), elucidates the Augustinian Rule and routines.

26. See, for example, Barbara Diefendorf, "Rethinking the Catholic Reformation: The Role of Women," in Kostroun and Vollendorf, *Women, Religion and the Atlantic World,* and Lux-Sterritt, "Between the Cloister and the World," 247–68.

27. Morin, *Histoire simple et veritable,* 100–105.

28. Morin, *Histoire simple et veritable,* 178–79.

29. Morin, *Histoire simple et veritable,* 250.

30. Morin, *Histoire simple et veritable,* 262.

31. Morin, *Histoire simple et veritable,* 262

32. Clark, *Voices from an Early American Convent,* 126.

33. In the 1660s one of the Jesuit priests apparently made a covert attempt to chastise Marie de l'Incarnation. During convent recreation hour, a curiously folded note arrived, and she began reading it aloud to the Ursulines amid some amusement, as the letter

turned out to be an exhortation to mortify her self-love and submit to those over her. Scholars believe that the letter was not the work, as purported, of a young boy Marie de l'Incarnation had befriended and who had subsequently gone to live with the Jesuits. The phraseology and the familiarity with the writing of St. Francis de Sales evident in the missive strongly suggest that the anonymous sender was a Jesuit. The incident appears in Joyce Marshall, *Word from New France* (Toronto: Oxford University Press, 1967), 24, and in more detail in Guy-Marie Oury, *Marie de l'Incarnation,* vol. 2 (Québec: Presses de l'Université Laval, 1973). In 1635, while the mystic was still in Tours, her spiritual advisor Dom Raymond responded to her dream of going to New France with a criticism of the presumptuousness of such a great ardor for a design too elevated for those of her sex. Guy-Marie Oury, *Correspondance: Marie de l'Incarnation, Mère, 1599–1672* (Québec: Presses de l'Université Laval, 1973), 46. On the widespread uneasiness about Ursulines and other women who adopted an active ministry whose "ambiguous status and . . . incursions into public spaces were disturbing" to early modern society, see Linda Lierheimer, "Redefining Convent Space: Ideals of Female Community among Seventeenth-Century Ursuline Nuns," *Proceedings of the Western Society of French Historians* 24 (1997): 213.

34. Enlightening on this subject are Bridget Hill, *Women Alone: Spinsters in England, 1660–1850* (New Haven: Yale University Press, 2001); Amy Froide, *Never Married: Singlewomen in Early Modern England* (Oxford, U.K.: Oxford University Press, 2005); and Karin Wulf, *Not All Wives: Women of Colonial Philadelphia* (Philadelphia: University of Pennsylvania Press, 2005).

35. Notarized documents survive of seigneurial purchases by several sisters who signed in their official positions such as superior, assistant superior, director of novices, *discrette,* or *dépositaire.* So do documents signed by numerous nuns who gathered under the convent bell for formal agreements about specific dowries, some even specifying how those several thousand *livres* would be invested in a mill or other communal project. For a sample Hôpital-Général contract, see Library and Archives of Canada, Colonial Series C11A 1720, vol. 107, folios 423–25. Subsequent citations of this archival source are preceded by C11A.

36. Karen M. Morin and Jeanne K. Guelke, introduction, *Women, Religion, and Space: Global Perspectives on Gender and Space* (Syracuse, N.Y.: Syracuse University Press, 2007), xxii.

37. Oury, *Correspondance,* 802.

38. Oury, *Correspondance,* 809.

39. Some of these sources are discussed in Jacques Ducharme, "Les revenus des Hospitalières de Montréal au XVIIe siècle," in *L'Hôtel-Dieu de Montréal, 1642–1973,* ed. Michel Allard (Montréal: Hurtubise, 1973), 232; see also *L'Hôpital-Général de Montréal 1692–1821,* 2 vols (Montréal: n.p., n.d.), 1:204–13.

40. Clark, *Voices from an Early American Convent,* 77–78. Sister St. Stanislaus was the name in religion of Marie Madeleine Hachard.

41. The figures are extrapolated from the text and map furnished in Dinet-Lecomte, *Soeurs hospitalières,* 21, 475.

42. Clark, *Voices from an Early American Convent,* 71.

43. When the Québec Hôtel-Dieu cared for the sick who embarked from the ship *Rubis,* for example, two nuns died and many others fell ill. In the epidemics of 1756–57, ten nuns from the Québec Hospice lost their lives caring for stricken soldiers and sailors.

44. Wheelwright's biography is found in *Dictionary of Canadian Biography,* vol. 4 (Quebec and Toronto: Laval and Toronto University Presses, 1966–). Also useful is Ann Little, chap. 4, *Abraham in Arms: War and Gender in Colonial New England* (Philadelphia: University of Pennsylvania Press, 2007); and William Henry Foster, *The Captor's Narrative: Catholic Women and their Puritan Men on the Early American Frontier* (Ithaca, N.Y.: Cornell University Press, 2003), 64–72. The foundational compilation of captive stories, which describes a number of individuals who lived for periods of time in convents, is Charlotte Alice Baker, *True Stories of New England Captives Carried to Canada during the Old French and Indian Wars* (Cambridge, Mass.: E. A. Hall, 1897), and Emma Lewis Coleman's expanded 1925 edition of same.

45. Clark, *Voices from an Early American Convent,* 82.

46. Clark, *Voices from an Early American Convent,* 74, 82, records this work in 1728; Clark, *Masterless Mistresses,* 134, notes the later work. Clark links literacy among New Orleans blacks to the Ursulines.

47. C11A 1731, vol. 54, folios 93–96.

48. C11A 1734, vol. 61, folios 135, 147.

49. For an overview of the literature and the controversies regarding hôpitaux and poor relief in Europe, see M. H. D.van Leeuven, "Logic of Charity: Poor Relief in Preindustrial Europe," *Journal of Interdisciplinary History* 24, no. 4 (1994): 589–613. Jacques Mathieu, *La Nouvelle-France: les Français en Amérique du Nord, XVIe-XVIIIe siécles* (Québec: Presses de l'Université Laval, 1991), 189, writes that the Québec Hospice "contrairement aux organismes de la métropole . . . n'est pas considerée comme une maison d'enfermement mais comme une institution de charité."

50. Clark, *Masterless Mistresses,* 98–103.

51. Clark, *Voices from an Early American Convent,* 79. There was a smaller class difference between day students and boarders in Québec, where students who lived in town and could return to their homes after class tended to do so, while boarders usually came from farther away.

52. Micheline D'Allaire, *L'Hôpital Général de Québec, 1692–1764* (Montréal: Fides, 1977) attributes the upsurge of postulants in the 1750s to desire for a safe haven in wartime, a theory also expressed by Bishop Briand. On the manufactory, see C11A 1717, vol. 106, folio 446; on the renown of the Hospice school, see P-G Roy, *La Ville de Québec sous le régime français* (Québec: Redempti Paradis, 1930), I, 528.

53. C11A 1734 vol. 62, folios 296–97.

54. Lorraine Gadoury, *La Noblesse de la Nouvelle France* (Montréal: Hurtubise, 1991), 68, gives lower figures than D'Allaire's 45.9 percent for percentages of sisters who were noble (1700–1760), perhaps the result of calculating on the basis of the whole convent, including lay sisters, rather than on the percentage among choir nuns. Gadoury's figures on nobles are these: Québec Ursulines 20.7 percent, Québec Hôtel-Dieu 17.2 percent, Québec Hôpital-Général 22.4 percent; Montréal Hôtel-Dieu, 19 percent.

55. Hierarchy pervaded the cloisters. Lay sisters (*converses*) addressed even adolescent choir nuns as "Mother." Choir nuns, drawn from the higher classes, passed much of their day in prayer, meditation, and song, though they spent some time in the wards and teaching the poor. The physical work of the convent was largely done by lay sisters, who were typically illiterate daughters of the working class. Their dowries were much lower. While choir nuns wore shoes, they wore clogs. Their bed linen was coarser.

Required to be healthy, robust, and docile, converses took care of the barnyard and did the heavy work in garden, laundry, and stable. These "Cinderellas of the convents" could not sing in the choir or vote in convent elections. D'Allaire, *L'Hôpital Général de Québec,* 152–53.

56. For sketches of the superiors see Joseph Trudelle, *Les jubilés et les églises et chapelles de la ville et de la banlieu de Québec, 1608–1901* (Québec: Le Soleil, 1904), 116–19. The Juchereau Duchesnays, a bourgeois family that was later enobled, made major contributions. Mother Geneviève de St. Augustine ruled as a superior for a decade. Her younger sister Mother Marie-Joseph de l'Enfant-Jesus became her assistant superior at twenty-one. She officiated nearly twenty years as superior, another twenty in such offices as hospital director, depositary, and discrète. Their niece, Mother Marie-Catherine de St. Ignace, wrote the Hôtel-Dieu annals. P-G Roy, *La famille Juchereau Duchesnay* (Levis, Québec: n.p., 1903), 1, 178–86, 221. On Mother St. Claude, see "Ramezay, Marie Charlotte de," *Dictionary of Canadian Biography,* vol. 3, and Jan Noel, "Caste and Clientage in an Eighteenth Century Québec Convent," *Canadian Historical Review* 82, no. 3 (2001).

57. Clark, *Voices from an Early American Convent,* 79.

58. On visits and other points of contention between the Vaudreuils and the Bishop see C11A 1721, vol. 124, folio 469; C11A 1722, vol. 24, folio 466–70; and C11A 1725, vol. 47, folio 452. See also Francis Hammang, *The Marquis de Vaudreuil* (Bruges: Université Louvain, 1938), 78; and Noel, "Caste and Clientage," 483.

59. These were said to amount to 200,000 livres (C11A 1738, vol. 70, folio 225–26). For more information on holdings of the Ursulines and the Hospice see C11A 1737, vol. 70, folios 204–7v, folio 400. For signs of favoritism, see C11A 1750, vol. 119, folios 369ff.

60. On ecclesiastical infighting and its negative effect on convents see Henri Tetu, *Les Eveques de Québec* (Québec: N. Hardy, 1889), 175–76. See also Dale Standen, "Politics, Patronage and the Imperial Interest: Charles Beauharnois's Disputes with Gilles Hocquart," *Canadian Historical Review* 60, no. 1 (1979): 19–40.

61. "Geneviève St. Augustin Superière à Votre Grandeur," October 4, 1728C11A 1728 vol. 50.

62. Soeur Agnes to the Minister, October 19 1728, C11A 1728, vol. 50.

63. Dosquet to Maurepas, 1730, C11A, volume 53, folios 379–80. He also requested that the Hospice Augustinians be placed under control of those at the Hôtel-Dieu. The governor and intendant observed that Dosquet's absolutism alienated most Canadian religious communities, adding that it did not help that he was neither French nor noble. C11A 1725, vol. 107, folios 231–32; see also 1731, vol. 56, folios 186–87.

64. The Crown did not remove the appointee; but Mother Duchesnay's younger sister was elected Superior in 1732, and for the rest of the time until the conquest, the superior was always a noblewoman. Nor was there further complaint of ecclesiastics interfering in elections. See C11A, 1731, vol. 54, folios 36–39 (January 15 and October 3–6). D'Allaire, *L'Hôpital Général de Québec,* identifies a spirit of independence as the nuns' foremost trait, 173. For supportive letters from Governor and Intendant see C11A 1731, vol. 56, f.175–88; C11A 1732 vol. 57 (October 1732); C11A 1735–36 vol. 107 (October 26, 1735, October 6, 1736).

65. Information about this incident comes from a letter from the Québec Hôspice that survived in the Augustinian archives at Rennes and is cited in D'Allaire, *L'Hôpital Général de Québec,* 176.

66. Marguerite Jean, *Evolution des Communautés religieuses de femmes au Canada de 1639 a nos jours* (Montréal: Fides, 1977), 199, 295, provides context and summarizes various cases where nuns sometimes won and sometimes lost disputes with ecclesiastics.

67. "Juchereau de la Ferté, Jeanne-Francoise," *Dictionary of Canadian Biography,* vol. 2. Securing retired Bishop Laval as her intermediary, she managed to ward off Bishop St. Vallier's plan to transfer twelve additional nuns from the Hôtel-Dieu to the Hospice.

68. Clark, *Masterless Mistresses,* 58.

69. For official musing that the sisters' independence may have sprung from the fact that the Québec communities predated the establishment of either bishop or royal government, see C11A 1730, vol. 52, folios 156–57. One official dispatch of 1665 suggested that at that point the bishop reviewed their accounts yearly (C11A, vol. 7, folios 63) but the colony subsequently experienced quite a few years of absentee bishops. Other imbroglios with the authorities included the Québec Hôtel-Dieu's five-year resistance in 1737–42 to returning soldier-patients' uniforms to the government and the convent's earlier attempts to restrict new nearby housing with windows which might disturb its privacy (see for example 1724 vol. 46, folios 328–31v; 1727, vol. 49, folios 124ff). There was disagreement too, about whether the nuns were required to accept as patients gentlewomen and servants as well as soldiers and the poor. On disputes, see also D'Allaire, *L'Hôpital Général de Québec,* 135.

70. D'Allaire, *L'Hôpital Général de Québec,* 217; see also 50, 117.

71. Oury, *Ursulines de Québec,* 47, 68, 73. They came from the dioceses of Tours, Paris, Rouen, and Vannes. On circulation of necrologies and the Ursulines French Procurer M. de Bernières, see Oury, *Ursulines de Québec,* 49, 78. On the Hôtel-Dieu nuns from France, see Rousseau, *La Croix et Le Scalpel,* 135. On New Orleans, see Clark, *Masterless Mistresses,* 265–66.

72. Oury, *Ursulines de Québec,* 94, 193.

73. This impact is developed in Keller-Lapp, "Floating Cloisters and Heroic Women."

74. C11A 1743 vol. 80, folio 186; C11A 1745, vol. 83, folio 248, and vol. 84, folio 77; C11A 1748, vol. 92, folio 201. Money collected by Mother St. Geneviève de l'Enfant Jesus for food they provided to sick seamen between 1733 and 1736 is recorded in C11A 1736, vol. 68, folio 46. There is an instructive 1755 balance sheet from the Québec Hôtel-Dieu that lists as the largest single source of revenue (more than 2000 livres) fruits and vegetables from their garden. Other sizeable amounts came from their seigneurial properties, from urban rents or interest payments, from their own convent livestock and harvests, and from sale of butter and cheese. Rousseau, *La Croix et Le Scalpel,* 152.

75. C11A 1731, vol. 56, folios 178–79; C11A 1732, vol. 58, folios 38–41; C11A 1740, vol. 114, folio 288; C11A 1745, vol. 115, folio 207.

76. Clark, *Masterless Mistresses,* 209

77. C11A 1734, vol. 61, folio 159.

78. See the account of Jacques Ducharme, "Les revenus des Hospitalières de Montréal au XVIIIe siècle," in *L'Hôtel-Dieu de Montréal, 1642–1973,* ed. M. Allard (Montréal: Hurtubise, 1973), 232.

79. Allard, *L'Hôtel-Dieu,* esp. 40–45 and 238–39. This institution experienced severe overcrowding during the war, accommodating a hundred patients in buildings designed for forty by co-opting the chapel and even some of the sisters' dormitory space. On

relations with General Amherst, see also Soeur Jeanne Bernier, *Trois siècles de charité a l'Hôtel-Dieu de Montréal, 1642–1692* (Montréal, 1949), 85.

80. Clark, *Masterless Mistresses,* 209

81. See Marie-Claude Dinet-Lecompte, "Les hospitalières françaises en Amérique aux XVIIe et XVIIIe siècles," *Revue d'Histoire de l'Eglise de France* 84 (1998): 261–82. In France the hospital work in Canada became firmly associated with suffering. Québec Hôtel-Dieu Mother St. Augustin informed a relative in Bayeux that she was "attached to the Cross by three nails"—namely, God's will, salvation of souls, and her vocation to live and die in Canada. French hospitalières of St. Joseph in Montréal characterized a Canadian posting as "l'éloignement de toutes satisfactions des sens, la mort continuelle de tout l'humain." Cited in Dinet-Lecomte, *Les soeurs hospitalières en France aux XVIIe et XVIIIe siècles: La charité en action* (Paris: Honoré Champion, 2005), 420–21.

82. Clark, *Masterless Mistresses,* 199–200, utilizing her own Dieppe comparison and the more general findings of C. Fairchild for Aix-en-Provence. Clark's chapter 6 surveys New Orleans convent sources of revenue in town and country.

83. See D'Allaire, *L'Hôpital Général de Québec,* 32ff., and Helena O'Reilly, Monseigneur de Saint-Vallier et l'Hopital-general de Quebec (Quebec: C. Darveau, 1882).

84. A. Doughty and G. W. Parmelee, *The Siege of Québec and the Battle of the Plains of Abraham* (Québec: Dussault and Proulx, 1901), 2:164. Of Wolfe's successor General Murray, the French commissary Bernier wrote to Chevalier de Lévis in October 1759, "Il paroit vouloir protéger toutes les Maisons des Dames religieuses." See *Lettres de Divers Particuliers au Chevalier de Lévis* (Québec: Demer, 1895), 28.

85. Figures available for the period 1800–1823 indicated government compensation for services amounting to about a thousand British pounds per annum. *Journal of the Legislative Council of Lower Canada*, 1824, appendix 1, "Report of the Special Committee . . . for . . . Insane . . . Foundlings . . . sick and infirm Poor," 2–3.

86. Clark, *Masterless Mistresses,* 126, 135–47, 157, 210–11.

87. Clark, chapter 7, *Masterless Mistresses,* elaborates on the developments described in this paragraph.

88. On this subject, see Nancy Lusignan Schultz, *Veil of Fear: Nineteenth-Century Convent Tales by Rebecca Reed and Maria Monk* (West Lafayette, Ind.: Purdue University Press, 1999).

89. Elizabeth Lehfeldt, *Religious Women in Golden Age Spain: The Permeable Cloister* (Aldershot, U.K.: Ashgate, 2005), 13.

Configuring and Reconfiguring Cathedral Space in the Spanish Atlantic

1. Manuel González Galván, *Trazo, proporción y símbolo en el arte virreinal: antología personal* (México D.F. [Mexico City]: Universidad Nacional Autónoma de México, 2006), 40.

2. Judith Etzion, "Spanish Music as Perceived in Western Music Historiography: A Case of the Black Legend?" *International Review of the Aesthetics and Sociology of Music* 29, no. 2 (1998): 95.

3. The years of recorded construction: Avila, 1160; Cuenca, ca. 1197; Burgos, 1222; Toledo, 1226;, Leon, 1255; Seville, 1402. From John Harvey, *The Cathedrals of Spain* (New York: Hastings House Publishers, 1957).

4. Alfonso Jiménez Martín, "Las fechas de las formas. Selección crítica de fuentes documentales para la cronología del edificio medieval," in *La catedral gótica de Sevilla: fundación y fábrica de la obra nueva* (Sevilla [Seville, Spain]: Universidad de Sevilla, 2005), 15–114.

5. Begoña Alonso Ruiz, *Arquitectura tardogótica en Castilla: Los Rasines* (Santander, Spain: Universidad de Cantabria, 2003), 114.

6. Norbert Nusbaum, "Space and Form Redefined: Paradigm Shifts in German Architecture from 1350–1550," in *La piedra postrera. Simposium internacional sobre la Catedral de Sevilla en el contexto del gótico final,* ed. Alfonso Jiménez Martín (Sevilla: Tvrris Fortíssima, 2007), 305. For a survey of contemporary practices relating to the study of "Gothic architectures," see Michael T. Davis, "Sic Et Non: Recent Trends in the Study of Gothic Ecclesiastical Architecture," *Journal of the Society of Architectural Historians* 58, no. 3 (1999): 414–23.

7. Robert Branner and Shirley Prager Branner, *The Cathedral of Bourges and Its Place in Gothic Architecture* (New York: Architectural History Foundation, 1989). The profundity of the influence of Bourges on the design of Toledo was called into question by Michael Wolfe and Robert Mark in "Gothic Cathedral Buttressing: The Experiment at Bourges and Its Influence," *Journal of the Society of Architectural Historians* 33, no. 1 (1974): 17–26. Relating to the religious-political stance of Ximénez de Rada, see Patrick Henriet, "Political Struggle and the Legitimation of the Toledan Primacy: The Pars Lateranii Concilii," in *Building Legitimacy: Political Discourses and Forms of Legitimacy in Medieval Societies,* ed. Isabel Alfonso, Hugh N. Kennedy, and Julio Escalona (Leiden, Netherlands: Brill, 2004), 291–318.

8. Ann Raftery Meyer, *Medieval Allegory and the Building of the New Jerusalem* (Cambridge, U.K.: D. S. Brewer, 2003), 94.

9. Ricardo Izquierdo Benito, "La construcción en Toledo en la baja edad media: situaciones conflictivas," in *La ciudad medieval de Toledo: Historia, arqueología y rehabilitación de la casa el edificio Madre de Dios,* ed. Jean Passini and Ricardo Izquierdo Benito (Cuenca, Spain: Universidad de Castilla la Mancha, 2007), 54.

10. "No cabe duda por tanto, que la apropiación de esos lugares era una de las máximas expresiones de la apropiación del territorio conquistado, y máxime cuando el edificio, por su historia o por su calidad y vistosidad, encerraba evidentes significados simbólicos para el vencido. Era, en cierto modo, una forma de privarles de parte de su identidad." Antonio Almagro Gorbea, "De mezquita a catedral. Una adaptación imposible," in *La piedra postrera. Simposium internacional sobre la Catedral de Sevilla en contexto del gótico final,* ed. Alfonso Jiménez Martín (Sevilla: Tvrris Fortíssima, 2007), 25. For a less architectural and more sociopolitical analysis, see Julie A. Harris, "Mosque to Church Conversions in the Spanish Reconquest," *Medieval Encounters* 3, no. 2 (1997): 158–72.

11. Almagro Gorbea, "De mezquita a catedral," 25; María José Lop Otín, "Los 'espacios' de la Catedral de Toledo y su funcionalidad," in *Sacra Loca Toletana: los espacios sagrados en Toledo,* ed. Juan Carlos Vizuete Mendoza and Julio Martín Sánchez (Cuenca, Spain: Ediciones Universidad de Castilla La Mancha, 2008), 229.

12. Almagro Gorbea, "De mezquita a catedral," 36.

13. The controversy arises over the fact that Alfonso VI had promised to retain the mosque as a place of Islamic worship as part of the city's capitulation agreement. To maintain the honor of Alfonso VI, great-grandfather of Ximénez de Rada's close ally Alfonso

VIII, Ximénez de Rada retold the story whereby Alfonso VI was supposedly absent from Toledo when de Sedirac used the opportunity to seize the mosque in the name of Christianity. Lop Otín and many other scholars saw Ximénez de Rada's account of the story highly improbable; given the enormous significance of such an act, it would not have gone unsanctioned by the king. "En realidad, no parece probable que Alfonso V.I. fuera ajeno a una decisión de tanta transcendencia; más lógico es pensar que deseara hacer ostentación pública de su control sobre la ciudad." Lop Otín, "Los 'espacios,'" 230.

14. Fernando Chueca Goitia, "Prólogo," in *La Catedral de Sevilla* (Sevilla: Ediciones Guadalquivir, 1991), 16.

15. Pedro Navascués Palacio, *La Catedral en España. Arquitectura y liturgia* (Lunwerg: Madrid, 2004), 54.

16. Diego Ortiz de Zúñiga, *Anales eclesiasticos y seculares de la muy noble y muy leal ciudad de Sevilla . . . que contienen sus mas principales memorias desde el año de 1246 . . . hasta el de 1671 . . . formados por Diego Ortiz de Zuñiga* (Madrid: en la Imprenta Real: Iuan Garcia Infançon, 1677), 249, 265.

17. "Hagamos una iglesia tan grande, que los que la vieren acabada nos tengan por locos." Ortiz de Zúñiga, *Anales eclesiásticos,* 265.

18. "El Templo Catedral, que se consagró en la primera Mezquita de los Moros, con la antiguedad, y daño que recibió en los terremotos en los años antecedentes, y la continuación de la urgente necesidad de reparos grandes, inducia deseos de nueva fabrica, cuando aun sin las causas que la pedian, la magnificencía de los animos Sevillanos sus ilustrísimos Capitulares, no cabía en aquel (aunque no pequeño) estrecho Templo, respecto de la numero du su Clero, y majestad de los divino Oficios." Ortiz de Zúñiga, *Anales eclesiásticos,* 265.

19. Magdalena Valor Piechotta and Miguel Ángel Tabales Rodríguez, "Urbanismo y arquitectura almohades en Sevilla. Caracteres y especificidad," in *Los Almohades: problemas y perspectivas,* ed. Patrice Cressier and Luis Molina (Madrid: Casa de Velázquez, 2005), 205.

20. Antonio Collantes de Terán Sánchez, "Una ciudad, una catedral." in *La catedral gótica de Sevilla,* 115–46 (Sevilla: Universidad de Sevilla, 2006), 119.

21. Chueca Goitia, "Prólogo," 16.

22. Begoña Alonso Ruiz, "El laboratorio arquitectónico: La huella de la Catedral de Sevilla en la arquitectura religiosa del tardiogótico hispano," in *La piedra postrera: Simposium internacional sobre la Catedral de Sevilla en el contexto del gótico final,* ed. Alfonso Jiménez Martín (Sevilla: Tvrris Fortíssima, 2007), 275.

23. Fernando Chueca Goitia, *La Catedral Nueva de Salamanca: Historia documental de su construcción* (Salamanca, Spain: Universidad de Salamanca, 1951), 82.

24. Luis G. Serrano, *La traza original con que fue construida la Catedral de México por mandato de Su Majestad Felipe II* (México: Universidad Nacional Autónoma de México, 1964), 18.

25. Luis Javier Cuesta Hernández, "Sobre el estilo arquitectónico en Claudio de Arciniega," *Anales del Instituto de Investigaciones Estéticas* 76 (2002): 65.

26. José Luis Pano Gracia, "El modelo de planta de salón: origen difusión e implantación en América," in *Arquitectura religiosa del siglo XVI en España y ultramar,* ed. María del Carmen Lacarra Ducay (Zaragoza, Spain: Institución Fernando el Católico, 2004), 42.

27. Pano Gracia, "El modelo de planta de salón," 53.

28. Jacqueline E. Jung, "Beyond the Barrier: The Unifying Role of the Choir Screen in Gothic Churches," *Art Bulletin* 82, no. 4 (2000): 622–57; Dawn Cunningham, "One Pontile, Two Pontili: The Choir Screens of Modena Cathedral," *Renaissance Studies* 19, no. 5 (2005): 682.

29. João Adolfo Hansen and Alcir Pécora, "Literatura del siglo XVII en Bahía," in *Barroco*, ed. Pedro Aullón de Haro (Madrid: Verbum Editorial, 2004), 1124.

30. Florian Nelle, "Telescope, Theater, and the Instrumental Revelation of the New Worlds," in *Instruments in Art and Science: On the Architectonics of Cultural Boundaries in the 17th Century*, ed. Helmar Schramm, Ludger Schwarte, and Jan Lazardzig (Berlin: Walter de Gruyter, 2008), 63.

31. José Antonio Maravall, *Culture of the Baroque: Analysis of a Historical Structure*, trans. Terry Cochran, Theory and History of Literature (Minneapolis: University of Minnesota Press, 1986), 85.

32. Paolo Cherchi, "Marino and the *Meraviglia*," in *Culture and Authority in the Baroque*, ed. Massimo Ciavolella and Patrick Coleman (Toronto: University of Toronto Press, 2005), 64.

33. Jan Lazardzig, "The Machine as Spectacle: Function and Admiration in Seventeenth-Century Perspectives on Machines," in Schramm, Schwarte, and Lazardzig, *Instruments in Art and Science*, 160.

34. Maravall, *Culture of the Baroque*, 58.

35. José Jaime García Bernal, *El fasto público en la España de los Austrias* (Sevilla: Universidad de Sevilla, 2006), 422–32.

36. María Teresa Sánchez Albarracín, "El templo catedralicio oriolano: Transformaciones e interacciones derivadas a la religiosidad popular y sociedad del Antiguo Régimen," in *El comportamiento de las catedrales españolas del barroco a los historicismos*, ed. Germán Ramallo Asensio (Murcia, Spain: Universidad de Murcia, 2003), 53–63.

37. José María Prados García, "El retablo mayor del siglo XVIII de la Catedral de León," *Archivo Español del Arte* 55, no. 20 (1982): 334.

38. Alfonso Rodríguez G. de Ceballos, "Liturgia y configuración del espacio en la arquitectura española y portuguesa a raíz del Concilio del Trento," *Anuario del Departamento de Historia y Teoría del Arte (U.A.M)* 3 (1991): 18.

39. Rodríguez G. de Ceballos, "Liturgia y configuración," 46.

40. Nelle, "Telescope, Theater, and the Instrumental Revelation," 61.

41. Lazardzig, "The Machine as Spectacle," 153.

42. *Diccionario de la lengua castellana, compuesto por la Real Academia Española, reducido a un tomo para su más fácil uso* (Madrid: Joaquín Ibarra, 1780), 606–7.

43. J. Javier Aparicio Maydeu, *Calderón y la máquina barroca: escenografía, religión y cultura en el José de las Mujeres* (Amsterdam: Rodopi, 1999), 15.

44. In 1554 Archbishop Montúfar wrote to Viceroy Luis de Velasco I, stating, "La traza que se ha elegido de mayor parecer, es la de Sevilla porque S.M. por real cédula, manda que se haga suntuosa como a ciudad e yglesias metropolitanas conviene." Four years later he wrote again, stating "que por los serios inconvenientes no convenía que fuese tan suntuosa como la Catedral de Sevilla—y añadía—Por tanto me parece que así lo he consultado con vuestro Visorrey, que bastará para esta Ciudad, una Iglesia como la de Segovia o Salamanca . . . y de esta manera se dará remedio al gasto tan excesivo." Luis G. Serrano,

La traza original con que fue construida la Catedral de México por mandato de Su Majestad Felipe II (México, D. F.: Universidad Nacional Autónoma de México, 1964), 18.

45. Justino Fernández, "El Ciprés de la Catedral Metropolitana," *Historia Mexicana* 6, no. 6 (1956): 89.

46. "Y que podria yo decir en abono de las tremendas caxas y dobles fachadas de los dos órganos . . . que tanto atormentan la vista del inteligente. . . . Nada á la verdad. Mas la catedral de Sevilla podrá responder lo mismo que las de Toledo y de Leon acerca del monstruoso transparente de la primera, y del ridículo retablo mayor de la segunda. Teniendo necesidad estas iglesias de construir aquellas obras, en principios del siglo XVIII, quando las bellas artes estaban en la mayor decadencia, no hallaron en España un profesor de mas fama que Narciso Tomé, discípulo de Churriguera, y propagador de su secta en Castilla; y la de Sevilla no encontró otro de más mérito y habilidad en 1724 para executar estas, que Luis de Vilches, discípulo de Barbás, el heresiarca de la arquitectura en Andalucía." Juan Agustín Ceán Bermúdez, *Descripción artística de la Catedral de Sevilla* (Sevilla: en la casa de la viuda de Hidalgo y sobrino, 1804), 52–53.

47. Juan Miguel Serrera, "Los ideales neoclásicos y la destrucción del barroco: Ceán Bermúdez y Jerónimo Balbás," *Archivo Hispalense* 73, no. 223 (1990), 135–60.

48. An *estípite* is a column or pilaster which is generally square in section and tapers from the top of the fust to the base.

49. For a definitive work on the *estípite* and the *retablo* of the Seville school, see Francisco Javier Herrera García, *El retablo sevillano en la primera mitad del siglo XVIII: evolución y difusión del retablo de estípites* (Sevilla: Diputación de Sevilla, 2001).

50. Kelly Donahue-Wallace, *Art and Architecture in Viceregal Latin America, 1521–1821* (Albuquerque: University of New Mexico Press,), 7.

51. Juan Anaya Duarte, *El templo en la teología y la arquitectura* (México, D.F.: Universidad Iberoamericana, 1996), 30.

52. Maravall, *Culture of the Baroque,* 144.

53. José Ramón Alonso Pereira, *Introducción a la historia de la arquitectura: de los orígenes al siglo XXI* (Barcelona: Editorial Reverté, 2005), 163.

54. Allen S. Weiss, *Mirrors of Infinity: The French Formal Garden and 17th-Century Metaphysics* (New York: Princeton Architectural Press, 1995), 59.

Emigration, Transatlantic Communication, and Methodist Identity in Nineteenth-Century Ontario and Québec

1. *Watchman,* March 20, 1855, 94. For a more detailed discussion of the themes addressed in this chapter, see Todd Webb, *Transatlantic Methodists: British Wesleyanism and the Formation of an Evangelical Culture in Nineteenth-Century Ontario and Québec* (Montréal: McGill-Queen's University Press, 2013), 17–42.

2. Some colonials continued to ask the same questions in the twentieth century. See, for example, J. G. A. Pocock, "History and Sovereignty: The Historiographical Response to Europeanization in Two British Cultures," *Journal of British Studies* 31, no. 4 (1992): 358–61.

3. Richard Carwardine, *Transatlantic Revivalism: Popular Evangelicalism in Britain and America, 1790–1865* (Westport, Conn.: Greenwood, 1978), 28–39; Marguerite Van Die, "'The Double Vision': Evangelical Piety as Derivative and Indigenous in Victorian English

Canada," in *Evangelicalism: Comparative Studies of Popular Protestantism in North America, the British Isles, and Beyond, 1700–1990,* ed. Mark A. Noll, David W. Bebbington, and George A. Rawlyk (New York: Oxford University Press, 1994), 256–58; Marguerite Van Die, "'A March of Victory and Triumph in Praise of 'The Beauty of Holiness': Laity and the Evangelical Impulse in Canadian Methodism, 1800–1884," in *Aspects of the Canadian Evangelical Experience,* ed. George A. Rawlyk (Montréal: McGill-Queen's University Press, 1997), 77–79; Elizabeth Jane Errington, *Emigrant Worlds and Transatlantic Communities: Migration to Upper Canada in the First Half of the Nineteenth Century* (Montréal: McGill-Queen's University Press, 2007), esp. sections dealing with Methodist Peters and Pashley families.

4. For examples of this narrative, see the two standard studies: Goldwin French, *Parson and Politics: The Role of the Wesleyan Methodists in Upper Canada and the Maritimes from 1780 to 1855* (Toronto: Ryerson Press, 1962); and Neil Semple, *The Lord's Dominion: The History of Canadian Methodism* (Montréal: McGill-Queen's University Press, 1996).

5. This discussion of the Atlantic World paradigm is based on David Armitage and Michael J. Braddick, eds., *The British Atlantic World, 1500–1800,* 2nd ed. (Basingstoke, U.K.: Palgrave Macmillan, 2009). The quotation is from David Armitage, "Three Concepts of Atlantic History," in Armitage and Braddick, *British Atlantic World,* 14. Carla Gardina Pestana's chapter on religion is insightful, but like the rest of the contributors in the book, she confines her attention to the period before 1800. See Carla Gardina Pestana, "Religion," in Armitage and Braddick, *British Atlantic World,* 71–91.

6. J. G. A. Pocock, "The New British History in Atlantic Perspective: An Antipodean Commentary," *American Historical Review* 104, no. 2 (1999): 493–94; J. G. A. Pocock, "British History: A Plea for a New Subject," *Journal of Modern History* 47, no. 4 (1975): 620, 626. See also the essays collected in J. G. A. Pocock, *The Discovery of Islands: Essays in British History* (Cambridge, U.K.: Cambridge University Press, 2005); and David Armitage, "Greater Britain: A Useful Category of Historical Analysis?" *American Historical Review* 104, no. 2 (1999), 427–45, which criticizes Pocock's approach as an "attempted . . . revivification of British history as an imperial history, both within Britain and Ireland and across the oceans" (431).

7. David J. Bodenhamer, John Corrigan, and Trevor M. Harris, introduction, *The Spatial Humanities: GIS and the Future of Humanities Scholarship,* ed. Bodenhamer, Corrigan, and Harris (Bloomington: Indiana University Press, 2010), vii; Edward L. Ayers, "Turning toward Place, Space, and Time," in Bodenhamer, Corrigan, and Harris, *Spatial Humanities,* 3, 6. See also Trevor M. Harris et al., "Challenges for the Spatial Humanities: Toward a Research Agenda," in Bodenhamer, Corrigan, and Harris, *Spatial Humanities,* 167–76.

8. J. G. A. Pocock, "Commentary," in *The Treaty of Paris (1783) in a Changing States System,* ed. Prosser Gifford (Lanham, Md.: University Press of America, 1985), 205.

9. John Wesley to John Mason, January 13, 1790, in *Letters of John Wesley,* ed. John Telford (London: Epworth, 1931), 8:196. See also John C. Bowmer, *Pastor and People: A Study of Church and Ministry in Wesleyan Methodism from the Death of John Wesley (1791) to the Death of Jabez Bunting (1858)* (London: Epworth, 1975), 111–12, 163–67; Edmund Grindrod, *Compendium of the Laws and Regulations of Wesleyan Methodism,* 8th ed. (London: Wesleyan Conference Office, 1865), 1–11, 29–42, 61–62; Michael R. Watts, *The Dissenters: The Expansion of Evangelical Nonconformity* (Oxford, U.K.: Oxford University Press, 1995), 361–62, 466–68.

10. Frank Baker, "The People Called Methodists—3. Polity," in *A History of the Methodist Church in Great Britain,* ed. Rupert Davies, A. Raymond George, and Gordon Rupp (London: Epworth, 1965–88), 1:222–24, 230–33.

11. Baker, "People Called Methodists—3. Polity," 1:222–23, 226–29, 236–42; Henry Rack, *Reasonable Enthusiast: John Wesley and the Rise of Methodism* (London: Epworth, 1989), 245.

12. John Wesley to John Clayton [?], March 28, 1739 in *The Works of John Wesley: Letters,* ed. Frank Baker (Oxford, U.K.: Oxford University Press, 1980–81), 1:616 (emphasis in original); John Wesley to John Smith, March 22, 1748, quoted in V. H. H. Green, *John Wesley* (Lanham, Md.: University Press of America, 1987), 91.

13. Frank Baker, "The Trans-Atlantic Triangle: Relations between British, Canadian, and American Methodism during Wesley's Lifetime," *Bulletin of the United Church Archives* 28 (1979): 17–19; John Walsh, "Methodism at the End of the Eighteenth Century," in Davies, George, and Rupp, *History of the Methodist Church,* 1:301–2; John Vickers, *Thomas Coke: Apostle of Methodism* (London: Epworth, 1969), 311–13; Watts, *Dissenters,* 6.

14. Russell E. Richey, *The Methodist Conference in America: A History* (Nashville: Abingdon, 1996), 35–39; Jesse Lee, *A Short History of the Methodists, in the United States of America* (Baltimore: Magill and Clime, 1810), 363.

15. Peter Marshall, "Americans in Upper Canada, 1791–1812: "'Late Loyalists' or Early Immigrants," in *Canadian Migration Patterns from Britain and North America,* ed. Barbara Messamore (Ottawa: University of Ottawa Press, 2004), 38; Nancy Christie, "'In These Times of Democratic Rage and Delusion': Popular Religion and the Challenge to the Established Order, 1760–1815," in *The Canadian Protestant Experience, 1760–1990,* ed. George A. Rawlyk (Burlington, Ontario: Welch, 1990), 10–11; Semple, *Lord's Dominion,* 40–43.

16. Phillip Buckner, "Making British North America British, 1815–1860," in *Kith and Kin: Canada, Britain and the United States from the Revolution to the Cold War,* ed. C. C. Eldridge (Cardiff: University of Wales Press, 1997), 17.

17. J. M. Bumsted, "Scots," in *Encyclopedia of Canada's People,* ed. Paul R. Magosci (Toronto: University of Toronto Press, 1999), 1124–27; Bruce S. Elliott, "Irish Protestants," in Magosci, *Encyclopedia of Canada's People,* 766, 775. Wesleyan Methodism was never a strong force in Lowland or Highland Scotland.

18. Bruce S. Elliott, "English," in Magosci, *Encyclopedia of Canada's People,* 469, 470–72, 481–82.

19. Bruce S. Elliott, "Regional Patterns of English Immigration in Upper Canada," in Messamore, *Canadian Migration Patterns,* 58–59, 63, 74; K. D. M. Snell and Paul S. Ell, *Rival Jerusalems: The Geography of Victorian Religion* (Cambridge, U.K.: Cambridge University Press, 2000), 124–26.

20. For the complaints, see Jabez Bunting to Edmund Grindrod, August 10, 1831, John Rylands University Library of Manchester (JRULM), Methodist Archives and Research Centre (MARC), Jabez Bunting papers, MAM PLP 18.14.8; William Squire to Joseph Taylor, September 23, 1830, United Church Archives (hereafter UCA), Wesleyan Methodist Missionary Society Correspondence (WMMC-C), Box 14, File 88, #7.

21. John DePutron to Richard Watson, September 16, 1822 (journal entry for February 27, 1822), UCA, WMMS-C, Box 6, File 48, #38; Anson Green, *The Life and Times of Anson Green, D.D.* (Toronto: Methodist Book Room, 1877), 51–52.

22. James Wilson Papers, Autobiography, 11, UCA.

23. Henry Pope to James Wood, February 11, 1817, UCA, WMMS-C, Box 2, File 27, #5.

24. James Booth to Joseph Taylor, August 4, 1823, UCA, WMMS-C, Box 7, File 52, #25; John Carroll, *Case and His Cotemporaries; or, the Canadian Itinerants' Memorial* (Toronto: Samuel Rose, 1867–77), 3:351, 2:322, 2:365–6; John Borland to Robert Alder, July 7, 1837, UCA, WMMS-C, Box 21, File 137, #15.

25. William Bennett, John Strong, and Richard Williams to James Buckley, July 10, 1816, UCA, WMMS-C, Box 2, File 23, #24; James Booth to Joseph Taylor, November 23, 1819, UCA, WMMS-C Box 3, File 35, #32; James Knowlan to George Morley, February 5, 1826, UCA, WMMS-C, Box 10, File 64, #2.

26. Henry Ruttan et al. to the Secretaries of the WMMS, January 12, 1820, UCA, WMMS-C, Box 4, File 39, #16; Thomas Catterick to the Secretaries of the WMMS, September 10, 1820, UCA, WMMS-C, Box 4, File 39, #29; Leaders and Stewards of Kingston to the Secretaries of the WMMS, May 17, 1841, UCA, WMMS-C, Box 25, File 169, #35.

27. Members of the Montréal Society to the Secretaries of the WMMS, November 11, 1815 (emphasis in original), UCA, WMMS-C, Box 1, File 20, #12; Henry Ruttan et al. to the Secretaries of the WMMS, January 12, 1820, UCA, WMMS-C, Box 4, File 39, #16.

28. This contest to define British identity is discussed in Todd Webb, "How the Canadian Methodists Became British: Unity, Schism, and Transatlantic Identity, 1827–54," in *Transatlantic Subjects: Ideas, Institutions, and Social Experience in Post-Revolutionary British North America,* ed. Nancy Christie (Montréal: McGill-Queen's University Press, 2008), 159–98.

29. For Methodism and the rebellions of 1837–38, see Colin Read, *The Rising in Western Upper Canada, 1837–8: The Duncombe Revolt and After* (Toronto: University of Toronto Press, 1982), 191–92; Todd Webb, "Faiths of '37: Methodism and Anti-Catholicism in Rebellion-Era Canada," *Canadian Society of Church History, Historical Papers* (2009): 105–11.

30. *Christian Guardian,* October 16, 1833, 194 (emphasis in original), May 7, 1834, 103.

31. *Minutes of the Annual Conferences of the Wesleyan-Methodist Church in Canada, from 1824 to 1845, inclusive* (Toronto: Anson Green, 1846), 113, 178; *Minutes of Twelve Annual Conferences of the Wesleyan Methodist Church in Canada, from 1846 to 1857 inclusive* (Toronto: Anson Green, 1863), 76; *Minutes of Several Conversations between the Ministers of the Wesleyan Methodist Church in Canada* (Toronto: Anson Green, 1862), 95.

32. *Minutes of several conversations between the preachers late in connexion with the Rev. Mr. Wesley* (London, 1818), quoted in *History of the Methodist Church,* 4:357 (emphasis in original). See also G. G. Findlay and W. W. Holdsworth, *The History of the Wesleyan Methodist Missionary Society* (London: Epworth Press, 1921–4), 1:73–75, 1:167. In 1841 the Mission House moved from 77 Hatton Garden to the more spacious Centenary Hall at 17 Bishopsgate Street Within, London.

33. Joseph Taylor to Richard Williams, July 6, 1820, UCA, WMMS-C, Outgoing Correspondence.

34. John Beecham to John Berry, April 25, 1834, UCA, WMMS-C, Outgoing Correspondence; Robert Alder to Jabez Bunting, July 17, 1838, JRULM, MARC, Robert Alder papers, MAM PLP 1.36.6; Elijah Hoole to Jabez Bunting, August 18, 1847, JRULM, MARC, Elijah Hoole papers, MAM PLP 55.32.45.

35. Richard Williams to Joseph Taylor, June 16, 1820, UCA, WMMS-C, Box 4, File 39, #22.

36. J. C. Arnell, *Transatlantic Mail to and from British North America from the Early Days to U.P.U.* (Hamilton, Ontario:: J. C. Arnell, 1996), 1, 5.

37. Circulars, Fiche #1986, August 10, 1823, School of Oriental and African Studies (SOAS), Methodist Missionary Society Archives (MMSA), WMMS, Home and General; Robert Alder to Jabez Bunting, September 9, 1839, JRULM, MARC, Robert Alder papers, MAM PLP 1.36.8.

38. John Beecham to Jabez Bunting, December 22, 1832, JRULM, MARC, John Beecham papers, MAM PLP 7.2.4.

39. John DePutron to Joseph Taylor, July 5, 1821, UCA, WMMS-C, Box 5, File 44, #27; William Martin Harvard to Thomas Jackson, August 22, 1837, JRULM, MARC, William Martin Harvard papers, MAM PLP 50.59.35; Robert Alder to Matthew Richey, March 25, 1844, UCA, Matthew Richey papers, Box 1, File 2.

40. James Booth to Joseph Taylor, May 29, 1820 (emphasis in original), UCA, WMMS-C, Box 4, File 39, #18; James Knowlan to Joseph Taylor, August 24, 1822, UCA, WMMS-C, Box 6, File 48, #22; James Knowlan to Joseph Taylor, May 31, 1825, UCA, WMMS-C, Box 9, File 59, #16.

41. Robert Alder to George Morley, June 4, 1827 (emphasis in original), UCA, WMMS-C, Box 11, File 70, #11; William Martin Harvard to Robert Alder, February 13, 1844, UCA, WMMS-C, Box 28, File 194, #4.

42. William Lunn to Robert Alder, October 31, 1834, UCA, WMMS-C, Box 18, File 112, #16; William Lunn to Robert Alder, March 1, 1836, SOAS, MMSA, WMMS, Home and General, Home Correspondence, Fiche #205; John Mathewson to Robert Alder, June 28, 1842, UCA, WMMS-C, Box 26, File 178, #16.

43. Joseph Stinson to Robert Alder, March 2, 1846, UCA, WMMS-C, Box 30, File 216, #11; Egerton Ryerson to Jabez Bunting, December 11, 1844, UCA, Egerton Ryerson papers, Box 3, File 68.

44. William Lunn to Richard Watson, February 3, 1824, UCA, WMMS-C, Box 8, File 56, #3; William Lord to Robert Alder, December 31, 1834 (emphasis in original), UCA, WMMS-C, Box 18, File 119, #11; Benjamin Slight to the Secretaries of the WMMS, October 13, 1848, UCA, WMMS-C, Box 29, File 226, #28.

45. Robert Alder to Matthew Richey, March 25, 1844, UCA, Matthew Richey papers, Box 1, File 2.

46. Arnell, *Transatlantic Mail to and from British North America,* 2–3.

47. Matthew Richey to Robert Alder, March 26, 1846, UCA, WMMS-C, Box 29, File 210, #8; Enoch Wood to John Beecham, May 22, 1854, UCA, WMMS-C, Box 38, File 281, #21; William Scott to Egerton Ryerson, March 13, 1856, UCA, Egerton Ryerson Papers, Box 4, File 110; John Hunt to the Secretaries of the WMMS, July 5, 1865, UCA, WMMS-C, Box 44, File 328, #19.

48. Anson Green to Robert Alder, November 20, 1846, UCA, WMMS-C, Box 30, File 209, #11; Enoch Wood to Elijah Hoole, George Osborn and William Arthur, June 28, 1856, UCA, WMMS-C, Box 40, File 291, #13; Frederick Jobson, *America, and American Methodism* (New York: Virtue, Emmins, 1857), 351–2; Enoch Wood to George Osborn, October 25, 1858, UCA, WMMS-C, Box 40, File 296, #17.

49. Joseph Stinson to William Arthur, March 13, 1859, UCA, WMMS-C, Box 41, File 300, #1; Enoch Wood to Elijah Hoole, [1859], UCA, WMMS-C, Box 41, File 300, #9; Enoch Wood to Elijah Hoole, July 2, 1863, UCA, WMMS-C,Box 43, File 316, #7.

50. Richard W. Vaudry, *Anglicanism and the Atlantic World: High Churchmen, Evangelicals, and the Québec Connection* (Montréal: McGill-Queen's University Press, 2003), 13–38.

51. Donal Lowry, "Ulster Resistance and Loyalist Rebellion in the Empire," in *'An Irish Empire'? Aspects of Ireland and the British Empire,* ed. Keith Jeffery (Manchester, U.K.: Manchester University Press, 1996), 191–209; Pocock, "British History," 628.

Confessional Spaces and Religious Places

Chieko Maene spent many hours creating the maps for this essay, for which I am forever in her debt. Hans-Christoph Rublack and Robert Scribner, each of whom shaped my thought on the Lutheran Reformation, died before this essay found its way into print. The essay and its author suffer from their absence.

1. Martin Luther, "Against the Murderous, Thieving Hordes of Peasants" (1525), available online at *History Guide: Lectures on Modern European History,* http://historyguide.org/earlymod/peasants1525.html ; Peter Blickle, *The Revolution of 1525: The German Peasant's War from a New Perspective,* trans. Thomas A. Brady Jr., and H. C. Erik Middlefort (Baltimore: Johns Hopkins University Press, 1985).

2. John Corrigan, "Qualitative GIS and Emergent Semantics," in *The Spatial Humanities: GIS and the Future of Humanities Scholarship,* ed. David J. Bodenhamer, John Corrigan, and Trevor M. Harris (Bloomington: Indiana University Press, 2010), 76–78.

3. David Blackbourn, "'Conquests from Barbarianism': Taming Nature in Frederick the Great's Prussia," in *Nature in German History,* ed. Christof Mauch (New York: Berghahn, 2004), 10–30.

4. John Gaddis, *The Landscape of History* (New York: Oxford University Press, 2002), 25–29; Bodenhamer, Corrigan, and Harris, *Spatial Humanities,* xi-xiii.

5. Edward Ayers, "Turning toward Place, Space, and Time," and Gary Lock, "Representations of Space and Place in the Humanities," in Bodenhamer, Corrigan, and Harris, *Spatial Humanities,* 1–13, 89–108.

6. Frederick Jackson Turner, *The Frontier in American History* (1920), available online at http://www.gutenberg.org/files/22994/22994-h/22994-h.htm ; Richard White, *The Middle Ground: Indians, Empires, and Republics in the Great Lakes Region, 1650–1815* (New York: Cambridge University Press, 1991); Bernard Bailyn, "A Domesday Book of the Periphery," in *The Peopling of British North America: An Introduction* (New York: Vintage, 1986).

7. Richard White's Middle Ground posits a negotiated cultural amalgam across racial, national, and cultural groups not far north from the geographic space in which Lutherans negotiated across religious, national, and cultural groups. The comparison of racial and religious tension in the eighteen-century middle colonies of Delaware, New York, New Jersey, and Pennsylvania is particularly useful.

8. For a detailed history of the earliest Lutherans in New Sweden, see Israel Acrelius, *A History of New Sweden; or, The settlements on the River Delaware,* trans. and intro. William M. Reynolds (Philadelphia: Historical Society of Pennsylvania, 1874). See also Carol E. Hoffecker, Richard Waldron, Lorraine E. Williams, and Barbara E. Benson, eds., *New Sweden in America* (Newark: University of Delaware Press, 1995).

9. See Susan Karant-Nunn, "The Reality of Early Lutheran Education: The Electoral District of Saxony—a Case Study," *Lutherjahrbuch* 57 (1990): 128–46; Elizabeth Lewis Pardoe, "Education, Economics, and Orthodoxy: Lutheran Schools in Wuerttemberg,

1559–1617," *Archiv fuer Reformationsgeschichte/Archive for Reformation History* 91 (2000): 285–315; Bruce Tolley, *Pastors and Parishioners in Wuerttemberg during the Late Reformation, 1581–1621* (Stanford, Calif.: Stanford University Press, 1995).

10. For more on Kelpius and theosophical beliefs, see Julius Friedrich Sachse, *The German Pietists of Provincial Pennsylvania, 1694–1708* (Philadelphia: Printed for the author, 1895). For Justus Falckner's involvement, see also Julius Sachse, *Justus Falckner: Mystic and Scholar, Devout Pietist in Germany, Hermit on the Wissahickon, Missionary on the Hudson* (Philadelphia: Printed for the author, 1903), 24–37; and Delber Wallace Clark, *The World of Justus Falckner* (Philadelphia: Muhlenberg Press, 1946), 13–17.

11. Julius Sachse does not provide any sources for his claim that "it is said that even a few Quakers and Indians were attracted to the church, and enhanced the picturesqueness of the scene." Sachse, *Justus Falckner,* 64.

12. "IMPRINT / of a MISSIVE / TO Tit: Lord D. henr. Muhlen, / From Germanton in the AMERI / CAN Province of Pennsylvania, otherwise / New Sweden, the First of August, in the Year / of out salvation One Thougsand, seven hundred / and one / CONCERNING THE condition of the CHURCHES / in AMERICA. / MDCCII." Sachse, *Justus Falckner,* 41.

13. Sachse, *Justus Falckner,* 41.

14. Sachse, *Justus Falckner,* 41–42. For more on the nature of pietism see Sachse, *German Pietists of Provincial Pennsylvania,* esp. 49–64.

15. Sachse, *Justus Falckner,* 42–43.

16. Sachse, *Justus Falckner,* 43–44.

17. Sachse, *Justus Falckner,* 44.

18. The irony of seeking quiet and providing loud music seems to have escaped him. Sachse, *Justus Falckner,* 45.

19. Sachse, *Justus Falckner,* 45. The Lutherans had a long tradition of hoping to capture the souls of children and then send them home to reform their parents. See Lewis Pardoe, "Education, Economics, and Orthodoxy."

20. Sachse, *Justus Falckner,* 45–46. For more on Luther's attitudes toward music see Sachiko Kusukawa, *The Transformation of Natural Philosophy: The Case of Philip Melanchton* (Cambridge, U.K.: Cambridge University Press, 1995).

21. Sachse, *Justus Falckner,* 49–71.

22. Sachse, *Justus Falckner,* 78–82.

23. Sachse, *Justus Falckner,* 83–83.

24. Sachse, *Justus Falckner,* 112.

25. For more on tailors as schoolmasters see Karant-Nunn, "Reality of Early Lutheran Education," and Lewis Pardoe, "Education, Economics, and Orthodoxy."

26. See Blickle, *Revolution of 1525.*

27. Sachse, *Justus Falckner,* 113–38. See also Walter Knittle, *The Early Eighteenth Century Palatine Emigration: A British Redemptioner Project to Manufacture Naval Stores* (Philadelphia: Dorrance, 1936).

28. Letter for the Church Council of the Lutheran Church in New York City to the Lutheran Churches in Holland and Elsewhere, New York City, December 11/22, 1723, in *Lutheran Church in New York and New Jersey, 1722–1760: Lutheran Records in the Ministerial Archives of the Staatsarchiv, Hamburg, Germany*, trans. Simon Hart and Harry J. Kreider (Ann Arbor, Mich.: United Lutheran Synod of New York and New England, 1962), 1–2 (hereafter *LCNYNJ*).

29. The Lutheran Consistory at Amsterdam to the Lutheran Ministerium of Hamburg, Amsterdam, March 2, 1724, *LCNYNJ*, 2–3.

30. Minutes of the Lutheran Ministerium of Hamburg, Concerning Candidate Wilhelm C. Berkenmeyer. Meeting held February 9, 1725 and Minutes of the Lutheran Ministerium of Hamburg, Concerning Candidate Wilhelm C. Berkenmeyer, meeting held May 8, 1725, *LCNYNJ*, 5.

31. Berkenmeyer continued: "The barn, however, was filled with fruit during that week, so that on Sunday morning they had no idea where the services were to be held, until they decided to have the services in a Reformed church, which was also a barn." Report, the Reverend Wilhelm C. Berkenmeyer to the Very Reverend Johann Friedrich Winckler, Senior of the Lutheran Ministerium of Hamburg, Loonenburg, N.Y., September 17, 1734, *LCNYNJ*, 56.

32. Petition from the Lutheran Congregations at Albany, The Camp [Germantown], Rhinebeck, Newtown [West Camp], and Tarbush [Manorton], to the City Council of Hamburg, New York City, November 18, 1726. *LCNYNJ*, 7.

33. Articles of the Call for a Pastor from the Elders of the Lutheran Parish at Raritan, New Jersey, to the Lutheran Ministerium of Hamburg. September 13, 1731, *LCNYNJ*, 14–16; Berkenmeyer to Winckler, September 24, 1731, *LCNYNJ*, 17–19.

34. *The Albany Protocol: Wilhelm Christoph Berkenmeyer's Chronicle of Lutheran Affairs in New York Colony, 1731–1750*, trans. Simon Hart and Sibrandina Geertruid Hart-Runeman, ed. John P. Dern (Ann Arbor, Mich., 1971), xxix–xxx.

35. In a letter to the Hamburg ministerium, Berkenmeyer complains that "Michael Schutz (Van Dieren's father-in-law . . . went to London to flood the whole of Europe with letters filled with lies) to call a hellish fanatic with the promise of 40 Pounds in salary and 20 pounds traveling expenses, and to undertake I do not know what kind of begging enterprise." The Reverend Wilhelm C. Berkenmeyer to the Very Reverend Johann Friedrich Winckler, Senior of the Lutheran Ministerium of Hamburg. New York City, November 4–6, 1731, *LCNYNJ*, 21.

36. *Albany Protocol*, 1–22 (manuscript pp. 1–12).

37. *Albany Protocol*, 48–49 (manuscript p. 30), esp. footnote 3.

38. *Albany Protocol*, 60–61 (manuscript pp. 8–39).

39. The niece must have been Daniel Falckner's daughter, which would explain her husband's enmity. *Albany Protocol*, 64–65 (manuscript pp. 42–43).

40. *Albany Protocol*, 66 (manuscript pp. 43).

41. First, he instructed Kurtz to ask Spahler to perform the baptism. Only if Spahler declined would Berkenmeyer conduct the service. When Spahler agreed to baptize the child, Berkenmeyer went to visit him "and told him that living in enmity this way was the work of Satan, who would break up our congregations because of it." Spahler declined the peace offering, which was conditional upon his acceptance of "fraternal relations" with Knoll. Berkenmeyer concluded that Spahler was "an obstinate man, a man who thinks himself wiser than all the rest of the people in the world, since he said that he could see as much with two eyes as another could with four." When one of his parishioners forced Spahler to visit Berkenmeyer at home two months later, Spahler began by trading insults with Berkenmeyer and his wife. Berkenmeyer seemed offended that Spahler intended to "request the Governor of Bermuda to give him a Negro." After two glasses of wine and a declined invitation to spend the night, Berkenmeyer began to discuss church

constitutions. Spahler "jumped up" and threatened to leave "more than ten times" during the conversation. At last, when a neighbor entered, Spahler "dashed out of the room and jumped into the canoe without saying goodbye." However, "he shouted back that he had absolutely no desire to make peace in the presence of [his] Church Council or to accept the [Amsterdam] constitution." *Albany Protocol,* 74 (manuscript p. 48), 75–76 (manuscript p. 49).

42. Letter to the Church Councils of the Germans at East Camp, Tarbush, Rhinebeck, and Beekmans Mills and to Magister Spahler, May 23, 1734, in *Albany Protocol,* 78–82 (manuscript pp. 51–52).

43. *Albany Protocol,* 85 (manuscript p. 55).

44. "He told me about the above mentioned Hoyer and his circumstances, stating that years ago he had run off with the wife of a man in Norway, who was still living and wanted to have her back, and that he [the husband] had written letters to Hoyer several times about this." The Reverend Michael Knoll to the Reverend Wilhelm C. Berkenmeyer. Hackensack, N.J., February 25, 1733, *LCNYNJ,* 28.

45. "You have been a genuine Benoni and son of pain to both your dear sainted parents, who have shed innumberable tears over you, so that you certainly have reasons to be in tears day and night and pray to God to forgive you for this grievous sin, to repent in sackcloth and ashes and to live your whole life in true repentance, keeping in mind that even if one should escape the judgment of worldly courts, he cannot escape the divine, which is always awaiting one who does not truly repent." The Reverend Andreas E. Elers to Erich Hoyer of Hackensack, N.J., Rendsburg in Holstein, Denmark, January 20, 1732, *LCNYNJ,* 23.

46. The Reverend Michael C. Knoll to the Reverend Wilhelm C. Berkenmeyer, Hackensack, N.J., February 25, 1733, *LCNYNJ,* 28.

47. Knoll to Berkenmeyer, February 25, 1733, *LCNYNJ,* 29–30.

48. Thomas Robisheaux, *Rural Society and the Search for Order in Early Modern Germany* (Cambridge, U.K.: Cambridge University Press, 1989), 96–98.

49. Robisheaux, *Rural Society and the Search for Order,* 95–146.

50. *LCNYNJ,* 43.

51. *LCNYNJ,* 29; the Rev. Michael C. Knoll to the Reverend Wilhelm C. Berkenmeyer. Hackensack, N.J., April 29, 1733, 36. In Europe the Lutheran church learned early on that "marital discipline" was a form of moral regulation that parishioners welcomed, precisely because it helped settle internecine disputes over inheritance. In Hoyer's case, Knoll was confident that he had indeed committed adultery because his family had left his deceased father's estate intact instead of having to yield Hoyer's portion to the Crown. However, Berkenmeyer wondered whether the relatives had concocted the story of Hoyer's adultery as a way of keeping his inheritance. Hoyer's children's status as illegitimate would in turn ensure that they could never place a claim on the inheritance either. For German practice, see Robisheaux, *Rural Society and the Search for Order,* 95–146.

52. *LCNYNJ,* 34.

53. *LCNYNJ,* 35.

54. *LCNYNJ,* 35–36.

55. Simensen's relationship to Catharina's sister is mysterious. Simensen finally had gotten the divorce from Catharina because he "wanted to marry a widow." Given that the sister had forced the marriage on Catharina and inherited the entirety of Simensen's

estate, one surmises that she was the widow Simensen wished to marry. The Reverend Michael C. Knoll to the Very Reverend Johann Friedrich Winckler, Senior, of the Lutheran ministerium of Hamburg, New York City, November 25, 1733, *LCNYNJ*, 44.

56. Knoll to Winckler, November 25, 1733, *LCNYNJ*, 45.

57. The Lutheran Ministerium of Hamburg to the Reverend Michael C. Knoll and his Church Council at Hackensack, N.J., Hamburg, May 7, 1734, *LCNYNJ*, 47–49.

58. The Lutheran Ministerium of Hamburg to the Reverend Michael C. Knoll. Hamburg, May 7, 1734 *LCNYNJ*, 49–50.

59. *Albany Protocol*, 103 (manuscript p. 59).

60. *Albany Protocol*, 114 (manuscript p. 67). This was not the only illegitimate child in Berkenmeyer's parish. In 1737 Samuel Bekman, the lay reader and schoolmaster in Loonenburg, ran off with the daughter of Jan Van Loon by whom he fathered at least the first of her two illegitimate children (*Albany Protocol*, 218 [manuscript p. 141]). One of Van Loon's other daughter's wished to marry Beckman's successor, but the Church Council first had to suffer through a prolonged investigation of how his first marriage had come to an end (*Albany Protocol*, 232–51 [manuscript pp. 152–68]). Berkenmeyer himself was accused and acquitted of fathering the illegitimate child of his biracial housemaid (*Albany Protocol*, 439–64 [manuscript pp. 320–46]). Berkenmeyer also baptized illegitimate children, to whom Van Dieren refused to give the sacrament (*Albany Protocol*, 188–190 [manuscript pp. 117–19]).

61. *Albany Protocol*, 112–13 (manuscript pp. 66).

62. *Albany Protocol*, 114–15 (manuscript pp. 67).

63. *Albany Protocol*, 115–16 (manuscript pp. 67–68).

64. Berkenmeyer's evidence for her good conduct is rather interesting: "As an example of this, it can be noted among other things that although she was separated from her previous husband for seven years and both parties could hardly state any reasons for it other than that they did not like to run after and seek each other, upon the very first admonition from her pastor she nevertheless joined her husband again and lived with him in peace until his death." Berkenmeyer does not note how long after this supposedly peaceful reconciliation her husband departed this life. In any case, it would seem Christina had her own experience of a bad marriage and would have been sympathetic to Lucas's plight. *Albany Protocol*, 119 (manucript p. 69).

65. *Albany Protocol*, 117–19 (manucript pp. 68–69).

66. *Albany Protocol*, 118–27 (manucript pp. 69–72). Christina refused to leave Lucas and was indeed excommunicated. However, she repented and rejoined the Lutheran Church after his death. *Albany Protocol*, 210–11.

67. Henry Melchior Muhlenberg, *The Journals of Henry Melchior Muhlenberg*, vol. 1, trans. Theodore G. Tappert and John W. Doberstein (Philadelphia: University of Pennsylvania Press, 1942), 107. Hereafter cited as Muhlenberg 1, followed by page numbers.

68. *LCNYNJ*, 96.

69. According to Muhlenberg, Berkenmeyer only resented his efforts. "Now that the business had come to an end, Mr. Berkenmeyer began to storm out against us in a long letter in which he cries and laughs and groans, and calumniates and slanders and reviles, and threatens to enter a complaints against me before the Reverend Consistory of Hamburg." Muhlenberg 1:108.

70. *Albany Protocol*, 164 (manuscript p. 100).

71. *Albany Protocol*, 247.

72. Muhlenberg 1:75–80; Beverly Prior Smaby, *The Transformation of Moravian Bethlehem: From Communal Mission to Family Economy* (Philadelphia: University of Pennsylvania Press, 1988), 3–9.

73. Muhlenberg 1:66–67.

74. Muhlenberg 1:68.

75. Tranberg had first served in the Swedish congregations in New Jersey but asked to be moved to the Christina church as he and his children grew older and desired a more cultivated environment. Having left the rural parishes open, the Swedish Lutherans soon found themselves under attack from the Moravians, who provided Swedish-speaking preachers to fill their empty pulpits. Acrelius, *History of New Sweden*, 327–33.

76. Muhlenberg had refused to help Kraft ordain "a worthless schoolmaster" and warned Kraft to stop the practice. Official Lutheran practice required a panel of three ordained ministers to examine and ordain students. Muhlenberg 1:69, 74–75.

77. Muhlenberg 1:75–76. For more on the widespread violence of the Moravian-Lutheran conflict see Aaron Fogelman, Jesus Is Female: Moravians and Radical Religion in Early America (Philadelphia: University of Pennsylvania Press, 2008).

78. Muhlenberg 1:76–77. These synods include the one Conrad Weiser attended. See Elizabeth Lewis Pardoe, "The Many Worlds of Conrad Weiser: Mystic Diplomat," *Explorations in Early American Culture* 4 (2000): 113–47.

79. Muhlenberg I:80–82. Muhlenberg's success was by no means a foregone conclusion. When Zinzendorf labeled Muhlenberg an "arch-pietist," he leveled a serious charge, one Muhlenberg could not easily deny. Muhlenberg trained under August Francke at the Prussian University of Halle, arguably the greatest pietist university and ministerial project in eighteenth-century Germany. There he absorbed the premise that theological learning without personal piety and moral behavior meant nothing. Muhlenberg lived according to these principles and passed them on to his students in the orphans' school at Halle as well as to his later congregations. Because he was a pietist, orthodox principalities prohibited Muhlenberg from preaching and drove him from villages in much the same way that he would later dispatch Moravians.

The Moravians' forefathers, the Bohemian Brethren, predated the Lutheran Reformation. The Brethren's fifteenth-century leader, Jan Hus, adhered to the reforming theology of England's John Wycliffe. Hus died at the stake as a heretic, and a full blown Hussite revolution failed. However, Bohemia did not return to orthodox Catholicism until 1620, when Catholics defeated Protestants at the Battle of White Mountain at the beginning of the Thirty Years War. Starting in 1722 Count Zinzendorf offered protection to those few remaining Protestants from Bohemia and Moravia who had survived secretly in the mountainous borderlands. Zinzendorf considered himself a Lutheran pietist, although he had also studied with French Catholics. In 1737 Zinzendorf became the second bishop in the revitalized Moravian church. Zinzendorf's actions caused all pietists to be impugned as Moravians by orthodox Lutherans. Pietists, in turn, felt an urgent need to criticize Moravians as a means of underlining their own Lutheranism. Muhlenberg 1:12–14, 69, 80–82, 84–85; Smaby, *Transformation of Moravian Bethlehem*, 3–9.

80. Muhlenberg 1:87, 94–95. For more on what the author calls Muhlenberg's "bricks and mortar" ministry, see A. G. Roeber, *Palatines, Liberty, and Property: German Lutherans in Colonial America* (Baltimore: Johns Hopkins University Press, 1993).

81. Muhlenberg was accused of keeping whores in Philadelphia, but the woman who brought the charges publicly retracted them. Muhlenberg 1:96–97.

82. Muhlenberg wrote Halle: "While all this was still in progress, the Moravian preacher, Pyrlaeus, presented his *complaints,* saying that it was not at all right for him [Weiser] to give his daughter to me for his child could have done much better amongst them. *Caetera transeant.* The whole affair was the occasion of talk and gossiping, pro and con, throughout the country. But our congregations are very well satisfied and they extend to my wife many proofs of love and regard." Muhlenberg 1:103.

83. Muhlenberg 1:104–5.

84. Muhlenberg 1:105–11.

85. Muhlenberg 1:111–15.

86. Muhlenberg 1:115, 140–42, 149–66, 199–201.

87. Muhlenberg 1:154, 185.

88. Muhlenberg 1:167.

89. Muhlenberg 1:202–2; *Documentary History of the Evangelical Lutheran Ministerium of Pennsylvania and Adjacent States Proceedings of the Annual Conventions from 1848 to 1821* (Philadelphia: General Council of the Evangelical Lutheran Church in North America, 1898), 3–8.

Confessional Spatiality in the Puritan Atlantic

1. Parts of the argument here have appeared in somewhat different form in the introduction and chapters 3 and 5 of my book *Faithful Bodies: Performing Religion and Race in the Puritan Atlantic* (New York: New York University Press, 2014).

2. Michael Wigglesworth, *The Day of Doom: Or, a Poetical Description of the Great and Last Judgment,* [2nd] ed. (Cambridge, Mass., 1666). *Day of Doom* was first published in 1662, but no copies of that edition have survived.

3. Michael Wigglesworth and Edward Wigglesworth, Notebook, in Wigglesworth Papers (R. Stanton Avery Manuscript Collection, New England Historic Genealogical Society, Boston, Mass.: 1658–1794).

4. On puritanism in Bermuda, see Gregory Edwin Shipley, "Turbulent Times, Troubled Isles: The Rise and Development of Puritanism in Bermuda and the Bahamas, 1609–1684" (Th.D. diss., Westminster Theological Seminary, 1989), 93, 288–89, 300–301; Michael J. Jarvis, "'In the Eye of All Trade': Maritime Revolution and the Transformation of Bermudian Society, 1612–1800" (Ph.D. diss., College of William and Mary, 1998), 4, 93–94, 236; Babette M. Levy, "Early Puritanism in the Southern and Island Colonies," *Proceedings of the American Antiquarian Society* 70 (1960): 69–348; Louise Timko, "Puritans in Bermuda, 1612–1650" (Ph.D. diss., Drew University, 1996); Charles McLean Andrews, *The Colonial Period of American History,* vol. 1 (London: Oxford University Press, 1934), 214–35; Alison Games, *Migration and the Origins of the English Atlantic World* (Cambridge, Mass.: Harvard University Press, 1999), 56–60, 132–38.

5. Joseph Roach, *Cities of the Dead: Circum-Atlantic Performance* (New York: Columbia University Press, 1996); David Hall, *Lived Religion in America: Toward a History of Practice* (Princeton, N.J.: Princeton University Press, 1997); Diana Taylor, *The Archive and the Repertoire: Performing Cultural Memory in the Americas* (Durham, N.C.: Duke University Press, 2003); Maaike de Haardt and Anne-Marie Korte, introduction, *Common Bodies: Everyday Practices, Gender and Religion,* ed. de Haardt and Korte (Münster,

Germany: Lit, 2002), 1–10. Andreas Reckwitz, "Toward a Theory of Social Practices: A Development in Culturalist Theorizing," *European Journal of Social Theory* 5, no. 2 (2001): 243–63, allows for more individual action than Pierre Bourdieu's encompassing cultural system of the "habitus" in *Outline of a Theory of Practice* (New York: Cambridge University Press, 1977). Michel de Certeau, *The Practice of Everyday Life* (Berkeley: University of California Press, 1984), articulated how daily or near-daily actions encode and create religious meaning.

6. Owen Stanwood, "The Protestant Moment: Antipopery, the Revolution of 1688–1689, and the Making of an Anglo-American Empire," *Journal of British Studies* 46, no. 3 (2007): 483n8; Mark A. Peterson, "*Theopolis Americana:* The City-State of Boston, the Republic of Letters, and the Protestant International, 1689–1739," in *Soundings in Atlantic History: Latent Structures and Intellectual Currents, 1500–1830*, ed. Bernard Bailyn and Patricia L. Denault (Cambridge, Mass.: Harvard University Press, 2009).

7. On trans- and circum-Atlantic connections of dissenting Protestants of many types, including Puritans, Quakers, and Huguenots, see Charles Hambrick-Stowe, *The Practice of Piety: Puritan Devotional Disciplines in Seventeenth-Century New England* (Chapel Hill: University of North Carolina Press, 1982); Francis J. Bremer, *Congregational Communion: Clerical Friendship in the Anglo-American Puritan Community, 1610–1692* (Boston: Northeastern University Press, 1994); Frederick B. Tolles, *Quakers and the Atlantic Culture* (New York: Macmillan, 1960); Phyllis Mack, *Visionary Women: Ecstatic Prophecy in Seventeenth-Century England* (Berkeley: University of California Press, 1992); and Andrew R. Murphy, *Conscience and Community: Revisiting Toleration and Religious Dissent in Early Modern England and America* (University Park: Pennsylvania State University Press, 2001).

8. Patrick Collinson's "hotter sort of protestant," denoting an intense and loudly voiced commitment to further reforms away from Catholic practice, emphasizes the existence of a spectrum of practice, as well as connections outside of England to the like-minded Dutch. See Collinson, *The Elizabethan Puritan Movement* (Berkeley: University of California Press, 1967), esp. 22–28.

9. On the specific influences of a Puritan worldview, see Charles Cohen, *God's Caress: The Psychology of Puritan Religious Experience* (Oxford, U.K.: Oxford University Press, 1986); and Robert Middlekauff, *The Mathers: Three Generations of Puritan Intellectuals, 1596–1728* (New York: Oxford University Press, 1971). Cornelia Hughes Dayton has argued that for most of the seventeenth century, colonists in New Haven and Connecticut attempted to enact a "Godfearing society" in all aspects of life, including the court system. See Dayton, *Women before the Bar: Gender, Law, and Society in Connecticut, 1629–1789* (Chapel Hill: University of North Carolina Press, 1995). More recently, see Martha Finch, *Dissenting Bodies: Corporealities in Early New England* (New York: Columbia University Press, 2010).

10. Karen Ordahl Kupperman, *Providence Island, 1630–1641: The Other Puritan Colony* (Cambridge: Cambridge University Press, 1993); Levy, "Early Puritanism in the Southern and Island Colonies"; Faren Siminoff, *Crossing the Sound: The Rise of Atlantic American Communities in Seventeenth-Century Eastern Long Island* (New York: New York University Press, 2004); Michael Jarvis, "Maritime Masters and Seafaring Slaves in Bermuda, 1680–1783," *William and Mary Quarterly* 59, no. 3 (2002): 590.

11. On the scholarly tendency to reduce the religious life of non-Europeans to something imaginary, see Kenneth M. Morrison, *The Solidarity of Kin: Ethnohistory, Religious*

Studies, and the Algonkian-French Religious Encounter (Albany: State University of New York Press, 2002), 20–35.

12. When discussing the English specifically—and to streamline syntax—I follow Karen Kupperman's and Michael Winship's adoption of Collinson's lowercase puritan, signaling the inclusion of a variety of fluctuating beliefs and practices while acknowledging their relatedness. See Kupperman, *Providence Island,* xiii; and Michael P. Winship, *Making Heretics: Militant Protestantism and Free Grace in Massachusetts, 1636–1641* (Princeton, N.J.: Princeton University Press, 2002).

13. Carla Gardina Pestana, *Quakers and Baptists in Colonial Massachusetts* (New York: Cambridge University Press, 1991).

14. J. William Frost, "Quaker Versus Baptist: A Religious and Political Squabble in Rhode Island Three Hundred Years Ago," *Quaker History* 63 (1974): 39–52; Sydney V. James and Theodore Dwight Bozeman, *John Clarke and His Legacies: Religion and Law in Colonial Rhode Island, 1638–1750* (University Park: Pennsylvania State University Press, 1999).

15. Mark A. Peterson, "The Practice of Piety in Puritan New England: Contexts and Consequences," in *The World of John Winthrop: Essays on England and New England, 1588–1649,* ed. Francis J. Bremer and L. A. Botelho (Boston and Charlottesville: Massachusetts Historical Society; Distributed by the University of Virginia Press, 2005), 81.

16. For southern Algonquian life and culture in the century before extended English settlement and through the early decades of sustained contact, see Kathleen Bragdon, *Native People of Southern New England, 1500–1650* (Norman: University of Oklahoma Press, 1996).

17. Sydney V. James, *Colonial Rhode Island: A History* (New York: Charles Scribner's Sons, 1975), 59–64; Jenny Hale Pulsipher, *Subjects unto the Same King: Indians, English, and the Contest for Authority in Colonial New England* (Philadelphia: University of Pennsylvania Press, 2005), 28–29, 37–69.

18. John Hutchins Cady, *Rhode Island Boundaries, 1636–1936* (Providence: Rhode Island Tercentenary Commission, 1936), 5–13.

19. Michael Jarvis, *In the Eye of All Trade: Bermuda, Bermudians, and the Maritime Atlantic World, 1680–1783* (Chapel Hill: University of North Carolina Press, 2010); Kopelson, *Faithful Bodies,* chaps. 8–11. Helpful syntheses of the vast literature on the demography of the slave trade include David Eltis and David Richardson, eds., *Extending the Frontiers: Essays on the New Transatlantic Slave Trade Database* (New Haven, Conn.: Yale University Press, 2008); and Paul Lovejy, "Trans-Atlantic Transformations: Origins and Identity of Africans in the Americas," in *The Atlantic World: Essays on Slavery, Migration, and Imagination,* ed. Wim Klooster and Alfred Padula (Upper Saddle River, N.J.: Pearson/Prentice Hall, 2005), 126–46.

20. Stanwood, *The Empire Reformed: English America in the Age of the Glorious Revolution* (Philadelphia: University of Pennsylvania Press, 2011).

21. T. Dwight Bozeman, *To Live Ancient Lives: The Primitivist Dimension in Puritanism* (Chapel Hill: University of North Carolina Press, 1988); Avihu Zakai, *Exile and Kingdom: History and Apocalypse in the Puritan Migration to America* (Cambridge, U.K.: Cambridge University Press, 1992); Katharine R. Firth, *The Apocalyptic Tradition in Reformation Britain, 1530–1645* (Oxford, U.K.: Oxford University Press, 1979).

22. John Russell Bartlett, ed., *Records of the Colony of Rhode Island and Providence Plantations in New England* (Providence, R.I.: A. Crawford Greene and Brother, 1857),

1:474; Joshua Micah Marshall, "Settling Down: Labor, Violence and Land Exchange in the Anglo-Indian Settlement Society of Seventeenth-Century New England, 1630–1692" (Ph.D. diss., Brown University, 2003), 41; Lynn Ceci, "Native Wampum as a Peripheral Resource in the Seventeenth-Century World System," in *The Pequots in Southern New England: The Fall and Rise of an American Indian Nation,* ed. Laurence M. Hauptman and James D. Wherry (Norman: University of Oklahoma Press, 1990), 48–63; Marshall Becker, "Wampum Use in Southern New England: The Paradox of Bead Production without the Use of Political Belts," in *Nantucket and Other Native Places: The Legacy of Elizabeth Alden Little,* ed. Elizabeth S. Chilton and Mary Lynne Rainey (Binghamton: State University of New York Press, 2010), 137–58.

23. Colin Calloway, ed., *After King Philip's War: Presence and Persistence in Indian New England* (Hanover, N.H.: University Press of New England, 1997); Jean O'Brien, *Dispossession by Degrees: Indian Land and Identity in Natick, Massachusetts, 1650–1790* (New York: Cambridge University Press, 1997); Ann Marie Plane, *Colonial Intimacies: Indian Marriage in Early New England* (Ithaca, N.Y.: Cornell University Press, 2000); Daniel Mandell, *Tribe, Race, History: Native Americans in Southern New England, 1780–1880* (Baltimore: Johns Hopkins University Press, 2008); Bragdon, *Native People of Southern New England, 1650–1775;* Christine DeLucia, "The Memory Frontier: Uncommon Pursuits of Past and Place in the Northeast after King Philip's War," *Journal of American History* 98, no. 4 (2012): 975–97.

24. John J. McCusker and Russell R. Menard, chap. 5, *The Economy of British America, 1607–1789* (Chapel Hill: University of North Carolina Press, 1985); Richard S. Dunn, *Sugar and Slaves: The Rise of the Planter Class in the English West Indies, 1624–1713* (Chapel Hill: University of North Carolina Press, 1972). On Africans in New England more generally, see Lorenzo Johnston Greene, *The Negro in Colonial New England, 1620–1776* (Port Washington, N.Y.: Kennikat Press, 1966); Robert C. Twombly and Robert H. Moore, "Black Puritan: The Negro in Seventeenth-Century Massachusetts," *William and Mary Quarterly* 24, no. 1 (1967); Ira Berlin, chap. 2, *Many Thousands Gone: The First Two Centuries of Slavery in North America* (Cambridge, Mass.: Harvard University Press, 1998); Dinah Mayo-Bobee, "Servile Discontents: Slavery and Resistance in Colonial New Hampshire, 1645–1785," *Slavery and Abolition* 30, no. 3 (2009): 339–60; Wendy Anne Warren, "'The Cause of Her Grief': The Rape of a Slave in Early New England," *Journal of American History* 93, no. 4 (2007): 1031–49.

25. Jarvis, *In the Eye of All Trade,* 102–9, 145–56.

26. James, *Colonial Metamorphoses,* 159; John A. Sainsbury, "Indian Labor in Early Rhode Island," *New England Quarterly* 48, no. 3 (1975): 378–93; Margaret Newell, "The Changing Nature of Indian Slavery in New England, 1670–1720," in *Reinterpreting New England Indians and the Colonial Experience,* ed. Colin G. Calloway and Neal Salisbury (Boston: Colonial Society of Massachusetts, 2003), 106–36; Ruth Herndon and Ella Wilcox Sekatau, "Pauper Apprenticeship in Narragansett Country: A Different Name for Slavery in Early New England," in *Slavery/Antislavery in New England,* ed. Peter Benes and Jane Montague Benes, Dublin Seminar for New England Folklife Annual Proceedings (Boston: Boston University, 2003); Marshall, "Settling Down"; Jay Coughtry, *The Notorious Triangle: Rhode Island and the African Slave Trade, 1700–1807* (Philadelphia: Temple University Press, 1981).

27. On shifts within Puritanism, see Mark Valeri, *Heavenly Merchandize: How Religion Shaped Commerce in Puritan America* (Princeton, N.J.: Princeton University Press,

2010). For a detailed study of this process in Connecticut, see Dayton, *Women Before the Bar,* 8, 10. On the increasing power of common law and professional lawyers, see Martha J. McNamara, *From Tavern to Courthouse: Architecture and Ritual in American Law, 1658–1860* (Baltimore: Johns Hopkins University Press, 2004); and Mary Sarah Bilder, *The Transatlantic Constitution: Colonial Legal Culture and the Empire* (Cambridge, Mass.: Harvard University Press, 2004).

28. An older article that surveys the Crown's proceedings against colonial charters, with a particular focus on Massachusetts and Bermuda, is Philip Haffenden, "The Crown and the Colonial Charters, 1675–1688: Part I," *William and Mary Quarterly* 15, no. 3 (1958): 297–311.

29. Lisa Brooks, *The Common Pot: The Recovery of Native Space in the Northeast* (Minneapolis: University of Minnesota Press, 2008), 3–8; Stephanie Fitzgerald, "'I Wunnatuckquannum, This Is My Hand': Native Performance in Massachusett Language Land Deeds," in *Native Acts: Indian Performance, 1603–1832,* ed. Laura Mielke and Joshua Bellin (Lincoln: University of Nebraska Press, 2011), 145–67.

30. Pulsipher, *Subjects Unto the Same King;* Daniel Richter, *Facing East from Indian Country: A Native History of Early America* (Cambridge, Mass.: Harvard University Press, 2001).

31. James David Drake, *King Philip's War: Civil War in New England, 1675–1676* (Amherst: University of Massachusetts Press, 1999), 80, 119–20.

32. The concept of identity has appeared in increasing numbers of scholarly articles published in history, literature, and postcolonial studies during the past twenty-five years; see Frederick Cooper, *Colonialism in Question: Theory, Knowledge, History* (Berkeley: University of California Press, 2005), 8, and chap. 3, "Identity," cowritten with Rogers Brubaker.

33. On skin color and changing markers of human difference generally, see Lisa Lampert, "Race, Periodicity, and the (Neo-) Middle Ages," *Modern Language Quarterly* 65, no. 3 (2004): 391–421; and Valentin Groebner, "*Complexio*/Complexion: Categorizing Individual Natures, 1250–1600," in *The Moral Authority of Nature,* ed. Lorraine Daston and Fernando Vidal (Chicago: University of Chicago Press, 2004), 359–83. For only a brief sampling of more recent scholarship on the competing explanations for human difference and the meaning of race as a cultural construct in the seventeenth and eighteenth centuries, see Joyce Chaplin, *Subject Matter: Technology, the Body, and Science on the Anglo-American Frontier* (Cambridge: Harvard University Press, 2001); Colin Kidd, *The Forging of Races: Race and Scripture in the Protestant Atlantic World, 1600–2000* (New York: Cambridge University Press, 2006); James H. Sweet, "Mistaken Identities? Olaudah Equiano, Domingos Álvares, and the Methodological Challenges of Studying the African Diaspora," *American Historical Review* 114, no. 2 (2009): 279–306; Franklin Knight, introduction, *Assumed Identities: The Meanings of Race in the Atlantic World,* ed. John D. Garrigus, Christopher Morris, and Franklin W. Knight (College Station: Texas A&M University Press, 2010), 1–18; and Rebecca Goetz, *The Baptism of Early Virginia: How Christianity Created Race* (Baltimore: Johns Hopkins University Press, 2012).

34. Kathleen Wilson, introduction, *The Island Race: Englishness, Empire, and Gender in the Eighteenth Century* (New York: Routledge, 2003); Roxann Wheeler, *The Complexion of Race: Categories of Difference in Eighteenth-Century British Culture* (Philadelphia: University of Pennsylvania Press, 2000) .

35. Stephen Greenblatt, "Mutilation and Meaning," in *The Body in Parts: Fantasies of Corporeality in Early Modern Europe,* ed. David Hillman and Carla Mazzio (New York: Routledge, 1997), 221–41.

36. See, for example, Kathleen Brown, *Foul Bodies: Cleanliness in Early America* (New Haven, Conn.: Yale University Press, 2009); and Finch, *Dissenting Bodies.*

37. Karen Ordahl Kupperman, *Indians and English: Facing Off in Early America* (Ithaca, N.Y.: Cornell University Press, 2000), 15, cautions against reading hard racial lines back into a period when they did not exist. See also Ania Loomba, *Shakespeare, Race, and Colonialism* (Oxford, U.K.: Oxford University Press, 2002), 4–7; and Dennis Britton, *Becoming Christian: Race, Reformation, and Early Modern English Romance* (New York: Fordham University Press, 2014).

38. In *Forging of Races,* Colin Kidd terms this body of learning "ethnic theology." On the links between the origins of people, providential reasoning, and the justification of European empires, see Alfred A. Cave, "Canaanites in a Promised Land: The American Indian and the Providential Theory of Empire," *American Indian Quarterly* 12, no. 4 (1988): 277–97; and Gordon M. Sayre, "Prehistoric Diasporas: Colonial Theories of the Origins of Native American Peoples," in *Writing Race across the Atlantic World: Medieval to Modern,* ed. Philip D. Beidler and Gary Taylor (New York: Palgrave Macmillan, 2005), 51–75.

39. Puritan settlement of New England was not driven by a desire to bring on the millennium. Puritans wished to create a new society based on pure biblical precedent, a precedent that in England and elsewhere in Europe had been distorted by centuries of human-inspired change; see T. Dwight Bozeman, *To Live Ancient Lives: The Primitivist Strain in Puritanism* (Chapel Hill: University of North Carolina Press, 1988). For John Eliot's belief that Natives had Jewish origins, see, for example, Kristina Bross, *Dry Bones and Indian Sermons: Praying Indians in Colonial America* (Ithaca, N.Y.: Cornell University Press, 2004), 48–49. However, the notion of Natives as one of the Lost Tribes persisted into the nineteenth century, rather than perishing by 1660 as Bross would have it. See Daniel Mandell's review of Bross, *Journal of Colonialism and Colonial History* 5, no. 3 (2004), Project MUSE, doi:10.1353/cch.2004.0079; and Richard W. Cogley, *John Eliot's Mission to the Indians before King Philip's War* (Cambridge, Mass.: Harvard University Press, 1999), 12–18, 76–104, and "The Ancestry of the American Indians: Thomas Thorowgood's *Iewes in America* (1650) and *Jews in America* (1660)," *English Literary Renaissance* 35, no. 2 (2005): 304–30.

40. Peter Lake and Michael C. Questier, *The Anti-Christ's Lewd Hat: Protestants, Papists and Players in Post-Reformation England* (New Haven, Conn.: Yale University Press, 2002).

41. On the Huguenot diaspora, see Neil Kamil, *Fortress of the Soul: Violence, Metaphysics, and Material Life in the Huguenots' New World, 1517–1751* (Baltimore: Johns Hopkins University Press, 2005); Bertrand van Ruymbeke, *From New Babylon to Eden: The Huguenots and Their Migration to Colonial South Carolina* (Columbia: University of South Carolina Press, 2006); Bertrand van Ruymbeke and Randy J. Sparks, eds., *Memory and Identity: The Huguenots in France and the Atlantic Diaspora* (Columbia: University of South Carolina Press, 2003); and Keith Luria, *Sacred Boundaries: Religious Coexistence and Conflict in Early Modern France* (Washington, D.C.: Catholic University of America Press, 2005).

42. On the role of anti-Catholicism in the Glorious Revolution, see Stanwood, *Empire Reformed.*

43. For the central role of religious categories in developing ideas about race as inherited characteristics linked to skin color in Virginia, see Goetz, *Baptism of Early Virginia.* Her inclusion of Bermuda as a similar example relies primarily on incomplete printed records; see Kopelson, *Faithful Bodies.*

44. Caroline Walker Bynum, *The Resurrection of the Body in Western Christianity, 200–1336* (New York: Columbia University Press, 1995); Jonneke Bekkenkamp and Maaike de Haardt, eds., *Begin with the Body: Corporeality, Religion and Gender* (Leuven, Belgium: Peeters, 1998); Haardt and Korte, *Common Bodies;* Janet Moore Lindman and Michele Lise Tarter, introduction, *A Centre of Wonders: The Body in Early America,* ed. Lindman and Tarter (Ithaca, N.Y.: Cornell University Press, 2001); Nancy Shoemaker, *A Strange Likeness: Becoming Red and White in Eighteenth-Century North America* (New York: Oxford University Press, 2004), 3–4; Finch, *Dissenting Bodies,* 29–46.

45. Laura Gowing, *Common Bodies: Women, Touch and Power in Seventeenth-Century England* (New Haven, Conn.: Yale University Press, 2003).

46. Richard Bauman, *Let Your Words Be Few: Symbolism of Speaking and Silence among Seventeenth-Century Quakers* (Cambridge, U.K.: Cambridge University Press, 1983), 24, 27; Michele Lise Tarter, "Sites of Performance: Theorizing the History of Sexuality in the Lives and Writings of Quaker Women, 1650–1800" (Ph.D. diss., University of Colorado at Boulder, 1993), 33.

47. "Appendix to the Letter; Containing Advice more Practical," in *A Letter from some aged nonconforming ministers, to their Christian friends, touching the reasons of their practice. August 24. 1701. Third edition corrected and enlarged* (London, 1704), 60; Shoemaker, *Strange Likeness,* 126.

48. MS 344 (John Penington Miss., 4), Friends' Library, 59, 111, cited in Krista J. Kesselring, "Gender, the Hat, and Quaker Universalism in the Wake of the English Revolution," *Seventeenth Century* 26, no. 2 (2011): 314.

49. Kesselring, "Gender, the Hat, and Quaker Universalism," 312; Mack, *Visionary Women,* esp. 285, 292; Elaine Hobby, "Handmaids of the Lord and Mothers in Israel: Early Vindications of Quaker Women's Prophecy," *Prose Studies* 17, no. 3 (1994): 91; Larry Ingle, "A Quaker Woman on Women's Roles: Mary Penington to Friends, 1678," *Signs* 16, no. 3 (1991): 593.

50. John Calvin, *Institutes of the Christian Religion,* ed. John T. McNeill, Library of Christian Classics (Philadelphia: Westminster Press, 1960), book 4, chap. 12, sec. 1; Stephen M. Johnson, "'The Sinews of the Body of Christ': Calvin's Concept of Church Discipline," *Westminster Theological Journal* 59, no. 1 (1997): 87–100.

51. E. Brooks Holifield, *The Covenant Sealed: The Development of Puritan Sacramental Theology in Old and New England, 1520–1720* (New Haven, Conn.: Yale University Press, 1974), 193–94.

52. John Winthrop, "A Modell of Christian Charity (1630)," in *Winthrop Papers* (Boston: Massachusetts Historical Society, 1931), 288–89.

53. Winthrop, like Fox in the following paragraph, was quoting Ephesians 4:16.

54. Winthrop, "Modell of Christian Charity," 288–89.

55. Winthrop, "Modell of Christian Charity," 292.

56. George Fox, *The Man Christ Jesus the Head of the Church* (London, 1679), 26.

57. Robert Blair St. George, *Conversing by Signs: Poetics of Implication in Colonial New England Culture* (Chapel Hill: University of North Carolina Press, 1998), 151.

58. The idea of the king's two bodies primarily applied to the political and symbolic reach of the monarchy; see Ernst Hartwig Kantorowicz, *The King's Two Bodies: A Study in Mediaeval Political Theology* (Princeton, N.J.: Princeton University Press, 1957). On the king's two bodies in a French colonial context, see Joseph Roach, "Body of Law: The Sun King and the Code Noir," in *From the Royal to the Republican Body: Incorporating the Political in Seventeenth- and Eighteenth-Century France,* ed. Sara E. Melzer and Kathryn Norberg (Berkeley: University of California Press, 1998), 113–30.

59. St. George, *Conversing by Signs,* 151.

60. Paul Kléber Monod, *The Power of Kings: Monarchy and Religion in Europe, 1589–1715* (New Haven, Conn.: Yale University Press, 1999).

61. Stanwood, *Empire Reformed,* esp. 20, 97, 143–46.

62. St. George, *Conversing by Signs,* 151; David George Hale, *The Body Politic: A Political Metaphor in Renaissance English Literature* (The Hague: Mouton, 1971); Jonathan Gil Harris, *Foreign Bodies and the Body Politic: Discourses of Social Pathology in Early Modern England* (Cambridge, U.K.: Cambridge University Press, 1998).

63. David G. Silverman, *Faith and Boundaries: Colonists, Christianity, and Community among the Wampanoag Indians of Martha's Vineyard, 1600–1871,* rev. ed., Studies in North American History (New York: Cambridge University Press, 2005); Bragdon, "*Native People of New England, 1650–1775* (Norman, University of Oklahoma Press, 2009; Linford Fisher, *The Indian Great Awakening: Religion and the Shaping of Native Cultures in Early America* (New York: Oxford University Press, 2012); Edward Andrews, *Native Apostles: Black and Indian Missionaries in the British Atlantic World* (Cambridge, Mass.: Harvard University Press, 2013).

64. The significance of body parts in English discourse was not limited to conflicts between the body politic and the body of Christ; see David Hillman and Carla Mazzio, *The Body in Parts: Fantasies of Corporeality in Early Modern Europe* (New York: Routledge, 1997). Sometimes the body parts were all too corporeal; see Andrew Lipman, "'A Meanes to Knitt Them Togeather': The Exchange of Body Parts in the Pequot War," *William and Mary Quarterly* 65, no. 1 (2008): 3–28.

65. James Muldoon, "Spiritual Freedom—Physical Slavery: The Medieval Church and Slavery," *Ave Maria Law Review* 3, no. 1 (2005): 69–93.

66. In 1618 the council overseeing doctrine for the Dutch Reformed Church left the decision of baptizing slaves up to the local ministers, allowing them to refuse baptism to the enslaved. It also allowed ministers to own slaves themselves. Some ministers in New Netherland continued to baptize the enslaved, who then pressed for their freedom and the freedom of their children based on church membership. By 1664 in New Netherland, about one in five people of African descent achieved hereditary freedom that would pass to their children; see Graham Russell Hodges, *Root and Branch: African Americans in New York and East Jersey, 1613–1863* (Chapel Hill: University of North Carolina Press, 1999); and Ira Berlin, "From Creole to African: Atlantic Creoles and the Origins of African-American Society in Mainland North America," *William and Mary Quarterly* 53, no. 2 (1996): 270. See also Evan Haefeli, *New Netherland and the Dutch Origins of American Religious Liberty* (Philadelphia: University of Pennsylvania Press, 2012).

67. The six were Maryland, Virginia, North Carolina, South Carolina, New York, and New Jersey. Marcus W. Jernegan, "Slavery and Conversion in the American Colonies," *American Historical Review* 21, no. 3 (1916): 506–7, 513–14; "Memorial . . . by many Ministers of the Gospel," May 30, 1694, *Acts and Resolves, Public and Private, of the Massachusetts Bay Colony* (Boston: Wright and Potter, 1895), 7:537.

68. Herndon and Sekatau, "Pauper Apprenticeship in Narragansett Country"; Newell, "Changing Nature of Indian Slavery."

69. Brooks, *Common Pot.* The maps are available in digital form at http://www3.amherst.edu/ ~lbrooks/map3.html (accessed January 5, 2017).

70. "Settlement Patterns in the Connecticut River Valley," Pocumtuck Valley Memorial Association, http://1704.deerfield.history.museum/maps/crv.html (accessed July 31, 2014).

71. Bragdon, *Native People of Southern New England, 1650–1775*, 205. See chap. 7; for figures, see 207–9.

CONTRIBUTORS

RICHARD J. CALLAHAN, JR., is associate professor of religious studies at the University of Missouri. He received his Ph.D. at the University of California, Santa Barbara, and is the author of *Work and Faith in the Kentucky Coal Fields* and editor of *New Territories, New Perspectives: The Religious Impact of the Louisiana Purchase.* Callahan's research explores the intersections of religion and cultures of work in the United States, and lately he has focused on the global oceanic networks of the nineteenth-century whaling industry.

LUCA CODIGNOLA is senior fellow at the University of Notre Dame's Cushwa Center for the Study of American Catholicism, adjunct professor at Saint Mary's University (Canada), and professeur associé at Université de Montréal. Formerly a professor of early North American history at Università di Genova (Italy), he has recently published *Little Do We Know: History and Historians of the North Atlantic, 1492–2010* (2011) and the six-volume *Calendar of Documents Relating to North America (Canada and the United States) in the Archives of the Sacred Congregation "de Propaganda Fide" in Rome 1622–1846* (2012).

JOHN CORRIGAN is the Lucius Moody Bristol Distinguished Professor of Religion and professor of history at Florida State University. His writings about the spatial humanities include three books coedited with David Bodenhamer and Trevor Harris: *The Spatial Humanities: GIS and the Future of the Humanities* (2010), *Deep Maps and Spatial Narratives* (2015), and *Making Deep Maps: Foundations, Approaches, Methods* (forthcoming). He is the editor in chief of the *Oxford Encyclopedia of American Religion* and editor of the Chicago History of American Religion book series.

ELIZABETH MADDOCK DILLON is professor of English and the codirector and cofounder of the NULab for Texts, Maps, and Networks at Northeastern University. She is the author of *New World Drama: The Performative Commons in the Atlantic World, 1659–1859* (2014), which received the Barnard Hewitt Award for Outstanding Research from the American Society of Theatre Research, and *The Gender of Freedom: Fictions of Liberalism and the Literary Public Sphere* (2004), which won the Heyman Prize for Outstanding Publication in the Humanities at Yale University. Together with Michael Drexler, she is coeditor of *The Haitian Revolution and the Early United States: Histories, Geographies, and Textualities* (2016).

LAUREN E. KOHUT (Ph.D., Vanderbilt) is the Andrew W. Mellon Postdoctoral Fellow in the Department of Sociology at Tougaloo College. Her current research focuses on colonial warfare and ecological change in the Colca Valley of the southern Peruvian highlands.

HEATHER MIYANO KOPELSON earned her Ph.D. in history from the University of Iowa in 2008. She is an associate professor in the Department of History at the University of Alabama, where she is also affiliated with the Department of Gender and Race Studies. Her book *Faithful Bodies: Performing Religion and Race in the Puritan Atlantic* (2014) examines race, religion, gender, performance, and the politics of the archive in the early modern Atlantic.

BRANDON MARRIOTT recently completed his doctorate at the University of Oxford in early modern European history and is the author of *Transnational Networks and Cross-Religious Exchange in the Seventeenth-Century Mediterranean and Atlantic Worlds* (2015), along with multiple articles on religion in the early modern world. He is currently working on a cross-religious history of Gog and Magog.

GEORGE EDWARD MILNE is associate professor of history at Oakland University and the author of *Natchez Country: Indians, Colonists, and the Landscapes of Race in French Louisiana* (2015). His work focuses on the interactions between Native Americans and European colonists during the seventeenth and eighteenth centuries and particularly on the relationships that developed in the Lower Mississippi Valley between the French and the Natchez, Chickasaw, and Choctaw peoples. His research has been supported by grants from the American Philosophical Society, the Huntington Library, and the American Historical Association.

JAN NOEL received her Ph.D from the University of Toronto and joined the History Department there in 1990. She has published some forty books, chapters, and articles on colonial history. Her work on aboriginal women in the fur trade received the New York State Historical Association's Kerr Prize in 2014, and her earlier work *Canada Dry: Temperance Crusades before Confederation* won the Canadian Historical Association's Macdonald Prize. Noel's most recent book is *Along a River: The First French Canadian Women* (UTP 2013).

ELIZABETH LEWIS PARDOE is director of the Office of Fellowships and a faculty affiliate in the Department of History and the Program in American Studies at Northwestern University. She earned master's degrees in European history as a Marshall scholar at the University of Cambridge and her doctorate in American history from Princeton. Her essays on early modern ethnic and religious pluralism have appeared in German and American journals.

KYLE B. ROBERTS is an associate professor of public history and new media and director of the Center for Textual Studies and Digital Humanities at Loyola University Chicago. He has published on eighteenth- and nineteenth-century print culture and religion, most recently in *Evangelical Gotham: Religion and the Making of New York City, 1783–1860* (2016). From 2009 to 2011, he co-authored *Dissenting Academies Online: Virtual Library System* (http://vls.english.qmul.ac.uk/), and in 2012 he launched the Jesuit Libraries Provenance Project (http://jesuitlibrariesprovenanceproject.com/), a collaborative effort to create a visual archive of provenance marks from historic Jesuit college libraries. He is at work on a history of nineteenth-century Catholic book and library culture in the midwestern United States.

SING D'ARCY, Ph.D., is a senior lecturer at the Faculty of Built Environment, UNSW Australia. His research areas include early modern Spanish ecclesiastical architecture, the nexus of music and architecture—particularly the role of the pipe organ, and the history of Australian interior design. Publications relating to Spanish architectural history include "Ecclesiastical Architecture and the Castilian Crisis of the Seventeenth Century: Seville Cathedral and the Church of the Sagrario," "Espacio, música y emoción: la arquitectura y el órgano en la España barroca," and "Painted Cloth and the Transformation of Seville Cathedral for the 1671 Festivities of the Canonization of Saint Ferdinand III."

TODD WEBB is an associate professor of history at Laurentian University. He holds a Ph.D. from York University (Canada). His book, *Transatlantic Methodists: British Wesleyanism and the Formation of an Evangelical Culture in Nineteenth-Century Ontario and Québec* (2013), was short-listed for the Canadian Historical Association's Sir John A. Macdonald Prize.

STEVEN A. WERNKE earned his Ph.D. at the University of Wisconsin in 2003. He is an associate professor of anthropology and director of the Spatial Analysis Research Laboratory at Vanderbilt University. His recent publications include *Negotiated Settlements: Andean Communities and Landscapes under Inka and Spanish Colonialism* (2013) and "Beyond the Basemap: Multiscalar Survey through Aerial Photogrammetry in the Andes" (with Gabriela Oré, Carla Hernández, Aurelio Rodríguez, Abel Traslaviña, and Giancarlo Marcone) in *Mobilizing the Past: Recent Approaches to Archaeological Fieldwork in the Digital Age*, edited by Erin Walcek Averett, Jody M. Gordon, and Derek B. Counts (2016).

INDEX